SEAMUS
HEANEY'S
REGIONS

SEAMUS HEANEY'S REGIONS

RICHARD RANKIN RUSSELL

University of Notre Dame Press
Notre Dame, Indiana

Copyright © 2014 by University of Notre Dame
Notre Dame, Indiana 46556
www.undpress.nd.edu
All Rights Reserved

Manufactured in the United States of America

Library of Congress Cataloging-in-Publication Data

Russell, Richard Rankin.
 Seamus Heaney's Regions / Richard Rankin Russell.
   pages   cm
  Includes bibliographical references and index.
  ISBN 978-0-268-04036-9 (paperback) — ISBN 0-268-04036-2 (paper)
  1. Heaney, Seamus, 1939–2013—Criticism and interpretation.   I. Title.
  PR6058.E2Z866   2014
  821'.914—dc23
                                                              2014002684

∞ *The paper in this book meets the guidelines for permanence
and durability of the Committee on Production Guidelines
for Book Longevity of the Council on Library Resources.*

To my son, Aidan Samuel Russell,

whose playful joy

amazes and delights me.

Contents

	List of Abbreviations	ix
	Acknowledgments	xi
	Introduction	1
One	The Development of Northern Irish Regionalism	41
Two	Recording Bigotry and Imagining a New Province: Heaney and BBC Northern Ireland Radio, 1968–73	66
Three	Heaney's Essays on Regional Writers: The 1970s	101
Four	Wounds and Fire: Northern Ireland in Heaney's 1970s Poetry	130
Five	Darkness Visible: Irish Catholicism, the American Civil Rights Movement, and the Blackness of "Strange Fruit"	162
Six	Border Crossings: Heaney's Prose Poems in *Stations*	187
Seven	Joyce, Burns, and Holub: Heaney's Independent Regionalism in *An Open Letter*	212
Eight	Affirming and Transcending Regionalism: Joyce, Dante, Eliot, and the Tercet Form in *Station Island* and *The Haw Lantern*	240
Nine	The Northern Irish Context and Owen and Yeats Intertexts in *The Cure at Troy*	279
Ten	Guttural and Global: Heaney's Regionalism after 1990	310

Eleven	"My Ship of Genius Now Shakes Out Her Sail": The Spirit Region and the Tercet in *Seeing Things* and *Human Chain*	356
	Afterword. Visiting the Dead and Welcoming Newborns: *Human Chain* and Heaney's Three Regions	393
	Notes	405
	Bibliography	461
	Index	487

Abbreviations

The following abbreviations are used in the text and notes for books by Heaney that are frequently cited. Full publication information is given in the bibliography.

AOL	*An Open Letter*
CP	*Crediting Poetry*
CT	*The Cure at Troy*
DC	*District and Circle*
DD	*Door into the Dark*
DN	*Death of a Naturalist*
EL	*Electric Light*
FW	*Field Work*
HC	*Human Chain*
HL	*The Haw Lantern*
N	*North*
OG	*Opened Ground*
S	*Stations*
SI	*Station Island*
SL	*The Spirit Level*
SS	*Stepping Stones*
ST	*Seeing Things*
WO	*Wintering Out*

Acknowledgments

I am grateful to the many people who have answered questions, offered suggestions, and given emotional, mental, and spiritual support during the writing of this book. A portion of it originated in my dissertation on Northern Irish literature and identity, which was directed by the beloved Weldon Thornton at the University of North Carolina, Chapel Hill, to whom I will always be thankful for his belief in me and my work, and for his own sterling example of teaching and scholarship on Irish literature. Most of this project, however, is based upon new research on Heaney that I have conducted in the last several years. A sabbatical from Baylor University's College of Arts and Sciences in the fall semester of 2010 enabled much thinking, researching, and writing. I am very grateful to the university's committee on research leaves and to Dean Lee Nordt of the College of Arts and Sciences for that sabbatical and to my chair in the Baylor English Department, Dianna Vitanza, for her sustained support of my work. Many thanks also go to my former provost, David Lyle Jeffrey, and former chair, Maurice Hunt, for reducing my teaching load several years ago so that I might have more time for scholarship.

The gifted Northern Irish artist Colin Davidson graciously allowed me to use one of his evocative pencil sketches of Seamus Heaney's face for the cover of this book.

I am very thankful to Henry Hart and Bernard O'Donoghue. Professor Hart's deep knowledge of Heaney, Robert Frost, and Ted Hughes and his numerous suggestions for the manuscript helped me to make a much more informed and sustained argument. Professor O'Donoghue's extensive thinking and research on Heaney, along with his insightful comments about the manuscript, have inspired me and enabled my greater understanding of Heaney's work.

I offer gratitude to Sir Christopher Ricks, who suggested to me at the 2009 meeting of the Association for Literary Scholars and Critics that I expand my paper on Heaney's *The Cure at Troy* into an essay and offered me several very helpful suggestions for doing so.

Earlier versions of portions of this book appeared as articles in several journals, whose editors and outside readers helped improve the clarity of my prose and overall argument. In particular, I would like to thank Nicola Presley, assistant editor of *Irish Studies Review*; Keith M. Dallas, managing editor of *Twentieth-Century Literature*; and Seamus Perry, coeditor of *Essays in Criticism*.

A portion of chapter 2 first appeared in "Imagining a New Province: Seamus Heaney's Creative Work for BBC Northern Ireland Radio, 1968–1971," *Irish Studies Review* 15, no. 2 (Spring 2007): 137–62, and appears with permission.

Part of chapter 3 was first published in "Seamus Heaney's Artful Regionalism," *Twentieth-Century Literature* 54, no. 1 (Spring 2008): 47–74, and appears with permission.

An early version of chapter 9 came out in "Owen and Yeats in Heaney's *The Cure at Troy*," *Essays in Criticism* 61, no. 2 (April 2011): 173–89, and appears with permission.

I am very grateful to Seamus Heaney for permission to quote from his archival material at Emory University's Manuscript, Archives, and Rare Book Library. After this book went into production, Heaney passed away in Dublin on August 30, 2013. The shock and sadness from his passing continue to reverberate throughout the poetry community and the world. I remain thankful not only for his creative work but also for his generosity, kindness, and thoughtfulness. He has enlarged our imaginative lives so considerably that it is hard to imagine "keeping going" without him. Yet his example nevertheless continues to inspire us with hope and joy.

Thanks to Evelyn Ellison at the BBC Northern Ireland Radio Archives in Cultra, Northern Ireland, for permission to reproduce a quotation from "Seamus Heaney—Poetry International."

Thanks to Professor Kevin Young for very helpful information about the holdings on Heaney and also to the members of staff at Emory's MARBL for their assistance during my time there in May 2012.

Thanks to the staff of the Henry C. Pearson Collection of Seamus Heaney at the University of North Carolina, Chapel Hill, for their help during my visit in May 2012.

Many thanks to the Centennial Professor Committee at Baylor for awarding me the 2012 Baylor Centennial Professor Award, which enabled me to conduct research at Emory and Chapel Hill and helped me purchase much Heaney material for my classroom and scholarly use. Additional thanks go to the Baylor Class of 1945, which funds the Centennial Professor Award.

Grateful thanks to Barrie Cooke for permission to reproduce three of his lovely charcoal images from the 1975 Rainbow Press edition of Heaney's *Bog Poems*.

All other quotations from Heaney's poetry are covered by the principle of Fair Use.

Many thanks to Stephen Little, acquisitions editor of the University of Notre Dame Press, for a thorough, thoughtful, and speedy publishing process.

Many thanks to the staff of the Press for their help in publicity, editing, proofreading, and other work on my book. I am especially grateful for Elisabeth Magnus's superb copyediting job.

I appreciate my undergraduate and graduate students at Baylor University for their own thoughts on Seamus Heaney's poetry, prose, and drama over the years, which have aided my own understanding of these rich works. The students in my graduate seminar "Yeats and His Successors" in fall 2008, along with the undergraduate students in my senior-level "Major Authors" course on Heaney and Brian Friel in Spring 2009, created particularly congenial and rigorous classroom environments and helped me think differently and better about Heaney.

Additional thanks to George S. Lensing, University of North Carolina, Chapel Hill, who has encouraged my work on Heaney over the years; Bryan Giemza, Randolph-Macon College, for his gift of friendship and sustained emotional support of my work and life; Marilynn Richtarik, Georgia State University, for her advocacy of my scholarship beginning during my time in Chapel Hill and continuing to this day; my church family at Redeemer Presbyterian, Waco; and my Baylor colleagues James Barcus, Mona Choucair, Mike DePalma, Luke Ferretter, Sarah Ford, Joe Fulton, Greg Garrett, Clement Goode, Maurice Hunt, Kyle Irwin, Joshua King, Vicki Klaras, Coretta Pittman, Emily Setina, Lisa Shaver, Betsy Vardaman, Dianna Vitanza, and William Weaver, all of whom support me in innumerable ways and make Baylor University the best kind of home for me and my family.

I am also grateful for the sustenance of my family in Tennessee—my father, Paul L. Russell; sister, Marjorie Levy; brother-in-law, Herb Levy; and nephew, Vincent Levy—and in North Carolina, my in-laws, Tim and Glenda Gray, and sister-in-law, Gretta Gray.

As always, my deepest gratitude must go to my wife, Hannah, and my two sons, Connor and Aidan. For the daily gift of themselves, for their grace, joy, and love, for Connor and Aidan's "letting Daddy get his work done," I am forever grateful. No man could ask for a more supportive and wonderful family.

Academic work is inherently lonely, yet I have been privileged to be a member of the above communities, leading me to conclude with Yeats,

> We must laugh and we must sing,
> We are blest by everything,
> Everything we look upon is blest.
> ("A Dialogue of Self and Soul")

INTRODUCTION

> *While a literary scene in which the provinces revolve around the centre is demonstrably a Copernican one, the task of talent is to reverse things to a Ptolemaic condition. The writer must re-envisage the region as the original point.*
> —Heaney, "The Regional Forecast"

> *Each person in Ulster lives first in the Ulster of the actual present, and then in one or other Ulster of the mind.*
> —Heaney, *Place and Displacement: Recent Poetry of Northern Ireland*

SEAMUS HEANEY'S REGIONAL IMAGINATION

Seamus Heaney observed, "John Keats once called a poem [of his] 'a little Region to wander in,'"[1] and notions of the region lie at the heart not only of his concept of poetry but also of his understanding of politics, culture, and spirituality. Regional voices from England, Ireland, and Scotland inspired

1

the 1995 Nobel Prize winner to become a poet, while his home region of Northern Ireland produced the subject matter for much of his poetry, which explores, records, and preserves both the disappearing agrarian life of that region and the dramatic rise of sectarianism and then the outbreak of the "Troubles" there beginning in the late 1960s and continuing through the late 1990s. At the same time, Heaney consistently imagined a new region of Northern Ireland where the conflicts that had long beset this region, and by extension the relationship between Ireland and the United Kingdom, would be synthesized and resolved. There was a third region he committed himself to explore—the spirit region, that world beyond our ken—and many of his poems, essays, and other works also probe the boundaries of this region. Heaney's regions—the first, geographic, historical, political, cultural, linguistic; the second, a future where peace, even reconciliation, might one day flourish; the third, the life beyond this one—offer the best entrée into and unified understanding of his tremendous body of work in poetry, prose, translations, and drama. There is a rough trajectory across these three regions toward the spiritual, which seems natural, as the poet had aged and survived a major stroke in August 2006, but often these three regions interpenetrate and inform each other. In his early seventies, for instance, he continued to write of his childhood region along with incidents in the Northern Irish Troubles, even as he dreamt of rapprochement in the North and imagined the spirit region in the long sequence from *Human Chain* (2010) entitled "Route 110." In Heaney's hands notions of the region and regionalism reached their fullest and most profound development in literary history, as he explored these three regions through a variety of genres and forms, perhaps most supremely through his adaptation of Dante's inherently regional form of terza rima into his particular tercet variant on that form, which itself became his chosen "region" to dwell in.

In 1983, Seamus Deane, a contemporary of Heaney's from Northern Ireland, argued in an important, albeit somewhat misleading essay, "The Artist and the Troubles," that writers of Heaney's generation, particularly those from the Catholic minority in the North, faced particular pressures to engage with the recent conflict in the province. He further held that Heaney, in particular, had done so by drawing on both an immediate concept of the region and a transcendent one:

Seamus Heaney's work, which began in a regionalism of the kind which had seemed to have passed with [painter William] Conor and [novelist and short-story writer Michael] McLaverty, suddenly expanded into the historical dimension with *Wintering Out* (1972) and *North* (1975) with such incandescent energy and force that it was immediately clear that here, in this work, the Northern imagination had finally lost its natural stridency (replaced by patience) and had confronted its violent origins. Heaney's best work is a contemplation of root and origin—of words, names, stories, practices, of violence itself. In him, Ulster regionalism realizes itself most fully and, in so doing, transcends itself.[2]

Unfortunately, Deane's contention that Heaney's first two books were essentially ahistorical is patently false: both *Death of a Naturalist* (1966) and *Door into the Dark* (1969) do not celebrate a bucolic, timeless ideal of Ireland but bear witness to its nightmarish history. The narrative of that particular violent history of the North of Ireland is then amplified and expanded in *Wintering Out* and *North* as Heaney turns increasingly to other northern societies such as ancient Denmark, in order to draw parallels with the intimate violence then being committed within and outside the "tribes" of contemporary Northern Ireland. Deane does not clarify or elucidate his last, telling remark about Heaney's best work being the apogee of Ulster realism yet also transcending it, but I would posit that a truer sentence has never been written about Heaney's regionalism. As Heaney himself stated, "Each person in Ulster lives first in the Ulster of the actual present, and then in one or other Ulster of the mind."[3]

This project takes up Deane's articulation of how Heaney's earlier work enables the fullest realization of "Ulster regionalism" and transcends it, a crucial endeavor not only for fully appreciating the trajectory of Heaney's work but also for understanding, by extrapolation, how it both reflects the peril and promise of divided Northern Ireland and anticipates its eventual emergence from the dark days of the Troubles into a less divided society that nonetheless remains riven with sectarianism. This sort of regionalism accords with that called for by the poet John Montague: "The real position for a poet is to be a global-regionalist. He is born into allegiances to particular areas or places and people, which he loves, sometimes against his will. But then he also happens to belong to an increasingly accessible world. . . .

So the position is actually local and international."[4] As Dennis O'Driscoll has observed, "This attitude is alert to the political, economic and environmental upheavals which uproot people and force them into new imaginative relationships with their native places. The universal informs the particular and vice versa."[5] Regionalism as Heaney imagined it played a crucial role in this devolution of the North of Ireland/Northern Ireland and in the development of his own work.

Writing in the mid-1980s about the poet John Crowe Ransom, who hailed from the American South, Heaney precisely articulates why he has devoted so much of his literary criticism to the work of regional writers— to affirm his own regional body of work and to connect it to that of other regional writers. He first points out that "Ransom was at a detached angle to what he cherished. He was in two, maybe three places at once: in the parochial south, within the imposed Union, and inside the literary 'mind of Europe.'"[6] So too had Heaney been at such a "detached angle": he was fully of his local parish, but he grew up within the "imposed Union" of Northern Ireland and the rest of Great Britain and increasingly dwelled within the "literary 'mind of Europe,'" as his later deep reading in the work of the Italian poet Dante and the Polish poet Czesław Miłosz shows. Because he occupied such places, sometimes simultaneously, Heaney found it helpful to turn to similar writers who had done so successfully, like Ransom. In this same essay, he further argues that because of his peripheral position the southern poet took on "poetic challenges and their resolutions [that] were tactical, venturesome, and provisional," concluding, "His plight was symptomatic of the double focus which the poet from a regional culture is now likely to experience, caught between a need to affirm the centrality of the local experience to his own being and a recognition that this experience is likely to be peripheral to the usual life of his age. In this situation, the literary tradition is what links the periphery to the centre— wherever that imaginary point may be—and to other peripheries."[7] Thus the poet from a region with such multiple allegiances must turn to "the literary tradition" to affirm the importance of "local experience" that is often rendered peripheral, especially in our own increasingly homogenized and homogenizing world—and to link that experience to those of others who similarly value local culture.

Although Heaney's immersion in the local rural life of southern County Derry in the 1940s and 1950s likely contributed more than any other factors to his positive, complex view of the region, regional literary exemplars such as Robert Frost (with some qualifications), Gerard Manley Hopkins, Patrick Kavanagh, and Ted Hughes actually led him to start writing poetry seriously in the 1960s and to consider his home ground as a positive and natural source for that poetry. In the 1970s, he pointed out that "several poets in the English tradition have nurtured me—Frost, Hopkins[,] and Ted Hughes, for example."[8] Later, in his lecture *Room to Rhyme*, he related the story in the Venerable Bede's "Ecclesiastical History of the English People" about the first English poet, Caedmon, who received his call to become a poet relatively late in life and linked his own vocation to hearing regional voices from Ireland and Britain:

> At the relatively advanced age of twenty-three, I heard the equivalent of the voice [from Caedmon's dream] telling me to make room to rhyme and to sing. This happened when I began to read contemporary Irish and English and Scottish and Welsh poets, people like Patrick Kavanagh and Ted Hughes and R[.] S[.] Thomas and Norman MacCaig and George Mackay Brown, and began to feel that my own experience was fit material to work with. Suddenly I felt that my own voice could make itself heard as it was, a voice with a local accent, but like the voices of those mummers [he has earlier discussed the Irish Christmas mummers' tradition] one that had inherited something of [the] language of the Globe and of the Irish language that English had long since replaced.[9]

Susan Stewart's reading of Caedmon's discovery of his vocational calling illuminates our understanding of Heaney's likening of his own call to that of the earliest English poet, whom he perceived as the first regional poet, as we will see below. She argues that "Caedmon's legend gives an account of poetic suasion that is reciprocal—the demand precedes the composition and is not an artifact of composition.... When poet and listener are engaged in this scene, they turn to the intersubjective task of making significance, of pointing to meaning."[10] Such poetry, like Heaney's, eschews solipsism in meaning making and thus establishes an inherently ethical position in its appeal to the Other. This ethic undergirds my entire regionalist argument about Heaney's writing in this study, which assumes that his work always seeks to make meaning and to communicate that meaning to others, forming provisional communities of writer and audience.

Heaney's call to poetry, then, stems from and is freighted with an ethical sense of his obligation to others to communicate meaning and form community, whether in the actual region of the North of Ireland, an imagined future North, or the spirit region.

At this point, the New England poet Frost, who spent significant time early in his career in England and who has been placed in the tradition of the regionally oriented Wordsworth and Hardy in valuing local culture, was important to Heaney, even as he admitted some reservations about Frost's public persona and acknowledged that Frost had a troubling tendency toward literary self-consciousness.[11] Frost's assertion in 1918 that "the colloquial is the root of every good poem" exemplified a salutary position for Heaney, despite his later insistence that "even Frost, for all his insistence on his own accent, cleared his throat, as if to remind English poetry that he had read his Virgil."[12] Similarly, he told Karl Miller that "there was a stand-up performer's patter that became tedious, a way of not caving in to academic jargon."[13] Nevertheless, Heaney's earliest and more recent readers have noticed Frost's presence throughout his poetry. For instance, Robert Buttel, author of the first monograph on Heaney, argues that Frost offered "the validation he required" because of his excellence "at rendering physical detail and sense experience," his facility with handling "traditional forms but [ones] charged with the rhythms of natural speech," his balanced view of malign and benign forces at work in nature, the "human pain and tragedy" of rural people, the combination of "matter of fact with transcendental inclinations," and "the appreciation of native skills and disciplines which have their correspondences to the art of poetry."[14] And as Daniel W. Ross has observed, "Frost was not, for Heaney, an acquired taste: even his earliest essays contain praises for Frost that indicate an early and pervasive influence."[15] Heaney himself noted that "when I first came to his poetry, the side of Frost that absolutely riveted me was his resolute down-to-earthness—the Frost of things-as-they-are."[16] The directness of Frost in his steadfast gaze at daily life, replete with all its tragedies and joys and expressed in his perspicuous language, confirmed for Heaney that he could employ direct language to reflect the ordinary life of his region.

Frost's great pleasure in rural labor also spoke to Heaney, who similarly enjoyed the hard work of agrarian tasks such as cutting hay with a scythe on his parents' farm. For instance, he has praised Frost's "Mowing," recalling,

> I myself had recently learnt to mow and took pride in my ability to sharpen and handle a scythe. Come to think of it, there was a special kind of scythe shaft they often used in County Derry—and Frost of course was a Derry boy too—another connection there—a scythe that had a shaft with a curve in it. This curved handle was for some reason called a "Yankee sned" and it gave you a longer, lower sweep and cut. Anyway, I loved to mow, and I loved to hear and watch other people mow, even when I had to fall in behind and lift and bind oats or grass-seed at the heels of the mower—the "swale," as Frost called it. So his poem meant a lot to me just because it described the particular sound of the blade in grass.[17]

Thus Frost modeled and affirmed for the young Heaney a connection to the earth, particularly the pleasures of hard rural labor—and the unique sounds of that work—that he was learning in the late 1940s and early 1950s. Yet in *Stepping Stones* Heaney told Dennis O'Driscoll that despite his appreciation for Frost's "primal reach into the physical" and his "covenant with the reader, an openness, an availability" (*SS*, 453), "I don't think of him as genetically important to my voice—Hopkins was far more important" (454). He even admitted that by the time he was reading Frost's poetry such as "Out, Out—," in his second or third year at Queen's University, "I was already a slave to Hopkins" (36).

And indeed, in terms of finding his voice and adjusting it to reflect local speech in his native province, he noted, "What had put me in step with myself and tuned my performance was what I heard coming through in poems by Hopkins, Ted Hughes and Patrick Kavanagh, things spoken in a way I might have heard them spoken in my own *provincia* by people who would hardly so much as open a book."[18] In "Feeling into Words," Heaney therefore observed that "the result of reading Hopkins at school was the desire to write, and when I first put pen to paper at university, what flowed out was what had flowed in, the bumpy alliterating music, the reporting sounds and ricocheting consonants typical of Hopkins's verse."[19] Recalling an early, uncollected poem of his entitled "October Thought," and comparing it to Hopkins's unique music, he lamented, "Some frail bucolic images foundered under the chainmail of the pastiches: 'Starling thatch-watches, and sudden swallow / Straight breaks to mud-nest, home rest rafter . . .' and then there was 'heaven-hue, plum-blue and gorse-pricked with gold' and 'a trickling tinkle of bells well in the fold.'"[20] Heaney's recourse to Hopkins's tendency to jam nouns together would later reinforce his desire to translate the Old English epic *Beowulf* (and to insist on its essentially regional nature), which revels in such grammatical features. Despite his self-critique here, however, he insists that "there was a connection, not obvious at the time, but, on reflection, real enough, between the heavily accented consonantal noise of Hopkins's poetic voice, and the peculiar regional characteristics of a Northern Ireland accent."[21] Musing further, he observes that accents in Northern Ireland are "energetic, angular, hard-edged, and it may be because of this affinity between my dialect and Hopkins's oddity that those first verses turned out as they did."[22]

In his essay on Hopkins, Heaney privileges his "philological and rhetorical passion," pointing out that, like Ben Jonson's poetry, "his verse is 'rammed with life,' butting ahead instead of hanging back into its own centre."[23] Going on to praise Hopkins's "masculine powers of powerful and active thought," Heaney finally argues that "his own music thrusts and throngs and it is forged. It is the way that words strike off one another, the way they are drilled, marched, and countermarched, rather than the way they philander and linger among themselves, that constitutes his proper music."[24] Many years later, Heaney would praise Hopkins's "sense of the powerline of English language trembling under the actual verse line. The sense of big voltage."[25] So going back to his earliest attempts at writing poetry in the 1950s and continuing through his days at Queen's University, when he "used to carry around the old Penguin edition of Hopkins's poems edited by W. H. Gardner" (*SS*, 39), Heaney valued the Victorian poet's philological underpinnings and passion along with the way he controlled that power through his precise forms. Hopkins's influence on Heaney has been downplayed and generally neglected in the extensive criticism on the Nobel Prize winner, but Heaney consistently viewed Hopkins's example as essential for finding his own regional voice, tuned to the rough energies and cadences of Northern Ireland speech.[26]

Moreover, Heaney found in Hopkins's poetry a reclamation of pre-Reformation rural English Catholicism, which confirmed him as a Catholic poet from the countryside. He said that despite Hopkins's scholarly bent, his poetry "is grounded in the insular landscape which, in the month of May, blooms and greens in a way that is still Marian, sacramental, medieval English Catholic."[27] For a poet beginning to devote himself not only to promoting his home region but also to recovering the Catholic subculture of that region, Hopkins's example was doubly salutary.

Heaney identified 1962 as the year in which he first read both Patrick Kavanagh and Ted Hughes. He recalled that "I was sort of pupped out of Kavanagh. I read him in 1962, after I'd graduated from Queen's and was teaching at St. Thomas's, where my headmaster was the short-story writer Michael McLaverty. He lent me Kavanagh's *Soul for Sale*, which includes 'The Great Hunger,' and at that moment the veil of the study was rent: it gave me this terrific breakthrough from English literature into home ground."[28] Kavanagh was himself from the old nine-county region of Ulster (County Monaghan), and his grittiness and specific attention to the local resonated deeply with Heaney. He told Seamus Deane in 1977 that Kavanagh had given him and other Irish writers "a confidence in the deprivations of our condition. It is to do with an insouciance and trust in the clarities and cunnings of our perceptions.... [Kavanagh modeled] the need to be open, unpredictably susceptible, lyrically opportunistic."[29] Heaney wrote multiple essays about Kavanagh, and the Monaghan poet helped inspire his interest not only in the cultural and geographical region but also in what I have termed elsewhere his "mental regionalism," a "new, imagined country of the poet's mind [that] offers a potential site of deep rapprochement and reconciliation . . . a proleptic correlative to a realistic region where the province's inhabitants might live in harmony."[30]

Kavanagh's proclivity for including dialect words and typically Ulster speech patterns in his poetry also affirmed Heaney in his similar inclinations. Heaney's well-known last line from "Digging," collected in *Death of a Naturalist*, about his desire to use his pen as a writer—"I'll dig with it"—suggests his fine ear for local speech by stressing "it" more than any word in the line (*DN*, 2). The Australian poet Les Murray has said that he told Heaney, "You couldn't say that in English English," meaning standard spoken English, and that Heaney agreed with him. Murray further observed that Heaney was putting his "own stamp of Ulster English on" the poem with this concluding emphasis on "it."[31]

While Kavanagh's savage antipastoral "The Great Hunger," combined with his well-known embrace of parochialism, including the living local language, led Heaney to examine his "home ground" with both affection and skepticism, Hughes's "live energy" convinced Heaney he could inject a similarly rough voltage and confidence into his own verse about local culture—and that he could use the English language to do so.[32] Shortly after Hughes's death, Heaney connected him explicitly to Caedmon through their shared northern English regionalism, observing sagely that "this modern poet from Yorkshire who published in the 1960s a poem called *The Bull Moses* would have had no difficulty hitting it off with Caedmon, the first English poet, who began life as a farmhand in Northumbria, a fellow northerner with a harp in one hand and a bundle of fodder under the other."[33] Heaney deftly renders Caedmon as the original regional poet here even as he links Hughes to him—and by extension himself to both poets. Noting that "in 1962 the current began to flow," he remembers "taking down Ted Hughes's *Lupercal* from the shelves of the Belfast public library and opening it at 'View of a Pig,' and immediately going off and writing a couple of poems that were Hughes pastiches almost."[34] Moreover, if Kavanagh led Heaney to write about his home ground, Hughes enabled him to feel at home in the English language with all its roughness and echoes of Anglo-Saxon cadences. Heaney told John Haffenden that Hughes's "energy comes out in the quality of the diction, powerful, violent diction, and there's a kind of anger at work. Hughes's voice . . . is in rebellion against a certain kind of demeaned, mannerly voice. . . . The manners of that speech, the original voices behind that poetic voice, are those of literate English middle-class culture, and I think Hughes's great cry and call and bawl is that English language and English poetry is longer and deeper and rougher than that."[35] Elsewhere, Heaney likened Hughes to the *Gawain* poet, arguing that Hughes's "diction is consonantal, and it snicks through the air like an efficient blade, marking and carving out fast definite shapes"; furthermore, he noted that his "consonants . . . take the measure of his vowels like calipers, or stud the line like rivets."[36] Hughes's home county of Yorkshire, on the periphery of the London-centered literary culture, likely also exemplified for Heaney the way off-center and out-of-the way places could be their own literary and cultural fields of force. Moreover, Hughes's rejection of the university as a teacher enabled him to speak "within the terms of his own world," and staying a "free-lance writer from his student days[,] . . . he always retained that sense of being at the edge."[37]

Hughes was not only a model writer for Heaney but an active collaborator with Heaney on three important projects: the limited-edition volume *Bog Poems*, lavishly produced by Hughes and his sister Olwyn's Rainbow Press in 1975; *The Rattle Bag*, a 1982 anthology of poems that sold very well; and its successor, the 1997 *School Bag*. Hughes, then, served as both publisher and editor to Heaney, along with writing early poems that enabled him to find his voice.

Hughes's importance as an enabling regional writer for Heaney cannot be overestimated: when he died, Heaney opened his funeral eulogy by lamenting, "No death in my lifetime has hurt poets or poetry more than the death of Ted Hughes. And no death outside my immediate family has left me feeling more bereft."[38] Heaney speaks here certainly out of his grief at the loss of such a good and valued friend but also out of the loss of a poet who seems to have embodied the most salutary notions of the region. Thus he recapitulates the language and thrust of his discussion above in his lecture *Room to Rhyme*, implicitly arguing that enabling regional voices are akin to the voice speaking to Caedmon in his dream. After terming Hughes a "keeper," in the various senses that word suggests, Heaney continues: "[He had] something indeed that the word 'Caedmon,' the name of the first English poet also embodies, a sense of being close to the first strata of the land and the language, close to Lindisfarne and Lamb Bank, Sir Gawain and the Gododdin, Flanders trenches and fustian."[39] By iterating these largely northern English place and literary names, and further, by alliterating them, Heaney pays homage to Hughes's northern English origins and suggests his exemplary closeness to the wellsprings of English language and literature.

Finally, Hughes's regionalism was not merely confined to recovering and affirming his northern English dialect and roots that he wrote about in his essay "Myths, Metres, Rhythms"; it also functioned for Heaney as an exemplary model of cultural and linguistic connection between oppositions. Henry Hart has noted that Heaney's 1998 elegy "On His Work in the English Tongue" seems to represent Hughes as "a bridge that connected . . . the opposed factions in Heaney's background: Protestants and Catholics, British culture and Irish culture, Anglo-Saxon verse and post-Chaucerian verse, rural dialect and official English."[40] Despite the perception in other quarters of Hughes as personally or even culturally polarizing, Heaney has always seen him as a reconciler of divided languages and cultures upon whom he could draw for his own such attempts.

For Heaney, moreover, the region is synonymous with the local culture epitomized both in the story of the Irish St. Kevin and in the unidentified Greek poet he singles out in his 1995 Nobel Prize speech, *Crediting Poetry*. His poem "St. Kevin and the Blackbird," collected in *The Spirit Level* (1996), relates how St. Kevin's outstretched hand, held out as he prayed, was made into a nest for a blackbird and how the saint kept that posture until the eggs hatched. He states that the story's "trustworthiness and its travelworthiness have to do with its *local setting*," arguing further that the carved relief of Orpheus, a bird, and a beast that he found in a museum in Sparta was similarly about a state of rapture and that "the description on the card moved me also because it gave a name and a credence to that which I see myself as having been engaged upon for the past three decades: 'Votive panel,' the identification card said, 'possibly set up to Orpheus by *local poet. Local work* of the Hellenistic period'" (*CP*, 21, 22; my emphases). Despite the possibility that the local can "quickly degrade into the fascistic, our vigilance on that score should not displace our love and trust in the good of the indigenous per se" (*CP*, 22). Going on to cite Yeats's Nobel Prize speech, Heaney argues that "he came to Sweden to tell the world that the local work of poets and dramatists had been as important to the transformation of his native place and times as the ambushes of guerrilla armies" (*CP*, 24). So has the work of Heaney and his contemporaries been for contemporary Northern Ireland, he suggests, urging his audience "to do what Yeats asked his readers to do and think of the achievement of Irish poets and dramatists and novelists over the past forty years, among whom I am proud to count great friends" (*CP*, 25). The work of the local writer thus can create a commonwealth of art where mutually opposed inhabitants might meet and converse and form community; such a state prefigures and may lay the groundwork for the emergence of a similar reality on the political level. Elsewhere, Heaney terms Yeats a "public poet," or "a political poet in the way that Sophocles is a political dramatist. Both of them are interested in the polis," and further suggests that "the whole effort of the imagining is towards inclusiveness. Prefiguring a future."[41] So too with Heaney, and the ground of that imagined future is the region.

One of the earliest theorists of regionalism, the English writer F. W. Morgan, argued in a seminal 1939 article, "Three Aspects of Regional Consciousness," that regionalism is marked by "a developing consciousness of the smaller units of the earth."[42] W. J. Keith argues further, citing the rural English writer H. J. Massingham's *Remembrance: An Autobiography* (1942), that regionalism attains specificity in the completeness of its presentation analogous to a work of art, and that the region so presented actually is art.[43] Seamus Heaney's artful rendering in his drama, prose, and poetry of his chosen region of Northern Ireland deserves critical recognition as art. This study thus seeks to redress the relative neglect of this important project by celebrating its distinctive features and analyzing them, charting Heaney's real and imagined region of the North, and finally exploring how his chosen late form of the tercet epitomizes his desire to dwell in the spirit region beyond our ken.

Tom Paulin, himself a poet and critic from Northern Ireland, has convincingly argued that "at some deep, culturally inherited level, it would appear that the European imagination perceives a secret kinship between art and the state."[44] Paulin cites Nietzsche's contention in *Thus Spake Zarathustra* that *state* "is the name of the 'coldest of all cold monsters,'" pointing out that although the German philosopher rejects the violent origins of the modern nation-state, "By offering us a metaphor, Nietzsche has moved the state out of a mechanically rational into an imaginative reality."[45] While Paulin is concerned to explore the often English Protestant imagining of the nation-state in poets from Milton through Peter Reading, many Catholic Irish have long imagined Ireland as a helpless female, variously figured as a young maiden or as an old woman (Kathleen Ni Houlihan, the Shan van Vocht), who needs rescuing from a rapacious British state. Heaney invokes both Paulin's formulation of the specifically Protestant state as monstrous and the imagined Irish nation as woman in his "Ocean's Love to Ireland," from his 1975 volume *North*:

> Speaking broad Devonshire,
> Ralegh has backed the maid to a tree
> As Ireland is backed to England
>
> And drives inland
> Till all her strands are breathless:
> "Sweesir, Swatter! Sweesir, Swatter!"
> (*N*, 40)

By line 4, then, Ralegh is transformed into the unstoppable sea, as we realize in reading stanza 3: "He is water, he is ocean, lifting / Her farthingale like a scarf of weed lifting / In the front of a wave" (40). Casting Ralegh/Britain as the penetrating, aggressive, masculine ocean and Ireland as a violated, passive, feminized land enables Heaney to imaginatively suggest Ireland's historical helplessness in the growing surge of British colonialism that finally resulted in the Act of Union in 1800.[46]

In his "Act of Union," also from *North*, Heaney's speaker movingly meditates on the births of Northern Ireland in 1920 and the Irish Free State in 1921 by assuming the voice of "imperially / Male" Britain in a bifurcated poem of two parts, which itself signifies the rupture effected by Britain's colonization of Ireland.[47] As the poem opens, the speaker acknowledges "a first movement, a pulse, / As if the rain in bogland gathered head / To slip and flood: a bog-burst, / A gash breaking open the ferny bed" (*N*, 43). When Ireland was forced to become part of the British state, he suggests, something was born and is struggling to get out of the "gash." The speaker then personifies Ireland, again focusing on how its back remains toward Britain: "Your back is a firm line of eastern coast / And arms and legs are thrown / Beyond your gradual hills" (43). A still interested Britain "caress[es] / The heaving province where our past has grown" (43). Figuring Ulster as a "heaving province" posits it as a site for further political upheaval, as indeed it was periodically throughout the nineteenth and twentieth centuries (and of course had been since the Jamesian plantations in Ulster during the early 1600s), which laid the sectarian groundwork for the contemporary "Troubles" of Northern Ireland. As the first section concludes, Britain "grow[s] older / Conceding your half-independent shore / Within whose borders now my legacy / Culminates inexorably" (43). Notice the emphasis again, as in "Ocean's Love to Ireland," on the inexorable: Britain's forcing itself upon Ireland results in a series of inevitable processes, including the birth of Ireland and the Northern Irish state, along with the beginnings of the conflict within that region.

Stanza 2 of "Act of Union" perceives Britain as a somewhat sympathetic variation on Nietzsche's "coldest of all cold monsters," as the speaker seems to lament "leaving you with the pain, / The rending process in the colony, / The battering ram, the boom burst from within" (43). He acknowledges Ireland's ongoing rupture, specifically within Northern Ireland, stemming from that original split or incursion accomplished by a series of brute force actions over hundreds of years. Now Britain fears what he has fostered in his "act" with her—not a Minotaur but a miniature monster in the form of a rebellious Protestant region:

> The act sprouted an obstinate fifth column
> Whose stance is growing unilateral.
> His heart beneath your heart is a wardrum
> Mustering force. His parasitical
> And ignorant little fists already
> Beat at your borders and I know they're cocked
> At me across the water.
> (43)

Heaney's pejorative language in describing an abstracted, Protestant-majority Northern Ireland as a bellicose male baby still shocks, especially because he often has promoted an imagined, inclusive Northern Irish regionalism as an artistic model that might be eventually actualized in a peaceful new Northern Irish state. Heaney's belligerent, "ignorant" baby has largely grown up now: Northern Ireland is an autonomous region with a coalition government of Protestants and Catholics established by the Good Friday Agreement of 1998. Recently, he has even suggested that the long interaction between Irish and English cultures and languages has resulted in positive examples; certainly his own life and work suggest how receptivity to this relationship can be very fruitful.[48] But how did this child with "ignorant little fists" grow into adulthood? Did the writers of Northern Ireland such as Heaney, have anything to do with it?

Heaney's persistent attempts to both describe the existing, conflicted region of Northern Ireland and imagine a new, more peaceful and inclusive region form the first and second strands of this book's argument. It thus follows Heaney's contention to Patrick Garland in 1973 that landscape could be both described and imagined: "The landscape, for me, is image, and it's almost an element to work with as [much as] it is an object of admiration or description."[49]

Chapter 1 surveys attempts in the North of Ireland to formulate regionalism by analyzing the short-lived Ulster Literary Theatre and several waves of regionally focused literary journals, including *Rann, Lagan, Threshold*, the *Honest Ulsterman, Forthnight*, and *Phoenix*. Such efforts resulted in a multifaceted concept of Northern Irish regionalism across the arts that included many voices. When he emerged as a poet in the 1960s and early 1970s, Heaney took to the airwaves of BBC Northern Ireland to promote his inclusive concept of regionalism with a series of broadcasts that feature crucial early poetry and some unappreciated radio plays, the subject of chapter 2. These radio plays culminate in the angry 1971 radio play *Everyman*, which bemoans Protestant bigotry in terms that anticipate his very unfavorable picture of Protestant Northern Ireland in "Act of Union."

Chapter 3 offers a series of readings of Heaney's regional exemplars, writers ranging from Patrick Kavanagh, John Hewitt, Louis MacNeice, and W. R. Rodgers in Northern Ireland, to Wordsworth, Larkin, and Hughes in England, to R. S. Thomas in Wales, to Edwin Muir, Hugh MacDiarmid, and George Mackay Brown in Scotland. Heaney's underappreciated prose essays on these regional writers confirmed him in his desire to continue dreaming of and imagining an autonomous, inclusive region of Northern Ireland even as the contemporary province descended further into violence, into "the big pain / That leaves you raw, like opened ground, again," as he puts it in the concluding lines of "Act of Union" (*N*, 44).

By then, Northern Ireland was beginning its slide into civil war, and chapter 4 shows how a negative strand of Heaney's poetry written during the 1970s focuses on images of burning and woundedness as he portrays Northern Ireland as a region of despair. His exploration of this more negative regionalism enacts a dialectic with his more positive regionalism of the period, in which he articulates a largely unifying Northern Irish dialect in certain poems from his 1972 volume *Wintering Out*, which I have analyzed elsewhere.[50] Specifically, this chapter examines Heaney's uncollected poems like "Intimidation," along with a series of poems about the Vikings, particularly those from *North*. Chapter 5 takes up the issue of race in the North of Ireland, arguing that Heaney perceived significant correspondences between Catholics and their civil rights movement in Northern Ireland and American blacks and their civil rights movement. He explored these similarities in his essays from the early 1970s, in poetry from the period, and in a critically underappreciated poem, the only sonnet among the bog poems in North, "Strange Fruit." Using archival evidence, I show

how this poem evokes the song sung by American Billie Holiday about lynchings of black men in that country and links specific deaths from lynchings to the Celtic cult of the severed head, the bog girl's head featured in the poem, the Irish Catholic martyr St. Oliver Plunkett, and the death of a Roman official at the hands of Egyptians. Chapter 5 concludes by showing the uncanny afterlife of "Strange Fruit" in Heaney's Dantesque poem "Ugolino," from *Field Work* (1979). Chapter 6 focuses on how the prose poems from *Stations* (1975) both reify images of sectarian Northern Ireland and, by virtue of their hybrid genre and some of their contents, seek to transcend them.

Chapter 7 explores Heaney's conflicted sense of regionalism in the early 1980s as part of his membership in the Field Day Theatre Company and through his writing of his Field Day pamphlet *An Open Letter*, which I show is heavily influenced by the stanza developed by Robert Burns to convey irony, James Joyce's angry broadside poems "Gas from a Burner" and "The Holy Office," and Czech poet Miroslav Holub's conception of the independent artist. Along with chapter 7, chapter 8 plumbs Heaney's increasing interest in Joyce as a regional writer, manifested both at the end of his central sequence in *Station Island* (1984) and in his seminal essay from 1989, "The Regional Forecast." Chapter 8 also articulates how Heaney moved formally from the blocky quatrains that constrain many of his bog poems from the 1970s to the more open and airy tercets that make up much of "Station Island" and "Sweeney Redivivus," the second two parts of *Station Island*. Heaney's deep interest in Dante as a regional writer led him to begin constructing his own variations on Dantean terza rima, a vernacular form that would later become his dominant stanza as he increasingly wrote of spiritual visitations and, eventually, of his own approaching death.

Chapter 9 focuses on Heaney's 1990 adaptation of Sophocles' *Philoctetes*, *The Cure at Troy*, in which he again returns to the image of the wound seen in "Act of Union" and other earlier poems to explore sectarianism in Northern Ireland through the figure of the wounded Greek hero Philoctetes, who represents the lonely and isolated unionist and nationalist communities in the North and their solitary pain. In famous stanzas Heaney then imagines a qualified "sea-change" in relations across the province by incorporating a series of intertextual references to the exemplary, independent figures of the English Wilfred Owen and the Irish W. B. Yeats into his adaptation.

Chapter 10 treats a variety of regionally oriented endeavors by Heaney beginning in the early 1990s and continuing up to his death in his translations of *Beowulf* and Robert Henryson's *Cresseid* and in crucial essays, including his study of the English poet John Clare, "Frontiers of Writing," "The Guttural Muse in a Global Age," and his approving discussion of the historian Hugh Kearney's conception of "Brittanic," not "British," history, all of which informed Heaney's devolutionary artistic project.

Chapter 11 returns to a consideration of the tercet form and charts its evolution in Heaney's poetry beginning in *Seeing Things* (1991) and continuing through *Human Chain* (2010), where it fully manifests itself as a supraregional form for poetry of departures (the deaths of old friends, Heaney's own stroke) and arrivals (Heaney's grandchildren, his own return to a life free from the temporarily debilitating effects of his stroke). This last chapter thus shows how Heaney's third strand of regionalism, which explores the spirit region in the world beyond this one, has been achieved through a particular, mediating form.

Finally, the Afterword meditates upon how book 6 of Virgil's *Aeneid*, particularly Aeneas's quest for his father Anchises, informs seminal poems from *Human Chain* where Heaney seeks the shade of his father, such as "The Riverbank Field" and "Route 110," the last of which is a summation of Heaney's career and of the trajectory of Northern Ireland during his lifetime. "Route 110" ends on the riverbank of Heaney's Ulster Elysium, where he converses with the shades of the past and welcomes his new granddaughter, Anna Rose, "talking baby talk" (*HC*, 57). With "'The Door Was Open and the House Was Dark,'" Heaney's tribute to his musician friend David Hammond, and "A Kite for Aibhín," a poem for another granddaughter styled partially after Giovanni Pascoli's "The Kite," the volume elegizes one last departed friend and imagines Heaney's own passing, respectively, even as he wishes for this granddaughter to soar.

Throughout this study, I try to recover and emphasize Heaney's considerable achievements in genres other than poetry because of the great value of his work in these other genres and their relative neglect by critics in favor of the poetry. Heaney undeniably privileged the power of lyric poetry; as Steven Matthews has recently argued, "He was (and is) an adherent of the Yeatsian belief in the primary power of the creative imagination, as manifested in the single lyric poem."[51] Such a judgment, however, reflects the tendency of many literary critics to focus on particular lyrics and downplays Heaney's sustained work in other genres. Critics who focus on the lyric poetry to the exclusion of Heaney's other artistic endeavors thus circumscribe his imaginative power by confining him to the category of "lyric poet." Moreover, my own *Poetry and Peace: Michael Longley, Seamus Heaney, and Northern Ireland* offers a sustained, chronological analysis of many major poems by Heaney up through *District and Circle* (2006), and the present study thus does not attempt to replicate such a trajectory.[52] My attention to these other genres signals what I hope will become part of a critical trend—a renewed effort to illuminate Heaney's considerable interests in other genres and to show how this work, too, has achieved considerable imaginative power that he has in turn wielded for great societal good.

When I do turn to the poems, I emphasize their formal dimensions in a way rarely done in previous studies of Heaney. Jason David Hall has recently observed that "most critical engagements with the formal dimensions of Heaney's poetry are incidental, merely means to other ends."[53] The poetry certainly does not get short shrift: my second chapter, on Heaney and BBC Northern Ireland, for example, examines crucial poems that he broadcast in the 1960s, and chapters 4, 5, 7, 8, 10, 11, and the Afterword analyze other significant poetry in the contexts of Heaney's developing theories of regionalism. But I have tried to put the poetry in play, as it were, with his much less well-known forays into the broadcast radio essay, the radio play, the prose poem, and the drama, along with his lesser- and better-known literary critical essays, to show how, even as he imagined a province that transcended the artificial boundaries established in 1920, he himself was breaking through what he conceived of as the formal boxes into which he had been put—lyric poet, Catholic, Irish writer, Northern Irish writer—and exploring other genres. For an artist long committed to overcoming political and regional boundaries, crossing such aesthetic divisions became an essential part of his fluid art.

Heaney's discussion of the bifurcation of Ireland into two distinct regions and the implication for inhabitants of the province in his essay "Frontiers of Writing" is especially relevant for my purposes and suggests that this historical reality has been adapted into a mental survival technique: "The whole population are adepts in the mystery of living in two places at one time. . . . They make do with a constructed destination, an interim place whose foundations straddle the areas of self-division, a place of resolved contradiction, beyond confusion. A place, slightly to misquote Yeats, that does not exist, a place that is but a dream."[54] This is a crucial moment in Heaney's criticism, as he transcends this binary and suggests that forward-thinking people in the province do as well. Here he is implying that everyday survival in Northern Ireland, on both a mental and a spiritual level, can be achieved through the imagining of a space—which he achieves through his own forays into multiple genres, spaces other than the poem, while not leaving the poem behind—that both recognizes and negotiates between the realities of split religious and political loyalties and transcends them. In this sense, my entire study shares Roland Barthes's contention that "a little formalism turns one away from history, but a lot brings one back to it."[55]

THE TURN TO REGIONALISM IN RECENT LITERARY THEORY

There is a critical tendency to conceive of regionalism as largely a twentieth-century creation, and indeed the last century saw the articulation of the most coherent and interesting formulations of regionalism, but R. P. Draper helpfully reminds us that regionalism emerged first in the late eighteenth century as a response to industrialism. Crucially for the argument of this study, he holds that "regional consciousness was not so much escapist as critically aware of the dangers of anonymity and desiccation attendant on the new forces; if it was characterized by a regretful recognition of the loss which inevitably accompanies change, it was also prompted to a fuller awareness of the complex reality of what was under threat and a desire to preserve its essentially human value."[56] So it is with Heaney's works, which are never escapist but are inherently liminal, Janus-faced, looking backward and forward, seeking to preserve and carry into an uncertain future the best aspects of traditional rural culture while jettisoning its regressive qualities.

Eric Falci has recently observed that "it is no surprise that British and Irish poetry after World War II is fretted with concern about place and space," and indeed, the "spatial turn" in geography and literature, to name but two fields, includes and draws on a wide range of concepts, as "the assumed immobility of place [has been] infused with the indeterminacy and activity of space."[57] As Falci goes on to argue, drawing in part on the Irish poet Patrick Kavanagh's well-known distinction between a mimetic provincialism and an original "parochialism" that attempts to "short-circuit the center-periphery model by re-centering the periphery," such a maneuver "becomes a powerful heuristic" that enables us "[to] trade the metropolitan internationalism of high modernism for a poetry of the hinterlands" and also to refigure poets like Basil Bunting and David Jones as enablingly regional.[58] Thus "The 'region' becomes not only the zone for an alternate politics, but also an imaginative space that can be made to enact temporalities and scales that differ from metropolitan rhythms. Regionality becomes a stance for poetry as well as a site for poems."[59] I share Falci's salutary characterization of regionalism and would emphasize that this study assumes an imaginative, propulsive character to the regionalism articulated and developed over the decades by Heaney.

Starting in the eighteenth century, and continuing through the nineteenth and twentieth centuries, originally because of nostalgia for the rapidly dwindling rural areas of England as their population continued to migrate to cities, the concept of regionalism was first invoked in theories about English rural literature.[60] The literary devolution that constitutes the largely untold story of twentieth-century "English" literature suggests the viability of regionalism generally and a decline in the dominance of literature and politics centered in London and even Dublin. The process of the "break-up of Britain" that Tom Nairn described in his 1977 book of the same name stemmed at least in part from nationalist movements "that exerted [an] enormous centrifugal force within British culture halfway between the end of World War II and the close of the twentieth century."[61]

This emphasis on literary devolution as a process is crucial to apprehending and articulating a thoughtful definition of regionalism that differs from stereotypical renderings of it in literary works that are static and hearken back to a nostalgic age. For example, in his introduction to his *Regions of the Imagination: The Development of British Rural Fiction*, W. J. Keith points out that "a common complaint against the regional novel ... is that it tries to ignore time and change, initiating what Raymond Williams has called 'a sustaining flight to the edges of the island, to Cornwall or to

Cumberland,' an escapist retreat to the backwaters where the illusion of a stable regional world could still be kept up."[62] Certainly, as Keith allows, using Thomas Hardy as his test case, there are early novels—*Under the Greenwood Tree* and *Far from the Madding Crowd*—that express this sort of nostalgia, but as he argues, "Hardy's main concern in his Wessex novels is change (generally decline) in the agricultural world," and he concludes, "It is not unreasonable to assert that the best regional novels are concerned not with a static rural society but with a countryside in process."[63]

Yet Raymond Williams's objection against regionalism as ahistorical persists in some contemporary theorizing about it. For example, Roberto M. Dainotto, in his *Place in Literature: Regions, Cultures, Communities* (2000), argues that "regionalism remains primarily the metaphor of a desire for an original and free literariness that has survived the instrumental impositions of nationalism and politics alike. 'Regional' is a pastoral sensibility untouched by the evils of history and sheltered from the latter within the 'boundaries of some sort' of place. To put it bluntly, regionalism is the figure of an otherness that is, essentially, otherness from, and against, history."[64] But invoking the pastoral form to denigrate regionalism is itself a problematic move because, as Bernard O'Donoghue has pointed out, "the pastoral itself was from its origins a contested form."[65] In perhaps the best discussion of Heaney and the pastoral form, Henry Hart argues that "Heaney's pastoral dialectic moves from a childhood Eden of repressed awareness to its antithesis, a self-conscious, narcissistic relishing of antipastoral slime and desolation, and finally to a candid appraisal of 'things as they are' beyond the pasture's walls."[66] Heaney's mixed attitude toward the pastoral suggests while it has been an important mode for him, its limitations ensured that the more elastic concept of the region would be the unifying force in his work.

Heaney has addressed the pastoral mode explicitly in his 1975 review "In the Country of Convention: English Pastoral Verse"; implicitly in both his and Ted Hughes's approach to including vernacular poetry in their 1982 anthology *The Rattle Bag* and in his 1990 review "The Vulgar Muse"; and in his 2002 Royal Irish Academy lecture "Eclogues *in Extremis*: On the Staying Power of Pastoral." This early review of John Barrell and John Bull's edited volume, *The Penguin Book of English Pastoral Verse*, distinguishes pastoral poetry in England from the concept of the region. Heaney calls it "a packed and well-groomed book, not so much a region to wander in as an estate to be guided through."[67] Thus contrasting the collection with his approving description of Keats's notion of "Endymion" as a "region to wander in" given above, he faults the editors for pruning the "informing, influencing voices" of Theocritus, Virgil, Horace, Mantuan, and Marot in translation and thus beginning "in the middle of things English, with Barnabe Googe, Sidney, Spenser, Raleigh [*sic*], and Drayton."[68] By the conclusion of his review, Heaney reclaims John Clare as a regional, not a pastoral, writer, arguing that "it was the unique achievement of John Clare to make vocal *the regional and particular*, to achieve a buoyant and authentic lyric utterance at the meeting-point between social realism and conventional romanticism."[69] At first seeming to admit that "one almost agrees with the editors' brisk dismissal of its further possibilities," Heaney points out the "diminution of force in the nineteenth century" of the pastoral, yet closes by making a case for including a series of twentieth-century writers such as Edward Thomas, Edwin Muir, Hugh MacDiarmid, A. E. Housman, David Jones, John Synge, Patrick Kavanagh, and John Montague. Mischievously, he asks, "Or are these latter works held at bay in the term 'frontier pastoral'?"[70] By including such a number of exemplary writers he would often call "regional" in the most positive sense of that word, Heaney is questioning the continued value of employing a term like *pastoral*, since it has not kept step with the energies and enabling peripheral position of these writers working beyond the pale of the university and the more genteel English pastoral tradition.

Nor has it usually employed the type of local language that Heaney has long valorized and that he praises often in his criticism, and implicitly so in a project like his and Hughes's anthology *The Rattle Bag*. Steven Matthews has held that the editors' approach to this collection of rejecting arrangement by theme or chronology in favor of an alphabetical list of single lyric poems "enables Heaney and Hughes to put forward an unpredictable range of the radical vernacular energies of English-language poetry, from folk songs, to versions of Anglo-Saxon done by Heaney, to Shakespeare, Wordsworth, John Clare, Hopkins, Lawrence, Yeats, and translations from the contemporary poets from Eastern Europe favored by Hughes and by Heaney in his turn."[71] Indeed, Heaney has recalled that in assembling the volume he and Hughes "knew that the humblest and most unlikely material could lie behind the officially sanctioned selections in the prescribed texts and we were therefore prepared, as anthologists, to lie down with Yeats, where all the ladders start, in the old rag-and-bone shop of the heart—that is to say, in the unofficial as well as the official cultural deposits."[72]

Even the title of *The Rattle Bag* sonically suggests a cacophonous assemblage that is loose, not ordered, connoting vibrant artistic energies found in regional poetry, energies that perhaps Heaney anyway may have slyly intended to offset the considerable passions then still being invested into sectarian activities in Northern Ireland. Hughes recommended that the anthology take its name from "a strange roguish poem translated from the Welsh of Dafydd ap Gwilym," a poem about "an instrument that sounds more like an implement, a raucous, distracting, shake, rattle-and-roll affair that disturbs the poet and his lover while they lie together in the greenwood.... We were wanting to serve notice that the anthology was a wake-up call, an attempt to bring poetry and younger people to their senses."[73] But there is a further hint of the type of regionalism Heaney favored, inclusive and forward-looking, in the use of "rattle," given that three years earlier he had collected in *Field Work* an elegy, entitled "A Postcard from North Antrim: In Memory of Sean Armstrong," that employs the present participle of that verb as a term of praise. Robert Sean Armstrong was a Protestant social worker who "worked for Voluntary Services International and organized cross-community children's parties and holidays"; he was shot by a member of the Ulster Defense Association/Ulster Freedom Fighters, a paramilitary group, on June 30, 1973.[74] In "A Postcard from North Antrim," Heaney characterizes Armstrong's voice as "independent, *rattling*, nontranscendent / Ulster—old decency" (*FW*, 20; my emphasis). Given Armstrong's efforts to bring children from Protestant and Catholic communities into contact and Heaney's praise of him here with such phrases, the title of *The Rattle Bag*, along with its strategy and contents, may obliquely recall the ecumenical Armstrong and implicitly use his example as a model for emphasizing vernacular poetry over against "official" English language and literature even while putting those bodies of work into conversation with each other.

A typical example of Heaney's privileging of this kind of unofficial, vernacular language occurs in his later review of Tom Paulin's *The Faber Book of Vernacular Verse*. He remarks there that "vernacular" includes the oral and anonymous verse of different regional and ethnic communities, and extends to dialect, folk song, blues talk and all kinds of linguistic frolics and relics. Graffiti, sampler rhymes, street cries, dandling rhymes, weather saws and sea chanties are all here, jostling for position with far more canonical matter: alliterative Langland, turbulent Shakespeare, Whitman in spate and the Bible in Scots. Add to this a host of other poets you'd expect (Barnes, Burns, Clare, Hardy, MacDiarmid and Harrison) . . . and you have one of the best anthologies in years, a big, feisty gathering.[75]

Heaney's list of authors here almost all constitute examples of regional poets he has turned to time and again in his criticism and poetry, and he clearly values the barbaric yawp expressed in their work as both a welcome addition to the received canon and a riposte to, quoting Paulin, "the often censoring effects of standard diction and accent."[76] Heaney then muses that "most of us . . . are children of 'the rhubarbarians,' Tony Harrison's name for the mob who were assigned the foggy gutturals of rhubarb, rhubarb as their only mode of self-expression. For generations, the idiom of this mob was treated not so much as human language as a typesetter's headache."[77] He goes on to remark that when such writers' works are finally written down rather than merely lingering on the tongues of their speakers, "Subcultural energy gets raised to cultural power, and the whole world is the better for it. As the recalcitrant enters the domain of the received, there is always a salutary shock of recognition. I remember, for example, my first encounter with the writings of Patrick Kavanagh and Brendan Behan every bit as clearly as hearing the news of Kennedy's assassination."[78] Such statements accord with Heaney's lifelong affirmation of regional voices— whether they be rural or urban. Too often, pastoral with its rigid conventions elides such voices and eviscerates the living words of the English language that he so values.

In "Eclogues *in Extremis*," Heaney continues to interrogate the pastoral convention, noting that because it "usually involves a self-consciously literary performance . . . it becomes vulnerable to accusations of artificiality"; thus he raises the question of "how successfully the mode has continued to account for itself."[79] Taking his contemporary Michael Longley's poem "The Beech Tree" as his first example, Heaney finds that in part through its allusions "to the first poem in Virgil's *Eclogues* and the last one in his *Georgics*," Longley's poem concentrates on personal and natural worlds, rejecting the violent recent history of Northern Ireland: "For decades it was the great outdoors of life in Northern Ireland that clamored for attention, asking that its unremitting violence be treated in terms dictated by the old sectarian and ideological divisions, but Longley on the whole resisted these expectations and put his faith in images of the peaceable kingdom of flora and fauna. So when he sets his beech tree deliberately in line with the ones in poems by the young Virgil, he is also putting his faith in the staying power of pastoral as a mode."[80] "What keeps a literary kind viable," Heaney quickly adds, "is its ability to measure up to the challenges offered by new historical circumstances, and pastoral has been confronted with this challenge from very early on."[81] Longley's reclamation of the pastoral mode has offered an important countervailing trajectory of the personal and the intimate to the impersonal and large-scale acts of atrocity in Northern Ireland.[82] Heaney, on the other hand, while admitting "the staying power of pastoral as a mode," has, with some few exceptions such as "Virgil: Eclogue IX" and "Glanmore Eclogue" from *Electric Light* (2001), chosen to retain pastoral's emphasis on the local yet largely jettison its artificial conventions such as its sometimes stilted language, its acknowledgment of earlier practitioners, and its figures of sheep and shepherds.

The central poem under consideration in "Eclogues *in Extremis*" is Czesław Miłosz's "The World," the title and thrust of which offer an outline of Heaney's own abiding interest in the region. Although Heaney calls the poem "definitely a version of pastoral, since it is in a strict sense idyllic," he also describes it as extending beyond the pastoral in its treatment of place, citing the poem's fourth stanza:[83]

> Now, past the curve, you can see the red roof:
> Father leans on his hoe in the front garden,
> Then bends down to touch a half-opened leaf;
> From his tilled patch he can see the whole region.[84]

The last line of this stanza, opening out from the local to the region, suggests, in its outward gaze, something very close to Heaney's concept of the region—anchored yet panoramic. Elsewhere, perhaps thinking of "The

World," Heaney has argued that Miłosz demonstrates a dual epistemology: "He manages to combine two ways of knowing. . . . One is through the long perspective, whether through history or philosophy, and the other is through the intimate grasp of the particular detail. Too much of the long perspective leaves us out of touch with the usual life, too much of the nose-to-the-ground limits and lessens our vision."[85] The region, epitomized by Heaney's description of Miłosz's vision, thus gives both "the intimate grasp of the particular detail" and "the long perspective."[86] Opting for a more expansive range of form and content in his regionally driven poetry than the pastoral can give, Heaney has employed the region as an expansive concept that has accommodated both the profound changes in Northern Irish culture, politics, and history and his own evolving poetry.

While Sidney Burris, in his fine study *The Poetry of Resistance: Seamus Heaney and the Pastoral Tradition*, confines himself to "chart[ing] Heaney's definition and portrayal of the rural Catholic community in Northern Ireland" in its political and historical context—and that only through Heaney's 1987 volume, *The Haw Lantern*—the present study articulates concepts of the region before his career began and throughout that career. Heaney's use of pastoralism and antipastoralism has been well covered in the criticism, and such finally binary usage is subsumed into his much more important emphasis on the region, a term with dynamic meaning that has driven much of his poetic and critical agenda, as we will see.[87] I thus both attend to rural Northern Irish culture's particularity and put that region into conversation, as it were, with regions throughout the world and even beyond—for instance, through Heaney's attention to the "spirit region."

To return briefly to Roberto Dainotto's "argument" against regionalism above: it represents an astonishing moment in a long screed against regionalism where the concept is abstracted and essentialized and seemingly put in its place for having the effrontery to survive the twentieth century in all its supposed homogeneity. Undoubtedly, the lingering impact on European consciousness of the German emphasis on regionalism in the 1920s and 1930s that led to the rise of the fascist dictators Hitler and Mussolini drives his criticism, but as Peter Nicolaisen has shown, "What appealed to the National Socialists was not the idea of regionalism as such—in fact, they quickly managed to eradicate most regional differences existing in Germany—but the strong racist element present in most German regionalist writing of the early twentieth century."[88] Furthermore, as Nicolaisen readily admits, "Most of the German agrarians . . . were in many ways deeply a-historical and called forth a mythic 'Germanic' past which lacked any kind of historical grounding."[89] The agrarian/regionalist movement in the American South that culminated perhaps in the publication of *I'll Take My Stand*, a collection of agrarian writings by the "Twelve Southerners" in 1930, was certainly more historically informed than German agrarianism but also was marred by most of its adherents' racist leanings. The agrarians' regionalist focus on the American South did, however, admit international influences. And the recent turn away from the nation-state and toward a more inclusive regionalism such as that articulated by Falci above surely is salutary. For example, can Dainotto really believe that even critical regionalism, a movement pioneered by the architectural historian Kenneth Frampton, envisages "the inside of a region . . . as a homogenous whole—one that is not divided within. The dialectic of history, we are told, annihilates 'marginal, subaltern,' powerless cultures. Regionalism, instead, annihilates history. What is left for us to contemplate is only idyllic regions and their perfect communities"?[90]

Clearly, as Frampton articulates in his important essay "Towards a Critical Regionalism," critical regionalism is self-conscious and flexible in its relationship to local places and attentive to history: "The fundamental strategy of Critical Regionalism is to mediate the impact of universal civilization with elements derived indirectly from the peculiarities of a particular place. . . . Critical Regionalism depends upon maintaining a high level of critical self-consciousness. It may find its governing inspiration in such things as the range and quality of the local light, or in a tectonic derived from a peculiar structural mode, or in the topography of a given site."[91] Furthermore, Frampton argues that "it is necessary . . . to distinguish between Critical Regionalism and simple-minded attempts to revive the hypothetical forms of a lost vernacular" because such attempts could lead us to "confuse the resistant capacity of a critical practice with the demagogic tendencies of Populism."[92] Thus Frampton's critical regionalism, properly understood, embraces the particular and veers away from the sort of abstraction that could lead to populism. Although I can find no evidence for Seamus Heaney's having read Frampton, his own evolving and devolving concept of regionalism certainly shares the "critical self-consciousness" of critical regionalism and nimbly responds to the inspiration evoked by particular places even as it refuses to simply be anchored in one bounded place.[93] Cheryl Herr, one of the few critics to employ Frampton's critical regionalism in relationship to literature, argues in her fine study of Ireland and the American Midwest that "critical regionalism marks less a space-and-place opposition than one that allows for understanding places seeking some form of relation beyond that woven by capital.... The key to a critical regionalist methodology for cultural studies is the relationality of regionalism."[94] Heaney's fluid sense of the region is inherently relational—both internally, as it seeks rapprochement between Catholics and Protestants in Northern Ireland, and externally, as it seeks connection between the region of the North and other regions.

To be sure, as Kevin Whelan has pointed out in his 1992 essay "The Bases of Regionalism," "The very idea of regionalism, with its emphasis on inherited rather than acquired identities[,] force-feeds the atavistic appetites of tradition.... In Burke's formulation, the region represents the integrity of traditional society and its local loyalties, and it can be set against abstract universalizing claims, which violate the customary affections and rooted relations which make society adhesive and stable."[95] Interestingly, however, such a formulation implicitly rebukes Dainotto's own abstraction of regionalism by virtue of its appeal to "local loyalties" and specificities. But the whiff of Burkeanism has continued to emanate from concepts of regionalism until our recent turn toward space and postmodernism's rejection of master narratives. As Whelan puts it, regionalism has thrived lately because of "post-modernism's concern to disperse and decentralize power, its willingness to conjugate past and present, its emphasis on spatial as much as temporal analysis."[96]

The regional literature that Heaney and his contemporaries and earlier Northern Irish writers created can be placed alongside that developing in Scotland, Wales, and parts of England outside the home counties, such as northern England. Draper has discussed how, during the course of the twentieth century, "if London remained at the heart of publishing and reviewing, places like Liverpool, Manchester, Newcastle and Hull became much more the regional capitals of a still urban, but no longer London-based literary activity. Many of the best English poets came from the regions and maintained a non-metropolitan, or even anti-metropolitan outlook."[97] Even beyond England, however, regionalism flourished in Scotland, Wales, and Northern Ireland. As Robert Crawford has shown in *Devolving English Literature*, until fairly recently the term *English literature* has not been questioned, and this has led to a totalizing of "all the constituents of English Literature . . . as both traditional literary history and post-structuralist criticism have done all too often."[98] When such an abstraction is practiced, "we perform an act of naïve cultural imperialism, acting as if books grew not out of particular conditions in Nottingham, Dublin, St. Lucia, or Salem, Massachusetts, but out of the bland uniformity of airport departure lounges."[99] While Crawford's book deals mostly with the rise of Scottish literature (although he does write engagingly and incisively of Heaney as a regional writer in the best sense of the term), much work remains to be done on the rise of Northern Irish literature. We can easily add Belfast to Draper's catalog of regional literary activity in the United Kingdom, for example, although it is an anomaly, geographically detached from the British mainland and profoundly bicultural in a way that no other major British city is, including Glasgow.

Sean O'Brien remarks in his introduction to his 1998 collection *The Firebox: Poetry in Britain and Ireland after 1945* that "progress towards devolution in each of the peripheral nations of the United Kingdom had contributed to a 'cultural assurance' for their poets, and to a collective voice and identity, which might justly have been envied by their English neighbours."[100] We might quibble with O'Brien's too-easy assumption that political devolution preceded literary devolution—in fact literary and cultural devolution often antedated and laid important groundwork for political devolution—but clearly, a marked "cultural assurance" is present in regional poets writing after 1945 such as Heaney.

IRISH/NORTHERN IRISH REGIONALISM

In Ireland, the historical geography practiced by both E. Estyn Evans at Queen's University and Tom Jones Hughes at University College, Dublin, in the mid- to latter part of the twentieth century helped bring French concepts of regionalism into Ireland, as Whelan notes: "Under the tutelage of Evans and Jones Hughes, landscape became a Braille over whose surface the geographical mind passed the tips of its understanding and sympathy to arrive at a reading of what lay behind the landscape. Such perspectives succeeded in revealing a rich mosaic of regional diversity, even in the relatively confined space of a small island."[101]

Regionalism across Ireland/Northern Ireland is thus a thoroughly modern, not Burkean notion, which nonetheless has deep roots in the past and has gradually accrued a series of articulate theorists such as Evans and Whelan and John Wilson Foster, upon whom this study draws. Part of the continuing appeal of regionalism may lie in its Janus-faced character, looking back and drawing upon layers of linguistic, geographic, and historical strata, even while looking forward along the general political, cultural, and literary trajectory toward decentralization. The mind that imagines and re-creates the past is well conditioned for reimagining the future, whether it be in a Europe of the regions that forms the framework of Whelan's argument or a literature of the regions that forms the basis of Seamus Heaney's own regionalism.

What if there were a region whose writers registered eruptions of violence; delineated fault lines of religious affiliation; evoked centuries of history rather than annihilating it? What if there were a heterogeneous region, nearly evenly divided between a so-called "settler" group (whose descendants have now been there some five hundred years) that looked east for its identity and a native population that looked south for its identity? What if such a region—or at least its intellectuals—slowly turned inward and found commonalities between these populations that might bind rather than divide them? What if such a region—caught between two nation-states and essentially homeless—oscillated among multiple shades of political, cultural, and religious identities? The region exists, has long existed, but since 1920 only in a truncated, artificial form called Northern Ireland.

The imaginative efforts of a series of Northern Irish writers beginning in the early twentieth century have led to the establishment of a regional, bicultural, and finally transcultural literature that has devolved aesthetically, albeit as a special case, from British and Irish literature in such a way as to anticipate and imagine a new region of Northern Ireland. In ways that are only just now beginning to be realized, the best writers from Philip Hobsbaum's Belfast Group (1963–66), such as Seamus Heaney, Michael Longley, Stewart Parker, and Bernard MacLaverty, have articulated a regional literature that interacts fruitfully with regional literatures all over the British and Irish archipelago, including Scottish, Welsh, and regional English writing, and with regional writers from America such as Robert Frost.

As John Wilson Foster has argued in "Radical Regionalism," a seminal article for understanding Northern Irish culture, politics, and literature,

> In face of the forces of deregionalization, can we persist in trying to imagine Ulster? The *ideal* uses of regionality are obvious. In our political culture it would provide Catholic and Protestant Northerners with a common allegiance. It would provide Protestants with a buffer between them and the Republic while satisfying their desire for Irishness and (at least semi-) autonomy. It would locate Catholic (and indeed Protestant) loyalty centrally in Ulster, not in England; the governmental centrality of England is as great an imposition on nationalists as the centrality of the Republic would be to unionists. In our general culture it would resist successfully the unacceptable international features of society while admitting and absorbing the desirable features. Unlike, say, Patrick Kavanagh's parochialism, it would be no cloistered virtue but traffic with the wide world, for some aspects of international and American culture are, and will be, liberating for corners of the globe like this one.[102]

I cite Foster at such length here because there is so much salutary about what he says. His persistence, moreover, in trying to continue imagining an ideal Ulster in 1989, as the conflict in Northern Ireland dragged on, is exemplary. Heaney's "The Regional Forecast," delivered to the first International Conference on the Literature of Region and Nation at the University of Aberdeen in August 1986, but not published till 1989, calls for "the writer" to "re-envisage the region as the original point," but why?[103] Why would Heaney, who would win the Nobel Prize for Literature less than a decade after this essay was delivered to a conference on regionalism, and who is thought, with some few exceptions, to have left the region far behind, still emphasize it—and in such striking, even urgent language— in 1986? And how can regionalism, sometimes thought to be a benighted and exclusivist term (*pace* Dainotto and David Lloyd), possibly be expansive and "traffic with the wide world," as Foster so aptly puts it?[104] Surely such a regionalism *would* be an imagined, even impossible condition? But maybe not.

In part because of the recent conflict, Northern Irish regionalism and writing have had an outsized impact on "English literature" in proportion to the province's tiny size (roughly 1.8 million inhabitants). As evidence of the influence of Northern Irish culture upon English culture, Neil Corcoran argues in *English Poetry since 1940* that the Northern Irish Troubles have been "the single most influential factor on the subsequent history... of contemporary 'English' poetry."[105] Far from being provincial, Northern Irish literature is actually regional in an expansive sense of the term, astonishingly plural and cosmopolitan in ways that far surpass some Irish and English literature. Only time will tell if the province will be incorporated into the Republic of Ireland, but for now its literature exists in a fragile and fascinating moment, redolent with hope for its future.

In one of the most searching and comprehensive explorations of regionalism in Ireland, Kevin Whelan has both anticipated objections to the current project and suggested how a reinvigorated regionalism is actually salutary politically, culturally, and, by extension, ecologically:

> Any argument for conservation of landscape and of the rural communities which sustain them always runs the risk of being a retreat into provincialism, or a conservative clarion-call to the faded nationalist pieties of hearth and home, blood and land. However, an alternative argument might seek to support regional distinctiveness which, in European terms, is frequently encoded in landscape. Stripped of meta-narrative and divested of Herderian melodrama, regional cultures are a powerful vernacular force. The valency of the vernacular derives from its salubrious democratic tendency. The stress on the region is potentially a stress on multi-culturalism. And diversity in culture may be just as necessary and healthy as diversity in ecology.[106]

Whelan's argument, based in part on postmodernism's embrace of decentralization, is made in the context of Ireland's role within the European Community in the early 1990s. In the course of his seminal essay, he discusses how various regions can be formed in particular areas of Ireland, analyzing, for example, four traditional regions of fiddling within southwestern County Donegal alone.

Whelan's description of the fiddling throughout this overall area is crucial to one element of this project's thesis—how Seamus Heaney's poetry performs and celebrates both the very existence of his home region of Northern Ireland, warts and all. "That music," Whelan suggests, "evolving out of the local environment and spontaneously transferred between generations, connected the community to its own place and its own history, and became then, as with any great art form, a celebration of the community's existence."[107] This type of music seems a particularly apt analogy for Heaney's poetry, which is grounded in a recognizable region of Northern Ireland, has evolved and fluctuated over time, shows how his fictional communities and their real-life counterparts are anchored in particular places and histories, and ultimately celebrates the survival of such communities over the generations, even as it often mourns their imminent demise. Such a regionalism is, then, intensely celebratory and performative of place as an event, even as it elegiacally records its passing and transformation.

Heaney's region of Ulster has historically had a tremendous amount of integrity because of its geography. E. Estyn Evans has noted that the northern part of Ireland historically "tended to form a distinct cultural region or group of regions, behind its frontier belt of drumlins," and that this relative geographic and cultural isolation and integrity gives the lie to "the idealistic model of a nationally united island" that "had existed from time immemorial."[108] Evans sees the "personality of Ulster" as "a strong regional variant, in habitat, heritage, and history," and points out that while often the term *the Two Irelands* signifies the traditionally wealthier East and poorer West, "the differences of outlook between north and south have been the most critical."[109]

Whelan has suggested that many smaller regions in Ireland than the large regions, or the traditional four provinces, "survive in popular consciousness although they are not administrative units.... Such regions have a fascination because they are organically derived, with a durable sense of identity based on the interaction between a human culture and an environment over time. They obviously also offer a humane and comfortable sense of scale and attachment, which is not imposed from without but arises from within a community's own sense of a shared identity."[110] Although regions are often thought to be rural only, they certainly can be composed of cities or industrialized areas, especially in literature: W. J. Keith argues, for example, that Arnold Bennett's Five Towns and D. H. Lawrence's Eastover/mining countryside are regions in their own right.[111]

Evans, whose *The Personality of Ireland* found its first audience as a series of lectures given at Queen's University, Belfast, in the early 1970s as the Troubles were flaring fiercely, argues that the "two communities in the north, however deeply divided by religion, share an outlook on life which is different from that prevailing in the south and which bears the stamp of a common heritage."[112] He goes on to audaciously claim that "they are alike in their intransigence. The epigrammatic concision of Ulster speech, most evident in the negative brevity of the notorious wall slogans, has been described as an essentially Gaelic quality. Dialectal expressions are direct, earnest, decisive and often cynical. . . . Both communities shared the benefits of what was known as the Ulster Custom, tenant right, and its bellicose spirit has outlived farm ownership."[113] Heaney, however, has pointed out the problems with conceiving of the contemporary province of Northern Ireland as "Ulster": "Ulster shrinks to a six-county region, its hero is not Cuchulainn but Carson, and its Great O'Neill not a rebellious chieftain from sixteenth-century Tyrone but a Unionist guards officer from Co. Antrim."[114] His pejorative reading of *Ulster* as signifying how Protestant loyalists and some unionists have articulated an exclusive version of Ulster regionalism coterminous with the modern statelet of Northern Ireland that excludes Catholics over against the ancient, more inclusive region of Ulster suggests the problems inherent with using the term in any discussion of the regionalism of the northern part of Ireland. Although I occasionally use the term *Ulster* in this study, I more often refer to *the North of Ireland* to signify this older, nine-county region or *Northern Ireland* to signify the political province that was established in 1920.

Perhaps no commentator writing on the special problem of Northern Ireland as a region both continuous with certain characteristics of the traditional Irish province of Ulster and discontinuous with that region has offered more insight on the issue than John Wilson Foster. In "Radical Regionalism," Foster shows the particular problems inherent in Northern

Irish regionalism as conditioned by the existence of the Northern Irish state. These problems have been perhaps lessened by the power-sharing agreement in Northern Ireland that has been operating since 2007, but rehearsing them is necessary for articulating and understanding Heaney's particular artistic attempts to speak to such a peculiar region. As Foster asks,

> Is a mutually acknowledged regional culture in Ulster possible? Two conditions are required. The first is that the Ulster identity be distinct from all other cultures in the world. But what might a regional culture of the future look like? How will the local express itself, if not only through inferior versions of international or American prototypes? Whereas international culture will increasingly render Catholic and Protestant similar, it won't render them distinctive in their mutuality. I want to set these questions aside for another occasion and turn instead to the implications and difficulties of the second condition, that Catholic and Protestant feel, equally, *of* Ulster.[115]

One major way in which Catholics in the North were made to feel "of Ulster," in Foster's phrase above, was through the formation of the Social Democratic Labour Party, or SDLP, in the 1960s. Michael Parker, whose work not only on Heaney but also on Northern Irish literature from the mid-1950s through the mid-2000s admirably blends literary and cultural/historical analysis, has pointed out that the SDLP, the more moderate alternative in Northern Irish nationalist politics to the harder-edged Sinn Fein party, embraced and articulated a common heritage among the two dominant communities in the province. For example, the SDLP's constitution includes wording in paragraph 6a that "pledges the new party to 'the promotion of culture and the arts with special responsibility to cherish and develop all aspects of our native culture.'"[116] Parker rightly claims that "the inclusion of this clause attests to the growing vibrancy and confidence in northern cultural life over the previous decade, and acknowledges the crucial role cultural regeneration might in future perform within a new Ireland."[117] As he further argues, the phrase "our native culture" by virtue of its use of "first person plural, the singular noun, and ambiguous adjective collectively suggest[s] that both traditions share in a heritage which predates partition."[118] Since the SDLP's ultimate agenda was a united

Ireland, Parker believes that its appeal to a transcendent northern heritage conflicted with "the regionalist thinking promulgated by government-funded institutions like the Arts Council of Northern Ireland and BBC Northern Ireland, and within the pages of such new literary journals as *The Honest Ulsterman*."[119] But certainly Heaney, himself an SDLP supporter, hoped his embrace of such venues as BBC Northern Ireland would enable him to promote a regionalist heritage for inhabitants of the North of Ireland, perhaps eventually leading to a united Ireland. Heaney thus drew both on the unifying rhetoric of the SDLP (he often praised its best-known leader, John Hume) and on the burgeoning tradition of Ulster regionalism that had been promoted for some decades in the province by a series of open-minded writers in literary journals and anthologies.

It is worth citing Parker's claim about the supposedly brief life and death of Ulster regionalism. He notes that

> while keen to maintain and voice the distinctiveness of their locale, exponents of 1960s regionalism were also committed to pluralism, inclusivity and reconciliation, values consonant with ecumenism in the religious sphere and O'Neillite rhetoric in the political sphere. They imagined—indeed continue to imagine—a higher, collective, cultural space, a fictive "common ground" where divisions might be accommodated and neutralized within existing constitutional structures. Once Stormont, backed by the British government, resorted to increasingly repressive, desperate measures to stem the violence, the SDLP—along with the vast majority of people from the nationalist tradition, including its foremost writers—withheld consent from those structures, and distanced themselves from [the] regionalist enterprise.[120]

I quote this passage at such length both to be fair to Parker and to show how he inadvertently shows exactly what I have just claimed about Heaney: that the SDLP's pursuit of a local agenda and Ulster regionalism actually had much in common, even if some proponents of Ulster regionalism may have desired the continued union with Britain, and that Heaney had both a regional political model and a regional literary model for a time in the 1960s. Moreover, his final claim here about the "foremost" nationalist "writers" distancing "themselves from regionalist enterprise" after the

Stormont regime's repressive attempts to stop the violence in the province founders on the evidence: John Montague's *The Rough Field*, a seminal volume of poetry for Heaney and other northern writers, was published in 1972, the year Stormont collapsed, and Heaney himself, easily the foremost nationalist writer in the North, continued to espouse versions of Ulster regionalism for virtually the rest of his career. But Parker's description of Ulster regionalism bespeaks the general attitude toward it, with a few significant exceptions, when it is addressed at all, in Irish Studies: it flowered in the 1960s—he calls it "1960s regionalism"—and quickly withered soon after the outbreak of the Troubles. But variants of Ulster regionalism—the vast majority of them the pluralistic, ecumenical kind—blossomed throughout the years leading up to and after partition, even though their most eloquent advocate, Heaney, did not appear on the scene until the 1960s.

Regionalism itself as artistically imagined by John Hewitt, among earlier Northern Irish writers, certainly prepared the way for Heaney's own work in this regard. Peter McDonald argues that Heaney's career, along with those of Michael Longley and Derek Mahon, "drew real benefits from the sense of local worth and literary legitimacy which Regionalism (and Hewitt in particular) promoted: when the 'Ulster Renaissance' made itself apparent at the end of the 1960s, it was on ground which Ulster Regionalism had prepared."[121] At the same time, Heaney's sense of the region went far beyond that of Hewitt, which, as McDonald admits, failed at the level of politics: "The attempt to make literary capital out of an insistence that the writer 'must be a rooted man' at the very least complicated, and perhaps fatally compromised, any espousal of liberalism, since it relied on the kind of allegiance which, in Northern Ireland, is inevitably and unavoidably divisive in political terms. 'Ulster,' that is, means different things to a Protestant and to a Catholic in Northern Ireland."[122] Hewitt's geographically confined regionalism, moreover, seems somewhat staid in comparison to the imagined communities composing Heaney's nearly limitless concept of regionalism.

Literary and cultural critics have weighed in on the debate over Northern Irish regionalism, many of them resorting to political terms instead of imaginative or literary ones. For example, Foster discusses a host of possibilities for Northern Irish regionalism, including "a power-sharing devolved administration," "a regional parliament for Northern Ireland within a federal Ireland," and a "federal kingdom of England, Scotland, Wales and Northern Ireland."[123] To his credit, as Foster admits, this second option was Hewitt's second choice behind devolution proper.[124] There is also the possibility, Foster notes, of developing the present situation: "For some time, Northern Ireland has been a region of the European Community."[125] The proposal submitted in 1994 by Richard Kearney and Robin Wilson to the Opsahl Commission details the many benefits of the province's fuller involvement as a European political region in this regard.[126]

As evidence of the province's uniqueness as a region, a characteristic it must have to be separate from "all other regional cultures in the world," Foster argues that "Ulster is distinguished by its inability to decide whether it is primarily a region of Ireland or a region of Britain. It is of course both, a fact that has yet to assume unique cultural form." Moreover, he holds that "for a long time the Ulster people have suffered the twin psychological colonialisms of Irish nationalism and British nationality that have falsified their consciousness and diverted them from the true task of self-realization. . . . No final peace can settle on Ulster until these ideas, which I believe most Ulster people feel to be untrue, are cast off."[127] At the same time, by attempting to jettison the influence of the Irish and the British states on the region, Foster runs the risk of defending a region of nothing. For if the province is not both British and Irish, what is it? "Ulster" has a history marked by what he terms those "twin psychological colonialisms," and that seems both its peril and its promise.

Perhaps a more plausible imagined alternative to the often political versions of Northern Irish regionalism that Foster sketched in 1989 is the 2002 proposal by Hilary Mantel, herself a regional writer from northern England: "The greatest hope of minorities, I think, is that they can find a refuge in an imagined Europe of the regions: not in a superstate, a Europe created on the model of past nation states, but within a Europe of diversity in which plural identities can flourish. . . . Meanwhile I think it is the role of writers and artists to make sure that the idea of a nation is not regressive, not repressive, not injurious to the freedom of others."[128] Northern Irish writers, not wed to either the British or the Irish state, and thus conditioned to being stateless but not regionless, are particularly well placed to articulate "an imagined Europe of the regions" in which their province might flourish.[129] Such a possibility is with us now. Edna Longley's assessment anticipates Mantel's argument: "Northern Ireland is potentially a diversified European region where you can live in three places at once (Ireland/Britain/'Ulster')—a liberating condition—not a place that fails to be two other places."[130]

Given the development of regionalism as a valid and unifying cultural and literary concept in Northern Ireland, Heaney employed subtle language to generate often politically unanticipated solidarities. He clearly believed in the efficacy of poetry and imaginative literature. To wit, writing in 1972, during one of the worst years of the Troubles, he stated unequivocally, "Finally I disagree that 'poetry makes nothing happen.' It can eventually make new feelings, or feelings about feelings, happen, and anybody can see that in this country for a long time to come a refinement of feelings will be more urgent than a re-framing of policies or of constitutions."[131]

Even as Heaney's regionalism expanded, his clear preference for a particular poetic form contracted. Understanding his actual and imagined Northern Ireland and the third strand of his regionalism—the spirit world—enables a particularly nuanced reading of his wintry yet magnificent volume *Human Chain* and the emergence of the tercet as his final poetic home. To return to Seamus Deane's contention that "the exploration of a central, if forbidding, feature of the community's experience" during the years of the Troubles has been "an essential homelessness," Heaney's last poetry reveals that he had settled the vexed question of homelessness occasioned by his divided cultural heritage and that he dwelled happily in his chosen regional form, the airy yet grounded tercet that he adapted from Dante's terza rima.[132] Such a dwelling place enabled him to figuratively straddle the boundary of the living and the dead, to connect the past and the present of Northern Ireland, and to explore the spirit region.

Chapter One

THE DEVELOPMENT OF NORTHERN IRISH REGIONALISM

As John Wilson Foster has recently observed, "Many college students of Irish Literature, clamoring to write their essays on Seamus Heaney and 'the North,' apparently believe that Northern Irish literature began *ab ovo* with the publication of *Death of a Naturalist* in 1966.... But then, only recently (say in the past quarter-century) did serious criticism discover that there were Irish writers of the Revival other than Yeats, Synge, O'Casey, and Joyce who merited extended discussion, so the understandable small tyranny unwittingly exerted by the Major Figure may also be in play."[1] Notwithstanding the outstanding scholarship by Foster himself and other critics who place Heaney in the proper context of Northern Irish literature and culture, there are many examples of Heaney criticism that, besides a perfunctory invocation of Kavanagh or Hewitt, treat his work to the exclusion of his regional literary influences. While the current study centrally concerns the Major Figure of Heaney, this chapter treats the flourishing of a heterogeneous Northern Irish regionalism in the first two-thirds of the twentieth century in the theater and especially through a variety of small magazines. In his invaluable history of the Irish literary periodical from 1923 to 1958, Frank Shovlin argues that "there continues to exist a relative critical neglect of Irish literature in the first forty years after Partition. Neglect of that period's literary magazines has been especially acute."[2] While many of these movements and journals were short-lived, in aggregate they helped create the conditions for the foundation of Northern Irish writing that was crucial for the development of the justly more famous writers such as Heaney who emerged from Philip Hobsbaum's Belfast Group.

Scholars of Irish literature have been considerably reluctant until very recently to admit or discuss the existence of something called "Northern Irish literature," by and large for very good reasons. Primary among these is probably the desire to assert Irish literature as a distinct entity over against British literature, a natural desire given the centuries of Britain's domination over Ireland and given the past tendency by British and American scholars to term "British" such authors as Yeats and Joyce. Northern Irish literature, with its plurality of styles and cultural implications, complicates the picture of "Irish" literature fruitfully, but this possibility is seldom admitted and it is treated as a special, disturbing center of literary activity: Irish literary scholars tend to suspect that literature from the political province of Northern Ireland is linked inextricably with the conflict there and that once the conflict peters out so will the literature. As this chapter demonstrates, however, Northern Irish literature has a deep-rooted existence that easily antedates the current conflict and should eclipse it.

Although it is difficult to say when a Northern Irish literature began, it is tempting to start with partition in 1920. However, it is dangerous and simplistic to try to plot a trajectory of something as varied and organic as Northern Irish literature on a linear history of the province. The articles and editorials drawn from journals and collections that emerged from the province often, but not always, anticipate qualities evident in Heaney's poetry: a deep and affectionate, though sometimes cynical, attachment to either the historic or the political province of "Ulster," a fidelity to the imagination, and a surprising receptivity to a mixture of political, cultural, and religious affinities, rather than an unquestioning acceptance of the unifying bonds of a particular community.

By far the most visible institutional proponent of a regionalized identity in the North was the Ulster Literary Theatre (ULT). Eugene McNulty's book-length treatment of it, *The Ulster Literary Theatre and the Northern Revival*, has become essential reading for anyone interested in appreciating this regional counterpart to the much better known Abbey Theatre and Irish Literary Revival. As McNulty has argued, "Many at the heart of the Ulster Literary Theatre saw it as a forum for realigning the cultural life of the North in order to break down some of the political divisions that had grown stronger in the years of Home Rule. . . . [It] took as one of its central goals the combating of . . . cultural bigotry; in its place its members hoped to discover in the theatre unifying codes for a society defined by boundaries of one sort or another (class, religious, political)."[3] Moreover, as Laura E. Lyons has persuasively argued, the ULT offered two substantive articulations of regionalism: "Its members recognized the critical differences among the four provinces of Ireland to be one of the nation's greatest strengths, and they were critical of those regional factors, particularly Orangeism, that prevented Ulster from playing its full role in the formation of a new nation. In other words, the ULT actively promoted a regional nationalism, a way of imagining the nation's strength and homogeneity in terms of its regional diversity, rather than a false homogeneity."[4] Although this "regional nationalism" eventually was subsumed by a focus solely upon Ulster's uniqueness, its importance for this current study ultimately lies in its reimagining of the historic province of Ulster as a verifiable and distinct entity unto itself and in its attempt at cultural unity. The ULT's regionalism would be molded and shaped by later artists such as John Boyd, John Hewitt, and Heaney. These later writers would imagine a new type of province united by a shared regional culture.[5]

Despite the short-lived cultural success of the ULT, politics in the northeastern part of Ireland had become increasingly sectarian well before partition in 1920.[6] Richard Kirkland has argued that "before partition, Northern nationalist culture can be identified as an increasingly self-confident force mobilizing itself around a considerable number of interlinked organizations, journals and coteries."[7] Other early Northern Irish writers generally evinced a fidelity to the imagination that enabled them to rise above their often-prejudiced religious and cultural upbringing. Perhaps surprisingly, given the hardening of sectarianism in the Protestant community leading up to and after partition, a number of these writers are from that same community and display progressive attitudes toward Catholics. All of these authors reimagine the political and cultural situation in the northern part of the island in fascinating ways. Taken together, the work of these earlier Northern Irish writers charts the varying dimensions of a broad province of the mind in stark contrast to the emerging culturally and politically restrictive statelet of Northern Ireland. Since the close reading of a number of primary works is beyond the scope of this chapter, its emphasis is descriptive rather than analytical—delineating and tracing the positions taken in articulating Northern Irish literature mainly in editorials and essays of significant anthologies and journals and exploring the aesthetic stance of literary coteries in the region.

The new province languished culturally until it acquired other literary journals to replace *Uladh*, the journal of the ULT. *Uladh*'s successor finally appeared in 1942 when the *New Northman*, a revitalized version of the long-running Queen's University newsletter the *Northman*, was launched by John Gallen and Robert Greacen. As Conor O'Malley points out, the *New Northman* eventually reverted to its original, nonliterary form and was defunct by 1951.[8] More important, the founding of the literary journal *Lagan*, edited by John Boyd, was a crucial, though short-lived printing experiment in the North that also aligned itself with *Uladh*.[9] This journal flourished during the war years of the 1940s. As Boyd writes in the second volume of his autobiography, *The Middle of My Journey*, both Bob Davidson and Sam Hanna Bell convinced him to be editor, and Bell, anyway, had "the notion that if Dublin could produce a lively literary magazine like *The Bell*, we three in Belfast might be able to produce something just as good."[10] Bell's assertion suggests that the embryonic journal was founded as a Northern Irish counter to the popular and well-respected journal to the south and demonstrates just how far the region's literary movement had come since the ULT, which had been founded specifically to promote a united Ireland. *Lagan* intended, however, to focus on unifying the province culturally.

Although it ran for only four issues, it was very popular: the two thousand copies of the first issue were quickly snapped up. Boyd told the present author in conversation that its policy was to "get in touch with established writers like MacNeice. [They were] always paid a fee. [We wanted] always to discover new literature."[11] The final issue appeared in 1946 but did not sell even five hundred copies, probably because, as Boyd speculated, a large part of its audience, American soldiers stationed in and around Belfast during World War II, had departed by then.[12] Though short-lived for financial reasons, *Lagan*'s success indicated that high-quality publishing and writing could flourish in the province. It also provided local poetry a focal point. For example, in the history of Northern Irish poetry he contributed to *Causeway: The Arts in Ulster*, Michael Longley points out the presence of "a group of poets who were closely associated with the magazine *Lagan*, Maurice J. Craig, Roy McFadden, Robert Greacen and John Hewitt."[13] Although Boyd cautiously held in his first two editorials that there was no renaissance in Ulster writing, *Lagan*'s success in establishing this coterie marks the beginning of poetry in Northern Ireland.[14] *Lagan* also importantly "shared John Hewitt's regionalist ethos," which will be explored shortly.[15]

Robert Greacen's first attempt to anthologize "Ulster" poetry at this time is helpful in understanding how it was linked to other regional poetry in Britain, while his second and third attempts mark an effort to distinguish Ulster poetry from these same other regional poets. In 1942, he coedited a collection called *Lyra: An Anthology of New Lyrics* with Alex Comfort. John Wilson Foster argues convincingly that the Irish poets represented in this volume (all from Northern Ireland) such as Greacen himself and Roy McFadden were implicitly linked with the British neoromantic poets Comfort and Vernon Watkin, who were regularly published in *Poetry Quarterly* (whose editor Wrey Gardiner published the anthology), "home to many of the 1940s neo-Romantics." As Foster asserts, "On the evidence of *Lyra*, Ulster poetry in the 1940s written by the newcomers was hardly distinguishable from British neo-Romanticism at large, even though they wrote out of a discouraging wartime in Belfast." Neoromantic poets from Ulster, Scotland, and Wales all equated "regionalism with Romantic Celticism," against which the British Movement poets in the 1950s would react.[16]

Two of the first important collections of writing from the province also appeared during the war, both assembled by Greacen, who felt, unlike Boyd, that Ulster was experiencing a renaissance in the arts. Tellingly, while *Lyra* had featured verse from throughout the regions of Britain, Greacen's 1942 pamphlet *Poems from Ulster* and his 1944 anthology *Northern Harvest: An Anthology of Ulster Literature* make the case for Ulster regional writing's uniqueness.[17] *Northern Harvest* presented the work of established and lesser-known writers in fiction, poetry, and belles lettres from the province. Greacen's literary importance in Northern Ireland was by then well established through his poetry and through his editing of the journal the *New Northman*. In his introduction to *Northern Harvest*, he first references "the new awakening in Ulster writing, which has taken place since the War started," noting that "thanks to the widespread interest which that renascence has aroused, I have felt for some time that a critical selection was called for."[18] In his second paragraph, Greacen sets Northern Irish literature over against that written in the Republic, unfortunately drawing on popular stereotypes of the dour Scot and the excitable Irishman in the process:

> But there is a further purpose inherent to the design of this book. It has been made by Ulstermen: and it is my fervent hope that, by means of this evidence of the creative spirit, we may win a sympathetic audience in Great Britain, as well as strengthening the interest of our own people in the affairs of the Province. Probably our Scots ancestry goes far in explaining the reserve, the lack of display, the unwillingness to "shoot a line" or to talk about ourselves, all of which traits characterize the Northern Irish and which stand in such contrast to the exuberant, colourful and, above all, voluble make-up of our fellow-Irishmen South and West of the Border. Whatever the reasons, the life and character of the North-East have had for long an unmerited obscurity: it is high time that at least the edges of the veil were lifted, so that the world may have a few glimpses of the kind of people we are.[19]

The political, geographic, and cultural vacillations in this paragraph are striking. Greacen notes that the new political province looks to Britain, Scotland, and even within for its identity, which he bases upon the allegedly reserved temperament of "Ulstermen." This identity is in stark contrast to what he sees as the overexcitable temperaments of citizens in Ireland. Strangely, though, he then calls people in the other twenty-six counties "fellow-Irishmen." His invocation of the "North-East," meant to stand for Northern Ireland, not "Ulster"—which would signify the traditional nine-county province—as a distinct cultural, even racial entity, however, is disturbing and attuned more to divisive political realities than to a potentially unifying literary culture.

The other important passage from this introduction for our purposes shares an expressed affinity for religious and cultural inclusion with that cited earlier from the original editorial of *Uladh*, while nonetheless resorting to a somewhat strident unionist message that reinforces partition. Additionally, while both the first and second editorials from *Uladh* evince a desire to articulate an Ulster theater within the confines of a united Ireland, Greacen here and throughout the introduction makes clear that postpartition writing in the northern part of the island is emphatically not Irish but Northern Irish:

> It must be pointed out that these essays, stories and poems are presented in no exclusive or arbitrary manner, that every viewpoint from Unionist to Nationalist, whether explicit or implicit, has been given its chance to speak out. Mr. Hugh Shearman defends the case for the majority of Ulster men and women; and I do feel that it is time for that case to be stated unemotionally and vigorously, freed from the dogmatic principle which is its chief enemy.[20] On the other hand, in the work of Mr. McLaverty and others, Catholic Nationalism is treated with the objectivity and sympathy that must inform all good writing. Whatever may be the solution to our political and social problems—which War conditions have, if anything, intensified—let us pay them the tribute of honesty and frankness. That has been my attitude, however much it offends certain armed camps. I need hardly state that any opinions expressed are those of the respective contributors and that the sole criteria for inclusion have been suitability and artistic merit.[21]

Greacen's attempt to be inclusive here can only be considered a failure, not least because he has already imposed received political and cultural, even racial, labels on the writers. While this imposition may be understandable in the case of a propagandist like Shearman, it cannot apply to an imaginative writer of the power of Michael McLaverty, whose work rises above simplistic sectarian tags. The inclusion of other writers such as St. John Ervine, Forrest Reid, Sam Hanna Bell, W. R. Rodgers, Roy McFadden, and John Hewitt suggests that the real value of the anthology lies in the individual stories, poems, and some essays, each of whose particular emphases deflates Greacen's broad generalizations in his preface.

Additionally, while Greacen's impulse to gather a rich harvest of writing from the province was exemplary, especially given the inevitable wartime limits on printing in Belfast, his recourse to stereotypes and overassertion of Ulster as a distinct entity, peopled by "Ulster men and women," smacks of exclusion for the sake of a superficial unity not supported by actual conditions in the divided province. The rhetoric of Greacen's introduction represents a negative conception of regionalism, which would easily be challenged and supplanted by Northern Irish writers such as Hewitt and Rodgers, and later by a new generation represented by Michael Longley and Heaney.[22]

The publication of literary journals such as the *New Northman* and *Lagan*, along with anthologies such as Greacen's *Poems from Ulster* and *Northern Harvest*, suggests the variety of regional voices emerging from the province and their polyphonic challenges to traditional notions of Protestant and Catholic political identities in the province, although Richard Kirkland correctly points out that "regionalism was a phenomenon located almost entirely within the realm of culture and its superstructural institutions, and was rarely found elsewhere" such as in politics.[23]

Peter McDonald asks a question pertinent to our exploration of imagined cultural identity in the province and the corresponding emergence of Northern Irish literature: "Does regionalism give birth to the individual artist, or does the artist create for his community the viable concept of regionalism?"[24] Certainly John Hewitt's conception of regionalism would not have been given nearly the credence it eventually gained had not the province of Northern Ireland been created in 1921. For instance, it took several decades for Hewitt and his coterie of Sam Hanna Bell, John Boyd, Roy McFadden, and other writers to consciously define the parameters of Northern Irish literature beginning somewhat formally in 1950, with the founding of the New Literary Dinner Club. As Gillian McIntosh has shown, the forums of the BBC and PEN (Playwrights, Poets, Editors, Essayists, and Novelists) enabled these Northern writers to formally and informally begin articulating their view of Northern Irish literature at least as early as the late 1940s.[25]

Hewitt, a crucial exemplar for Heaney in his formulations of regionalism, attempted to articulate a viable, culturally cohesive Ulster regionalism, while acknowledging the particular intractability of his province to a vibrant literary culture. Gillian McIntosh terms him "the linchpin of the

Northern Irish literary scene" through his efforts to promote Northern Irish literature.[26] Hewitt outlined his philosophy of regionalism in a radio piece broadcast on BBC Northern Ireland in November 1945:

> Ulster is not a nation, yet she has ceased to be just a colony, for those of us who are of English or Scots extraction, have been here long enough to form a distinct people together with descendants of earlier immigration.... But now, although there are many surface differences and some fairly deep ones among our people, we have lived long enough together to be more like each other than unlike.... We are not big enough to form a nation, but we have our own attitude of mind, our own place on the map.... We are compelled to preserve our emotional and, dare I say, spiritual integrity, to turn our hearts and our intimate affections to some unit smaller than the nation—but larger than the townland—to what is called the Region. In our own case to Ulster.[27]

Regionalism, for Hewitt, provided a permanent entry for Ulster Protestants into the history and contemporary culture of the province while ideally also transcending sectarian differences.[28] As John Wilson Foster points out, Hewitt purposely refrained from delineating the county boundaries for his region of Ulster in hopes of attracting support for his conception from both Catholics and Protestants. If he had argued for the traditional nine-county Ulster, "current Protestant withholding of allegiance to that entity [would] match current Catholic withholding of allegiance to the entity of Northern Ireland. The problem was not to be solved by immediately adding back three counties [Cavan, Monaghan, and Donegal] to Northern Ireland."[29]

For Hewitt, a regionalist political philosophy required and could be galvanized by a literary component. In fact, because his political plan for Ulster to become part of a federated British Isles failed, his imaginative aesthetic and geographic community is all the more striking, as Kirkland points out. Kirkland argues, however, that this seemingly aesthetic formulation centered on the individual artist and thus that Hewitt's theory could easily be read as a political unionist conception:

> Hewitt allows the problematic relationship between the individual ... and the communal "emotional unity" to be reconciled only through the

paradigmatic figure of the artist: an ideology which accords at least as well with the nationalist thinking of the nineteenth-century Young Ireland journal the *Nation* as it does to any of the regionalist thought to which he more obviously subscribes. . . . By never clearly recognizing which community he was serving or writing for, the absolute concept of Hewitt's Ulster regionalism was always open to the misreadings and political appropriations that its ambiguity sought to foreclose. As his contemporary Roy McFadden noted, "I suspected that the Ulster Regionalist idea could be used to provide a cultural mask for political unionism or a kind of local counter-nationalism. I was also troubled by Hewitt's use of the word 'Ulster,' which he did not clearly define."[30]

Kirkland's characterization of remarks like these as "misreadings and political appropriations" is itself perhaps the best refutation of the paranoia rife in McFadden's comment. Hewitt's sympathy for Northern Irish Catholics, coupled with his ambiguous formulation of Ulster as a region identical with the historic province of Ulster, suggests strongly his exemplary attempt to present regionalism as a unifying solution to the cultural, political, and religious divide in the province.[31]

Both Hewitt and his fellow Ulster poet W. R. Rodgers had long evinced an interest in regionalism, especially Hewitt through his sojourns to various socialist summer schools scattered mostly over the British Isles.[32] Frank Ormsby believes the wartime travel restrictions beginning in 1939 led to Hewitt's increasing explorations of the province. Hewitt noted that at this time "I felt very enclosed and segregated, and then my thinking turned inwards"; he later summed up his interest in regionalism as "a reaction to the isolationism of the war years."[33] Patrick Walsh argues convincingly, however, that Hewitt's inward turn did not preclude heightened interaction with his and his wife's summer neighbors in the predominantly Catholic Glens of Antrim during their holidays there from 1945 to 1965. In fact, "The Hewitts were frequent visitors to Catholic churches both at home and abroad," visited a local mass rock chapel in the Glens, and evinced a "growing tolerance for religious feeling."[34] In allowing himself to be doubly displaced "as an urban interloper and as a Protestant" in the Catholic Glens, and in his fascination with poems of this era that allude to "the rituals of Catholic religious practice with its richly textured symbolism," Hewitt displayed a clear openness to the ideas and faith of Northern Irish Catholics, although Heaney later would come to believe that for Hewitt Catholics were finally Other and perhaps unassimilable into his imagined region of Ulster.[35]

Always seeking to develop regional writing in Ulster, Hewitt would cajole local creative and critical talent to recognize the excellent literature issuing from the province for many decades, just as Michael Longley would later in the century through his position with the Arts Council of Northern Ireland beginning in 1970. Hewitt recognized regional literary developments in Scotland and Wales and sought analogies in Ulster regionalism, while acknowledging his province's lack of a creative literary culture. For example, in his 1945 essay "The Bitter Gourd: Some Problems of the Ulster Writer," first published in John Boyd's third issue of *Lagan*, Hewitt opens by discussing the regionalism of Wales and Scotland and contrasting their status as "geographical and national entities" with that of the regions of the West of England and Ulster, which are not as clearly defined.[36] Besides the vexed question of the geographic makeup of "Ulster," Hewitt quickly goes on to argue that while "Scots has been a literary instrument since the days of Dunbar and Gawain Douglas," Ulster has no similar heritage: "We have no such literary heritage, no such ancient languages. Scotsmen, Englishmen and Irishmen have here in Ulster become clofted in an uneven and lumpy mixture."[37] This mixture has produced brilliant scientists such as Lord Kelvin, but the province remains "deficient in creative genius."[38] Additionally, "Ulster's position in this island involves us in problems and cleavages for which we can find no counterpart elsewhere in the British archipelago. Scotland has its Lowlands and its Highlands still with shreds and vestiges of historical, linguistic and even religious divergences, but on nothing approaching the scale with which we are faced here."[39] Hewitt finds the American region of New England to have the most affinities with modern Northern Ireland, especially because of their shared inheritance of Protestant nonconformity. After noting the similarities of Ulster and New England writing—"the careful rejection of the rhetorical and flamboyant, the stubborn concreteness of imagery, the conscientious cleaving to the objects of sense"—he argues, however, that the cultural conditions in each region have so radically altered that no contemporary analogies can be drawn between the two.[40]

He then links the development of the Ulster mind with the Scottish Enlightenment and the corresponding rise of industrialism, noting that creative writing was the sole province of the weaver poets.[41] He sees William Carleton, an exemplar for Heaney in *Station Island*, as the apogee of this period of Ulster writing: "The very best peasant work, indeed among the very best Ulster work of all time, was that of the drunken Carleton, in prose not verse."[42] But for many years after Carleton's passing, Hewitt argues, "the province failed to support or even harbour writers of any quality," and those who remained and had sensitive minds, "finding themselves in an extroverted stubborn inarticulate society with well defined material values and, for the most part, a rigid creed, revolted against their condition" and left the province.[43] The solution for the current crop of writers in the province, as Hewitt saw it, was to draw on their local surroundings for their art; the Ulster writer "must be a *rooted* man, must carry the native tang of his idiom like the native dust on his sleeve; otherwise he is an airy internationalist, thistledown, a twig in a stream."[44]

Finally, Hewitt argues that Queen's University has a significant role to play in promoting Northern Irish writing, though because of its mainly English and Scottish faculty "it has remained culturally a foreign oasis among us."[45] Citing various British university literary groups from the past, including "Marlowe and his fellow pioneers" and "the Auden group," Hewitt notes that these groups constitute a haven for the sensitive minded from the rampant materialism of the larger society: "The importance of these groups resides, of course, in the bringing together of young keen contemporary minds enjoying for a period some measure of social security and not yet involved in and conditioned by openly economic demands and their superstructure of material ideals."[46] No notable coteries of this sort have arisen at Queen's, he concludes, which "at various times had its groups, but they have been infrequent, drawing only a tiny membership and producing little work of significance."[47] Within twenty years, the emergence of Hobsbaum's Belfast Group at Queen's would answer Hewitt's call for Queen's to support "the bringing together of young keen contemporary minds." In the meantime, Northern Irish writing would flourish largely on the basis of the work of its professional writers such as Hewitt and in a series of short-lived journals.

The poetry journal *Rann*, founded by Roy McFadden, published local talent starting in 1948 but finally folded in 1953. Although Frank Kersnowski has argued that the journal failed "to instill a sense of community among Ulster writers, to produce a literature," *Rann*, despite its short run, certainly raised the level of consciousness about the existence of a largely nonsectarian and dynamic Northern Irish literature among fellow writers and other intellectuals.[48] Citing McFadden's editorial in the first issue of *Rann* in 1948 that "we are offering this region an opportunity to find its voice and to express itself in genuine accents in these pages," Heather Clark suggests that "McFadden's repeated emphasis on 'genuine accents' shows just how seriously *Rann* took the idea of regionalism, despite its Irish name," although she also notes how McFadden's review of Louis MacNeice's *Collected Poems, 1925–1948* reductively criticized MacNeice for neglecting the issue of place in his poetry: "[While] regionalists were trying to combat parochial attitudes towards literature and culture, they could sound as provincial in their opinions as those they criticized."[49]

The final issue of *Rann* provides several crucial midcentury assessments of the growth of Northern Irish literature along with a much-needed bibliography of this work.[50] Even this last issue's cover bespeaks the attempted inclusiveness of Northern Irish writing at the time, since it features the hero of the ancient province of Ulster, Cuchulainn. The brief introduction by Barbara Hunter and McFadden builds upon this image by arguing for an Ulster literature inherited from the Ulster mythological cycle: "This issue of RANN will help towards providing a balanced picture of the recent past and the present in what we call Ulster writing: and may perhaps indicate certain qualities that are native to writers nurtured in the province of Deirdre and Cuchulainn."[51] This rhetorical gesture should not be confused with the recent spurious revisionism undertaken by Ian Adamson; instead it should be understood as a unifying image for mid-twentieth-century Ulster writing.[52]

Such an outlook undermines Frank Shovlin's contention that although it was "not as narrowly regional in its thrust as its predecessor *Lagan* . . . , *Rann* none the less attempted to demonstrate the existence of a unique artistic strain in Northern Ireland. . . . The journal, by its very nature, was a political statement. Its reluctance to look beyond the narrow field north of the border stands in stark contrast with the efforts of Sean O'Faolain and Peadar O'Donnell at *The Bell*."[53] But clearly, the journal's overall attempt to promote the old nine-county province of Ulster shows how Shovlin misreads its editorial stance by wrongly attributing a partitionist mentality to it. Furthermore, a number of important articles in this crucial last issue bespeak *Rann*'s commitment to an inclusive concept of regionalism.

Indeed, the volume's opening essay, Howard Sergeant's "Ulster Regionalism," argues for regionalism's openness toward different cultures, contrasting it with the cultural narrowness of nationalism, which he notes, runs the risk of cultural isolation. Sergeant begins by arguing that "true regionalism is a movement towards a future in which a balanced life in every community has become the source of local self-respect and human dignity. It arises out of a natural affection for or an attachment, conscious or unconscious, to a particular environment, and finds expression through a language, outlook and manner of life, of the people concerned, adapted to the intellectual and emotional experience of the individual."[54] Sergeant's regionalism accords with Hewitt's in that it too calls for attachment to the writer's immediate surroundings, but it supersedes Hewitt's in its calls for "local self-respect and human dignity," properties that were probably latent but were not expressed in Hewitt's regionalist formulations and that anticipate Heaney's position on regionalism from the beginning of his career onward.

While Hewitt claimed in "The Bitter Gourd" that Ulster regionalism suffered in comparison to Welsh and Scottish regionalism, Sergeant, writing eight years later in 1953, praises Ulster regionalism for being free of the pernicious aspects of nationalism usually associated with regionalism in those areas: "There is considerable danger that the economic and political elements [in regions that can be characterized as nations] will be over-emphasized at the expense of the cultural, with the result that critical standards are lowered and a superficially nationalist content becomes the primary criterion of value. And if, as it frequently is, the attitude is confined to a vociferous minority, whose opinions are unacceptable to their fellows, there will also be an inclination towards the development of an aggressive self-consciousness."[55] As Sergeant further articulates, regionalism is inherently outward looking, while nationalism is inward looking and constitutes the real provincialism: "The principal difference between the two is that while regionalism offers its contribution to the whole culture of a nation or comity of nations, nationalism is more conducive to cultural isolation. The history of Irish literature and drama provides a clear example of the inter-relationship and counteraction of these predominant forces."[56] Before surveying the poetry of MacNeice, Greacen, Maurice Craig, McFadden, Rodgers, and Hewitt, Sergeant insightfully points out the individuality of these poets and the way in which Ulster regionalism has produced them "without fostering a special movement."[57] Partly "because there is no specific 'school,' as there is, say, in the case of the young Scottish poets, dominated by the ideas and Anglophobia of Hugh MacDiarmid, because there are no 'pragmatic and ruthless attitudes,' . . . their work has not been given the attention it deserves."[58] A final reason for this lack of critical attention paid to the midcentury Ulster writers, and one that both Heaney and Longley would address, "is that there is little or no emphasis upon Gaelic as the appropriate poetic language; nor is there any equivalent to Lallans or 'synthetic' Scots."[59] Sergeant might be the most eloquent and articulate advocate of Ulster regionalism during the 1950s. His call for human dignity amid competing aggressions fostered by nationalisms would be echoed later by Heaney as he would formulate his own regionalist ethos amid the most aggressive forms of republicanism and loyalism the province had seen since its founding.

The other essays in this last volume of *Rann* were no less impressive in both their scope and their openness to defining "Ulster" writing. Two articles, on Ulster poetry and Ulster theater, do just that. For example, Daphne Fullwood and Oliver Edwards contributed a long article, "Ulster Poetry since 1900," that is commendable for both its historical sweep and its inclusiveness. They claim the nineteenth-century authors Samuel Ferguson and the Donegal writer William Allingham as Ulster writers, along with A. E. (George Russell), whom they term "the most distinguished member of what someone in *Rann* 15 called the Pseudonymous Generation,— roughly the Ulster writers born between 1860 and 1890, most of whom, for one reason or another, preferred to hide or at least to veil their artistic being from a world they sense to be hostile to that side of their being."[60] They also discuss in greater detail the verse of Richard Rowley, Hewitt, Rodgers, Kavanagh, Michael McLaverty, MacNeice, Maurice Craig, and McFadden. They note that they have limited themselves "strictly to the Ulster-born" and lament the exclusion of Gaelic Donegal poets because of the language barrier: "(Ignorance of Gaelic keeps us from the new poets in Irish of Donegal, who should be here: as Hewitt says, historic Ulster goes 'back to Columcille')."[61] Reappropriating the loyalist slogan "Not an inch," they inclusively assert earlier in the essay that "however many counties there may be in Northern Ireland, there are Nine Counties in Ulster.... Our intellectual attitude in respect of the Three Counties of Ultonia irredenta is Not an inch."[62]

Finally, Hewitt's expansive essay "The Course of Writing in Ulster" argues for Ulster's historical and literary uniqueness, invoking the historic province's resistance to the English and the subsequent "racial juxtaposition and intermingling" that he believes "must have had effects upon the literary arts practiced in this area, which should to some degree have produced differences from and modifications of the same arts in the rest of these islands."[63]

In this essay, Hewitt charts the growth of printing in the province beginning in 1700 and articulates the development of two poetic schools, the Colonial, associated with "standard" English, and the Vernacular, associated with Scottish settlers: "the Colonial, based on contemporary or near-contemporary English usage, and written normally by Church of Ireland clergymen, medical doctors, town schoolmasters and the daughters or sisters of these; and the Vernacular, which, although still colonial, because of its dispersal over the Scots planted districts and its exercise by handloom weavers, small farmers, and country schoolmasters, began, by comparison with the English colonial, to appear a rooted activity."[64] In true regionalist fashion, Hewitt notes that "each of these [vernacular] poets was strongly local. Man and place were knotted together."[65] Their politics were "radical and democratic," and they were "liberal in their Presbyterianism," all qualities that appealed to the radical socialist himself.[66] He argues that their decline was caused by the cessation of the rural economy upon the introduction of industrialism and "the establishment of National Schools which, by concentration on standard English spelling, bred up generations unable to read the vernacular and somewhat ashamed to speak it."[67] Hewitt upholds Samuel Ferguson, William Allingham, and Thomas Caulfield Irwin as "three good poets of Ulster birth and planter stock [who] were in full creative vigour" outside the province.[68] Always prescient, Hewitt's characterization in this essay of Ulster writers who emigrated from the province, such as Ferguson, Carleton, John Mitchel, and A. E., anticipates the continuing emigration in the twentieth century of writers such as MacNeice, Brian Moore, Heaney, Derek Mahon, Stewart Parker, and Bernard MacLaverty, all of whom have written consistently about their native province from outside it. The great growth of writing in the province led Hewitt to conclude this article in an optimistic vein similar to that of John Boyd in his essay on the Ulster novel,[69] but unlike Boyd he sees the rise of this literature in a regionalist context: "Having ceased to be a colony, and having become, whether we like the word or not, a region, there are signs that we are already expressing ourselves in a distinctive literature."[70]

Despite the importance of *Lagan* and *Rann*, they were both short-lived publishing ventures with no real literary permanence, although many ideas they expressed concerning Ulster regionalism have a valid and continuing circulation, and they fostered a growing sense of literary community in the province. The province needed journals that would last for decades in order to promote Northern Irish literature on a more permanent basis. Two were soon born: *Threshold* and the *Honest Ulsterman*. In February 1957, *Threshold* was founded by the Lyric Players Theatre in Belfast. Its attempts to reach all parts of Ireland and its connection to a Northern theater place it "firmly in the tradition of *Uladh*," as Conor O'Malley notes.[71] In its Ireland-wide appeal, *Threshold* contrasts strongly with the regionalism of the *New Northman*, *Lagan*, and *Rann*. O'Malley cites an early foreword (vol. 1, no. 4) in which "a wide perspective was taken, [but] the relevance to the local scene was manifest": "The writer has a special responsibility in every community. His work cannot be entirely isolated from the immediate environment. Strong political, religious or social tensions present a dilemma. A conscious attitude of detachment or of selective involvement is liable to restrict vision and interest. Engagement without compromise may provoke serious opposition or censorship. The approach of the writer, however, to this dilemma, is an indication of the health of a community and of its cultural standard and achievement."[72] This editorial statement makes clear the degree to which *Threshold* saw its role in promoting new writing. Its base in the province undoubtedly attuned it to the cultural intricacies of life there and the responsibility of writers throughout Ireland to be involved in the community through their work, whatever approach they might choose. The strength and diversity of artists (and by implication, those of the community as well) then, lie in their presumably varied approaches to the dilemma of choosing between utter detachment from, selective involvement with, or whole-scale engagement with political, religious, or societal problems.

O'Malley argues that while "theatre and poetry criticism tended to be progressive in tone and outlook with contributors stressing the need for innovation, experiment and new artistic horizons," the "short prose fiction published in the early *Threshold* was pessimistic and defeatist in attitude."[73] Beginning with the sixteenth issue, the quarterly journal became published occasionally and was guest edited. At this time, "creative writing begins to dominate," as short stories by Patrick Boyle and Brian Friel were published.[74] Later important issues were issue 21, given over to the work of "Ulster" writers, including pieces by Heaney, MacNeice, and Montague; issue 22, edited by Heaney, which "showed the beginnings of a new creative energy in the North"; and issue 23, the "Northern crisis" issue, edited by Montague, which featured the first appearance of Heaney's important poem "The Tollund Man."[75] O'Malley concludes that the journal's real value lay in its criticism, not its creative work: "The issue on the Northern troubles stands out for its original material, and for its creative response to the historical moment. Overall the amount of creative work of quality is relatively small. On the other hand the standard of literary and historical criticism is particularly high and reflected progressive trends in Irish society."[76] Frank Kersnowski, on the other hand, praises *Threshold* for both "sensible criticism and responsible imaginative writing" and singles out John Hewitt's role as poetry editor of the journal as having done "much to effect the remarkably high level of verse published there."[77]

Writing in 1964, however, Heaney was scathing in his criticism of *Threshold*. In his essay "Our Own Dour Way," he opens by stating, "It is high time the North had another literary magazine."[78] While praising the editors of and contributors to *Lagan* and *Rann* in the previous two decades, he argues that *Threshold* has not carried on those journals' tradition "because it is not essentially a northern magazine. It might as well be published in Dublin. In fact put a copy of *Threshold* inside a *Kilkenny Magazine* cover and very few people could tell the difference. Moreover, it relies on established reputations."[79] Heaney obviously felt not only that *Threshold* was not sufficiently regional but also that it was not doing enough to promote the emergence of new writers in the North.

But John Hewitt certainly promoted the reputation of local poets such as Heaney in other periodical outlets beyond *Threshold*. By the mid- to late 1960s, Hewitt clearly believed Heaney was pursuing a regional project similar to his own. On May 19, 1966, the *Belfast Telegraph* published a review by Hewitt of *Death of a Naturalist* that favorably compared Heaney with other Northern Irish writers such as Patrick Kavanagh (from the old Ulster county of Monaghan) and Michael McLaverty: "Reading these poems, I have sometimes been reminded of the gritty cadence of Patrick Kavanagh, but more often and more deeply of those good prosemen, Michael McLaverty's prismatic vision, [Donegal novelist] Peadar O'Donnell's sly rhetoric, [Armagh author] Michael J. Murphy's folk-piety, the late [Northern Irish author of *Come-Day, Go-Day*] John O'Connor's gentle sensitivity: for these also inhabit the same region of our national feeling."[80] Placing Heaney on the map of the historic province of Ulster along with other talented Ulster writers was consistent with Hewitt's continuing regionalist concerns, and his praise seems genuine, especially when he immediately argues, "Seamus Heaney's awareness that human pity must exist within the indifferent context of a pitiless nature edges his thought beyond that estimable company."[81] Hewitt clearly felt that Heaney would be a major Northern Irish poet because of this paradox and because of a concern common to both poets—language.

Thus Hewitt praises the younger poet for his use of active verbs, concrete nouns, and the ways in which the "poems are grounded on, but reach beyond, the farm, the barn, the flax dam, the smells and rhythm of churning, the digging of potatoes, the ploughman's accurate gift, the water diviner's gift, the trout in the stream."[82] That sense of the particular and the universal evoked by "grounded on, but reach[ing] beyond" perfectly accords with Kavanagh's philosophy of parochialism, but it also coheres with Hewitt's belief, in his seminal essay on regionalism, "The Bitter Gourd," that the Ulster writer "must be a rooted man, must carry the native tang of his idiom like the native dust on his sleeve; otherwise he is an airy internationalist, thistledown, a twig in a stream," and the corresponding belief that that rootedness enables such a writer to reach a worldwide audience.[83]

By 1972, Heaney had returned the favor, praising Hewitt's *Collected Poems, 1932–1967* (1968) in an essay published in *Threshold*. Besides admiring "Hewitt's own tense care in the handling of metre, rhyme, and stanza," Heaney approves of the poetry's quietness, noting that "the verse itself rarely raises its voice, relying on tone, understatement and oblique reference to make its more astringent points."[84] More important for Heaney's own burgeoning interest in regionalism, he then argues that Hewitt displays a "stubborn determination to belong to the Irishry and yet [is] tenaciously aware of a different origin and cast of mind," citing Hewitt's well-known poem "The Colony," which "converts the Ulster planter's experience into a Roman situation where the citizens of the colony are on the verge of turning native."[85] By the early 1990s, in his Oxford lecture "Frontiers of Writing," Heaney would come to reject Hewitt's regionalism as not sufficiently inclusive of the lingering Gaelic (and Catholic) presence in the province, but here he approvingly charts the older poet's evolution from the "mask for what he wished to be—faithful to a heritage, rooted within a tradition," to "a man without a mask. The verse has become free, the statements grope towards something irreducible . . . the kind of authority without dogma that poets stand for."[86] That Heaney published this review in *Threshold*, which he had previously dismissed as a regional Northern journal, suggests he may have been trying to infuse Hewitt's thoughtful, regionalist ethos into that venue, along with promoting the elder poet's work.

Other regional magazines in the province such as the *Honest Ulsterman* and *Fortnight* allowed local writers to have a venue protected from the periodic attempts by some magazines based in the South to amalgamate Northern Irish writing into a nationalist Irish literary tradition.[87] As Richard Kirkland points out, one of these southern magazines that tended to dismiss or deny Northern Irish writing and co-opt it into an utterly homogenous Irish national literary tradition was *Hibernia*: "Until its closure in 1980 *Hibernia* observed the activities of Northern Irish culture from its Dublin base with a subtle mixture of bewilderment, condescension and denial. By regularly publishing articles on the state of Irish letters by Desmond Fennell, Sean Lucy and John Jordan, it fought a rearguard action for the forces of national literary tradition and editorially was inclined to co-opt Northern writing into a coherent Irish tradition as a matter of faith. For these reasons *Hibernia* often became a key journal of oppositional definition for Northern magazines such as *The Honest Ulsterman* or *Fortnight*."[88] As I have already argued, certain cultural continuities across the island undoubtedly exist, but attempts to read Northern Irish literature *solely* as part of Irish literature are simply not attuned to the intricacies and complexities of Northern writing. Primarily, such an attempt would ignore what John Wilson Foster has termed the androgynous identity of "the Ulster people" (especially, for him, Northern Protestants)—their ability to be attuned to at least two different cultures at once.[89] However, even the *Honest Ulsterman*, at least early on, was not necessarily an ideal venue for promoting a broadly based Northern Irish aesthetic. For example, Kirkland argues that "in [editor James] Simmons's essentially Protestant visionary outlook is a provincial world-view centred on the actuality of partition and on the particular realizable perfection of the conceptual 'Honest Ulsterman': Simmons himself."[90]

While Kirkland further claims that the *Honest Ulsterman* was construed less as a dissent from "Dublin writing" than as "more intimately tied to the canon of British literature and Northern Ireland's problematized cultural relationship with the rest of the United Kingdom," such an assertion fails to fully convey the attempted independent regionalist ethos of the *Honest Ulsterman*.[91] Heather Clark points out that "though it was to be a literary magazine, it was also a way to voice opposition to Ulster's conservative cultural establishment: Queen's, the BBC, the Ulster Museum, and *Threshold* were all targets."[92] Indeed, though editor Simmons bizarrely claimed to be starting a revolution based on his own steps of autobiographical confession undertaken "to reach the desired form of individuated essentialism," he nonetheless conceived of the magazine as a liberally enlightened regionalist venue for its writers and its audience.[93] At the same time, Simmons was no consistent emissary of harmonious regionalism: the journal became a way for him "to challenge the Heaney-Longley-Mahon trio."[94]

In his inaugural editorial, after devoting three pages to the necessary free will of the individual (which he links to the "Honest" and the "man" terms of the journal's title), Simmons argues for it as an explicitly regional magazine:

> The emphasis on Ulster seems easy to understand; the magazine originates in Ulster, it provides a special opportunity for Ulster writers and Ulster readers. It will be read here and there about the world; but if it has any profound effects they are most likely to be seen in Ulster.... Just as it is necessary for each individual to claim his own freedom and make his own decisions, so it is important for the regions, small manageable social units, to establish their independence. They say it makes economic

sense for Ulster to keep step by step behind England; but it makes no other sort of sense. I look to a new flowering when not only men and women but towns and counties will assume their real, unique personalities. Ulster education, politics and architecture will be as distinctive as our police force.[95]

Simmons may not have realized how jarring his last sentence here would be for Catholics in Northern Ireland, since the various incarnations of the police in Northern Ireland have, until very recently with the attempt of the Police Service of Northern Ireland to recruit Catholics, been heavily Protestant. Yet the rest of this editorial and indeed the journal itself have often included Catholic voices from the province, including those of Heaney and Bernard MacLaverty. The *Honest Ulsterman*, moreover, consistently published a broad range of Northern Irish writers, enlarging the admittedly small group of writers associated with the Belfast Group coterie into a more provincewide one. For example, just a few years after its founding, Michael Longley clearly felt that Simmons was promoting a wide variety of writers from the province: "Simmon's [sic] two main achievements as an editor are to have brought out *The Honest Ulsterman* almost every month—a unique record in the annals of Irish literary magazines!—and to have discovered and encouraged many new talents, most of them under twenty-five. Indeed he has inaugurated what might almost be termed The Honest Ulsterman School of Poets. These he published in small pamphlets which accompanied the magazine."[96]

Further evidence that Simmons conceived of his magazine as a promoter of regional Northern Irish writing can be found in the advertisements he took out in similarly oriented journals such as *Phoenix* from the same period. For example, the inside front page of the Summer 1970 double issue of *Phoenix* contains the following opening statement from Simmons about the journal: "It is a regional magazine in that it is dedicated to keeping the writers of a region in touch with the readers of a region; but in fact the editor cannot resist printing the work of good writers from other regions when he gets it, and even good translations from Russian and Polish etc. . . . The region needs to know something of what is happening in other regions."[97] Simmons goes on to cite the following authors and critics who have already appeared in the journal's pages: John

McGahern, Stevie Smith, Roger McGough, W. Price Turner, Tony Harrison, Mahon, Montague, Hewitt, Gavin Ewart, Heaney, and Walter Allen. Under a series of editors including Simmons and Frank Ormsby, the *Honest Ulsterman* published the best in Northern Irish writing from May 1968 to 2003, including more than thirty poetry chapbooks, such as Paul Muldoon's first publication, *Knowing My Place*.[98]

An addition to this wealth of journals featuring largely writing from Northern Ireland was Harry Chambers's magazine *Phoenix*, which was based in Belfast for its first two issues and which published many local writers in the late 1960s and early to mid-1970s. *Phoenix*'s first issue was a "Special Arts in Ulster Issue" that came out in March 1967 and featured poems by Longley, Heaney, Arthur Terry, and Iris Bull, all Belfast Group writers, as well as poems from Derek Mahon, who was not connected with the Belfast Group. This first issue also featured two reviews grounded in a recognition of regionalist writing, editor Chambers's review, "Festival Poetry Pamphlets," about the work published by mostly Belfast Group writers for the Belfast Festival of 1965, and Edna Longley's review, "Northern House Pamphlet Poets," about the work of several prominent northern English poets such as Geoffrey Hill, whose poetry Heaney would later praise as exemplifying regionalist writing in his 1976 essay "Englands of the Mind." Chambers's review notes that "the series as a whole has unity and point: each of the poets represented either comes from Northern Ireland or has at some time lived and worked in Belfast."[99] He lauds the oft-linked trio of Heaney, Longley, and Mahon, declaring them to be "three of the best poets in the whole of Ireland writing at the present moment," and disparages the lack of attention they received in England, noting that "the English literary periodicals and little magazines have generally ignored the whole series," indicating the general refusal of the English establishment and even its cultural fringe to recognize the ways in which the United Kingdom's regions were devolving.[100] Yet while this contention may have been true about the poetry pamphlets published in 1965 by these three men, by the time Chambers's review appeared in print, Heaney had been asked to submit *Death of a Naturalist* to Faber and Faber in London, which published it in 1966, and he actually garnered some criticism in Northern Ireland because he received so much attention from English reviewers for this volume. By the next year, Mahon would publish his first full-length volume, *Night-Crossing*, with Oxford University Press, and Michael Longley's poems would be published in a pamphlet entitled *Three Regional Voices: Iain Crichton Smith, Barry Tebb, Michael Longley*, by Poet and Print Press in London, and in *Secret Marriages*, by Chamber's own publishing venue, Phoenix Pamphlets Poets Press. Longley's first full-length volume, *No Continuing City*, was published by Macmillan in 1969, and Heaney's second such volume, *Door into the Dark*, the same year. Chambers is to be commended for his early advocacy of these three poets, but they have received considerable critical attention, even to the detriment of many fine poets from the Republic of Ireland, beginning in the mid- to late 1960s and since.

Edna Longley opens her review with a very clear regionalist affirmation: "I have long felt that the aesthetic conscience of England is to be found in the North—an unexpected form of Pennine backbone. The Northern House pamphlets, a beautifully presented series first produced in Leeds about three years ago, exhibit as a venture an integrity which confirms this impression. They take for granted standards only intermittently honoured in the metropolitan poetry world."[101] Her articulation of a northern English regionalism complements Chambers's delineation of the emerging Northern Irish regionalist poets such as Heaney, Michael Longley, and Mahon. Even after *Phoenix* moved to Manchester, Chambers continued to feature many writers from Northern Ireland, indicating his continuing recognition of regional literature issuing from the province, while he was publishing regional writers from England, such as Philip Larkin.[102]

This proliferation of literary journals in the province makes Gilbert Marshall Irvine's despairing lament for a Northern Ireland–based literary journal in 1929 seem highly pessimistic to us today, though it was completely realistic at the time: "How necessary it seems that a community capable of producing any thought worth recording should have a journal for that purpose! Yet Ulster has none, and outside the influence of Queen's University has no chance apparently of ever having one."[103] Heaney himself could look back in 1983 and praise a series of Irish literary magazines including the *Honest Ulsterman* and note that "they gave generations of writers a forum where their work entered more or less topically into the common culture and the culture was in turn affected by them."[104]

Other literary publications and local cultural endeavors in the late 1950s helped create an impetus for Ulster regionalism. Blake Morrison traces this movement to the 1957 appearance of *Irish Folk Ways*, by the cultural anthropologist E. Estyn Evans, "a book that documented the actual material of traditional peasant life."[105] Other significant cultural endeavors in this promotion of Ulster regionalism included the beginning of work on the *Ulster Dialect Dictionary* (a project that is still uncompleted); the revival of traditional Irish music; the historical research of J. C. Beckett, A. T. Q. Stewart, and F. S. L. Lyons; and the official opening of the Ulster Folk Museum, which had been initiated in 1958.[106]

This overview of earlier Northern Irish theories of regionalism reveals a significant foundation for Heaney's own regionalism as he was emerging in the 1960s and beginning to try to understand his own relationship to the North. Thus there was an organic tradition of imaginative literature and critical literature in Northern Ireland that explicitly considered and articulated with varying degrees of success the multifaceted concept of regionalism that would influence Heaney as he sought both to describe Northern Ireland as it was and to imagine it as it might be.

Chapter Two

RECORDING BIGOTRY AND IMAGINING A NEW PROVINCE

Heaney and BBC Northern Ireland Radio, 1968–73

THE EVOLUTION OF BBC NORTHERN IRELAND AND HEANEY'S WORK FOR THE SCHOOLS PROGRAM

Commentators on Heaney's work have generally not acknowledged his earlier dramatic work that preceded his translation of Sophocles' *Philoctetes, The Cure at Troy,* in 1990. For example, in an otherwise fine essay from 1992, Alan Peacock claims that *The Cure* "is in a number of ways a latest stage in the realization of certain key aspirations in his poetry. Heaney has always, in one way or another, been moving further [*sic*] towards some kind of appropriate public mode, genre or form which might fully accommodate the ever-widening purview of an internationally minded poet."[1] This statement, however, ignores how Heaney had commanded a significant public audience since the 1960s through not only his poetry but also his radio work and dramas for BBC Northern Ireland. Certainly he periodically worried throughout his career about his responsibility to the public and about his commitment to the essentially private form of lyric poetry, but he consistently embraced public genres such as radio drama and newspaper articles.

In "A Sofa in the Forties," Heaney recalls imaginatively "riding" a childhood sofa with his brothers and sisters: "All of us on the sofa in a line, kneeling / Behind each other, eldest down to youngest, / Elbows going like pistons, for this was a train" (*SL*, 7). In the third section, he describes how they heard the BBC radio news as they rode:

> We entered history and ignorance
> Under the wireless shelf. *Yippee-i-ay*,
> Sang "The Riders of the Range." HERE IS THE NEWS,
>
> Said the absolute speaker. Between him and us
> A great gulf was fixed where pronunciation
> Reigned tyrannically. The aerial wire
>
> Swept from a treetop down in through a hole
> Bored in the windowframe. When it moved in wind,
> The sway of language and its furtherings
>
> Swept and swayed in us like nets in water
> Or the abstract, lonely curve of distant trains
> As we entered history and ignorance.
>
> (8)

The abrupt tonal shift in the poem from airy imaginings to the authoritative voice of the "absolute speaker" announcing the beginning of the broadcast is striking. Heaney and his siblings were quickly brought out of their reverie and clearly experienced a lack of linguistic connection (the "great gulf" of the poem) between their rural Ulster accent and the "proper King's English" of the announcer. Previously united in their imagination, they were subsequently linguistically united through their shared dialect. They would not have known the full extent of their marginalization at the time, but the grown poet is certainly reminded of their distance both geographically and ideologically from the metropole of London and of their exclusion from full citizenship in the Protestant-controlled province of Northern Ireland. Heaney's later remarks about this time in which he was exploring his imagination while listening to the official language of the radio suggest why he turned to broadcasting some of his early poems and plays on BBC Northern Ireland Radio: to "adjudicate between" the various "promptings" and pressures he was feeling as a minority poet committed both to his art and to achieving full Catholic civil rights in the 1960s.[2]

Through its focus on how the imagination of the early Heaney interacted embryonically with cultural education, "A Sofa in the Forties" provides an entry into understanding how his radio work for BBC Northern Ireland reveals his efforts to balance his first allegiance, his dedication to the integrity of his art, with an articulation of his righteous anger at the treatment of Catholics in the province as the civil rights movement in the province encountered violent resistance from Protestant loyalists. This struggle would lead him to promote reconciliation through his conception of Northern Irish regionalism, an aesthetic grounded in part on the shared culture and dialects of many Catholics and Protestants. Heaney had contributed work to the station starting in 1966; this chapter focuses on three later radio pieces he wrote and broadcast on the station: an imaginative script for the series *Explorations* (1968), which is replete with important early poetry, and the radio dramas *Munro* (1970) and *Everyman* (1971). It concludes with a brief assessment of Heaney's 1973 radio script on Sam Thompson's drama *Over the Bridge*. Only one of these works, *Munro*, has been published, although all of them had a wide broadcast audience throughout Northern Ireland at the time. An examination of his early radio scripts yields considerable insight into the variable cultural and political role this regional BBC station played in the province at this time. After a history in which it had featured relatively few representations of the Catholic community in the province, BBC Northern Ireland shifted gears in the 1960s and allowed many Catholic voices on the air as part of its developing regionalist plan to stress commonalities between Catholic and Protestant communities in the province.

In his July 1, 1966, essay for *New Statesman*, "Out of London: Ulster's Troubles," Heaney admitted that the sectarian tension growing in the province after the Ulster Volunteer Force shot three youths and killed one of them could lead writers either to go into exile or to explore the dramatic situation: "It might concentrate a man's energies on the immediate dramatic complex of tension and intrigue."[3] Despite his great caution about representing the rise in sectarianism in his poetry at this time, which would not emerge clearly and definitively until the poems of *North*, Heaney was nonetheless considering for himself the possibilities afforded drama by the violence on the streets of the province. He clearly wanted not merely to reflect the violence but to shepherd such energies into the arts, particularly the theater, since in this essay he goes on to praise the work of the Lyric Theatre and the Circle Theatre, noting that the Circle Theatre is putting on "four new Ulster plays."[4] Yet he also goes on to praise the Arts Council of Northern Ireland, various art galleries, the *Northern Review*, the emergence of Philip Hobsbaum's creative writing group, and the appearance of a series of poetry pamphlets for the Queen's Festival sponsored by Michael Emmerson. Heaney concludes by observing, "In all these activities... a liberal atmosphere prevails. The possibility of a cultural life here is the possibility of salvation."[5] This statement is one of his earliest recorded iterations of his belief that poetry and the arts could have an ameliorating effect on the violence in the province—could save it from a descent into a sectarian hell. Although that did not happen, Heaney nonetheless strove mightily to effect such a deliverance, and his involvement with BBC Northern Ireland Radio over the next several years constitutes an untold chapter of a crucial period in the development of his artistic and political interest in the region.

Heaney's interest in evoking a common linguistic and cultural heritage among Northern Irish Protestants and Catholics thus dovetailed well with John Hewitt's continued espousal of a regionalist agenda in the mid- to late 1960s, a period of great turbulence but also great hope as the Northern Irish Civil Rights Association was founded on February 1, 1967, and pressed for equal rights for Catholics. The untitled BBC Northern Ireland Radio script from 1968 suggests Heaney's commitment to imaginative exploration despite what would shortly become intense pressure on him to become a propagandist for nationalists, while *Munro*, *Everyman*, and the script about *Over the Bridge* show the perniciousness of sectarianism, even while registering the poet's anger at the treatment of Northern Irish Catholics in *Everyman*. These scripts achieve a balance between the life of the mind and social activism, a position from which the poet articulates, in *Everyman*, a tentative vision of reconciliation between Northern Irish Catholics and Protestants. In the process, he avoided what Timothy Kearney has argued are the two temptations of the Northern Irish poet: first, "the seductiveness of the Yeatsian vision of culture, of setting oneself up as the vatic spokesman of one's tribe," and second, "the temptation to flee from such intense cultural confusion into an introverted lyrical cul-de-sac."[6] He thus proved himself capable of both remaining faithful to his powerful artistic imagination and offering cultural alternatives to the atrocities being committed in the province by the late 1960s and early 1970s. As Helen Vendler has argued, he was "forced, by the place and time into which he was born, to take on, within the essentially private genre to which he was called, the representation of an unignorable social dimension."[7] Complicating this task that Vendler outlines in the context of his "essentially private genre" of poetry was the more public arena into which he entered through his BBC Northern Ireland transmissions.

Heaney's deft use in these broadcasts of the medium that had been home for so long to the imperial English that had so troubled and transfixed the young child in "A Sofa in the Forties" enabled him sonically to create an imagined regional community of the sort described by Benedict Anderson, a new province where the contributions of both Catholics and Protestants would be honored. Anderson claims that "much the most important thing about language is its capacity for generating imagined communities, building in effect *particular solidarities*."[8] Heaney's imagined community of a province of Northern Irish Catholics and Protestants living in harmony with one another is all the more striking, given the nationalist sentiment, growing in Northern Ireland during the late 1960s and reaching an apogee by the early 1970s, that the "Six Counties" must be reunited with the Republic, and given the increased desire among unionists at the same time that the union with Great Britain be maintained. Heaney realized that, as Martin McLoone has pointed out, in the twentieth century, "broadcasting has been the primary site for the mediation, promotion and maintenance of collective identity."[9] Although McLoone notes that the BBC was mobilized to promote a general sense of British identity, he shows how the organization operated as an instrument of both hegemony and impartial autonomy, the latter of which gave Heaney a medium to register the presence of Northern Irish Catholics and also to incorporate them into an imagined, pluralized province:

> Public service broadcasting has always operated a form of masking, forging links by denying (or at least playing down) difference.... On one

hand, in its pursuit of hegemony, it has operated as a rather blunt instrument, legitimizing (and marginalizing) forms of public discourse by patrolling the boundaries of accepted social, political, and cultural behavior. And yet since its formative days . . . , it has always striven to maintain its autonomy from government interference and from the influences of the market place. Thus in its commitment to impartiality and its obligation to represent all sections of society it has also provided a space for the kinds of dissident or minority opinion which in its hegemonic role, it sought to disavow.[10]

These contradictory impulses were especially strong at BBC Northern Ireland, but by the time Heaney began broadcasting in the mid-1960s its trajectory was toward a "commitment to impartiality" that provided a cultural platform for the young poet who sought to educate the province's populace about the need for multiple cultural and political voices in a complex society.

Language was the medium Heaney chose to promulgate this cultural dialogue and regional devolution, which is nowhere more fully explored than in the Ulster dialects he sees Northern Irish Protestants and Catholics sharing in his 1972 volume *Wintering Out*. The present chapter does not develop this claim about radio scripts that were broadcast orally, but clearly the dissemination of Heaney's own dialect on the air powerfully signaled his determination to suggest the range of similar Northern Irish dialects as a common "language" for the variety of inhabitants in the province.

The "British Broadcasting Company," as it was first known, had nine local, separate radio stations in the 1920s, with each of these covering "about twenty miles in radius—although the exact distance depended [on] whether one was listening on a valve or crystal set."[11] Matthew Linfoot has described how the new regional stations were limited by transmitter locations: "[When] the Company became a Corporation these early local stations were gradually replaced by the 'Regional Scheme.' From 1929 onwards, national output from London was complemented by six Regional services for London and the South-East, Birmingham and the Midlands, the North of England, Scotland, Wales and the West of England and Northern Ireland. The only problem was, these regions were defined not by the people, places and characteristics of the geographical areas, but by the physical landscape that determined where the transmitters could be sited."[12]

What would become BBC Northern Ireland, or "2BE," as it was then known, remained a very limited service because of its continuing restricted reception, the corresponding general exclusion of many in the province, and its lack of local staff members. Rex Cathcart, whose history of the BBC in the North from 1924 to 1984 remains an invaluable study, points out that the 1934 BBC *Year Book* noted in its report on Northern Ireland that the region's "character, from the cultural point of view, is still in the process of formation, and broadcasting has been called upon to play its part."[13] But while BBC Northern Ireland may have been willing to play such a role, its signal reached only a "thirty-mile radius of Belfast" and was criticized for excluding the residents of the vast majority of the province.[14] In the years before World War II, almost the entire BBC NI staff was English and Scottish "and felt alien and insecure" living in Belfast, and there was no discussion of politics on the air, to the gratitude of its staff, who "somewhat inevitably . . . tended to support the Unionist regime because their existence in Ireland depended on it."[15]

After the war ended, a gradual momentum built up within the service to feature more local programming, and gradually discussion of politics crept into the broadcasts. Cathcart has argued that "the memo which the Controller Andrew Stewart issued in 1949 to all programme staff in Broadcasting House, Belfast, is the most important statement on regional policy to originate in Northern Ireland."[16] The two main policy points the network adopted that year suggest a more purposeful attempt to cover the Northern Irish region than ever before, while even sending out local programs to the BBC: "to operate the Northern Ireland Home Service by drawing fully on the resources of the Region and, in the main, on other BBC Home Services. The programmes should reflect the character and taste and inform the thought of listeners in Northern Ireland" and "to supply the BBC with Northern Ireland programmes."[17]

However, as a member of the Catholic minority growing up in the 1940s and 1950s, Heaney distrusted BBC Northern Ireland because, as he recalled in a lengthy conversation with Karl Miller, it had historically excluded Irish Catholic culture: "The only 'Irish' as opposed to 'British' thing that appeared on the Northern Ireland Home Service was a Saturday evening programme called 'Irish Rhythms,' which had the BBC Northern Ireland Orchestra playing Irish jigs. There was a fiction maintained that everything was homogeneous and British. . . . There was a suppression of whatever nationalist culture was, and for my own generation of Northern Catholics, one of the needs was to intrude upon that, and to put Irish culture-speak in there."[18] Heaney's distrust of the BBC lingered into the 1960s, despite his positive experiences with Protestants at Queen's University such as those he met and interacted with in Hobsbaum's Belfast Group.[19] BBC House in Belfast was an imposing building staffed mainly by Protestants, many of whom were committed to maintaining their political and cultural dominance of the province. Longtime BBC radioman and playwright John Boyd, a socialist from the Protestant community in East Belfast who was committed to easing sectarian tensions in the province, articulates this intense local exclusion of Catholics in the second volume of his memoirs:

> Broadcasting House in Belfast was a part of the *British* Broadcasting Corporation and the ethos was definitely non-Irish. The emphasis was almost entirely on the "Ulster" way of life, and "Ulster" was defined as the Six Counties only, and the Six Counties were predominantly Protestant. The staff in Broadcasting House contained only a few Catholics, of whom none held senior posts, and none were producers. This was no accident but a deliberate policy of exclusion. Catholics were considered to be untrustworthy for posts of responsibility, and many years had to pass before the question of religious discrimination was confronted, as I'm told it now has been.[20]

Moreover, BBC Northern Ireland was not just a site of class polarization and Unionist inertia. The controversies in the 1960s that resulted from attempts to stage the liberal Protestant playwright Sam Thompson's *Over the Bridge* (1959) and to broadcast Boyd's radio drama *The Blood of Colonel Lamb*, both of which attacked sectarianism in the province, provide striking evidence of the degree to which the Unionist government occasionally colluded with BBC Northern Ireland to censor local cultural productions.[21] When I asked Boyd about BBC Northern Ireland's rejection of his play, he pointed out the danger of writing something controversial as an employee of the network: "The play was a kind of skit on Paisleyism. You're supposed to be objective. You cannot be partial to the Labour Party or Communist Party. It was a dangerous play"; he then admitted that he had distanced himself from the play to some degree, since "I was afraid I'd get kneecapped because I took the mickey out of Paisleyism."[22] At this time, fundamentalist preacher Ian Paisley of the Free Presbyterian Church was becoming quite popular among certain segments of the Protestant community for his strident verbal attacks on Catholicism, rhetoric that drastically worsened sectarianism in the province.

I mean to suggest, not that BBC Northern Ireland itself was a puppet of the varying Unionist governments over the decades, but rather that on several occasions, notably in the late 1950s and 1960s, it did censor creative work critical of the Unionist establishment. Ritchie McKee, chairman of the board of directors of the Ulster Group Theatre, which demanded significant changes to Thompson's play that forced him finally to withdraw it, was the brother of Cecil McKee, then Unionist lord mayor of Belfast, and on the board of governors at BBC Northern Ireland. Hagal Mengel notes that McKee brought Harry McMullan, head of programs at the BBC, to speak with Thompson, and although "he was present in his capacity as one of the eight directors of the Group Theatre" it became clear that "despite the conciliatory attitude of McMullan . . . McKee had invited him to the meeting in order to make the point that Thompson was in some danger of biting the hand that fed him, namely that of the BBC."[23] BBC Northern Ireland, as Gillian McIntosh has pointed out, "was neither a crude promoter of unionism, nor was it a champion of any distinctive version of 'Irish' culture. It reacted to, and reflected, the state's social developments and political pressures and throughout this formative period [1924–49] it walked a political tightrope in terms of the image of the state it reflected to its domestic audience and to the wider British public."[24] The political pressure brought to bear upon BBC Northern Ireland, however, does reflect the degree to which Unionist politicians attempted to quash criticism of their policies, particularly from Northern Irish Protestants.

The BBC Northern Ireland's bigotry in refusing to produce Boyd's play *The Blood of Colonel Lamb* was a lingering remnant of a formerly restrictive policy on broadcasting dramatic material related to the province.

Cathcart has also pointed out that the 1949 policy memo specifically addressed the need to incorporate not only local music (including traditional Irish music) on the air but also drama by playwrights in Northern Ireland. The memo states that "the work of Ulster playwrights should have first call upon attention and help. Plays by other Irish authors, in which character or situation could emerge in Ulster, should be considered on merit, as should plays with close Ulster parallels from other parts of the United Kingdom, or from other countries."[25] So by 1949, two years after the educational act that would send many Northern Irish Catholics such as Heaney to university by the 1950s, BBC Northern Ireland was, at least in principle, committed to broadcasting dramatic material by local writers. This commitment preceded the formation of the Schools Department at the service, but both the articulation of this dramatic policy and the establishment of a Northern Ireland Schools Department would enable Heaney to begin broadcasting for BBC NI's schools programs and to have his own radio dramas produced by the late 1960s.

Forty years after other regions in Britain received their own Schools Departments to broadcast regional material, BBC Northern Irish Radio finally acquired its own Schools Department in 1960. As Marilynn Richtarik notes, Unionist politicians had previously viewed such a department as too closely linked with Irish nationalism: "The reason for the delay was political: Unionist officials resisted the creation of a broadcasting entity whose *raison d'etre* would be to focus on 'Irish' subjects, which were associated in their minds with republican views."[26] She further argues that the fears of both unionists and nationalists (the latter group naturally skeptical of an entity with *British* as its primary adjective) were unfounded because the Northern Irish Schools Department strove vigorously to promote a shared Northern Irish culture. It aims were to "induc[e] the future decision-makers of the province to acknowledge, respect, and even appreciate Northern Ireland's diversity and to recognize the intertwining strands of a shared Northern Irish culture."[27]

The major public controversy that resulted from the Group Theatre's cancellation of Thompson's play after Ritchie McKee's public rejection of it in the *Belfast Telegraph* in May 1959 made the Northern Ireland members of the School Broadcasting Council press hard for noncontroversial productions as part of their grudging assent to the Council's 1960 decision to form a Schools Department. As Cathcart has pointed out, the pressure brought to bear "on the School Broadcasting Council to establish local production in Belfast increased until finally in 1960 the Council conceded. The three Northern Ireland representatives on the Council resisted the development to the very end, giving in with poor grace and demanding assurances that nothing controversial would ever be broadcast."[28] However, by 1965, a potentially controversial series on modern Irish history entitled *Two Centuries of Irish History* was broadcast. This series "was welcomed unanimously and won extensive publicity north and south."[29] As Cathcart goes on to note, the relative jubilation associated with such BBC Northern Ireland programming, coupled with the seeming liberalizing tendencies of Northern Irish prime minister Terence O'Neill, made the BBC leadership believe that a watershed in cultural relations in the province had occurred: "In the mid-1960s there was a measure of euphoria in broadcasting circles. Rapprochement externally and internally in Northern Ireland seemed to have been achieved. One member of the Advisory Council, Sam Napier, could even speak in 1966 of 'integration' in Northern Ireland's society."[30] Already that summer, however, the First Belfast Battalion of the Ulster Volunteer Force, which was founded in 1913 by Sir Edward Carson, Ian Paisley's personal hero, announced a campaign of violence against the IRA and its splinter groups, and although republican paramilitaries were basically moribund at the time, five murders were carried out against Catholics, four of whom were shot after leaving a pub called the Malvern Arms.[31] Although the leadership of BBC Northern Ireland turned out to be wrong about the sea change they had foreseen coming in provincewide cultural relations, their vision of inclusivity was a significant cultural contribution to artistic efforts to reconcile the divided communities.

It is important to recognize this promotion of a shared Northern Irish culture and literature through the BBC Northern Ireland schools program in its proper context, as part of the regionalist agenda the studio had pursued since the end of World War II. As Gillian McIntosh has observed, "There was also a drive [after the war] by BBC NI to recruit more local people, a move which drew in creative writers such as Sam Hanna Bell and John Hewitt.... Local music and the arts were given a platform in series such as *In Ulster Now*, while *Writing in Ulster* provided a forum for the work of Northern Irish writers."[32] It was thus more natural than it might have first seemed for Heaney, as the leader of a new generation of

Northern Irish writers, to broadcast on BBC Northern Ireland; after all, his literary forebears such as John Hewitt had been doing so for some time. Nevertheless, he was the first prominent Northern Irish writer from the Catholic community to do so.

Hence, despite the BBC Northern Ireland–led refusal to broadcast John Boyd's drama, the Northern Ireland schools programs demonstrated that a progressive and ecumenical trajectory for the network was developing. It would eventually move toward its current strategy, "which requires the broadcasters to reflect the whole of society in Northern Ireland as it is, in its negative and its positive aspects."[33] Despite lingering resistance to imaginative work attacking sectarianism and an abiding distrust of lower-class artists (not to mention Catholic artists and Catholics generally), BBC Northern Ireland's artistic programming became more culturally representative and innovative as the 1960s progressed. It was thus perfectly suited for Seamus Heaney's early explorations about the imagination and about how regional literature might begin to imagine healing cultural divisions in the province. Fittingly, he used the Northern Irish schools program to imaginatively and culturally educate the next generation of the province in a nondidactic but moral manner.

Michael Parker has pointed out that the poet's association with BBC Northern Ireland resulted from his friendship with the Northern Irish Protestant singer and broadcaster David Hammond, who, upon joining the station at the end of 1965, "approached Heaney, and asked him to contribute some radio scripts. The result was *Over to You*, a series for E.S.N. pupils throughout Britain."[34] Parker notes that although there were many protests in London "about the number of regional accents and Irish references in the programmes . . . they became increasingly popular with teachers and pupils, because they dealt with powerful themes and did not talk down to their listeners."[35] Unlike many Northern Irish Protestants, Hammond shared a strong sense of Irishness with the Catholic Heaney; more important, the two men shared "a passion for 'the hidden Ulster,' for the folk customs and culture of their forebears, and sought through teaching and learning to sensitise their countrymen and themselves to their past and present inheritance."[36] Heaney returns repeatedly in his essays and poetry to the phrase "the hidden Ulster," which not only signifies a substratum of Catholic and Irish culture that he sought to recover but also suggests for him the necessary first step to putting Irish Catholic culture and British Protestant culture in the province on equal footing so that there might be a rapprochement between them. Heaney and Hammond increasingly came to promote an awareness of Northern Irish regionalism through their work together at BBC Northern Ireland. Both men seem to have felt that a shared sense of their common regional identity and culture might unite Catholics and Protestants.

Their work together in other venues similarly sought to explore and express a unifying Northern Irish regional culture. In 1968, the same year that Heaney's important radio transmission on the imagination was broadcast as part of BBC Northern Ireland's *Explorations* series, Heaney, Hammond, and Michael Longley traveled together around the province on a tour they called "Room to Rhyme." The Catholic Heaney and the Protestant Longley recited their own poems, and Hammond sang many folk songs of Northern Ireland. It was a success, in part because, according to Heaney, "wherever we went, it tended to be a mixed audience, people with an interest in hearing poems and songs, hence people with a certain ability to read not just the content but the codes in what was being presented" (*SS*, 117). Heaney recalls that "what we had was the beginnings of pluralism rather than the same old primness," and although he quickly admits that "my recollection of that moment may be too rosy, too subject to political as well as personal nostalgia," he finally argues that "the content and conduct of our programme were symptomatic of a change for the better" (118), implying how a shared regional identity could begin imagining solutions to sectarianism.[37]

After the success of his first radio scripts for schoolchildren, Heaney wrote a piece on the imagination, perhaps with the hopes of sparking an interest in schoolchildren who were growing up in a relatively static educational culture of homogeneous, segregated schools. His remarks about education in his 1983 lecture dedicated to the memory of his former teacher John Malone are particularly apposite with regard to his work for the schools program on BBC Northern Ireland. As he observes in that lecture, "The educational process is a matter of sympathetic recognition. The learning experience is both challenge and liberation."[38] Even by the 1960s, Heaney felt that an increased emphasis on imagination generally might lead to an imagined province where Catholics and Protestants could engage in "sympathetic recognition" by expressing and even celebrating many aspects of their shared identity as Northern Irish. He had already formally prepared to teach; now he sought to educate in a more informal but still important venue. He had previously trained as a teacher at St. Joseph's College of Education in Belfast from 1961 to 1962 and, as part of the course, had taught under the Northern Irish writer Michael McLaverty at St. Thomas Intermediate School in Belfast. McLaverty reinforced Heaney's desire to promote a shared regional Northern Irish identity, as did the presence of an array of Northern Irish poets that were featured on BBC Northern Ireland between 1945 and 1966.[39] Heaney, in his turn, sought to educate schoolchildren throughout the province about their common cultural heritage through a medium that had a wide appeal across generations, classes, and denominational affiliations in the province.

It is difficult for audiences outside Ireland to imagine the intensity with which the Irish listened to radio, but Christina Hunt Mahony makes clear that radio listening was a crucial part of Irish cultural life at the time: "Long after radio's introduction, radio listening also continued to be something of a ritualized practice, as the device was turned on at certain times of the day or week for specific programs, and family schedules fell into an established rhythm.... Early listeners focused all their attention on radio listening, unlike today's listeners, who hear radio in their cars, in elevators, in doctors' offices as background noise that only occasionally impinges in a lasting or meaningful sense."[40] For audiences in Northern Ireland, the radio occupied a crucial position in the cultural life of the province, and weekly programs were eagerly anticipated. Cathcart points out that even when television became more widespread, Northern Irish audiences "remained loyal to the older medium," at least in part because "television for long lacked any significant local component whereas radio continued to supply a regional service."[41] He also notes that listener research proved Northern Ireland to be the only region in Britain where more people listened to their regional Home Service than to the Light Programme.[42] Heaney himself has recalled in his essay "The Regional Forecast" the avidity with which his family listened to the weather forecast for the region of Northern Ireland: "If an angel had passed or a mighty wind had arisen or tongues of flames descended, the occasion could not have been more prepared for or more expectant."[43] This intense interest in radio was heightened by the poor economic conditions of both the Catholic minority in the province and the working-class Protestants, for whom television was a luxury not to be enjoyed for some time.

HEANEY'S *EXPLORATIONS* RADIO SCRIPT AND THE IMAGINATION

The untitled work Heaney contributed to the station was part of the BBC Northern Ireland series entitled *Explorations*; it was broadcast on BBC Northern Ireland Radio Four on Wednesday, May 1, 1968, from 2:20 until 2:45 in the afternoon. Later that year, the Northern Irish Civil Rights Association (NICRA) would begin explorations of a different sort as it held its first civil rights march from Coalisland to Dungannon to protest discrimination against Catholics. Before and even for a brief time after this largely peaceful march was held, to be followed by later marches, such as the infamous one of October 5, in which the Royal Ulster Constabulary attacked protesters in Derry with batons and water cannons, a window of opportunity existed for NICRA to make common cause with supportive Protestants, including those from the working-class ghettos.[44] Heaney's radio script features a running commentary on the imagination interspersed with some of his own poems. The critical interest in the piece is twofold: it offers a window into Heaney's early thinking about the imagination and also allows us to understand the political pressure on him to desert his fidelity to it that was enabling him to conceive of the province as a pluralist region and instead to comment on the growing tensions in the province and anti-Catholic discrimination.

The opening remarks are from Heaney's narrator and explicitly link the piece's title to geographic and mental exploration:

> I suppose our first images of exploration come from the comic strip or the adventure story: those intrepid Britishers with short pants and long socks, sweating their way beneath cork helmets and a tropic sun.... You can explore inwards as well as outwards, obviously. Your head is a world that contains oceans, continents, the lonely constellations. It can make room for constellations to come, galaxies that have not yet been named. Your head may come to house the far side of the moon, and the strangest

zones of Mars. Its dark spaces can recede to encompass each new found land. And which, I wonder, is the more powerful summons to discovery, the dark on the map or the dark inside your head?[45]

Crucially and surprisingly for a minority Catholic in Ulster, Heaney lends a specific cultural identity to this outward exploration in approvingly recalling "those intrepid Britishers," although the use of the demonstrative pronoun suggests that he sees them as outsiders in some respects.

After a general narrative about global historical exploration, the narrator speculates about the instruments by which we discover new lands, then suggests instruments that will help us discover ourselves and the minutiae of experience:

The captain at the deck-rail with his telescope, the scout scanning the plain through his poised binoculars: These might seem emblems of the explorer's quest.... I would try to think of other means of discovery and loss. I would add the mirror and the microscope. The mirror opens worlds in my own eyes, my eyesockets look out dark as gaps in a jungle. The microscope reveals worlds under my own nose: the fly's wing turns brilliant as a distant star. Then, by looking hard we travel from ourselves; you can disappear into the thing you look at. You and I were often lost in thought. We explore lives not our own by our attention.[46]

All these are instruments of the Enlightenment and its accompanying emphasis on the material, but Heaney manages to transform two of them—the mirror and the microscope—into powerful aids to self-discovery and insight about others. He implicitly argues that the imagination can lead to appreciation of "lives not our own," a powerful first step in promoting his notion of a plural yet united province. Properly balanced vision partakes of both inward contemplation and the outward gaze, a liminal position the poet himself was then trying to achieve in being true to himself, yet keeping an eye on events transpiring in the province.

In this untitled radio piece, Heaney certainly affirms the viability of looking inward, but at the same time he sounds a cautionary note about becoming too self-absorbed and losing touch with one's community. Toward the end of the script, he invokes a frogman—an in-between, amphibious person—and suggests this creature has drifted too far inward, away from the earth: "He has lost touch with the dry land where they know him. He pokes around in the rich darkness of the riverbed the way I poke around inside myself when I begin to write. The further I go in my own head, the more I lose the sense of those around me. I wonder when we carry exploration too far?"[47]

In its echo of his famous early poem "Digging," Heaney's introduction to the poem that follows, "Frogman," offers another profound image of the imagination—metaphorically digging, this time, in the rich soil of the riverbed for fertile ideas.[48] But whereas in the earlier poem the poet remains firmly (and literally) above ground and rooted to the communal land, Heaney's frogman as a symbol of himself has become cut off from the land, too subterranean; he has come to love the water too much:

The air's a slap
In the face. He always

Walks home late now
In rubber and goggles.[49]

The concluding solitary image at the end of stanza 4 of the frogman walking home late every night—disturbingly, still in his outfit—suggests his obsessiveness and warns against self-absorption. The monitory "Frogman" thus resonates with both "Death of a Naturalist," a poem featuring the boyhood poet's awakened sexual fears raised by angry frogs, and "Personal Helicon," which warns against overimmersion in the imagination specifically (*DN*, 3–4, 57). In the context of Heaney's Northern Ireland, "Frogman" thus may imply that an imagination divorced from the reality of the actual conditions on the streets and in the neighborhoods of the province would be a solipsistic entity unable to attend to pressing and specific political and cultural concerns.

The narrator follows this discussion by reading Heaney's poem "The Plantation," which would be collected in his second volume of poetry, *Door into the Dark* (*DD*, 36–37).[50] This poem continues his emphasis on balance, suggesting through three images of circles in its first three stanzas the possible fruitlessness of walking in an enchanted wood:

Any point in that wood
Was a centre, birch trunks
Ghosting your bearings,
Improvising charmed rings

Wherever you stopped.
Though you walked a straight line
It might be a circle you traveled
With toadstools and stumps

Always repeating themselves.[51]

By the end of the poem, the speaker observes that

You had to come back
To learn how to lose yourself,
To be pilot and stray, witch,
Hansel and Gretel in one.[52]

The necessary balance between action and contemplation is suggested beautifully by the pair of "pilot," with its directional connotation, and its obverse, "stray." To underscore his message, the poet intensifies that pair by coupling it with the fairy tale trio. The point is that the imagination must remain balanced between delightful meandering and traveling toward a destination. Its proper path lies between utter self-absorption, characterized by wandering, and complete engagement with the world, symbolized by rigid linearity.

Carl Jung's distinction between directed and nondirected thinking has special bearing for this point. In his essay "Two Kinds of Thinking," Jung holds that "directed or logical thinking" is "reality-thinking, a thinking that is adapted to reality, by means of which we imitate the successiveness of objectively real things, so that the images in our mind follow one another in the same strictly causal sequence as the events taking place outside it."[53] In contrast, nondirected thinking is "effortless, working as it were spontaneously, with the contents ready to hand, and guided by unconscious motives. The one [directed thinking] produces innovations and adaptation, copies reality, and tries to act upon it; the other turns away from reality, sets free subjective tendencies, and, as regards adaptation, is unproductive."[54] Given the growing political pressures in Northern Ireland, Heaney's imagination would soon be sorely tested. He seems to be steeling himself in "The Plantation" for such a test, while also encouraging the schoolchildren of the province to develop an imagination supple enough to cope with rapid change and dislocation, even the intimate horror of familial and outside violence, as the Hansel and Gretel reference suggests.

The narrator concludes by speculating more on journeys, finally employing the physical metaphor of a diver to privilege similarly courageous mental movements: "The journey backwards is in memory to childhood, the journey forward in imagination towards death. Are all our actions only preparation for the last expedition? Is the poet's journey through imagination and the astronauts [sic] orbit into outer space and Columbus's attempt to find the edge of the world, is all this only a metaphor for the final departure into the dark? Like the diver at the end of the springboard, man braces himself and leaps into action, makes his best showing before going under. It takes courage and gaiety to make the most memorable actions."[55] Heaney himself would soon come to display the courage and gaiety that his diver on the springboard does as he began entering the controversy around the NICRA marches.[56] His artistic courage and his gaiety in this context are Yeatsian qualities the younger poet would evince in the face of the violence that would soon erupt in the province, even though he would confess periodically his cowardice, perhaps most famously in poems such as "Punishment" from *North* (*N*, 31).[57]

In this seminal BBC radio program broadcast in May 1968—just months before his fellow Catholics would be vilified and persecuted for their burgeoning civil rights movement—Heaney is exploring and stretching the limits of the dichotomy between contemplation and the outer world of action. As the conflict in Northern Ireland accelerated, he would increasingly wonder how detached he should remain—how much he should look inward like his frogman does before his utter self-absorption—and to what degree he should get involved in the external affairs of his province. His exemplar, Yeats, had struggled with this question throughout his career, as Ireland sought to gain its independence from Britain. Heaney eloquently articulated how Yeats's imagination filtered these events and enabled him to write poetry about them, if he so chose, that was not reportorial or immediate but meditative and thoughtful:

> He did record direct responses to some events in Ireland, most notably in his poem "Easter 1916," but generally the poems did not arise from the immediate stimulus of happenings or from a desire to set down the story. They arose, rather, from the resonance that the happenings produced within his consciousness and from the meditated meaning they engendered there. Obviously, then, although the historical shocks that ran through the world did affect Yeats, his imagination did not function like an obedient seismograph. Indeed the whole force of his thought worked against those philosophies which regarded the mind's activity as something determined by circumstance and which consequently limited its possibilities to empirical discovery.[58]

Much the same statement could be made about Heaney's own creative work: while it remained engaged with life in Northern Ireland and in the Republic, it was always written out of intense imaginative contemplation that was attentive to political and historical events but not subservient to them. Heaney, like Yeats, refused to let his poetry become mere political propaganda, preferring instead to let his imagination, not political instigation, guide him. John Wilson Foster has perhaps best expressed Heaney's position in this regard: "He has tried to dedicate his central allegiance to Poetry and make that art his candid but chivalrous battlefield.... It is as if Poetry has been Heaney's conscience, preventing blatant partisanship or propaganda, keeping him in the political no-man's land as fidelity to Poetry dictates."[59]

At the same time, as the Catholic minority in the North struggled for equal rights, including an end to gerrymandered voting districts, fair housing, and increased employment opportunities, Heaney realized that his vocation was inextricably intertwined with such issues yet still desired full poetic integrity. This recognition epitomizes what Edna Longley, writing in the mid-1980s, characterized as the Northern Irish poet's inability to be let "off the hook of general or particular 'responsibility' toward political events" as a part of the process of preserving imaginative sovereignty:

"The price of imaginative liberty is eternal vigilance."[60] Along with his sense of responsibility in writing about cultural and political problems, Heaney's interest in what Dillon Johnston has termed "rural violence and the country attitude toward death" in his first two volumes prepared him to some degree for artistically dealing with the upsurge of mostly urban violence and deaths when the contemporary Troubles began in the fall of 1968.[61]

THE UNITED IRISHMEN, THE CIVIL RIGHTS MOVEMENT, AND *MUNRO*

Heaney was long fascinated by the United Irishmen and often praised their actions. For instance, he once recalled acting as a blacksmith who "forged pikes for the United Irish insurgents" in Bellaghy, "probably 1959 or 1960," as part of a "melodrama based on a novel called *The Hearts of Down*, about Betsy Gray ... [who] figures in the lore of the 1798 Rebellion in County Down as a kind of local Joan of Arc" (*SS*, 92). And he fondly remembered the image of Wolfe Tone hanging in the local hall: "Wolfe Tone, our enlightenment revolutionary and founding father of Irish Republicanism ... the figure in tight-fitting white trousers and braided green coat whose large profiled nose stared out over the audience."[62] That image accorded well with another image of Tone he found in the late 1940s of the man "dressed in an open shirt and dark breeches, his arms folded, staring into a shaft of light that struck into his prison cell from a high barred window. Again, this image of a noble nature stoically enduring had a deeply formative effect on my notion of the United Irishmen, the 1798 rebellion, and the whole tradition of Irish separatism."[63] Nobility, stoicism, endurance, and a propensity to ecumenism thus were all characteristics of Tone that appealed to Heaney and colored his view of the United Irishmen and their uprising in 1798.

Early in the Troubles, Heaney was commissioned by BBC Northern Ireland to write a verse play for its radio series *Books, Plays, and Poems* about Henry Munro, who was one of several County Down Protestant leaders of the United Irishmen sympathetic to Catholics during the 1798 rebellion. After the rising in Down started with an attack on Saintfield on

June 9, 1798, the ill-trained and poorly equipped rebels were insubordinate and threatened to leave the field at any time. The next day, Henry Munro, a Lisburn linen draper, was appointed the commander of the rebel army of Down, which was based at Creevy Rocks, just south of Saintfield. But Munro, who had hoped to rally his men to a great victory at Ballynahinch on June 11, was deserted by hundreds of his recruits on the eve of the battle. Marianne Elliott argues that partly because of this desertion, and partly because of Munro's "absence of military acumen," the United Irishmen lost the battle at Ballynahinch.[64] No one, however, disputes "Munro's courage and honour,"[65] and these qualities, along with his desire to attain civil and political rights for Catholics, are what Heaney celebrates in his verse play.

Kenneth L. Dawson points out that Munro joined the first company of Lisburn Volunteers shortly after its formation in 1778 and notes that "the Volunteers were at the forefront of radical politics in Ulster, and, in the early 1790s, when they revived as proxy vehicles for the dissemination of United Irish propaganda, the Lisburn companies were doing their bit to bring about a unity of Catholic, Protestant and Dissenter in the town."[66] Seeking to downplay the ecumenical force of this movement, Roy Foster has suggested that Ulster radicalism has been generally overestimated outside Counties Antrim and Down, which, while generally supportive of Catholic emancipation, had "very few Catholics and a strong New Light Presbyterian tradition," while "the old siege mentality was still much in evidence in most of the province."[67] And yet Down had the largest number of rebelling Catholics in the historic nine-county province of Ulster during the uprising. The so-called "New Light" Presbyterians had seceded from the Presbyterian Synod over the Westminster Confession during the First Subscription Controversy in the 1720s and had formed the separate Presbytery of Antrim. They were "latitudinarians" and "represented the libertarian tradition within Presbyterianism," manifesting a "more radical, less austere form of Presbyterianism" that "created a climate for the flowering of Protestant radicalism in the Volunteers, in the first [G]aelic [R]evival, and in the United Irishmen."[68] Even though "the bulk of Protestant opinion in the North" evinced a "preference for gradual emancipation" of Catholics, "Presbyterian libertarianism pushed the north-east in the other direction" and "Belfast defiantly opened Volunteer ranks to Catholics in May 1784."[69] Dawson observes that "Monro's political outlook was . . .

shaped by his membership of the Freemasons, a movement that was in the vanguard of the European Enlightenment and, locally, of the principles and ideals espoused by the United Irishmen. The lodge allowed Protestants and Catholics to meet as equals, as brothers without religious distinction."[70] Some Freemasons were not radicals, but because of their secretive practices individual lodges could "act subversively," and the presence of such radicals as Bartholomew Teeling, "son of Luke Teeling, the Poleglass [linen] bleacher and leading radical," along with Munro himself, ensured that Lodge 193's "agenda was shaped by people like Bartholomew Teeling, and [that] Monro [*sic*], as master of this lodge, would have been at the forefront of any radical or seditious activities in which it was involved."[71] Munro, then, held long-standing radical opinions and was firmly committed to achieving ecumenism between Catholics and Protestants and to obtaining the franchise for Catholics.

Heaney's radio drama, simply titled *Munro*, and broadcast by the BBC on January 14, 1970, portrays the Presbyterian leader in an admirable light, focusing on his ecumenical qualities that stemmed from his deep Christian faith. The play takes place before Munro, whose severed head was later placed on a spike in Lisburn town square, was hanged by General Nugent, commander of the British troops that eventually put down the rebellion, and it centers on Munro's dialogue with the general as they discuss his part in the rebellion. After Munro invokes his motto of "Sword, Bible and purse: / Righteousness the just course" in the midst of his oral last will and testament, Nugent argues that "sword, Bible and purse / Abused by citizens are a curse."[72] As their dialogue continues, Munro eloquently defends the rebellion in language borrowed from the New Testament (invoking grace) and the French Revolution (exalting the rights of man), claiming the essential inclusiveness of the rising:

> This was a commonwealth where all was level.
> In the mailed fist of your laws they saw a devil
> And their obsequious ways were a shield of grace
> To hold against that hard official face.
> The Catholic and the Presbyterian
> Can demonstrate the ways of God to men
> Without paying tithes, without discrimination.

We have a stake forever in this nation
That landlords and a crooked parliament
And an army that can boast the excrement
Of England never will uproot.
The rights of man are the banner we salute.
Religious freedom, the butts from which we shoot.[73]

Although Heaney began writing poems as a youth with blank verse imitations of the English Puritan John Milton, he has generally not engaged with Milton's work;[74] here, however, his lines "The Catholic and the Presbyterian / Can demonstrate the ways of God to men" suggest that he has Munro impute the authority given God in Milton's theodicy *Paradise Lost* to Irish Catholics and Presbyterians as conscious, Christlike agents, cocreators "of a commonwealth where all was level."

As he and Nugent continue to argue about rebellion versus authority, Munro finally invokes other rebels with whom he identifies: "Brutus and Rousseau stand with me. / And Christ. And Luther."[75] The act of publicly invoking and praising the name of the founder of the Protestant Reformation in a favorable context in 1970 would have been anathema to many Northern Irish Catholics, who felt persecuted by Protestant fundamentalists, such as Ian Paisley's Free Presbyterians. Indeed, Heaney himself had written an essay in July of 1966 criticizing the bigoted Protestant preacher and leader for his threat to the stability of Northern Ireland.[76] But Heaney held that Paisley's distortion of Presbyterianism was just that, a distortion, and instead believed in a more ecumenical view of radical Presbyterianism in the northern part of Ireland, epitomized by what he understood to be the commitment of Presbyterians like Munro—whom he aligned with Luther and even Christ—to Catholic emancipation in the late 1790s. While a series of historians such as Roy Foster have recently shown that "the desire to merge the rising in Ulster into that in Wexford . . . meant ignoring the drift of Northern opinion against the [formation of the] French Republic by the later 1790s, and basic structural differences too," Heaney focuses on the radical nature of the United Irishmen in County Down, Munro's home, as springing from a radical Presbyterian commitment to protonationalism and Catholic civil rights, influenced in part by his hope that such a commitment would arise again in the 1960s.[77]

As the play concludes, Munro settles the accounts of his linen shop from the gallows and makes his peace with his savior, looking forward to his heavenly reward. His execution, however, does not bode well for Catholic-Protestant relations in the northern part of Ireland. The final ominous words of the play belong to the Singer, who relates a vision of revenge taken by Munro's sister:

> Then up came Munro's sister, she was all dressed in green
> With a sword by her side that was well sharped and keen
> And she gave three cheers and away she did go
> Saying "I'll be revenged for my brother Munro."[78]

Letting the obviously Protestant singer, who is tellingly cloaked in the nationalistic color of green, have the last word instead of Munro may seem to work against the ecumenical thrust of this drama, but Heaney understands well just how quickly martyrdom can be appropriated for sectarian ends. Thus he subtly evokes the conflated image of Kathleen Ni Houlihan here as Munro's sister "all dressed in green / With a sword by her side that was well sharped and keen," simultaneously suggesting and critiquing the rise of especially militant nationalism in the wake of the failed uprising, in part for the sake of the ecumenical Munro.

Heaney's sympathetic portrait of the failed 1798 rebellion indicates his bittersweet awareness of the lost potential for Catholic-Protestant harmony after that rising failed and of the now-vanishing hope for that present accord represented by the then-foundering Northern Ireland civil rights movement. The cautious optimism he had expressed only fifteen months earlier in his essay on the contemporary civil rights movement, "Old Derry's Walls," had largely disappeared at this point. In "Old Derry's Walls," he could state hopefully that "a real change is taking place under the thick skin of the Northern Ireland electorate. Catholics and Protestants, Unionist and Republican, have aligned themselves behind the civil rights platform to examine the conscience of the community." He describes this new alignment as "the renaissance of an interest in the rights of man which began here (and was effectively ended, of course) with the United Irishmen in the latter part of the 18th century."[79] As Elliott points out, in the aftermath of the rising, relationships between lower-class Catholics and Protestants in Ulster were the most divided they had been the entire century: "For the first time that century the bulk of lower-class Catholics were disaffected, the bulk of lower-class Protestants and Presbyterians were loyalist."[80] Some disaffected Catholics joined the militant Ribbonmen, which "perpetuated lower-class Catholic sectarianism into the nineteenth century,"[81] while secretive sectarian Orange societies flourished and attracted scores of lower-class Protestants. After the relative optimism for changed Catholic-Protestant relations in the North during the early and mid-1960s, especially through the cultural reconciliation taking place through BBC Northern Ireland's commitment to representing both major cultures in the province, the militant nationalism that was reborn there in the early 1970s in the face of growing Protestant loyalist brutality must surely have reminded Heaney of the same hardening of the divide that took place after 1798.

That Heaney published the text of his radio play in a special issue of *Everyman: An Annual Religio-Cultural Review* on the situation in Northern Ireland also bespeaks his ecumenical intentions but through a specifically literary/humanist appeal. This short-lived journal, on whose editorial board Heaney served, was published by the Servite Priory at Benburg in County Tyrone, Northern Ireland. This order, as it notes on the inside front cover of the third issue of *Everyman* in which Heaney published *Munro*, focuses on "parishes, foreign missions, teaching, parish missions and retreats, the written word."[82] And indeed, Cyril Farrell's editorial in this issue muses upon the power of negative words such as sectarian slogans and the potentially liberating power of positive words of reconciliation. He opens by noting that "as our last Editorial was being written students were marching towards Burntollet. Their march is now history. It has been a good year for historians, but a bloody awful year for those who made the history of Northern Ireland."[83] Farrell goes on to observe that "millions of words have been written: quick dispatches to beat deadlines; reasoned exposés from an objective distance. . . . But they have solved nothing. Then why go on adding to the words and the pictures? For different reasons, I suppose: the hope that we are helping; the salving of our consciences; the settling of scores. In this issue we are adding to the multitude of words and pictures, simply because we feel compelled."[84] He contends that "it is the ignorance, the misconceptions, the deafness to the voices of the others that must be cleared away," arguing that "this is not a political problem, nor even a religious one. It is a merely human problem" that "demands" that we use "the common sense that is given to most humans, and us[e] the higher aspirations of which most humans are capable."[85]

Farrell finally appeals to the reader in terms of this rationalist outlook, concluding that the volume's contributors, including Heaney, have written pieces that are "not the 'hot news' of last night's riots, but their considered reflections. Words, words, words, if you choose to look at it that way. Put all their thoughts together and there may not be yet the term of a solution. Or there may be—if you, reader, would listen.... How many people must die, how many houses must be burned, before people will begin to listen, and reflect on what they hear? And act according to their deep convictions instead of following slogans?"[86] Farrell's appeal to humanist literacy and contemplation as a possible solution to the burgeoning violence in the province by 1970 chimes well with *Munro*'s focus on the 1798 rebellion. Roy Foster notes that "the traditions of Enlightenment debate were diffused through Belfast 'society'...; this encouraged the fashion for Paine (seven Irish editions of the *Rights of Man* between 1791 and 1792) and the full newspaper reports of Convention debates."[87] Munro's invocation of "the rights of man" in the long passage from the play I cite above suggests the ecumenical thrust of Heaney's portrayal of this 1798 leader, and that ecumenism is repeatedly conveyed through an emphasis on Munro's able use of rhetoric. When Nugent, for example, calls the 1798 soldiers "wasps," Munro turns to the rhetoric of the neoclassicists of the eighteenth century, who themselves often drew on the image of bees and honey to convey order and peace: "My harmless bees, they prayed their honey thrive, / And rain in harvest, frost in spring, were all their fears."[88] He concludes that particular speech with a trinitarian procession of phrases again designed to portray his soldiers as peaceful farmers and speakers of sweet rhetoric: "In their honeycombs of thatch—the word of song / The word of gossip and the word of God. / Their blades were for the briar and the sod."[89]

Such an evocation of the 1798 rebels as countrymen who loved the words of song, gossip, and God indicates Heaney's own deep connection to them through his own biography. John Hobbs has convincingly argued in his suggestive essay about Heaney and the United Irishmen that because Heaney was a "rural Northerner," a major reason that "the Rebellion engaged Heaney's imagination was the heavy involvement of countrymen, while the [1916 Easter] Rising was an urban event" and did not similarly stir him.[90] Thus, when Munro recalls his recruits as "busy drones" who desired only "a well-ploughed rood, a well-mowed swathe," Heaney clearly sanctions their commitment to rural farmwork and particularly to agriculture, just as his carefully crafted poems still reflect his own aesthetic commitment to cultivating verse.[91]

Finally, Munro's casting of all of his speeches in the play as "my last will and testament" and particularly the last moving scene, during which his "last request" is "that you will send in to my desk / For my two ledgers, my pens and my inkwell," further suggests that Heaney was drawn to portray Munro because of his facility with the pen.[92] In Heaney's November 27, 1969, review of Thomas Pakenham's influential study about the 1798 rebellion, *The Year of Liberty*, Heaney interprets Munro's settling of accounts on the gallows as "a retreat into solitude, at least a retreat from partisan politics, a last frail attempt at healing the community."[93] Even though Munro was a linen draper and was literally settling his outstanding business accounts while on the gallows, Heaney clearly approves of the link between Munro and writing. For instance, when Munro's ledgers, inkwell, and pens are being retrieved, he sarcastically tells Nugent, "You will excuse me if I blot this solemn occasion / With a few strokes from my chosen weapon. / You did remind me, General, after all, of counter and pen."[94] Heaney sonically signals his approval of Munro's association with the pen and writing more generally by Munro's breaking into couplets in this long speech—full couplets in many places and near couplets otherwise. His 1963 essay "Our Own Dour Way" contextualizes his famous poem "Digging" and the hope held before the Troubles broke out by Heaney and some of his contemporaries in Northern Ireland that cultural and political relations were changing for the better. Thus, just as his famous early poem "suggests a version of the old saw, 'The pen is mightier than the sword,'" so does this verse play's endorsement of Munro's commitment to the pen, even though he had taken up arms in a just cause.[95]

Heaney's attempt to publicly appeal to a great section of the citizenry in Northern Ireland at this time is further signified not only by his publishing a play about what he understood to be the ecumenical aspect of the 1798 rising but also by publishing it in a journal called *Everyman*, which titularly appeals to everyone. The morality play *Everyman* was much on Heaney's mind in the 1970s: he would cite it in his analysis of Philip Larkin in "Englands of the Mind,"[96] and he would give his next radio play this title. If his earlier radio work for BBC Northern Ireland's schools program grew out of Heaney's core conviction that teachers foster "the ideal of 'self-cultivation' " to help the individual to "come to a sense of his powers and skills" so that he might be "freed into some new independence, readied for commitment and truly active selfhood," his radio scripts of *Munro* and *Everyman* stress the cultivation of cultural and political literacy so that Northern Irish society, already teetering on the brink of utter collapse, might look to thoughtful, reflective rhetorical engagement to prevent further chaos.[97]

EVERYMAN: A CONTEMPORARY MORALITY PLAY FOR NORTHERN IRELAND

Even as the province descended into greater violence, Heaney did not despair, again looking to his imagination for alternatives to seemingly intractable sectarian divisions, this time through his radio play entitled *Everyman*. This drama was transmitted on Thursday, March 11, 1971, on BBC Northern Ireland Radio Four from 9:55 to 10:15 a.m. By the end of 1970, there had already been thirty-nine deaths and close to three hundred shootings in the province.[98] NICRA had conducted a series of marches protesting political discrimination against Catholics. Heaney himself had participated in some of these marches and recalled "the indignation and determination of the civil rights marchers" in Derry on the October 5, 1968, march in his article "Old Derry's Walls."[99] And, on July 3, 1970, a twenty-four-hour curfew was imposed on the Lower Falls Road of Belfast, a noted Catholic enclave. During the curfew, both wings of the IRA—the older Official IRA and the new Provisional IRA—exchanged fire with the British Army. Many commentators believe that this curfew represented a turning point in relations between working-class Belfast Catholics and the British Army: from then on, this community no longer viewed the army as their protectors. On February 9, 1971, two BBC Northern Ireland engineers and three building workers were killed by a land mine as they worked on a transmitter in County Tyrone.[100] The regional BBC affiliate was increasingly seen by republicans as a mouthpiece for the British government, despite the station's periodic efforts to cultivate cultural harmony. It was all the more daring, then, for Heaney, who was increasingly, if often unwillingly, viewed as a spokesman for the nationalist tribe in the province, to write a radio play for the company at this time.

BBC Northern Ireland's efforts toward cultural reconciliation had also spurred protests by unionists and loyalists, who increasingly attacked the BBC verbally and even physically. Cathcart notes that the radio company's promotion of Irish culture in the late 1960s created "stirrings of dissatisfaction and opposition in various sections of the unionist community."[101] Loyalists led by Ian Paisley seriously injured a BBC cameraman during coverage of the Armagh civil rights march, and "The open aggression shown to BBC men on the ground was paralleled by an unprecedented level of abuse [from Northern Irish Protestants] in calls and in letters to Broadcasting House, Belfast."[102]

Long interested in medieval drama,[103] Heaney treats the role of art in ameliorating cultural strife as he explicitly critiques the tradition of Protestant Orangeism and laces this morality play with references to the contemporary Troubles. Part of the BBC Northern Ireland series *Here in Ulster*, *Everyman* is called "a fairytale for radio,"[104] but its subversive potential cannot be ignored. Heaney had previously contributed some protest lyrics about the abuses committed against civil rights marchers to a program on Raidió Teilifís Éireann, the official Irish state radio and television network, at the behest of the composer Sean O'Riada and was moving into a new phase in his radio work with those angry lyrics and the fiery protests at Protestant intolerance of Catholics in *Everyman*.[105] The play thus displays Heaney's growing anger at the treatment of the civil rights marchers and registers the Catholic presence in the province even while continuing to promote reconciliation. It features three characters: Everyman, a Guide, and a Boy. There are also a "Reader" and "Children." Always concerned with rhythm, Heaney chose here to contrast the destructive beat of music associated with Protestant Orange bands with the peaceful rhythm of more unifying music.[106]

As the play opens, Everyman approaches a playground, where the presumably Protestant children chant verses about "Our Queen." They scatter at his approach, but one boy stays behind and finally hums three verses of "Green Gravel" at Everyman's urging. He too, fades away, as the noise of clashing symbols harshly intrudes. Now the Guide enters and makes Everyman reflect on the songs of his childhood; although he claims this was a peaceful time, the Guide reminds him of "another dance— / Around the bonfire, following bands," and then "Lillibulero," a traditional Ulster Protestant triumphal song, is begun on a flute.[107] Heaney had been reflecting on loyalist bonfires in the province for some time and had published an uncollected poem entitled "Intimidation" the previous year in the *Malahat Review* that resentfully criticizes the bonfires and triumphalism associated with Protestant celebrations around July 12 in Northern Ireland.

Everyman now muses, "Some way or other, nowadays / The country's always in a mess, / Bombs exploding and CS gas—."[108] But as another phrase of "Lillibulero" is played, the Guide chastens him with a short speech in almost perfect rhyming couplets: "You carried the strings and dirtied your tongue. / You caught the poison-speech when young, / And never disinfected your mouth— / Just don't forget your dancing youth."[109] This last line is double-edged, recalling the origins of religious and cultural prejudice in Everyman's youth and also referencing the dancing youth of the play. As the song finishes, Everyman recalls the lift to his heart that the Orange parades caused. Again, he is brought up short by the Guide, who contrasts Everyman's unrhymed speech with another pair of couplets to aurally emphasize his point: "O, everybody loves a band. / But does every person in the land / Rally and march to the tunes you played? / What was the cause of the music you made?"[110] Everyman claims the cause "doesn't matter" and celebrates as the noise of lambeg drums crashes around them. He then asks the Guide, "Now isn't that music you'd want to hear?" but the Guide answers quietly, "That is a music I sometimes fear, / For there's a voice can come out of the drum / That's nothing to do with dance and joy / But anger and threats and power / to destroy."[111] Still scoffing, Everyman is now momentarily bewitched by the Guide, as the music of Irish *uileann* pipes is heard. Finally rejecting this music as foreign, Everyman then claims, "The fife and drum / Will be my death march and requiem."[112]

Heaney's critique of these Protestant triumphalist songs was very different from BBC Northern Ireland's efforts to promulgate cultural understanding by appreciatively playing the same Protestant tunes along with those sung by Catholic nationalists after Orange and Green marches, respectively, in the late 1960s, as Cathcart remarks:

> Between the summer of 1966 and the summer of 1968 Broadcasting House, Belfast, pursued a determined policy of opening up broadcasting and of helping to improve community relations. . . . While coverage of the Orange Twelfth of July marches and of the Ancient Order of Hibernians' marches on 15 August was by now customary, a new departure in 1968 was the transmission in the evenings after the marches of special traditional music programmes which presented the ballads and tunes associated with the day. *Orange Folk* and *Green Folk* involved producing music which might have been expected to provoke a torrent of abuse from viewers. There was no public reaction [however] and some favourable press comment.[113]

The burgeoning Catholic civil rights movement that fully got under way by late summer of 1968 and the violent reactions by Protestant mobs obviously would have made both Orange and Green anthems inappropriate for later radio broadcast. By 1971, the date of transmission for Heaney's radio play, Orange marching tunes would have been considered anathema by Northern Irish nationalists—hence his criticism of them and the violence associated with them by then in his script.

Immediately after Everyman embraces the music of the fife and drum, sounds of street violence are heard, interrupted periodically with a staccato series of questions from the Guide: "Is this the drum beat of your life? / Is the whistling bullet to be your fife? / Must killing become an act of faith? / Why are you caught in this dance of death?"[114] Everyman's prejudice crumbles, and the Guide tells him his vision of music bringing the world together harmoniously: "I want all people to dance as brothers."[115] The play ends with Everyman asking the Boy about the dances and games he participates in, a moment of cultural reconciliation. As a modern morality play, *Everyman* recalls the original intent of the medieval morality plays, which was to dramatize and urge the forgiveness of sins, an essentially unifying Christian function, as Robert Potter points out: "The traditional morality play is not a battle between virtues and vices, but a didactic ritual drama about the forgiveness of sins. Its theatrical intentions are to imitate and evoke that forgiveness."[116] Through its generic modeling of Christian forgiveness in a topical context, *Everyman* offered a powerful message to the Catholics and Protestants of Northern Ireland. The unifying moment between Everyman and the Boy anticipates Edna Longley's powerful claim that the arts in Northern Ireland can create a cultural corridor through which intransigent elements of the province can meet.[117] The power of Heaney's imagination thus managed to register his righteous anger at the injustices being committed against Northern Irish Catholics at the time and to envision cultural healing through the arts across generations. He sought to effect that healing through an artistic radio script focusing on the culturally beneficial properties of another art, music.[118]

Yet by 1973 Heaney would write a retrospective radio essay on Sam Thompson's *Over the Bridge*, again for the BBC Northern Ireland Radio series *Explorations*, that suggests how sectarianism poisons our relationships and, further, how the passivity of those who refuse to take a stand against such hatred exacerbates the situation. A profound irony of Heaney's using the network to critique bigotry in the province arises from his looking back fourteen years to a play that a representative of BBC NI had helped prevent from being staged for a year. He had praised Thompson in 1966, observing that his "anger at hypocrisy in high places and ... passion for justice transfigured plays that might otherwise have been regarded as clumsy or old-fashioned into urgent tracts for the times."[119] In his script, he points out the similarities of Thompson's play, in both situation and character, to William Golding's *The Lord of the Flies*, a novel that young people listening to the program would know well:

> [There are] men whose stubbornness drags the whole organization, the whole community, into conflict. This is brought out early in the play in the dislike between Peter O'Boyle and Archie Kerr: the sectarian feelings which have them at one another's throats threaten to stir up the whole union. Now in a way, this sectarian anger which ends up in violence and death again links *Over the Bridge* with *Lord of the Flies*. The union's way of dealing with division, as represented by Davy Mitchell, is a democratic, reasonable way. He attempts to persuade and reason with the men. Davy therefore is like Ralph, appealing to the better side of human nature. But the mob leader, who leads a crowd against Peter O'Boyle, at the end of

the play, corresponds to Jack in *Lord of the Flies*. He calls on people's violent instincts. He plays on their fears. He suggests that there is only room for one point of view, and that is his own and that of the people who see eye to eye with him. The climax of the play comes when the mob, who personify intolerance and selfishness, come face to face with Davy and Peter, who are standing on the union principles of unity and tolerance. [Davy is killed by the mob.][120]

By the time this script was broadcast, Heaney and the rest of the province had experienced the horrors of both Bloody Sunday on January 30, 1972, perpetrated on members of NICRA in Londonderry/Derry by the British Army's renegade Para 1 Regiment, and Black Friday, carried out by members of the Provisional Irish Republican Army all over Belfast on July 21 of that same year. Increasingly, sectarian divisions had hardened in the province, and the emphasis on "unity and tolerance" that had been espoused by NICRA had been largely forgotten. Heaney closes his script by meditating on Baxter's cowardice in Thompson's drama to obliquely warn what can and will happen in Northern Ireland if people who want peace stand by and do nothing: "Baxter, who had little enough faith in human nature all along, is distressed by the way people reacted when Davy was killed. Yet in a way these people who turned their back and closed their eyes to what had happened were following their own selfish instincts for self-preservation. They didn't want to get involved. They felt that Davy's death was none of their business. They did not want to have to face the ugliness of what their fellow workers had done and their own failure in allowing the men to do it."[121] Such a warning applied to the poet himself and he knew it. As the 1970s advanced and the catalog of atrocities committed in the province rose, Heaney knew he could not say nothing and increasingly spoke out, through his radio work, poems, prose poems, and prose, to protest the province's descent into civil strife. He became increasingly committed to the notion that art could at least open a space for dialogue between opposing factions, even if it could not immediately stop conflict and heal its underlying poisonous hatred.

Seamus Heaney's early work for BBC Northern Ireland suggested that a conciliatory cultural vision expressed through a medium that encouraged attentive listening offered a richer and subtler way of imagining the possibilities between disparate groups of people in Northern Ireland than had been offered by often calcified political conceptions of Northern identity. By drawing upon the shared cultural heritage of Northern Irish Catholics and Protestants, he imagined a united province that would celebrate both of its major cultural traditions while critiquing disabling aspects of those communities. Despite having moved to the Republic of Ireland by 1972, he remained fully committed to his regionalist project, and his work antedated the call by critics such as Edna Longley in the aftermath of the 1998 Good Friday Agreement for "a shared regional locus of allegiance [that] must evolve."[122] He explicitly argued that during this turbulent time "we probably felt that if we as poets couldn't do something transformative or creative with all that we were a part of, then it was a poor lookout for everybody," quickly musing that "what was envisaged and almost set up by the Good Friday Agreement was prefigured in what I called our subtleties and tolerances—allowances for different traditions and affiliations, in culture, religion and politics" (SS, 123). As part of its heightened efforts toward cultural reconciliation in the province, BBC Northern Ireland enabled Heaney to make several important early literary contributions to this end through articulating his unifying concept of regionalism even as sectarian conflict tragically broke out again.

Chapter Three

HEANEY'S ESSAYS ON REGIONAL WRITERS
The 1970s

This chapter draws upon Heaney's substantial essays and book reviews on Northern Irish, Scottish, Welsh, English, and even American regional writers from the 1970s, as he continued to suggest how an expansive concept of regionalism, set in a dialectic with other emerging regional writing from the Atlantic archipelago, might prove an inclusive, viable concept to which those in the North might give allegiance, rather than to party factions or terrorist groups. The current state of Northern Ireland retains only six of the original nine counties from the traditional Irish province of Ulster because of successful Protestant efforts before partition to exclude those three counties for fear of their majority-Catholic population. Thus Counties Donegal, Monaghan, and Cavan became part of the Irish Republic in 1922, while only Counties Fermanagh, Antrim, Tyrone, Londonderry, Armagh, and Down formed the new province of Northern Ireland. Heaney has often recognized the contribution of writers to literature from the North from these three excluded counties, such as Patrick Kavanagh, who grew up in and devoted his early poetry to writing about County Monaghan. Heaney also drew upon the work of significant regional writers from contemporary Northern Ireland such as

101

John Hewitt, John Montague, W. R. Rodgers, Louis MacNeice, and Michael McLaverty, along with Robert Frost and authors from Wales, Scotland, and England, including R. S. Thomas, Norman MacCaig, Hugh MacDiarmid, George Mackay Brown, Edwin Muir, William Wordsworth, Thomas Hardy, Philip Larkin, Geoffrey Hill, and Ted Hughes. Thus, in its transhistorical, transcultural, and transterritorial nature, his regionalist project bursts the bounds of contemporary Northern Ireland—an implicit riposte to monolithic notions of identity inscribed by religion, culture, and politics there.

Although Heaney is a powerful literary critic, the critical tendency has been to devalue his criticism in favor of his poetry or, at best, to assume that the criticism should be read primarily to explain his own poetry. Thankfully, a countervailing trajectory has gradually emerged, beginning with Arthur E. McGuinness's long chapter on the prose in his 1994 study, *Seamus Heaney: Poet and Critic*; in Neil Corcoran's penetrating chapter in his 1998 analysis, *The Poetry of Seamus Heaney: A Critical Study*; and in several subsequent studies.[1] Here I follow Eugene O'Brien, who argues that the poet's prose is "central to his developing project" and should be considered as such, rather than following the usual procedure, which is to see it as "a meta-commentary on his poetry."[2]

NORTHERN IRISH REGIONAL EXEMPLARS

In the 1960s, as Heaney was learning to write poetry thoroughly grounded in the actual conditions of Northern Ireland, he not only interacted with other Belfast Group poets but also turned naturally to older literary exemplars from the province. That he was engaged in promoting Northern Irish literature is evident from the influence of "Ulster" writing generally upon him, through the Northern Irish literary journals he contributed to in the 1960s and 1970s, and in his recognition of the emergence of other regional literatures across the British and Irish archipelago and even in America. By 1989, he could look back and proclaim, in his suggestively titled essay "The Regional Forecast," that "I have a sense that nowadays the writers on the outskirts know more about one another than ever before and have begun to take cognizance of each other in ways that are fortifying and illuminating."[3]

Even before Heaney looked to other regional writers, however, he looked out onto his local County Derry landscape, reading it through a series of essays such as "Mossbawn." The first part of that extended essay, called "Omphalos," read by Heaney on BBC Radio 4 in 1978, which shows his continued dedication to the medium of radio to convey his regionalist views, suggests how he felt simultaneously comforted and exposed by dwelling in such a culturally and historically conflicted landscape. For example, after praising the "green, wet corners, flooded wastes, soft rushy bottoms" as giving him "an immediate and deeply peaceful attraction," he notes that "the rattle of Orange drums from Aughrim Hill sets the heart alert and watchful as a hare. For if this was the country of community, it was also the realm of division. Like the rabbit pads that loop across grazing, and tunnel the soft growths under ripening corn, the lines of sectarian antagonism and affiliation followed the boundaries of the land."[4] And in "Belfast" Heaney famously discusses the multiple meanings of the family farm's name, "Mossbawn," in a way that suggests how he grew up among three different ways of reading landscape: "*Moss*, a Scots word probably carried to Ulster by the Planters, and *bawn*, the name the English colonists gave to their fortified farmhouses. Mossbawn, the planter's house on the bog. Yet in spite of this Ordnance Survey spelling, we pronounced it Moss bann, and *bán* is the Gaelic word for white. So might not the thing mean the white moss, the moss of bog-cotton? In the syllables of my home I see a metaphor of the split culture of Ulster."[5] As he goes on to remark in the conclusion of this essay, "My quest for definition . . . is conducted in the living speech of the landscape I was born into."[6]

Heaney's tendency to read his landscape through its local and imported linguistic markers suggests how his writing on place anticipated the gradual shift away from a supposedly more objective stance to a more subjective one. As Patrick J. Duffy has argued, whereas the "empiricist" approach to Irish landscape, symbolized by the well-known Ordnance Survey project of the 1830s, relies on quantitative sources of information including measurements and archival data, the second, "subjective" approach "reflects a critique of the older emphasis on material landscapes and a move away from morphology towards representation, meaning[,] and the experience of landscape. . . . This [view] is based on the belief that landscape does not speak for itself, it is 'read' by its viewers, its inhabitants, visitors, tourists, or scholars."[7] For Duffy, Heaney's home ground of Mossbawn exemplifies this second, superior approach: "His 'Mossbawn' is a place of sounds and smells, light and dark textures, as well as a geographical location on a map. Heaney's is a very particular rendition of the power of place, especially local place, in our lives and expresses a kind of organic link between people and place, where time and space are inextricably interwoven in memory and experience."[8] Heaney's recovery of the significance of his local terrain through the often buried or half-submerged substrata of myth and language would serve him well in formulating his evolving concept of regionalism, which, even in its earliest contours, repudiates the new Northern Irish state and includes the old Gaelic dispensation.

Heaney's essay on Ulster literary magazines in 1962 brought him into contact with writers such as W. R. Rodgers and John Hewitt, who had also, like [Patrick] Kavanagh, "created a poetry out of their local and native background."[9] He has recalled the importance of this essay to his regionalist project: "What I got from doing the essay was a demonstration that the local was workable literary matter and a hint that I myself might be able to work *with* it" (*SS*, 79). Four influential Northern writers for Heaney's early conception of regionalism were Kavanagh, from Monaghan, part of the historic province of Ulster; John Montague, born in New York but raised in rural County Tyrone, part of present-day Northern Ireland; Hewitt, born in Belfast; and the novelist and short story writer Michael McLaverty, from Monaghan.

Although Richard Kirkland has recently bifurcated Northern Protestant and Northern Catholic writing in the second half of the twentieth century along alleged differences in their literary concerns, particular writers from these two communities, which are themselves more varied than Kirkland allows, have shared salient characteristics that proved salutary for them.[10] Heaney, for example, has long cited the Catholic Kavanagh's influence on his poetry. The introduction by Peter Fallon and Derek Mahon to *The Penguin Book of Contemporary Irish Poetry*, however, strangely refuses to recognize the existence of Northern Irish poetry,[11] then dubiously overstates Kavanagh's contribution to contemporary Irish poetry while nonetheless helpfully pointing out his major influence on later writers:

More than MacNeice, more than Yeats, Kavanagh may be seen as the true origin of much Irish poetry today. One poem, the sonnet "Epic," gave single-handed permission for Irish poets to trust and cultivate their native ground and experience:

I have lived in important places, times
When great events were decided, who owned
That half a rood of rock, a no-man's land
Surrounded by our pitchfork-armed claims.
I heard the Duffys shouting "Damn your soul"
And old McCabe stripped to the waist, seen
Step the plot defying blue cast-steel—
"Here is the march along these iron stones"
That was the year of the Munich bother. Which
Was more important? I inclined
To lose my faith in Ballyrush and Gortin
Till Homer's ghost came whispering to my mind.
He said: I made the Iliad from such
A local row. Gods make their own importance.[12]

The editors go on to cite the influence of Kavanagh's advice in his short essay "The Parish and the Universe" for Irish poets to write about the parochial, not the provincial. Both of these terms are freighted with negative connotations today, but as Kavanagh used them the difference is crucial—the provincial poet always mimics the metropole, but the parochial poet, confirmed in the validity of his endeavor, writes about the local in such a way as to convey universal truths and concerns.

Hobsbaum had stressed Kavanagh's emphasis on the parochial to the Belfast Group to such a degree that Heaney even recalls Hobsbaum in terms usually associated with the elder Ulster poet: "He [Hobsbaum] emanated energy, generosity, belief in the community, trust in the parochial, the inept, the unprinted."[13] Heaney would enact Kavanagh's emphasis on the parochial through lovingly and intensely meditating on the particularized objects and landscape of his rural Derry childhood. When asked in the 1960s why he had dedicated no early poems to Kavanagh, Heaney replied, "I had no need to write a poem to Patrick Kavanagh; I wrote *Death of a Naturalist.*"[14] And in his autobiographical sequence "Singing School" from *North* (1975), Heaney began his first lyric, "The Ministry of Fear" with a quotation from Kavanagh: "Well, as Kavanagh said, we have lived / In important places" (*N*, 57). If those poems testify to the Monaghan poet's influence on Heaney to trust his immersion in the local landscape of rural South Derry, so do two of his early essays—the first on Kavanagh's Monaghan landscape and the second on place more generally.

In the first of these, "From Monaghan to the Grand Canal: The Poetry of Patrick Kavanagh" (1975), Heaney praises the public quality of Kavanagh's work in articulating a rural Catholic consciousness in aquatic terms he previously reserved for his own poetry's focus on the imagination in poems such as "The Diviner" and "Personal Helicon" from *Death of a Naturalist* (1966), along with "A Lough Neagh Sequence" and "Bogland" from *Door into the Dark* (1969):

> There is what I would call an artesian quality about his best work because for the first time since Brian Merriman's poetry in Irish at the end of the eighteenth century and William Carleton's novels in the nineteenth, a hard buried life that subsisted beyond the feel of middle-class novelists and romantic nationalist poets, a life denuded of "folk" and picturesque elements, found its expression.... Kavanagh forged not so much a conscience as a consciousness for the great majority of his countrymen, crossing the pieties of a rural Catholic sensibility with the *non serviam* of his original personality, raising the inhibited energies of a subculture to the power of a cultural resource.[15]

Thus Kavanagh's poetry brought submerged Northern Catholicism into public literature and culture, an instructive move for the young Catholic poet from rural Derry and one he would emulate often in his own verse. An important difference, though, between the two is that while Kavanagh's poetry often focuses on the brutality and weariness of rural life, Heaney generally focuses on its life-affirming and renewing aspects. At the same time, though, Duffy has pointed out how Kavanagh, "like Carleton . . . represented a busy, well-peopled countryside, in spite of the emigration which had emptied many houses and farms since Carleton's time. His landscapes are full of the sounds of people and animals, cans clattering, cart-wheels rattling along roads, calves bawling, dogs barking, people calling to each other over fields, intimate representations of a small-farm countryside in a pre-mechanized age."[16] He argues, drawing on Heaney's essay "Mossbawn," that his "remembered Ulster landscape has the same texture about some of its description" and goes on to cite a passage from that essay featuring dogs barking and a litany of local place names that is Kavanaghesque.[17]

Perhaps more important for Heaney was Kavanagh's poetic imagination and the way in which he was able to constantly renew it. Employing the same terms he had employed in his seminal essay "Feeling into Words," Heaney praises Kavanagh for his elevation of "technique" over "craft": "There is, we might say, more technique than craft in his work, real technique which is, in his own words, 'a spiritual quality, a condition of mind, or an ability to invoke a particular condition of mind . . . a method of getting at life.'"[18] Significantly for Heaney, Kavanagh enabled him to dwell upon local landscapes to such a degree that they became mental states as well. Indeed, as he states here in his comments upon Kavanagh's *Tarry Flynn*, "What we have in these poems are matter-of-fact landscapes, literally presented, but contemplated from such a point of view and with such intensity that they become 'a prospect of the mind.'"[19] Heaney's landscape poems similarly dwell in both the actual and the abstract, and Kavanagh's supple linkage of outer and inner terrain, including his increasingly spiritual bent, would influence Heaney's later career, as we will see in my analysis of Heaney's essay "The Placeless Heaven: Another Look at Kavanagh" in chapter 11.

In 1977, two years after he wrote his first essay devoted to Kavanagh, Heaney praised him more specifically for his articulation of "parochialism" in "The Sense of Place." He argued there that Kavanagh's work was closer to the lives of the majority of Irish people than was Yeats's because of "Kavanagh's fidelity to the unpromising, unspectacular countryside of Monaghan and his rendering of the authentic speech of those parts."[20] Citing Kavanagh's seminal poem "Epic" and his essay "The Parish and the Universe," he argues that he "cherished the ordinary, the actual, the known, the unimportant."[21] For all his intense scrutiny of the local, however, Heaney believed at the time, although he would later significantly revise this view, that Kavanagh remained on the landscape's surface and that his place names were "denuded of tribal or etymological implications."[22]

John Montague's poetry, on the other hand, was rife with the cultural and political implications that Heaney believed Kavanagh's poetry lacked. In his 1973 review of Montague's influential 1972 volume *The Rough Field*, Heaney observes how the collection explores and celebrates "what might be called a tribal consciousness," even as it is "at the same time an elegy for that consciousness," particularly for the "submerged memories and emotions of the Irish Ulstermen" represented by "the Flight of the Earls, and in particular the exile of the Chieftain of Tyrone in the early 17th century." He terms Montague's "inspiration" a "matter of northern sunlight on broken columns, fragments cherished after the ruins," and concludes by praising "the most luminous moment in the book": "when the poet climbs to the source of a mountain stream that 'defines his townland's shape' and slips his hand under a rock to find the heart of the spring, the pulse of his region and the pulse of his imagination."[23] Heaney, always seeking to put his finger on the pulse of his same region, found in Montague's work, particularly *The Rough Field*, a salutary concern with language, culture, geography, and politics that he might emulate in his own poetry.

Heaney praises Montague's poetry for its deep concern with the landscape and history of the North of Ireland immediately after his discussion of Kavanagh's poetry in "The Sense of Place." Employing aquatic terminology he typically uses to laud poetry of the highest order, Heaney argues that Montague's place names are "sounding lines, rods to plumb the depths of a shared and diminished culture. They are redolent not just of his personal life but of the history of his people, disinherited and dispossessed."[24] Although both poets are evoking a buried culture in the province, Montague's exploration goes much deeper, suggesting the acute loss of pagan and Gaelic civilization: "Both Kavanagh and Montague explore a hidden Ulster, to alter Daniel Corkery's suggestive phrase, and Montague's exploration follows Corkery's tracks in a way that Kavanagh's does not. There is an element of cultural and political resistance and retrieval in Montague's work that is absent from Kavanagh's. What is hidden at the bottom of Montague's region is first of all a pagan civilization centred on the dolmen; then a Gaelic civilization centred on the O'Neill inauguration stone at Tullyhogue."[25] The common feature, then, in both poets' work that drew Heaney to them was their evocation of the hidden cultures that they rendered through differing ways of poetically gazing on their local terrain.[26]

The problem with Heaney's reading of Montague's sense of place, however, has been clearly identified by John Lucas, who points out its reductive qualities and tendency to revert to a rural idyll that rejects the city: "Such a culture is heavily dependent on stock images and attitudes and . . . it thus conspires with the sense of diminishment it wishes to discover. . . . The trap is sprung by what can fairly be regarded as a dangerous myth of dwelling, where that affirms a commitment to 'roots' and 'stability' and 'history' against those who shift about, 'like some poor Arab tribesman and his tent.' . . . For this dream of contact with the soil turns into a regressive ruralism which must necessarily regard the city as the antitype of true civilization."[27] This is a difficult charge to refute and one worthy of extended exploration. One is tempted to say that Heaney's immersion in the Belfast of the late 1960s and early 1970s that was rapidly descending into violence justified his view of the city as "the antitype of true civilization," but of course many sectarian murders were committed in rural parts of the province as well, most notably by the loyalist Protestant gang called the Shankill Butchers in the mid- to late 1970s.

Heaney's supposedly "regressive ruralism," however, is actually grounded in his religious understanding of the countryside where he grew up, which forms an essential component of his rural regionalism. This landscape recalls that of the playwright John Synge's Aran Islands, where both in real life and in Synge's re-creation of that life in plays such as *Riders to the Sea* (1904) islanders easily moved between belief in Catholic rituals and belief in local spirits such as witches. Heaney recalls this syncretistic terrain in his native southern County Derry in his essay "The Poet as a Christian": "There, if you like, was the foundation for a marvelous or magical view of the world, a foundation that sustained a diminished structure of lore and superstition and half-pagan, half-Christian thought and practice. Much of the flora of the place had a religious force, especially if we think of the root of the word religious in *religare*, to bind fast."[28] The allure of the countryside, then, for both Heaney and Montague as read by Heaney is its evocation of this syncretistic, half-buried world signified by its plants and trees.[29] This blend of pagan/Christian rootedness confounds binary attempts to categorize Heaney's regionalism, including those marked by sophisticated theoretical forays into his work.[30]

While a sectarian-minded poet would perhaps have been content to register the influence of two fellow Northern Irish Catholic poets upon his own developing sense of regionalism, Heaney concludes "The Sense of Place" with a discussion of the Protestant John Hewitt's poetry, lauding Hewitt for his "bifocal" regionalism in contrast to Montague's "monocular" outlook in seeking to reclaim Catholic culture in Ulster. Heaney's reclamation of Hewitt silently builds on Montague's similar praise of Hewitt's regionalism, which he published in an essay that appeared in a 1964 issue of *Poetry Ireland* that also contained Heaney's uncollected poem "The Indomitable Irishry."[31] Montague praises Hewitt for his concentration on the peculiar situation of divided Northern Ireland at the beginning of his article, observing, "The Ulster question is the only real outstanding political problem in this country: to live in the province and ignore it would be like living in Mississippi, without questioning segregation."[32] He also admires Hewitt for beginning "to suggest the necessity for Planter and Gael in coming to terms" in poems such as 1953's "The Colony" and singles out his 1954 verse play, *The Bloody Brae*: "This dialogue between a Cromwellian veteran and the ghost of a Catholic neighbor he has killed is almost intolerably moving."[33] Hewitt's bicultural regional stance partaking of an English and Ulster tradition was more helpful to Heaney in developing his theory of regionalism at this point in his career than Montague's regional reclamation of a "pagan civilization centered on the dolmen; then a Gaelic civilization centered on the O'Neill inauguration stone at Tullyhogue."[34] Hewitt thus appealed to Heaney as a Northern Irish writer also living between British and Irish cultures. As an example, Heaney details the significance of their archaeological symbols:

> When Montague's vision founds itself on the archaeological, it is on Knockmany Dolmen, on the insular tradition. When Hewitt searches for his primeval symbol, it is also megalithic; "a broken circle of stones on a rough hillside, somewhere," is the destination of his search for a "somewhere," and his note tells us that that somewhere is a refraction of two places. "'Circle of stones': for me the archetype of this is the Rollright Stones on the border of Oxfordshire, mingled with the recollection of 'Ossian's Grave,' Glenaan, Co. Antrim.'" Oxfordshire and Antrim, two fidelities, two spirits that in John Donne's original and active verb, interanimate each other.[35]

Heaney's praise of Hewitt in "The Sense of Place" signifies how he continued to look favorably not only upon Hewitt's theory of regionalism in the late 1970s but also generally upon Northern Irish regionalism. Such an attitude suggests how misleading, even fallacious, Bruce Stewart's recent narrative is about Heaney's relationship to Ulster regionalism and to both Hewitt and Kavanagh. Stewart believes that Heaney had only a "brief involvement in the crusade of Ulster regionalism," which he suggests stopped in 1969 with Heaney's editing of the special Ulster issue of *Threshold*, noting that his list of contributors in that issue suggests that "the 'Ulster literary tradition' idea had not been entirely abandoned, if leavened with some others (Lavin and Kinsella) whose Northern connections were as negligible as anything that Heaney had critiqued in earlier issues of the journal.... Hewitt had just published his *Collected Poems* (1968) ... and his absence from Heaney's *Threshold*, if purposed, was unkind."[36] Unfathomably, Stewart then claims, "At the time of editing that issue, however, Heaney was rapidly moving towards the formulation of a new theory for Irish literature and, when he delivered this as 'The Sense of Place' at the Ulster Museum in 1977, Kavanagh was crucial to the argument he framed."[37] Besides the fact that "The Sense of Place" was delivered eight years after Heaney edited the special issue of *Threshold* (not exactly evidence that Heaney was "rapidly moving" toward this theory of place), both the special issue and the essay are not separate, unrelated events but clearly outgrowths of Heaney's thinking about regionalism in the North, the former about Northern regionalism and the latter about Irish literature. Moreover, Heaney treats Kavanagh as a Northern Irish poet, not an Irish one, in both "From Monaghan to the Grand Canal," when he writes of him "raising the inhibited energies of a subculture to the power of a cultural resource," and in "The Sense of Place," when he remarks that he (and Montague) "explore a hidden Ulster." Finally, as we have seen, while Kavanagh *is* important to Heaney's argument in "The Sense of Place," his thinking on landscape and cultural issues concerning the North was not "crucial," because not as important as Montague's, whose views, in turn, were not as important as Hewitt's to Heaney. For Stewart to also argue that "The Placeless Heaven," Heaney's 1985 essay on Kavanagh, "reveals a gradual process of disentanglement from the hegemonic authority of English literary culture associated with the curriculum he followed as an undergraduate, then a brief flirtation with Ulster regionalism as an alternative to that somewhat alienating canon, before full immersion in the idea of Irish literature as the objective correlate of his own mind and the minds of the people to whom he gave his primary allegiance," shows a surprising ignorance not only of Heaney's relationship to English literary culture (which he repeatedly appreciates in his criticism) but also of his long "entanglement," if you like, in the matter of Ulster regionalism.[38] There is no question that Heaney gradually retrieved and learned the history of Irish literature, but his engagement with "Ulster regionalism" was much longer-lasting than Stewart claims.

Clearly, Heaney privileges Hewitt above both Kavanagh and Montague in "The Sense of Place," a position that is consistent with his stance five years earlier in his 1972 book review of Hewitt's *Collected Poems, 1932–67*. There, Heaney admiringly articulated the terms of Hewitt's biculturalism when he discussed his "two-way pull, back into the grave and eloquent mainstream of English and out into the shifting, elaborate, receding currents of the Irish experience."[39] Certainly, Heaney had been reading Hewitt for some time. He has remarked that before Hewitt's poetry was collected, "his stuff was hard to get and he'd given me several privately printed pamphlets," further noting that "I'd read some of his poems early on, in a Faber anthology of contemporary Irish poetry done in the 1950s—one of the few poetry books in the Magherafelt library" (*SS*, 330). Michael Allen recalls Heaney lending him his "well-thumbed review copy of Hewitt's *Collected Poems* in 1968."[40] Heather Clark has convincingly argued that during the late 1960s Heaney was much drawn to Hewitt's aesthetic of "simplicity, sobriety and measure," "recognizable virtues of country life" that transcended Heaney and Hewitt's religious differences and also "resonated with his self-image, characterized by Michael Allen as that of 'a humble worker-craftsman.'"[41] Allen has concluded that especially on the evidence of the poems of *Wintering Out*, "Heaney needed the earthing mask of that careful, honest, slow-speaking 'North of Ireland' identity as modeled by Hewitt."[42]

Heaney has recently noted in *Stepping Stones* that "Hewitt was a poet to be grateful for, whether you were a Protestant or a Catholic. He tilted the lens a fraction. The Northern Ireland situation was allowed its historical dimension: he recognized that it was a colonial predicament and hence 'The Colony' remains an important intervention by a poet. Politically, he was gruffly the democrat, committed to equality and civil rights for everybody" (*SS*, 331). Heaney's involvement with Hewitt's poetry and engagement with his formulation of Ulster regionalism thus runs at least four decades—dating from the 1950s and continuing into the 1990s—as we will see in the penultimate chapter's discussion of Hewitt's regionalism in Heaney's Oxford lecture "The Frontiers of Writing."

Although Richard Kirkland sees Heaney's developing regionalism as stopping short of "Hewitt's call for a 'more autonomous political life,'" in point of fact Heaney's emphasis on regionalism as a context for evoking a shared culture and language in the province was always a first step for reconciliation on a political level, which process might well later involve a more devolved government, as Northern Ireland now has in the Good Friday Agreement, and eventually a united Ireland.[43]

Hewitt's regionalism, however, while often salutary for Heaney, may finally be too bound up with place and thus too restricted for the younger poet. Clark has shown that Heaney's "The Peninsula" (1969) displays a debt to Hewitt's "Glenarriffe and Parkmore" (1948), which is definitively grounded in the Glens of Antrim. At the same time, Heaney's more universal poem, with its desire to "uncode all landscapes," reveals that "he may also have already been experimenting with a different kind of regionalism— the kind that did not depend on allegiance to place but rather on a profound respect for the sanctity of place itself."[44] For Clark, Heaney's "The Peninsula" "is the site of non-ownership, and, perhaps by extension, sectarian reconciliation. It is as if Heaney is refining Hewitt's conception of regionalism, purifying it of its cultural assumptions and biases, offering a revised version based upon universality rather than locality, submission rather than ownership."[45] Clark's reading of Heaney's relationship to Hewitt's regional project helps us understand how Heaney both lauded Hewitt's regionalism and gradually came to enlarge it.

While Hewitt attempted to unify the two dominant cultures in the province through his regionalist project (even though Heaney himself would eventually consider this regionalism limited because of his sense that it could exclude Catholics), the poets W. R. Rodgers and Louis MacNeice engaged in different though no less important work that enabled them to critique received notions of identity. John Wilson Foster has contrasted Rodgers's exuberant embrace of Irishness with Hewitt's more careful articulation of it: "Rodgers was a blithe spirit in claiming without reservation his Irishness and it is in sober contrast that we read Hewitt's careful exploration of his cultural traditions, his self-questioning[,] and the slow march of doubts; it is a contrast between Rodgers's cavalier assurance and Hewitt's roundhead conscience."[46] Gerald Dawe, like Foster, another expert commentator on culture and literature in Northern Ireland, also appreciates Rodgers's interest in the Republic of Ireland but claims that for Rodgers the South became an idealized third space: "Ireland became an imaginative home-place or cultural alternative, ironically distanced from the London axis, of which Rodgers had become part, but separate, too, from the cramped provincialism of what he called the north, 'a backwater of literature out of sight of the running stream of contemporary verse.'"[47]

Both Rodgers and MacNeice shared with Hewitt a revulsion to religious narrowness, which attitude surely appealed to Heaney. As Michael Longley approvingly writes in his introduction to Rodgers's *Poems*, "Like his friend Louis MacNeice, Rodgers was motivated by strong anti-puritan feelings. The vividness they share was projected partly as an assault on religious narrowness and cultural restriction."[48] Rodgers's position as a Presbyterian clergyman until he took a leave of absence in 1943 enabled him to speak to his own community's biases against Catholics, though his views were never received very well in that milieu. Heaney similarly has seen Rodgers in a positive light, arguing that his "understanding of himself as being between London, Loughgall [in Northern Ireland], and the [Scottish] Lowlands" is fruitfully tricultural, "analogous to the triple heritage of Irish, Scottish, and English traditions that compound and complicate the cultural and political life of contemporary Ulster."[49]

As Peter McDonald has argued, MacNeice's emigration from Northern Ireland to London did not enable him to be accommodated within Hewitt's regionalism and "made MacNeice something of a sapless hybrid in the Hewitt circle."[50] However, MacNeice, much the more famous poet than Rodgers, is in many ways the ideal Northern Irish writer for understanding Heaney's regionalism because, as Michael Longley has stated, anticipating Heaney's explanation of Rodgers's mixed cultural heritage, he "was never able to align himself wholeheartedly with any aesthetic, political, or religious creed" and cannot be categorized with a received national label: [he] "is a difficult figure to pin down and label. To the Irish he is an exile, to the English something of a stranger. He was an Ulsterman, and Ulster is a limbo between two (three?) cultures."[51] Yet it was not until the early 1990s that Heaney explicitly articulated MacNeice's influence as salutary, even putting him at the point of a quincunx of an "integrated literary tradition" in Ireland.[52] MacNeice's own chameleonic nature and the variety of theme and form in his verse have been a striking example of literature's varied and vigorous imaginative power to successive generations of writers. Thus both MacNeice and Rodgers rejected a monovalent Northern Irish Protestantism and embraced other aspects of their region with an ecumenical spirit that helped Heaney negotiate an inclusive regionalism that drew on both dominant cultures in the province while registering the "hidden Ulster" of Northern Catholicism.[53]

The final Ulster regionalist influence upon Heaney is one pointed out by Hewitt in his review of *Death of a Naturalist*, Michael McLaverty.[54] In McLaverty, who supervised Heaney's teacher training at St. Thomas's Intermediate School, Belfast, in 1962, Heaney found another example of a rooted Catholic Northern Irish writer who, like Kavanagh, also gazed intensely upon his parish. In his obituary for McLaverty, Heaney fondly points out that "his work was valued by readers and writers alike for its fidelity and detail in the treatment of common experience."[55] Heaney dedicated "Fosterage," the fifth poem in the sequence "Singing School" from *North*, to McLaverty. The speaker concludes by recalling that McLaverty "fostered me and sent me out, with words / Imposing on my tongue like obols" (*N*, 65). In his 1978 introduction to McLaverty's *Collected Short Stories*, Heaney praises him in terms similar to those he would employ in his obituary—for his "fidelity to the intimate and the local" and "his sense of the great tradition that he works in, his contempt for the flashy and the topical, his love of the universal, the worn grain of unspectacular experience, the well-turned grain of language itself."[56] In a way similar to Kavanagh, McLaverty taught Heaney disdain for the ephemeral and respect for the lasting. These values would stand him in good stead as he mostly resisted the urge to comment immediately upon the violence in the province beginning in the late 1960s. And like Kavanagh, McLaverty, with his deep affection for local landscape, gave Heaney another example of a Northern Irish writer who successfully developed a rich country of the mind out of a geographic one. Heaney thus concludes his introduction to McLaverty's *Collected Stories* by observing the way in which McLaverty's physical region became internalized through his loving observation of it, using the same phrase, "a prospect of the mind," that he had used to describe Kavanagh's contemplation of his landscape in "From Monaghan to the Grand Canal": "There is, of course, a regional basis to McLaverty's world and a documentary solidity to his observation, yet the region is contemplated with a gaze more loving and more lingering than any fieldworker or folklorist could ever manage. Those streets and shores and fields have been weathered in his affections and patient understanding until the contours of each landscape have become a moulded language, a prospect of the mind."[57] McLaverty's regionalism suggests a model of patience for Heaney, who was still trying to contemplate Northern Ireland lovingly and lingeringly as the Troubles wore on.

REGIONAL INFLUENCES BEYOND NORTHERN IRELAND:
ROBERT FROST, WELSH AND SCOTTISH POETS, ENGLISH POETS

Heaney also perceived Northern Irish literature as participating in dialogues with other regional literature of the period. Perhaps the most lasting of these has been with the American poet Robert Frost, a major transatlantic regionalist influence on Heaney's developing regional aesthetic, whose example is more fully explored in the introduction to this study. Heaney wrote a series of essays on Frost over the years and observed that "I felt at home in the world of his poetry—the New England farm world, the people, the idiom that was used" (*SS*, 453). Rachel Buxton's study of Frost's influence on Heaney and Paul Muldoon carefully and helpfully traces the details of Heaney's reading of Frost's poetry, starting at Queen's University under Laurence Lerner.[58] Heaney's interest in Frost was confirmed by Hewitt, whose essays Heaney read as a graduate student at Queen's when he was writing his extended essay on Ulster literary magazines in 1962. Hewitt cites Frost in the conclusion of "The Bitter Gourd," in particular his "rural portraits," "his avoidance of ornament and rhetoric," and his "unhurried and sinewy wisdom."[59] After suggesting the applicability of Frost's "The Gift Outright" to the situation in Northern Ireland,

Hewitt concludes by noting that "some of us . . . are endeavouring to re-create that story, that art, that enchantment, drawn from and firmly rooted in what Ulster was and is, and playing our parts in helping to make her, what first in fitful glimpses but now more and more by a steady light, we realize she should and can become."[60] Frost's poem, then, portrays a land that can be enhanced by the gift of ourselves that involves an outpouring of literature and the arts. Hewitt suggests that the landscape of Northern Ireland, similarly, is a sort of palimpsest that can be instructively written upon by artists in the present. Heaney, however, specifically criticizes Hewitt's endorsement of Frost's poem in "Frontiers of Writing," pointing out that in Hewitt's article "he dropped the line about the deed of gift being many deeds of war, an understandable and tactful suppression of the conquest element behind the planters' at-homeness. But he kept the line about the land being 'unstoried, artless, unenhanced' until the [American] colonists surrendered to it, and in so doing he participated in Frost's unconscious erasure of native American stories and arts and enhancements, and made a similar colonial erasure of the original native culture of *Uladh*."[61]

Despite his protest at what he perceives as Hewitt's and Frost's erasure of native culture, their close relationship to the land (along with Kavanagh's and Montague's) was otherwise salutary to the development of Heaney's regionalism, and he singles out Frost in particular for his close relationship to farming as helpful in expressing his adopted New England regionalism. He has thus recalled how Frost's "credentials as a farmer poet," even if Frost, by his own admission, was a lackadaisical and unsuccessful farmer, showed in his poetry: "how forkfuls of hay were built upon a wagonload for easy unloading later, when they have to be tossed down from underfoot."[62] Heaney's own accurate portrayals of rural life in poems such as "Digging" obtain something of their documentary immediacy from his immersion in Frost's clear-eyed farming poems as well as his own immersion in the life of his family's farm. As he says in "Above the Brim" about the "grim accuracy" of Frost's poem "Out, Out—," "I was immediately susceptible to its documentary weight and did not mistake the wintry report of what happened at the end for the poet's own callousness."[63] In her brief discussion of Heaney's terming Frost a "farmer poet" in "Above the Brim," Edna Longley argues that this phrase "places Frost between Kavanagh, more genuinely a farmer, and Hughes, then more exclusively a poet. This fits Heaney's own inside/outside relation to the environment he evokes or constructs."[64] Longley's construction of Heaney as insider/outsider perfectly captures the spirit of such early poems as "Digging" and reveals the way in which he has drawn on his regional influences, yet reconfigured them for his own poetic and cultural purposes to offer an imagined Northern Ireland where seemingly disparate religious and cultural groups might meet and engage in productive encounters, simultaneously reinscribing "the original native culture of *Uladh*" and writing its future along with other enabling regional writers.

Closer to home, Heaney was drawn to the poetry of the Welsh poet R. S. Thomas, although Thomas did not become the lasting influence Frost did. Michael Parker cites a little-known review of Thomas's first volume of poetry, *The Bread of Truth* (1963), published in *Trench* in June 1964, in which Heaney enthusiastically praises the Welshness of the elder poet's work: "Welsh religion, Welsh landscape, Welsh characters are the thongs tightening his imagination and intelligence.... The physical features of the Welsh hill country and its inhabitants are presented in pungent detail, so that a self-contained world gradually evolves in the imagination.... The sensibility that informs this work is instinctive, fermented in the dank valleys of a country imagination.... To regard this poet as regional ... is to blind oneself to the blush of the universal on his gaunt Welsh features."[65] Heaney is concerned to not diminish Thomas's considerable achievement by describing it negatively as "regional," which often connotes provincialism and narrowness. That he saw Thomas's distinctive Welsh poetic project as having both particular and universal qualities confirmed the regionalist program he was himself pursuing to render specific aspects of Northern Ireland universal.[66] Heaney respected Thomas's considerable achievements in poetry so much that he gave an address at his memorial service at Westminster Abbey, on March 28, 2001. He clearly affirmed the Welshman's poetry as an inspiration for his own region-based poetry, observing, "When I first read R. S. Thomas, I valued him for his truth to the bleak life of the hillfarmers to whom he ministered. The people in the poems reminded me of small farmers and farm labourers I myself had known, and his poems were therefore among those that helped me to get started on my own writing."[67]

Norman MacCaig's and Hugh MacDiarmid's Scottish regionalism further confirmed the young poet. Employing *parochial* in a manner reminiscent of Kavanagh's use of the term in "The Parish and the Universe" to describe MacCaig's influence on Heaney, Michael Parker argues that "no doubt MacCaig's world with its epiphanies spilling easily from local, parochial experience, gave confidence to Heaney as he allowed his bucket to plummet into the well."[68] Besides being influenced by MacCaig's parochial epiphanies, Heaney has praised him for his art, explicitly recognizing in the Scot's poetry the central analogy of his own work between fishing and poetry in seminal poems such as "Casualty" from *Field Work*: "He was a great fisherman, master of the cast, of the line that is a lure. And the angler's art—the art of coming in at an angle—is there in his poetry too. He could always get a rise out of the subject. He made it jump beyond itself."[69]

More important than MacCaig, though, in developing Heaney's concept of regionalism was the Scottish poet Hugh MacDiarmid, the subject of two different Heaney essays, the first of which was published in the 1970s (the second will be discussed in chapter 10 of this study). In a review of *The Hugh MacDiarmid Anthology*, originally published in *Hibernia* in 1972, Heaney explicitly links Wordsworth and MacDiarmid through their common regionalist projects based on everyday language: "Both professed a diction that was deliberately at variance with prevalent modes."[70] Heaney further develops the connection between the two poets by articulating MacDiarmid's particular incorporation of Lallans, or Scots, into his poetry, just as Wordsworth incorporated the language of the Cumbrian peasants who lived around him in the Lake District: "Again like the young Wordsworth, MacDiarmid has a sense of an enervating cultural situation—he saw Scottish civilization as damned and doomed by influences from south of the Border—that is intimately linked with his linguistic obsessions. . . . Lallans, his poetic Scots language, is based on the language of men, specifically on the dialect of his home district around Langholm in Dumfrieshire, but its attractive gaudiness is qualified by the not infrequent inanities of his English, for he occasionally speaks a language that the ones in Langholm do not know."[71] Those "not infrequent inanities of his English" were too stylistically ornate for Heaney and he himself has not indulged in them. Yet he continues, praising MacDiarmid's "Water Music" in specifically regional terms for the way in which "the Scots and the Latinate English furl together in a downpour of energy." He argues that in this poem "the local and the indigenous, which were Joyce's obsession also, are affiliated to oral and instinctive characteristics of the region and the intensity and volubility of the regional diction."[72] MacDiarmid's successful fusing of Scots and Latinate English in "Water Music" undoubtedly confirmed for Heaney the validity of the mixed dialects of Northern Irish and Irish English he incorporated—even made the subject of—in several important poems in *Wintering Out* such as "Broagh," "Nerthus," and "Traditions."

Also important for Heaney in developing his Ulster regionalist poetry grounded in the particular dialects of his region were the Orcadian Scottish authors George Mackay Brown and Edwin Muir, whose work in *An Orkney Tapestry* Heaney reviewed in the *Listener* on August 21, 1969.[73] Michael Parker reads this review as expressing a type of retreat into the recesses of Heaney's mind from the burgeoning violence in the province,[74] but Heaney's comparisons of the poetry of Brown and Muir to that of the regional English writers William Barnes and Thomas Hardy suggests he views Scottish, Northern Irish writing, and English literature from outside London as constituting a matrix of regional literature. Additionally, as he attempted to keep his own poetry and Northern Irish poetry generally from being seen as too narrow and negative, especially in light of the accelerating conflict in the province, Heaney may well have identified with what John Holloway has called the "almost visionary hopefulness and exploratory imagination" of Muir's writing from the 1950s.[75] If Muir's late verse gave Heaney hope and a widening imaginative compass, Mackay Brown's own anthropological impulse must surely have confirmed Heaney's continued documentation of traditional crafts in rural Ulster.[76]

In a recent interview, Heaney has confirmed the importance of such Scottish voices. He told Susan Mansfield of the importance of Norman MacCaig, Iain Crichton Smith, Hugh MacDiarmid, Sorley Maclean, George Mackay Brown, and Edwin Morgan to him. As she noted,

> There was a kinship right from the start, he says, between the speech of Scotland and Northern Ireland. He grew up with Burns recitations and Jimmy Shand records, a "sense of at-homeness with that part of the other isle. . . . There was a sense of relationship [among the poets], a sense of access, fraternity if you like. When a poet says 'Och' instead of 'Oh dear,' . . . it domesticates the art in a different sort of way. Poetry is

always slightly mysterious, and you wonder what is your relationship to it. So to have established writers who could be your neighbours in terms of attitude, speech and so on, that's corroboration."[77]

Heaney has long felt a pull to reclaim "a hidden Scotland" and bring Scottish speech more into the purview of his work, just as he previously sought to retrieve "a hidden Ulster" by bringing the historic region of Ulster, including its Catholics, into his elastic concept of regionalism. Thus he has long been thankful for the "corroboration" these established Scottish writers gave him.

Four other examples of poets who confirmed Heaney in his regionalist aesthetic were William Wordsworth, Thomas Hardy, Philip Larkin, and Ted Hughes—English poets whose work Heaney convincingly reappropriated as regionalist because of their locations far from the Home Counties, their successful poetic infusion of local dialect (in the case of Wordsworth, Hardy, and Hughes), and their urge to preserve vanishing aspects of English cultural and agricultural traditions (all four poets) in their poetry. We have seen above in my discussion of Heaney's first essay on MacDiarmid how favorably he looked upon Wordsworth's romantic verse for employing the language of the common man to ward off the pernicious cultural influence of English verse far south of the Lake District. J. H. Alexander has suggestively argued that Wordsworth abhorred provinciality and instead achieved a "profound regionalism which breaks free of spatial and temporal restrictions to offer a radical challenge to *metropolitan* complacencies, snobberies, and denials of true life."[78] Wordsworth is an enabling regional writer to whom Heaney has returned often. For instance, he wrote an early essay, "The Makings of a Music: Reflections on Wordsworth and Yeats," that was collected in *Preoccupations: Selected Prose, 1968–1978*; he edited a selection of Wordsworth's poems for Faber; and he treated Wordsworth in a series of other essays.[79]

Additionally, the influence of Thomas Hardy as an exemplary regionalist for Heaney cannot be overestimated. Hardy noted that he invented the term *Wessex* for the region of England about which he wrote "because there was no available word for the area which he recognized as forming a distinct entity but which extended over parts of at least six modern counties."[80] Heaney has explicitly affirmed Hardy's regionalism as speaking both to his local area and beyond, noting that "Thomas Hardy . . . widened his knowledge and the range of his philosophical reading as he grew up, but it would have been a total error, artistically and psychologically, for Hardy to start repudiating his doleful Dorset understanding of the world for some more metropolitan, clued-in, intellectually tuned-up way of seeing things."[81] Instead, Hardy, according to Heaney, knew that "what travelled, what reached across the Dorset border and beyond the Wessex landscape and the local language was a truth to life below or above the ethnic and the regional. . . . Just because you bear the markings of a particular cultural milieu doesn't mean that your work can only be appreciated within that milieu. It's crazy to think of a poem existing in a state of cultural or ethnic protectionism."[82] Such clear affirmations of particularized but finally transcendent regionalism by Heaney here suggest that real regionalism reaches a series of widening, heterogeneous audiences.

In recalling his early reading in poetry, Heaney noted the sterility and removed quality of much literature he explored at that time, which he then contrasted with Hardy's fiction: "Somehow the world of print was like the world of proper and official behavior among strangers. . . . There was no dirt on your boots and you had washed your hands."[83] As he thankfully recalled, "It was not until I read the novels of Thomas Hardy in my teens that what was actual at home and what was actually in print encountered [each other] inside my head."[84] Similarly, in Heaney's Richard Ellmann Lecture, "The Place of Writing: W. B. Yeats and Thoor Ballylee" (1989), he discusses Hardy country and the way in which "the Hardy birthplace embodies the feel of a way of life native to the place. It suggests a common heritage, an adherence to the hearth world of Wessex."[85] Heaney has recalled mentioning Hardy to Kavanagh one of the two times he met the older poet, noting, "I either commended Thomas Hardy or asked what he himself thought of Hardy" (*SS*, 73). Clearly, Heaney was linking one regional exemplar from the North of Ireland with another one from England in this moment.

Larkin's example would prove even more powerful for Heaney, and while it is beyond the scope of this chapter to trace his various influences on Heaney, Heaney's sense of Larkin as a regional poet was certainly positive overall. He would later write two major essays on Larkin, "The Main of Light," in 1982, and "Joy or Night: Last Things in the Poetry of W. B.

Yeats and Philip Larkin," in 1990, which would focus on Larkin's more spiritual qualities and final slide into nihilism, respectively, but in the 1970s he was more taken with Larkin's affirmation of the region.[86] Unfortunately, criticism on Heaney's relationship to Larkin has generally tended either to draw direct comparisons and contrasts between the poetry of each or to explore the positions articulated in these latter two essays and neglect how Larkin exemplified fidelity to a chosen region.[87]

In his lecture "Englands of the Mind," Heaney discusses how Larkin, Hughes, and Geoffrey Hill attempt to preserve age-old continuities in England through the distinctive language of their poetry. He opens with another affirmation of the region: "All . . . treat England as a region—or rather treat their region as England—in different and complementary ways."[88] For Heaney, each poet retrieves certain aspects of England's past worth preserving. For instance, "Hughes relies on the northern deposits, the pagan Anglo-Saxon and Norse elements, and he draws energy also from a related constellation of primitive myths and world views," while Hill employs "a scholastic imagination founded on an England that we might describe as Anglo-Romanesque, touched by the polysyllabic light of Christianity but possessed by darker energies which might be acknowledged as barbaric."[89] Larkin's "proper hinterland is the English language Frenchified and turned humanist by the Norman conquest and the Renaissance, made nimble, melodious and plangent by Chaucer and Spenser, and bosomed clean of its inkhornisms and its irrational magics by the eighteenth century."[90] And yet, Heaney will conclude the essay by musing about Larkin's poetic laments for an English "pastoral hinterland," a phrase suggesting that Larkin's perspicuous language, drawn from various aspects of the English literary tradition, made him one of the most articulate proponents of saving rural regions of England.[91]

One of the few critics to analyze Heaney's treatment of Larkin as a regional poet, Raphaël Ingelbien, has challenged Heaney's account of Larkin's "quasi-tribal sense of nationhood which he ascribes to Hughes and Hill: Larkin is 'the insular Englishman, responding to the tones of his own clan.'"[92] Ingelbien focuses upon Heaney's citation of Larkin's "The Importance of Elsewhere," which he sees as "a strategic choice for Heaney, since the poem deals with Larkin's experience of living in Belfast in the 1950s."[93] He points out that the conclusion of Larkin's poem actually suggests the English poet's "existential strangeness" living in England, "a temptation to refuse which did not make sense in terms of national identity."[94] Yet Ingelbien misses much of the thrust of Heaney's discussion treating Larkin, not realizing that he stresses Larkin's (and Hughes's and Hill's) defense of a vanishing England, as when he muses upon their "desire to preserve indigenous traditions, to keep open the imagination's supply lines to the past, to receive from the stations of Anglo-Saxon confirmations of ancestry, *to perceive in the rituals of show Saturdays and race-meetings and seaside outings, of church-going and marriages at Whitsun, and in the necessities that crave expression after the ritual of church-going has passed away*, to perceive in these a continuity of communal ways, and a confirmation of an identity which is threatened—all this is signified by their language."[95] The wistful tone and the language here recall Heaney's similar lament in an autobiographical sketch he wrote, likely around the time *Death of a Naturalist* was published in 1966: "The old traditional community which I knew as a child has disappeared. Farming and dealing have become dehumanized—there is no longer co-operation among farmers to save crops, no longer gatherings at potato and harvest time; machinery has killed this. Fairs are no longer in existence."[96] He published an uncollected poem, "Fair (A Progress Report)," in 1963, when this concern was much on his mind. That poem features "raw-jawed mountain hill farmers [who] dander / Among trailers to drive hard grudged bargains." Even though the poem's speaker concludes, "Men gaunt as ancestral photographs reflect / That horse-fairs have died out," he concedes that "on the humped street / Tractor fumes have not killed the sheep-reek, / And among these shepherd's [*sic*] cheques are suspect."[97] The defiant tone of that poem has disappeared by the time he collected several poems in *Death of a Naturalist* that mourn that vanished world, perhaps none more so than "Ancestral Photograph," whose title draws on the almost verbatim phrase from "Fair (A Progress Report)," and which compares Heaney's father's skills as a cattle herder to those of his father's uncles. It then concludes, "Father, I've watched you do the same / And watched you sadden when the fairs were stopped. / No room for dealers if the farmers shopped / Like housewives at an auction ring" (*DN*, 13–14). Heaney articulated a similar elegy, this time, for the vanishing practice of hand-digging turf for peat in a program he wrote and broadcast for BBC Television, likely in the early 1970s: "The blade of the spade has yielded to the blades of the machine, the closed circle of natural process has been finally broken up by the modern urge towards productivity but peoples' feelings and attachments are still fragrant with the memories of that older, slower, poorer, peaceful way."[98] The passage above from "Englands of the Mind" thus implies how much Heaney has internalized and sympathizes with Larkin's poems lamenting this disappearing England (and by extension Heaney's own disappearing Ulster) such as "Show Saturday," "To the Sea," "Church Going," and "The Whitsun Weddings."

Heaney was one of the earliest critics to appreciate Larkin as a sort of amateur environmentalist—a poet of the modern age, no doubt—but one who elegiacally enshrined the remnants of centuries-old traditions in poems such as "Going, Going." Part of Larkin's sense of "existential strangeness" living in a rapidly modernizing England stemmed from his continuing backward look at unifying cultural traditions such as those hymned in these stirring poems. Such a perception accords with Heaney's contention that Larkin's "trees and flowers and grasses are neither animistic, nor hallowed by half-remembered druidic lore; they are emblems of mutabilitie. . . . His landscape is dominated neither by the untamed heath [as in Hughes] nor the totemistic architectures of spire and battlement [as in Hill] but by the civic prospects, by roofs and gardens and prospects where urban and pastoral visions interact as 'postal districts packed like squares of wheat.'"[99] The clash of such visions animates much of Larkin's poetry, as does his "stripped standard English voice," whose "ancestry begins . . . when the Middle Ages are turning secular."[100] Larkin's plain-spoken attention to the disappearing rural areas of England—if anything a cause for his unease living in urbanizing England—drives the conclusion of the essay toward a recognition of a unifying preservationist urge in Larkin particularly, but also in Hughes and Hill. Heaney does not quote Larkin's "The Importance of Elsewhere" in isolation but links it instead to the concern of "Going, Going." Here are the two sentences that yoke the two poems together and are left conveniently out by Ingelbien: "Larkin's England of the mind is in many ways continuous with the England of Rupert Brooke's 'Grantchester' and Edward Thomas's 'Adlestrop', an England of customs and institutions, industrial and domestic, but also an England whose pastoral hinterland is threatened by the very success of these institutions. Houses and roads and factories mean that a certain England is 'Going, Going.'"[101]

Larkin is increasingly perceived as a regional or provincial writer in the most enabling sense of those terms. R. P. Draper, for example, has argued this case, noting that Larkin's "slightly aggressive-defensive Englishness is provincial rather than nationalist. It has a strong Midlands-cum-North-of-England flavor, as befits a man who was born in Coventry and worked as a librarian in Wellington, Shropshire, in Leicester and in Hull."[102] And in Belfast for five years in the 1950s! Even more convincingly, Robert Crawford, in his revealing discussion of Larkin in *Devolving English Literature*, argues that Larkin's "provincialism" (not in Kavanagh's negative sense of the term) was influential in Heaney's development as a regional writer:

> Hull gave Larkin a valued provincial status as a place that can only be reached, in the language of his poem "Here," by "Swerving" aside from the main flow of the traffic, and this provincial status of Larkin's was to be of use to such writers as Seamus Heaney, able to see Larkin as one of the modern English poets "now possessed of that defensive love of their territory which was once shared only by those poets whom we might call colonial—Yeats, MacDiarmid, Carlos Williams." By seeing Larkin as, in some sense, a "colonial" writer, Heaney is able both to identify and compete with Larkin, the poet of "English nationalism" ["Englands of the Mind," 151, 167]. If Larkin's "English nationalism" is really very much of a provincial variety, that makes him all the closer to the Northern Ireland-born Heaney.[103]

In "Englands of the Mind," after citing Larkin's "Going, Going," Heaney argues that "that sense of an ending has driven all three of these writers into a kind of piety towards their local origins, has made them look in, rather than up, to England."[104] Here we see Heaney implicitly linking his own urge to explore and preserve the local folkways and traditions of the historic province of Ulster and to accomplish this aim in part through rendering the various Ulster dialects.

Although he approves of the languages employed by each of these three important poets in their verse, Heaney particularly seems to approve of Ted Hughes's language, if not his steeping of his poetry in violence. He explicitly recognizes and lauds Hughes's incorporation of his heavy native West Yorkshire dialect into his poetry, noting that its "sensuous fetch, its redolence of blood and gland and grass and water, recalled English poetry in the fifties from a too suburban aversion of the attention from the elemental; and the poems beat the bounds of a hidden England in streams and trees, on moors and in byres."[105] His articulation of Hughes's evocation of a "hidden England" in this May 1976 lecture seemingly accords with his articulation of Kavanagh's and Montague's exploration of "a hidden Ulster" in "The Sense of Place," already discussed. Yet Hughes did sometimes employ metaphors of carnage in a way that indicated he relished the violence he associated with these cultures. While Heaney clearly distinguishes between good and evil in the hidden cultures he retrieves from the Ulster landscape as part of his ethical regionalism, Hughes was more interested in tapping into the "elemental power circuit of the universe" that lies beyond good and evil.[106]

The general trajectory—but not its primal violence—of Hughes's "hidden England" thus affirmed Heaney's general subterranean urges in this period, often expressed through his desire to burrow into the depths of his mind in poems such as "North," or through his fascination with the "bog bodies" found in northern Europe in poems such as "The Tollund Man" from *Wintering Out* and "Punishment" and other bog poems in *North*. More important, Heaney's recognition of a "hidden England" and a "hidden Ulster" signals his growing awareness of how the regional poetry in the British and Irish archipelago represented a powerful, enduring path down which poetry in the English language might continue moving. As he notes in his conclusion to "Englands of the Mind," "The loss of imperial power, the failure of economic nerve, the diminished influence of Britain inside Europe, all this has led to a new sense of the shires, a new valuing of the native English experience."[107]

In his 1972 review of Hughes's *Selected Poems*, Heaney anticipates the language he would use about the Yorkshire poet's recovery of a "hidden England" in "Englands of the Mind" when he suggests that "Hughes brought back into English poetry an unsentimental intimacy with the *hidden country*. Probably not since John Clare had the outback of hedge and farmyard been viewed so urgently."[108] Hughes's closeness to the land was exemplary for Heaney, but perhaps even more so was his distinctly northern English voice: "Into the elegant, iambic and typically standard English intonations of contemporary verse he interjected an energetic, heavily stressed, consciously extravagant and inventive northern voice."[109] Heaney was drawing on ten years of reading Hughes by then. Henry Hart argues that Heaney's reading of Hughes's *Lupercal* "bound him back to his rural home ground, confirmed his sometimes uncertain trust in his rural imagination and subject matter ..., and encouraged him to articulate his pastoral preoccupations in a sensuous, down-to-earth, alliterative voice that was different from the urbane voice favored by Movement poets at the time."[110] Hughes's peripheral position—both geographically and linguistically—from England's political, cultural, and poetic center of London appealed to the young Ulster poet, who loved the tradition of English literature but also long had felt deep affinities with the margins of that tradition.

Despite Heaney's clear approval of regional English literature in "Englands of the Mind," Edna Longley, continuing in her conviction that Heaney's *North*, published the year before, reifies and mystifies the rituals of Irish republicanism, strangely reads this lecture as a manifestation of Heaney's hidden nationalism. Longley thinks that Heaney's remark about Hughes's "hidden England" recalls Daniel Corkery's nationalistic study *The Hidden Ireland*, as no doubt it does. But she is wrong to infer from that reference that Heaney "encourages in Hughes ideas of cultural recovery similar to those associated with a particular form of Irish nationalism.... Heaney ... restores to England, via Northern Ireland, nineteenth-century ethno-critical concepts. In particular, his response to Hughes as Saxon/Protestant Other disregards the historical contingencies (post-war, post-religious, post-industrial) that engender and inform Hughes's myth. This reproduces the Jacobite a-historicity that conditions Heaney's own thinking about Northern Ireland."[111] This is a misreading of Heaney's lecture, especially since Longley does not recognize its place in the context of his clear approval of other regional literatures. This approval may well be because "Heaney is as alert as Hewitt (for complementary reasons) to those aspects of postwar England that bespeak imperial decline and the dismantling of Protestant Britishness,"[112] but Heaney's regionalist ethos, while it may celebrate Britain's imperial decline, is more oriented toward unifying the disparate communities in the province and often recognizes "Protestant Britishness" as an aspect of his Ulster inheritance, even as he is concerned to reclaim and evoke the Irish Catholic subculture of his region.[113]

Heaney's ongoing regionalist project consistently retrieves unifying cultural elements, particularly dialects and languages, from the landscapes of his long-divided province and other regions. Eugene O'Brien remains one of the few critics besides the present one to ascribe ethical implications to Heaney's sense of place, even terming all of "Heaney's descriptions of place" as particular "gestures towards an ethical revelation or unveiling."[114] In this sense, Heaney's repeated geographic explorations of place in these essays on regionalist writers, which, taken together, attain the status of art, carry an implicit ethical charge: landscape functions as a repository of cultural and religious signifiers that must be read closely to determine how regionalism has powerful and potentially liberating effects on cultural consciousness.

To return briefly to Kenneth Frampton and his theory of critical regionalism that I mooted in the introduction, Frampton's contrast of two differing ways of preparing a building site for a structure illuminates Heaney's practice in his regionalist essays: "The bulldozing of an irregular topography into a flat site is clearly a technocratic gesture which aspires to a condition of absolute *placelessness*, whereas the terracing of the same site to receive the stepped form of a building is an engagement in the act of 'cultivating' the site."[115] Rather than charging into the literal and literary landscape of the region of Ulster/Northern Ireland and attempting to create a *tabula rasa*, Heaney wisely recognized the irregularities of this contested landscape and cultivated the site by adapting and transforming his regionalist ethos in the light of his readings of literary exemplars. Having been built upon their shoulders, his regionalism is grounded yet flexible and future-looking, attuned to particularities and peculiarities, and constantly attentive to new influences from outside the geographic region of Ulster. Because of Heaney's artistic rendering of an actual, yet imagined province, influenced by regional Northern Irish, American (especially Frost), Scottish, Welsh, and regional English writers, his 1970s prose explorations of regionalism analyzed here offer a wonderful paradigm of rapprochement and inclusiveness for a province that is still beset with cultural and political misunderstandings.

Chapter Four

WOUNDS AND FIRE
Northern Ireland in Heaney's 1970s Poetry

My own poetry is a kind of slow, obstinate papish burn, emanating from the ground I was brought up on.
—Seamus Heaney, "Unhappy and at Home"

Heaney told Seamus Deane in 1977 that "my first attempts to speak, to make verse, faced the Northern sectarian problem. Then this went underground and I became very influenced by [Ted] Hughes and one part of my temperament took over: the private County Derry part of myself rather than the slightly aggravated young Catholic male part."[1] That "slightly aggravated young Catholic male part" of the poet had reared its head by the early 1970s in reaction to the brutal assaults perpetrated by the police, the loyalists, and finally the British Army against civil rights marchers. If Heaney used his prose essays in the 1970s to promote his unifying concept of regionalism, representing what he calls in this same interview "the obstinate voice of rationalist humanism," his early hopes for a province taking steps to become more united through language and culture were placed in a dialectical relationship with a more negative conception of the province as literally and metaphorically wounded and burned in a series of significant poems that arise from the other part of his temperament—the "slow, obstinate papish burn."[2] Such poems include the uncollected "Intimidation" and a poem called "Nocturne" that Heaney revised into the first poem of the sequence "A Northern Hoard" for *Wintering Out*, along with collected poems such as "Linen Town," "The Last Mummer," and "Servant Boy," also from that volume, and "Belderg," "Funeral Rites," "Viking Dublin: Trial Pieces," "Bone Dreams," and "Kinship" from *North*. By offering readings of these poems that show how Heaney figures Northern Ireland as wounded, I demonstrate how he draws upon images not only from the violent, dark past of Scandinavia and its Viking invaders who eventually came to Ireland but also from the land itself as alluring yet dangerous, going back to his childhood memories of bogs in Northern Ireland.

WINTERING OUT AND THE NORTH'S TURN TOWARD VIOLENCE

The positive regionalism Heaney had been promoting since the 1960s is reflected in the largely unifying poems employing dialects common to the province that he published in the 1972 volume *Wintering Out*, as I have argued elsewhere.[3] Another poem from that volume, "Linen Town," which is subtitled "High Street, Belfast, 1786," continues to explore Heaney's fascination with the potential of what might have happened in history—an interest epitomized by the poet's belief in the cultural and political possibilities raised by the 1798 Rising, some supporters of which sought to achieve equal rights for Irish Catholics, as we saw in my discussion of his verse play *Munro* in chapter 2.[4] In "Linen Town," Heaney encapsulates a moment in time in Belfast, capital of the linen industry in Ireland. Ireland and Belfast especially were in dire straits economically then because of the departure to America of so many of Ulster's Protestant citizens. Jonathan Bardon has pointed out that by the late 1770s the Irish depression was exacerbated by Ulster's support for the American colonists against the British and by government trade embargoes. Additionally, "Linen sales continued to plummet, as William Brownlow, MP for Co. Armagh, told the Irish Commons in February 1778: 'The last September market was bad, this is worse. This may be seen at the Linen Hall: a great quantity of linens are unsold.'"[5]

In the opening lines of the poem, a horseman rides into one of the alleyways or entries in Belfast,

> Coming perhaps from the Linen Hall
> Or Cornmarket
> Where, the civic print unfrozen,
>
> In twelve years' time
> They hanged young McCracken—
> (*WO*, 38)

Heaney's judicious use of the dash brings the poem to an abrupt halt so that the potential of the moment can be examined. Henry Joy McCracken has not yet been hanged—the United Irishmen would not even be formed for five more years—and the "civic print" is still fluid, anything can happen (38).

Then, as if the print somehow foreclosed on any other possibility occurring,

> Pen and ink, water tint
>
> Fence and fetch us in
> Under bracketed tavern signs,
> The edged gloom of arcades
> (*WO*, 38)

The lines of ink in the print from the future and the signs and buildings in the present close off this shining moment of potential, and we are left with two stanzas that offer little respite from the coming doom:

> It's twenty to four
> On one of the last afternoons
> Of reasonable light.
>
> Smell the tidal Lagan:
> Take a last turn
> In the tang of possibility.
> (38)

Smell, taste, and sight coalesce here to present a dramatic picture of what might have been. This is Heaney's poetic recognition of the moment of possibility in history for Catholic enfranchisement—and for a subsequent diminution in nationalist agitation later in Ireland—if the United Irishmen attained their political objectives.

Besides the retrospective hope of the poem, there is an additional linguistic optimism. Implicit in the name of "Belfast" is a linguistic duality that for Heaney signals both the possibility of progress out of Northern Irish tribalism and the possibility of regress, both in the late eighteenth century and in the current situation. Heaney points out this potential in a 1972 BBC Northern Ireland Radio program that opens with his reading the lyrics of a song, "May the Lord in His Mercy Look Down on Belfast." He then observes,

> Belfast itself was once known as "The Athens of the North." That was in the late eighteenth century. Before that, it was known as *Beal Feirste*, which is the Irish for "the mouth of the Farset." And I suppose in the two names, in *Beal Feirste* and in "The Athens of the North," you have two directions in which you can approach or be caught up in the question of Ireland and particularly at the moment, the question of Northern Ireland. You can look and be lured backwards into a kind of native bog of lore and facts and resentment and political aims. Or, Athens of the North, you can stand to the side and say, "Of course, in the twentieth century, this kind of thing is quite archaic, quite barbaric, these energies should be dead long ago." And anybody living in Belfast, living in Ireland at the minute, is pulled in those two directions. Anybody writing poetry is also pulled, I think, anybody writing.[6]

Heaney's explicit equation of the Irish place name for the city with "a kind of native bog of lore and facts and resentment and political aims" indicates his transcendence of half of his own linguistic heritage and his willingness to admit the dark side of cultural nationalism, an admission that beautifully balances his affirmation of the Hibernicized place names "Anahorish" and "Broagh" in those largely unifying poems from *Wintering Out*. At this point in his career, Heaney had already found one of his most powerful later emphases—the *potentia* inherent in the imagination generally and specifically in poetry—but here he seems constrained by the burden of history, which was probably increased by the heightening of violence in the province during the writing of the poems of this volume.

A similar poem from *Wintering Out*, "The Last Mummer," sets the unifying, likely Catholic figure of a mummer against an uncertain future in the province. Heaney has remarked that mumming was a tradition that transcended sectarianism and gathered entire communities in his childhood Ulster together. He admitted to Dennis O'Driscoll that while "the last mummer is . . . an alter ego of sorts. He too is resentful and impenitent," mumming, like cockfighting, "cut across the sectarian divide" (*SS*, 130, 131). Academic studies of mumming agree with Heaney's assessment of the practice as a nonsectarian, inclusive practice; although it was carried out mainly by Catholics, the mummers visited both Catholic and Protestant homes. For instance, Henry Glassie, in his classic study *All Silver and No Brass: An Irish Christmas Mumming*, points out that "generally, all of the mummers were Catholics, though a few Protestants might travel along with them, but they went to Protestant homes as well as Catholic ones and acted with particular politeness at houses where they had heard they were not welcome."[7] And in his review of the 2007 volume of essays *Border-Crossing: Mumming in Cross-Border and Cross-Community Contexts* Mike Pearson notes that "throughout, a persuasive case is made for regarding rhyming as crossing social classes and ethnic and religious groupings, as well as national boundaries."[8] Pearson further observes that despite its performative anarchy and "moments of crisis," which led to its being "regarded as a potential threat to social order" (by the 1950s, mummers in Northern Ireland had to apply to the Royal Ulster Constabulary for a permit), mumming's "purpose, or effective outcome, is regarded by a number of authors as nurturing inclusiveness and communal adhesion."[9] Heaney's approval of mumming's cross-border appeal in every sense of that phrase and similar affirmation of its created anarchic revelry starkly contrast with his growing dismay and disapproval of the anarchy on the streets of the province that by the early 1970s was increasingly separating Catholics and Protestants. Glassie conducted his study in the district of Ballymenone, County Fermanagh, a border area of Northern Ireland, against the backdrop of the Troubles during the same time that Heaney wrote "The Last Mummer." Glassie asked one of his subjects, Peter Flanagan, a former mummer, whether "mumming [had previously] helped hold the community together," and Flanagan's response is revelatory: "Aye surely.

It was to bring unity amongst them and to show the opposite number that there was no harm in them. We would go to the houses of the people of Protestant persuasion and they were delighted. Often and often they would give more than what the Catholic people would. . . . It broke down a lot of barriers. It changed public opinion altogether. If the mummin [*sic*] had spread—if people had become more mixed—it really wouldn't have developed as it has at the present time. I really think that."[10]

Mummers' plays in Ireland, in England, and across Europe arose from midwinter rites conducted by pagans who feared the imminent disappearance of the sun and thus would plead with the gods for its strength to be restored. Thus the nonsectarian mummers' tradition as represented in "The Last Mummer" suggests that even though the volume's title, *Wintering Out*, drawn from an agricultural term that connotes hanging on through a hard winter in the hope of the revivifying spring, betokens hope for an end to wintry, hardened sectarian relations in Northern Ireland, Heaney correctly feared that the interventions that might thaw those relations were doomed. And they were not just any interventions, but particularly artistic ones: after all, mummers were so called because in earlier mummers' plays they would sometimes mime, and in later plays they would murmur or mutter. They were artists trained in singing, masking, dancing, and deception. The disappearance of the last mummer ostensibly recalls many such poems about dying rural crafts from the 1960s such as "Digging" and "Thatching"; more ominously, it suggests that by 1972 Heaney was beginning to fear that art of any kind would not be able to halt the seemingly interminable sectarian winter that the region of Northern Ireland was experiencing.

The central feature of the mummers' play was a struggle between two figures that represented light and darkness. The dark figure, representing the death of the old year, would fall to the ground but would then be miraculously revived by a doctor character who would restore life to the dead body, which would then represent the coming new year. In Ulster, the masked tradition of mumming may be more than 2,500 years old.[11] Heaney's poem, with its images of "St. George, Beelzebub and Jack Straw" (*WO*, 18), conveys a thorough familiarity with the tradition, which he employs to suggestively offer the possibility that in the continuing present of the Troubles in 1970s Northern Ireland there will be no miraculous solution to conflict—that bodies will continue to litter the streets with no hope of revival and that masked fiends, not playfully masked mummers, will run rampant in committing sectarian atrocities.[12]

This tripartite poem opens with a roving mummer who "carries a stone in his pocket, / an ash-plant under his arm," which seem to be talismans that signify his charmed ability to move through the countryside unmaligned and connote his complementary penchant for enchanting those he encounters (*WO*, 18). Even though "the luminous screen in the corner / has them charmed in a ring," the mummer patiently waits, seemingly gathering his energy so that his own, ancient magic can successfully compete with the modern television (18). Shortly before he "starts beating / the bars of the gate," he becomes "shrouded," slipping on his mask so that his own identity will not be known (18). This mummer's insistence on entering the modern community of this household implies that what he brings to them is still needed in a time when ancient sectarianism is rearing its ugly head.

Heaney has even remarked that the rhymes of the "Christmas Rhymers," as they were called in his part of County Derry, were "spoken in the local accent, but they were spoken with a ritual force that wouldn't have disgraced the actors in Shakespeare's Globe Theatre. Indeed, the accent itself bore some relation to the accents you'd have heard in the Globe, because then and now Co. Derry was also Co. Londonderry, the place to which the English planters of the early seventeenth-century Plantation had also brought the English speech of Elizabethan and Jacobean London."[13] Thus the mummers' very speech bore in it traces of conquest and division, yet they were finally a culturally unifying force in their regionalist accents and their sense of drama's ritualistic, magical powers.

In the second section of "The Last Mummer," we are told that the mummer's position as masked entertainer enables him to pick "a nice way through / the long toils of blood // and feuding" (*WO*, 19). His ability to negotiate such intimate hatreds also stems from his adept use of his tongue, his instinct for an opening, and his manners:

His tongue went whoring

among the civil tongues,
he had an eye for weather-eyes

at cross-roads and lane-ends
and could don manners

at a flutter of curtains.
His straw mask and hunch were fabulous

disappearing beyond the lamplit
slabs of a yard.
(*WO*, 19)

The outrageousness of the mummer's "whoring" tongue releases the pent-up energies behind the country people's "civil tongues," the polite language they would speak in the open. Presumably, his slyly suggestive speech would open their own mouths and enable a free speech among those he met. Swooping into a closed community, the mummer could create a suspension of animosity as he enabled a free-wheeling clatter of talk and revelry through his masking and position as figure of fun.

But that participle "disappearing" in the last two lines of this section also indicates the decline of mumming in Northern Ireland by the time Heaney reached young adulthood and the concomitant disappearance of a space where Protestants and Catholics could meet on equal terms and engage in spirited laughter and conversation. As a verbal replacement for this tradition, the poet dreams not only "a cricket in the hearth / and cockroach on the floor" but also "a line of mummers / marching out the door //as the lamp flares in the draught" (*WO*, 19). He tells us that the "melted snow off their feet / leaves you in peace" (19–20), two lines that signify how the approach of mummers could temporarily melt sometimes-frozen relations between Catholics and Protestants in Ulster. As the poem ends, "He makes dark tracks, who had // untousled a first dewy path / into the summer grazing" (20). The withdrawal of this charmed and charming mummer through the making of his "dark tracks" hints at the spreading darkness Heaney and many other residents of Northern Ireland were faced with as the 1970s wore on and violence exploded on an unprecedented level.

That darkness is represented perhaps most famously in *Wintering Out* through "The Tollund Man," whose appearance continued a series of bog poems that began with "Bogland," from *Door into the Dark* (1969), and would culminate in the well-known bog poems from *North*. But the much less well-known "Intimidation" and the only slightly better-known "Northern Hoard" represent Heaney's fears for the province much more directly than the myth-inflected "The Tollund Man." "Intimidation" and "Nocturne," the latter an earlier version of what would become Part I of "A Northern Hoard," entitled "Roots," were published together in January 1971 in the *Malahat Review*. Until now, Neil Corcoran and Michael Parker are the only commentators to delve even briefly into "Intimidation."[14]

While the masked man in "The Last Mummer" is welcomed into the lamplit intimacy of country communities because he brings laughter and revelry to them, the subject of "Intimidation" fears the disturbing revelry associated with the triumphalism of the annual July 12 bonfires lit throughout Northern Ireland by Protestants to celebrate the victory of King William over the Catholic King James at the Battle of the Boyne in 1690. The intimidated and increasingly exasperated speaker, presumably a Catholic, both fears and is mentally spurred by the actions of the loyalists who burn their annual bonfire near his house. The "architecture" of the poem consists of four quatrains, Heaney's favored form in his 1970s poetry; he has recalled using them like augers boring down into subterranean depths.[15] The actual architecture portrayed in the poem, however, focuses upon the "gable" of the speaker, which is "scorched" by this fire in the opening line and "blackened" in the concluding line.[16] The poem is thus framed by images of blackness that signify the darkness of hatred the speaker associates with the assembled loyalists outside every July 12.

Always keen to ring multiple meanings on crucial words, Heaney employs three words charged with varying registers of significance in "Intimidation" to convey the atmosphere of hate. The first of these is *tumulus*, used in line 3 when the speaker "kick[s] through" in line 2 "a tumulus of ash."[17] *Tumulus* has the most common meaning of "an ancient sepulchral mound, a barrow."[18] The way Heaney employs this first meaning of the word is indeterminate: it seemingly connotes that the speaker feels figuratively buried in the ash of this triumphalist bonfire, but in rereading the poem with the speaker's vow in stanza 3 that these loyalists will "taste their ashes yet," we see that the speaker could perceive their behavior as self-destructive or as inviting destruction, perhaps by republicans.

Following the phrase "tumulus of ash" in line 3 is the appositional phrase of line 4, which freights the former phrase with additional meaning. "A hot stour in the moonlight" invokes a martial image that may be particularly resonant in the context of sectarian relations in Northern Ireland.[19] *Stour* denotes an armed combat; a stiff, even bold resolve; and a deposit of dust.[20] It thus connotes that the bonfire outside is brazenly violent. But in another sense, it softens the hardened sense of *tumulus* into an easily dispersed dust. Most interestingly, the meaning of the word as "stiff" or "bold" may play upon the vaunted staunchness of Ulster Protestant loyalists, whose vow "No priest, no pope, no surrender" signifies their refusal to accommodate Northern Irish Catholics politically or otherwise. Heaney uses the phrase "so staunch and true" to signify such a recalcitrance in some of the opening lines of *The Cure at Troy* (*CT*, 1).

Finally, by calling the assembled loyalists "a nest of pismires / At his drystone walls" at the end of stanza 2, the speaker connotes both their appearance to him as ants, or insignificant creatures, and their persistence, their working away at hatred time out of mind. He rests in the strength of those stony walls, perceiving them as pests that will not topple his house—which is finally figured as permanent—while casting them as temporary invaders from the "Ghetto."[21]

Whereas a common dialect potentially unites inhabitants of the province over against the English in poems such as "Broagh" from *Wintering Out*, here the Catholic speaker draws boundary lines around his presumably isolated home, and the threat of dispossession lingers in the air. "Intimidation" traffics in the language of ownership, with the speaker clearly believing that he is the grounded native and the assembled "burners" outside the interlopers. The poem begins by contrasting the plural possessive of the loyalists with the singular possessive of the speaker: "*Their* bonfire scorched *his* gable."[22] In stanza 2, the speaker describes "*their* midsummer madness," while stanza 3 observes darkly, "They'll come streaming past / To taste *their* ashes yet." Stanza 4 pictures the speaker sitting in darkness with soot drifting off "*his* blackened gable."[23]

Heaney would have likely never sympathized with such a stance, which is rendered just as bigoted as that of the loyalists by the speaker's pejorative appellation of "Ghetto rats!" for the gathered Protestants and his vow that they will die by tasting "their ashes."[24] At the same time, he probably felt he should at least ventriloquize this attitude because so many young men were then joining the IRA in response to loyalist attacks on Catholics. He has never collected the poem, probably out of fear that its anger and threatened violent reprisal might be linked to his own attitude at the time.

The companion poem to "Intimidation" in the January 1971 issue of the *Malahat Review*, "Nocturne," seems at first a tranquil, domestic counterpoint to the sectarian activity and hatred of the former poem, but it too is eventually penetrated by violence from the outer world. "Nocturne" rejects the favored Heaney quatrain of the canonical poems of the early to mid-1970s in favor of a fifteen-line stanza followed by an eight-line stanza, although when he revised it for the first section of "A Northern Hoard" he rendered it in quatrains, a form he has explicitly associated with the poems of *Wintering Out*.[25] The sinuous effect of the original lineation and stanzaic pattern, which is heightened by Heaney's indentation of line 10, invites us into a poem that appears at first to be a classic example of a nocturne with its calm, meditative tone, a peacefulness that is eventually shattered with the introduction of "gunshot and siren" in line 11:

> Leaf membranes lid the window.
> In our streetlamp's glow
> Your body's moonstruck
> To drifted barrow, sunk glacial rock.
> Sleeping beauty, the touch of love
> Operative as faith to move
> Your small mountains
> And shift your gradual plains
> Is stilled.
>   Above each slated terrace
> Gunshot and siren dwindle towards us
> Like well-timed noises off.
> The fault is opening at last—my love,
> How should we love our old Gomorrah?
> We petrify or uproot now.[26]

This poem, written several years before Heaney's "Act of Union," works in the opposite direction in terms of its evocation of human body and geographic landscape. The speaker in "Nocturne" portrays his sleeping lover's beauty in topographical terms, dwelling on her "small mountains" and "gradual plains,"[27] while the speaker in "Act of Union" will render the Irish landscape feminine, as we saw in my introduction.

I use the word *penetrated* above because "Nocturne" muses upon the potential act of sexual penetration and the entrance of violence into the speaker and lover's domestic world and ponders an imagined uprooting of self and family and their reinsertion into another landscape. As line 9 abruptly is "stilled" with a full stop, line 10 abruptly enters the poem, but its entrance is mitigated by a prepositional phrase that serves to indirectly and gradually introduce the noise of the "gunshot and siren."[28] As they hear those sounds, the speaker observes, "The fault is opening at last— my love. . . ," a splendidly rendered example of how the dash can visually interrupt a line of poetry and, here, signify the growing chasm in the province.[29] At first we might believe that the speaker is about to make love to his companion, but then we realize the question of love he raises here about "our old Gomorrah" and petrifaction references contemporary Northern Ireland as refracted through the Old Testament narrative of Lot and his family, who were warned by the Lord not to look back on Sodom and Gomorrah as they fled those sites of iniquity in Genesis 19. Heaney's allusion to this Old Testament passage teasingly suggests that Northern Ireland is essentially God-forsaken and given over to great sin and will be punished with fire from heaven.

Because Heaney and his family would move to the Republic of Ireland the next year after this poem was published, it seems reasonable to assume that the question posed here had already assumed a real urgency and resonance for them. They may well have feared becoming petrified in the figurative sense of the word if they stayed: for example, Heaney undoubtedly was frustrated by the conditions on the ground in the province after he returned there from his academic year spent at the University of California, Berkeley, in 1970–71. As he notes in a short passage from the preface to his 1975 prose poem pamphlet *Stations*, "On my return a month after the introduction of internment my introspection was not confident enough to pursue its direction. The sirens in the air, perhaps quite rightly, jammed those other tentative if insistent signals."[30] The "gunshot and siren" that sonically interrupt the meditative calm of "Nocturne" must have not only "jammed" his attempts to write in the new subgenre of prose poetry but also led at least in part to his and his wife Marie's decision to leave the fractured North.[31]

The last stanza of "Nocturne" makes clear that the speaker has made the decision to "uproot" himself and his family from wounded Northern Ireland, as he portrays himself using a mandrake, "lodged human fork, / Earth sac, limb of the dark" to "wound" the "damp smelly loam" of a shrub in a dream, and then "stop[ping] my ears against the scream."[32] According to the mythology that has accrued around this odd, sometimes human-shaped plant, if it is uprooted it will scream, and that sound will kill all those within hearing. This strange action must be meant to be an erotic parallel to the wound that the "pale sniper" in this same stanza will inflict on an unsuspecting victim. But why would Heaney portray himself in this way? Is he likening his family to a mandrake and attempting to stop the inevitable scream of protest if he uproots them, then replants them in unfamiliar ground, perhaps figuratively "killing" them and himself in the process? And what do we make of his likely allusion to the story of Leah and Rachel from Genesis 30:14–23?

Rachel was Jacob's second, infertile wife who bargained with her sister Leah (who had had four children by Jacob but who had herself been infertile for a time) for the mandrake roots that Leah's and Jacob's son Reuben found in a field. In exchange for the mandrake roots that Leah gave to Rachel, who hoped they would make her fertile according to the legendary promise of the plant, Rachel promised Leah she could sleep with Jacob that coming night. Leah slept with Jacob and conceived another son, Issachar, and then later a sixth son, called Zebulun, and finally a daughter, called Dinah. Rachel did not conceive a child for several years after Leah's final three children were born. Heaney's exact use of this allusion is unclear, but by introducing the mandrake along with perhaps alluding to its use in this narrative from Genesis he also may be suggesting that if he uproots himself from his native province, partly to find enhanced poetic fertility, he may become a Rachel figure and have to wait for some time until he can conceive poetry again.

Thus "Nocturne" ends with a sort of imagined, dreamlike trial run whereby the speaker, whom I take to be the poet himself here, imagines uprooting himself and family from hearth and home, a potentially murderous wounding that he hopes he can stop their ears against. But such a voluntary wounding, despite the potential for temporary, poetic death, seems preferable to lingering in the North, where "the fault is opening at last" and they may be swallowed up in the increasing violence.

Wounds and Fire   143

When Heaney was assembling the poems for *Wintering Out*, he rewrote and incorporated "Nocturne" into his five-part lyric sequence "A Northern Hoard," which offers a treasure trove of images featuring wounds. These images contrast the images of light that will signify the liberating imagination in his later poem "North," one of the seminal poems from that later volume that feature the poet tuning himself to hear and heed the voices of "those fabulous raiders" (*N*, 10) warning him not to lose himself in contemplating violence and instead to dwell on illuminating treasure dug from deep within his mind (10–11).[33] Wounds open and fester throughout "A Northern Hoard," and the speakers in the various lyrics seemingly cannot escape them and certainly cannot heal them; in one striking example, a speaker even becomes an amputated limb himself.

Richard Kearney has argued in one of the seminal articles on the playwright Brian Friel that "the festering wound of the North is a constant reminder for Friel that the body politic of the Irish nation is deeply hemorrhaged" and thus that "an amputated Ulster acts as a phantom limb haunting his work."[34] In much the same way, Heaney's sense of Ulster as "amputated" from "the body politic of the Irish nation" haunts the content of his work, particularly these poems from the early 1970s that employ such images of dismemberment. More surprisingly, perhaps, woundedness often colors their style as well. Using the language of blood, Heaney has even observed that "the battened-down, hunched-over, self-defensive position that people adopted to survive the early days of the Troubles is reflected in the stylistic *clots* and clinches of those particular poems."[35]

For example, in the tersely articulated "No Man's Land," the second lyric in "A Northern Hoard," the "deserted" speaker opens by noting, "I shut out / their wounds' fierce awning," in the opening three-line stanza, then concludes by asking, "Why do I unceasingly / arrive late to condone / infected sutures / and ill-knit bone?" (*WO*, 40). And the last line of the third lyric, "Stump," ends disturbingly with the statement, "I'm cauterized, a black stump of home" (41). Seemingly unable to speak because of this, he asks in the previous line, "What do I say if they wheel out their dead?" (41). The speaker implies he has been charred by lingering in the body of the blackened province, an interesting transformation of the images of the female lover who is rendered in topographic terms in "Nocturne." This horrific image thus may answer the question the poet poses to himself in "Nocturne": "How should we love our old Gomorrah?" If he does not uproot and leave the province, he fears a stopped voice, a figurative amputation. Yet Heaney certainly remained poetically fertile in the 1970s, and the Troubles may well have helped wound him into further creativity once he reached his rural retreat in County Wicklow and got some literal and figurative distance from the province. This concern that drives "Nocturne" and many later poems from the decade anticipates his interest in exploring the character of the wounded Philoctetes in *The Cure at Troy*, leading us to realize he could not escape dwelling on the wounded condition of Northern Ireland despite his exile from there. Moreover, he was likely somewhat dismayed that this "wound" could be fertile and empower him artistically.

The final two lyrics in the sequence, "No Sanctuary" and "Tinder," feature images of "the turnip-man's lopped head" and "tinder, charred linen and iron," respectively (42, 43). Even though the speaker is ostensibly musing upon Halloween in the first poem, the image of the dismembered head calls to mind the cauterized amputation of "Stump." And the catalog of "tinder, charred linen and iron" in "Tinder" references, not fire making per se, but the history of manufacturing in the North, including its linen industry, which has now been effectively "replaced" by the tools used to spark the flames of violence that have raged throughout the earlier poems. "Tinder" ends with the collective speakers "squat[ting] on old cinder," "with new history, flint and iron, / Cast-offs, scraps, nail, canine" (44). We are back to the ashy tumulus first portrayed in "Intimidation" and the cycle of reprisal violence—ashes to ashes, dust to dust.

Heaney's interest in writing poems about wounds had deep roots: he has admitted that his childhood immersion in Irish mythology, particularly the stories about Cuchullain and Ferdia, "sank deep, those images of wounds bathed on the green rushes and armour clattering in the ford."[36] In the early to mid-1960s, he wrote an unpublished poem called "Amputation" that he read aloud to Philip Hobsbaum's Belfast writing group, a sonnet that described a quarry worker who "wakes now at night in the pain-charged ward / With white hell throbbing in a sawed-off knee."[37] "Stump," from "A Northern Hoard," would draw on the image of the amputated quarry worker in "Amputation" who "fingers the stanched stump."[38] He also composed two poems about cockfighting during this time that feature disfigured onlookers and cocks alike brought together. One of these features "the blind, the maimed, the deaf dementedly / Easing the daily pain with daily blood."[39] *Door into the Dark* features a decapitation nightmare entitled "Dream," whose speaker uses "a billhook" to cut down "a stalk / Thick as a telegraph pole" but realizes upon swinging again that there was "a man's head under the hook" (*DD*, 15). That poem concludes with the terse lines, "Before I woke / I heard the steel stop / In the bone of the brow" (15).

But these incidents were drawn from rural life, bereft of any sectarian context.[40] By the 1970s, with the festering and spreading violence in Northern Ireland, wounds were much on Heaney's mind as part of his thinking about his region and nation; he has even recalled that after Tom Flanagan led him deeper into readings of Yeats and Joyce and Irish history and culture during his California sojourn, "I was starting to see my own situation as a 'Northern poet' more in relation to the *wound* and the work of Ireland as whole" (*SS*, 143; my emphasis). The image of woundedness in Heaney's creative work would culminate in his 1990 adaptation *The Cure at Troy*, but during most of the 1970s he would write repeatedly and evocatively about rifts, faults, severings—all to signify how Northern Ireland was essentially sundered from both Britain and Ireland and was slowly turning in on and wounding itself as the Troubles accelerated. Such continued preoccupation with wounds and Heaney's repeated interrogation of them give the lie to David Lloyd's unsubstantiated and hyperbolic claim that Heaney's "poetic offers constantly a premature compensation, enacted through linguistic and metaphorical usages which promise a healing of division simply by returning the subject to place, in an innocent yet possessive relation to his objects."[41]

NORTH TOWARD VIKING VIOLENCE AND THE TROUBLES

Some of these poems about violence and oppression find their origins in the dark violence of far northern lands and narratives distant from contemporary Ireland—Scandinavia, with its Old Norse sagas, and ancient Jutland, or contemporary Denmark, and the saga *Beowulf*. Heaney has consistently argued that such narratives contain human truths we can learn from in the present. In his 2005 address at Silkeborg, Denmark, whose museum houses the body of the Tollund Man, to mark the opening of an exhibition featuring material associated with Scandinavian sagas,

Heaney pointed out that "if the stories of Odin and Thor and Ragnarok are not the truth, there is nonetheless truth in them. Or to put it another way, the myths are true not because they give factual information, but because they have been effective, because they once had an effect on human behavior."[42] There is a mysteriousness and otherness to these narratives that Heaney privileges as well when he compares the activity of discovering and making poetry to an archaeological dig: "Like the archaeologist, the poet can only work when she or he senses that there's something hidden just out of reach, something just waiting to be discovered."[43] These two statements together explain the logic of Heaney's poetic explorations of the violent North in the world of the Scandinavian sagas, the retrieval of which registers an alterity, yet finally an intimacy comparable to the discovery process of poetry and its truths.

The first such "Northern" poem Heaney published was "Shoreline" from *Door into the Dark*. As he muses upon the often-invaded shoreline of Ireland and hears the tide, he creates a picture of past invading voyagers washing up on the Irish coast:

> Listen. Is it the Danes,
> A black hawk bent on the sail?
> Or the chinking Normans?
> Or currachs hopping high
>
> On to the sand?
> (*DD*, 38–39)

Heaney knew his Irish history very well indeed and began in "Shoreline" to explore how this history was characterized by waves of invaders, a project that would culminate in his ongoing investigation of the English and Scottish settlers of the Jamesian plantations whose arrival in the northern part of Ireland would lead to the friction that lingers today between them and the local Catholics, many of whom the Protestant settlers dispossessed.

While in *Wintering Out* he finds many reasons to celebrate the resulting mix of languages in the ancient province of Ulster because of these invasions, in *North* Heaney continues his etymological project he began there but now draws upon such linguistic clashes to illustrate the cyclical violence in the province. For instance, in "Belderg" he realizes that his childhood family farm's name, "Mossbawn," contains "older strains of Norse" (*N*, 14). More important, in "Funeral Rites," which draws directly on the Old Norse *Njáls saga*, the poem concludes with a vision of the saga's dead hero, Gunnarr Hámundarson,

> who lay beautiful
> inside his burial mound,
> though dead by violence
>
> and unavenged.
> Men said that he was chanting
> verses about honour . . .
> . . . .
> . . . as he turned
> with a joyful face
> to look at the moon.
> (9)

As one commentator has pointed out, Heaney's version differs completely from that in the saga, since there Gunnarr is revenged.[44] Through his imagination, Heaney allows "the reader to suppose that the vision of Gunnarr offers hope and affirmation following violence. . . . Indeed, the longer-term prospects in the saga are desperately bleak: though the violence set in train by the death of Gunnarr does finally dissipate, this does not happen until the killings have engulfed the lawyers and the politicians, a shockingly pessimistic analogy to the Troubles in Northern Ireland."[45] In this sense, "Funeral Rites" can be read as an exploration into and rejection of the utter unhealthiness of funeral customs past and present, despite their promise to placate violence. Particularly in the Northern Irish context, such events have often occasioned further violence, as did the massacre of Catholic mourners by loyalist Michael Stone at Milltown Cemetery on March 16, 1988.[46] Such reprisals, as Michael Wood has argued, combine "causality and chance. There is a reason why this is happening, but no reason why it is happening to you. . . . The unruly, excessive actions of soldiers or gunmen are both unpredictable and calculated. Reprisals offer . . . a narrative that doesn't know its own limits or procedures, and so isn't entirely a narrative; a logic that seems broken even before it starts to operate."[47]

Later, in the title poem, the speaker finds himself facing "the unmagical / invitations of Iceland, / the pathetic colonies of Greenland," and somehow the voices of those "fabulous raiders, / those lying in Orkney and Dublin," come alive and warn him to take refuge in the linguistic ore of his brain and avoid Northern violence (*N*, 10).[48] Such raiders and their art are fully displayed in "Viking Dublin: Trial Pieces," which focuses upon a series of found art objects to meditate upon how violent men still turn to art and how the fragments of such culture have washed up in Dublin, a city figured as a heart of darkness by the poet. The opening section describes "a small outline" (12) cut into a bone or even harder object that Heaney first imagines as a "swimming nostril" (12) that is then transformed into "a migrant prow / sniffing the Liffey [River], // swanning it up to the ford, / dissembling itself / in antler combs, bone pins, coins, weights, scale-pans" (13). The keel sticks into the riverbank mud, "its clinker-built hull / spined and plosive / as *Dublin*" (13). By italicizing the city's name, Heaney draws our attention to its dark connotations, since "*Dubh*" is Irish for "black." Such a linguistic "find" in the midst of a volume purporting to investigate Northern violence in ancient Scandinavia and closer to home, in contemporary Northern Ireland, brilliantly brings the Republic of Ireland and its own bloody history into the volume's compass and shows how the entire island is united by its bloody past.

In the fourth section, the speaker becomes "Hamlet the Dane, / skull-handler, parablist, / smeller of rot // in the state," not so much the indecisive Hamlet as the investigative character determined to discover and then out his father's killer, a maneuver that Heaney employs as an opportunity to finally move into the intimate killings then occurring in Northern Ireland. As the speaker invites us to "come fly with me, / come sniff the wind" (14) and nose out such murders, a compressed quatrain follows that juxtaposes these atrocities by situating them in a familiar, Scandinavian and (Northern) Irish context:

Neighbourly, scoretaking
Killers, haggers
And hagglers, gombeen-men,
Hoarders of grudges and gain.
(15)

Reading this part of "Viking Dublin" in the context both of Heaney's earlier "The Tollund Man," which concludes with his unhappy recognition of how "at home" he will feel "out there in Jutland / In the old man-killing parishes" (*WO*, 48), and of "North," with its iteration of "thick-witted couplings and revenges, // the hatreds and behindbacks / of the althing" (*N*, 10–11), suggests the "neighborly," intimate context of such vengeful killings in the Scandinavian past and the Northern Irish present. "Funeral Rites" also presents "each neighbourly murder" in such a context (7). Heather O'Donoghue points out that the Icelandic word *althing* (literally, "general assembly") "conjures up the alterity of medieval Icelandic life, but in fact, the Althing was nothing strange or exotic; it was a precociously and precariously democratic parliamentary and legal institution.... The similarities between saga society and the domestic violence of the Ulster troubles constitute an even more disquieting issue."[49] Here, instead of dwelling in the "word-hoard" of his art as the longship advises the speaker to do in "North" (11), he muses upon the "Hoarders of grudges and gain," those murderers who greedily nurse their treasure, revenge, and then act with swift violence. These "scoretaking" killers indicate the hard men of the paramilitaries in Northern Ireland who exact revenge for real and alleged attacks and slights, but it also may specifically refer to the British paratroopers who murdered thirteen Catholics on Bloody Sunday, January 30, 1972, with a fourteenth later dying of his wounds. One of those soldiers wrote later that day on a wall in Derry, "PARAS THIRTEEN ... / BOGSIDE NIL," a grotesque grafitto incorporated into Heaney's later poem "Casualty" (*FW*, 22).

The following stanzas of "Viking Dublin: Trial Pieces" chillingly describe a complex image cluster: an allusion to "blood-eagling" from a passage of Old Norse verse, to the Shankill Butchers, a Protestant murder gang of the mid- to late 1970s that abducted many Catholics in Belfast at random and killed them with butcher knives and other weapons, and to the Greek myth of Dedalus and Icarus, this last as it is appropriated by James Joyce.[50] Heather O'Donoghue argues that it is unclear whether the Vikings actually took the lungs from a dead or dying body and spread them out "in a gruesome parody of wings, so that the victim apparently becomes a sacrifice to Óðinn, the Norse god of battle associated with birds of carrion such as eagles or ravens," but that Heaney's "allusion presents the Vikings as not merely mutilating the corpses of their victims, but transforming them into pagan sculptures, a gross extension of the aesthetic impulse."[51] Heaney turns to the Icarus myth to approach their dark actions, showing how the Vikings may have mutilated their victims and how the Shankill Butchers killed with similar savagery:

> With a butcher's aplomb
> they spread out your lungs
> and made you warm wings
> for your shoulders.
> (15)

The Shankill Butchers are figured as Dedalian artists of sorts at the beginning of the next stanza, when the speaker implores them, "Old fathers, be with us" (15). But he makes clear they are "artists" of atrocity whose designs kill those who are unlucky enough to cross their paths. The prideful, Protestant triumphalist killers viewed Catholics as beneath them just as the prideful Icarus flew too close to the sun in an attempt to be godlike. Additionally, Heaney references the end of Joyce's *Portrait*, when Stephen Dedalus unwittingly casts himself as Icarus about to fly too close to the sun when he writes in his last diary entry, "Old father, old artificer. . . ."[52] Satan himself is often referred to as the "Father of Lies," and Heaney's conflation of the Shankill Butchers with the Icarus myth and with Satan, who also fell flaming and later brought sin into the world, suggests how violence spirals out of control and festers, fomenting further violence. These stanzas in the fifth section finally function as Irish *dinnseanchas* ("place lore") of the Troubles, where "old cunning ancestors / of feuds and of sits / for ambush or town" lead us to gaze upon sites of atrocity (15).

But rather than muse more upon such Northern killings, "Viking Dublin" concludes with a disturbing series of skulls displayed at the City of Dublin Museum: "White skulls and black skulls / and yellow skulls, and some / with full teeth, and some / haven't only but one," according to the story told by Jimmy Farrell to the speaker (15). Farrell also relates that the museum has the brain pan of "an old Dane, / maybe, was drowned in the Flood" (15). Heaney's speaker-as-"Hamlet the Dane" (14) thus follows Viking art into the violent past of Dublin and ends up "hunting / lightly as pampooties / over the skull-capped ground" (16) in his search for artifacts of violence, fragments he has unearthed to demonstrate the violent history of Ireland, South and North, past and present.

In the sequence of lyrics Heaney entitles "Bone Dreams," he continues his archaeological search for relics of past Northern violence to illuminate the darkness, beginning with an invocation of a "small ship-burial" (19), which Bernard O'Donoghue observes is an "allusion to Sutton Hoo, or to Scyld's funeral with which *Beowulf* opens (and which Heaney will translate in *The Haw Lantern* as 'A Ship of Death': *HL* 20)."[53] Sutton Hoo is the latest in a series of portrayals of treasure in these early poems from *North*, and once again, as he did in "North," Heaney links literal Scandinavian treasure to the linguistic riches of the English language, itself drawn from and infused by its Northern, Anglo-Saxon origins. "Bone Dreams" explores the English language itself, as the speaker now linguistically investigates the past through "push[ing] back / through dictions, / Elizabeth canopies" (20). He goes back further still, through "Norman devices," all the way to the "ivied latins / of churchmen" until he reaches "the scop's / twang, the iron / flash of consonants / cleaving the line" (20). Now he is fully in the world of the Anglo-Saxons, whose word-hoard he renders as martial with its consonants like cutting implements "cleaving the line," scoring meaning onto it. This stanza indicts the origins of the English language for its inherent violence and harshness. If some 80 percent of our current words in English come from Old English, as is commonly thought, then Heaney, writing in English, suggests that our own language is stained and scored with violence—that it is essentially contaminated, blackened. "Bone Dreams" ends at Hadrian's Wall in northern England and in Devon, where the poet finds a dead mole and blows on its fur as he touches it: as he does, the mole's geography leads him to touch "small distant Pennines, / a pelt of grass and grain / running south" (23).

Having drawn on the geography of northern climes ranging from Iceland and Greenland to Jutland and other parts of Scandinavia to situate and contextualize the contemporary violence in the North of Ireland, Heaney turns to the so-called suite of "Bog Poems" to investigate further the intimate tribal killings from the past that he found portrayed in P. V. Glob's *The Bog People* and that fueled his exploration of similarly personal murders in Northern Ireland.

The "Bog Poems" were originally published together in a limited edition by Ted Hughes and his sister Olwyn's Rainbow Press in 1975, featuring gruesome images by Heaney's friend Barrie Cook. This beautifully produced volume with its marbled paper boards lettered in gilt and quarter-bound in maroon Moroccan leather belies its horrific content to some extent (figure 1).

Its artistry and charcoal illustrations suggest, however, the terrible beauty of these bog bodies for Heaney, an issue that I have addressed elsewhere in my discussion of their content and that I characterize as a dynamic that potentially imperils the observer and compels our ethical judgment.[54] The title page features what looks like two bones with bulbous protusions framing the title (figure 2).

Other illustrations set the tone for these disturbing poems, such as the one that seemingly depicts a coiled spinal column suggestively heightening the noose imagery in "Punishment," "Strange Fruit," and "Bog Queen" (figure 3).

Bog Poems features "Bone Dreams," "Come to the Bower," "Bog Queen," "Punishment," "The Grauballe Man," "Tête Coupée" (an earlier title of "Strange Fruit"), "Kinship," and "Belderg."[55] In *North*, Heaney includes these same poems but arranges them in a different order and without Cooke's evocative illustrations.

Heaney's note at the beginning of *Bog Poems* conveys the importance for his work not so much of the bog bodies as of their black landscape, the bogs of Denmark and Ireland. To wit, he remarks, "'Bog' is one of the few borrowings in English from the Irish language: the Irish word means 'soft,' and one of its Irish usages has survived in the Hiberno-English as 'soft day.' Where I grew up, however, we called the bog 'the moss,' a word with Norse origins that was probably carried to Ulster by Scottish planters."[56] Heaney's sense of this landscape's profound yet disturbingly fearful beauty and its continuity forms an important, relatively unexplored subject in criticism of *North*.

More specifically, he has explicitly likened a cut bank of turf to a wound to suggest how the Irish landscape itself is cut open and revealed where bogs abound: "The dark wound of a turf-bank or the sturdy form of a turfstack were almost natural works of art."[57] The artistic appearance of such turf banks and turf stacks thus works in his bog poems to frame

Figure 1

Figure 2

Figure 3

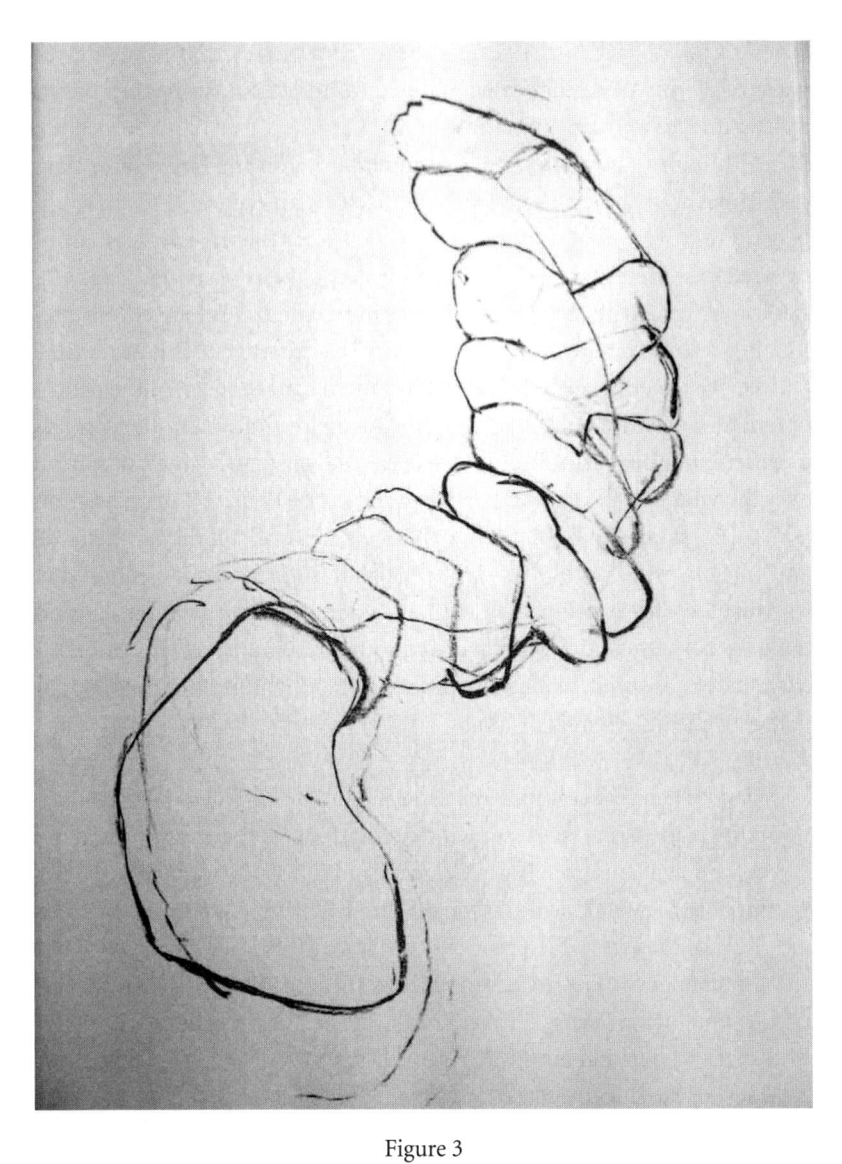

other works of "art"—the severed heads and bodies that populate the pages of *North*. An aesthetically rendered wounded landscape thus begets artistic images of other human wounds.

Although I and many other commentators on the bog poems have previously focused on the bodies themselves, an epigraph Heaney appended to the original draft of *North* makes clear that he is at least as interested in representations of the land because it has remained relatively stable over time while the people groups in Ireland have changed. He cites J. C. Beckett's "The Study of Irish History" to this effect: "But at no time between the twelfth century and the twentieth can we speak of the people of Ireland as a single political community—at one time or another, groups of different cultural traditions have exercised varying degrees of control over the whole or part of the island, in more or less direct subrodination [*sic*] to England. We have, therefore, an element of stability—the land, and an element of instability—the people. It is to the stable element that we must look for continuity."[58] Heaney had interviewed Liam de Paor on the Northern Ireland Home Service, Radio 4, about Beckett's book on Irish history, *Confrontations*, in January of 1973, and in the transcript of that conversation he reflects that

> Liam de Paor's observation that land and cattle constitute a kind of continuity in the Irish experience is interesting, because the great epic that has come down to us from Pagan Celtic Ireland concerns a war between territorial armies, and the war is fought about cattle. This epic, known as the *Tain Bo Cuailnge* which translates as the Cattle Raid of Cooley, is about the attempt of Queen Maeve and the armies of Connacht to steal a fabulous bull from Ulster. The hero of the epic is Cuchullain, the Hound of Ulster, who maintains the defence of Ulster's borders, single-handed, for most of the story. And there are obvious parallels here between this early Ulster saga and certain aspects of the contemporary Ulster psyche.[59]

Heaney is thus drawn to both J. C. Beckett's and Liam de Paor's insistence on land as a continuity in the Irish experience. Part of that perdurance of his childhood landscape stems from the isolation of the traditional province of Ulster from the rest of Ireland because of its geography, including the drumlin belt. Heaney's appreciation of Cuchullain as a defender of Ulster, alone and outnumbered, and his application of this figure's mentality to "certain aspects of the contemporary Ulster psyche" imply how he understands—but does not condone—the position of Protestant loyalists who perceive themselves as defending the "Gap of the North" from Catholics. In "Funeral Rites," he describes a funeral procession that "drags its tail / out of the Gap of the North" (*N*, 8). Clearly, along with the Norse sagas and P. V. Glob's narratives of bog bodies unearthed in Jutland, the great Ulster saga *Táin Bó Cúailnge* was another source for the poems about retribution and revenge in Part I of *North*. Heaney's onrushing style that drives the catalogs of atrocities in many of the enjambed lines from poems like "North" echoes the breathless narration of the *Táin*.

"Kinship," the last of the bog poems in *North*, gets to the heart of Heaney's fascination with the boggy landscape of Northern Ireland and the way he figures his region as layered in past violence. As the speaker walks, "the bog floor shakes, / water cheeps and lisps," and he reaches a turf bank, a sort of altar where he stops to marvel at its mystery:

> I love this turf-face,
> its black incisions,
> the cooped secrets
> of process and ritual
>   (33)

Despite their evocation of this mysterious landscape, images of the bog bodies as Other dominate the earlier bog poems in *North*, but "Kinship" shows how deeply Heaney feels related to this landscape, intimately connected to its sensuous, sucking power.

In the second section, he begins sounding the etymology of this terrain through a series of stanzas that offer a running catalog of synonyms for the bog: "Quagmire, swampland, morass: / the slime kingdoms," followed by "bog / meaning *soft*," and "ruminant ground," "deep pollen-bin" (34). Drawing on the compound coinings of the Anglo-Saxon poets called kennings, Heaney delightedly chants,

> Earth-pantry, bone vault,
> sun-bank, embalmer
> of votive goods
> and sabred fugitives.

Insatiable bride.
Sword-swallower,
casket, midden,
floe of history.
    (34)

Speaking in 1997 about a bog painting by Hughie O'Donoghue, Heaney similarly praised it for its evocation of the bog's textures: "The pigment recalled you to the tones of the bog, the benign murks and mosses and brackens and the grags, the fragrant earth . . . the spreadfields and bog banks."[60] His penchant for piling up kennings and alliterative synonyms for the bogs in these different venues indicates both his ongoing admiration for their mysterious properties and his inability to finally capture those ineffable qualities in words.

He concludes this section by explicitly connecting the bog to his own psychic terrain:

Ground that will strip
its dark side,
nesting ground,
outback of my mind.
    (35)

Heaney has long argued for a connection between his mind and his native landscape, perhaps nowhere so strongly and directly as in "Mossbawn," an essay where he admits both the danger and the allure of the bog. He was fascinated by its creatures such as "mosscheepers," of whom he asked, "What was a mosscheeper, anyway, if not the soft, malicious sound the word itself made, a siren of collapsing sibilants coaxing you out towards bog pools lidded with innocent grass, quicksands and quagmires?"[61] And yet, although the bog was "forbidden ground," he quickly admits, "To this day, green, wet corners, flooded wastes, soft rushy bottoms, any place with the invitation of watery ground and tundra vegetation . . . possess an immediate and deeply peaceful attraction."[62] As he goes on to recall, he became one with this landscape as a child with another boy and he went skinny-dipping "in a moss-hole, treading the liver-thick mud, unsettling a smoky muck off the bottom and coming out smeared and weedy and darkened. . . . somehow initiated."[63] This passage goes to the heart of Heaney's lifelong attraction to the bog: through his immersion in this South County Derry "moss-hole," he becomes a sort of living bog body himself, covered with the bog's preserving mud and "somehow initiated," even baptized, we might say, into a new life obsessed with the dangerous, deadly power of the bog.

The first part of *North* thus not only catalogs and charts a series of bog bodies found in Jutland and Ireland but also implies how Heaney's own psychic terrain is intimately connected to such dark places and their alluring beauty. And this terrain is expressed through his dark poetry in this section of the volume, proving the truth of his contention about poetry articulated elsewhere: "A poem is, among other things, a process of coming to for the first time in a place which nevertheless feels like the psyche's home ground. That being so, you would think it should be easy for poets to remember where they are, but in fact it usually takes a while for the familiar to sink in deep enough for it to be able to resurface in a way that renders it finally imaginable."[64] The bogs of his native landscape sank to such an imaginative depth that it took years for them to swim to the surface of his mind in the bog poems. When they did, they resulted in some of the most powerful poetry in the second half of the twentieth century cast in a transregional context.

"Kinship" finally revises Heaney's original image of the bog in the earlier "Bogland." Whereas that poem ends with the redolent phrase "The wet centre is bottomless," implying the limitless depth of the bog and presumably the unfathomable depths of Heaney's own mind (*DD*, 42), the fourth section of "Kinship" directly challenges that claim. The speaker claims, "This centre holds / and spreads," going on to show how the bog gathers in "the mothers of autumn / [that] sour and sink, / ferments of husk and leaf" and becomes a sort of omnium gatherum for all natural life around it (*N*, 36). When he concludes this section,

> I grew out of all this
> like a weeping willow
> inclined to
> the appetites of gravity[,]

he admits how he has fed upon this landscape, metaphorically drinking in its muddy waters just as a young Wordsworth "drank in" the beauty of his native Lake District (37).

In the fifth section, he recalls how he insinuated himself into the rituals of the bog, making a god of the man who rode upon the turf cart, perhaps his grandfather that he recalls in "Digging." He claims, "I was his privileged / attendant, a bearer / of break and drink," and functioned as "the squire of his circuits" (37). There, he grew in local status: "we were abroad, / saluted, given right-of-way" (37). And he grew in understandable pride as a fellow worker with him: "Watch . . . / . . . / my manly pride / when he speaks to me" (38). The bog thus gave him standing in both his grandfather's and the community's eyes as he traversed it during turf-cutting season.

Yet after canvassing his love of the bog and the ways in which he grew into and up in it for the first five sections of the poem, Heaney concludes by offering a sixth section that now reads the bog figuratively as the killing ground of his home region, Northern Ireland. "Our mother ground / is sour with the blood / of her faithful," he states, and quickly shows further how this feminized landscape has been stained with the blood of Catholics who have died fighting for a united Ireland in the very next stanza:

> they lie gargling
> in her sacred heart
> as the legions stare
> from the ramparts.
> (38)

The tender evocation of the sacred heart of Jesus, a symbol that was commonly found in Catholic households all over Ireland at the time, but especially in Northern Ireland, whose Catholics had long been oppressed by the British, is cleverly juxtaposed with the hardened stares of British soldiers, figured as Roman legions, staring down at them from the many military observation towers that littered the Northern Ireland landscape at the time.

But lest we think Heaney endorses such a binary trope, he concludes the poem by sarcastically now ventriloquizing the Irish republican mindset: "how we slaughter / for the common good" (38) and "shave the heads / of the notorious" as "the goddess swallows / our love and terror" (39).

Such a *summa* of the preceding bog poems such as "Punishment," which concludes by meditating on the punishment of tar-and-feathering given by the IRA during the Troubles to Catholic women who consorted with British soldiers, gives the lie to the unfair charges that he endorsed republican violence in *North* levied at Heaney from some quarters. Instead, he incisively articulates how Irish republicanism essentially adheres to a pagan cult of goddess worship that privileges helplessness in the face of a British imperialism that follows a male cult of dominance. He says as much in "Feeling into Words" when he writes of the conflict in Northern Ireland that "to some extent the enmity can be viewed as a struggle between the cults and devotees of a god and a goddess.... Mother Ireland, Kathleen ni Houlihan, the poor old woman, the Shan Van Vocht ... and her sovereignty has been temporarily usurped or infringed by a new male cult whose founding fathers were Cromwell, William of Orange and Edward Carson, and whose godhead is incarnate in a rex or caesar resident in a palace in London."[65] Roman imperialism forms a continuum with British imperialism in this formulation as a politics of conquest, while Irish republicanism is figured as feminized victim, helpless to fight back. But fight back it did, of course, during the Troubles, and the bog poems not only deplore the British Army's tactics in Northern Ireland but also the murderous response by the IRA and other republican groups, who often killed Catholics along with members of the security forces and meted out horrible punishments against members of their own community. The region of Northern Ireland as wounded, amputated from the rest of Ireland, haunts these poems from *Wintering Out* and *North*, but so too do images of blackness. The next chapter analyzes how such images are employed to connote Catholics in the North as "black" analogues to their oppressed American counterparts whose civil rights movement inspired the similar one in the province.

Chapter Five

DARKNESS VISIBLE
Irish Catholicism, the American Civil Rights
Movement, and the Blackness of "Strange Fruit"

BLACKNESS AND RACE IN NORTHERN IRELAND

The blackness of that cauterized limb in "Stump" from "A Northern Hoard" forms part of a whole host of other images of blackness in additional poems from *Wintering Out* and *North* that are often connected to the trope of woundedness. I draw on these images and other statements by Heaney during the 1970s to show how he subtly implies the cultural and political blackness of Northern Irish Catholics. He obliquely meditates on the oppression of African Americans in the United States, most daringly within one of his most revised and important poems, the neglected sonnet "Strange Fruit," to suggest how his own Catholic "tribe" has been historically considered "black" and mistreated by the British and by some Protestants in Northern Ireland, who metaphorically have "fed" on them.

In *Wintering Out*, black images are far apart, then gradually appear more often: the "black, / long-seasoned rib" of the titular wood in "Bog Oak" (*WO*, 14); the "stepping stones like black molars" in "A New Song" (33); the "limb of the dark" (describing the mandrake) in "Roots," the first section of "A Northern Hoard"; the "black stump" in "Stump"; the "peat-brown head" of the Tollund Man (47). After "The Tollund Man," they largely disappear. But notice how in almost every case the images of blackness are personified until Heaney finally writes about the "stained face" of an actual body, the Tollund Man (47). Through his emphasis on revivifying and humanizing objects such as bog oak, stepping-stones, mandrake root, and turnip, he is lifting such inanimate objects into luminosity, a typically Heaneyan maneuver. But in so doing, he is preparing us for his real project of revivification—that of reanimating the bog bodies, as it were, and sympathetically launching himself imaginatively into their past lives.

Heaney's implicit emphasis on race in such poems might sound unusual given that until very recently Irish literature has been written almost entirely by persons of Caucasian descent, but there is a long history of treating the Irish as "black," and his interest in the subject and poetic explorations of it beginning in the mid-1960s and especially those from the early to mid-1970s form a compelling and unexplored episode in the burgeoning conversation about Irish literature, Irish culture, and race. In 1965, Heaney remarked favorably on the American poet John Berryman's character Henry in *77 Dream Songs*, praising Henry as "a kind of American negro Teresias [*sic*]."[1] Heaney is especially interested in how "the dream songs reverberate in his [Henry's] echo-chamber imagination," marveling that "the subjects that swim up from Henry's subconscious are various, ranging from racial discrimination and nuclear disaster to the death of poets like Roethke and Frost."[2] In much the same way, the poems of *North* swim up from Heaney's own Catholic imagination: violence and racial discrimination rear their ugly heads time and again in that volume. In Heaney's privileging of the black Henry's position as Tiresias retrieving and commenting upon the dream songs of his hard life, we glimpse the young Irish poet, better educated and acculturated than Henry, yet still concerned to sing his songs of discrimination and sectarianism.

John Brannigan has recently argued that while race is "a central figure in the debates concerning the location and provenance of Irish studies . . . perhaps because of its insinuative forms, it remains relatively underexplored as an affective agent in Irish culture."[3] Brannigan's book helpfully traces how racialized discourse underpinned the founding of the modern Irish state and many literary explorations of Irish consciousness in twentieth-century Irish writing. As he has shown, "The struggle for national self-determination re-enacted in conceptual terms the assertion of Irishness as a white ethnicity in the racial politics of nineteenth-century America."[4] Writing from within Northern Ireland, then the Republic of Ireland, however, Heaney instead drew on images of blackness and wounding borrowed from the African American civil rights movement in the United States of the 1960s and early 1970s in part to represent the then-contemporary Northern Irish Catholic struggle for self-determination and agency against the neocolonial British state. While it lies beyond the scope of this chapter to address, his similar interest in how the mixed-race Caribbean poet Derek Walcott sought a poetic form "to bleed off the accumulated humors of his peculiar colonial ague" in his drama and poetry implies he found striking correspondences as a minority member of his society to Walcott's position as a neocolonial subject emerging into political and poetic independence.[5]

Heaney has remarked upon his interest in the ongoing civil rights movement in America for both African Americans and Native Americans during his time at the University of California, Berkeley, in 1970–71, and that concern merged with the ongoing struggle for Catholic civil rights in Northern Ireland, although many Catholic demands actually had been met by that time. For example, he told Dennis O'Driscoll that "coming from the minority in Northern Ireland, I couldn't not be in sympathy with the Civil Rights movement, the whole clamour for social justice that was resonating through the black American community, and starting up among the Native Americans" (*SS*, 145). And in an interview from 1974, he has pointed out that "Catholicism as a set of doctrines and beliefs is not what being a Roman Catholic means in Northern Ireland. It's almost a racist term, a label for a set of cultural suppositions."[6] His sympathy for black Americans, however, even his potential empathy with them as a member of a perceived nearly racial minority—Catholics in Northern Ireland— has not usually been registered in any well-developed critical readings of these 1970s poems. Instead, many commentators (including myself) have focused on how Heaney's meditations on the bog bodies represented in P. V. Glob's *The Bog People* enabled him to refract the contemporary victims of violence in Northern Ireland through the light of mythology, in the process showing how intimate and tribal violence has always been with us. Existing critical accounts of these "bog poems," however, have neglected how Heaney also imbricated those bog bodies with a darkness that he likely absorbed through his observation of the black experience in America during his time in California. Such portrayals reach their apotheosis in his masterful sonnet "Strange Fruit," which draws upon four levels of violent murder—the ancient hanging of a Roman by Egyptians, the Celts' practice of decapitating their enemies, the violence done to the actual bog body in the poem, and the penchant for lynching black men in America through the mid-twentieth century.

In his important book on racism in America, *The Hidden Wound*, Wendell Berry has observed that "*within* the language [spoken by white people] there was a silence, an emptiness, of exactly the shape of humanity of the black man.... One could, by a careful observance of the premises of the language, keep the hollow empty and thus avoid the pain of the recognition of the humanity of an oppressed people and of one's guilt in their oppression."[7] Such an emptiness, he argues, is the hidden wound, into which he finally decided to speak "speech of another and more particular order, so that the hollow begins to fill with the substance of a life that one must recognize as human and demanding."[8] Heaney, too, has recognized such a space in his divided society, and he writes of it in poems from *North* such as "Whatever You Say Say Nothing," a lyric that attempts to speak truth into tired clichés but does not fully succeed. Much has been made of Heaney's immersion in a Northern Irish culture that perforce historically valued taciturnity: Blake Morrison, for example, argued in an early, influential book on Heaney that "the community Heaney came from, and with which he wanted his poetry to express solidarity, was one on which the pressure of silence weighed heavily. It was not only rural, renowned like all rural communities for its inwardness and reserve, but also Northern Irish and Catholic, with additional reasons for clamming up."[9] Asserting one's identity as Catholic could lead to verbal or even physical violence, and thus the presence of a significant minority in Northern Ireland that suffered widespread discrimination over the course of the Stormont regime from 1921 to 1972 was occluded and often rendered silent. Northern Ireland was officially British, not Irish; the province was unofficially Protestant, not Catholic. The hidden wound of the Catholic presence in the North gaped ever wider as the century wore on, and, even after the gains of the civil rights movement and toward the end of the Troubles, the increasingly religiously divided population of the province made it easy to ignore this wound.[10]

Heaney explicitly connected the African American civil rights struggle in the United States with the Catholic civil rights movement in Northern Ireland in an essay entitled "Christmas, 1971," that was originally published in the *Listener* that year and was later collected as part of the longer essay "Belfast." In discussing the Protestant vigilante groups that had sprung up in the province by then, he notes that these defensive group members may not agree "with the sentiments blazoned on the wall at the far end of the street" but observes that "'Keep Ulster Protestant' and 'Keep Blacks and Fenians out of Ulster' are there to remind me that there are attitudes around here other than defensive ones."[11] While loyalists may have linked Catholics and "Blacks" in this pejorative way—as interlopers into an imagined, "pure," Protestant Ulster—by the end of this essay, Heaney positively links these Catholics and black Americans by recourse to Martin Luther King Jr.'s famous "I Have a Dream" speech. Recalling that he read an excerpt from that speech "last Sunday, at an interdenominational carol service in the university," he cites a hopeful part of the speech but quickly balances that optimism with a disturbing image of a wounded man he had dreamed while in California:

> "I have a dream that one day this nation will rise up and live out the full meaning of its creed"—and on that day all men would be able to realize fully the implications of the old spiritual "Free at last, free at last, Great God Almighty, we are free at last." But, as against the natural hopeful rhythms of that vision, I remembered a dream that I'd had last year in California. I was shaving at the mirror of the bathroom when I glimpsed in the mirror a wounded man falling towards me with his bloodied hands lifted to tear at me or implore.[12]

Here Heaney places in dialectic the hopefulness of King's "dream"—a vision in which black Americans could be truly free and enter into full rights as U.S. citizens—with his own nightmare about the wounded, bloodied man falling toward him. The festering wound of the North, gaping ever wider, thus was displacing Heaney's hopeful dream of an imagined North where Catholics would finally achieve full civil rights.[13]

"The Last Mummer" reflects Heaney's interest in representing the consciousness of the enslaved and outcast other at this time because it features a masked character that recalled to Heaney the mumming he had witnessed "in my early days when neighbours' youngsters would blacken their faces and dress up in old clothes" (*SS*, 131). The energy and resentfulness Heaney associates with this practice that occurred during the blackness of the long winter night, along with the blackened faces of the mummers, further associates them with the minority Catholic consciousness in Northern Ireland, as he says explicitly when he notes that "the last mummer, is like the servant boy, an alter ego of sorts. He too is resentful and impenitent. He carries a stone in his pocket. He beats the bars of a gate with his stick. He fires a stone up at the roof of the [*sic*] 'the little barons'" (130). So, while the reception of mummers was an important symbol for the poet of crossing the sectarian divide in Northern Ireland, Heaney also sees the practice of mumming as symbolizing his own angry, minority self and by extension that of the Catholic population in the North.

Yet Heaney knew the danger of getting carried away by righteous anger into violence, and he deplored the atrocities starting to be committed by both the Official Irish Republican Army and the newly fledged Provisional IRA, along with the threatened violence by the Black Panthers in America. In an essay written at the end of 1970, he muses upon the various manifestations of the peace movement during his year in Berkeley, yet segues into pondering the growing violence in Northern Ireland and in America: "We read of . . . the desultory spluttering of the Belfast fuse. We read *The Black Panther* on New York slumlords: 'Every door the fascists attempt to kick down will put them deeper into the pit of death. Shoot to kill. All power to the people.' The rough beast still slouches painfully to Bethlehem but the second coming is hard to expect. The violence of the Panthers' rhetoric is shocking. 'Subversive' isn't quite the word. It is grotesquely violent, without irony, without concessions of any kind, meant to scare while it indoctrinates."[14] Repelled by the Black Power movement in America, Heaney chose instead to privilege the nonviolent civil disobedience Martin Luther King Jr. and the Southern Christian Leadership Conference had waged in America and the similar campaign then being waged in his home region by the Northern Ireland Civil Rights Association.

Even more important in illustrating his brooding upon the consciousness of outcast others such as black Americans at this time is his poem

"Servant Boy," from which the title of the earlier volume *Wintering Out* is drawn. Heaney has told Dennis O'Driscoll that the figure of the servant boy was "based on an old man called Ned Thompson who used to visit our house once or twice a week.... From him I *did* hear talk about different masters, about sleeping in the loft, about the ones who fed him well and the ones who didn't, about having to walk for miles home and back on a Sunday" (*SS*, 130). Lest we suppose that such a character was consigned to the distant past in the poet's mind, he quickly goes on to state:

> The servant boy in the poem, however, is also meant as a portrait of a minority consciousness, a minority artist's consciousness even: "carrying the warm eggs" is what a servant boy would have had to do in the morning... but it's also an emblem of the human call to be more than just "resentful and impenitent," even while injustices are being endured. In the poem, the servant boy "kept his patience and his counsel" while he was wintering out; whatever he said, he said nothing; he knew the score, bore the brunt and bided his time. But by the time of the Civil Rights marches his stoop had begun to be straightened and his walk, I would like to think, was being braced by the poem in which he appeared. (130)

White men in the American South commonly called grown black men "boy" to emasculate them and keep them subjugated, and "Servant Boy" likely draws upon the employment of such an appellation there as well—not just its use for servants in Ireland and Britain.[15] I cite this quotation at such length because it signifies not only that by the very early 1970s Heaney was writing poems about "minority consciousness" but also that he perceived the minority Catholic population as coming into its own by then and straightening up and walking taller, as it were.

When asked specifically about the effect of sectarianism on him in his boyhood days, Heaney did recall resenting "the overall shape of things because you... knew that the Orange arches erected in the village and at various crossroads were what the Romans might have recognized as a form of *jugum* or yoke, and when you went under the arches you went *sub jugum*, you were being subjugated, being taught who was boss, being reminded that the old slogan, 'a Protestant parliament for a Protestant people,' now had real constitutional force" (*SS*, 133).[16] He knew from his reading and his time spent in America the real subjugations—and worse, such as the practice of lynching—also visited on blacks and sympathized with them. So although Heaney was largely sheltered from overt acts of discrimination in his childhood, as he moved into adulthood in first Derry, then Belfast, the increasing sectarian violence in the North penetrated his consciousness fully and linked up with his childhood memories of sectarian practices, issuing forth some terrific poems about terrifying subjugation, none more horrific than "Strange Fruit."

THE BLACKNESS OF "STRANGE FRUIT" AND "UGOLINO": FEASTING ON WOUNDED HEADS

"Strange Fruit," a poem little discussed in Heaney criticism, stands out in *North*, even among the poems reading Northern Ireland's conflict in the context of past Scandinavian struggles and the bog poems' similar juxtaposition of ancient bog bodies with contemporary victims from the province. It is the only bog poem not cast in quatrains, and its unrhymed sonnet form suggests that it was of particular importance to him, even though other bog poems such as "Punishment" and "The Tollund Man" have garnered much more critical attention. Existing drafts of earlier, much different versions of the poem show that it was originally considerably longer and at one point formed a portion of "Part I" of a tripartite sequence entitled "Triceps."[17] Heaney's extensive revisions of this poem, beginning as early as December 19, 1972, and continuing through sometime in 1975, themselves suggest its importance to him.[18] Helen Vendler dismisses "Strange Fruit," however, arguing that it "relies too heavily on lavish but conventional adjectives: 'Murdered, forgotten, nameless, terrible / Beheaded girl.'"[19] She does not seem to recognize the possibility that Heaney purposely employs these adjectives to show his own inability to properly capture the preserved girl in his poetry, as he does with his adaptation of the sonnet form. Even Edna Longley, who greatly disliked most of *North* because she felt it was too concentrated "on the Catholic psyche as bound to immolation," and who described it as "a book of martyrs rather than tragic protagonists," approves of the passage in "Strange Fruit" that Vendler questions: "The frank adjectives capsize what has previously been a rather decorative dawdle of a sonnet."[20]

Heaney's eventual turn toward the Petrarchan sonnet form of two quatrains and a concluding sestet (if not its rhyme scheme), which had traditionally been used for love poetry, is also formally subversive: he employs this structure to lead us to apprehend and then condemn a series of violent acts against victims so that we might appreciate their humanity more fully. At the same time, as Bernard O'Donoghue has observed, "*North* attempts to chart moral absence, the abdication of the responsibility of judgment,"[21] and thus "Strange Fruit" also seeks to reinscribe and remind us of our responsibility to judge those who would kill others they have stereotyped. Yet the poem brilliantly turns even on us by its conclusion, suggesting how we feed on images of violence by recapitulating them. Remarkably, it achieves an agency for the murdered girl whereby her gaze outlasts our own stare and remains beyond our ken.

In his careful formal meditation on the girl's preserved head, Heaney imaginatively enters her brokenness through the broken sonnet shape, offering her, as it were, to us, through a form that reflects, even honors, her dismemberment, even as it is presented to us in a single block of seemingly impenetrable text. This form accords with Vendler's brief reading of her as "like an uninterpretable residue" and suggests how Heaney adroitly melds form and content here.[22] Jason David Hall has mused that Heaney's concern with sonnets throughout his career suggests that some of his "most poignant poetry, some of his most revelatory personal and cultural commentary, has been expressed in sonnet form."[23] I would argue that of all the bog poems, "Strange Fruit" lays claim to being one of Heaney's most moving and revelatory poems in his oeuvre, which is signaled in part by his employment of the sonnet form. Whereas casting the other bog poems in quatrains may have enabled Heaney to proceed in a series of formally contained attempts to describe the preserved body in question and meditate upon its relevance for the vexed situation in the North of Ireland, the broken sonnet form of "Strange Fruit" visually appears as a single block of dark text that echoes the figurative blackness of the various murderous deeds referenced in the poem, which were in turn committed against the sacrificed, "black" other, and suggests how violence, once engaged in, spreads like an ink blot across lives and generations.

In his poems featuring inanimate black objects from this period, Heaney is greatly concerned to revivify them, and that penchant is supremely displayed in "Strange Fruit" by his titular allusion to the American practice of lynching black men who had been dehumanized, made into objects, by white culture. This practice has informed many major American works of art, but most significantly for Heaney's purpose it inspired Jewish writer Abel Meeropol's "Strange Fruit," most famously sung by Billie Holiday beginning in 1939 (strangely enough, the year of Heaney's birth).

Before I explore how this intertext informs Heaney's poem, I would point out the food motif in "Strange Fruit" that is continued from other bog poems. The poem's title and three of its opening images render the girl's body as figurative food that her oppressors have gazed upon, then fed on to satiate their desire for visiting violence upon the helpless. Many images of food are lodged in Heaney's other bog poems: these occur in "The Grauballe Man," where he likens "the ball of his heel" to "a basalt egg," and "his hips" to "the ridge / and purse of a mussel, / his spine an eel arrested / under a glisten of mud" (*N*, 28); in "Bog Queen," whose bog body speaker observes the "bruised berries under my nails" (25); and in "Punishment," where Heaney describes the body's head as shaved "like a stubble of black corn" (30). But because of the concentrated focus of his broken sonnet form in "Strange Fruit," and that poem's explicit likening of the body to fruit, this poem, of all the bog poems, reminds us uncomfortably that our bodies are flesh that others visually may feast upon, which in turn, may lead to the commission of nearly unspeakable acts of violence in which our bodies turn into "strange fruit," literally inedible but satisfying the blood lust within us. By likening the girl's head to "an exhumed gourd" and in the very next line mentioning that she is "prune-skinned" and has "prune-stones" for teeth (32), Heaney extends the resonance of the title, suggesting through images of the inedible how she has been figuratively feasted upon by violent perpetrators.

He shocks us even further by suggesting through the adjectives *prune-skinned* and the verb *unswaddled*, respectively, that the young woman has been "born" out of the bog, replete with wrinkled skin like a newborn baby, her hair having been slowly unwrapped as a baby would be unswaddled for our viewing by archaeologists. Yet this imagery itself is preceded and complicated by the adjective *exhumed*, which together with *prune-skinned* and *unswaddled* connotes that the head of this girl, preserved in the fluids of the womblike bog, seemingly alive, has been "exhumed" for us to gaze upon her "leathery beauty." Finally, "leathery beauty" complicates and completes our sense of her features again, implying that although the process of her recovery and indeed her first appearance and presentation together make her seem akin to a newborn, she actually is greatly aged. The combination then, of the newborn and ancient imagery make us pause and want to gaze longingly at such a fragile, "perishable treasure" (32) with the attentive care it deserves.

The poem was heavily Catholic and devotional in many drafts and even carried the title "Reliquary" at one point.[24] For instance, an early typewritten draft features these later-excised stanzas:

We have uncarpeted
her fragrant sanctuary,
let air consume
her censers of pressed flowers.

Gathered the broken cruet.
Her tabernacle is unroofed,
her veil pulled off.
~~Here is her leathery head~~, [Then a holograph correction]:
   This is a monstrance
for her leathery beauty,

. . . .
~~This was her body.~~
~~This was her blood.~~
~~This was a monstrance~~
~~for her exposition.~~[25]

Heaney has remarked about reading and viewing the bog bodies in P. V. Glob's book *The Bog People*, and then later visiting Denmark and seeing the actual head of the Tollund Man at Silkeborg and the Grauballe Man's body at Aarhus, that "what I was experiencing in my very bones and being was a feeling of reverence. . . . My sense of reverence was also compounded of feelings derived from my Catholic background, with its stories of saints whose bodies stayed un-decomposed and fragrant in death because of their sanctity in life; and as well as this there was the sheer physical mildness and refinement of the Tollund Man's face, a certain Christ-like resignation which gave him the aura of a redeemer."[26] Such a markedly strong sense of reverence experienced in the photographic and then literal presence of these remains lies behind the reverential Catholic language in this early draft of what would become "Strange Fruit," which in another draft also carried the title "My Reverence" and termed the "bog-stained head" of the girl "an after-image // Of Veronica's napkin."[27] He obliquely evokes the image of St. Oliver Plunkett's severed head that resides in St. Peter's Church at Drogheda when he vows, in a crossed-out passage from this draft,

> Or I will nail my articles to door the door
> At Drogheda
> Of Oliver's church
> Or else revoke beatification. . . ."[28]

Plunkett was the last Catholic to be martyred in England when he was hung, drawn, and quartered on July 1, 1681. In one of the great ironies of Irish history, Plunkett operated the first nonsectarian institution of learning in Ireland, a Jesuit college to which Protestants were also admitted, which surely must have appealed to Heaney, who went to the "mixed" elementary school Anahorish. Thus, in its original references to Catholic worship practices, to transubstantiation, to Veronica, and to Plunkett, "Strange Fruit," despite its catalog of atrocities across time and cultures, partakes of both Catholic hagiography and ecumenism.

It is difficult to know why Heaney excised this explicitly Catholic language, but he may have feared running the risk of over-reverencing the girl's head by conflating it with Christ's body and blood and thus committing blasphemy. He may also have decided to extend the range of references in the poem and lift it out of a solely Catholic context, widening its compass to include not only Europe but also America. So gradually, he largely jettisoned that Catholic devotional language and emphasized instead the pagan Celtic cult of the human head, which, late in the composition process, he would link to the lynching of black Americans in the United States. Somewhat surprisingly, Heaney's focus on the girl's head inscribes the severed-head motif of Celtic mythology within a poem ostensibly about a Jutland girl's head. Evidence for this reading comes from both the poem's composition and periodical history and Heaney's long-standing interest in this mythology.

In the draft of "My Reverence," he explicitly wants to "drive past Drogheda to where / Cuchullain poled the heads of enemies."[29] Heaney was preoccupied with this Celtic fetish for years beginning in the late 1960s and continuing through the 1970s. Certainly, he read about it and viewed an image of it in John Montague's *The Rough Field*.[30] He has even written about Louis le Brocquy's painting *James Joyce Study 69* that one of its distinguishing characteristics is "symbolic allusion (to the cult of the head in Celtic iconography)."[31] The poem we now know as "Strange Fruit" was published in Heaney's limited edition *Bog Poems* in May of 1975 and entitled "Tête Coupée," translated "The Severed Head," a title connoting a transnational Celticism that situates the poem in a wider European context, rather than solely the American racial context that its final title finally gave it. Helen Litton has observed that for the Celts, "The human head was of almost sacramental importance.... The head was seen as the residence of the soul; taking a man's soul implied control of his spirit."[32] Heaney realized the importance of the severed head in Celtic religion after he had written "The Tollund Man," the disturbing poem from *Wintering Out* that focuses its first section on characteristics of that ancient body's head. As he has recalled, when he wrote "The Tollund Man," "I had a completely new sensation, one of fear. It was a vow to go on pilgrimage and I felt as it came to me ... that unless I was deeply in earnest about what I was saying, I was simply invoking dangers for myself."[33] After then going to Jutland on this pilgrimage to view the Tollund Man in person, Heaney discovered Anne Ross's discussion of the centrality of the severed-head motif to Celtic religion in her *Pagan Celtic Britain: Studies in Iconography and Tradition*. He quotes a long passage from her chapter on the pagan Celts, including the crucial portion for our purposes in assessing the awestruck attitude the speaker adopts in viewing the girl's head in "Strange Fruit": "the symbol of the severed human head ... [stands for] the hard core of Celtic religion. It is indeed ... a kind of shorthand symbol for the entire religious outlook of the pagan Celts."[34] He then immediately notes that "my sense of occasion and almost awe as I vowed to go to pray to the Tollund Man and assist at his enshrined head had a longer ancestry than I had at the time realized."[35]

Apprehending the reverence given to the dead Jutland girl's head through the Celtic fixation on the severed head heightens our imagined perception of victims of this fetish, her face, the faces of dead black men in the United States, hanging from trees, and the also-imagined face of the Roman lynched for killing a cat holy to Egyptians in Diodorus Siculus's history. A series of unseen faces therefore stare back at us through the dead girl's gaze; they reflect layers of atrocity throughout history and the perverse religious practices associated with them. Moreover, through adapting images undoubtedly drawn from Meeropol's song "Strange Fruit," Heaney invokes local involvement at lynchings in the United States, suggesting that such murders and the community's affirmations of them were akin to a secular "religion" in white racist American society.[36] The poem implicitly connects such crimes to other murders committed in religious contexts—such as the severing of heads in Celtic regions and the ancient Egyptians' murderously protective reverence of cats. But while the poem urges us to tenderly and compassionately view these present and past faces in our mind's eye, it also finally rejects our reverencing them, as the girl's gaze (and by implication the gaze of African American men who were lynched, victims who had their heads severed by the Celts, and the Roman who was lynched by the Egyptians) outstares both the speaker and her various audiences—the visitors to the museum where she is displayed, us as readers of the poem.

Heaney's most shocking decision in the poem, to link this bog body to the images of black men hanging from trees in the American South and elsewhere from Meeropol's song, widens the arc of his references to other blackened bodies from other periods of history in the bog poems and, more specifically, implicitly posits Catholics in Northern Ireland as "black" victims who are captured, tortured, and then sometimes killed in intimate fashion by members of their own community. Despite its compact form, "Strange Fruit" has the widest frame of reference of any of the bog poems, incorporating references to atrocities in the United States (through its title), Egypt (through the invocation of a narrative from Diodorus Siculus), Celtic lands, and Jutland.

I reprint Meeropol's song lyrics here to refamiliarize readers with them and remind us how he brought attention to the plight of black men in the American South who were often unfairly convicted of imagined crimes (like the rape of white women), castrated, sometimes tarred and feathered, publicly hanged by lynch mobs, then often burned. Meeropol, a high school teacher from the Bronx in New York City, was probably inspired to write "Strange Fruit" after seeing Lawrence Beitler's photograph of the August 7, 1930, lynching of Thomas Shipp and Abram Smith in Marion, Indiana. While others performed the song before Billie Holiday, after she performed the song in 1939 it became a regular feature of her live performances, and the recording of it became her best-selling record. In a December 1999 editorial, *Time* magazine called it "the song of the century."[37] "Strange Fruit" was inspired by Heaney's viewing of the particular photograph of a "bog girl" published in Glob's book and by Meeropol's song, which was itself inspired by the picture of Shipp's and Smith's lynching.

Although Heaney's sonnet dispenses with stanzas and is rendered as one block of text, the impact of Meeropol's song lyrics accrues through the repetitions and music of three quatrains in rhyming couplets. Notice that the song approaches the sonnet length—twelve lines—an experimental form for Heaney very early in his career with "October Thought."[38] Here are the complete song lyrics of "Strange Fruit":

> Southern trees bear strange fruit,
> Blood on the leaves and blood at the root,
> Black bodies swinging in the southern breeze,
> Strange fruit hanging from the poplar trees.
>
> Pastoral scene of the gallant south,
> The bulging eyes and the twisted mouth,
> Scent of magnolias, sweet and fresh,
> Then the sudden smell of burning flesh.
>
> Here is fruit for the crows to pluck,
> For the rain to gather, for the wind to suck,
> For the sun to rot, for the trees to drop,
> Here is a strange and bitter crop.[39]

Meeropol's song displays a strong command of formal poetic techniques. Note the "envelope alliteration" at the beginning of the first quatrain's first and fourth lines—"southern" and "strange"—along with the alliterative "blood" and "black bodies" of lines 2 and 3, the alliterative "the" and "then" of lines 6 and 8, and the exact repetition of "for" in lines 10 and 11 and "here" in lines 9 and 12.

Although Heaney himself is obviously not racially black, his growing consciousness of himself upon matriculation at Queen's University in 1957 and after as a political minority "other" in Protestant-dominated Northern Ireland shares salient features with the now-classic descriptions of black consciousness articulated by Frantz Fanon in his 1967 work *Black Skin, White Masks*. Of course, certain elements in England had long stereotyped all Irish as "negroid" or black, as Perry Curtis, the author of *Apes and Angels*, has shown.[40] After the Free State of Ireland was formed in 1921 and instituted in 1922, Catholics there slowly gained a sense of themselves as agents of their own destiny (despite lingering ties of all sorts to Britain), but this racialized identity for Irish Catholics lingered in the Northern Irish state. This racialized consciousness was largely subdued during the safety of Heaney's rural upbringing, then early education at the ecumenical school Anahorish, a period he described with great affection in the poem "Anahorish" and in several interviews.[41] While I doubt the full efficacy of applying a postcolonial model based on literal ethnic and linguistic differences between white colonizer and black colonized to "minority" (Northern) Irish Catholic writers such as Heaney, as Declan Kiberd and others have done, I believe that Heaney was consciously courting an analogy between the Irish Catholic experience throughout Irish history and continuing under the Stormont regime (1921–72) and the African American struggle for equality in the southern United States through his intense focus on images of blackness and objectification and in many of the poems I have discussed from *Wintering Out* and *North*, particularly "Strange Fruit."[42]

Perhaps the strongest evidence for such an analogy comes from Heaney's repugnance he expresses in the early drafts of the poem at the murder and excessive punishment to the body of the innocent St. Oliver Plunkett by hanging, drawing, and quartering, which in turn may have led him to the lynching motif he came to articulate in the final draft of

178 SEAMUS HEANEY'S REGIONS

the poem. Although Plunkett is mentioned only in passing in "My Reverence," he became the focus of the opening two stanzas in the tripartite draft entitled "Triceps" and a crucial part of the draft called "Reliquary." The speaker in "Triceps" recalls,

> I once knelt
> Where our martyr's head reposes
> Under its dome,
> On a side-altar.
>
> He kept the faith for us,
> this Oliver.
> We name our sons for him
> and call him blessed.[43]

In "Reliquary," the link between the girl's blackened head and Plunkett's severed head is even clearer. Immediately after describing her "eye-holes black as pools in the old workings—," he immediately states in this same second stanza,

> I recall a perishable jewel,
> A pash of tallow under its glass dome.
> I once knelt where the martyr's head reposes
>
> On a side altar in Drogheda.
> We smuggled what remains from Tyburn Tree
> To name our sons for him and call him blessed,
> And priests still celebrate his sacrifice
> Robed in the scarlet from his spouting trunk.
>
> So my reverence for the seasoned kernel
> Of her beauty comes naturally.[44]

What seems to be a fairly late draft thus retains the martyrology for Plunkett that Heaney would have been immersed in from a young age and links the head of that "black" or supposedly treasonous Catholic (for allegedly conspiring against the English crown) to the severed, blackened head of the dead girl and both by extension to the "strange fruit" of the lynched black men connoted by the title. The girl's head alone becomes the "perishable jewel" in the final draft of the poem, covertly recalling the now-elided reference to Plunkett's fragile head, but also signifying how her head became a trophy for those who removed it, much like the trophies collected by lynch mobs in the United States. Furthermore, her dismemberment and objectification suggest how the dominant white gaze has depersonalized people of color with devastating psychic and physical results.

Fanon writes movingly and convincingly of his growing sense of his body in the white world, noting that in that milieu, "the man of color encounters difficulties in the development of his bodily schema. Consciousness of the body is solely a negating activity. It is a third-person consciousness."[45] One day, he relates, "I took myself far off from my own presence, far indeed, and made myself an object. What else could it be for me but an amputation, an excision, a hemorrhage that spattered my whole body with black blood?"[46] Such a rhetorically visceral passage anticipates Heaney's very similar language in "Amputation" and "Stump," above. The type of extreme divorce from one's own body he relates here was potentially deadly, as Fanon suggests, but a less extreme version of adapting a double-consciousness, to use W. E. B. DuBois's term in *The Souls of Black Folk*, was apparently a near-daily exercise for many people of color in segregated societies, including the American South.[47] Successful negotiating of daily life involved protecting their inner identity, their true sense of themselves, from white society's external gaze.[48] Unless this true identity were preserved, the identity foisted upon the black "other" by white oppressors could become dominant, leading to at least psychic death.

Fanon articulates such a burdensome, forced identity in exacting language: "In terms of consciousness, the black consciousness is held out as an absolute density, as filled with itself."[49] Heaney's "Strange Fruit" fills the page in what I think is a textual attempt to represent the "absolute density" of black consciousness that Fanon identifies here:

Here is the girl's head like an exhumed gourd,
Oval-faced, prune-skinned, prune-stones for teeth.
They unswaddled the wet fern of her hair

> And made an exhibition of its coil,
> Let the air at her leathery beauty.
> Pash of tallow, perishable treasure:
> Her broken nose is dark as a turf clod,
> Her eyeholes blank as pools in the old workings.
> Diodorus Siculus confessed
> His gradual ease among the likes of this:
> Murdered, forgotten, nameless, terrible
> Beheaded girl, outstaring axe
> And beatification, outstaring
> What had begun to feel like reverence.
>
> (N, 32)

Very late drafts of the poem show Heaney casting it into a three-part structure typical of the Petrarchan sonnet, if without that form's particular rhyme scheme.[50] The final text, however, collapses that structure and is so tightly bound outwardly by its overall shape and internal, multiple stopped lines that we at first experience only its blackness, its impenetrability, a process that Heaney purposely attempts to put us through in order to vicariously attain a temporary sense of encountering the other—here the mystery of the poem itself, which is bound up with the blackness of its many victims and their heinous treatment. Its shape, moreover, resembles a series of enclosing forms—the first eight lines form an enclosure on the right side of the poem, as do lines 8 through 10 and lines 10 through 14—visually suggesting the tightness of the noose implied in the poem's title.[51]

Heaney likely drew upon his knowledge of lynching to imagine the public pain of being literally black in "Strange Fruit." For example, he decries the way in which "they unswaddled the wet fern of her hair / And made an exhibition of its coil, / Let the air at her leathery beauty" (N, 32), even as he cannot help gazing at her himself. Along with the use of the title from Meeropol's song, Heaney brilliantly suggests the lynching rope used to hang African American men in the United States by the "coil" of the dead bog girl's long hair. He was already thinking about lynchings in the previous poem in North, "Punishment," which concludes with the very public punishment of tarring and feathering naked Catholic women for consorting with British soldiers and leaving them chained to railings, when he adverts to "her noose" (30). Black men in America were often tarred and feathered before they were castrated, lynched, and burned.[52] By drawing on the repetitious phrase of "Here is" in lines 9 and 12 of Meeropol's song in his opening line, "Here is the girl's head like an exhumed gourd" (32), Heaney borrows from the song's articulation of the publicly humiliating punishment of lynching that created the "strange fruit" hanging on trees and indicts himself and us all for our desire to watch outrageous, murderous behavior practiced in public. Such a "crop," the poem suggests (as does the song), is left for nature to devour, the assembled mob and onlookers having been satisfied visually, even sexually, with the horrific spectacle.[53]

Although we have no idea why the young girl in "Strange Fruit" was decapitated, she may well have sexually transgressed the rules of her tribe. Coming immediately after "Punishment" and its depictions of Catholic women tarred and feathered and chained naked to railings in public for keeping company with British soldiers, the poem invites a sexual reading. The way in which her hair is unwrapped and displayed and the general air of voyeurism in the poem on the part of the speaker give a sexual frisson to the poem.

Although the subject is clearly a girl, through Heaney's employment of his resonant title and the procession of images of blackness she stands in for black men in America who were sexually humiliated, often castrated, before being "punished" in other ways, usually for real or imagined "offences" of pursuing white women. Trudier Harris has shown the explicitly sexual nature of lynching during which black males were stripped of their sexuality, often through castration, then hung over a fire with a rope around their necks. As she observes, "The climactic release began with the crackling of fire against flesh, with the gathering of souvenirs, and with the cries of the victim; it concluded in the yells of the crowd when they knew the victim was dead, yells which gave way to the silence of complete (sexual) purgation, the ultimate release from all tension."[54] Heaney's poem courts a series of parallels with such lynchings but does so in passive language indicating a series of completed actions. Rather than describing a black man's genitalia being severed with a razor or knife, Heaney "displays" the ancient girl's severed head. Rather than describing the roaring fire of lynching, he likens her body to a candle: "tallow" (*N*, 32). Rather than showing a vociferous crowd baying for blood, he quietly shows how she is capable of being objectified by breaking her body down into its constituent parts, including "her broken nose" and "her eyeholes" (32). Rather than the "trophies" of a charred body hanging from a tree, the "strange fruit" implied by his title referring to the song sung by Billie Holiday, we are left with only the severed head and "her leathery beauty."[55]

Finally, by virtue of his reference to an incident in Egypt recorded by Diodorus Siculus, Heaney inscribes another religiously inspired murder within the text of his poem—that of the unnamed Roman who was hanged by Egyptians for killing a holy cat. Siculus notes that during a trip to Egypt by Italian embassy representatives, "one of the Romans killed a cat and the multitude rushed in a crowd to his house[;] neither the officials sent by the king to beg the man off nor the fear of Rome which all the people felt were enough to save the man from punishment, even though his act had been an accident."[56]

Heaney likely knew that Siculus wrote about the importance of severed heads to the Celts, and thus he subtly links this Jutland girl's death with the murder of this unnamed Roman and with the Celts' general practice of severing the heads of their enemies.[57] When he writes that "Diodorus Siculus confessed / His gradual ease among the likes of this" (*N*, 32), he chillingly suggests that the historian's repeated viewing of violent images—from the lynching of the Roman in Egypt to the common Celtic severed-head fetish—desensitized him to the point that he became accustomed to such sights and not revolted by them. By extension, he implies that any habitual gazing at violence or the product of violence can lead audiences to a disturbing ease with such sights—whether in ancient Egypt, Jutland, modern America, or contemporary Northern Ireland.[58]

"Strange Fruit" finally mourns multiple linked, representative murders committed with religious or near-religious motivations—those committed by the Celts; the murder of the unnamed bog girl herself; the lynchings of the black men Thomas Shipp and Abram Smith in Indiana in 1930; and the Egyptians' hanging of the unnamed Roman for killing a holy cat—even as it admits its inability to do so fully. Heaney's poem concludes by privileging the gaze of the dead girl. Neil Corcoran argues convincingly in this regard that "outstaring axe and reverence, she is also outstaring him [the poet]; refusing, in that redeemed cliché of the poem's fourth line, to be 'made an exhibition' of."[59] The poem thus brilliantly reverses a series of poetic gazes in previous bog poems, including Heaney's reverential description of the body in "The Tollund Man" from *Wintering Out*—"a saint's kept body" (*WO*, 47)—and his lingering gaze that makes him an "artful voyeur" (*N*, 31) of the body in "Punishment." St. Oliver Plunkett, who had featured so prominently in many drafts of "Strange Fruit," was beatified in 1920 and canonized in 1975 (as the first new Irish saint for nearly seven hundred years) when Heaney was still working on the poem. The girl thus "outstares" not only our own and Heaney's attempts to reverence her, but also probably the reverence still given to Plunkett in Ireland; her gaze may offer also a riposte of sorts to Irish Catholics for overly reverencing him. There is a further habitual gaze in the background of "Strange Fruit" itself that is now negated as well—that portrayed in the photographs taken of lynchings in America and made into postcards featuring "grinning spectators, good churchgoing citizens . . . , posing for a camera with the backdrop of a naked, charred, mutilated body hanging from a tree."[60] The agency is therefore transferred from the Celtic killers of their victims, from the original murderers of the girl who killed her out of religious reverence, from the murderers of Thomas Shipp and Abram Smith, from the Egyptians who killed the unnamed Roman cat-killer, and finally even from the poet who recognizes he could be seen as violating and reverencing her by writing about her—to the murdered girl by virtue of her lingering gaze.

Such a series of transfers resonates well with the ancient Celtic belief that to own and display a particular head "was to retain and control the power of the dead person" and the related belief that "the head, once freed from its captor or his successor, would be able to work against them."[61] Heaney's conclusion thus indicates that he has temporarily "possessed" this head through his artistic "presentation" of it in the majority of the poem to us: his releasing it, signaled by his move from the passive verbs associated with the girl earlier in the poem to the repeated active verb "outstaring" in two of the last three lines, both enables her to acquire power and agency and potentially endangers him by exposing him and his readers to her penetrating vision.

The strangeness of such public punishments elegized in "Strange Fruit," meant as examples for others who would violate the taboos of the tribe, became so Other to Heaney that the entire poem, from its title, to its broken sonnet form, to its language, presents this blackness to us as still mysterious and impenetrable and, most strange of all (to recover another sense of its title), nourishing to those who create such images and those who feed upon them. Heaney does run the risk of doing further violence by casting such atrocities in language. As Slavoj Žižek points out, "Language simplifies the designated thing, reducing it to a single feature. It dismembers the thing, destroying its organic unity, treating its parts and properties as autonomous."[62] Certainly the poem's catalog of various body parts of the girl—her head, her teeth, her hair, her nose, her eye-sockets—comports, literally so, with Žižek's claim. Yet I contend that by the poem's end the "terrible / Beheaded girl" is restored to a condition of mysterious alterity, if not wholeness, that outstrips language's power to describe her by breaking her into constituent parts and acquires a visual, re-membered denseness that finally resists language. In this sense, it embodies James Longenbach's conception of poetry's resistance: "Especially when it has something urgent to say, a poem's power inheres less in its conclusions than in its propensity to resist them, demonstrating their inadequacy while moving inevitably toward them."[63] For Longenbach, the best poetry wounds us through its "composed wonder—wonder produced by poetry's mechanisms of self-resistance: syntax, line, figurative language, disjunction, spokenness. Without these mechanisms, poems would be vehicles for knowledge, explanations of experience that would threaten to dispel its wonder. They would be useful, then disposable."[64] The wonder of Heaney's "Strange Fruit" stems from its internal formal resistance to fully communicating its mysteries or the richness of the life of the dead girl (or of the other bodies from various eras that it mourns); in this resistance, it bodies forth those individuals from the past, rendering them radiantly mysterious and indispensable—although their societies disposed of them savagely and suddenly—while also proving itself worth keeping.

"Strange Fruit" has an uncanny and heretofore unrecognized afterlife in Heaney's terrible and strange translation from Dante's *The Divine Comedy*, "Ugolino," the concluding poem in *Field Work*, which shows how he understood Northern Ireland as a region "amputated" from the rest of Ireland. Several commentators have argued that this translation and "The Strand at Lough Beg," also in *Field Work*, began a long interest in Dante for Heaney,[65] but while such poems are deeply Dantesque, Heaney had been reading the Italian poet since 1972,[66] and in another sense, "Ugolino" marks the conclusion of the blackness and woundedness that characterize much of his poetry from the decade. By exploring a horrific image from cantos 22 and 23 of Dante's *Inferno* in "Ugolino," he shows how hellish punishment can involve a literal feeding upon another, a fascinating extension of his portrayals of our need to visually feed upon victims of violence in many of the bog poems such as "Punishment" and "Strange Fruit."

In the memorable opening stanza, the poet spies Count Ugolino feeding upon Archbishop Roger as Roger's punishment for causing Ugolino's and his children's cruel death by starvation, although Heaney's Ugolino perversely allows his children to die from starvation to establish himself as a victim. Heaney employs a variation of the phrase "strange fruit" when he depicts Ugolino "Gnawing at him where the neck and the head / Are grafted to the *sweet fruit* of the brain, / Like a famine victim at a loaf of bread" (*FW*, 61; my emphasis), injecting an Irish dimension into these lines with the Great Famine simile. He then immediately likens Ugolino to "the *berserk* Tydeus" who gnashed and fed / Upon the severed head of Menalippus / As if it were some spattered carnal melon" (61; my emphasis).[67] Heaney had already written of the image of a "holmgang / Where two *berserks* club each other to death / For honour's sake, greaved in a bog, and sinking" in the fourth lyric of "Summer 1969," from his sequence "A Singing School" in *North* (*N*, 64; my emphasis). By employing the language of madness in referring to "the berserk Tydeus," recapitulating and transforming the image of the girl's head "like an exhumed gourd" in "Strange Fruit" with his phrase "spattered carnal melon" in "Ugolino," and obliquely linking the girl's severed head from "Strange Fruit" and the "lopped head" of the turnip in "No Sanctuary" from "A Northern Hoard" to the possibly future severed head of Archbishop Rogers and the dismembered head of Menalippus, Heaney recalls the blackness of the human heart he explored so thoroughly in *North*, reminding us that just as his poems are often subtly connected, so are we to each other. More specifically for Heaney's purposes in depicting the graphic and intimate violence of his native region at this time, Joseph Heininger shows that Heaney's translation "connect[s] the sectarian violence of the Northern Ireland of the 1970s with the fates of Archbishop Roger and Count Ugolino because the everlasting hatred they represent for Dante is replicated morally and emotionally by the Irish betrayers and slayers of children."[68]

Our need for each other can become twisted and perverted as we participate in punishments that go beyond all sense of decency for imagined and actual crimes. In the focus on this need, expressed through the wounded and blackened images running from the uncollected "Intimidation" to the more canonical poems of his successive three volumes in that decade, Heaney hoped to shock us and himself into recognizing our common humanity and our common bent toward sinfulness. Maurice Harmon has noted that in 1974 Heaney said his poetic role "was to give a true picture of man's inhumanity to man, and for that he found the Icelandic sagas a good parallel, 'dealing as they did with a tightly knit community, reciprocal feuding and murder which did not shock anyone too badly.'"[69] The last phrase of Heaney's quotation indicates that he did indeed aim to shock us, to jolt us out of our ordinary perceptions and into a series of emotional responses—outrage, anger, even fear. Fleeing Northern Ireland mostly for artistic purposes, but surely also out of some shock and fear, Heaney would land in County Wicklow by 1972, looking back to his home region, remembering and lamenting contemporary and ancient atrocities.

Chapter Six

BORDER CROSSINGS
Heaney's Prose Poems in *Stations*

If Heaney's poems from the 1970s, expressed in the form of the quatrain or, much less often, the sonnet, drew extensively on images of woundedness and blackness to convey his negative impression of Northern Ireland as a region and of Northern Catholics as "black," he was also experimenting with an altogether more experimental and malleable form during the early to mid-1970s—the prose poem. Many of the prose poems that were eventually collected in the 1975 volume *Stations* were originally planned for inclusion in *North*, as an early draft of that volume shows. Although *Stations* has been critically neglected and has never been reprinted, Heaney himself thought enough of it to reproduce fully a third of the contents—seven of the twenty-one prose poems—in his *New Selected Poems, 1966–1987*. These are "Nesting-Ground," "England's Difficulty," "Visitant," "Trial Runs" (which he used as the new title of "Trial Runs: Welcome Home, Ye Lads of The Eighth Army"), "Cloistered," "The Stations of the West," and "Incertus." Later, he would choose to include nine of the twenty-one prose poems from *Stations* in his *Opened Ground: Selected Poems, 1966–1996*: "Nesting-Ground," "July," "England's Difficulty," "Visitant," "Trial Runs" "The Wanderer," "Cloistered," "The Stations of the West,"

187

and "Incertus." He also considered choosing "The Wanderer" as one of two poems he read to sum up his lifetime achievement in poetry when he was awarded the prestigious David Cohen Prize for Literature in 2009.[1] Finally, Heaney continued to write more prose poems in succeeding decades, suggesting even more strongly that he approved of the subgenre. Thus he felt that these prose poems were significant parts of his canon, although only Henry Hart, Jonathan Hufstader, and Anne Stevenson have written extended discussions of them. Adopting the freer form of the prose poetry in *Stations*, in contrast to the many quatrain-driven poems from *Wintering Out* and *North*, enabled Heaney to remember and re-create images from his childhood, thus suggesting his movement from Wordsworthian innocence into a Blakean experience signified by his exposure to sectarianism. In the process, he registered his autonomy as a poet and affirmed how his nimble mind would continue to record past and present sectarianism in his region of Northern Ireland and also to imagine it as an expansive region, a site of rapprochement and community for Catholics, Protestants, and perhaps even outsiders.

In his nuanced book-length reading of Heaney's prosody, Jason David Hall has observed that "certainly one of the more powerful contrasts—or counterpoints—to Heaney's 'well-made' metres, quite possibly a more powerful contrast even than his 'free' verse, is his attempt to forsake the line as a fundamental organizing unit."[2] While Hall regards "Heaney's 'prose genres' to be sufficiently distinct, in formal terms, and sufficiently anomalous in his oeuvre" from his lyric poetry and thus does not treat them in his important study, Heaney has turned to prose poetry often. This formal dialectic between regular quatrain poems and prose poems that emerged during the 1970s indicates that he wanted to surprise his readers with a variety of forms that cross aesthetic boundaries, perhaps in part to model how his readers might themselves cross personal, religious, cultural, and political boundaries and, in the process, began suturing the open wound of sectarianism in Northern Ireland.

Thus Heaney's turn to prose poetry as a hybrid genre evinces both a desire to register the divide in Northern Ireland between Catholics and Protestants through an inherently divided form and his further attempt to connect the two traditionally distinct genres of prose and poetry, perhaps as a formal model for cultural connection in the province. The commentary on this genre suggests its potential ability to straddle and join traditionally separated genres, even as it subverts and disrupts more traditional literary expectations. For instance, Margueritte S. Murphy suggests that "the prose poem is involved in many 'mockeries': among them, the mockery of the concept of fixed genre. . . . It calls for the abandonment of set forms and conventions, and has played a central role in the trend toward dissolution of genre that began with romanticism."[3] Stephen Fredman, on the other hand, argues that "the prose poem can be thought of as . . . proposing to unite two of the basic categories of literature that have remained as distinct sparring partners since ancient Greece."[4] In applying his reading of the prose poem "England's Difficulty" to *Stations* as a whole, Henry Hart memorably suggests that "the prose poem, which stalks the border between genres like a double agent, disguising the identities of both by blending them, depends on the sort of freedom Heaney must have felt in California and Wicklow. Removed from direct confrontation with the Troubles, he could experiment with a new form that, as he states in a letter, 'the rather stricter, mocking and self-mocking atmosphere of Belfast would not have allowed.'"[5] Heaney has articulated this view consistently, arguing that beginning in the late 1960s and continuing during his year in Berkeley, in 1970–71, he had "already begun to slacken those braces" of his quatrains, aided in part by William Carlos Williams, but that "conditions in the Belfast I returned to [from Berkeley] would soon tighten them up again. Lines that were beginning to waver out like antennae in *Wintering Out* (1972) pulled back and curled themselves into the harder stanza-formations of the first part of *North* (1975)."[6] The bunker mentality of strife-torn Belfast thus seems to have enforced a restricted form on Heaney that he had been trying to escape. Drawn already to subversive yet unifying forms of performance such as the tradition of mumming, Heaney thus found himself similarly attracted to the prose poem because of its boundary-crossing form and its suasive power. In this regard, poet Russell Edson's observation that "the prose poem allows the individual to create his or her own boundaries. It's kind of a naked way to write" suggestively hints at the risk the writer of prose poetry takes even as he may revel in the relative freedom of the form.[7]

When asked by Dennis O'Driscoll, "I wonder if it makes sense to suggest that the conversational writing in Part II [of *North*] represents a compromise of sorts between the short-lined intensities of Part I and the looser conventions of the prose poem?" Heaney responded that the poems of *North* and the prose poems of *Stations* sprang from "different impulse[s]":

> I don't think it was a question of compromise. The prose poems started from a different impulse. Some of them were autobiographical, some emblematic. I believe it was after I handed in the manuscript of *North* that I took them up again and at that stage I went from dealing with the pre-reflective life of Mossbawn to pieces backlit by awareness of the historical moment or the political circumstances—there's one about the demobbed Evans brothers arriving on our doorstep with the rosary beads for my father, one about the German prisoner of war stationed at the local aerodrome, and one about encountering the Loyalists in the Gents of a Belfast hotel. (*SS*, 180)

Notice that Heaney emphasizes the arc of *Stations* as moving from the "pre-reflective" to the consciously reflective, particularly in light of the province's sectarianism. In his careful, thoughtful reading of this suite of prose poems, Hart posits their origins as "pre-reflective," pointing out that Heaney "offers a ritual design that is archetypal rather than idiosyncratic, a trial run over a fractured territory that maps old wounds as if for the first time."[8]

When O'Driscoll goes on to remark to Heaney in this same interview, "Judging by *Stations* and by your subsequent prose poems, you seem to conceive of the form as a Joycean 'epiphany,'" Heaney agrees with him but quickly makes a striking connection to the liminal form employed by the Welsh poet David Jones in his major work:

> That's fair enough. It's a way to pounce on material that has been in my memory for so long it has almost become aware of me and has begun to be wary of being chosen for verse. It's not that the subjects treated aren't amenable to verse, more that they came into my sights at a time when I was in the prose habit. I'm not sure, by the way, that the things should be called "prose poems"; maybe it would be better to use David Jones's word "writings" about them. Each is a making over into words that are more self-conscious than the usual prose record and yet not justified as verse. (*SS*, 180)

Heaney is likely referencing Jones's comment in his preface to his 1937 volume, *In Parenthesis*: "This writing is called *In Parenthesis* because I have written it in a kind of space in between—I don't know between quite what—but as you turn aside to do something; and because for us amateur soldiers, (and especially for the writer, who was not only amateur, but grotesquely incompetent, a knocker-over of piles, a parade's despair) the war itself was a parenthesis—how glad we thought we were to step outside its brackets at the end of '18—and also because our curious type of existence here is altogether in parenthesis."[9] Heaney's allusion to Jones's word for this hybrid genre—"writings"—suggests that perhaps he first turned to such a form in the midst of warfare as Jones did, likely in the hope that the conflict in Northern Ireland might turn out to be a type of parenthesis in his own life that he could "step outside" within a short time, a hope that was, of course, sadly disappointed as it dragged on for at least twenty-five years.[10]

In Heaney's introduction to *Stations*, he articulates two reasons he abandoned his prose poems for a time after having started them during his year in Berkeley: because he believed Geoffrey Hill's *Mercian Hymns* were better than his own prose poems and because the current events in Northern Ireland prevented him from accessing the sectarian childhood events hovering at the back of his mind:

> These pieces were begun in California in 1970/71 although the greater part of them came rapidly to a head in May and June last year [1974]. The delay was partly occasioned by the appearance of Geoffrey Hill's *Mercian Hymns*: what I had regarded as stolen marches in a form new to me had been headed off by a work of complete authority. But a second, less precisely definable block was in the air when I came back to Belfast: those first pieces had been attempts to touch what Wordsworth called "spots of time," moments at the very edge of consciousness which had lain for years in the unconscious as active lodes of nodes, yet on my return a month after the introduction of internment my introspection was not confident enough to pursue its direction. The sirens in the air, perhaps quite rightly, jammed those other tentative if insistent signals. So it was again at a remove, in the "hedge-school" of Glanmore, in Wicklow, that the sequence was returned to, and then the sectarian dimension of that pre-reflective experience presented itself as something asking to be uttered also.

I think of the pieces now as points on a psychic *turas*, stations that I have often made unthinkingly in my head. I wrote each of them down with the excitement of coming for the first time to a place I had always known completely.[11]

Turas, Gaelic for "journey," is a crucial word for *Stations* and the orbit of Heaney's early life that they describe and inscribe. Heaney published many of these prose poems in two different installments during 1975, and one grouping of them—"Cauled," "Hedge-School," "Nesting Ground," "Sinking the Shaft," "Water Babies," "Patrick and Oisin," "England's Difficulty," "A Visitant," "The Wanderer," "Cloistered," "Turas," "Ballad," and "Alias"—was published in two volumes of the journal *Exile* that year under the title "From Turas."[12]

In their indispensable bibliography of Heaney, Rand Brandes and Michael J. Durkan note that Heaney also published "The Sabbath-Breakers," "An Ulster Twilight," "England's Difficulty," "Sweet William," "The Gents," "Kernes," "Ballad," and "*Mo Thuras Go Rann Na Feirste*" in the *Irish Times* on July 8, 1975, and collectively titled them "Autobiographical Borings."[13] Heaney's introduction to them in that venue is revealing: "I don't know if these can be called prose poems. They could be regarded as autobiographical borings, narrow shafts let down into one stratum of a northern consciousness, bits to drill the compacted years of G. A. A. [Gaelic Athletic Association] sports days and *ceilidhe* bands, that embattled culture of *feiseanna* and *Gaeltacht* scholarships, family rosaries and Faith of our Fathers. They do not form a complete sequence but are extracted from a pamphlet collection of similar pieces which is to appear from *The Honest Ulsterman* later this year."[14] Interestingly, Heaney employs the same sort of language of drilling down that he has associated with the narrow quatrain form for in *Wintering Out* and *North*.[15] His uncertainty about whether these "autobiographical borings" are even prose poems suggests his tentativeness about the form that he was starting to practice, but clearly he intended to use them in an effort to recover some latent autobiographical memories. Prose poetry, as many commentators have suggested, is particularly well suited to this process because of its tendency to deeply reflect on language. So Stephen Fredman argues: "In the most ambitious poet's prose [his term for prose poetry], the poetic faculty is turned back upon its own medium, language, resulting in an investigative, exploratory poetry rather than a poetry of striking images encapsulated in tightly crafted lines."[16]

In this sense, the prose poems of *Stations* are companion poems to the autobiographical sequence "Singing School" in *North*, which Heaney introduces with two epigraphs—one from book 1 of Wordsworth's *The Prelude* and another from Yeats's *Autobiographies*. Moreover, in a draft of *North*, Heaney had included a section entitled "Seed-Time," consisting of twelve prose poems—some that would be published as part of *Stations* and others that would remain uncollected—which comes after a draft of "Singing School." This earlier draft of *North* therefore suggests how fully he himself saw the prose poems as integrated with his lyrical poetry.[17] The Wordsworth epigraph that precedes both "Seed-Time" and the published version of "Singing School" stresses beauty and fear as formative elements in that great poet's life: "Fair seedtime had my soul, and I grew up / Fostered alike by beauty and by fear."[18] Reading the prose poems of *Stations* through this passage from Wordsworth suggests that they are autobiographical explorations of how Heaney, too, was fostered by both beauty and fear. Indeed, as we will see, some of these pieces, such as "Sweet William," feature elements of both beauty (the flowers of that name) and fear (the loyalist connotations evoked by images of "King Billy" in Northern Ireland). But the epigraph from Yeats also draws the specter of sectarianism—the "Orange rhymes" (*N*, 57) of the stable boy—into the orbit of Heaney's prose poem sequence because he was originally considering publishing "Singing School" and "Seed-Time" together in *North*.

Heaney also interwove the lyric "A Constable Calls," the prose poem "July," the lyric "Orange Drums, Tyrone, 1966," and the prose poem "Inquisition" for a 1977 collection of material simply entitled *Seamus Heaney* and published in Denmark. Although he identifies each of these as coming from either *North* or *Stations*, his grouping of them suggests how he continued to think of them together and not divided by genre, particularly since each registers the fear created in the minority Catholic population of Northern Ireland when confronted with reminders of Protestant dominance (in "A Constable Calls") and outright bigotry (in the last three pieces).[19]

Heaney scholars have never known that he originally intended an entire long section of prose poems to be part of *North*, nor have they fully explored or explained the close relationship between *North* and *Stations*, particularly between the "Singing School" sequence and *Stations* in this Wordsworthian context of beauty and fear, but Heaney himself certainly was experimenting with the relationship between prose poetry and lyric poetry in the early to mid-1970s. For example, he places one strange prose poem, "The Unacknowledged Legislator's Dream," as the first poem in Part II of *North*. He has observed recently about this piece that "it's a free-floating invention, that one," noting further that the poet (the unacknowledged legislator) in the poem "is fit as a fiddle, his spirit blithe, his audience in great fettle . . . but he happens to be a kind of a joke in the eyes of his captor and he's aware that he has simply become a part of some new political spectator sport" (*SS*, 181). Clearly, this prose poem with its conclusion featuring someone watching the imprisoned poet enacts an uncomfortable conversation with the earlier bog poems in Part I of *North* such as "Punishment," whereby the poet who gazes at the various bog bodies found in Jutland in those poems is now being watched himself.

More tellingly for our understanding of his fluid sense of the relationship between lyric poetry and prose poetry, Heaney would rewrite a prose poem entitled "Romanist" as the lyric "Freedman," which he would publish in Part II of *North* the next year, and he would similarly transform what was originally a prose poem, "A Constable Calls," into a lyric that was published in "Singing School." Both of these works originally published as prose poems appeared in Padraic Fiacc's *The Wearing of the Black: An Anthology of Contemporary Ulster Poetry*, which Blackstaff Press in Belfast brought out in 1974. Heaney included these prose poems in Fiacc's anthology, along with the prose poem "July," which would later appear in *Stations*, the previously collected "The Tollund Man," and other lyrics such as "Whatever You Say, Say Nothing" and "From Singing School," but his later exclusion of the prose poems from *North* suggests that he came to believe that this particular form was more suitable for writing directly about sectarianism and the Troubles than was the lyric, which he employed for more indirect critiques of the violence in *North*.[20]

Clearly, Heaney as poet is more self-conscious in the prose poem through his use of "I," as we can see in the transformation of "Romanist" into "Freedman." The original prose poem is worth reprinting for purposes of comparison with its latter, now canonical incarnation:

I was subjugated under arches, manumitted at a graduation ceremony, for years a humble client at the lattice of confessionals. My murex was the purple of lent on a calendar patterned with fish-days.

I knelt to take the impress of the celebrant's ashy thumb, a silk friction, the spread palps of his fingers cold as mushrooms at my temples. An infinitesmal [sic] fall of dust itched down over my nose. Stipple of the first spadeful. *Momento homo quia pulvis es et in pulverem reverteris.*

Caste-marked annually, I went among the freemen of the city for their inspection. In forum and theatre I felt their gaze bend to my mouldy brow and fasten like a lamprey on the mark. In vain I sought it myself on the groomed *optimi*, on the hammerheads of lictor and praetorian. I was estimated and enumerated with my own, indelibly one with the earth-starred denizens of catacomb and campagna.[21]

In contrast, "Freedman" is a model of concision and economy in its four quatrains:

Subjugated yearly under arches,
Manumitted by parchments and degrees,
My murex was the purple dye of lents
On calendars all fast and abstinence.

"*Memento homo quia pulvis es.*"
I would kneel to be impressed by ashes,
A silk friction, a light stipple of dust—
I was under the thumb too like all my caste.

One of the earth-starred denizens, indelibly,
I sought the mark in vain on the groomed optimi:
Their estimating, census-taking eyes
Fastened on my mouldy brow like lampreys.

Then poetry arrived in that city—
I would abjure all cant and self-pity—
And poetry wiped my brow and sped me.
Now they will say I bite the hand that fed me.

(*N*, 55)

The poem is obviously an important one for Heaney, as indicated by its extensive revisions, the change from prose poem into lyric, and his addition of an epigraph (from R. H. Barrow's *The Romans* on slavery and the early Roman Empire) for "Freedman" as it was printed in *North*. Despite the addition of the new content of the fourth stanza in "Freedman," that lyric is only 113 words long, whereas "Romanist" is 153 words.

The change in title from "Romanist" to "Freedman" titularly signifies the speaker's transformation from enslavement to the British (Protestant) Northern Irish state and the Irish Catholic Church—both symbolized by imperial Rome—to freedom through education, but more particularly, in "Freedman," through poetry. After the mostly pararhyming earlier quatrains, the move into rhyming couplets in the last quatrain of "Freedman" suggests Heaney's songlike rejection of such enslaving institutions as the Roman and British Empires and the imperial Catholic Church. "Freedman" thus emphasizes poetry's agency and liberating power for the poet and, by extension, for everyone, while "Romanist," despite its experimental form, seems resigned to entrapment in a series of imperial systems untouched by poetry, even though its elaborate images ("lattice of confessionals"), length, and repeated use of "I" convey the poet's desire for freedom in form and selfhood.

A biblical text that the scripturally well-informed Heaney may have been contemplating while writing "Romanist" and later transforming it into "Freedman" is Galatians 5:1–15. Paul opens this chapter in his letter to the Galatians by stating plainly, "For freedom Christ has set us free; stand firm therefore, and do not submit again to a yoke of slavery."[22] The retention of "subjugated" in both versions of the poem, which derives from the Latin *subjugo*, "to yoke," is significant in this regard and replicates Paul's language here. Because he saw Catholics in Northern Ireland as similar to African Americans, Heaney chooses to once again subtly link his Catholic "caste" with both the history of black Americans' slavery and emancipation and the history of slaves in Roman times and the promised freedom of belief in Christ.

Unlike Heaney's intent in his poem(s), Paul's intent is not to subvert the Catholic Church, which of course did not even really exist at that time, but to urge the new Christians to avoid being enslaved to the laws and customs of their time and place and instead to revel in the freedom that Christ purchases for them. Such a freedom would ideally lead to voluntary service to others and to the formation of a Christian community based on self-sacrifice and love. Paul goes on to exhort these Galatian Christians in 5:13–15, "For you were called to freedom, brothers. Only do not use your freedom as an opportunity for the flesh, but through love serve one another. For the whole law is fulfilled in one word: 'You shall love your neighbor as yourself.' But if you bite and devour one another, watch out that you are not consumed by one another."[23] Rereading Heaney's "Romanist" and its transformation into "Freedman" with this passage from Galatians in mind, we can see how the hopes for reconciliation in Northern Ireland between Catholics and Protestants that Heaney often voiced (as he did in his address to the ecumenical church gathering in Belfast on Christmas 1971, cited in the previous chapter) resonate strongly with his sense of Christianity's emphasis on loving our neighbors as ourselves.[24]

During the writing of the collection that became *Wintering Out*, from 1969 to late September 1971, this belief led him to think that "a time of renewal—whether national, political, or cultural—might be at hand," as he told Michael Parker in a 2004 interview.[25] He also began writing the prose poems that would constitute *Stations* in this optimistic state of mind. But, as he acknowledges in his suggestive preface to that volume, the majority of those prose poems "came rapidly to a head" in May–June 1974, the time of the infamous Ulster Workers' Strike in Northern Ireland that brought down the hopeful Sunningdale Agreement. So although *Stations* began in hope, the majority of its prose poems must have been written out of a deep despair at what by June of 1974 seemed an intractable situation in the province.

Sunningdale had a lasting impact on Northern Irish writers such as Stewart Parker, and Heaney's *Stations* enacts an interesting "conversation" with Parker's 1974 radio play *Iceberg* and his 1987 stage play *Pentecost*, particularly in their joint focus on children. In *Pentecost*, Parker employs "dispossessed, dead, and still-born babies to lament the haunting death of the power-sharing executive in May 1974—another lost moment of potential reconciliation" like, for him, the failure of the 1798 Rising, which he wrote about in his 1984 play *Northern Star*.[26] Heaney too writes of childhood in these prose poems, many of which plumb a child's first perceptions of sectarianism through a Wordsworthian emphasis on "spots of time."[27]

But as he remembers his childhood in *Stations*, Heaney takes another type of journey that recalls that of another romantic poet who is rarely mentioned in studies of Heaney—William Blake and his poetic representations of the change from innocence to experience.[28] Indeed, Heaney's early poem "Death of a Naturalist," with its turn from the innocent young boy's point of view in Part I to his gradual realization of the sexual life of frogs and all of nature in Part II, rehearses in miniature the movement from innocence to experience in *Stations*. Heaney suggests such a trajectory when he writes above in his preface about "the sectarian dimension of that pre-reflective experience [that] presented itself as something asking to be uttered also." Thus we should read *Stations* both as a Wordsworthian recovery of moments of being fostered by both beauty and fear during what was largely an idyllic Catholic childhood and as a movement from that time of innocence into experience, which is signified largely by Heaney's early encounters with representatives of Protestantism and the British state in Ulster in the 1940s and early 1950s. In the context of his developing concept of regionalism in the 1970s, then, this volume should be interpreted as an investigation of sectarianism and how that bigotry might be subsumed into a larger, more unifying web of provincial relations in which prejudices are aired openly and somewhat deflated by virtue of this articulation, as they seem to be in both "Welcome Home Ye Lads of the Eighth Army" and "Inquisition."

Heaney made clear in an interview from this period how he identified himself in the wider context of Irish trauma and rebellion and was viewed pejoratively as a Northern Ireland–born Catholic by some Protestants in the province. These remarks amplify the reasons he would have written at such length about this background and the prejudices against Northern Irish Catholics in *Stations*. He mused, "I think if you look at my poems with [the bias against Catholics] ... in mind then you will see that when I think about my territory and my hinterland and my past I am thinking in terms of Ireland as a whole and the history of the famine and the rebellion. Within Northern Ireland having that set of myths for yourself and your nation is what it means to be a Catholic. My poetry is not sectarian but is [*sic*] has been deeply affected by the smells of sectarianism."[29] Although many of the lyrics in *North* treat sectarianism, they do so in a more indirect context colored by the history of violence in northern

Europe more generally, and outside of the poems in "A Singing School" Heaney seems to have reserved his most direct treatment of that plague for his prose poems, especially the ones collected in *Stations*.

The lack of lineation and the relative lack of adornment common to the prose poem establish more direct conversations with readers than traditional, lineated poems, and Heaney likely turned to this form to enact a conversation with readers about sectarianism, in prose poems such as "Welcome Home" and "Inquisition." Prose poem practitioner Jay Meek points out this attribute of the subgenre when he remarks that "I admire the prose poem for its ability to face readers head on, an attitude less often found in verse poems."[30] Poet Gary Young has similarly remarked that the prose poem's "very lack of expectation" makes it "supremely subversive and supple; the reader may be seduced in wholly unanticipated ways. By eschewing the ornamental apparatus of received poetic forms, the prose poem must rely wholly on the music and honesty of its own utterance."[31] Young goes on to note that "what I treasure most about this form is the moral pressure it exerts. The prose poem encourages a particular kind of modesty. It might even at times achieve a certain humility, a humility which may, through grace, be reflected back upon the poet's own heart."[32] In this sense, while Heaney resorts to the solid quatrains of the bog poems in *North* to implicitly read contemporary Northern Irish sectarianism through the lens of tribal violence going back to ancient Jutland, in *Stations* he writes in the form of the prose poem to render his outrage at sectarianism in Ulster more directly and to exert a kind of moral pressure through luring us into the sinuous rhythms of his undulating prose. This pressure stems from what Mary Ann Caws has delineated as one of the major characteristics of the prose poem: the way in which "emotion is contracted under the force of ellipsis, so deepened and made dense."[33]

Several commentators on the prose poem have suggested how it is especially suited to conveying the workings of the unconscious mind. For example, Michael Benedikt points out how it "attend[s] to the priorities of the unconscious," observing that "this attention to the unconscious, and to its particular logic, unfettered by the relatively formalistic interruptions of the line break, remains the most immediately apparent property of the prose poem."[34] More recently, Morton Marcus has remarked that "the most identifiable aspect of the modern Western prose poem" is "its following of the spontaneous twists and turns of the mind at work,"[35] and certainly Heaney's remarks in his preface to *Stations* about how the prose poems recall his "pre-reflective experience" and function as "points on a psychic *turas*" reflect his own interest in contributing to a hybrid form that allows perhaps greater rumination than lyric poetry offers, yet still gives a focus that prose cannot provide.

One of the early prose poems in *Stations*, "Sinking the Shaft," is a Wordsworthian meditation on the wound created in the ground outside Heaney's childhood home where some workmen sank the family's pump when they installed it. He describes it as "a big wound in front of the back door. Backs and elbows skylined at ground level but by the afternoon, nothing but a light spray of sand that dribbled gold and capped the dark heap at the rim" (*S*, 8). Invited down by the workmen to gaze at the newly installed pump, the young boy marvels at the seeming stability of this device for bringing water to the surface, musing, "Snouted, helmeted, the plunger like an active gizzard, the handle dressed to a clean swoop, set on a pediment inscribed by the points of their trowels, I suppose we thought it never could be toppled" (8). This positive re-creation of a wounded landscape that seemed a sacred site of wisdom innocently prefigures the later prose poems in the collection about wounds caused by sectarian actions he came to know in his childhood, wounds he also explored in his poems from this period.[36]

Because of the prose poem's unique qualities, it is well suited to emphasizing just such metaphors as the wound. Greg Boyd has noted, "I take particular delight in how the very shape of the prose poem lulls and attracts the unsuspecting reader, who often wades into it expecting the calm waters of the familiar, only to find himself caught in a linguistic riptide. An unleashed metaphor will wander, tail wagging, from place to place."[37] Benedikt more precisely points out that "in pursuit of its own independent internal logic, the prose poem will frequently make an unusual use of metaphor and analogy in determining internal structuring, so that these elements are actually given an outstanding focus, relative to verse norms" (47). Reading "Sinking the Shaft" through Benedikt's and Boyd's insights reveals how carefully structured this early prose poem and indeed the entire volume are.

The first "paragraph" of the piece is flush left (as with all the prose poems in *Stations*), and the following five units all are indented. Because the phrase "It was a big wound in front of the back door" appears in the first line of the first indented "paragraph," and because it is the longest such unit overall in the poem, it receives the most readerly attention, leading us to ponder and even reread that line again. Because "Sinking the Shaft," like the other prose poems in *Stations*, invites us to read both sequentially and, by virtue of its form, to construct an overall spatial reading of it according to its indentations and emphasis on certain phrases, it exemplifies what Matei Calinescu has articulated as the "double reading" that can occur in "certain circumstances" during the first reading of a work when we also realize we are engaging in "a retrospective logic of rereading."[38] Thus even as we read the sentence "It was a big wound in front of the back door" linearly, we are already "shadowing" this first reading with an eye toward the structure of the poem as a whole.[39] Of course, lyric poems generally may occasion such a double reading because of their easily apprehended "architecture," but it does seem that prose poems, particularly Heaney's carefully crafted ones in *Stations*, lend themselves to such bilevel readings and therefore have an especially charged opportunity to convince us of the truth of their message.

The metaphor of the wound wanders from place to place throughout *Stations*, lulling us at first, as Boyd observes the prose poem can do, in the lovely images that adorn the opened ground for the pump—the aestheticized "light spray of sand that dribbled gold," the "clean swoop" of the pump handle—then tries to suck us into itself in subsequent prose poems that explore the pain and suffering experienced by Catholics in Northern Ireland at the hands of bigoted Protestants.

But in "The Sabbath-Breakers," Heaney recalls how he and his Catholic friends could also cause offense to Protestants, as he writes of how they marked out a field of play for a forthcoming game (perhaps Gaelic football or hurling, another Gaelic game) on a Sabbath, a day on which local Protestants would have reverently rejected such an emphasis on sports. The phrase "Sabbath-breaker" is an important one for Heaney: he will use it again in the opening poem from the titular middle section of *Station Island* to refer explicitly both to his childhood neighbor Simon Sweeney— "I know you, Simon Sweeney, / for an old Sabbath-breaker / who has been dead for years" (*SI*, 61)—and implicitly to himself as a Sabbath-breaker by virtue of being a poet.[40]

The significant phrase in "The Sabbath-Breakers," the one that begins both paragraphs, is "Call it a pattern." In the first paragraph, that phrase introduces the way in which Heaney and his friends set up the field of play for the tournament: "Call it a pattern. We called it a tournament" (S, 13). He follows with a series of images that signify how united in their preparation the friends were, and they are finally pictured walking home, "a band of brothers high with anticipation" (13). The reference to Shakespeare's St. Crispin's Day speech in *Henry V* interestingly qualifies the Gaelic/Catholic versus British/Protestant binary that this prose poem playfully explores. For King Henry V and his men won a nearly impossible battle at Agincourt in 1415 that led to his marriage to the French princess Catherine and peace for the rest of their short lives. Surely, however, "The Sabbath-Breakers" is not seriously intending to offer this childhood tournament as a step toward peace in the province! Much more likely, Heaney intended to show with this Shakespearean phrase how he and his friends were similarly inspired in preparation for this tournament. As further evidence for this reading, we are told that when they hear a nearby dog barking, "we thought of Setanta's feats at hurling and our steps trampolined along the glimmer" (13). Taking the Gaelic hero Cuchulain (known also as Setanta until he killed the guard dog of Culain the blacksmith) as their inspiration, they dream of adding to the sporting lore he was known for, but their dreams are briefly dashed by the destruction visited upon their carefully prepared field of battle, as recalled in the next paragraph.

Now we see how the opening phrase, "Call it a pattern," acquires a negative, more religious and political connotation: "Call it a pattern. We can hardly call it a pogrom" (13). Looking back to the first paragraph, we see that local Protestants might have perceived the disrespect Heaney and his Catholic friends showed on the Sabbath as "a pattern," while he and his mates thought of their preparations that Sunday as preparation for a tournament. The response of Protestants who must have had this perception is somewhat charitably described by Heaney to be consistent with a pattern of Protestant reaction to Catholic expressions of identity, and certainly not to be anything nearly so strong as a "pogrom." Immediately following these opening two sentences, Heaney cleverly offers a trinitarian sentence to suggest the vested authority of Protestants who saw themselves as maintainers of the Sabbath: "The next morning the goalposts had been felled by what roundhead elders, what maypole hackers, what choristers of law and liberty" (13). Referring to these Protestants by nicknames given to supporters of parliamentary rights against the absolutist right of the king during the English Civil War allows Heaney to suggest that although they are not inflicting violence as Oliver Cromwell and his men did, they are acting in the same spirit as the Cromwellians, who, despite their initial rebellion against tyranny, eventually became despotic themselves.

Heaney and his friends respond to this destruction by playing their tournament anyway, recalled in a remarkable series of lines: "Undaunted we threw in the ball, manned the gap of danger match after match, raised a tricolour in the chestnut tree and faced it proudly for the anthem. We lived there too. We stared into the pennanted branches and held the tableau. **In spite of dungeon, fire and sword.** Implacable" (13; Heaney's bolding). The "gap of danger" refers to what Cuchulain always defended in Irish mythology—the gap between Ulster and the rest of the province—and by using this phrase, Heaney suggests that he and his friends are mock-heroically the true defenders of the North of Ireland. Notice how the response of the "roundhead elders," couched in a series of three linked, appositional noun phrases, is matched and superseded by a group of four verbal phrases here: Heaney and his friends "threw," "manned," "raised," and "faced." That procession of verbs is then reinforced by three more, "lived," "stared," and "held," for a total of seven verbs, a veritable wall of active Catholic resistance to Protestant disapproval of their tournament preparation on a Sunday. Finally, the bolded phrase, "In spite of dungeon, fire and sword" adds a religious sanction to their playing: that phrase comes from the English Catholic hymn "Faith of Our Fathers" (1849), which was adapted in Ireland to have a nationalistic third verse: "Faith of Our Fathers, Mary's prayers / Will keep our country true to thee. / And through the truth that comes from God / Ireland shall then indeed be free."[41] This hymn originally alluded to the so-called Catholic recusants in England who refused to convert to Protestantism after the Reformation, yet also refused to engage in any sort of martial rebellion to reestablish Catholicism as England's dominant faith and overthrow the monarchy. Heaney's employment of "Faith of Our Fathers" casts his and his friends' action in a presumably mock-heroic mode, as the latest in a long line of Catholic martyrs, a position that he has already undermined by noting at the beginning of the paragraph, "We can hardly call it a pogrom," which was indeed what was visited upon Catholics in England after the Reformation. "The Sabbath-Breakers" thus casts these young Catholic boys as inspired by a strand of Gaelic mythology epitomized by Cuchulain; by the English battle of Agincourt, for which at least one English Catholic recusant's family has been given a medal of valor; and by Irish Catholicism's emphasis on nationalistic self-determination as expressed in their adapted use of "Faith of Our Fathers."[42] Heaney playfully suggests that they are the true loyalists—loyal to the North of Ireland, to the spirit of Henry V, and to Catholicism.

And yet as the true loyalists, Heaney renders himself and local Catholics as Other through the virtue of the prose poem genre here and elsewhere in *Stations*. Margueritte S. Murphy has suggested that "because of its marginality, its situation on the 'borderline of prose' (T. S. Eliot's phrase), it must continually subvert prosaic conventions in order to establish itself as authentically 'other.'"[43] As he looked back to childhood discriminations against himself and other Catholics, Heaney likely was drawn to signify this oppression through this genre that has been traditionally marginalized in favor of the "clearer" genres of poetry, drama, and prose.

The spirit of resistance to the dominant Protestant culture in Northern Ireland occurs in a number of other prose poems from *Stations*, including "Sweet William," "Kernes," "Welcome Home, Ye Lads of the Eighth Army," "July," and "Inquisition." It is significant that Heaney retained only "Welcome Home" and "July" out of these six angrier poems (including "The Sabbath-Breakers") in the prose poems from *Stations* that he reprinted in *Opened Ground*, undoubtedly in an effort to tone down some of this indignation. As Jonathan Hufstader has noted, Heaney's decision to omit such poems chronicling the oppressiveness of Protestant culture in the North for Catholics from his *Selected Poems* "give[s] the impression that the prose poems chronicle the writer's evolution up and away from the anti-Protestant and anti-British provincial mentality which nurtured him. . . . [But] taken together the omitted poems provide an intriguing and complex representation of a culturally determined, but nevertheless individual, state of mind, one which combines attraction and repulsion, pride and humiliation, a need to belong and a need to flee."[44] Such antinomies are perhaps best expressed by the prose poem form, a form that is divided against itself even as it seeks to borrow the best properties from both prose and poetry.

"Sweet William" ostensibly portrays the beautiful flower of that name, but an ominous note quickly intrudes in the first sentence of the first paragraph: "their blooms infused themselves into the eye like blood in snow, as if the clumped growth had been spattered with grapeshot and bled from underneath" (S, 11). Immediately, the next paragraph transmutes the flower imagery into that of a loyalist banner celebrating King William, hero of Ulster Protestants, who still celebrate his victory over Catholics in the Battle of the Boyne every July 12, as we saw in my earlier discussion of "Intimidation":

> Sweet William: the words had the silky lift of a banner on the wind, where that king with crinkling feminine black curls reached after the unsheathed flare of his sword—and that was heraldry I could not assent to. And the many men so beautiful called after him, and the very flowers, their aura could be and would be resisted. (11)

Despite the tactile and visual appeal of the flower, because of the loyalism Heaney quickly associates with it, he vows to refuse assenting to that "heraldry." Hufstader shows that the child's resistance is signified by Heaney's purposeful "spoiling [of] a line of pentameter (perfect through the first four feet) with a verb ("assent") learned from catechism: "and thát was héraldrý I cóuld *not assent to*."[45] Heaney's nimble use of parataxis at the end of the penultimate sentence of this paragraph and at the beginning of the last sentence adroitly yokes his young self's continuing resistance not only to Ulster loyalism but also, hyperbolically, to Protestant men in the province named after King William and to the flower itself.

In "Kernes," the fairly abstract resistance to loyalism expressed steadfastly in "Sweet William" and "The Sabbath-Breakers" continues but takes on a personal edge as the poet recalls his schoolmate Dixon's practice of declaring supremacy over his Catholic schoolmates as he places "his hand to" the "true wood" of the "newly painted flagpole" that is "candystriped red, white and blue": "I could beat every fucking papish in the school!" (14). By including this snatch of oral declaration and a later one in the same prose poem—"No surrender! Up King Billy every time!"—Heaney courts readers' approval of his and his friends' actions when they prepare to pelt Dixon with "a small arsenal of sods from the green verge" (14). By virtue of employing the prose poem to convey the thrust of this incident, Heaney draws upon the way in which "this amorphous genre has been and continues to be a vehicle for the introduction of nonliterary prose into 'poetic' discourse—the prose of the street . . . the political arena, . . . and so on."[46] After the boy pedals through their midst singing "God Save the King," the final one-line paragraph simply informs us that "one by one we melted down lanes and over pads, behind a glib he hadn't even ruffled," further casting the boys as "kernes" and returning to the resistant resonance of this prose poem's title. Heaney famously calls himself "a wood-kerne / Escaped from the massacre" toward the end of his poem, "Exposure," from *North* (*N*, 67). While a "wood-kerne" denotes an "Irish outlaw or robber," a "kerne" was a "light-armed Irish foot-soldier,"[47] and thus his use of this obsolete word combined with the actions of him and his friends in the final line suggests their collective identity in defending themselves against the verbal attacks of the triumphalist Protestant Dixon and then disappearing with their dignity intact. Heaney had read and reviewed John Montague's *The Rough Field* (1972) by the time he wrote both this prose poem and "Exposure"; Montague's explicit references to and illustrations from John Derricke's *A Discoverie of Woodkarne* (1581) in that volume likely led Heaney to also employ it in his etymological reclamation of the word *kerne* to signify a marginalized Catholic.[48] Moreover, their identity as specifically Irish versus the proudly British/Protestant identity of Dixon is enhanced by Heaney's use of *glib*, which in normal usage conveys a smoothness of manner but also means "a thick mass of matted hair on the forehead and over the eyes, formerly worn by the Irish."[49] By embracing a metaphorical hairstyle sometimes worn by wood-kernes, Heaney mock-heroically contrasts his and his friends' martial, outlaw status here with the "law-abiding" status of their schoolmate Dixon and of the "roundheads" in the earlier "The Sabbath-Breakers."[50]

But the implacable resolve expressed by the poet and his fellow Catholics in the schoolboy games of "The Sabbath-Breakers" and "Kernes" is replaced by a creeping, spreading fear in "July" and "Inquisition," prose poems where the mock-heroic, playful mode disappears. The visually striking elements of the dominant Protestant culture that colored "Sweet

William" and "Kernes" are subsumed at first by the Orangemen's drumming in the first three paragraphs of "July." This drumming "didn't murmur, rather hammered," leading the poet to note in the third paragraph that "the hills were a bellied sound-box resonating, a low dyke against diurnal roar, a tidal wave that stayed, that still might open" (*S*, 15). Since the first sentence informs us that "the drumming started in the cool of the evening," presumably the "diurnal roar" that the drumming holds at bay is the vocal opposition Catholics sometimes have voiced against what they perceive as a sectarian music (15). If prose poems explore the edges of consciousness, as Heaney and other practitioners of the genre have repeatedly affirmed, then "July" itself seamlessly fuses its form with its content, as the Orangemen's march and drumming are portrayed at a liminal time of day, "sunset," and assure the loyal hearers of their elect status as true believers: "Through red seas of July the Orange drummers led a chosen people through their dream" (15).

Heaney represents the province of Northern Ireland as an ignorant, bellicose infant in "Act of Union" from *North*, and the very next sentence in "July" suggests a corresponding imagery of bloody birth that grows progressively bloodier and monstrous: "Dilations and engorgings, contrapuntal; slashers in shirt-sleeves, collared in the sunset, policemen flanking them like anthracite" (15). By the next paragraph, the Orangemen have effectively colored the night air "dark, cloud-barred, a butcher's apron," and we are told that "the night hushed like a white-mothed reach of water, miles downstream from the battle, skeins of blood still lazing in the channel" (15). It is as if these men, these "slashers in shirt-sleeves," have bled the Catholic populace with the violence of their drums and then washed that figurative blood off in the river.[51] Such imagery resonates with Heaney's portrayal of this same practice in "Whatever You Say Say Nothing," in the passage where the speaker wryly notes, "Last night you didn't need a stethoscope / To hear the eructation of Orange drums" (*N*, 53) and in "Orange Drums, Tyrone, 1966": "The goatskin's sometimes plastered with his blood" (62). And whereas the eager audience in "Orange Drums" is represented by "every cocked ear, expert in its greed" (62), in "July" Heaney simply and quietly concludes, "And so my ear was winnowed annually," suggesting how his own hearing became gradually more attuned to the sectarian nature of such drumming and thus able to discard it as chaff, as he also does in his

BBC Northern Ireland Radio play *Everyman* while presumably also clinging to the grain of music that affirmed him, like "Faith of Our Fathers," featured in "The Sabbath-Breakers" (*S*, 15).

While the Protestant intransigence that Heaney critiques in "July" is represented by the orange drumming, the "old news" of "**Remember 1690** and **No Surrender**" (Heaney's bolding) in "Trial Runs: Welcome Home Ye Lads of the Eight Army," the phrase beginning "Welcome Home Ye Lads" has been "painted along the demesne wall, a banner headline" over those older messages and seems to signal a greater rapprochement for a time between Heaney's neighbor, returned home from World War II, and his father (*S*, 18). That moment of great intimacy and familiarity, even fun, is thus the "new news" (my phrase) and its representation in direct dialogue suggests an easy give-and-take between the elder Heaney and this neighbor:

"Did they make a papish of you over there?"
"O damn the fear! I stole them for you, Paddy, off the pope's dresser when his back was turned."
"You could harness a donkey with them."

(18)

This prose poem ends with a resonant sentence that bespeaks a tentative hope in such continuing good relations with this neighbor: "Their laughter sailed above my head, a hoarse clamour, two big nervous birds dipping and lifting, making trial runs over a territory" (18).[52] Henry Hart reads this prose poem somewhat negatively, holding that "their friendly, two-faced masks are donned for the sake of peace," while Helen Vendler offers a more positive reading.[53] Whereas Heaney and his friends picture themselves at the conclusion of "Kernes" as disappearing birdlike "behind a glib" that their Protestant schoolmate Dixon "hadn't even ruffled" (14), here the avian language bespeaks the cautious flight of language between Patrick Heaney and the neighbor in a way that conveys their exposure of their deep-rooted fears and prejudices and the promise that their ensuing laughter may augur a deeper intimacy between them in future, although presumably that relationship was already strong.[54]

This conversational ease and laughter are gone, however, from the disturbing prose poem "Inquisition," the penultimate poem in the volume, as the young speaker is harassed and interrogated by some loyalists in the jakes of a pub. He is significantly left out of their "porter drinkers' laughter" and "back-thumping" brotherhood (23). One of the men "barred the door" and another "caught my hand in a grip alive with some pincer alphabet" (presumably a Masonic handshake); when he cannot respond properly, they know that he is likely a Catholic, but one of them "thumped my back again," saying, "Ah, live and let live, that's my motto, brother. What does it matter where we go on Sundays as long as we can still enjoy ourselves. Isn't that right, brother?" (23). But instead of lingering and engaging with them animatedly as his father and the neighbor do in "Trial Runs," we are told simply that "the door was unexpectedly open and I showed them the face in the back of my head" (23), a watchful, cowed response that ends the poem in the fearful silence these men have engendered in him.

Stations therefore engages in a profound series of examinations of the trajectory of the young Heaney from innocence to experience as he began observing, absorbing, and even participating in sectarian activities as a boy growing up in Northern Ireland. Hart has convincingly argued that "Heaney's obsessive theme, which the prose poems stylistically underscore, is the anguish that a man feels when he persistently crosses between two camps." He believes finally that the "ideal of organic unity" throughout the volume "provides a model for a democratic state in which different factions work in creative proximity, just as contrary sympathies do in his mind and poems." By being so "doggedly self-reflexive, Heaney in *Stations* offers a spiritual autobiography that amounts to a self-crucifixion."[55]

In the constant replaying of old memories that *Stations* rehearses, and through the process by which we doubly read these prose poems in both a linear and a more spatial way, Heaney is attempting to facilitate our own deep engagements with such debilitating experiences and to thereby show us how such (re)readerly meditations might lead to kinder treatment of others, perhaps exemplified in the passage from Galatians 5 that I quoted earlier in the context of my explication of "Romanist" and "Freedman." In this sense, *Stations* functions as a literary/spiritual approximation of going through the Catholic stations of the cross in a ritualistic fashion. An illuminating remark by Matei Calinescu suggests how rereading leads us into the spiritual realm: "The attention proper to reflective rereading may give us a hint as to what Proust meant, in one of his essays on Ruskin, when he stated that reading, while not yet a spiritual act (as Ruskin thought), could be at once a form of self-understanding and a preparation or training for the spiritual."[56]

Stations reminds us that immersing ourselves in the past repetitively through an in-between, inherently liminal form such as the prose poem can retrieve moments of oppression, even as Heaney would eventually escape from Northern Ireland's entrapping narratives. His emphasis on remembering through the form of the prose poem remains a lasting contribution to investigations of memory and how it shapes us and in turn is shaped by us. To quote again from his interview with Dennis O'Driscoll above about why he chose this form for this psychically resistant material, "It's a way to pounce on material that has been in my memory for so long it has almost become aware of me and has begun to be wary of being chosen for verse." Heaney's affirmation of poetic agency to retrieve submerged, "wary" material suggests his embrace of authorial power even as he realizes how authority does not confer perfection on the art realized from remembering. As Edward Casey reminds us in his magisterial study *Remembering*, "I regain the same past anew even as I return to it continually in the same act-form of remembering. No wonder we keep coming back to the past in memory . . . without finding it in the least boring! As autonomous rememberers, we are generating our own ever-differing versions of the same past."[57]

Even as he sought to explore some of the most searingly sectarian moments of his own wounded past in the early to mid-1970s, Heaney often did so through the hybrid genre of the prose poem, which can "effect what Octavio Paz calls 'the mixture and ultimate abolition of genres.'"[58] In so doing, he may have been adumbrating how the dominant factions in his home region of Northern Ireland might be brought together—through tentative, exploratory language shot through with honesty, even though it might be colored with a lingering rancor. Both Richard Terdiman and Margueritte S. Murphy have argued for the way in which the prose poem imagines a more democratic society, Terdiman from a Marxist standpoint and Murphy from a more postmodern, Bakhtinian position. Terdiman holds that what he terms "the counter-discursive," his term for the prose poem, "imagines the liberation of the whole realm of social discourse from such essentially defensive and oppositional structures. Its horizon—in Mallarmé's period as in our own—is the plenitude and the cultural richness of a freer discursive economy, in which something more like authentic democracy might prevail."[59] Citing this insight by Terdiman, Murphy believes that "one might go so far as to affirm that the prose poem already enacts this more 'authentic democracy,' at least in some instances, through the conflicting discourses orchestrated in some of its more polyphonic examples."[60] As the conflict in Northern Ireland dragged on, Heaney plunged into controversy with his pamphlet-poem *An Open Letter*, which he published under the auspices of the Field Day Theatre Company. Yet he continued to autonomously plumb the fluctuating waters of his memory to articulate an expansive, more unified region of Northern Ireland where Catholics, Protestants, and others could meet on common ground and imagine the future together.

Chapter Seven

JOYCE, BURNS, AND HOLUB
Heaney's Independent Regionalism
in *An Open Letter*

Heaney critics commonly argue that his supposed conversion to focusing on spiritual subjects and turning away from the messy matter of the region of Northern Ireland in the 1980s is heralded by his increasing interest in W. B. Yeats. Heaney himself contributed to this belief, noting in his 1988 lecture "The Place of Writing: W. B. Yeats and Thoor Ballylee" that "the poetic imagination in its strongest manifestation imposes its vision upon a place rather than accepts a vision from it."[1] As I have written elsewhere about Heaney's declaration in this essay, "Although he is speaking of the poetic imagination of the later Yeats, after age fifty, the approval implicit in noting that Yeats's late 'poems have created a country of the mind rather than the other way round' suggests Heaney's own desire to invert the terms of his earlier relationship to region, to no longer be, as Yeats in his earlier career was, 'a voice of the spirit of the region.'"[2] But how do we square this affirmation with statements in Heaney's little-known 1989 essay "The Regional Forecast" such as "Talent.... has to take thought and be born again, responsible and independent, exposed to the knowledge that while a literary scene in which the provinces revolve around the centre is demonstrably a Copernican one, the task of talent is to reverse things to a Ptolemaic condition. The writer must re-envisage the region as the original point"?[3] Joyce, not Yeats, is the supreme regional writer for Heaney in this essay: Heaney even states, "When it comes to seeking the regional redeemer, Joyce is crucial. Just how indispensable his achievement was and how corroborating it continues to be is demonstrable in a thousand ways."[4] If Yeats's "country of the mind" becomes one component of Heaney's increasingly mental regionalism in the 1980s and beyond, then Joyce's regionalism, which is predicated upon independence and linguistic fluidity, forms another, heretofore largely unrecognized component of Heaney's increasingly elastic concept of regionalism.

After showing the influence of Joyce on Heaney's thinking about regionalism beginning in the early 1970s, this chapter analyzes the context and content of his poem-pamphlet for the Field Day Theatre Company, *An Open Letter* (1983), showing that Joyce's broadside poems "Gas from a Burner" and "The Holy Office" may well have inspired the genre and tone of that poem, while the Burns stanza and its characteristic irony likely inspired the *aaabab* form of it. Moreover, Heaney's allusion to the Czech poet Miroslav Holub's "On the Necessity of Truth" for the last narrative he tells in *An Open Letter* suggests his recognition of an essentially regional quality in eastern European poets writing behind the Iron Curtain. By turning to the work of Joyce, Burns, and Holub, Heaney's broadside demonstrates the independence of these regional poets for his own evolving regionalism, which enabled him to cast a somewhat cold eye upon the poetry anthology enterprise and the literary academy more generally. Thus this chapter finally shows that more than merely register Heaney's discontent at his work's inclusion in the now-infamous anthology of British poets edited by Blake Morrison and Andrew Motion, *An Open Letter* constitutes a subtle meditation about his Northern Irishness in the context of his evolving concept of regionalism, which was becoming expansive and elastic, ranging far beyond Northern Ireland.

In a little-remarked-upon passage from his 1984 lecture *Place and Displacement: Recent Poetry of Northern Ireland*, Heaney reads the poetry of his younger contemporary Paul Muldoon through late Joycean style, pointing out that for Muldoon, "Language is his resolving element, his quick-change gear, his vehicle for get-away. James Joyce, who could invest the very names of punctuation marks with historical riddles when he addressed his people as 'Laities and gentes, full-stoppers and semi-colonials,' the Joyce of *Finnegans Wake* who melted time and place into a plasm of rhythms and word-roots, puns and tunes, a slide-show of Freudian slips for the Jungian type-setter, this Joyce would recognize the verbal opportunism of Muldoon as a form of native kenning, *a northern doubling*, a kind of daedal fiddling to keep the home fires burning."[5] Linking Muldoon to Joyce through the phrase "a northern doubling" suggests Joyce's doubleness for Heaney as a writer neither fully English or Irish, a "semi-colonial," living between countries and cultures, and thus exemplary for Heaney, who similarly had dwelt between these entities.

Heaney's interest in Joyce, in both his poems and his prose, was long-standing because he saw him as an exemplary regional writer. Heaney's epigraph to "The Wool Trade," originally collected in *Wintering Out* (1972) but left out of *Opened Ground: Selected Poems, 1966–1996*, comes from Stephen Dedalus's lament in *A Portrait of the Artist as a Young Man* after encountering the dean, who rejects Stephen's use of the word *tundish*: "How different are the words 'home,' 'Christ,' 'ale,' 'master,' on his lips and on mine" (*WO*, 37). As I have argued elsewhere in my analysis of this poem, Heaney links the dean's use of these monosyllabic words to similar words in line 4 of "The Wool Trade," which describes the Protestant artisanry of wool making: "To shear, to bale and bleach and card."[6] Stephen's later realization that *tundish* is part of the English language leads him to revel in the possibilities of writing in English, just as Heaney's Joyce will later suggest similar potential for working in English to the poet at the end of the twelfth section of "Station Island." *Tundish*, a disyllabic word with a mellifluous ending, may have lingered in Heaney's mind and recalled the same ending of "Anahorish," the site of his ecumenical primary school in Northern Ireland, which is remembered in another poem of that title in *Wintering Out*. Heaney has told Dennis O'Driscoll that his emphasis on phonetics in that volume must have been inspired subconsciously by Joyce: "Joyce must have been at work downstairs. The first paragraph of 'The Sisters,' maybe, where there's this dreamy caress of words like 'gnomon' and 'simony,' or the little deliquescent hymn to the word 'suck' early on in *A Portrait of the Artist*" (*SS*, 124). Although Joyce lived in the heart of the "Hibernian metropolis" in Dublin and would leave Ireland by 1904, and Heaney would be born in rural Northern Ireland at the beginning of the Second World War, moving south to the Republic by 1972, Joyce's embrace of languages and wordplay has always inspired Heaney, and by the time he wrote *Station Island* Joyce's example, along with that of Dante, would become paramount to him as he attempted to "re-envisage the region as the original point," as he would later state in "The Regional Forecast."

In his June 1983 John Malone Memorial Lecture, *Among Schoolchildren*, Heaney offers his most cogent and thorough reading of the tundish passage and its aftermath in Joyce's *A Portrait*, confirming that in the early 1980s he still considered Joyce a regional author because of his reliance on dialect and his independence. Although his address references Yeats's famous poem in its title and in his opening and closing remarks, the thrust of it really concerns how Joyce became an enabling regional writer for Heaney. He praises "specifically the Joyce who wrote about Stephen Dedlus's linguistic self-consciousness in *Portrait of the Artist as a Young Man*."[7] He then references Stephen's lament by quoting most of the passage from *A Portrait* that he used as the epitaph for "The Wool Trade." Crucially, he distinguishes Stephen's feeling of linguistic displacement at the time with Joyce's at-homeness in the English language: "But that was Stephen's view and not necessarily the view of his creator, James Joyce himself. Stephen, the character, looks with envy at the unity of culture and possession of a shared language and a unified myth which ratifies English identity. Joyce, the writer, did not necessarily look with the same envy at this state of affairs. He accepted the universe of Ireland as a different, if also a desperate state, with its own integrities and destinies which had to be defined and resolved in accordance with their own structures and idioms."[8] Heaney quickly reveals Stephen's discovery that *tundish* was a valid word in English, noting that "what had seemed disabling and provincial is suddenly found to be corroborating and fundamental and potentially universal. To belong to Ireland, to speak its dialect, is not necessarily to be cut off from the world's banquet because that banquet is eaten at the table of one's own life, savoured by the tongue one speaks."[9] Significantly, Heaney claims not so much that Joyce's style is regional but that his reproduction of dialect words like *tundish* marks him as regional and exemplifies artistic freedom for him and for his characters like Stephen.

But to his great credit, Heaney refuses to stop there, going on to argue,

> Joyce ... is also exemplary in refusing to replace that myth of alien superiority by the myth of native superiority. If the coherence of English

culture is a fruitless aspiration, equally fruitless is the dream of a Gaelic order restored. Joyce is against all such alibis. What Stephen called in the diary entry "our own language" is, after all, the English language modified by its residence in Ireland. If he has gone to the trouble of freeing his mind from the net of the English myth, he is also intent on deconstructing the prescriptive myth of Irishness which was burgeoning in his youth and which survives in various sympathetic and unsympathetic forms to this day.[10]

Heaney then proceeds to attack an example of the "prescriptive myth of Irishness" found in the Gaelic poet Sean O'Riordain's "Come Back Again," concluding by refusing to reject his English literary heritage as O'Riordain advises his readers to do in the poem.[11] But almost immediately he swerves to attack the Ulster loyalist position, noting that if O'Riordain "would obliterate history since Kinsale, the loyalist imagination at its most enthusiastic would obliterate history before Kinsale."[12] While he admits that the loyalist's fidelity can be "a holding, grounding, utterly necessary exercise in self-definition and self-respect" in its preference for "the dream of a mainland home" and the maintenance of "solidarity with our traditional values," it can also display the "neurotic intensity" that O'Riordain's exclusivist poem does and be "in danger of turning conceptions and loyalties within the Unionist tradition into refusals and paranoias."[13] This address reveals that for Heaney, James Joyce, caught between the Gaelic past and the English present and future, was *the* exemplary regional writer because he was fruitfully torn in his use of Irish and English culture and language, particularly speech, and in his independent artistic stance.

As further evidence that by the early 1970s Heaney was considering Joyce a regional writer, in the most positive senses of that term, we should recall that he invokes him in his 1972 review of *The Hugh MacDiarmid Anthology*, "Tradition and an Individual Talent: Hugh MacDiarmid." There, in his reading of MacDiarmid's "On a Raised Beach," he points out the "uncertainty about language" in the poem, which he sees as "peculiar not just to MacDiarmid, but to others who write generally in English, but particularly out of a region where the culture and language are at variance with standard English utterance and attitudes."[14] Only two sentences later, he invokes Joyce favorably as the pattern for a successful regional writer wrestling with writing in a language imposed upon him: "Joyce made a myth and a mode out of this self-consciousness, but he did so by taking on the English language itself and wrestling its genius with his bare hands."[15] He then notes how MacDiarmid cites "this Joyce of *Finnegans Wake* in the opening lines of 'Water Music,'" concluding that "in the poem, the local and the indigenous, which were Joyce's obsession also, are affiliated to oral and instinctive characteristics of the region and the intensity and volubility of the regional diction."[16] Clearly, Heaney viewed regionalism as a positive term that connoted attention to local culture, particularly its speech. But by embracing the urban Joyce, he was already expanding traditional definitions of regionalism that usually consider it rural and peripheral. Dillon Johnston's succinct assessment that "by turning away from the country and the countryman, Joyce opened up the city as a legitimate Irish landscape" is apposite for appreciating Heaney's sense of Joyce as a regional writer.[17] Joyce's Dublin was inherently local and still marginalized in the British Empire, and thus Heaney's recognition of Joyce's "regionalism" was both continuous and discontinuous with the more usual, enclosed, and often rural characteristics of regionalism that the poet continued to renovate and reimagine as his career evolved.[18]

Without terming Joyce a regional writer, Robert Crawford has shown that he, among others, forged "a diction so polylingual and sophisticated that it tops and outflanks the English cultural centre."[19] This practice, which Heaney does not recognize in much of his criticism on his predecessor, preferring instead to evoke the Joyce who privileges dialect words, as we have seen in Heaney's repeated references to the tundish episode in *A Portrait*, also marks Joyce as a regional writer. Crawford cites what he calls the "continual presence of the demotic in *Ulysses*" that "is matched by its thorough diffusion throughout the word-carnival of *Finnegans Wake*, in which the ground-rhythms of common Irish speech are given their head," further arguing that the "Irish demotic in particular is used to give his voice at once a local, provincial as well as an international, cosmopolitan accent."[20]

Indeed, in 1990 Heaney would remark, in language redolent of Joyce, upon his attempts in the early 1970s to maintain a middle passage between his Irish and English poetic predecessors:

> A few months earlier [before 1972], I had proposed a somewhat oversimplified programme for the poetry I thought I wanted to write. In an

attempt to sail between the Scylla of "the Irish mode" originally sponsored by Thomas MacDonagh and maintained as a literary category by later writers such as Robert Farren in his book *The Course of Irish Verse* (1949), and the Charybdis of a more standardized, New Lines-ish, iambic English, I devised a conceit in which Irish experience was to equal vowels and the English literary tradition was to equal consonants, and my poems were to be "vocables adequate to my whole experience." It was, admittedly, a fairly Euphuistic conception, but even so, one which has been endemic to Irish writing and whose solution always represents a definite moment in a poet's development.[21]

Heaney would come to modify this formulaic solution to representing both his Irish and his English literary heritage, yet his urge to remain true to this dual heritage remains at the heart of all of his poetry. As his career progressed and as he continued to read Joyce, Heaney gradually began articulating a simultaneously regional and cosmopolitan Joyce, at times stressing one aspect of the dialectic over the other.

In "Joyce's Poetry," originally published in 1982 as "Come into the Chamber of Dreams," Heaney negatively contrasts Joyce's poetry such as "Ecce Puer" with "the great poetry of the opening chapter of *Ulysses*," which he argues "amplifies and rhapsodizes the world with an unlooked-for accuracy and transport. It gives the spirit freedom to range in an element that is as linguistic as it is airy and watery."[22] Here Heaney is clearly articulating his view of Joyce in the 1980s, whose work inspired, in part, *An Open Letter*, and who appears at the end of "Station Island," a writer characterized by freedom, exile, and wateriness.

Heaney would make his verse contribution to the Field Day Theatre Company in the form of *An Open Letter*, his poetry pamphlet from 1983 that revisits the metaphor of the birth of modern Northern Ireland that the introduction to this study explored and that Heaney again articulates to show his two-mindedness and bicultural identity as he rejects the label of "British" poet ascribed to him by his inclusion in *The Penguin Book of Contemporary British Poetry*, which Blake Morrison and Andrew Motion edited and published in 1982.

Field Day Theatre Company was a major occupation of Heaney for at least a decade, and its original purpose was primarily artistic rather than political. Founded in Londonderry/Derry in 1980 by Brian Friel and Stephen Rea to envision a fifth province of Ireland, Field Day's board of directors was ecumenically composed of three Catholics and three Protestants. After three of Brian Friel's plays were staged—*Translations, Three Sisters,* and *The Communication Cord*—the directors decided to add an academic element to the company and started a pamphlet series, with a set of three to appear every six months or so. The first set included Heaney's *An Open Letter,* Tom Paulin's *A New Look at the Language Question,* and Seamus Deane's *Civilians and Barbarians.* In *Acting between the Lines: The Field Day Theatre Company and Irish Cultural Politics, 1980–1984,* Marilynn Richtarik has an extended and powerful discussion of Heaney's *An Open Letter.*[23] Richtarik points out that Heaney's poetic objection here to being included in *The Penguin Book of Contemporary British Poetry* is not so surprising given the delicate situation of national affiliation in Northern Ireland: "Much of the delicacy of the problem stems from the anomalous position of Northern Ireland midway between two countries with different cultures, neither of which is fully committed to the province and to neither of which it entirely belongs."[24] Richtarik goes on to argue that "there are a great many people from Northern Ireland who consider themselves British, although Heaney does not happen to be one of them."[25] But this contention is too reductive: Heaney considered himself *both* British and Irish because of his dual linguistic and cultural heritage, and his expansive concept of regionalism based on Northern Ireland's potentially enabling blend of languages and cultures allowed him to claim both labels and transcend them.

An example of Heaney's emphasis on this dual affiliation occurs in his last Oxford lecture in 1993, "Frontiers of Writing," where he explicitly claims both his Irishness and his Britishness in commenting specifically upon *An Open Letter:*

> In that same letter, I wrote that my passport was green, although nowadays, it is a Euro-, but not an imperial, purple. I wrote about the colour of the passport, however, not in order to expunge the British connection in Britain's Ireland but to maintain the right to diversity *within* the border, to be understood as having full freedom to the enjoyment of an Irish name and identity within that northern jurisdiction.... There is

nothing extraordinary about the challenge to be in two minds. If, for example, there was something exacerbating, there was still nothing deleterious to my sense of Irishness in the fact that I grew up in the minority in Northern Ireland and was educated within the dominant British culture. My identity was emphasized rather than eroded by being maintained in such circumstances. The British dimension, in other words, while it is something that will be resisted by the minority if it is felt to be coercive, has nevertheless been a given of our history and even of our geography, one of the places where we all live, willy-nilly. It's in the language. And it's where the mind of many in the republic lives also.[26]

Heaney's statement here eloquently and cogently insists both on his right to be Irish within Northern Ireland, a colonial holding, *and* on his given Britishness, which, while he may not proclaim it loudly, is still there—in the language he writes and in his mental and physical geography. It is more accurate to say that Heaney's complaint was against the anthology's failure to recognize this "both and"—his dual linguistic and cultural heritage—and its easy (and wrong) characterization of him, however unwittingly, as *simply* British. It is a complaint that he inherited from Joyce.

Heaney took the stance he did in *An Open Letter* for an additional reason—his dislike of Margaret Thatcher and her resurrection of traditional notions of the British nation-state that effectively excluded Catholics and regions of Britain outside the Home Counties. In 1982, Thatcher led Britain into the Falkland War against Argentina, seen by many as a rearguard attempt to hold together remnants of the former British Empire. Additionally, she argued for a continuous sense of British history with the monarchy and the Anglican Church at the nation's center. As Hanne Tange has wryly observed, "This official myth of the nation has little room for alternative British identities of class, gender, region and race, however, because they are difficult to accommodate within a highly centralized state."[27] Feeling the erasure of his region, Irish culture, and childhood Catholicism under Thatcher, Heaney sought to reinscribe them in his pamphlet poem.

In his 2001 essay "Through-Other Places, Through-Other Times: The Irish Poet and Britain," Heaney would revisit *An Open Letter* by musing upon its epitaph by Gaston Bachelard: "What is the source of our first suffering? It lies in the fact that we hesitated to speak.... It was born in the moment when we accumulated silent things within us" (*AOL*, 5). In writing *An Open Letter*, Heaney felt some pressure in the wake of the IRA hunger strikes in the Maze prison in 1981 to again be a representative of the minority Catholic population in the North, although he had often previously been uncomfortable in this role. In his discussion of the context of *An Open Letter*, he points out in "Through-Other Places, Through-Other Times" that "we [Northern Irish Catholics] had escaped from Lord Brookeborough's sectarian Ulster only to be landed in Margaret Thatcher's. In the early 1980s, we were in the bitter aftermath of dirty protests and hunger strikes, in the middle of the IRA's campaign, and at that polarized moment the Morrison and Motion book was published. I had the feeling that if my British audience were not kept apprised of my stand-off with the 'British' nomenclature, and indeed if my unionist readers were not kept reminded of it, I would be guilty of more than evasiveness."[28] In both "Punishment" and "Whatever You Say Say Nothing" from *North*, Heaney had already condemned himself for not criticizing more publicly the sectarianism driving the conflict in Northern Ireland. For example, in "Punishment," he memorably says in relation to the bog body he believes was punished for adultery that he would have not spoken had he been there when she was being hurt ("I ... would have cast ... the stones of silence") and that he has been silent in the present ("I who have stood dumb") "when your betraying sisters, / cauled in tar, / wept by the railings" (*N*, 31). And in "Whatever You Say," Heaney again indicts himself for his silence on condemning violence in the province, blaming "the famous // Northern reticence, the tight gag of place / And times" (53). Many commentators have observed, however, that Heaney does criticize the violence in the North and its sectarian underpinnings in such poems.

But such critical self-flagellation is significantly different in its objective from Heaney's professed attempt to make a stand and embrace his conflicted Irishness in *An Open Letter*; indeed, he ran a risk in appearing somewhat sectarian himself by making the statements he does there. In some of the most infamous lines from the poem, in stanza 14, Heaney declaims, "be advised / My passport's green. / No glass of ours was ever raised / To toast *The Queen*" (*AOL*, 9). And he concludes his thirty-third and final stanza by noting, "But British, no, the name's not right. / Yours truly, Seamus" (13). In the sharply divided political climate in the North ushered in since Thatcher's decision to strip the inmates in the Maze prison in Northern Ireland of their political status, which resulted in the successive so-called "blanket" and "dirty" protests, then finally in the deaths of ten republican hunger strikers, such lines could be read as affirming solidarity with the republican prisoners and, by extrapolation, with the republican cause in general. These strikes and the deaths of the hunger strikers whipped Irish nationalist fervor into a state it had not experienced since the aftermath of Bloody Sunday in 1972, and Sinn Fein support rose dramatically in the North.

While he certainly felt obliged to remind his audience of his Irishness and his Catholic background in *An Open Letter*, Heaney himself has disavowed any overt republicanism on the part of himself and Field Day. In a 1994 BBC radio program to which he contributed, he recalled the negative image of Field Day and acknowledged the difficulty of its being taken as anything other than a representative of republicanism:

> Field Day began to be perceived as being a very nationalist-based, green organization. I remember a woman in Dublin saying to me "you're very green," as if that was a kind of doomed or forbidden hue. And there were terrible things said ... about Brian Friel's plays. He was ... more or less, accused of being an IRA propagandist, only because there was a refusal to yield, if you like, [to] an Irish past as a condition of a prefigured future. The minute you posit an Irish base for a movement, it's as if you are endorsing the Provisional IRA, and it's an extremely difficult position to survive in.[29]

Richtarik has pointed out that many reviewers disparaged all three of the pamphlets: "In Ireland the pamphlets were generally taken as straightforward nationalist statements and greeted with approbation or disgust depending upon the political opinions of the reader or reviewer."[30] However, several prominent critics did single out *An Open Letter* for special praise, both for its artistry and for its relative avoidance of nationalist sentiments.

Eavan Boland was a significant exception, writing in the *Irish Times* that "Seamus Heaney has been in and around anthologies of English poetry for nearly fifteen years. ... I cannot believe that the sudden appearance of the word 'British' on the title page came as a rude shock. He has either changed his mind or changed his friends, and neither process is completely safe for poets."[31] Boland was correct to point out that Heaney *had* been in a number of British poetry anthologies before the Morrison and Motion volume. One of these was *The Young British Poets*, edited by Jeremy Robson and published by St. Martin's in 1971, a year of crisis in the North and a period during which Heaney was still identifying himself as writing out of nationalist minority concerns. His bemused outrage in his pamphlet at his inclusion in a British poetry anthology appears late in coming and somewhat suspect, given the relatively nationalist slant Field Day was beginning to acquire and the political situation in the North at the time. No one seems to have thought to ask the obvious question: Would Heaney have been similarly outraged at being included in an anthology of Irish poetry, as indeed he has been numerous times? He never registered such an objection.

Yet in 2002, Heaney responded to Boland's remarks by observing,

> Times had changed, I had changed, everybody had changed. But working with Brian Friel and Seamus Deane and David Hammond in no way entailed change of friends. People were killing and being killed because of matters related to the British and Irish words. It was hardly out of order, in the circumstances, for a poet to do something not completely safe. . . . You'll understand I didn't write the letter as part of a "Brits Out" campaign. As a character says in *Translations*, confusion is not a dishonourable condition. I'd even say there was an element of the "confessional" involved. I may have been involved with Field Day, but what I felt when I published *An Open Letter* was more like solitude than solidarity. (*SS*, 418)

This statement is worth lingering upon because it shows both Heaney's sense of continuity (by having the same friends he had had for some time) and his realization of the risk he was taking in writing the poem. Perhaps more important, he suggests his own state of confusion by citing Friel's schoolmaster Hugh from *Translations*: Hugh's hybridity in speaking Irish but not retreating into Gaelic culture, along with his grudging acceptance of modernity and speaking English in that play, models Heaney's own hybridity and confusion about being so caught between two cultures.

Finally, Heaney's claim that he felt "solitude" not "solidarity" in publishing the poem resonantly suggests that he consciously was distancing himself from the Field Day coterie and also from others who had promoted his career, like Blake Morrison. Close friends and at least one Field Day colleague, Seamus Deane, perceived *An Open Letter* as breaking from Field Day. Deane felt that its being cast in verse was a personal maneuver that made the other Field Day pamphlets more polemical. Aidan O'Malley cites a "confidential commentary on the first series of pamphlets in 1983," in which Deane "took exception to Heaney's use of verse in *An Open Letter*. Deane felt this rendered Heaney's objection to being included in *The Penguin Book of Contemporary British Poetry* an entirely personal matter, and this perspective set *An Open Letter* apart from the other two pamphlets in the series, making them appear more strident in the process."[32] Heaney used very similar terms less than a year after *An Open Letter* was published in approvingly analyzing Derek Mahon's "A Disused Shed in Co. Wexford" in his August 1984 lecture, *Place and Displacement: Recent Poetry of Northern Ireland*. He concludes that lecture by noting that the voices of the insistent mushrooms begging for attention in that memorable poem "could not have been heard so compellingly if Mahon had not created the whispering gallery of absence not just by moving out of Ireland but by evolving out of *solidarity* into irony and compassion. And, needless to say, into *solitude*."[33] Heaney is implying here that Mahon broke from his early solidarity with his Ulster Protestant background and culture and gradually moved into a condition of solitude, an enabling state where one can retain agency and resist the siren song of the tribe. Presumably then, in looking back to the writing and publication of *An Open Letter* in September of 1983, Heaney felt that it had been a step in the direction of artistic independence ("solitude") even though it was heralded in many quarters as merely an affirmation of his Irishness ("solidarity"). Rand Brandes has even argued that *An Open Letter* was Heaney's first attempt to "recreate himself if he was to continue writing" given his recognition at having reached middle age and gained great success, a state of mind compounded with the guilt he felt at the death of his former neighbor Francis Hughes from the republican hunger strikes.[34]

Heaney's recollection of that time in "Through-Other Places" as a moment in his career when he felt he must speak out and claim his Irishness must be balanced with his more conciliatory statement from "Frontiers of Writing," also cited above, so that we may realize how Heaney's righteous indignation at being called simply "British" by virtue of his inclusion in the Morrison/Motion anthology of British poetry stems from his sense of himself as attempting to "maintain the right to diversity *within* the border, to be understood as having full freedom to the enjoyment of an Irish name and identity within that northern jurisdiction," as he emphatically says.[35]

Startlingly, Heaney may have been inspired to use the periodical format, the angry tone, and the couplet form he does in *An Open Letter* by his interest in Joyce's poems "Gas from a Burner" and "The Holy Office" that he cites at the end of his 1982 article "Joyce's Poetry." He observed in a 1983 interview about publishing his poem in a pamphlet format that "he sees the Field Day publication as helping revive the pamphlet as a means of stimulating discourse on political and artistic matters. . . . Pamphleteering was an important Irish tradition that seems to have lapsed somewhat in recent times."[36] While he may have been thinking of Jonathan Swift's pamphleteering, Joyce's broadside poems likely were on his mind as well. In the final paragraph of "Joyce's Poetry," Heaney notes that "'Gas from a Burner' and 'The Holy Office' may not be as self-consciously beautiful or as well finished as the lyrics but they are in earnest. The language has all the roused expectation of a loosed ferret. The thing may be hurried, but it has angry momentum. And it is a performance. The connoisseur of styles is showing off, but at the same time the hurt human being is giving vent to his rage. Significantly, this is the stuff that people tend to know by heart:

'Twas Irish humour, wet and dry,
Flung quicklime into Parnell's eye;
'Tis Irish brains that save from doom
The leaky barge of the Bishop of Rome
For everyone knows the Pope can't belch
Without the consent of Billy Walsh.
O Ireland my first and only love
Where Christ and Caesar are hand and glove!"
          ("Gas from a Burner")[37]

This angry passage cast in couplets and near-couplets indicts the Irish for betraying Parnell and the Catholic Church but also simultaneously expresses Joyce's exasperated love for his country, where he believed the Catholic Church and the British Empire essentially colluded with each other to keep the populace in line. The crucial preceding lines that Heaney leaves out here make clear Joyce's indictment of Ireland for sending its writers and political leaders into exile and betrayal: "This lovely land that always sent / Her writers and artists to banishment / And in a spirit of Irish fun / Betrayed her own leaders, one by one."[38]

When we recall that both "The Holy Office" and "Gas from a Burner" were published by Joyce as broadsides in 1904 and 1912, respectively, for circulation among his friends, Heaney's recourse to the pamphlet form and his decision to title the poem *An Open Letter*, which suggest a public forum, become more understandable. By using the more ephemeral form of the pamphlet, he could distribute his own satire, à la Joyce, to close friends, yet also do so under the academic imprimatur of Field Day, appealing to both populist and professional audiences. Even his admission to Dennis O'Driscoll about *An Open Letter* that "I'm sorry it's not shorter and punchier" (*SS*, 419) suggests he wanted the poem to be suitable for rapid public consumption and perhaps regretted that it was not as short as Joyce's two poems, which could each fit on a long broadside. And because he has never collected the angry poem, it has remained less known than many of his other ones and has never become part of his official canon.

Another way that Heaney registers his discontent with being termed "British" in *An Open Letter* is through his recourse to the six-line Burns stanza, rhyming *aaabab*, a form popularized by the Scottish writer in many of his dialect poems. Heaney would later praise Burns's ability to inscribe his profound Scottishness over against the monolithic entity of Britishness in his 1997 essay "Burns's Art Speech." That essay crystallizes Heaney's interest in Burns as a regional writer going back decades and suggests how Burns became a regional exemplar for the poet even in his schooldays. Robert Crawford has pointed out that "from earliest infancy Burns had been educated in two cultures—that of the [*A Collection of Prose and Verse, from the*] *Best English Authors* featured in [Arthur] Masson's anthology, and that of his family background, where his mother sang him Scots songs and he enjoyed listening with terror to the vast repertoire of supernatural tales which his mother's maid rejoiced in telling him."[39] Like Burns, Heaney early on learned to speak the language of hearth and home in domestic settings but quickly became adept at "standard" English, which he employed in his formal writing and speaking.

Masson's then-popular eighteenth-century anthology brings up the vexed issue of Heaney's being included in an anthology at all, although his work had been featured in earlier anthologies. While surely having his work anthologized was appealing on one level to Heaney, on another level there was a part of him that disdained the entire academic enterprise. This stance lingered despite his having personally and professionally profited through his long and varied association with a series of universities, including Queen's in Belfast; the University of California, Berkeley; Carysfort College in Dublin; and Harvard. This issue has never been addressed in criticism of *An Open Letter*, since the political issue has always been to the fore—indeed, Heaney himself has privileged it. Yet Heaney approved Burns's tendency to reject the academy and its tendency to pigeonhole and classify writers, which the Scottish poet felt lessened his conception of the poet as a rough bard brimming over with natural energy. Crawford has demonstrated that Burns fashioned himself as "the Scotch bard," occupying a space where "he was able to be admired by the literati even as he developed further a style of writing which was both outside and, in many ways, opposed to their strictures."[40] Such a stance appealed to the rural-born Heaney, who had always cast a somewhat skeptical eye on the sometimes elitist nature of the professional practice of literary study. Bernard O'Donoghue points this attitude out in his marvelous study of the poet's language: "He combines with his sense of poetic mission a strong suspicion that poetry is not the most important thing in the world.... In an interview with John Haffenden, he says of writing: 'there is indeed some part of me that is entirely unimpressed with the activity.... It's the generations, I suppose, of rural ancestors—not illiterate, but not literary. They, in me, or I, through them, don't give a damn.'"[41] Thus, realizing Heaney's recuperation of Burns's regional and antiacademy stance in *An Open Letter* contributes greatly to our understanding of its rough-hewn regionalism and independence from the sometimes elitist preserve of poetry.[42]

As T. V. F. Brogan has observed, the Burns stanza is particularly effective because of its precision, irony, and intricate rhyme: "Following the crescendo of the initial tercet, the short lines lend themselves well to effects of pointing, irony, and closure."[43] Although O'Donoghue believes that the

Burns stanza is a "genial medium" and "has a disarming friendliness to it," citing its tone in Auden's "Letter to Lord Byron" and John Fuller's *Epistles to Several Persons*, in fact, as we will see, Heaney's joking tone in the first draft of the broadside largely vanishes in the angrier, published version.[44] Thus Heaney employs the irony inherent in the Burns stanza combined with the angry tone he found in Joyce's broadside poems to signify his discontent with being labeled British when in fact he feels both British and Irish, a condition epitomized by his Northern Irishness.

Perhaps the strongest evidence of Heaney's commitment to regionalism in *An Open Letter* comes from his earlier draft of the poem, which has never been discussed in criticism. This draft illuminates how he originally juxtaposed a Northern Irish dialect with the formal properties of a traditional letter to rhetorically inscribe his regional affiliation in an indirect, colloquial, joking way that contrasts with the more direct, declarative, even angry, final version. For example, the original first stanza runs,

> Addressed to: The Editors,
> Contemporary British Verse,
> C/O Penguin Books. Dear Sirs,
>   (Or Hello youse—
> The format of the open letter's
>   All a ruse).[45]

The final, published stanza leaves out the dialect word "youse" and instead substitutes "muse," settling for a geographic reference to "furze," a plant common to the North of Ireland, to register the poet's Northernness:

> To Blake and Andrew, Editors,
> Contemporary British Verse,
> Penguin Books, Middlesex. Dear Sirs,
>   My anxious muse,
> Roused on her bed among the furze,
>   Has to refuse
>
>   The adjective. It makes her blush.
>   (*AOL*, 7)

The revised stanza, while it loses the colloquial Northern familiar term of "youse" and thus the original opening regional affirmation, intriguingly inscribes an English regional identity to Penguin Books by correctly locating it in Middlesex instead of the British capital of London, where most people probably think it is housed.

In the original second and third stanzas, which are completely missing from the revised, published poem, along with the original stanzas 4 through 6, Heaney's speaker continues in a jocular tone, proceeding to tell a sexual joke set in Northern Ireland, replete with more dialect words:

> Did you ever hear the one about
> The Antrim man, embarrassed at
> Explaining how the drawers he'd bought
>   Were far too small:
> Specifically, "shockin' tight"
>   Round crotch and fall.
>
> He asks the shopgirl, "Did I ever
> See you at a dance in Comber?"
> "Och," she says, "would you give over!
>   There's no ballroom there."
> "Exactly," says he, "what's the bother
>   With these things here."
>   ("AOL")

This sort of narrative approach to the sensitive subject of the North superficially recalls Heaney's customary attitude to the problems of the province in volumes such as *North* that indirectly critiqued sectarianism, for example, by musing upon violence in northern Europe. But here the joke firmly situates the reader from the start in specific locations in Northern Ireland—Antrim, Comber—and uses the dialect word *och* to register that northern location as well. We are distracted from the problem at hand—Heaney's offense at being included in a well-known volume of "Contemporary British Verse"—by having to pay attention to the play on words in the joke, which itself raises the question of perceived national constraint and confinement through the sartorial tightness of the man's "drawers."

The next two stanzas, 4 and 5 in the early draft of *An Open Letter*, effect a stuttering indecision at Heaney's having to protest his inclusion in the anthology. For instance, stanza 4 turns to the dialect of Dickens's *Great Expectations* and the indecision of Pip to suggest Heaney's own vacillation about the issue:

> Which, I mean ter say, old chaps—
> To quote Joe Gargery and relapse
> From Ulster Doric into Pip's
>   Suppressed Hodge-speak,
> Among the tongue-tied, twisting caps
>   And looking meek—.
>   ("AOL")

Stanza 5's first two lines continue in this vein, "Which I mean ter say, although / What's wrong is what I'm getting round to" ("AOL"). Heaney's speaker then invokes the famous reticence of American writer Herman Melville's Bartleby in his short story "Bartleby the Scrivener":

> The ones most deeply in the know
>   Are those who shy
> From talk of it. They prefer not to,
>   Like Bartleby.
>   ("AOL")

In the published version of the poem, Heaney instead condemns himself for silence. While he opens stanza 6 by vowing, "Anything for a quiet life. / Play possum and pretend you're deaf" (*AOL*, 8), he opens stanza 7 with lines of self-castigation: "And what price then, self-preservation? / Your silence is an abdication" (8). By the beginning of stanza 8, he concludes, "And therefore it is time to break / Old inclinations not to speak" (8).

Thus having established his own off-center, regionalist identity to London-centered Britishness by invoking Northern Irish dialectic, by telling a locally specific joke from the province, by recalling the dialect of the eastern English area of the Fens in a famous Dickens novel, and by commending the taciturn silence of the American clerk Bartleby, Heaney can turn to the matter at hand—not, as the published version of the poem leads us to expect, to his being included in an anthology of British poetry, but to the vexed issue of the region of Northern Ireland. This is the context for explaining his rejection of his work's inclusion in the Morrison and Motion anthology, which is really only a secondary issue in *An Open Letter*.[46]

Stanza 6 in the first draft stutters into life with a series of end-stopped phrases: "The north. Identity. Crisis. / *Deja-vu.* Notorious" ("AOL"). Heaney then cites Shakespeare's Macmorris, whom, along with Joyce's character Leopold Bloom, he had invoked positively to articulate a positive, inclusive definition of a nation in the poem "Traditions" from *Wintering Out*.[47] Having Macmorris say, "*Ish a pish,*" and "*Ish a rogue,*" Heaney concludes this stanza with "Still, I've a quarrel with that British. / End of prologue" ("AOL"). These first six joking, indecisive stanzas are entirely missing from the later, published version, which features a series of angry phrases.

For instance, instead of "I've a quarrel with that British," in stanza 6 of the original draft, Heaney concludes the published stanza 4 indignantly:

> As empire rings its curtain down
> > This "British" word
> Sticks deep in native and colon
> > Like Arthur's sword.
> > > (*AOL*, 7)

Moreover, even though Heaney unequivocally states in the first draft of the poem "be advised / My passport's green" ("AOL"), he immediately valorizes both Irish and British citizenship as a native of Northern Ireland in the twenty-first stanza, then rejects the IRA in the twenty-second stanza:

> Dual citizenship is prized.
> God Save the Queen,
>
> Meant to be God's and Ulster's voice
> Remains, in a deep sense, a choice
> Of anthem. And you realize,
> > Needless to say,
> To refuse her does not espouse
> > The IRA.
> > > ("AOL")

In the published version, Heaney rejects the British national anthem in the published fourteenth stanza: "be advised / My passport's green. / No glass of ours was ever raised / To toast *The Queen*" (*AOL*, 9), a much more straightforward disavowal of English identity. To soften the blow, as it were, he opens the published stanza 15 by vowing, "No harm to her nor you who deign / To *God Bless* her as sovereign," but quickly continues more negatively, "Except that from the start / her reign / Of crown and rose / Defied, displaced, would not combine / What I'd espouse" (*AOL*, 10).

Such examples should suffice to show how the final version of *An Open Letter* was, despite its retention of a self-conscious indecision about biting the British hand that had long fed Heaney through his being published by Faber and Faber, angrier than the more ambiguous and jocular original version, which concludes with a delightfully epistolary ending that invites immediate newspaper publication:

Things I wrote here I might delete
Unless I go to post. So stet
    Without revision.
P. S. Do you think is too late
    For the next edition?
        ("AOL")

By using the direct address throughout his poem, Heaney was aligning himself with Joyce's similar strategy in his two broadside poems; by highlighting his voice, he was performing an essentially regional maneuver according to his own definition of the term. Recall that his essays on MacDiarmid and Joyce repeatedly insist on their regionalism because of their use of dialect words and speech. And in the fifth stanza of the published version of *An Open Letter*, Heaney does just that, noting that he has "footered, havered, spraughled, wrought / Like Shauneen Keogh, / Wondering should I write it out / Or let it go" (*AOL*, 8). This procession of Hiberno-English dialect words suggests his great indecision through their onomatopoeia but also makes clear his embrace of his regional identity because only an Irish audience would have any real sense of their meaning. *Footer* denotes a "fidgety, awkward behaviour" and can even mean "to act in a bungling manner," while *haver* means "to talk foolishly."[48] *Spraughle* means to "clamber or walk awkwardly,"[49] and *wrought*, a past and past participial form of *work*, refers to working material (as iron is wrought) but here seems to carry the additional connotation that he is upset and overexcited like Synge's Shauneen Keogh in *The Playboy of the Western World*. Finally, although "Shauneen" is the diminutive form of "Shaun," Heaney may also be playing on a similar-sounding word in Hiberno-English, *shoneen* or *seonin*, which is a pejorative term for "a person more interested in English language and customs than Irish ones; a 'West Briton.'"[50] Perhaps here he is indirectly referencing Joyce again, this time, his indecisive, often foolish-feeling Gabriel Conroy in "The Dead," who is derisively called a "West Briton" by the hypernationalist Molly Ivors.[51]

But this admission of feeling awkward and foolish belies to some degree the anger in the poem, which hearkens back to Joyce's angry tone in his broadside poems that Heaney had been musing upon the year before *An Open Letter* was published. Puzzlingly, Marilynn Richtarik argues that "his tone throughout is self-deprecatory and apologetic," while Dennis O'Driscoll remarks on what he sees as the poem's "good grace and good humour."[52] Yet they base their judgment mainly on Heaney's twenty-ninth stanza, where he observes, "I hate to bite / Hands that led me to the limelight / In the Penguin Book" (*AOL*, 13). If he employed the angry tone of Joyce he found in "The Holy Office" and "Gas from a Burner" for *An Open Letter*, he did so for a very different effect. In both his satirical poems, Joyce attacks Ireland and the Catholic Church in vituperative language, but Heaney affirms the Irish side of himself, after opening with an apology to Blake Morrison, who had written an early book on his poetry, while again resorting to the language of woundedness in describing contemporary Northern Ireland. When we consider, however, that Joyce wrote "The Holy Office" shortly before leaving for exile on the European continent and "Gas from a Burner" eight years later, we gain even more of an appreciation for Heaney's sense of himself as an outsider in Northern Ireland, and then, after moving to the Republic, as an exile from Ulster—a conception that must have been exacerbated by the simplistic tag of "British" in the Morrison/Motion collection's title.

As he did in "Ocean's Love to Ireland" and "Act of Union," both collected in *North*, he resorts in *An Open Letter* to the language of birth as a wound in describing the emergence and condition of contemporary

Northern Ireland. To convey this birthing wound that continues to fester, however, he briefly resorts to incorporating language from Eliot's "The Waste Land" and Yeats's poem about Zeus's rape of Leda in "Leda and the Swan." At the end of stanza 21, the speaker mentions that he "long felt my identity / So rudely forc'd" and continues in the next stanza, "Tereu. Tereu. And tooraloo" (*AOL*, 11).[53]

Immediately after the "tooraloo" of line 1 in stanza 22, Heaney begins channeling Yeats's "Leda and the Swan": "A shudder in the loins. And so / The twins for Leda. And twins too / For the hurt North, / One island-green, one royal blue. / An induced birth" (*AOL*, 11).[54] Anticipating Declan Kiberd's reductive reading of Yeats's poem in *Inventing Ireland* as the metaphor of the imperial rape of Ireland by Britain, Heaney here reads Ireland as Leda, and Zeus as the male Britain forcing itself upon the feminized island.[55] He had already opened the poem by suggesting how the very appellation of him as "British" has made his feminized muse blush. Thus Heaney yokes together his feminized Irish muse, who previously acquiesced to the tag of "British" but who now refuses that term, with feminized Ireland, who has been ravished by Britain and has birthed the Republic of Ireland and Northern Ireland.

And yet whereas such language of imperial ravishing of the feminized colony of Ireland is simply uttered and apparently endorsed by the poet in the earlier lyric poems from *North*, in *An Open Letter* Heaney quickly goes on to reject such a reductive reading of the situation, again through a reference to Joyce, noting in the very next stanza,

> One a Provo, one a Para,
> One Law and Order, one Terror—
> It's time to break the cracked mirror
>   Of this conceit.
> It leads nowhere so why bother
>   To work it out?
>   (*AOL*, 11)

Highlighting his jettisoning of this binary politics, he resorts to a roughened language, another maneuver borrowed from Robert Burns. O'Donoghue reads this stanza in the context of Heaney's employment of the Burns stanza, arguing that "this metrical roughness of the provincial is matched by a crunching return to the long-abandoned harsh diction ('No way, my friends': stanza 18)," holding further that "the dialect at which this is adept is a very deliberate challenge to the urbane formalities of the well-wrought poem."[56] The "cracked mirror" phrase, of course, recalls Stephen Dedalus's comment in chapter 1 of Joyce's *Ulysses* after looking into "the mirror held out to him, cleft by a crooked crack," that "it is a symbol of Irish art. The cracked lookingglass of a servant."[57] Heaney, like Stephen, rejects this shopworn symbol, vowing to break the mirror. He thus draws upon Burns's, Stephen's, and Joyce's stance of independence in declaring his freedom, not just from labels and categories like "British," but also from clichéd conceits about Irish art.

Heaney begins the twenty-fourth stanza by articulating a phrase that had increasing relevance to his conception of regionalism in the 1970s, 1980s, and beyond: "The hidden Ulster lies beneath" (*AOL*, 11). This phrase "the hidden Ulster," had already appeared in his 1977 lecture "The Sense of Place," explored in chapter 3.[58] And only a few months before *An Open Letter* was published, in his lecture *Among Schoolchildren*, Heaney again used the term "hidden Ulster" similarly, reflecting on how reading Daniel Corkery's *The Hidden Ireland* had enabled him to appreciate his Gaelic past:

> Around this time ... I had a small experience which ratified this sense of a relationship to a *hidden Ulster* in a memorable and intimate way, and ratified Corkery's notion of loss and deprivation. I came across, in Dineen's Irish dictionary, a word with the letters *Doir* in brackets after it, a word which was thereby defined as one peculiar to the Irish spoken at one time in my own English-speaking County Derry. The word was "Lachtar," meaning a flock of young chickens. Suddenly I was animated with the fact of loss which Corkery had described. The word had survived in our district as a common and, as far as I had known until then, an English word but now I realized it lived upon our tongues like a capillary stretching back to a time when Irish was the lingua franca of the whole place. Suddenly the resentful nationalism of my Catholic minority experience was fused with a concept of identity that was enlarging and releasing and would eventually help me to relate my literary education with the heritage of the home ground.[59]

Later, Heaney would use this phrase again in relation to his place/language poems of *Wintering Out*, telling Dennis O'Driscoll that those poems that "harked back to the Irish language underlay and were laying claim to a *hidden Ulster*, the *Uladh* of *Doire Cholmcille* rather than the Londonderry of the Plantation and the Siege," but then immediately stating that "you're right to think of their energy as phonetic rather than political. . . . What happened in them was a kind of meltdown of memory-stuff and Ulster myths of belonging" (*SS*, 124–25; my emphasis).

In *An Open Letter* is Heaney therefore trying to again claim this "hidden Ulster" as a pagan site overlaid with Gaelic culture by invoking the phrase as he does in "The Sense of Place," or is it a more inclusive concept, an attempt "to do justice to all the elements of heritage in my natural speech" while still letting "the Irish . . . have its equal say," as he seems to affirm in his later use of the phrase "hidden Ulster" to O'Driscoll? The twenty-fourth stanza goes on to note, again borrowing the language of Yeats's "Leda and the Swan," that there after "a sudden blow, she collapsed with / The other island; and the South / 's been made a cuckold" (*AOL*, 11). Presumably his personification of the "hidden Ulster" as feminine suggests he continued to view it in the terms he had identified in "The Sense of Place" as the original pagan civilization overlaid with the Gaelic civilization in "Montague's region."[60]

And yet to suggest that both this "hidden Ulster" and "The other island" (Britain) collapsed after their encounter implies that both are unrecoverable because they are spent, exhausted; the fourth line of stanza 25, "All passion spent," confirms the point, while stanzas 26 and 27 show that there is no more living tradition of sectarian labels outside Ulster.

> Exhaustion underlies the scene.
> In Kensington, on Stephen's Green,
> The slogans have all ceased to mean
>   Or almost ceased—
> *Ulster is British* is a tune
>   Not quite deceased
>
> In Ulster, though on "the mainland"—
> Cf., above, "the other island"—

> Ulster is part of Paddyland,
> And Londonderry
> Is far away as New England
> Or County Kerry.
> (*AOL*, 12)

Heaney thus implies that the English perceive Northern Ireland as part of "Paddyland," or Ireland, and further suggests that even in the Republic of Ireland sectarian slogans are nearly meaningless. He also slyly implies that only Protestants in Northern Ireland still consider it British.

If Heaney is correct in noting that by the early 1980s the Republic of Ireland and England were largely neglecting the matter of Ulster (and there is ample evidence to suggest they were), why then does he make such a fuss over being included in an anthology of "British" poetry? By citing in stanza 29 Miroslav Holub's example of a man in the cinema who "yells out / When a beaver's called a muskrat / By the narrator," Heaney argues that he must set the record straight because "right names were the first foundation / For telling truth" (*AOL*, 12, 13).[61] But partly, too, because words matter, and even though he has chosen to write in English, he wants to be known as having a strongly Irish identity despite being raised in British Northern Ireland, especially given what he viewed as the Thatcher government's bungling of the conflict in Northern Ireland at the time of the poem's writing. By employing the periodical format and dialect words that characterized Joyce's two poetry broadsides "Gas from a Burner" and "The Holy Office," this Irish James makes clear that his regionalism has indelibly shaped his cultural and literary worldview, which compels him to protest at being termed simply "British."[62]

Indeed, the Holub allusion suggests that Heaney was drawing on the authority of regional literary exemplars beginning with Burns and Joyce to establish his own regionally inspired artistic independence. In this regard, Michael Molino argues that *An Open Letter* signifies Heaney's growing internationalism, observing that, "while he refuses to exclude his Irish voice, Heaney opens new vistas for himself and other writers when he speaks of a 'new commonwealth of art' and when he alludes to writers such as Miroslav Holub."[63] Beyond opening such vistas, Heaney must have been drawn specifically to Holub's independence, a quality he looked to both

Burns and Joyce for in writing *An Open Letter*. In his essay written in 1982 on Holub, "The Fully Exposed Poem," he approvingly points out "Holub's well-braced stance in the world, his suspecting weather-eye, the impression he gives of watchful self-reliance," which stem from his "bounded condition" that "makes him all the more anxious to preserve his inner freedom."[64] The phrases "suspecting weather-eye" and "watchful self-reliance" invoke the example of the independence of Louis O'Neill, Heaney's fisherman-friend whom he memorialized in "Casualty," and affirm Holub's independence as an artist working behind the Iron Curtain. Magdalena Kay has surprisingly little to say about Heaney's relationship with Holub— though Holub's artistic stance heavily influenced *An Open Letter* and occasioned the writing of "The Fully Exposed Poem"—but her general point about the appeal of Slavic poets in Britain, Ireland, and America in the 1970s suggests how their mysterious quality of Other was salutary for poets searching for a voice independent of inherited traditions. She argues that the "most obvious" reason for this "Slavic chic" involved the "mystery created by the metaphor of the Iron Curtain itself: Slavic countries were seen as definitely 'other' and took on the mystique of inaccessibility." More important, the high quality of these poets' work "was indubitable," and "*they*, too, underscored the separateness of their poetic tradition, particularly from that of the United States."[65]

Heaney's expanding sense of regionalism displayed in *An Open Letter* goes hand in glove with his growing realization that Irish literature and Irishness are part of international literature, the latter of which is signified by his review of Sean O'Tuama's and Thomas Kinsella's 1981 anthology of Irish poetry, *An Duanaire, 1600–1900: Poems of the Dispossessed*, when he observes, "We are led to the Irish poems not in order to warm ourselves at the racial embers but to encounter works of art that belong to world literature."[66] He specifically links himself and other poets from Northern Ireland to those from "Eastern bloc countries" like Osip Mandelstam when he observes that "there is an unsettled aspect to the different worlds they inhabit, and one of the challenges they face is to survive amphibiously, in the realm of 'the times' and the realm of their moral and artistic self-respect, a challenge immediately recognizable to anyone who has lived with the awful and demeaning facts of Northern Ireland's history over the last couple of decades."[67] Perhaps the way forward out of the continuing impasse in Northern Ireland in which citizens were too easily lumped into one of two abstract categories—Irish Catholic or British Protestant—might lie, not in trying to recover a "hidden Ulster," an entity that Heaney finally rejected in *An Open Letter*, but in trying to transcend national, religious, and cultural divides by evoking a concept of the region that was specific yet expansive, an "Ulster-yet-to-be," as it were.

Chapter Eight

AFFIRMING AND TRANSCENDING REGIONALISM

Joyce, Dante, Eliot, and the Tercet Form in
Station Island and *The Haw Lantern*

Station Island (1984) simultaneously registers the pervasive violence in Heaney's home region and seeks to articulate a wider regionalism, particularly by nearly framing the central, titular section through the literary figures of William Carleton and James Joyce (Carleton appears in the second lyric and Joyce in the twelfth and last lyric). It also gestures toward the third strand of Heaney's regionalism—the spirit region beyond our ken. Joyce's famous advice to Heaney to strike out on his own, however, creates the problem that the poet's developing concept of regionalism might remain part of a staid model of center/periphery, through which he would simply define himself as a marginal writer over against the cultural center. This chapter thus explores why Heaney meets Joyce at the end of the "Station Island" sequence and how Heaney's "The Regional Forecast," as well as his other essays on Joyce from this period, attempt to recover him as not merely an Irish writer but an enabling, transcultural writer who helped Heaney formulate regionalism in the 1980s and beyond as a condition that would prove exemplary for the evolving and finally devolving statelet of Northern Ireland. Joyce led Heaney almost ineluctably to Dante, and that great medieval poet gradually replaced Joyce as the dominant influence on Heaney's later poetry, although Joyce's shade continued to hover over Heaney. Bernard O'Donoghue has even claimed that "it is Dante above all who provides the larger scope, in language, politics and ethics, that warrants Heaney's making such great claims for the jurisdiction of poetry."[1] Heaney was increasingly drawn to Dante's emphasis on the vernacular in the form of terza rima, a local, yet transcendent form for Dante and then Heaney. Finally, T. S. Eliot's complicated influence as an apologist for regionalism was eventually an enabling stance for Heaney when writing "Station Island" and coming to develop his version of Dantean terza rima, which replaced Heaney's formerly favored quatrain as the poet's dominant form from the mid-1980s onward, even though he wrote occasionally in tercets after the early 1960s.

WHAT HEANEY LEARNED FROM WILLIAM CARLETON AND JOYCE ABOUT REGIONALISM

In the context of the inclusive theory of regionalism Heaney had been developing, the career of the nineteenth-century Ulster writer William Carleton is exemplary, if finally limiting. As John Wilson Foster argues in *Forces and Themes in Ulster Fiction*, Carleton's "courage and forthrightness have yet to be acknowledged."[2] He straddled "the deep divisions that lie like geological faults across the Irish, and particularly the Ulster, psychic landscape: those between nationalist and unionist, between Little Irelander and West Briton, between Protestant and Catholic, between North and South, between countryman and townsman."[3] After celebrating the peasant life of County Tyrone, Carleton later moved to Dublin. Additionally, he was raised Roman Catholic and converted to Protestantism. Carleton's position as a liminal writer mediating between polarities in politics, religion, and geography is striking and along with his courage in the face of religious and cultural discrimination constitutes his enduring literary legacy to the generations of Northern Irish writers who came after him, both before and after the partition of the province. Carleton's protean nature anticipates the sort of general openness needed in thoughtful Northern Irish writers throughout the twentieth century as they staked out important artistic positions that allowed them to stay faithful to their imaginations and *only then* powerfully and subtly to critique the entrenched political, religious, and cultural attitudes of the province.

Heaney claimed Carleton had exemplary regional qualities that derived from his early sense of the impoverished condition of Catholicism in the North of Ireland, despite his later conversion to the Church of Ireland, from his Irish-inflected English, and from his sense of quotidian life in the North. For example, in a 1980 essay, Heaney observes that Carleton's prose recollection of his pilgrimage to St. Patrick's Purgatory in the 1820s shows how "Carleton's country Catholic being responds in complete harmony to the humbled melodies of his own patient debilitated tribe. . . . [Carleton's significance lies in] the marks he bears in his sensibility and watermarks into his writing of experiences not archetypal but historical, not ennobling but disabling."[4] Even though "Carleton became a member of the Established Church and wrote at first to corroborate the attitudes of 'that lean controversialist,' Otway," he could not erase "the substance of what is being condemned: the music of that underworld which made Carleton was the music of his own humanity."[5] Heaney believes Carleton's "music" issued forth in his regional dialect: "His English does not consciously seek for Irish effects but has only recently emerged from the Irish language itself and if it has a less perfect finish than Synge's, it embodies what Synge admired in peasant speech—hyperbole, ebullience and range of intonation."[6] More recently, Heaney told Dennis O'Driscoll that William Carleton effectively auditioned for the part of guide through the sequence of spectral meetings in "Station Island" as Virgil did for Dante because of his intimate knowledge of not just Catholicism but Northern Irish Catholicism, and his subsequent break from that "tribe" and conversion to Anglicanism: Carleton, he points out, "was a cradle Catholic, a Northern Catholic, a man who had lived with and witnessed the uglier side of sectarianism, but still a man who converted to the Established Church and broke with 'our tribe's complicity' [a quote from Heaney's "Casualty"]. He had a wide-angle understanding of the whole Irish picture and a close-up intimacy with the vicious Northern side of it" (*SS*, 236).[7] By using the same language for Carleton that he did earlier in "Casualty" about Louis O'Neill's independent behavior after Bloody Sunday that resulted in his death from a bomb blast when he was drinking at a pub during a curfew the IRA had called, Heaney again calls attention to the constraining nature of Northern Irish Catholicism and privileges Carleton's escape from it as salutary.[8] Heaney also relates that after "I read the reissued *Autobiography* in the sixties, I felt I knew him inside out," and that his visit with his wife to Carleton's birthplace in County Tyrone confirmed that feeling because it "was like driving into our own yard at home, a whitewashed house, a door opening directly on to the street, a life that could have been your own going on inside" (*SS*, 236). This remark suggests that Carleton's own upbringing as a Northern Catholic and his home's location on the street kept him in touch with the intimate happenings of his surroundings, a quality reflected in his realistic use of an Hiberno-English dialect in his writing, just as Heaney felt similarly in touch with his own townland growing up in rural County Derry. The result of his immersing himself not only in Carleton's *Autobiography* (the edition that Heaney read was introduced by Patrick Kavanagh, Heaney's exemplar of parochialism) but also in *Traits and Stories of the Irish Peasantry* and Tom Flanagan's chapter on Carleton in his book about Irish novelists was that Carleton "turned into someone very strongly imagined, as much a *shuler* as a writer" (*SS*, 237).

Carleton thus appears in "Station Island" as a model regionalist writer because of his sure understanding of the intricacies of Northern Irish sectarianism and his rejection of them. He signifies Heaney's second strand of regionalism—the imagined, more ecumenical future Northern Ireland. Crucially, both he and Joyce appear to Heaney in a shower of rain, a positive sign of potential cultural and spiritual rebirth. Although Carleton is angry at Heaney for going on the same pilgrimage that the older writer immortalized in his *Lough Derg Pilgrim*, once "the air, softened by a shower of rain, / worked on his anger visibly," he confesses that "hard-mouthed Ribbonmen and Orange bigots / made me into the old fork-tongued turncoat / who mucked the byre of their politics" (*SI*, 65). The adjective *fork-tongued*, of course, has been used by Heaney himself in "Whatever You Say Say Nothing" to pejoratively refer to Northern Irish Catholics' doublespeak on the issue of the border, and his repetitions of this phrase here and close variations on it elsewhere suggest something of his own desire to go against his "tribe" in his work.[9] Here he rehabilitates the term from his earlier use of it in "Whatever You Say" to signify how Carleton betrayed both Catholic and Protestant fundamentalist bigots in a healthy way by joining the Church of Ireland.

Heaney quickly tells Carleton that "I have no mettle for the angry role" and notes that in his childhood years the Ribbonmen were reduced to "a frail procession / staggering home drunk on Patrick's Day // in collarettes and sashes fringed with green" (*SI*, 65).[10] He contrasts what he perceives as their lack of sectarianism with that of the Fenians: "Obedient strains like theirs tuned me first / and not that harp of unforgiving iron // the Fenians strung" (65–66). After he tells Carleton how much they have in common with their similar upbringings, Carleton agrees but replies that "you have to try to make sense of what comes. / Remember everything and keep your head" (66). This advice to remember the past but look forward to the future without losing one's mind is apposite for Heaney in the central section of a volume where he tries to do justice to several victims of the Troubles (among other friends he has lost) but also look forward to a future when he will not feel so constrained by the pressing sectarianism of Northern Ireland.

Even though the section concludes with Heaney switching tack by invoking the beauties of nature they both appreciated in the Northern Irish countryside, Carleton finally interrupts, arguing, "All this is like a trout kept in a spring / or maggots sown in wounds— / another life that cleans our element. // We are earthworms of the earth, and all that / has gone through us is what will be our trace" (*SI*, 66). Such language suggests that Heaney's Carleton deemphasizes the spiritual, focusing instead on the body and earth, the opposite position that Joyce takes in the concluding section by advocating fluidity and buoyancy to Heaney. Thus, despite all the positive connotations of Carleton's regionalism, particularly his rejection of tribal hatred, he finally is an earth-bound figure for Heaney who cannot help him expand his notion of regionalism beyond the example of other regional writers from the North like Kavanagh, Montague, Michael McLaverty, and others.

The spectral James Joyce in section 12 has traditionally been read as a being who frees Heaney from all manner of constraints, just as his creation Stephen Dedalus vowed to fly by the nets of nationality, language, and religion in *A Portrait of the Artist as a Young Man*.[11] I have previously argued that "Joyce, in the role of aesthetic priest . . . absolves Heaney from his enslavement to the past and from an absorption with 'postcolonial' musings,"[12] and I stand by that assessment, even as I now admit to a major reservation about Joyce's advice to Heaney. Although I am still convinced that both the ghostly Louis O'Neill in "Casualty" and Joyce's shade here function as "reminders for Heaney that his essential poetic posture is listening in isolation away from the alluring voice of the tribe," the geometric terms that Joyce employs when he warns, "Keep at a tangent. / When they make the circle wide, it's time to swim // out on your own" represent another net that by the 1980s Heaney found himself caught in and perhaps was turning to the eastern European poets to escape—the center/periphery binary (*SI* 93–94).[13] The difficulty in trying to escape the model that Joyce implicitly argues for here is compounded by his resemblance to Heaney's own father: Heaney describes him as using an "ash plant" for a walking stick as Heaney's own father did and even calls him "old father" (92). This phrase not only refers to Stephen Dedalus's final diary entry in *A Portrait* but also surely signifies that Joyce has become a father figure to him, a bond that is all the stronger given Heaney's feelings for his own father, who would die later in the 1980s. But whereas Stephen Dedalus surely does not realize that in writing "old father, old artificer" he is placing himself in the role of the soon-to-plummet Icarus, which suggests that his artistic plans will die, Heaney recognizes the danger of casting himself here as an Icarian figure who could fly metaphorically too close to the sun by absorbing himself in a given cause.[14]

In his brief analysis of Heaney's endorsement of "Joyce's solution: a self-confident redefinition of the centre-periphery relation," Hans-Werner Ludwig cites the phrase I already have cited as an epigraph to the introduction to this study from Heaney's "The Regional Forecast" about talent having to imagine reality from a Ptolemaic, not a Copernican condition.[15] Ludwig does not invoke Joyce's advice to Heaney to "swim out on your own" at the end of "Station Island," but that recommended trajectory also fits his articulation of the "centre-periphery" binary and gives additional weight to his closing remark that "Heaney is still arguing within the matrix of centre and periphery." The question he then poses for Heaney is one that he will wrestle with in the last section of *Station Island*, "Sweeney Redivivus," and afterward: "Under which conditions may it be possible to move completely beyond this frame of reference?"[16]

Heaney recognizes this center/periphery problem for regional writers who would define themselves simply against canonical English literature when he writes in one of his most important essays, "The Redress of Poetry," that "whether they are feminists rebelling against the patriarchy of language or nativists in full cry with the local accents of their vernacular, whether they write Anglo-Irish or Afro-English or Lallans, writers of what has been called 'nation language' will have been wrong-footed by the fact that their own literary formation was based upon models of excellence taken from the English language and its literature. They will have been predisposed to accommodate themselves to the consciousness which subjugated them."[17] Appropriately for our purposes in this chapter in understanding Joyce as a regional writer who modeled an attention to both the local and the wider world, Heaney quickly invokes Joyce a few passages later, noting that

> in any movement towards liberation, it will be necessary to deny the normative authority of the dominant language or literary tradition. At a special moment in the Irish Literary Revival, this was precisely the course adopted by Thomas MacDonagh.... With more seismic consequences, it was also the course adopted by James Joyce.... Joyce, for all his hauteur about the British Empire and the English novel, was helpless to resist the appeal of, for example, the songs and airs of the Elizabethans. Neither MacDonagh nor Joyce considered it necessary to proscribe within his reader's memory the riches of the Anglophone culture whose authority each was, in his own way, compelled to challenge. Neither denied his susceptibility to the totally persuasive word in order to prove the purity of his resistance to an imperial hegemony. Which is why both these figures are instructive when we come to consider the scope and function of poetry in the world. They remind us that its integrity is not to be impugned just because at any given moment it happens to be a refraction of some discredited cultural or political system.[18]

I quote this passage at such length because Heaney seems to stand so strongly behind this *apologia* for most poetry's inherently mixed nature in reflecting all the varying cultural, political, and literary influences upon it, and certainly upon his own poetry. He both denies "the normative authority of the dominant language or literary tradition" and at the same time defends poetry's use of suasive rhetoric from any inherited tradition.

Poetry that both denies the dominant literary tradition and draws upon it confounds the center/periphery model. Certainly, Heaney's decision to base "Station Island" on the St. Patrick's Purgatory pilgrimage continues and complicates a tradition that, as Conor McCarthy has suggested, animates the passage in which Hamlet wonders whether, "by Saint Patrick," his father's ghost has come from purgatory in English literature's central work, Shakespeare's *Hamlet*.[19]

Once again, Joyce proved exemplary for Heaney in this process as he attempted to become the same sort of visionary regional writer. In "The Regional Forecast," Heaney finally sees Joyce as a universal writer drawing on Aristotle, Thomas Aquinas, and the European literary tradition who did not seek "the sop of ethnic self-respect but an alternative literary tradition, which, with good luck, may some day become for others an indigenous one."[20] Heaney's own interest in the eastern European tradition was a powerful affirmation of the truthfulness of art in times of oppression, but more important here is his interest in the great Italian Dante, whose tripartite structure in *The Divine Comedy* underlies *Station Island* and whose series of meetings in that great work with shades of the underworld underlies the central section of Heaney's volume.

Heaney's search for a new poetic form coalesced with his evolving concept of regionalism at some time in the late 1970s and especially by the early 1980s with his turn away from his favored form through most of the 1970s, the heavy quatrain, and toward the lighter form of the tercet, which he had used periodically from the beginning of his career but not to the extent that he did starting at this time. Dante's use of terza rima must have influenced Heaney to himself begin using a modified type of that form in his recourse to the tercet in particular poems from the first two sections of *Station Island* and throughout "Sweeney Redivivus." This poetic unit, halfway between the blocky, enclosed quatrain and the terse couplet, formally signifies how Heaney had begun stripping himself of those constraining cultural dissonances he had inherited in Northern Ireland and indicates how he then began opening himself to a larger, yet nonetheless vernacular, tradition epitomized by a contemporary adaptation of Dante's terza rima. His formal adaptation of the tercet is thus, startlingly, a regional maneuver for him, in the most enabling and positive senses of the term.

HEANEY'S VARIED USES OF THE TERCET FORM

Heaney turned to a variation on Dante's terza rima when writing many poems from the middle and last sections of *Station Island* because of his conviction that that form was inherently vernacular, regional, and attentive not only to local politics, geography, and culture but also to the region that lies beyond this life. Surprisingly, Jason David Hall, in his excellent discussion of Heaney's prosody in *Seamus Heaney's Rhythmic Contract*, offers nothing substantive about Heaney's use of the tercet verse form, which, along with the quatrain, sonnet, and ottava rima, is one of his four favorite forms, and there is precious little critical discussion of Heaney's recourse to this form. Although Rui Carvalho Homem commends Heaney for his use of the form in sections of "Station Island," calling it a "simplified and fluent approximation of *terza rima*," he wrongly believes that Heaney turned to the tercet only at this point in his career, pointing out that the form "has had notable continuities in his poetry, when we consider the number of pieces in three-line groups (rhymed, unrhymed, assonantal) in all of his subsequent collections."[21] In fact, Heaney used the form in his earliest poetry and off and on throughout his later work until *Station Island*, when it became a dominant form. Moreover, what Neil Corcoran, usually one of Heaney's best and most sure-footed critics, has to say specifically on Heaney's tercet use in "Station Island" is inadequate for appreciating the complexity of the poet's skill in employing subtle variations on the form in that lyric sequence. Bernard O'Donoghue makes very helpful and thoughtful remarks on the same issue in his *Seamus Heaney and the Language of Poetry*, but there is no thoroughgoing assessment of the form in studies of Heaney.

He had long experimented with the tercet, going back even to his earliest poetry, particularly in poems that deal with fluidity and movement. For example, in *Death of a Naturalist* alone, he used the tercet form throughout "Saint Francis and the Birds," a poem that presages his later "St. Kevin and the Blackbird" in *Seeing Things*; "Waterfall"; "Mid-Term Break," about the death of a younger brother; "Lovers on Aran"; and "The Early Purges"; twice among the varying stanza lengths of "Digging"; and once in "At a Potato Digging," and in "Cow at Calf." He employs the form too in the early poems "Corncrake" and "May Day," also from this period. "Corncrake" is composed of nine lines—three three-lined stanzas—while "May Day" runs fifteen lines—five three-lined stanzas.[22] When Heaney would settle on his final "macro-form" for showing off his modified tercets, he would settle on a form exactly in between the lengths of "Corncrake" and "May Day"—twelve lines constructed out of four three-lined stanzas. Of all these early poems that use the tercet, "St. Francis and the Birds" most closely resembles terza rima in its use of that form's rhyme scheme: the rhyme "up" from the end of line 2 faintly anticipates the opening rhyme in the first line of the next stanza, "lips," which in turn is set in a faint pararhyme with "capes" at the end of that three-line stanza (*DN*, 40). The end rhyme of the second line of this second stanza, "head," roughly sets up the opening end rhyme of the third tercet, "played," which in turn rhymes fully with the third end rhyme in this stanza, "made." The end rhyme on line 2 of this stanza, "flight," then fully chimes with the rhyme in the "dangling" last line, "light" (40). Such usage of tercet variations on terza rima in his early and mid-1960s poetry that was grounded fairly specifically in his native region of Northern Ireland suggests that even then, unconsciously perhaps, Heaney saw it as a vernacular form that could carry and transmit well his regionalist sensibility through his continuing fidelity to the geographic and cultural region of Northern Ireland in all its linguistic complexity.

We see his continued usage of the form in "Undine" and "The Given Note," both from *Door into the Dark*, and perhaps most auspiciously in "The Other Side," Heaney's marvelous long poem about Catholic-Protestant relations in the North that was collected in *Wintering Out*. All three of these poems traffic in fluidity and transformation, whether the female water nymph having received a soul in "Undine" after she bears a man's child; the "spirit music" that "rephrases itself into the air" in "The Given Note" (*DD*, 34); or the way in "The Other Side" that the Protestant neighbor, who during the day dismisses the Heaneys by commenting about their land, "It's poor as Lazarus, this ground," but at nighttime deferentially waits to approach them until they are finished saying the rosary, signaling a potential model for a transcendence of calcified Catholic/Protestant relationships (*WO*, 34–36).[23]

Heaney's interest in the form stems from his long immersion in Dante's poetry. He delighted in the Italian poet's music and wordplay, and though he was not drawn to the descriptions of the torments of the dead being punished in hell, he observed that "for a while I was so exhilarated by the whole marvel of Dante that I was tempted to have a go at doing the complete *Inferno*—simply for its own imaginative splendor" (*SS*, 425). His joy in Dante reminds us of one of his greatest qualities as a writer— the desire to show others that same delight and have us experience it too. And he did actually translate and contribute three cantos to a 1993 collection of contemporary versions of the *Inferno*.[24] Interestingly, although Heaney would later take Eliot to task for not using language sufficiently local in his adaptation of Dante in "Little Gidding," his own translations of the first three cantos of the *Inferno* depart from Dorothy Sayers's insistence, in her introduction to her translation that was instrumental in leading Heaney deeply into Dante, that translators of the great poet be attentive to the variations in his style, including his use of the vernacular and colloquial. Her own translation "is considerably more local than Heaney's and more lyrical. She uses more alliteration and more colloquial, blunt Anglo-Saxon words," as one commentator observes.[25] When Heaney turned his hand to incorporating a modified form of terza rima into the central section of *Station Island*, however, he allowed the colloquial to reenter and impart color and a vernacular energy to his language, even though his tercet form takes considerable liberties with Dantean terza rima.

This existing motivation in Heaney to form extratextual communities of readers by evoking the "imaginative splendor" of Dante was likely reinforced in his reading of the specific encounters imagined in the *Commedia* by the Italian poet, who, as Susan Stewart has argued, invented what she terms "the poetry of meeting," which "involves a lived encounter or exchange and so includes an open possibility of transformation by means of language."[26] As she goes on to posit, "Visions and beholding may be involved in these poems of meeting; but because the speakers of such poems are not alone, sublime experiences do not lead to silence and speechlessness."[27] Heaney's portrayal of himself as silent in earlier poems—most anxiously in "Punishment," where he says that if he had been present at the scene of the victim's execution he "would have cast . . . the stones of silence," and throughout "Whatever You Say Say Nothing"—changes dramatically in the conversational poems of meeting that compose the sequence "Station Island." Even as he continued to look inward in assessing his vocation as a poet, he did so in the context of community in these poems that are indebted to Dante's great *Commedia* and its inherently conversational line.

Even more important, it was not until Heaney became a serious student of Dante that he realized he could use variations on terza rima that would evoke connotations beyond the literal region of Northern Ireland and further suggest the region of eternity, where flickering shades beckon the poet, especially in "Station Island," the long middle section of his volume bearing the same title. Heaney told Carla de Petris in 1989 that reading Sayers's translation of Dante in 1972 after his move to the Republic quickly drew him into the Italian poet's work.[28] By 1974, when he was led to the Neolithic settlement Seamus Caulfield had discovered underneath the bog at Belderg, Heaney was sufficiently immersed in *The Divine Comedy* to cast Caulfield as Virgil and himself as Dante and to draw a parallel between those Neolithic people and Dante's ghosts: "As we moved among the pattern of the stone age fields and the trunks of the primeval woods, the presences of the original diggers and dwellers materialized as powerfully out of the rain on the hillside as Dante's doomed shades out of the glimmer of the infernal regions."[29] Formally, Heaney's deep interest in Dante shows in both "The Strand at Lough Beg" and "Ugolino" in *Field Work*, which display modified versions of terza rima within their uneven, long stanzas. "The Strand" is preceded by an epigraph drawn from Sayers's translation of the *Purgatorio* (*FW*, 17).[30] After the first four unrhymed lines, this poem features a series of tercets with rhyming first and third lines, each of which contains a completely new set of rhymes, unlike true terza rima. Thus lines 5 and 7 conclude with the masculine rhyme of "track" and "pack"; lines 8 and 10 close with the feminine pararhyme of "squealing" and "stalling"; lines 11 and 13 finish with the masculine pararhyme of "gun" and "down"; and lines 14 and 16 conclude with the full masculine rhyme of "knew" and "yew" (17). There are a series of such tercets in the second half of the poem and two couplets. Likewise, the five sections of "Ugolino," Heaney's version of lines from the *Inferno*, cantos 32 and 33, similarly feature many full and pararhymed "buried" tercets that are disguised by virtue of their nondemarcated lineation and their interruption by extra, nonrelated rhymes. And significantly, the title poem, "Field Work," has two lyrics in its sequence of four lyrics that are lineated as terza rima, down to the dangling last line (52, 54), but these stanzas have no rhymes at all in them. After using the tercet to some extent in his 1960s poetry, Heaney was clearly experimenting with variations on Dantean terza rima by the late 1970s. Michael Parker even argues that "throughout *Field Work*, he enjoys *ulsterizing* Dante."[31] The poems of *Station Island*, then, should be seen as an outgrowth of this periodic experimentation, not as a completely new departure for Heaney.

Heaney has long been drawn to discussing rural crafts in Northern Ireland, such as digging, divining, thatching, and blacksmithing, to name but a few, as analogues to the making of poetry, and the emphasis on the local and vernacular in Dante, who lards his terza rimas that drive the *Divine Comedy* with references to the Florentine wool industry, must have appealed to him. As Robin Kirkpatrick has noted in his introduction to his translation of the *Commedia*, Dante "is inclined to describe words in terms drawn from the wool-making industry that dominated the Florentine economy: some words are silky, some are combed out and some are 'hairy,' as if they shared their characteristics with velvet or Harris Tweed. These are striking and even polemical metaphors. The Florence Dante hated depended on the trade in cloth; the fabric of Dante's poetry will offer a philosophical and linguistic alternative."[32] While Heaney certainly does not hate Northern Ireland as Dante grew to hate Florence before his exile from it, his ambiguous and complicated relationship to it is explored in two earlier poems, "The Wool Trade" and "Linen Town." Belfast's and Northern Ireland's historic dependence on the linen industry produced a high number of weavers and tailors in the eighteenth and nineteenth centuries; thus Heaney's interest in "the fabric of Dante's poetry" certainly may have emerged in part from his realization that historically, Northern Ireland, beset with divisions like Dante's Florence, shared with his regional exemplar par excellence a passion for cloth making.

That Heaney linked conflict to the tercet form is evidenced by the only tercet poem in *North*, "Ocean's Love to Ireland," and by "The Strand at Lough Beg" and "Ugolino," the two disguised tercet poems of *Field Work*. "Ocean's Love," surrounded as it is by the many quatrain poems of *North*, negatively expresses fluidity and transformation, as Ralegh, representing England, rapes the maid, representing Ireland. If, by the conclusion, "the ground" is "possessed and repossessed," the completely nonrhyming tercets of this poem about England's historic imperial domination of Ireland suggest a broken transformation of Ireland, a fracturing into "the plashy spots where he would lay / His cape before her" (*N* 41, 40). Similarly, Colum McCartney's murder by a loyalist death squad—his transformation from living, breathing human being into elegized shade—as portrayed in "The Strand at Lough Beg" is reinforced by that poem's habitual use of "hidden" tercets. And the horrific devouring of Archbishop Roger by Count Ugolino in the last of these three poems is also largely cast in disguised tercets, signifying the transformation of these former lofty personages into the linked, frozen-together pair that occupies the Ninth Circle at the bottom of the pit of hell, which holds traitors' souls. The closeness of the two bitter enemies likely also suggests the intimate enmity between victim and killer during the Northern Ireland Troubles. Heaney himself noted that "I translated 'Ugolino' in order for it to be read in the context of the 'dirty protests' in the Maze prison" in 1979 (*SS*, 425).

He was not alone, of course, in noting the applicability of Dante's *Commedia*, particularly the *Inferno*, to the troubled region of Northern Ireland: his younger contemporary, the Belfast-born poet Ciaran Carson, translated the entire *Inferno* and compares contemporary Belfast to Dante's medieval Florence because of their shared sectarian divisions in his introduction to that translation. Carson muses that as he hears a British Army helicopter hovering overhead while he writes, "I imagine being airborne in the helicopter, like Dante riding on the flying monster Geryon, looking down into the darkness of that place in Hell called Malebolge. 'Rings of ditches, moats, trenches, fosses / military barriers on every side': I see a map of North Belfast, its no-go zones and tattered flags, the blackened side-streets, cul-de-sacs and bits of wasteland stitched together by dividing walls and fences. For all the blank abandoned spaces it feels claustrophobic, cramped and medieval."[33] Well before Carson's translation, by the time of *Field Work* and *Station Island*, Heaney almost certainly knew and recognized an analogue to the close-fought conflict in Northern Ireland in the civil war between the Guelfs and Ghibellines and then later in the internecine strife between the so-called Whites and Blacks of the Canellieri family, eventually joined by the Florentine Guelfs, which led to "a whole series of disturbances, so that the city [of Florence] was divided into two armed camps."[34]

Heaney also likely identified with Dante's position as an exile from the dominant city of his region: Dante (involuntarily) from Florence by

1302 and himself (voluntarily) from Belfast in 1972. He likely approved and identified with Sayers's description of Dante's "fatal defect," which "was that of being insufficiently party-minded"; even though "he was born and brought up Guelf, and he liked the sturdy native quality of the Guelfs, their tang of the soil . . . their rooted republican constitutionalism and their modern liberal outlook . . . [,] he was drawn to the Ghibellines and liked their princeliness—the large mind, the magnificent aristocratic gesture; the patronage of art and learning . . . and later, he came to be passionately of their mind in desiring to see a united Italy as part of a united Empire, free from Papal interference in the political sphere."[35] There are too many differences between medieval Florence and contemporary Belfast to determine an exact correspondence between Dante's independence and Heaney's similar privileging of artistic autonomy. But surely Heaney, who was rooted in local, Catholic Gaelic culture like the Guelf-born Dante but who also drew on British liberalism and the English literary tradition, found a powerful exemplar of artistic autonomy in the exiled Dante.[36]

In his 1985 review of Tom Phillips's illustrated edition of Dante's *Inferno*, published only a year after his own experimentations in and deviations from terza rima in *Station Island*, Heaney noted that "the bell of the Italian language is necessarily muted in English. The lovely carillon of *terza rima*, its feminine endings, its linkages and deliquescence (which give the poetry its essential phonetic joyousness) cannot be properly sounded in an Anglo-Saxon register. It is usually best to settle for a good loping narrative pace and an unadorned but not untutored diction."[37] His approval of Phillips's work—"This is exactly what Tom Phillips has done in an excellent obedient new translation of *The Inferno*"[38]—suggests that Heaney himself is largely describing his own process in adapting terza rima into English in *Station Island*, even though he would later lament his own attempts at directly translating about three cantos or 429 lines from the *Inferno* because "I couldn't establish a measure that combined plain speaking with fluent movement. I just couldn't match the shapes that the bright container of the *terza rima* contained" (*SS*, 425–26).[39] The "good loping narrative pace and an unadorned but not untutored diction" that he describes in 1985 and the "plain speaking" diction "with fluent movement" that he privileges many years later in interview are qualities that his own versions of terza rima in *Station Island* share, and they reflect his sense that this, of all poetic forms, is the one most suited to presenting his re-

Affirming and Transcending Regionalism 255

gionalist concerns. Heaney's tercets thus reflect his love of the vernacular inherent in his conflicted home region of Northern Ireland, while they also imply, in the poems of "Station Island," a hope for a future, more peaceful region through his meeting with ghosts from the spirit region. This form therefore brings together his three strands of regionalism.

Although Dante is perhaps best known for his *Inferno* and Heaney chose to translate the first three cantos from it, he finally seems most interested in his *Purgatorio*, as the epigraph to "The Strand at Lough Beg" and the long central section of *Station Island* attest. This interest is another aspect of his affinity with Dante that has never been sufficiently explored in Heaney criticism, but two passages from Sayers's introduction to her translation of the *Purgatorio* may suggest why he prefers this part of Dante's epic. Sayers notes that this section is, for readers who come to the poem in English, both "the least known" and "the least quoted," noting further that "if one is drawn to the *Purgatorio* at all, it is by the cords of love, which will not cease drawing till they have drawn the whole poem into the same embrace." She believes it is the "tenderest, subtlest, and most human section of the *Comedy*."[40] Heaney, sick of the inferno of Northern Ireland by this point in his career, may have chosen to devote himself to meeting Dantean-like shades most directly in the second section of his own tripartite volume because of the *Purgatory*'s sheer tenderness and humanity, which would enable him to respond similarly to the ghosts from his and the province's past. He also realized, along with Sayers, that "in the matter of sheer artistry, the second *cantica*, by comparison with the first, displays a livelier invention, increased architectural skill, greater freedom of handling and technique, a smoother and more assured mastery of the verse.... The *Purgatorio* is, from the start, much more firmly consolidated; the poet is doing exactly what he chooses, as he chooses, and when he chooses, with perfect awareness throughout of what he is doing."[41] By calling his own volume *Station Island* and locating its middle part on St. Patrick's Purgatory in Lough Derg, traditionally thought to be the site of the entrance to Purgatory, Heaney calls attention to its *Purgatorio*-like title section, where he displays his own great freedom and artistry in handling and modifying Dantean terza rima.

If he was drawn to the *Purgatory* for these reasons, he was especially drawn to Sayers's translation because of her own lightsome handling of terza rima, and he departs further than did she from any strict version of this form in "Station Island," just as he did in earlier poems drawing on that form. Heaney pointed out how much he liked her translation and its terza rima, noting that "It has no pretentions to decorum. There is a touch of Gilbert and Sullivan in the rhyming—she's just sketching it out. The feeling is that she is saying to you: 'It goes more or less like this, and it rhymes more or less like this.' Its swiftness makes it very readable."[42] Such a reading of Sayers's terza rima suggests further how Heaney saw that her more strict usage of the form, which admittedly makes departures from true terza rima by some recourse to pararhyme, for example, gave him warrant for his own wider and more varied employment of the form. Corcoran has argued, however, in his overall assessment of Heaney's tercet use in *Station Island*, that "there are occasional uncertainties in the handling of verse form, particularly in Heaney's sometimes ragged variations on the Dantean *terza rima*," further holding that "the form is notoriously difficult in English, but Heaney's variations on it are bound to summon much too closely for comfort Eliot's tremendous imitative approximation of it in the second section of 'Little Gidding,' and Yeats's use of it in a poem Heaney admires in *Preoccupations*, 'Cuchulain Comforted.'"[43] Corcoran cannot have it both ways: to claim that Heaney's tercets are too imitative both of Eliot's handling of the form in "Little Gidding" and of Yeats's in "Cuchulain Comforted" misleads, since Heaney's tercets are actually not as close to Eliot's blank verse versions of terza rima as Corcoran believes, while Yeats's stanzas adhere fairly closely to the *aba bcb cdc*, etc. rhyme scheme of true Dantean *terza rima*, despite a few half-rhymes that he introduces. Heaney thus learned how to modify his own tercets, in part, from Eliot's tercet form in "Little Gidding" but also from Yeats's "Cuchulain Comforted," where he learned in what context he should use it: not only to plumb the intricacies of local places, but also to address situations involving last things and the apprehension of the spirit region.

ELIOT'S REGIONALISM AND TERZA RIMA

Heaney is well aware of the dangers of imitating Eliot, or, for that matter, the master himself, Dante. As we will see, however, he feels that Dante himself is a figure who took unorthodox positions and reveled in artistic freedom; imitating Dante for Heaney thus really is the highest form of flattery. To take the second literary figure first, Heaney would note in October 1986, in "The Government of the Tongue," one of his T. S. Eliot Memorial Lectures delivered at the University of Kent, about Osip Mandelstam's approach to Dante, that "a traditional approach to Dante . . . might involve some attention to the logical, theological and numerological significances which devolve from the number 3, there being three Persons in the Holy Trinity, three lines in each stanza of *The Divine Comedy*, three books in the whole poem, thirty-three cantos in each book, and a rhyme scheme called *terza rima*. All this can press upon the mind until Dante is gradually conceived of as some kind of immense scholastic computer."[44] The disapproval fairly drips off this last phrase and Heaney quickly hastens to tell us that Mandelstam rejected this notion of Dante "as the great example of a poet whose tongue is governed by an orthodoxy or system," observing that, for example, Mandelstam affirms Dante's terza rima not only by reclaiming the form as vernacular but also by suggesting that "the three-edged stanza is formed from within, like a crystal, not cut on the outside like a stone. The poem is not governed by external conventions and impositions but follows the laws of its own need."[45] This important last statement, and the general thrust of my argument below, together suggest that Heaney's use of a heavily modified terza rima, really better called "individually rhyming, self-contained tercets" (to coin a hugely awkward term), in the middle and third sections of *Station Island*, "follows the laws of its own need" and thus freely imitates and borrows from both Dante and Eliot, for that matter. Thus Heaney's only obedience in adapting Dante's terza rima and Eliot's variation on that form in "Little Gidding" for "Station Island" and "Sweeney Redivivus" is to the natural growth and need of the poems themselves.

Critically, Heaney's use of Eliot has often been invoked to illuminate his conception of the auditory imagination, a term that he explores at some length in his 1988 "Learning from Eliot" address, which becomes a crucial aspect of our understanding of Heaney's tercet use in *Station Island*. As part of his marked engagement with Eliot, Heaney has articulated an extremely complex and evolving view of him as a regional writer.

This turn toward Eliot is signaled by Heaney in a passage from "Little Gidding" that he originally was going to publish as an epigraph to *North* but then decided against. It begins, "This is the use of memory: / For liberation" and continues through "the faces and places, with the self which, as it could, loved them, / To become renewed, transfigured, in another pattern."[46] Although Anthony Cuda has argued in his analysis of this deleted epigraph that Eliot's use of memory enabled the younger poet to develop a "generative principle of love and self-renewal" as he began writing Part I of *North*, Heaney's original decision to employ it also suggests how even in the early 1970s he was looking toward Eliot to determine how that poet, of New England stock, born in the American Midwest, educated at Harvard, and settled in England, negotiated the various regions he occupied.[47] Heaney concludes his important, uncollected 1987 essay "Place, Pastness, Poems: A Triptych" by quoting the same passage from "Little Gidding" that he originally had planned to use as an epigraph for *North*. He leads into those lines via a discussion of how the American poet John Crowe Ransom negotiated his "regional culture" by employing a literary tradition to connect local and wider cultures at "that moment when, politically and culturally, the centre could not hold, when one place could no longer be proved more than another place, when St. Louis and Dublin and Wyncote, Pennsylvania could each affirm its rights to it all and Paterson, New Jersey could, with equal and opposite confidence, proclaim an independence of it."[48] "St. Louis" implicitly invokes Eliot, born and reared there, and to clarify his affirmation of Eliot as a regional poet Heaney immediately notes that "a quarter of a century after he had thought it all out in 'Tradition and the Individual Talent,' Eliot with equal authority but new and mind-sweetening simplicity, summed it all up." He then cites the "Little Gidding" passage about the use of memory.[49] Heaney's formulation of the region here, with its affirmation of local culture, confirms its (and Eliot's) centrality to his thought, its connection to the wider world, and finally, its independence from a slavish attachment to that larger, usually more homogeneous culture. By connecting his own regionalism to Eliot's in the now-deleted epigraph to *North*, elucidated by his essay, Heaney himself makes recourse to that tradition in the same way he believes the regional poets Ransom and Eliot did, yet in the process finally affirms his independence of them, although he will continue looking to Eliot especially to formulate his own developing concept of regionalism for decades to come.

Heaney's interaction with Eliot in a regional context continues with his 1980 review, "Treely and Rurally," of C. H. Sisson's translation of *The Divine Comedy* and George Holmes's *Dante*, which Henry Hart persuasively reads as an attack on Eliot for ignoring the parochial elements in Dante, a view that Heaney would further develop in his 1985 essay "Envies and Identifications: Dante and the Modern Poet."[50] There Heaney rejects what he sees as Eliot's refusal to make his tercets in "Little Gidding" more local and regional even as he simultaneously approves of Eliot's "indigenous language." Moreover, as I will argue later in a close reading of this essay on Dante, Heaney came to believe in terza rima and, by extension, variants on it as a liberating, vernacular form first articulated by Dante, and his praise of Dante and qualified praise of Eliot in that essay finally accord with his approval of Eliot's more general *apologia* for regionalism, although it took him some time to admit this. In his 1986 essay "The Impact of Translation," however, Heaney thoroughly rejects Eliot's tercets in favor of the Scottish poet Edwin Muir's reclamation of a vernacular European tradition in his poem "The Interrogation." But by 1989, in his essay "The Regional Forecast," Heaney privileges Eliot's defense of regionalism, drawing on important Eliot essays like "The Social Function of Poetry," "The Music of Poetry," and *Notes toward a Definition of a Christian Culture*.

I want to turn first to "The Impact of Translation," because its rejection of Eliot as a regional writer is so sweeping: there Heaney argues that Eliot's blank verse tercets in "Little Gidding" illustrate "how effective the beauties of the poetic heritage could be in keeping at bay the actual savagery of the wartime experience. There, in the Dantesque set-pieces of the dawn patrol, Hitler's Luftwaffe could be sent packing as a dark dove beneath the horizon of its homing, and the All Clear after an air raid could recompose the morning by recourse to matutinal airs which had once drifted from the dew of a high eastern hill towards the battlements of Elsinore."[51] Heaney's objection here uncannily parallels the criticism of his bog poems—that he revels too much in the beauty and mystery of those savagely killed victims that were transformed into such graphic images through the preservative properties of Danish and Irish bogs.[52] Is Heaney indirectly and retrospectively admonishing himself for a somewhat similar stance that some critics feel he condoned in *North*? It is difficult to tell, but he is clearly concerned here to defend regional poetry that he associates with an independent artistic stance, as he does when suggesting Holub's influence on *An Open Letter*, for instance. Eliot functions as a convenient whipping boy over against the Orkney-born Muir and the whole tradition of eastern European poets such as Czesław Miłosz, whose poem "Incantation" Heaney cites to begin "The Impact of Translation." For Heaney, Miłosz's poem typifies "work by many other poets, particularly in the Soviet Union and the Warsaw Pact countries, whose poetry not only witnesses the poet's refusal to lose his or her cultural memory but also testifies thereby to the continuing efficacy of poetry itself as a necessary and fundamental human act."[53] It seems, then, that Heaney finally faults Eliot's tercets in "Little Gidding" for not sufficiently registering in powerful, independent language both the atrocities of the Blitz and the necessity for continuing to write poetry in such a time. Although Heaney may have wished that Eliot had written a graphic war poem about London during the Blitz, the elder poet chose to write a wartime poem focusing on his Dantesque communion with ghosts, which was certainly his prerogative. Moreover, Heaney's critique of "the dark dove" imagery misleads. That dark dove is not so much "sent packing"; rather, Eliot's blank-verse tercets register its terrifying, destructive fire, which is then gradually transformed into the mystical, healing flames of the Holy Spirit by the conclusion.

While Corcoran cites Heaney's essay on Dante to illuminate how Heaney values Dante's emphasis on the local and particular, he curiously neglects how closely this article interrogates Eliot's use of Dante in the second section of "Little Gidding."[54] In his essay, Heaney explicitly charges Eliot with not being sufficiently attentive to the local conditions of London during the Blitz, which is consistent with his overall affirmation of Eliot's regionalism in "The Regional Forecast." In this sense, Heaney's real objection is to Eliot's abstract, artificially universal use of language in what he considers a local, vernacular form—his modified terza rima. For example, Heaney damningly notes that the "language conducts us away from what is contingent; it is not mimetic of the cold morning cityscape but of the calescent imagination. We can say, as a matter of literary fact, that the lines are more haunted by the flocks of Dante's *terza rima* than by the squadrons of Hitler's Luftwaffe."[55] Heaney quickly continues: "We can also say that the language of the poem is more affected by Eliot's idea of

Dante's language than it is by the actual sounds and idioms of those Londoners among whom Eliot lived and over whom he was watching during his 'dead patrol.' "[56] If we go along with Corcoran's contention, we could now say that Heaney's lines "are haunted more by the flocks of Eliot's *terza rima* variations" than by those of Dante, but that would be misleading because even if Heaney's actual tercets are closer in form to Eliot's than to Dante's, which, as it turns out, they are not, his word use within them is characteristically local, vernacular in the same way as Dante's language.

Three experts on terza rima, Steve Ellis, Ciaran Carson, and Michael Hurley, echo Heaney's contention above, in his 1985 review of Tom Phillips's translation of the *Inferno*, that the form must have "an unadorned but not untutored diction," and two of them, Carson and Hurley, additionally affirm with Heaney that the form must have "a good loping narrative pace." For example, in the introduction to his 1995 translation of the *Inferno* that he titles *Hell*, Ellis, who is from northern England, points out the poem's "regional dimension," observing that "the fact that Dante's poem used a specifically Florentine speech and language, that is, a dialect, has allowed me to draw on my own native Yorkshire background."[57] While Ellis generally eschews "individual dialect words and expressions" and has "drawn rather on this background for the basic speech-tones which are employed," he nonetheless affirms that "this translation is bonded within a particular speech community."[58] Carson, moreover, approves of both Dante's privileging of local, vernacular language and its walking rhythm, observing in his introduction to his translation of the *Inferno* that "the Italian or Florentine of the *Inferno* . . . has a relentless, peripatetic, ballad-like energy, going to a music which is by turns mellifluous and rough, taking in both formal discourse and the language of the street."[59] And Hurley has pointed out that "whereas Homer and Virgil had written their great epics in the stateliest diction, Dante chose the *vulgare illustre* (a marked departure even from his own pronouncements in the *Convivio*, where he assents to the medieval notion that Latin is the nobler and more rational language) and makes plain his purpose from the opening line. Confounding the epic convention, '*Nel mezzo del cammin di nostra vita*' alerts us to the immediacy of a story being told without fanfare or poeticized strain: it begins *in medias res*, and proceeds in the simplest terms."[60] Heaney's own *Commedia* begins similarly, with a description of himself and his wife running through a tunnel in the London Underground to get to the Proms at the Royal Albert Hall in London for a concert: "There we were in the vaulted tunnel running, / You in your going-away coat speeding ahead / And me" (*SI*, 13). Certainly, however, their joint running almost comically contrasts Dante's solitary fear at the beginning of the *Divine Comedy* when he panics before dangerous animals at the entrance to hell, from which no one ever returns.

Heaney's and his wife's running in this opening poem is replaced by his "walking barefoot" as contemporary Catholic pilgrims do through the stations of St. Patrick's Purgatory or Station Island on Lough Derg in County Donegal (*SI*, 122), and this pedestrian rhythm may have also drawn him to Dante's own more rigidly rhyming terza rima. In his essay on Dante, Heaney approvingly cites a series of passages from Mandelstam's 1979 "Conversation on Dante,"[61] and although he does not cite Mandelstam's description of "how the *Commedia* glorifies 'the human gait, the measure and rhythm of walking, the footstep and its form,'" he surely must have read this passage and realized the truth of Mandelstam's implicit affirmation, in Hurley's words, that "the fall of rhyme evoking the incremental progress of the pedestrian is at the heart of this concept of prosody."[62] Even though Heaney's rhyme scheme in his tercets in "Station Island" departs from Dante's true terza rima, as we will see, he nonetheless must have been drawn to Mandelstam's linkage of walking with terza rima, not only because it aptly describes that rhyme scheme and, in turn, its applicability to his own walking and praying pilgrimage on Station Island, but also because such an analogy echoes his ascription of Wordsworth's prosody to his habitual walking in the Lake District, a process that he calls attention to in his 1974 essay on Wordsworth, which also celebrates the poet as regional exemplar.[63]

Moreover, Heaney's language in "Station Island" conforms with his approval of Eliot's defense of "indigenous language" in "The Regional Forecast" and his rejection in "Envies and Identifications" of what he perceives as Eliot's mischaracterization of Dante's language as universal and as bearing "an almost allegorical force": in saying this, Heaney observes, "he does less than justice to the untamed and thoroughly parochial elements which it possesses. To listen to Eliot, one would almost be led to forget that Dante's great literary contribution was to write in the vernacular and thereby to give the usual language its head."[64] Heaney had already noted this quality of the Italian poet in "The Sense of Place": "Dante was very much a man of a particular place, [and] . . . his great poem is full of intimate placings and place names, and . . . as he moves round the murky circles of hell, often heard rather than seen by his damned friends and enemies, he is recognized by his local speech or so recognizes them."[65]

Heaney sees Eliot as having been influenced by Dante's emphasis on local culture and on the vernacular in particular some twenty years earlier than "Little Gidding," when he wrote "The Waste Land," and he cites the last stanza from the opening section of that poem beginning "Unreal city" to make his point: "The language is more allied to the Shakespearean-local-associative than to the latinate-classical-canonical."[66]

Even by 1929, just seven years after "The Waste Land" was published, Eliot, in his essay on Dante, neglects the great Italian master's privileging of vernacular language, according to Heaney. For example, Heaney says, in his reading of Dante's use of *smarrita* in the third line of the *Inferno*, that the English definitions of the word are "less particular, less urgently local than the Italian word, which has all the force of dirt hitting a windscreen. Eliot underplays the swarming, mobbish element in the Italian"; then he notes that a phrase from Dante's next stanza, "'*Selva selvaggia*[,]' is as barbarous as Hopkins."[67] Heaney consistently has praised Hopkins's singular language as influential for his own adoption of occasional Ulster dialect words into his poetry and thus as an affirmation for his earlier, more geographic conception of regionalism, which of course is still on display in *Station Island* even as he is shifting to a more expansive concept of regionalism in his varying adoptions of Dante's terza rima. For instance, he argued in his December 1974 lecture on Hopkins in similar terms, using Eliot's terms in *The Sacred Wood* in contrasting Shakespeare and Ben Jonson to contrast Keats's and Hopkins's styles: "Keats has the life of a swarm, fluent and merged; Hopkins has the design of the honeycomb, definite and loaded."[68]

Bernard O'Donoghue has tellingly remarked upon Dante's importance to Heaney's regionalism that "for Heaney, Dante is the epic of the parish, as Homer was for Yeats."[69] Heaney repeatedly uses the vernacular and colloquial in "Station Island," and in the rare instances where he does not do so he employs more formal language for a specific effect. Take

Corcoran's contention that in the seventh section, the elegy for Heaney's friend William Strathearn, Heaney employs a "heavy-handed" dialogue: "'Open up and see what you have got' and 'Not that it is any consolation, / but they were caught' seems stilted, especially in their context of deep emotional perturbation and distress."[70] In response to O'Donoghue's assertion that the "language of the exchange . . . is not rhetorically recast . . . but occurs unprocessed," Corcoran states, "Surely, at the very least, the verbs in these exchanges would be elided in unprocessed form: not 'you have' but 'you've'; and not 'it is' but 'it's.'"[71] Heaney certainly does imaginatively re-create or poetically "process" the conversation Strathearn had with his wife and the two waiting men below who will shortly murder him. Yet in all but those two examples and one additional instance in the poem, Heaney actually does employ contractions, as when Strathearn tells Heaney in the fifth stanza, "It's only me. You've seen men as raw / after a football match" (*SI*, 77), or when Strathearn's wife starts crying after the men call her husband to come down into the shop and he replies angrily, "Is your head // astray, or what's come over you?" (78). And when Strathearn asks, "What do you want? Could you quieten the racket // or I'll not come down at all," the men reply, "There's a child not well. / Open up and see what you have got—pills / or a powder or something in a bottle" (78). The offending line for Corcoran—"Open up and see what you have got"—occurs in the midst of a colloquial dialogue for contrast. Heaney thus marks their linguistic turn into formal speech here to show how they are masking their dishonorable intentions with unnatural speech. And his next instance of "stilted" dialogue in the poem, when Heaney tells Strathearn, "'Not that it is any consolation, / but they were caught,' I told him, 'and got jail'" (79), is a much more benign example of purposely formalized language that Heaney consciously offers his friend even while knowing that these words themselves cannot help Strathearn or his widow. Finally, after a great deal more colloquial dialogue between Heaney and Strathearn, when Heaney tells him, "Forgive the way I have lived indifferent— / forgive my timid circumspect involvement" (80), the poet is clearly admitting the inadequacy of what he feels at the time was his relative silence about the violence in the North by refusing to slip into contractions again and thereby giving his plea a certain gravity.

When we turn to Heaney's use of terza rima in this particular lyric from "Station Island," we actually find, moreover, *contra* Corcoran, that

Heaney's use of the form occupies a halfway house of rhyme between Dante's in *The Divine Comedy* and Eliot's in that crucial section of "Little Gidding." Occasional rhymes are featured in the tercets of that section from Eliot's poem, but they do depart from the regular *aba bcb cdc* rhyme scheme of the terza rima, as do Heaney's. But the difference is that while Eliot soon slips into a series of tercets with no end rhymes of any kind, Heaney maintains, by use of some pararhyme, a chiming of the first and third lines in each tercet throughout, although he does not use the rhyme of his initial second line to begin the rhyme of his second stanza as normal terza rima would do. The line endings of the first three tercets from Heaney's poem on Strathearn amply illustrate my point: "water," "it," and "barometer"; "reflection," "presence," and "concentration"; and "spoke," "reluctant," and "shock" (*SI*, 77). Therefore, Heaney establishes a new alternating rhyme scheme in each successive tercet in this particular section that departs from the hurtling rhyme scheme of true Dantean terza rima but certainly is far from Eliot's general lack of any rhyme in that famous section of "Little Gidding" and different again from Corcoran's other example that he feels Heaney's tercets too closely imitate: Yeats's fairly regular employment of actual terza rima (with some pararhyme exceptions) in "Cuchulain Comforted."

But if Heaney rejected Eliot's own neglect of Dante's precise and haunting use of the vernacular beginning in the English poet's lecture on the Italian master from 1929 and continuing through "Little Gidding," he still found Eliot's prose defense of regionalism in "The Social Function of Poetry," "The Music of Poetry," and *Notes toward a Definition of a Christian Culture* instructive.[72] In "The Regional Forecast," Heaney closes his essay, not by discussing Joyce further, but by invoking Eliot's defense of regionalism in his 1943 lecture to the British-Norwegian Institute, "The Social Function of Poetry," where he argues in the midst of World War II that, in Heaney's words, poetry remains "the last ditch of defense which Eliot can envisage" and captures "the fidelity of a region or a nation to its indigenous language, its poetry, and its particular religious sensibility."[73] Moreover, Heaney was likely drawn to other passages in Eliot's essay that specifically defend poetry in these terms, as when Eliot states, "Feeling and emotion are particular, whereas thought is general. It is easier to think in a foreign language than it is to feel in it. Therefore no art is more stubbornly national than poetry," and shortly thereafter, when he summarizes his argument: "Emotion and feeling, then are best expressed in the common language of the people—that is, in the language common to all classes: the structure, the rhythm, the sound, the idiom of a language, express the personality of the people which speaks it."[74]

Such convictions are consistent with Eliot's emphasis on the importance of living language in poetry that he expressed a year earlier in his 1942 W. P. Ker Memorial Lecture, "The Music of Poetry." In this talk, while admitting the necessity of dynamism in both speech and poetry (such as the development of free verse), he holds that "whether poetry is accentual or syllabic, rhymed or rhymeless, formal or free, it cannot afford to lose its contact with the changing language of common intercourse."[75] A few passages later, Eliot suggests that "while poetry attempts to convey something beyond what can be conveyed in prose rhythms, it remains, all the same, one person talking to another.... The immediacy of poetry to conversation is not a matter on which we can lay down exact laws.... No poetry, of course, is ever exactly the same speech that the poet talks and hears: but it has to be in such a relation to the speech of his time that the listener or reader can say 'that is how I should talk if I could talk poetry.'"[76] Finally, Eliot gives "common speech" and place as essential coordinates in defining his titular phrase: "The music of poetry, then, must be a music latent in the common speech of its time. And that means also that it must be latent in the common speech of the poet's *place*."[77] Thus when Heaney was setting up the particular soundscape of *Station Island*, Eliot's defense of poetry based on living speech as preserver of regional or national culture was salutary for him, and as we will see, in his essay on Dante it actually formed the basis of his particular rejection of Eliot's too-abstract language in his reading of "Little Gidding."

So, if Heaney is generally imitating Eliot's adaptation of Dantean terza rima more than Dante's own verse form in certain tercets from *Station Island*, he is doing so in part in an homage to the Anglo-American poet who defended regionalism, particularly regionalism as embedded in and embodied by the language of living poetry, as healthy for England, as well as for Ireland, Scotland, and Wales. In *Notes toward a Definition of Culture*, when Eliot argues that local culture is preserved by the so-called "satellite culture," he observes that "the satellite exercises a considerable influence upon the stronger culture; and so plays a larger part in the world than it could in isolation."[78] Given that Heaney's evolving sense of regionalism in the 1980s came to reject the center/periphery model because satellites must always rotate around something with a larger gravitational pull than themselves—the moon around the earth and in this case, Ireland around England—Eliot's word choice might have seemed offputting to him. Yet he probably affirmed the passage where Eliot argues that the "*absolute* value" of regionalism "is that each area should have its characteristic culture, which should also harmonize with, and enrich, the cultures of the neighboring area," followed immediately by his claim that "in order to realize this value it is necessary to investigate political and economic alternatives to centralization in London or elsewhere"; thus Heaney explicitly rejects the center/periphery model and suggests how he values the region's autonomy and influence upon the metropolis.[79]

Heaney also has continued to value Eliot's own soundscape. In "Learning from Eliot," he cites approvingly how he learned to listen to the older poet's "undulant cadences and dissolving and reining-in" in the "Death by Water" section of "The Waste Land," and to follow "the footfall of the word 'time'" in the opening lines of "Burnt Norton" from the "Four Quartets," where it "echoes and repeats in a way that is hypnotic when read aloud."[80] In a fashion that is beyond the scope of this chapter to demonstrate, Heaney establishes a similarly Eliotic macro-soundscape of repetitions and cadences that enables us to realize that while a later volume such as *Seeing Things* will often highlight visual instances of the marvelous through his use of tercets, in the early to mid-1980s Heaney's meetings with the shades on Station Island are characterized by his emphasis on the sonic qualities of vernacular words and the local form of his variation of Dante's terza rima in the most important sections: 2, 4, 7, a short stretch of 8, 11, and 12.

Thus Heaney's own sequence about his series of meetings with ghosts from the Northern Irish Troubles and from other parts of his life, set in a rural, marginalized area of the Republic of Ireland in County Donegal, a county nearly cut off from the Republic and separated by the border from Northern Ireland, drawing both on Dante's meetings with recognizable shades and on Eliot's singular meeting with a strangely familiar ghost in "Little Gidding," reimagines, resituates, and reinscribes his own experience so that we perceive, not Eliot's London, but Lough Derg as the literary/cultural/religious center of Britain and Ireland. In so doing, Heaney yokes his own poetry to the English tradition that Eliot came to represent and love, but he does so by rendering his own ghosts both intimate and identifiable in a verse form hauntingly familiar, mediated by Eliot's take on Dantean terza rima. Additionally, as Conor McCarthy has argued in suggesting how the English Cistercian H. de Saltrey's *Tractatus de Purgatorio Sancti Patricii* (1180–84) helped create the doctrine of purgatory in the Catholic Church and placed its actual entrance at Lough Derg, Heaney's audacious adaptation of Dante's *Commedia* "to a local Donegal context in 'Station Island'" enables him to "not just appropriat[e] Dante to a local context, but relocat[e] Dante to the site of an earlier medieval purgatory in Ulster."[81]

Another consequence of Heaney's departure from true Dantean terza rima in "Station Island" concerns his tercets' function as self-contained units of sound: in short, they lack the propulsion of the typical terza rima because the rhyme does not roll through the poem, becoming "a *perpetuum mobile* in which linkage and continuation are seamlessly articulated."[82] Starting a new rhyme in each tercet potentially creates a problem for his presentation of the series of meetings between Heaney and these ghosts; unlike Dante's meetings with his shades in his *Purgatorio*, where we are swept along by virtue of the terza rima's forward momentum, we are forced to imagine a series of freeze-frames of each subject in Heaney's tercet sections, but hopefully we in turn build up a collage of impressionistic images. Were each tercet end-stopped the effect would be too staccato and jerky, but Heaney's usual pattern in these poems blends a minority of end-stopped tercets with a majority of enjambed or only lightly stopped tercets (commas or colons) to form a series of tercets that make up several large units in each poem.[83] Within these units, of course, because of the new rhyme of the first and third lines in each tercet, we may linger on each particular stanza, which makes for a concentrating effect that is built up, stanza by stanza, and that coalesces at the end of each unit of end-stopped tercets.

Consider section 2, one of the most crucial sections, where Heaney meets William Carleton, first hearing, then seeing the fast-striding Carleton, then speaking to him, and finally telling him, "I'm on my road there now to do the station" (*SI*, 64). Heaney signals Carleton's aggression and furious pace by not end-stopping the final line of a tercet until the end of the sixth one, which naturally concludes this first unit of description.

A close reading of the next unit of three tercets suggests that Heaney uses a series of medial and nonmedial caesuras, indicated by a series of commas and colons, to indicate Carleton's brusqueness and jerky body motions, reinforcing the last two lines of the seventh tercet: "His head jerked sharply side to side and up / like a diver surfacing" (64). There are no fully end-stopped lines after a question from Carleton in line 1 of the seventh tercet—"O holy Jesus Christ, does nothing change?"—followed by more of Heaney's physical impressions of the man, until, at the end of the ninth stanza, Carleton states, "It is a road you travel on your own" (65). By end-stopping that line, Heaney focuses our attention on Carleton's rejection of Heaney's pilgrimage before he tells the younger poet why—because he rejected sectarianism in his lifetime and he views this pilgrimage as an example of Catholic sectarianism. To return to section 7, the poem about the murder of William Strathearn, Heaney end-stops only seven of twenty-eight stanzas (if one counts the dangling, enjambed last line as the twenty-eighth stanza), only about a fourth of the poem.[84] But overall, there are many more end-stopped lines in the first and second lines of particular tercets in this poem than in section 2, which Heaney utilizes perfectly to illustrate the confused, staccato series of reactions that Strathearn experienced the night he was killed.

Finally, in the famous section 12, where Heaney confronts Joyce, we have a series of tercets that are far closer to Dantean terza rima than any other lyric in the sequence,[85] seemingly suggesting that Heaney is sonically signaling his emergence from his often dissonant (sonically and thematically) meetings with other shades. He often resorts to pararhyme to achieve this modified terza rima, but a surprising number of these stanzas are nearly full terza rima. Consider: the "b" rhyme of "again" in line 2 chimes partially with the beginning "b" rhyme of the very next stanza, "mine"; and the new "c" rhyme in this second stanza, "guide," perfectly rhymes with the beginning "c" rhyme of the third stanza, "side" (*SI*, 92). I find that the first six stanzas approach the condition of terza rima through such slant and full rhymes and that the pattern briefly collapses when Joyce begins speaking in stanza 7, when the last word of the first line, "obligation," is only very faintly drawing on the sound of "clean" in the middle of the previous tercet (92). Such a near break from terza rima signals Joyce's abrupt speech, but once he fully launches into that speech, the concluding sound from the end of the second line in that seventh tercet, "rite," is perfectly echoed by "write," the concluding sound at the beginning of the eighth stanza. And then "work-lust," at the end of the next line of that eighth tercet, sets up a partial rhyme with "breast" to begin the ninth stanza, where "dangerous," at the end of the second line of that stanza, will be only faintly echoed by "ashes," to begin the tenth stanza. This mixture of broken and near and full terza rima sonically suggests Joyce's own multiplicity of styles and implies that at least some of what he says harmonizes (the near and full terza rima) with Heaney's growing conviction to become more independent of tribe and province. But when Joyce's first speech concludes with the end-stopped tercet, "You've listened long enough. Now strike your note," the full break in terza rima to Heaney's reflection on his advice ("forget" in the middle line of the tenth stanza does not set up the initial rhyme, "space," of the next stanza) signals his entrance into a space of foreknowledge, and he will soon start musing on Stephen's epiphany about the tundish at the end of *A Portrait*: "It was as if I had stepped free into space / alone with nothing that I had not known / already. Raindrops blew in my face // as I came to" (93). So the full break in terza rima in this part of the lyric sonically reinforces Heaney's pending epiphany, but Joyce soon rejects that realization in a long speech beginning in stanza 14 and continuing through stanza 18, five stanzas of near terza rima (the first three) and full terza rima (the last two), famously telling Heaney to "swim // out on your own and fill the element / with signatures on your own frequency" (93–94). All seems well, if we go along with the notion that with such nearly regular and regular terza rima Heaney is fully accepting Joyce's advice to leave the "tribe" behind and be fully independent. But that way lies solipsism, as I have suggested earlier, and by the very end of the poem, another dangling line (which could be the start of a nineteenth tercet or the end of the eighteenth, making that stanza actually a sort of fractured quatrain), implies Heaney's wariness of this charge, which is heightened by the only very faint rhyme of "tarmac" and "walk" (94).

This careful formal analysis of Heaney's tercets in three different lyrics from "Station Island" shows that his variations on Dantean terza rima are far from being "ragged," as Corcoran claims above, and proves that they are very carefully composed sound units that Heaney uses to variously signal conversational breaks (as in the second section on Carleton and the seventh section on Strathearn), mental vacillation (in both the seventh and the twelfth sections), and temporary epiphanies that are then dashed (twice in the twelfth section). Moreover, Heaney's tercet use in this middle section enables him to fully engage with two writers who were exemplars of regionalism for him—Dante (whom he comes to through Joyce, another major regional exemplar) with his use of both vernacular words and the terza rima form, and Eliot, with his employment of colloquialisms in his earlier poetry, recourse to the broken terza rima in the second section of "Little Gidding," and defense of regionalism, including Irish regionalism, in "The Social Function of Poetry" and elsewhere, which Heaney recognizes in his own essay, "The Regional Forecast." I agree with Bernard O'Donoghue that "great as these predecessors are [Eliot and Yeats], Heaney's *terza rima* in the sequence will come to be regarded as an equally impressive adaptation of the form to his particular purposes."[86] Heaney's modification of terza rima is a localized form that corresponds perfectly to his regional agenda in its focus on local culture and its evocation of the spirit world.

JOYCEAN ADVICE AND HEANEY'S FLIGHT FROM THIS OLD FATHER

Corcoran argues convincingly that Joyce's advice to Heaney in this final section, particularly the language beginning with "fill the element / with signatures on your own frequency," suggests how "the strong poet" is "decisively swerving from the admired but inhibiting precursor," arguing that "the nouns of the passage have a distinctively Heaney-like, rather than Joycean, quality," and finally holding that "this may well be read as an almost parricidal act, denying paternity even in the act of asserting it, making 'James Joyce' a function of the work of Seamus Heaney."[87] Moreover, when Heaney's Joyce argues, "That subject people stuff is a cod's game, / *infantile*, like your peasant pilgrimage" (*SI*, 93; my emphasis), "infantile" recalls the "swaddling band" (*FW*, 22) that tightened metaphorically around the Catholic community in Northern Ireland in the wake of the Bloody Sunday shootings. In "Casualty," Heaney's speaker seems to finally reject that constricting image of nationalism for the liberating independence of the slain fisherman Louis O'Neill, while at the end of this twelfth lyric of "Station Island" the speaker ventriloquizes Heaney's rejection of nationalism when it wallows in victimization, yet does not fully embrace solipsistic independence. Finally, his refusal to engage in anything approaching full terza rima in any of the many tercet-driven poems of "Sweeney Redivivus" further sonically proves his rejection of Joyce's specific advice given in irregular and regular terza rima, even if it is not a nearly "parricidal" move because he values Joyce's general affirmation of independence.[88]

In fact, Heaney's later decision to excise almost all of the original twelfth and thirteenth stanzas, the passages where he calls the poet "old father," and references Stephen Dedalus's diary entry about the tundish (*SI*, 93), suggests that within a few years he felt sufficiently comfortable with his rejection of Joyce's specific advice to not even fully register him as a literary father in this passage. Although Corcoran argues that "Heaney significantly revises the Joycean passage in the version of the poem he publishes in his *New Selected Poems 1966–1987* . . . in a way that suggests a continued uncertainty about the degree of self-aggrandisement that may be read into the encounter," his language here about "the Joycean passage" misleads:[89] Heaney cuts the entirety of his own speaker's speech in this section, which was expressed through his references to *A Portrait*, but retains with only slight revisions almost all of Joyce's dialogue. Certainly, Heaney's later excision of his reference to the tundish passage in the original 1984 version of this twelfth lyric in the "Station Island" sequence signifies that he has so fully incorporated the vernacular, both in diction and in his adaptation of the terza rima form here and elsewhere in the volume, that there is no longer (by 1987) even a need to rehearse Stephen's affirmation of the vernacular. The silence of those now-missing stanzas loudly suggests the truth of my argument, whereas Heaney's retention of almost all of Joyce's speech, with a few minor changes, earlier in the poem and in its conclusion implies that this shade's challenge to go out on his own still hovers in front of him. Significantly, Heaney's silence in both the 1987 and the 1998 versions of the poem (the latter in *Opened Ground: Selected Poems, 1966–1996*), suggests that Joyce's advice, "You've listened long enough. Now strike your note" (*SI*, 93; *OG*, 245), will not be heeded—that Heaney may continue to be a silent listener, another way to reject the center/periphery model. Keeping one's own counsel, as Heaney had lamented doing in significant metapoetic moments in his career ("Punishment," for example), had proven to be a salutary exercise, after all, and achieving such a stance through this textual revision indirectly privileges an independence that affirms the general thrust of Joyce's advice to embrace artistic freedom while it rejects Joyce's cataract of words characteristic of his late fiction (a form that is still to be named) in favor of a silent wisdom offered in the carefully rendered form of the tercet. Henry Hart has contended in this regard, "Joyce's literary direction was always toward greater verbal intricacy, greater abstraction from the vernacular. Heaney's is the reverse. His religious journey, like Eliot's, has simplified rather than complicated his diction."[90]

Had Heaney adopted Joyce's specific advice, his artistic trajectory would likely have resulted in a Stephen Dedalus–like artistic failure and simply reaffirmed the lingering center/periphery model that Ludwig correctly urged Heaney to reject in the late 1980s. Michael Molino's argument is especially helpful for understanding how Heaney, through his adoption of the Sweeney persona in the third section of the volume, escapes this model. Molino observes that "Heaney chooses not to follow Joyce's advice and launch out on an odyssey of his own; he does not attempt to make the circle wider nor to ask who might make it wider for him. Instead, like Sweeney who was stripped of his kingdom, his family, his dignity, his humanity, and his mind, Heaney begins to strip away the . . . cultural dissonance that constitutes the conscience of his race in order to start again . . . and to see things anew."[91] Molino's analysis of this process of cultural stripping away is exemplary and recommended to readers.[92] Another way that Heaney strips away such "cultural dissonance" is by dwelling upon the great European Dante and by doing his own translations of the first three cantos of the *Inferno*. Such exercises, along with his own "translations" of conversations with ghosts of his past and the Northern Irish Troubles, enabled Heaney to place his "Station Island" in the context of what he says in "The Impact of Translation" are the contributions of the eastern European and Russian poets such as Holub and Miłosz that he admires so much. As he claims, "The note sounded by translated poetry from that world beyond—pitched intently and in spite of occupation, holocaust, concentration camps and the whole apparatus of totalitarianism—is so credible, desolating, and resuscitative."[93]

Heaney generally breaks from any use of rhyme within the vast majority of the tercets in "Sweeney Redivivus," a change from his employment of the tercet in "Station Island." Their thematic lightness, then, is echoed and reinforced by his refusal to even write a series of tercets with a rhyme unique to each one, instead giving us free-verse tercets that largely float free of rhyme altogether. Such a decision perhaps shows how his Sweeney learned to see his punishment of tree-flitting as liberating rather than confining and, by extension, how Heaney used his former fixation on the physical and linguistic characteristics of Northern Ireland to spring toward an airier form and subject matter, one signaled by his continuing use of tercets in his later volumes.

Flitting rather than flying toward artistic freedom (with the attendant danger for the flying mythical Icarus he recognizes in his appropriation of Stephen Dedalus's invocation to "Old father" in section 12 of "Station Island"), Heaney nonetheless still expresses his typical tentativeness, despite the great optimism of many of the poems in "Sweeney Redivivus." In using an even more bare form of the tercet in this section than he did in the "Station Island" sequence, he may be sonically showing how he wants to leave behind entrapping narratives from his home region of Northern Ireland.

Heaney's tercet poem "The Disappearing Island," from his 1987 volume *The Haw Lantern* shows the continuing influence of Joyce as regional writer and highlights the issue of Heaney's continued commitment to imagining a new Northern Ireland despite his varied attempts to move away from treating the North in his work. In his April 1988 Richard Ellmann lecture, "Cornucopia and Empty Shell: Variations on a Theme from Ellmann," Heaney reads "The Disappearing Island," about the landing of St. Brendan the Navigator on "a barren but nonetheless welcome island in the western ocean," which turns out to be a sea monster who soon awakens and vanishes into the waves.[94] The poem meditates upon the relationship between place and the imagination and helps us understand how Joyce's art addresses these entities.

"The Disappearing Island" is composed in unrhymed tercets, like many other poems from the volume, including "From the Frontier of Writing," "The Stone Grinder," "A Daylight Art," much of "Parable Island," "From the Republic of Conscience," "Hailstones," "Two Quick Notes," "The Wishing Tree," and "A Postcard from Iceland." There is a distant echo of Dante's terza rima, though: the "b" rhyme of "shores" in the first stanza of "The Disappearing Island" is faintly recalled by the opening end rhyme of the second stanza, "hearth," while the first syllable, not the last, as is in traditional terza rima, of the second end rhyme from that second stanza, "firmament," is copied exactly for the end rhyme of the first line of the third and last stanza—"firm" (*HL*, 50). Only an extremely skilled wordsmith could ring such adroit changes on the chimes of the traditional terza rima, and Heaney seems to self-consciously proclaim his ability in this regard in using "know" three times during the course of the roughly similarly constructed three-stanza tercet poem "A Postcard from Iceland" (37). To return to "The Disappearing Island," on first glance, it looks rather solid in its three tercets, but the freedom he builds into his tercets here also signals formally to the cautious reader the hazardous condition of the island because there is no blocky, formal respite of the 1970s Heaney quatrain. The vigorous activity of St. Brendan and his fellow sailors in setting up camp, making fire, and praying all is for naught by line 6: "The island broke beneath us like a wave" (50). The first two lines of the final tercet suggest symbolically that sheer possession of a seemingly stable landscape can be illusory, with a clear application to the political situation in Northern Ireland: "The land sustaining us seemed to hold firm / Only when we embraced it *in extremis*" (50).

Were this the only tercet-driven poem in the volume meditating on particular landscapes or zones that seem familiar but disorienting to the speaker, it might be possible not to read "The Disappearing Island" in this manner, but the similar subject and theme in "From the Frontier of Writing," "Parable Island," and "From the Frontier of Conscience," indicate these four poems collectively form a cluster of visionary meditations on place and dispossession in a Northern Irish context signaled by the initial confrontation between the native speaker and the imperial British soldiers in "From the Frontier of Writing" and continued in the following poems. Corcoran points out that "From the Frontier of Writing" uses "a modified Dantean *terza rima*" and thus "may . . . be urging at the formal level the conception of writing as the place where you may move from an inferno of political subjection to a paradiso of imaginative enablement," while Helen Vendler argues similarly that "its material hellishness" in its "four opening tercets" and "its spiritual purgation" in its "four appended and almost identical tercets" are "emphasized by its rendition in a version of Dantesque *terza rima*."[95] The ideal of artistic autonomy free from groupthink in "From the Frontier" is reinforced negatively by the penchant for narrative dominance shown by the islanders of "Parable Island," who "yield to nobody in their belief / that the country is an island" and who are "always vying with a fierce possessiveness / for the right to set 'the island story' straight" (*HL*, 10, 11). The independence for the artist necessitated by such attitudes also colors "From the Republic of Conscience," in which the speaker, after returning from a visit to this republic where, significantly, "You carried your own burden" (12), is told by the customs clerk on the border that "I was now a dual citizen" and an "ambassador" for the republic of conscience (13), as indeed Heaney would become and as was recognized with his 1995 Nobel Prize for Literature. The perplexing last line of "The Disappearing Island"—"All that happened there was vision"—may be read as connoting that Brendan and his men's initial vision of being on *terra firma* was a necessary, temporary one that was quickly superseded by surprising reality. Reading this poem both in its own historical context and in the context of its three companion poems from *The Haw Lantern* thus suggests the curious ways in which seeming "reality" can lead to the marvelous, actual reality of the future. In such poems, Heaney implies that the tercet will be his visionary form, as indeed it is in *Seeing Things* and later volumes like *Human Chain* where he increasingly explores the spirit region.

Shortly after discussing "The Disappearing Island" in "Cornucopia and Empty Shell," Heaney argues that "Joyce moved like a great factory ship, unlooked for and inexorable, hoovering up every form of life on the seafloor of the Irish psyche, from the most evasive and scuttling dishonesties to the most hampered and crustacean petrifactions. In his exhaustiveness lies his exhilaration. By dividing the torpid consciousness of his race against itself, by giving it an affronting image of itself, he still fortified it even as he castigated it, and thereby justified the potentially overbearing claim he made to Grant Richards in 1906 that his literary purpose consisted in 'the spiritual liberation of my country.'"[96] But he quickly admits that for both Yeats and Joyce, "the drive to inflame people with a livable truth, was secondary to the artistic impulse itself."[97] Dillon Johnston, who has argued strongly for Joyce's stylistic influence on contemporary

Irish poets, agrees with Heaney's position on Joyce, citing Dominic Manganiello's criticism of the "spiritual liberation" passage from Joyce in that critic's *Joyce's Politics* to prove his point that "for Joyce, the freeing of the individual was the main issue, indeed the only one."[98]

If two of Heaney's greatest exemplars, Yeats and Joyce, were driven more by the artistic impulse than by this "spiritual liberationist" drive, what effect does this realization have on his agenda of indirectly and at times, directly, promoting a future, less conflicted Northern Ireland, the second strand of his regionalism? Heaney's thinking about Yeats and Joyce in "Cornucopia and Empty Shell" posits that they were not propagandists but independent because of their devotion to their art. But Heaney seems also to be admitting a certain selfishness, at least on the part of Joyce, as the price he paid for his art. It would be too much to claim that Heaney desired the spiritual liberation of Northern Ireland, but certainly he was much concerned to help imagine a future, less-divided North while not being willing to sacrifice his artistic independence to achieve such a state. Heaney was fundamentally communal, relational, in ways that Joyce was not, and Heaney long hoped for and attempted to imagine what a more communal Northern Ireland might look like. In this regard, we might think that Joyce's example was singularly unhelpful until we remember that Heaney approvingly cites the fairly inclusive definition of a nation given by Joyce's outcast Jewish character Leopold Bloom in the concluding lines of his poem "Traditions" from *Wintering Out*: "'Ireland,' said Bloom, / 'I was born here. Ireland'" (*WO*, 32).

Heaney is clearly daunted by Stephen Dedalus's famous vow at the end of *A Portrait*, but that does not mean he shrinks from what he came to see as a secondary task of the regional poet (the first obligation is always to the imagination) to conceive of a future region with considerable integrity for its inhabitants who hold much more in common than what has traditionally divided them. Robert Crawford has pointed out how Heaney cites Joyce at the conclusion of his 1974 lecture "Feeling into Words" on this very issue, "where, after writing of his view of poetry, and particularly of his own Irish poetry, as 'a restoration of the culture to itself,' Heaney ends with the statement that 'to forge a poem is one thing, to forge the uncreated conscience of the race, as Stephen Dedalus puts it, is quite another and places daunting pressures and responsibilities on anyone who would risk the name of poet.'"[99] So even as he recoiled from it, Heaney certainly considered something like Stephen's hyperbolic vow in writing about the collision of Irish and British culture and politics in Northern Ireland and attempting to use an ever-expanding concept of regionalism to both chart the source of the past and present disturbances there and explore ways forward, paths toward peace. First, however, he would turn to Greek mythology and the figure of the wounded Philoctetes for his 1990 Field Day play, *The Cure at Troy*, the most moving and extensive contemplation of the wounded condition of Northern Ireland he had yet essayed and simultaneously the most hopeful, albeit cautious, about the improving political conditions there.

Chapter Nine

THE NORTHERN IRISH CONTEXT AND OWEN AND YEATS INTERTEXTS IN *THE CURE AT TROY*

For a swoop on the classics to be successful, there needs to be surprise, amplification, some sense of potential being located and a path opened to the writer's underlying preoccupations.
—Heaney, "Seamus Heaney (January 2010)," interview by Jody Allen Randolph

Joyce (along with Dante), with his blend of local idiolects and cosmopolitanism, was a major regional exemplar for Heaney in the 1980s as his regionalism became gradually more expansive in its outlook. If Joyce desired to Hellenize the island of Ireland by using the Homeric parallels in *Ulysses*, Heaney would turn by 1990 to a Hellenized island— Lemnos—and Hibernicize it, finding parallels to its loneliness and the wounded condition of its lone inhabitant, Philoctetes, and the isolated feelings of Northern Ireland's inhabitants in his adaptation of Sophocles' *Philoctetes, The Cure at Troy*. Heaney has explicitly connected Joyce to Greece through his claim to be European and his sense of woundedness— which both stemmed from his being raised in the milieu of Irish Catholicism. He argues that Joyce took the position that "'okay, we may not have

279

had the Reformation, but weren't we lucky, we escaped all the consequences. We have direct access to Dante and direct access to Europe. We are actually Greek in a way. The Dubliner is a Daedalus. We really have bypassed the provincialism of that other island over there.'... His [Dante's] works are read in the context of international modernism.... But the wound of inferiority, and the wound of the Irish situation, is a *driving force*."[1] Thus Heaney's version of *Philoctetes* draws deeply on the locale of Londonderry/Derry, the home of the Field Day Theatre Company, and in so doing suggests how an inwardly turned, solipsistic regionalism could be wounding and crippling. Simultaneously, however, he implies how an outward-facing, receptive regionalism could be enabling and even inspiring for the citizens of Northern Ireland, who, well before 1990, were sick of their province being torn apart repeatedly by violent bigots.

Besides the analogies he draws between the Greek island of Lemnos and the city of Londonderry/Derry (and by extension, all of Northern Ireland), Heaney likely was influenced by his continuing belief in what he saw as Joyce's regionalist affirmation of local idiolect in the tundish scene in *A Portrait of the Artist* as he prepared to adapt Sophocles' resonant drama. In his 1999 exploration of the role of the translator, Heaney noted that Stephen Dedalus's discovery that *tundish* is listed in the dictionary as a proper English word affirmed his regionalist outlook by making him feel at home in that language: "By finding that his Dublin vernacular is related to the old English base, Stephen discovers that his own linguistic rights to English are, as it were, pre-natal. He may not be the true-born English man, but he is the new-born English speaker.... He realizes that his vernacular possessions are buried treasures, that his own word-hoard is the artistic equivalent of a gold hoard."[2] While Heaney made these remarks in the context of discussing his translation of *Beowulf*, his language here hearkens back to the poem "North," where the longship's tongue concludes that poem by telling the speaker to "'Lie down / in the word-hoard, burrow the coil and gleam of your furrowed brain'" and to "'trust the feel of what nubbed treasure / your hands have known'" (*N*, 11). If we read *The Cure at Troy* through these two affirmations of regional language, we realize how the play's insistence on artistic independence is consistent with his lifelong affirmation of it through a particular type of regionalism. Yet this privileging of the writer's agency would once again be put under

The Northern Irish Context and Owen and Yeats Intertexts 281

pressure by Heaney himself, as he added a series of lines to *The Cure* that suggest its public dimension for him.

Whereas Heaney's most-cited line during the Northern Irish Troubles was "Whatever you say say nothing," from the poem of that same name in *North*, that line has now been replaced with some of the chorus's closing lines in *The Cure at Troy*, which he retrospectively dedicated to the victims of the Real IRA bombing at Omagh, which occurred on August 15, 1998, killing twenty-nine people and injuring hundreds more. In *Stepping Stones*, Heaney admits the public quality of parts of this adaptation, noting that "there are writings of mine I'd think of as public in the megaphone sense of the term—things like the song I wrote after Bloody Sunday ['The Road to Derry'] and the 'Human beings suffer' chorus of *The Cure at Troy*" (*SS*, 385–86). This chorus specifically mentions "a hunger-striker's father" and a "police widow in veils," clearly incorporating details from the Northern Irish conflict (*CT*, 77).

Yet Heaney himself has cautioned against reading his adaptation (the full title is *The Cure at Troy: A Version of Sophocles' Philoctetes*) as solely connoting the recent Troubles in Northern Ireland, noting that "while there are parallels, and wonderfully suggestive ones, between the psychology and predicaments of certain characters in the play and certain parties and conditions in Northern Ireland, the play does not exist in order to exploit them. The parallels are richly incidental rather than essential to the *version*."[3] In another context, he has remarked about the process of translation that "the proper translation—'proper' in the Latin sense of belonging, belonging recognizably to the original and to the oeuvre of the translator—exists half-way between a crib and an appropriation."[4] He also points out "the liminal situation of the literary translator, the one standing at the frontier of a resonant original, in awe of its primacy, utterly persuaded, and yet called upon to utter a different yet equally persuasive *version* of it in his or her own words."[5] In its portrayal of Philoctetes stranded on Lemnos, *The Cure* evokes the isolated city of Londonderry/Derry that straddles the border of Northern Ireland and the Republic, and thus its liminal setting symbolically echoes Heaney's sense of the liminal or "half-way" role of the translator. Moreover, Heaney's likely ability to place himself psychographically back in the divided city when he was adapting Sophocles' play enabled him to gaze at the "resonant original" of the deathly situation in Northern Ireland while also imagining "a different yet equally persuasive version of it in his . . . own words," as we will see.[6]

Some of these allegedly "richly incidental" parallels raised in Heaney's remarks above actually purposefully evoke the troubled situation in Northern Ireland by tentatively raising the hope of an end to the violence in the decade of the 1990s, but they also probe a series of parallels to other conflicts—with World War I, especially as represented in Wilfred Owen's poetry, most supremely in "Strange Meeting" and "Insensibility"—and with the Easter Rising in Dublin during April 1916, particularly as explored by W. B. Yeats in "Easter, 1916." Both Owen and Yeats modeled the kind of artistic independence in the midst of conflict that Heaney desired. Whereas the thrust of Sophocles' original drama lies in the Greeks' attempt to convince Philoctetes to rejoin them so he can help them slaughter their enemies in the Trojan War, Heaney follows Edmund Wilson's lead in his classic essay about the play, "Philoctetes: The Wound and the Bow," and transforms the story into an allegory in which Neoptolemus represents the divided artist seeking independence and Philoctetes the isolated communities of unionists and nationalists dwelling on their suffering in Northern Ireland. I argue, against Paul Turner's suggestion that "the *Cure* gives no indication of any particular interest in the play that Sophocles wrote, or of the slightest respect for it," that Heaney's translation is deeply interested in Sophocles' play and respects it in part through employing its setting and situation to give us a moving, timeless meditation on loyalty and treachery, hope and hopelessness.[7]

HEANEY, THE FIELD DAY THEATRE COMPANY, AND NORTHERN IRISH VICTIMHOOD

Despite the immense critical attention Heaney's poetry has received for decades, his long-standing interest in drama has been given relatively short shrift critically, although he is the author of original radio plays for BBC Northern Ireland and two major translations, *The Cure at Troy* and *The Burial at Thebes* (2004), the latter a version of Sophocles' *Antigone*. Additionally, Heaney's version of *Sweeney Astray* for radio was transmitted by the BBC while the Field Day Theatre Company was staging *The Cure*, suggesting how Heaney was publicly voicing his theory of regionalism on the air and onstage in 1990.[8] Writing in 1992, Alan Peacock points out how, "in its critical notice," *The Cure* "was not generally treated in relation to the rest of his work," arguing that "this sideways displacement, though understandable, may in fact mask important continuities. In, for instance, its implicit canvassing of possible analogies between the matter of Philoctetes and the situation in Northern Ireland, the play continues an insistent trait in Heaney's work in seeking workable historical and other perspectives on this issue."[9] *The Cure at Troy* certainly displays this continuity with Heaney's earlier poems, radio dramas, and prose poems, yet it also should be read as an essentially regional drama through its specific applications to the Northern Irish situation, and it finally transcends mere geographic regionalism in its implications for divided societies globally.

Heaney has long been enamored of the drama and its power to enchant us, a primary effect that might eventually lead to a secondary process whereby the observer is changed. By 1957, for instance, he was enjoying hearing Professor Terence Spencer read and discuss Christopher Marlowe's *Tamburlaine* at Queen's University.[10] Significantly for appreciating the incantatory power of many passages in *The Cure at Troy*, he argues that in *Tamburlaine* "the reader or audience is in thrall to the poetic equivalent of a dynamo-hum, a kind of potent undermusic."[11] In the early 1960s, he developed his fascination with drama further during his teaching days at St. Joseph's Training College, Belfast, when he led a group of first-year teachers-in-training on Easter putting on the Passion section from the medieval Chester cycle of mystery plays.[12] He has also held that Caliban's description in Shakespeare's *The Tempest* "of the effect that Ariel's music produces in him could be read as a kind of paean to the effect of poetry itself. . . . 'Sounds and sweet airs, that give delight, and hurt not': that, as a description of the good of poetry and of literature in general, will do. It is not required that the experience of the sounds change Caliban into another kind of creature, or that it have a carry-over effect upon his behavior. The good of literature and of music is first and foremost in the thing itself."[13] Consistently throughout his career, Heaney has made this argument, which he always follows or precedes with a secondary one—that poetry or drama or art of any kind can actually make things happen if it is true to itself and its capacity to delight. For example, before he introduces this passage from *The Tempest*, he observes that "the paradox of the arts is that they are all made up and yet they allow us to get at truths about who and what we are or might be." He then muses, pondering how the Nazis, who loved the beautiful, nevertheless could "authorize mass killings and attend a Mozart concert on the same evening." Immediately, he claims, "Yet if it is a delusion and a danger to expect poetry and music to do too much, it is a diminishment and a derogation of them to ignore what they can do."[14] While he expounds on art's ability to enchant and delight in what follows, he has already admitted the possibility that it can tell us who we are or might become, thereby ascribing to art the potential power to change us.

The formation of the United Irishmen and their 1798 rebellion have long exerted an influence on Heaney, who sees those events collectively as the last historical moment for common cause between Catholics and Protestants in Ulster until the 1960s, when he would himself meet and befriend poets such as Michael Longley, raised Protestant, in Philip Hobsbaum's Belfast Group of writers. In 1983, Heaney fondly recalled his amateur acting as a schoolboy in plays about the 1798 rebellion: "Far from the elegances of Oscar Wilde and the profundities of Shakespeare, I was acting with the Bellaghy Dramatic Society in plays about 1798, now playing a United Irishman, a blacksmith forging pikes on a real anvil fetched from Devlin's forge at Hillhead, now playing Robert Emmet in a one-act melodrama and having my performance hailed in the crowded columns of the *Mid-Ulster Mail*."[15] In Heaney's 1798 play, *Munro*, his reading of that historical event focuses on the potential rapprochement between Catholics and Protestants in Ireland at that time as signified by Munro's use of his pen, which symbolizes the importance of writing in uniting seemingly disparate communities. Heaney's long-standing interest in 1798, his acting in the plays of his boyhood about that rebellion, and his dramatization of *Munro* for BBC Northern Ireland suggest his hopes in the 1960s for enhanced cultural understanding in contemporary Northern Ireland. After his radio play *Everyman* was broadcast by the network in March of 1971 and the province slid further into violence, he devoted himself to his poetry and prose until he became involved with the Field Day Theatre Company beginning in the early 1980s.

Heaney has recently observed that *The Cure at Troy* was "a partial fulfillment of Brian Friel's hope that Field Day would induce the poets to have a go at work for the stage" (*SS*, 420). Friel noted in a 1983 interview with Raidió Teilifís Éireann that "poets are essential" to the vision of Field Day "because in some way the poetic voice is the purest artistic voice. It's not diluted by audiences or by theatre tickets or by sale of paperbacks or that sort of nonsense."[16] Shortly after this statement, in the same interview, Heaney approvingly cites the motif of naming in Friel's 1980 play *Translations*, which launched Field Day, concluding that "one of the functions of the poetic imagination within any given reality or group or country is in some way to speak the name—the name of things as they are at the moment—to speak that reality. And I think Brian's welcome for the poet is really a solidarity with that idea, that that is the function of the poet and, secondly, that the function of Field Day is a poetic function."[17] Heaney's remarks in these two interviews suggest that *The Cure at Troy* was undertaken in a spirit that was faithful to the vision of Field Day, which sought to establish a fifth, imagined province (in addition to the four traditional provinces of Ireland), a space in which artistic commonalities throughout Northern Ireland could be explored. Although Friel, one of the two founders of Field Day along with actor Stephen Rea, was not the first to articulate this idea, he quickly adopted it, noting in the interview with Raidió Teilifís Éireann that "if we were to create, as somebody else has suggested, a fifth province; if there was a possibility of establishing *some* kind of centre ground—and I don't mean that in political terms or bridge building—but in some kind of artistic centre ground . . . we then might have something that would be of intense artistic value for the country."[18] In this same interview, Heaney goes further than Friel and predicts that a change in the grim situation in Northern Ireland is in the air, perhaps anticipating his adaptation of Shakespeare's resonant phrase in *The Tempest* later in *The Cure at Troy* about the possibility for a "sea-change" in Northern Ireland: "I think there's also a sense of a change—the relationship with the British thing. While politically there are still maintenances going on, there is in some deep place in the Unionist psyche, in the Northern Catholic Nationalist psyche, and in the psyche in the Republic—some deep place that knows—a sense of an ending."[19] As we have seen, Heaney's 1983 pamphlet for Field Day, *An Open Letter*, had garnered much attention for its rejection of his inclusion as a "British" poet in Blake Morrison's and Andrew Motion's *Penguin Book of Contemporary British Poetry* (1982).

The Cure at Troy, however, produced by Field Day just seven years after the publication of *An Open Letter*, rejects the kind of anger associated with political and cultural categories displayed by the poet himself in that very public poem. In 2005, Heaney would look back at Field Day and note that "there is no doubt that the plays it toured allowed the preoccupations of the times to strut and fret upon the stage, and to vex and invigorate in equal measure both local audiences and the literati."[20]

Heaney's translation does, however, display an impatience with intransigent factions on both sides of the major religious/political divide in Northern Ireland as he names "things as they are at the moment," to cite again his line quoted above in his comment about Field Day's function, indicting them both for stubbornness and an obsessed gazing at their own woundedness and victimhood. It is not often the case, as Michael Cavanagh has recently argued, that Heaney affirms "the idea of the poet as spokesperson for a group, whether that group be the tribe or all of humanity, and as one who sees the permanent conditions in which all people live, especially those involving suffering."[21] Heaney's chorus in *The Cure*, however, constitutes an exception to his fairly consistent desire for artistic autonomy, and it speaks explicitly for him in the opening and conclusion of the play, not only articulating the vexed, violent reality of the province at the time, but also voicing his hope that the conflict in Northern Ireland might end soon if its citizens reject the politics of victimhood.

But he notably chooses to cast his closing lines in the slant rhyme first modeled by Wilfred Owen, a writer whose poetic was based on pity. The irony of using Owen's rhyme scheme to express hope and reject an obsession with community and individual suffering, even while recognizing the reality of that suffering, is profound. Another poet, W. B. Yeats, haunts *The Cure at Troy*: Yeats, like Owen, charts the kind of independent course in his politics and poetry that Heaney himself has always striven to follow. Although Yeats disdained Owen's privileging of pity in his poetry, he himself nonetheless allowed that poetry could evoke strong emotion from its audience. The following discussion about the emotions of major characters in the play, specifically about the proper and improper use of pity and hope, accords with Heaney's belief, expressed in his contention about the concluding lines of Auden's "In Memory of W. B. Yeats," that poetry and, by extension, the creative arts generally are "on the side of life, and continuity of effort, and enlargement of the spirit."[22]

Heaney has recalled that he himself chose *Philoctetes* for production by the Field Day Theatre Company and noted that he had previously read about it in Edmund Wilson's "The Wound and the Bow," saying that "the main attraction was the material itself, in particular the way Sophocles explores the conflict experienced by the character Neoptolemus—the crunch that comes when the political solidarity required from him by the Greeks is at odds with the conduct he requires from himself if he's to maintain his self-respect. That kind of dilemma was familiar to people on both sides of the political fence in Northern Ireland. People living in a situation where to speak freely and truly on certain occasions would be regarded as letting down the side" (*SS*, 420). The translation repeatedly stresses Neoptolemus's need for independence, an analogue to that of the Northern Irish poet or any poet caught between two sides. Neil Corcoran notes that "the position of Neoptolemus as go-between, as a man in two minds who is also independent-minded, is continuous with the view of the action of poetry both in Heaney's work elsewhere and also in this play's opening chorus, where poetry is a 'borderline,' 'always in between / What you would like to happen and what will— / Whether you like it or not.'"[23]

Heaney's reading of Wilson's description of the struggle for Neoptolemus's loyalty by both Odysseus and Philoctetes must also have reinforced his sense of identification with Neoptolemus. Wilson argues that "though Philoctetes and Odysseus struggle for the loyalty of Neoptolemus, he himself emerges more and more distinctly as representing an independent point of view, so that the contrast becomes a triple affair which makes more complicated demands on our sympathies."[24] Like Neoptolemus, Heaney had long felt torn between political and cultural allegiances and had sought to remain independent. Corcoran has shown how in *Philoctetes* Heaney dispenses with the deus ex machina agency of Hercules, who helps Neoptolemus persuade Philoctetes to return with him. Instead, he points out, Heaney internalizes "the god as a function of Philoctetes' own consciousness and conscience . . . therefore making the acts of persuasion and response seem more humanly generated than they are in the original."[25]

Moreover, Heaney, especially in certain opening and closing lines, becomes at one with the chorus in *The Cure at Troy*, expressing hope for a sea change to take place both in the heart of Philoctetes and in the society of Northern Ireland. He acknowledged to the American poet Robert Hass that he "wrote in a couple of extra choruses" in the play because "the Greek chorus allows you to lay down the law, to speak with a public voice. Things you might not get away with in your own voice, in *propria persona*, become definite and allowable pronouncements on the lips of the chorus."[26] Similarly, he told Dennis O'Driscoll that "the choral ode, the choral mode, allows for and almost requires a homiletic note that you would tend to exclude from personal lyric. So the quotable element in the lines comes in part from that unrestrained rhetoric" (*SS*, 421). But when O'Driscoll asked Heaney about the stanza he had added late in the play that is explicitly about the Northern Irish conflict with its reference to the republican hunger striker and the widow of a presumably Protestant policeman, "Was there not a case for letting the timelessness of the play make its own mark?", Heaney immediately showed regret for his insertion of the topical, admitting, "There certainly was, and once the performances started I came to realize that the topical references were a mistake. Spelling things out like that is almost like patronizing the audience. But luckily it was the more quotable 'hope and history' line that caught on. Even [Sinn Fein leader] Gerry Adams went for the uplift factor" (421).

The Field Day Theatre Company originally produced *The Cure at Troy* at the Guildhall in the flashpoint city of Londonderry/Derry, long a site of sectarian tensions, on October 1, 1990. Like Friel's drama *Translations*, also produced at the culturally significant Guildhall, long the symbol of Protestant unionist domination in the city, *The Cure at Troy* suggests that dialogue, not violence, offers the only chance to unite former enemies. This small city sits on the border of Ireland and Northern Ireland and is a sort of island, like the Greek Lemnos in Sophocles' play, where both Protestants and Catholics have long felt isolated and besieged. Marilynn Richtarik observes that "Derry, although it is a large city, shares with remote western areas [in the Republic of Ireland] the problem of unemployment and the feeling of isolation," suggesting further that the city historically has been "central to both the unionist and nationalist consciousness. For unionists, Derry, which withstood a lengthy siege by James II in 1689 to make possible the continuation of Protestant rule, is a symbol of their determination to remain British. For nationalists, who constitute a majority in Derry but a minority in the North as a whole, the gerrymandering that kept a Protestant minority in power in the city stands out as one of the most egregious of the official and legal discriminations practiced against Catholics in Northern Ireland until recently."[27] The utter desolation and abandonment expressed often by Heaney's Philoctetes represents the cultural isolation felt by Protestants and Catholics throughout Northern Ireland, but especially in Derry, where its geographic marginality concentrates that dislocation. In this regard, Philoctetes' lamentations about his isolation in the play would resonate strongly with the isolated feelings of both Catholics and Protestants in Derry.[28] Philoctetes, who has been abandoned by the Greeks for years, tells Neoptolemus that he has experienced "absolute loneliness. Nothing there except / The beat of the waves and the beat of my raw wound" (*CT*, 18). Shortly after this lament, he proclaims, "This island is a nowhere. Nobody / Would ever put in here. There's nothing. / Nothing to attract a lookout's eye. / Nobody in his right mind would come near it" (18). Later, he calls the island "a home where I never was at home" (29).

Along with the excruciating mental pain of loneliness and abandonment that Philoctetes bears in the play, which would enable Northern Irish Catholics and Protestants to empathize with him, Heaney's portrayal of Philoctetes' agonizing physical pain through the suppurating wound in his foot also would have been familiar to those living in Derry at the time through its strange admixture of private and public suffering. In this sense, Philoctetes' woundedness corresponds to what Elaine Scarry has articulated about "the felt experience of physical pain, an almost obscene conflation of private and public," that "brings with it all the solitude of absolute privacy with none of its safety, all the self-exposure of the utterly public with none of its possibility for camaraderie or shared experience." She even explicitly mentions Sophocles' play in this regard: "The terrain of Sophocles' *Philoctetes* . . . is a small island of jagged rocks at once utterly cut off from homeland and humanity and utterly open to the elements."[29]

While Heaney's *Cure* generates feelings of sympathy and even empathy on the part of Northern Irish audiences for the isolation and physical pain of his Philoctetes, it also offers a stinging critique of enmity and sectarianism across history by condemning those who would parade their isolation and suffering as badges of honor. In its opening remarks, for instance, the chorus makes clearly critical statements about victims and perpetrators of violence in the context of the Troubles; although these comments begin by iterating the names of Philoctetes, Hercules, and Odysseus, the chorus quickly includes "heroes. Victims. Gods and human beings" (*CT* 1). These lines have not been recalled as those more hopeful ones at the end of the play have, probably because they are acerbic and indict both sides for perpetuating the conflict:

> People so deep into
> Their own self-pity, self-pity buoys them up.
> People so staunch and true, they're fixated,
> Shining with self-regard like polished stones.
> And their whole life spent admiring themselves
> For their own long-suffering.
> Licking their wounds
> And flashing them around like decorations.
> I hate it, I always hated it, and I am
> A part of it myself.
> (1–2)

In the context of the play, "Licking their wounds," a phrase that occurs on both page 2 to describe Philoctetes, Hercules, and Odysseus, and on page 74, used by Neoptolemus to describe Philoctetes alone, simultaneously signifies and rejects a deep self-absorption with personal trauma. In the context of the recent Northern Irish conflict, however, its broader meaning stuns us. It is tempting to assign Heaney's description of self-pitiers here to Northern Irish republicans who have, at times, been nearly solipsistic in their self-pity, and to read "People so staunch and true, they're fixated" as a description of Northern Irish Protestant loyalists who see themselves as true religious believers and true defenders of an imagined, purely Protestant "Ulster," but in fact these lines could equally apply to the other community's rhetoric.[30]

More expansively, Heaney uses the simile about "polished stones" to suggest the self-regard of both republicans and loyalists who, Narcissus-like, gaze at themselves unduly. That image of reflection is heightened, of course, by their "flashing them ["their wounds"] around like decorations." In Heaney's own essay on his translation of the play, "*The Cure at Troy*: Production Notes in No Particular Order," he admits that Neoptolemus's asking of Philoctetes "if he is going to stay there 'saying no forever'" echoes "the Ulster Unionist refusal of the Anglo-Irish Agreement in 1987," but he then goes on fairly quickly to point out, using the language of wounds, that "Philoctetes is not meant to be understood as a trimly allegorical representation of hardline Unionism. He is first and foremost a character in the Greek play, himself alone with his predicament, just as he is also an aspect of *every* intransigence, republican as well as Unionist, a manifestation of the swank of victimhood, the righteous refusal, the wounded one whose identity has become dependent upon the wound, the betrayed one whose energy and pride is a morbid symptom."[31]

Michael Parker has observed that "the imagery of wounds generally has political associations in Heaney's work," noting the "running sore" of "At a Potato Digging" in *Death of a Naturalist*, the "raw . . . opened ground" of "Act of Union" in *North*, and the wound in *The Cure at Troy*, "in which it is a key symbol and image for the Ulster condition."[32] But despite dwelling so deeply on Ulster as an amputated limb from the Irish body politic in significant poems from the early and mid-1970s, as we have seen earlier in this study, Heaney had never so prominently featured woundedness as the central condition for a literary work until this play. The chorus's opening lines attempt to articulate how such people who fixate on their woundedness isolate themselves from others even as that condition places language under extreme pressure to represent it.

When Heaney's Philoctetes experiences severe pain from his foot wound, he moans repeatedly (*CT*, 39–40); then says, "I'm being cut open" (40); then finally states, clearly drawing on Wilfred Owen's formulation of poetry, which I will explore later, "There are no words for it. Only *pity. Pity*" (41; my emphases). Alan Peacock has observed how woundedness was conveyed by the original Field Day production, noting that the "white sheeting" that shrouded the set at the beginning "was slowly pulled apart to reveal" a "visually startling group of red-clad figures from which the white sheeting slowly disengaged. . . . Subsequently in the production," after the audience views Philoctetes' "suppurating and bandaged leg, the pulling aside of the white sheets came, at one level, to represent an unbandaging—the figures dressed in stark red against the white set tokening blood in an open wound."[33] Heaney's understanding of such pain and this production's visual rendering of it enable him to depict it as a condition of isolation signifying that of both Catholics and Protestants in Northern Ireland, especially in the semantically and culturally divided city of

Londonderry/Derry. As Scarry argues in her masterful work *The Body in Pain*, pain, unlike every other psychic, somatic, and perceptual state we experience, "has no object. . . . It is itself alone. This objectlessness, the complete absence of referential content, almost prevents it from being rendered in language."[34] And indeed, as we have just seen, Philoctetes finally admits his pain cannot be expressed in language. In recognizing pain's objectless state, Heaney thus brilliantly employs the isolating power of Philoctetes' extreme pain as a metaphor for the condition of Northern Ireland, whose republican terrorists were long linked to the political party Sinn Fein (motto—"Ourselves alone") and whose loyalist terrorists often portrayed themselves similarly, as alone and outnumbered, "under siege."

The motifs of starvation and siege in *The Cure at Troy* also reflect Heaney's employment of a strong Northern Irish context ranging from the Siege of Derry in 1689 to the republican hunger strikes in the early 1980s. For example, early in the play, Philoctetes tells Neoptolemus about having "to keep alive" by "crawling and twisting / To get myself down for a drink of water" (18) and how he has experienced "ten years' misery and starvation—" (19). Later in the play, when Philoctetes believes Neoptolemus is going to take his bow away, he laments, "He's condemning me to a death by hunger. / I'm going to be a ghost before my time" (52). And after Odysseus and Neoptolemus temporarily leave him, Philoctetes wails, "I am going to die here, / I'm going to die of hunger" (59). Such lines would recall images for Derry audiences—and probably for audiences throughout Northern Ireland—of the starving city residents during the months-long Siege of Derry in 1689 by the Catholic King James II's forces. After negotiations with city residents collapsed in April 1689, Jacobite forces shelled the city and tried to slowly starve the residents into submission. Roughly ten thousand of the city's thirty thousand defenders died, and as Ian McBride has noted, "The most haunting image of the siege is that of the starving citizens reduced to a diet of horse flesh, dogs, cats, rats and mice, tallow and starch."[35] Over time, as McBride and other historians have shown, the Siege of Derry has gradually become the most powerful narrative in the Ulster Protestant psyche, particularly for loyalists. During the recent "Troubles" in Northern Ireland, the story of the siege was often "retold to reflect the disillusionment experienced by Ulster Unionists during that time period."[36]

At significant moments throughout the Troubles, loyalists in Northern Ireland, using the language of the siege, attempted to rally Protestants throughout the North to their cause, even threatening a UDI, or Unilateral Declaration of Independence, from Great Britain when they found that British support for maintaining Northern Ireland's union with Britain was waning. In 1985, five years before Field Day produced *The Cure at Troy*, the Anglo-Irish Agreement further suggested to loyalists that an accommodation with Catholics in Northern Ireland would be foisted upon them by Britain and Ireland, and loyalists throughout the province staged rallies against it. When Heaney's Philoctetes vows to the chorus late in the play, "Never. No. No matter how I'm besieged. / I'll be my own Troy. The Greeks will never take me" (63), he stands symbolically for a particular strand of Protestantism in Northern Ireland, particularly in Londonderry/Derry, adherents of which feared they would be forced into government with Catholics and, perhaps more pernicious to their minds, the possibility of their eventual relegation to minority status by a growing Catholic population in the North.

At the same time, Philoctetes also represents Catholics in Northern Ireland, especially in Derry, and most specifically, as the 1980s began and Heaney was contemplating writing a play for Field Day, the republican hunger strikers in the Maze prison, some of whom hailed from County Derry. These hunger strikers were much on his mind in the 1980s: he even began one of his Oxford lectures in the mid-1990s by discussing being at a college dinner at Oxford in May 1981 and realizing that a wake for a hunger striker, a local man from a neighbor's family back in County Derry, was taking place simultaneously, and noting that that knowledge "shadowed and questioned my presence at an otherwise perfectly jocund college feast."[37] Heaney would memorialize this young man, Francis Hughes, in the ninth lyric of the titular middle section of his 1984 volume *Station Island*. The republican hunger strikes were particularly devastating for the Thatcher administration, as ten young men died, including Bobby Sands, who was elected a Member of Parliament for his district of Northern Ireland while in prison. Murals of gaunt young men, replete with rosary beads and other aspects of Catholic iconography, were painted in working-class republican areas of Derry, Belfast, and elsewhere in the province, and thus a Christian sacrificial ethos became conflated with the hunger strikers' deaths. Heaney's translation features James Barry's painting *Philoctetes* on the cover of the American edition; although this depiction of the character looks muscular and well-fed, he is dressed in rags, which would remind readers of the hunger strikers' sartorial condition after months of wearing their blankets instead of the prison-issued uniforms as a protest against the British government's taking away of their political status. Disturbingly for constitutional nationalists like Heaney, the hunger strikes helped fuel the rise of Sinn Fein, the political party linked to the IRA, and "the thought of Sinn Fein becoming the voice of northern nationalism was enough to frighten London and Dublin alike into rescuing the [moderate nationalist] SDLP [the Social Democratic Labour Party] from the doldrums," as one prominent historian of Ulster Catholicism has pointed out.[38] Such a rescue was effected in part by the New Ireland Forum of 1983–84 and the aforementioned Anglo-Irish Agreement of 1985.

Therefore, in its employment of the images of starvation and language of siege common to Derry specifically and to republicans and loyalists in Northern Ireland generally, *The Cure at Troy* admits the reality of the still-intransigent divide in 1980s Northern Ireland, but in finally rejecting such imagery and rhetoric it embraces the gradual movement in the North away from violence and toward open discussion and the hope for peace. Again, the play shares Field Day's concern to create a fifth province of the mind where cultural dialogue can occur. Heaney thus draws on Sophocles' privileging of dialogue and trust over reprisal violence and duplicity by showing the real battle in a divided society like Northern Ireland as occurring in the hearts and minds of its citizens and emphasizing the importance of personal interaction in the characters of Neoptolemus and Philoctetes. Dishonest talk, as represented by Odysseus's plan for Neoptolemus to lie to Philoctetes—"Sweet talk him and relieve him / Of a bow and arrows that are actually miraculous"—is not a viable option (*CT*, 8).

THE OWEN AND YEATS INTERTEXTS: POSITIVE SOLITUDE

Whereas *The Cure at Troy* evokes and rejects this pejorative series of parallels to the loneliness of victimhood endemic in the republican and loyalist communities in Northern Ireland, symbolized by Philoctetes' incessant dwelling on his woundedness, it also creates and affirms a type of artistic solitude in its endorsement of the independent artistic stance and ability to unflinchingly record human suffering that Heaney found in his reading of Wilfred Owen and W. B. Yeats, troped in his character of Neoptolemus. Heaney long maintained, as he did in the opening of his essay on Dante when analyzing Yeats's description of Dante in the Irish poet's "Ego Dominus Tuus," that "When poets turn to the great masters of the past, they turn to an image of their own creation, one which is likely to be a reflection of their own imaginative needs, their own artistic inclinations and procedures."[39] Indeed, poets who merely dutifully record a portrait of a past master or attempt a strictly faithful translation that has not been transmuted somewhat through their imaginations are likely suffering from a paucity of imagination. Heaney, who has always evinced an allegiance to the imagination over church, politics, even country, always has managed to richly enlarge the context of his work on other authors through his web of intertextual references.

It is difficult, of course, to think of modern poetry without Wilfred Owen's famous dictum from his preface to his sole volume of poetry: "The Poetry is in the pity."[40] Citing this remark as evidence of Owen's overly sentimental verse, Yeats famously refused to include any of his poems in his introduction to his edition of the *Oxford Book of Modern Verse, 1892–1935* (1936), arguing that "passive suffering is not a theme for poetry."[41] Heaney directly rebuts Yeats's dictum in his elegy for Ted Hughes, "On His Work in the English Tongue," when his speaker asks, "Passive suffering: who said it was disallowed / As a theme for poetry?" (*EL*, 74). He often invoked Owen favorably when discussing the relationship between poetry and violence. For instance, the monitory voices of "those fabulous raiders" that "were ocean-deafened voices / warning me" away from violence (*N*, 19) recall Owen's description of the poet's job that Heaney affirmed more than once: "All a poet can do today is warn."[42] In fact, when asked by Dennis O'Driscoll, "To what extent would you accept Brodsky's contention 'the only thing politics and poetry have in common is the letter 'p' and the letter 'o'?" Heaney answered with an affirmation of poetry as political, citing Owen's famous dictum while transmuting it: "I'm always tempted to agree with it, but I cannot entirely. First of all, it takes the word 'politics' at its lowest evaluation. Secondly, it ignores the political reality of poems such as Alexander Blok's 'The Twelve' or Wilfred Owen's 'Strange Meeting' or Elizabeth Bishop's 'Roosters' or Allen Ginsberg's 'Howl'. . . . To transmogrify Wilfred Owen's famous line, I'd say that the politics are there in the poetry" (*SS*, 381, 382).

The usual critical maneuver when addressing Heaney's relationship to the World War I poets, however, is to cite Francis Ledwidge, who, after all, is the titular subject of Heaney's poem "In Memoriam Francis Ledwidge," which was collected in *Field Work*. Heaney also wrote the introduction to Dermot Bolger's 1992 edition of *Francis Ledwidge: Selected Poems* and had an essay on Ledwidge published in the *Irish Times* that same year entitled "Poet of the Walking Wounded."[43] Jim Haughey has argued that Heaney's elegy for this Irish Catholic poet who fought for the British in the Great War "shows how the war continues to be appropriated in order to consolidate tribal myths," holding further that in the context of the Northern Irish conflict, "Heaney's final image of Ledwidge interred with all the other 'true-blue ones' is a reminder that while a common thread of suffering unites these former adversaries, any hope of political reconciliation between nationalists and unionists depends on whether both sides can transcend their mutual obsession with their own martyr culture."[44] Such fixations drive the plot of *The Cure at Troy*, as Odysseus is determined to obtain Philoctetes' deadly bow and arrows through any means possible and as Philoctetes is fixated upon his festering foot wound and on revenge against Odysseus and the other Greeks who abandoned him on Lemnos ten years before the start of the play.

But if Heaney's relationship to World War I and its poets has been well but fairly narrowly explained through elucidations of his poem on Ledwidge, he himself has repeatedly invoked the example of Wilfred Owen in his own poetry, essays, and interviews, often to show how obsessive behaviors can be overcome. Several commentators have remarked upon Heaney's indebtedness to Yeats in his lyric sequence "Singing School" from *North*, but none has remarked upon the influence of Owen on the final poem in that sequence, "Exposure," whose title, freezing imagery, and theme of vocation, all directly recall Owen's wartime poem. Heaney may have been thinking of Owen's "Exposure" when he was writing *The Cure*: late in the play, when Philoctetes worries that "I am going to die here, / I'm going to die of hunger," he concludes that speech with a terse line recalling the dilemma for the freezing soldiers in Owen's poem and that poem's title: "Slow death by *exposure*" (*CT*, 59; my emphasis). More indirect echoes of Owen's poetry abound in later Heaney poems, such as his "In Memoriam Francis Ledwidge," "Ugolino," "The Song of the Bullets," and "On His Work in the English Tongue."[45] Heaney has been most drawn to Owen's "Strange Meeting" and "Insensibility," and *The Cure at Troy* contains many references to these poems.

Heaney's intertextual references to "Strange Meeting" set the tone of confusion, then gradual clarity that suffuses *The Cure*. The chorus articulates the theme of strangeness early in the play when it tells Neoptolemus, "We're in a maze. / We're strangers and this place is strange. / We're on shifting sand. It is all sea-change. / Clear one minute. Next minute, haze" (*CT*, 12). Much of *The Cure at Troy* concerns the blurring of boundaries between supposed enemies when Philoctetes and Neoptolemus encounter each other, in a "strange meeting" like that described in Owen's poem where the speaker, having entered hell, is greeted by the soldier he killed the day before, who tells him finally, "I am the enemy you killed, my friend."[46] The growing clarity of purpose on the part of both Neoptolemus and Philoctetes is enhanced with an understanding of Heaney's intertextual use of "Strange Meeting," which similarly moves from confusion on the part of the speaker to recognition. Moreover, Heaney's familiarity with Owen's poem allowed him to overlay his translation about the internal strife within a faction of Greeks with Owen's narrative about a recently dead English soldier meeting and being befriended by a ghostly German soldier he has killed, thus suggesting that nationality and enmity can be potentially transcended by a mutual recognition of suffering, from which friendship might flow. Owen's spectral German soldier reminds his English killer how he had intimately stabbed him, linking the two through a shared narrative of suffering. In *The Cure at Troy*, Neoptolemus manages to gain Philoctetes' trust by reciting his personal story of suffering in which he was denied the wearing of his father Achilles' armor because Odysseus had started wearing it (*CT*, 21–22).

Another way in which Heaney inserts the intertext of "Strange Meeting" into his translation is through his emphasis on the underground dwelling place of Philoctetes, which recalls the "profound dull tunnel" of hell in Owen's poem.[47] Odysseus tells Neoptolemus that Philoctetes lives in "a sort of den, / An open-ended shelter" (*CT*, 4). Later, Neoptolemus tells the chorus in reference to Philoctetes' lair that "his shake-down is up there / In a sort of roofed-in place under the rocks" (12). This underground lair functions psychographically as well because Heaney employs it, just as Owen does, to stage a meeting in which the central character has a crisis of conscience once he meets and recognizes the humanity of his supposed enemy. Heaney, of course, has long employed images of dark places, especially in his early poetry, to signify the depths of the unconscious; think, for example, of "Personal Helicon" from *Death of a Naturalist*, or "The Forge" from *Door into the Dark*. Recognizing how the hellish subterranean setting of Owen's "Strange Meeting" is interwoven into the text of *The Cure* makes us realize how vexed the internal struggle of Neoptolemus is as he wavers between his vow to Odysseus to take the deadly bow and arrows from Philoctetes and his internal morality, which urges him to comfort Philoctetes as he gradually perceives him as human, not monstrous.

Heaney identifies with both the chorus and Neoptolemus, the latter of whom represents his favored position of artistic independence. In "The Redress of Poetry," he approvingly refers to the independent stance taken by both Owen and Yeats when he states, "If you are an English poet at the front during World War I, the pressure will be on you to contribute to the war effort, preferably by dehumanizing the face of the enemy. If you are an Irish poet in the wake of the 1916 executions, the pressure will be to revile the tyranny of the executing power.... In these cases, to see the German soldier as a friend and secret sharer, to see the British government as a body who might keep faith ... to do any of these things is to add a complication where the general desire is for a simplification."[48] Heaney clearly references Owen's "Strange Meeting" in his approving use of the phrase "friend and secret sharer." Later in "The Redress of Poetry," Heaney stresses again poetry's need to complicate, to refuse reductiveness: "It should not simplify. Its projections and inventions should be a match for the complex reality which surrounds it and out of which it is generated."[49] In *The Cure at Troy*, Odysseus, with his obsessive desire to gain the bow and arrows of Philoctetes and leave that character behind, represents unalloyed hatred, while Neoptolemus, with his ability to be moved by Philoctetes' narrative of suffering, represents not only Heaney but also poetry itself, which shifts and sways in the currents and eddies of our minds, fluid and unable to be fully fixed.[50]

Heaney's Neoptolemus changes before our eyes as he muses upon the suffering experienced by Philoctetes in the last ten years of exile on Lemnos, a suffering Heaney explicitly evokes through recourse to Owen's emphasis on pity in his poetry, especially through direct repetitions of "pity" and more oblique references to Owen's "Strange Meeting." At the end of one of Philoctetes' longest speeches in the play, during which he urges Neoptolemus to take him with his crew of men, he concludes by invoking an Oweneque sense of pity, which is quickly echoed by the gathered chorus. "Count your blessings, / And always be ready to *pity* other people," he says to the younger man (*CT*, 27). The chorus quickly exclaims, "*Pity* him, sir, do. / The man's at breaking point. / Imagine he was your friend. / And you didn't take him then?" to which Neoptolemus soon replies, "I'll not have it said / I ever stopped a stranger being helped" (28; my emphases). This interchange commingles the language of friend and stranger, again echoing the trajectory from strangeness and confusion toward friendship and clarity in Owen's "Strange Meeting." Because of the pity that Neoptolemus feels for Philoctetes, he cannot leave him on Lemnos, as Odysseus wishes him to; Neoptolemus states explicitly that "I can't help it. There's something in me he touched / From the very start. I can't just cut him off" (53).

Heaney's Neoptolemus chooses not to remain insensible to his new friend's pain, and his sympathy for this wounded warrior draws generally both on Owen's theme of pity and specifically on his poem "Insensibility." The speaker in Owen's poem finishes by cursing men who "by choice . . . made themselves immune / To pity and whatever moans in man," concluding by musing how those insensible humans are unmoved by "whatever shares / The eternal reciprocity of tears."[51] This last line became a phrase employed by Heaney whenever he dwelt on atrocity. In his essay "The Atlas of Civilization," for example, he cites in full Polish poet Zbigniew Herbert's poem "Apollo and Marsyas," concluding afterward that it "manages to keep faith with 'whatever shares / The eternal reciprocity of tears.'" Indeed, this is just the poetry which Yeats would have needed to convince him of the complacency of his objection to Wilfred Owen's work (passive suffering is not a subject for poetry), although, in fact, it is probably only Wilfred Owen (tender-minded) and Yeats (tough-minded) who brought into poetry in English a 'vision of reality' the equal of this one."[52] And in response to Dennis O'Driscoll's question about Bloody Sunday and Bloody Friday being "crucial consciousness-raising events for you," Heaney reels off a list of atrocities, then invokes both Yeats and Owen to convey his reaction to them, stating, "The combination in your thought and feeling of what Yeats would have called abstract passion and its opposite, what Owen would have called 'the eternal reciprocity of tears.' Nothing I can say about it seems to get it right" (SS, 119). And after being asked about the role of the poet and about writing newspaper commentaries after major events during the Troubles and in their immediate aftermath, Heaney again invokes Owen's line from "Insensibility," arguing, "A poet does have a role and a responsibility. You're allowed, for example, to quote poetry— probably *expected* to quote it; in the wake of the Omagh bombing, I remember how grateful I was to invoke Wilfred Owen's line about 'the eternal reciprocity of tears'" (SS, 353).

If the tone of Owen's famous line is evoked through the pity that Neoptolemus evinces for Philoctetes in *The Cure at Troy*, then the opening lines of the chorus specifically reference "Insensibility," in which the "dullards whom no cannon stuns" in that poem's last stanza are compared to "stones" who "by choice they made themselves immune / to pity and whatever moans in man."[53] As noted earlier, the chorus links Philoctetes, Hercules, and Odysseus together in its opening speech, noting that their joint conviction of righteousness renders them "shining with self-regard like polished stones" (CT, 1). In Owen's terms, all three are insensible dullards because of their stony, stoic hearts, but of course, as we know, Philoctetes will experience a real change of heart as the play proceeds and will overcome his antipathy toward Odysseus and his own self-obsession.

To convey that change in Sophocles' title character, Heaney concludes his translation by employing two intermittently half-rhymed stanzas that recall Owen's use of half-rhyme epitomized by "Strange Meeting" and "Insensibility":[54]

Now it's high watermark
And floodtide in the heart
And time to go.
The sea-nymphs in the spray

Will be the chorus now.
What's left to say?

Suspect too much sweet talk
But never close your mind.
It was a fortunate wind
That blew me here. I leave
Half-ready to believe
That a crippled trust might walk

And the half-true rhyme is love.
(*CT*, 81)

These lines that Heaney added at the end of the play are significant for his cautious hope for Northern Ireland in their hopeful moderation. The specific form of these lines, an homage to Owen's poetry, expresses Heaney's privileging of a healthy sorrow, not pity, in his audience.

The anonymous writer for the *Guardian* concluded in his 1920 review of Owen's *Poems* that the device used in "Strange Meeting" is "neither rhyme nor assonance," further terming it "a subtly contrived escape from tonal completeness" that affects us "as the baffling elusiveness of a fugitive pun, or the half-foiled meeting of two stanzas of a sestina," finally holding that "just because of the baffling and the foiling it fails in its artistic purpose."[55] But later critics have been much more appreciative of Owen's innovative use of rhyme, including Heaney himself, who, citing the first stanza of "Strange Meeting," has approvingly pointed out that "Owen's mastery of half-rhyme combines with his memory of the fallen angels in Milton's *Paradise Lost* to present a typically Dantean encounter with the figure of his enemy, at once familiar and unexpected."[56] Heaney's formal recourse to Owen's pararhyme in these closing stanzas thus generates a combination of unfamiliar and unexpected feelings in ourselves, as we meet a rhyme scheme that soothes yet startles, much as Neoptolemus recognizes the humanity he shares with Philoctetes, whom he had believed an enemy.

One further way in which Owen's poetic proved exemplary for Heaney in his *Cure* involves his positive modeling of poetry as witness to atrocity in the role of truth-teller. In his famous preface, in much less often cited lines than the one equating poetry and pity, Owen states, "All a poet can do today is warn. That is why the true Poets must be truthful."[57] In "The Interesting Case of Nero, Chekhov's Cognac and a Knocker," Heaney, having already cited (twice) in the preceding pages this statement from Owen's preface, argues that Owen and the other World War I poets "are among the first of a type of poet who increasingly looms as a kind of shadowy judging figure above every poet who has written subsequently. The shorthand name we have evolved for this figure is the 'poet as witness,' and he represents poetry's solidarity with the doomed, the deprived, the victimized, the under-privileged. The witness is any figure in whom the truth-telling urge and the compulsion to identify with the oppressed becomes necessarily integral with the act of writing itself."[58] *The Cure at Troy* accords with Heaney's affirmation of the truth-telling function of the writer as he delineates it in this essay through its insistence on depicting the reality of Philoctetes' suffering and, by extrapolation, the suffering of those in Northern Ireland during the recent conflict.

In several of the remarks about Owen just cited, Heaney links Owen and Yeats together, and indeed, the two often form a complementary pair of exemplary poets for Heaney, although criticism on his work has usually sundered them, perhaps because of their differing nationalities and Yeats's antipathy to Owen's insistence on pity. Heaney clearly draws on both Owen and Yeats, however, in these crucial opening lines he invented for his chorus about people so obsessed with "their own self-pity, self-pity buoys them up" and who are "so staunch and true, they're fixated, / Shining with self-regard like polished stones" (*CT*, 1), lines that Heaney argues apply equally to republicans and loyalists. A further indication of the suitability of these lines to describe such mentalities lies in Heaney's adaptation of a striking simile from Yeats's "Easter, 1916." In the third stanza of that poem, Yeats, who has just catalogued some of the leaders of the Easter Rising and categorized them jointly as being obsessed, observes that "hearts with one purpose alone / Through summer and winter seem / Enchanted to a stone / To trouble the living stream."[59] The stoniness of the rebels' hearts indicates their fixation on Irish independence and Yeats's critique of that fixation, which he contrasts with the triple flux evoked in a striking image, also from stanza 3: "Minute by minute they change; / A shadow of cloud on the stream / Changes minute by minute."[60]

Moreover, the *Cure*'s use of the particular Yeatsian intertext of "Easter, 1916" corresponds with Yeats's rejection there of the Easter rebels' fixity in favor of fluidity and thus affirms Neoptolemus's ability to see multiple sides of the issue before him. Neoptolemus's protean ability to change sides and dwell in between the demands of both Odysseus and Philoctetes echoes Yeats's privileging of fluidity over fixity in "Easter, 1916" and in other poems such as "The Magi" (recall those disturbingly fixed eyes of the Magi) and its companion poem, "The Second Coming."[61]

Additionally, Yeats's ability to stand above the fray, to remain his own man, an independent artist like Owen, has been often cited by Heaney, and this stance of Yeats seems to hover behind Heaney's translation. In a little-known essay, "Yeats's Nobility," first delivered in 1989, a year before *The Cure at Troy* would be produced, Heaney, after pointing out Yeats's conflicting emotions toward the rebels in "Easter, 1916," argues that while Yeats was "daring in his arrogation to himself of the role of national poet" in that and later poems, speaking as "the voice of greatly representative imagination," he nonetheless "spoke not for any party or faction but utterly from himself and for himself."[62] In much the same way, as Heaney turned fifty in 1989 and was working on his translation, he increasingly became Ireland's national poet yet remained thoroughly committed to literature, not any ideologies.

While *The Cure at Troy* portrays suffering and simultaneously rejects the victim mentality, it also transcends its present moment of composition and performance by offering hope for an imagined end to the conflict in Northern Ireland. The most well-known lines of the translation were also not in Sophocles' original but added by Heaney:

History says, *Don't hope*
On this side of the grave.
But then, once in a lifetime
The longed-for tidal wave
Of justice can rise up,
And hope and history rhyme.

So hope for a great sea-change
On the far side of revenge.
Believe that a further shore

Is reachable from here.
Believe in miracles
And cures and healing wells.
(*CT*, 77)

Aidan O'Malley points out that this first six-line stanza "is the most frequently cited passage from the [Field Day Theatre] [C]ompany's entire output,"[63] an astonishing fact since Friel's *Translations* has become a much more anthologized text than Heaney's play.

Heaney changed the original title of *Philoctetes* because "we were going to be touring *Philoctetes* to audiences who wouldn't have much historical sense of the play or its place in Sophocles' oeuvre, so I believed a new title could work as a pointer, a kind of subliminal orientation. And this led to *The Cure at Troy*, since in Ireland, north and south, the idea of a miraculous cure is deeply lodged in the religious subculture, whether it involves faith healing or the Lourdes pilgrimage" (*SS*, 422). He himself is deeply drawn to the notion of poetry as leading to healing, as when he cites the concluding lines of Auden's "In Memory of W. B. Yeats" in an essay on poetry's function in the midst of war or atrocities:

In the deserts of the heart
Let the healing fountains start.
In the prison of his days
Teach the free man how to praise.

He observes that these lines "are a kind of prayer to the shade of the dead poet, asking him to ensure the continuation of poetry and to sponsor its constant work of transformation."[64] And yet Heaney holds a tough-minded attitude toward such transformations, especially given his deep knowledge of the deep-seated sectarian attitudes that still affect Northern Ireland.

This notion of a "miraculous cure" clearly spoke in 1990 to an exhausted Northern Irish populace, who by 1998 would affirm the Good Friday Agreement with 71 percent of the electorate voting to begin a power-sharing, devolved government with both Catholic and Protestant representation. However, Heaney purposely chose not to offer any regular rhyme scheme in these two stanzas, as if to avoid bestowing an air of sonic harmony and completion on the hoped for "sea-change": only two of six lines fully rhyme in the first stanza, and none fully rhyme in the second stanza.

Moreover, these lines occur several pages from the end of the play and are not the chorus's last words; instead, the chorus chants the concluding stanza beginning with "Suspect too much sweet talk" that I cited in my discussion of the Owen intertext in the play above. As I have argued elsewhere, "'Mind' and 'wind' are eye-rhymes but not true rhymes, while the only couplet, which rhymes 'leave' with 'believe,' is then undercut by the non-rhyming of the last two lines that tentatively advance a hope 'That a crippled trust might walk,' which is itself then mitigated by the statement that 'the half-true rhyme is love.'"[65] In the context of the play, these lines suggest the miraculous occasion signified by the crippled Philoctetes' decision to walk down to the waiting Greek boats and sail with them to Troy and help them defeat the Trojans. Philoctetes has been betrayed by Odysseus and the other Greeks ten years before when they cast him on Lemnos, and during the course of the play Neoptolemus, whom Philoctetes grows to trust, betrays him again by acquiring his deadly bow and arrows from him. But overcome by a crisis of conscience, Neoptolemus goes back to Philoctetes, returns his weapons, and promises to honor his original promise to take Philoctetes home. Only then, with significant prompting from the chorus, does Philoctetes freely choose to help the Greeks defeat Troy. As O'Malley has noted, however, the "cure" that Philoctetes' bow "brings about—the eventual end of the war—is only accomplished by the destruction of one side; a point that places an even larger question mark over the references to Northern Ireland in the Choral intervention."[66]

In the political context of Northern Ireland in 1990, in 1998, and now, the chorus's concluding lines may still suggest a cautious hope for the peace process if the truth is spoken in love; the line "a crippled trust might walk" implies that if even Philoctetes can overcome both his own obsession with his wound and the lack of trust he has in the Greeks, so might Northern Ireland as a society choose to walk away from their crippling wounds of the past and reach out in love to those on "the other side."[67] Moreover, Heaney's adoption for his epigraph of two stanzas from Auden's "As I Walked Out One Evening" that are spoken by the chorus of "all the clocks in the city" suggests both everyone's radical sinfulness and the imperative to love (and implicitly forgive) each other while there is still time.[68] Halfway through its seventh stanza, the clocks in the city of Auden's poem start speaking in an odal maneuver—"O let not Time deceive you, / You cannot conquer Time"[69]—and conclude with the two quatrains in Heaney's epigraph:

> O look, look in the mirror,
> O look in your distress;
> Life remains a blessing
> Although you cannot bless.
>
> O stand, stand at the window
> As the tears scald and start;
> You shall love your crooked neighbor
> With your crooked heart.[70]

The crucial adjective in the second stanza here, "crooked," may have led Heaney to his line about "a crippled trust" and confirmed in him our inability to fully trust or love another even though that reaching out should happen. His chorus likely echoes Auden's monitory clocks with their odal insistence and repeated verbs and adjectives that insist on a process of self-examination ("O look, look in the mirror") leading to an outward action (loving one's "crooked neighbor / With your crooked heart"). Although such a process is not ever fully achievable and likely not fully efficacious because of our own warped natures, it is still worth striving for.

But with his recourse to some of his favorite exemplars—Owen, Yeats, and Auden—is Heaney arguing that imaginative literature can heal such wounds, suture such divides? His chorus warns against such a reading late in the play, insisting, "No poem or play or song / Can fully right a wrong / Inflicted and endured" (*CT*, 77). Heaney has noted about Michael Longley's poem "Self-Heal" that the "action of poetry . . . is a self-healing process, neither deliberately provocative nor culpably detached."[71] Perhaps *The Cure at Troy* finally offers us, in its balanced condemnation of violence across the political and cultural spectrum in Northern Ireland, a vision of self-healing, as Philoctetes slowly hobbles to the boats of the waiting Greeks and as the citizens of the long-benighted province of Northern Ireland slowly, even miraculously, begin to trust again, although they cannot forget the hurts that have been visited upon them.

When asked in 2001 by an interviewer about his persistent interest in "the power of poetry and music to heal," Heaney confirmed this penchant, then immediately qualified it, stating,

> This power to heal will only affect those who come to poetry of their own accord, ready for it. Obviously poetry doesn't have the same power as an inoculation or an antibiotic. . . . The singular, individual, solitary, memory-marking, soul-settling experience of reading at an intimate individual level can have an effect. Very tiny, very delicate—like a change of the light on water. But those experiences and changes can become part of the memory system, part of the value system within an individual life. And if enough people attend like that within a society then there is a general strengthening of possibility and something that might be called healing, a growth of culture.[72]

Qualified though this statement may be, it nonetheless speaks volumes about his hope that individual reading can lead to gradual, accretive, cultural growth in society.

The simultaneously local and international thrust of the play, coupled with Heaney's contribution of lines from it to an ecumenical, humanitarian project that same year it was published and produced, reveals how his original conception of Northern Irish regionalism both deepened and widened its appeal beyond the borders of the province. Two instances illustrate this aspect of Heaney's regionalism in its transnational hope for justice, even healing—the first in England with the conviction and eventual release of the Birmingham Six and the second in South Africa with apartheid and its collapse.

The first of these concerns Heaney's recourse to some lines from *The Cure at Troy* as his response to the situation of the Birmingham Six. In the wake of the trial and continuing appeal process of these six wrongly convicted people, a number of prominent intellectuals and artists contributed to a limited-edition book entitled *The Birmingham Six: An Appalling Vista*, published in 1990. The case of the Birmingham Six began on July 14, 1974, when pubs in Birmingham, England, were bombed, killing nineteen and injuring 182 people. Six men were arrested and imprisoned for this crime and were convicted. During their trial, the prosecution admitted that all of them had been seriously assaulted while in custody. Their

1987 appeal was rejected by the Court of Appeal in London on January 28, 1988; the court dismissed "the idea that there ha[d] been a large-scale conspiracy by the police and that confessions had only been obtained by the police beating the men." Finally, on March 14, 1991, the six men, now known as the "Birmingham Six," were freed after a second appeal resulted in a trial that suggested there had been forgeries in West Midlands Police documents and false evidence given.[73]

Seamus Deane, Heaney's former classmate from St. Columb's College, wrote the introduction to *The Birmingham Six: An Appalling Vista*, succinctly indicting both the British judicial system and the "silence of us who now speak and then were *dumb*,"[74] a phrase that almost surely draws on Heaney's lines from "Punishment": "I who have stood *dumb* / when your betraying sisters, cauled in tar, /wept by the railings" (*N*, 31; my emphasis). As Heaney pointed out in "Whatever You Say Say Nothing," "Northern reticence" existed in the province during the time of the conviction of these innocent men (*N*, 53). Recall too his regretful epigraph from Gaston Bachelard to *An Open Letter*: "What is the source of our first suffering? It lies in the fact that we hesitated to speak. . . . It was born in the moment when we accumulated silent things within us" (*AOL*, 5). Deane's acknowledgment of the previous silence on the part of intellectuals and artists is powerful and humbling, while his insistence on the diversity of the contributors to the book speaks volumes about the eventual widespread outcry at the men's continued imprisonment: "When a range of writers and artists, journalists and intellectuals, individuals and organizations, as diverse as that represented here, can agree to speak with one voice against the conviction and imprisonment of the Birmingham Six, that is in itself a tribute to the strength of their case."[75]

Heaney's contribution to this volume is an excerpt from *The Cure at Troy* that begins with the chorus's—and by virtue of its inclusion here— Heaney's recognition that literature cannot fully right wrongs: "Human beings suffer, / They torture one another, / They get hurt or play hard. / No poem or play or song / Can fully right a wrong / Inflicted and endured" (*CT*, 77). The first line of the next stanza, "The innocent in gaols," certainly has special bearing on the case of the Birmingham Six, while the thrust of the remaining stanzas expresses "hope for a great sea-change" and the possibility of people hearing about the injustices committed (77).

Given the context of the reprinted passage, Heaney clearly supported the release of the Birmingham Six; his support for them indicates both traditional nationalist anxieties about the British judicial bias against Irish people and an increasing emphasis on human rights generally.

The second illustration of his qualified but tentative hope that *The Cure*'s dramatization of betrayal and forgiveness could augur improved social and cultural understanding not only in Northern Ireland but also beyond it stems from his own application of the play to the dissolution of apartheid in South Africa and the subsequent election of the long-imprisoned Nelson Mandela to the presidency of that divided country. When interviewed after his trip to South Africa in 2002 to receive an honorary doctorate from Rhodes University, Heaney recalled that he had been "involved with the anti-apartheid movement in Dublin for a number of years" and reflected upon Mandela's release from prison in February 1990, while he was teaching at Harvard:

> I was translating a play called *Philoctetes*, about how a marooned man comes back and helps the Greeks to win the city of Troy. The play is really about someone who has been wounded and betrayed, and whether he can reintegrate with the betrayers or not. Human sympathy says yes, maybe political vengefulness says no, but the marooned man in Sophocles' play helps the Greeks who betrayed him to win Troy. It seemed to me to mesh beautifully with Mandela's return. The act of betrayal, and then the generosity of his coming back and helping with the city—helping the polis to get together again.[76]

Heaney's likening Mandela to Philoctetes implies that with such contemporary and ancient heroes, healing can start only through their clear recognition of betrayal, then their gracious generosity to unify people. His progressive focus in *The Cure at Troy* on isolation, then liberation, and finally an outward-facing generosity suggests strongly the continuing evolution of his conception of regionalism in simultaneously continuing to dwell upon the vexed matter of Northern Ireland even as he imagined a more united province in the future and offered it as a potential model for redress of injustices worldwide.

Chapter Ten

GUTTURAL AND GLOBAL
Heaney's Regionalism after 1990

There is a healing and curative power, a kind of immunization, available from the old guttural accents that underlie our standardized speech, and it is this heaviness of glottal underlife that will save us from the weightlessness of the global babble that surrounds us.
—Heaney, "The Guttural Muse in a Global Age"

TOWARD THE QUINCUNX: HEANEY'S LATER
REGIONAL ESSAYS

The Cure at Troy's titular emphasis on miraculous healing, which is mitigated by the caution expressed by the chorus in the play's conclusion, remained alluring to Heaney in subsequent years even as he continued to reject such instantaneous cures for deep cultural and societal wounds. As we will see in this chapter, his second strand of regionalism— the decades-long attempt to develop a reinvigorated sense of the common literary, linguistic, and cultural heritage of Northern Ireland that might provide the basis for rapprochement between Catholics and Protestants there—did not wane after *The Cure at Troy* but rather attained a new complexity and resonance. These qualities stemmed from his continuing and growing conviction that his public role as writer compelled him to embrace justice and offer hope despite the suffering continuing in Northern Ireland and worldwide. Heaney's lifelong artistic emphasis on portraying suffering and injustice in his home region gradually broadened into his conviction to articulate the same in regions of violence throughout the world. This strand of his regionalism has a marked ethical, propulsive quality that seeks to startle us out of our complacency and inertia when faced with suffering, to condemn it, and perhaps to even seek to end it through pursuing justice and reconciliation. Through this process, a gradual cure for our ills—or at least a tentative model of such a cure—may slowly, haltingly, but inexorably begin within ourselves.

Even those critics who recognized the significance of Heaney's regionalist commitment in the 1960s and 1970s began to argue by the end of the twentieth century and beginning of the current one that he was gradually leaving regionalism behind. Yet such commentators generally relegate Heaney's regionalism to its first aspect—recording the rural traditions of his native province in highly wrought, local language—and do not apprehend how this part of his regionalism not only survives but becomes continuous with his desire to imagine a new Northern Ireland and to understand the spirit world beyond our own, the other two components of his regionalism. For instance, in 1999, R. P. Draper argued about Heaney's poetry of *The Haw Lantern* and after that "though Heaney continues to be a distinctively regional ... Irish poet, there is a noticeable de-emphasizing of this particular brand of commitment. The verse is less heavily charged with the accents of his 'guttural muse,' and there is a trend towards a limpidity and impersonality which seem the work of language using the poet, rather than the poet using language."[1] And while John Wilson Foster argued in 2009 that "Heaney is developing in his poetry an increasingly public, de-regionalized poetic voice," such views neglect his defiant and triumphant return to a reinvigorated regionalism that traffics with globalization in his later poetry, particularly in *District and Circle* (2006), along with his regionalist works in other genres in his latter years.[2] More convincingly, Michael Cavanagh, writing the same year as Foster, held that "much of the poetry in ... *Electric Light* and *District and Circle* ...

clings to the Ireland he grew up in."[3] And yet there is nothing defensive or embarrassed about that clinging; rather, Heaney has continued to explore his lifelong interest in regionalism as cohering in a distinct geopolitical identity through language—specifically in Irish and English and the idioms of Hiberno-English and Ulster English. This chapter treats a variety of Heaney's regionalist endeavors from 1990 onward, including his translations of *Beowulf*, *Sweeney Astray*, and Robert Henryson's *The Testament of Cresseid*; crucial essays on John Clare, John Hewitt, Hugh MacDiarmid, and Louis MacNeice as regional writers; and "The Turnip-Snedder," "The Harrow-Pin," and the sequences "The Tollund Man in Springtime," "Found Prose," and "District and Circle," all from his 2006 volume, *District and Circle*. These works suggest that Heaney continued to believe in the power of place, evoked through particular, often regional, language to gather people, memories, and even objects together in transtemporal communities.

As the last decade of the twentieth century progressed, Heaney continued to argue that poetry could exemplify the particularity of local cultures that politics should seek to emulate and establish. For instance, in his Nobel Prize speech, *Crediting Poetry*, he holds that "a trust in the staying power and travel-worthiness of such good ["the indigenous *per se*"] should encourage us to credit the possibility of a world where respect for the validity of every tradition will issue in the creation and maintenance of a salubrious political space," as he points out has occurred in Israel, South Africa, and eastern Europe (*CP*, 23). Reflecting on the continuing issue of the partition of Northern Ireland and Ireland, Heaney comments that "surely every dweller in the country must hope that the governments involved in its governance can devise institutions which will allow that partition to become a bit more like the net on a tennis court, a demarcation allowing for agile give-and-take, for encounter and contending, prefiguring a future where the vitality that flowed in the beginning from those bracing words 'enemy' and 'allies' might finally derive from a less binary and altogether less binding vocabulary" (23). The tennis court metaphor is compelling because of the porous quality of the net itself and the intimacy of the playing area where opponents meet at the net before, occasionally during, and after the match. A major portion of Heaney's poetry, prose, and translations from the late 1980s and beyond exemplifies such openness and intimacy with "the other" and in so doing offers models of this "agile give-and-take."

In the wake of the Iron Curtain being lifted in eastern Europe, the 1994 IRA and Combined Loyalist Command cease-fire in Northern Ireland, and the dissolution of borders throughout the world, poetry's ability to presage a less calcified politics was thus often on his mind. For example, in his 1997 essay, "Further Language," he discusses the role of poetry as an intermediary between "historical and subjective reality," then argues that the political culture should also function in this manner:

> The political culture should promote conditions where the imagined communities towards which people aspire can find their symbolic reflection. And this is why, for example, the appearance in a Northern Ireland context of the Irish Language on radio and television—and on official notices and street signs in certain areas—should be greeted as a positive historic development; it should not be regarded as a takeover bid by Irish nationalists, but as a timely *de facto* acknowledgement that in order to prefigure a workable future, a pluralist present has to be worked for and worked out. Use of the Irish language is how some people's imagined community finds its reflection, and the desire for such symbolic reflection should be taken as exactly that, and not as a form of subversion or an attempt to demean or occlude someone else's reflection.[4]

Heaney's language here about the "imagined community" is clearly borrowed from Benedict Anderson's *Imagined Communities*. Anderson makes a powerful case in his study for the evolution of communities and nations based on imagined ideas of themselves as expressed through the development of print languages. He argues that print languages helped lay the foundations for "national consciousnesses in three distinct ways. First and foremost, they created unified fields of exchange and communication below Latin and above the spoken vernaculars." Through this process, speakers became aware of many other speakers of this language and began to believe in an abstract notion of "the nationally imagined community to which they all belonged."[5] Additionally, "print-capitalism gave a new fixity to language," and "created languages-of-power of a kind different from the older administrative vernaculars."[6]

The obvious weakness in trying to apply Anderson's model to Heaney's description of the Irish-speaking community identifying itself with Gaelic street signs lies in Irish's essentially oral nature. Only recently has the government developed a standard written Irish; Irish speakers still generally express themselves orally, though there are certainly columns written in Irish in the republican newspaper *An Phoblacht* and in the *Irish Times*. The emphasis on the oral nature of the Irish language is implicitly affirmed by the reading of the Irish news in each of the three different dialects every evening on Raidió Teilifís Éireann. Heaney's model seems more appropriate for understanding the contemporary community that identifies itself with the Irish language than Anderson's, since it recognizes the historical existence of an Irish-speaking community and enables them to feel more at home through a belated written recognition of their language in a largely English-speaking, majority-Protestant province.

Heaney continued to enrich and develop his concept of a rooted, yet inclusive Northern Irish regionalism in other essays from the 1990s, such as his 1992 Oxford lecture "John Clare's Prog," one of his most important explorations and affirmations of the validity of local culture for contemporary poetry. In his recovery of such writers, his essays on them affirm Neil Corcoran's contention that his criticism "carries ... a strong ethical as well as aesthetic charge."[7] Heaney opens his essay on Clare by noting that his own poem "Follower" (*DN*, 12) originally opened with the line "My father wrought with a horse-plough" "because until recently that verb was the common one in the speech of mid-Ulster," but that he changed that local verb to "worked" in the final version.[8] Observing that *wrought* always "carried a sense of wholehearted commitment to the task" and that "the word implied solidarity with speakers of the South Derry vernacular and a readiness to stand one's linguistic ground," Heaney wonders, "Why, then, did I end up going for the more pallid and expected alternative 'worked'?"[9] He concludes that "I thought twice," ruefully musing that "once you think twice about a local usage you have been displaced from it, and your right to it has been contested by the official linguist censor with whom another part of you is secretly in league. You have been translated from the land of unselfconsciousness to the suburbs of the *mot juste*."[10] Heaney's formulation here conveys well his lifelong struggle to balance the pull of his childhood regional culture and dialect with the equal allure of his adopted academic culture and its idiom. In this particular instance, and in some subsequent ones, such as his decision to drop the adjective *bottomless* from his description of the monsters' mere in his 1999 translation of *Beowulf*, he seems to have given in to the "official linguistic censor," but in fact his agonized articulation of such linguistic struggles itself works to worry us into realizing how such situations can fruitfully lead us into preserving aspects of our regional culture, or at least into celebrating the more successful efforts of such regional writers as Clare.

"John Clare's Prog" returns to this concern repeatedly, even obsessively. Heaney casts Clare's brief but meteoric literary career in terms of an enabling fairy tale for subsequent writers like himself who hope to register the traces of their regional culture in their work: "Once upon a time John Clare was lured to the edge of his word-horizon and his tonal horizon, looked about him eagerly, tried out a few new words and accents and then, willfully and intelligently, withdrew and dug in his local heels. Henceforth, he declared, I shall not think twice."[11] Clare's "The Mouse's Nest" constitutes one of Heaney's examples of how the English poet did not think twice in cleaving to local speech. Pausing on the couplet, "The water o'er the pebbles scarce could run / And broad old cesspools glittered in the sun," Heaney sagely observes that here "the eye of the writing is concentrated utterly upon what is before it, but also allows what is before it deep access to what is behind it.... This typical combination of deep-dreaming in-placeness and wide-lens attentiveness in the writing is mirrored by the cesspools as they glitter in the sun. They too combine a deep-lodged, hydraulic locatedness within the district with a totally receptive adjustment to the light and heat of solar distances."[12] His description uncannily recalls his own attempt at utter concentration and "wide-lens attentiveness" in his "Bogland," which opens, "We have no prairies / To slice a big sun at evening—" and continues to also register "the light and heat of solar distances" with such lines as the one describing the bog as "crusting / Between the sights of the sun" (*DD*, 41).

Heaney's use of the phrase "the district" signals his approval of Clare's deep connection to his local Northamptonshire landscape and culture, because he often wrote of his own "district" in South Derry in his essays such as "The Bog" and would even incorporate the word *district* into the title of his 2006 volume, *District and Circle*, in a defiant proclamation of his continuing regionalism in the midst of contemporary culture's often dislocating trajectory. I point out this striking affinity between the two poets not so much to show how Heaney is reading Clare through his own regionalist project, although that is certainly true, but rather to demonstrate how in Clare Heaney found a fellow poet who also celebrated a culture that is ultimately transregional, just as he would come to see the *Beowulf* poet and his culture in this light. Heaney, like Clare, stands at "*the frontier of writing*, in a gap between the unmistakably palpable world he inhabits and another world, reached for and available only to awakened language."[13]

The phrase "frontier of writing," which is first mooted in the poem "The Frontier of Writing," from *The Haw Lantern*, acquired a rich significance in Heaney's work during the late 1980s and early 1990s, culminating in his last Oxford lecture, "Frontiers of Writing," which functions in part as an apologia for a grounded, yet inclusive regionalism. For Heaney to defend his version of regionalism as a unifying project, he felt compelled to finally register his discontent with its most famous Northern Irish defender, the poet John Hewitt, who had promoted Heaney's first volume, *Death of a Naturalist*, in his 1966 *Belfast Telegraph* review. While he admits that Hewitt "settled upon the region of Ulster itself as the first unit of his world, in the hope that a place that was both a *provincia* of the British imperium and an area of the ancient Irish province of Uladh or Ulster could command the allegiance of both Unionists and Nationalists," and while he terms such a maneuver "original and epoch-making, a significant extension of the imagining faculty into the domain of politics," he goes on to claim that "it could not wholly reconcile the Unionist mystic of Britishness with the Irish Nationalist sense of the priority of the Gaelic inheritance."[14] While defending Hewitt as "personally a man of the deepest tolerance and sympathy, principled in his sense of diversity, passionate for social justice," Heaney claims that "he could not include the Irish dimension in anything other than an under-privileged way.... The fact that Gaelic was a dying language was enough for Hewitt to absolve himself of any imaginative obligation to the Gaelic order. He was predisposed to write out rather than write in the native inheritance."[15] Later, Heaney would repeat this charge, claiming in *Stepping Stones* that "in John Hewitt's imagining, the Catholics in the North, and the Irish south of the border, remained definitively 'other.' He had a principled regard for them and would have fought for their rights, but nothing in him could altogether flow towards them" (*SS*, 331).

Certainly, poems such as "The Irish Dimension," from *Kites in Spring: A Belfast Boyhood* (1980) and "A Little People," one of Hewitt's last, written in June of 1986, bear out Heaney's sense of the older poet's distance from the Catholic population in the North and his fear that Ulster Protestants will eventually become outnumbered by Catholics in the province. In the first of these, Hewitt recalls meeting the new next-door neighbors and realizing "they were Catholics, / the very first I even came to know," and although he rejects calling them "Teagues or Micks," he admits how the boy particularly represented the "other" to him: "His magazines were full / of faces, places, named, unknown to me. / Benburb, Wolfe Tone, Cuchullain, Fontenoy. / I still am grateful, Willie Morrissey."[16] After discussing the characteristics of Ulster Protestantism in the opening stanzas of "A Little People," the poem's fifth stanza offers horribly negative images of Northern Irish Catholics, likely not Hewitt's own perceptions but certainly those held by certain Protestants in the North: "Among that other tribe, a myth-crazed clan, / oath-bound to serve their dream of nationhood, / cower in their covens secretly to plan / their future's chart in scrawls of tears and blood."[17] But to be fair, the poem also concludes that his "tribe" of Ulster Protestants has lost any redeeming rhetoric: "So now intransigently negative / our threadbare lexicon provides no scope / should one of our nay-sayers dare to give / some gentler phrase of mercy, grace or hope," and he concludes, "That only hope now is to tame our tongues, / trim them to truth, for all within the place / endure the same indignities and wrongs," finally desiring a time "when each may grasp his neighbor's hand as friend."[18]

Perhaps because of such poems, Heaney finally ruefully looks back on Hewitt's regionalism as a failed project, noting that "it just might have come into being, had the gerrymandered statelet of Brookeborough's era been transformed through the administration of Lord O'Neill and Brian Faulkner (with the help of agitation by the Civil Rights Movement) into an opener, more tolerant democracy. But that transition was not to happen, and what did happen jumped the political disposition of both minority and majority back into a renewed and desolate defensiveness."[19]

While Heaney came to reject Hewitt's regionalism, there is later evidence, coming in the form of his 2001 discussion of Hewitt's poem "The King's Horses" and at least one interview, that he continued to recuperate him as an exemplary Northern poet whose occasional unease and tentativeness helpfully modeled such an attitude during the time of iron certainties at the beginning of the Troubles in Northern Ireland. In "Through-Other Places, Through-Other Times: The Irish Poet and Britain," Heaney introduces Hewitt's poem as written "by someone who has often been treated more as a cultural witness or as some form of ethnic or anthropological symptom than as a poet per se."[20] He himself is guilty of exactly this treatment of Hewitt in "Frontiers of Writing," although his 1972 review of Hewitt's *Collected Poems* sought to analyze the poetry and its subtle silences and rhythms. Such guilt likely drives Heaney's attempt to recover "Hewitt the Poet," rather than "Hewitt the Failed Regionalist." He first offers what he terms "a tendentious argument claiming that Hewitt perceives himself as the shattered Humpty Dumpty in that he is a man divided against himself, a person with all the deep affiliations to British traditions that come with his Ulster planter background, and yet equally a man with a deep desire for regional separateness."[21] But he quickly rejects this reading, claiming that such a construction "would be to attribute to Hewitt a kind of literary and ideological deliberateness which is absent from this poem. In fact, one reason why I chose this particular poem of Hewitt's discussion is that for once Hewitt does not seem to know from the start where exactly he is going."[22] According to Heaney, Hewitt concedes here "that the civic part of him . . . is a disguise, a kind of false self. And that his real allegiance is to a 'pace and beat' that are 'utterly different,' namely the pace and the beat he knows and obeys as a poet." Heaney thus returns to his 1972 statement that Hewitt "is evolving into a man without a mask" and that later Hewitt establishes "the kind of authority without dogma that poets stand for."[23] In one of his interviews collected in *Stepping Stones*, Heaney repeats this assertion, observing, "I find him most convincing as a poet when he realizes the emotional cost of the stand-off, in poems as different as 'The King's Horses' and 'A Local Poet.' He's at his best when he gets away from his cut-and-dried, man-of-the-left decidedness and finds himself talking to no one but himself" (*SS*, 331). Heaney's solitary and adogmatic Hewitt thus stands uneasily in the divided North but achieves considerable authority in such poems, in contrast to his dogmatic, regionalist Hewitt, who is more firmly planted in the province.[24]

In "Frontiers of Writing," Heaney sees Louis MacNeice and, as we will see later, Hugh MacDiarmid as more inclusive modelers of regionalism than Hewitt. MacNeice's appearance as the central figure for an invigorated Heaneyean regionalism startles, especially given Heaney's long engagement with Hewitt's regionalism in essays such as his 1972 review of Hewitt's *Collected Poems, 1932–1967*, "The Poetry of John Hewitt," and his 1977 essay "The Sense of Place," along with his consistent, approving citation of Frost in his talks, readings, and essays. Moreover, earlier in his career, Heaney had claimed to be distanced from the older poet, noting that MacNeice's "poems arose from a mind-stuff and existed in a cultural setting which were at one remove from me and what I came from.... I envied them but I was not taken over by them the way I was taken over by Kavanagh."[25] Indeed, in "The Sense of Place," Heaney does not discuss MacNeice at all, preferring instead to discuss Kavanagh, Montague, and Hewitt. MacNeice has been invoked and claimed much more often by Heaney's fellow poets such as Derek Mahon, who wrote the classic poem about MacNeice, "At Carrowdore Churchyard," with its approving advocacy of the older poet's philosophy in the lovely lines, "The ironical, loving crush of roses against snow, / Each fragile, solving ambiguity."[26] Additionally, Michael Longley has written an early and powerful defense of MacNeice and edited a popular selection of his poetry.[27] Indeed, Heather Clark goes so far as to claim that Mahon and Longley especially, "by collectively establishing MacNeice as the doyen of Northern poetry, by promoting a selective canon, and by 'rewriting' many of his ideological and philosophical concerns in their own work (exile, origin, transience, self-division, humanism, scepticism, and social consciousness), . . . have placed him at the beginning of a line of an inheritance which is, by right, theirs."[28]

In his April 1988 Richard Ellmann Lecture at Emory, "The Pre-natal Mountain: Vision and Irony in Recent Irish Poetry," Heaney finally claims MacNeice as an exemplary figure for his poetics through first approvingly defending Paul Muldoon's inclusion of him in his 1986 anthology, *The Faber Book of Contemporary Irish Poetry*: "To include him in an anthology of Irish poetry is to affirm in a politically useful way that the category of Irishness is no longer confined to persons with the native blood-thrum but has been expanded to include people of Irish birth who wish to be allowed the rights to all the other dimensions integral to their memory and their heritage."[29] These dimensions arise, Heaney posits, from the two divisions within MacNeice—"the overarching Ireland/England one," and "the tension between the civil Anglo-Ireland of Nationalist sympathy and Connemara scenery from which his father sprang... and another Ireland, a Calvinist, abrasive and increasingly militant Ulster of Orange bands and stern-faced Unionist magnates, facing down the voluble resentments of the Catholic ghettoes."[30] MacNeice's emigration to England enabled him to transcend these divisions, providing "an example of how distance, either of the actual, exilic, cross-channel variety or the imaginary, self-renewing, trans-historical and trans-cultural sort, can be used as an enabling factor in the work of art in Ulster."[31]

In "Frontiers of Writing," citing MacNeice's poem "Carrick Revisited," which he had previously analyzed in "The Pre-natal Mountain," Heaney terms it "a poem written out of a need to straddle his areas of self-division, and to bring his inherited and acquired characteristics into congruence." He argues in an implicit riposte to Hewitt and Frost that "it was as if MacNeice combined within himself both the Yankee and the native American. He saw his Northern Ireland nativity—his given destiny, his bridgehead into reality—as something that was to be neither cancelled nor defensively fortified. Like Hewitt, he grew up in pre-partition Ireland, but, unlike Hewitt, he did not allow the border to enter into his subsequent imaginings: his sense of cultural diversity and historical consequence within the country never congealed into a red and green map. In MacNeice's mind, the colours ran—or bled—into each other."[32] Heaney's now well-known but misunderstood formulation of the quincunx of cultural and literary tradition across Ireland and beyond follows this discussion of MacNeice. While Neil Corcoran claims that Heaney "derives [the quincunx] from Sir Thomas Browne's *The Garden of Cyrus*," a more immediate source comes from the poet's reading of MacNeice's complicated cultural and political heritage.[33] Heaney anticipates the image of the quincunx and its ability to hold in equilibrium opposing forces when he argues in "The Pre-natal Mountain" that "In 'Carrick Revisited,' the whole parallelogram of cultural and ancestral forces operating in MacNeice's life is discovered and thereby to a certain extent redressed. What the poem calls 'the pre-natal mountain'... is an imaginary place held in equilibrium with two other places. First, the England of his schooling and domicile.... But second, and more important in its otherness from the dream-mountain, is the plumb, assured, unshakable fact of an Ulster childhood which cannot be shed."[34]

By the time he wrote "Frontiers of Writing," however, Heaney specifically and repeatedly identified the figure as a *diamond*, a figure that recalls the central area of Derry City, which he would memorably describe twice in his poem about his brother Hugh, "Keeping Going," and which likely also recalls Heaney's interest in the imaginary "fifth" province of Ireland that the Field Day Theatre Company, based in Derry, took as its abiding image. In the penultimate stanza of "Keeping Going," the speaker describes the horror of a sectarian assassination on the Diamond, while in the final stanza, he movingly recalls the joy of Hugh's trips to the Diamond, where "your big tractor / Pulls up at the Diamond, you wave at people, / You shout and laugh above the revs" (*SL*, 12). Although this poem was collected in *The Spirit Level*, which came out in 1996, three years after his essay was delivered in Oxford, he first published it on October 12, 1992, which suggests he was musing on the figure of the diamond in the poem around the same time he first mooted the figure of the quincunx in his Oxford lecture on MacNeice in late 1991, to which he returns in the 1993 lecture "Frontiers of Writing."[35] Given Heaney's birth and childhood in County Derry and his extensive involvement with Field Day, such a reading of his figure of the four-pointed diamond with its fifth, central tower shows that it is much more freighted with the matter of Derry specifically and Northern Ireland more generally—its horror, its joys, its potential—than it might at first seem. Derry continued to be much on his mind even by the end of the twentieth century. For instance, he wrote a preface for the 1999 collection of essays on County Derry for what has become the standard survey of counties on the island; in it, Heaney surveys his own sense of the county by drawing on his childhood and his awareness of the county's varying geology, history, topography, and religious cultures, concluding by observing, "Diversity wasn't a word that was much in vogue then, but Derry did—and does—give the concept real substance."[36] Such statements suggest Heaney's persistent belief even well into this century that a viable regionalism inheres in various diversities, not a monolithic or monoglot culture.

By virtue of its content, the diamond figure is also more than a symbol for Northern Ireland or an imagined fifth province of the imagination—and more even than simply a complex image of Ireland's literary and cultural heritage. In its complexity and diversity, it becomes Heaney's lasting model of the first strand of his regionalism, one that bursts the bounds of Northern Ireland and draws on regional traditions in Ireland, Britain, Europe, and even America as well.

Heaney's "integrated literary tradition" includes at its center "the tower of prior Irelandness, the round tower of original insular dwelling, located perhaps upon what Louis MacNeice called 'the pre-natal mountain.'"[37] He locates "at the southern point of a diamond shape Kilcolman Castle, Edmund Spenser's tower, as it were, the tower of English conquest and the Anglicization of Ireland, linguistically, culturally, institutionally," then places Yeats's tower, Thoor Ballylee, as the western point of this diamond, lauding his "poetic effort, which was to restore the spiritual values and magical world-view that Spenser's armies and language had destroyed."[38] Next, he locates the fourth tower, "on the eastern edge," as Joyce's Martello tower, where he attempted "to marginalize the imperium which had marginalized him by replacing the Anglocentric Protestant tradition with a newly forged apparatus of Homeric correspondences, Dantesque scholasticism and a more or less Mediterranean, European, classically endorsed world-view," an enablingly regional formulation that I have articulated in my previous chapters on the debt that Heaney's *An Open Letter*, *Station Island*, and *The Cure at Troy* owe to Joyce.[39] Heaney finally places MacNeice on the northern point of his imagined diamond at Carrickfergus Castle, claiming that

> this tower, once it is sponsored by MacNeice's vision, no longer only looks with averted eyes back towards the Glorious Revolution and the Mother of Parliaments, but is capable of looking also towards that visionary Ireland whose name, to quote MacNeice, "keeps ringing like a bell / In an underwater belfry." MacNeice ... by his English domicile and his civil learning is an aspect of Spenser, by his ancestral and affectionate links with Connemara an aspect of Yeats and by his mythic and European consciousness an aspect of Joyce.... He can be regarded as an Irish Protestant writer who managed to be faithful to his Ulster inheritance, his Irish affections and his English predilections. As such, he offers a way in and a way out not only for the northern Unionist imagination in relation to some sort of integral Ireland but also for the southern Irish imagination in relation to the partitioned north.[40]

Heaney evidently wishes that his own regionalist project will succeed to at least this degree so that we might term him in the future an Irish Catholic writer "who managed to be faithful to his Ulster inheritance, his Irish affections, and his English predilections," and thus a figure of similar cultural inclusiveness across Ireland and Britain.

In a potentially divisive maneuver, however, heretofore unrecognized in criticism treating his discussion of the quincunx, Heaney surely draws on the Catholic image of this pattern, which is associated with the cross and the five wounds of Christ. He may have been inspired to do so by one of his leading regional exemplars: Joyce uses the term *quincunx* in his short story "Grace" to describe the pattern that Mr. Kernan and his friends sit in at the religious retreat held at the Jesuit church on Gardner Street.[41]

But Heaney's goal is finally larger than simply inscribing Catholicism throughout the map of Ireland: by adding MacNeice to the quincunx, he "also admits a hope for the evolution of a political order, one tolerant of difference and capable of metamorphoses within all the multivalent possibilities of Irishness, Britishness, Europeanness, planetariness, creatureliness, whatever."[42] Thus he somewhat flippantly implies that his own construction of this quincunx and indeed the entirety of his regionalist endeavor prefigures not only the gradual political devolution of Northern Ireland but also a world where difference is affirmed in the embrace of singular cultures and where their contribution to human understanding and decency is celebrated.[43]

Although Heaney's quincunx has proven a useful figure for his thinking about the various interpenetrating and overlapping cultures in Ireland and Britain, the geometry of the triangle may be finally more applicable to his own ongoing recovery of his triple heritage. When he writes of the Northern Irish poet W. R. Rodgers that "in the triangulation of Rodgers's understanding of himself between [sic] London, Loughgall and the Lowlands, in that three-sided map of his inner being that he provided with its three cardinal points . . . there is something analogous to the triple heritage of Irish, Scottish and English traditions that compound and complicate the cultural and political life of contemporary Ulster," he is articulating his own gradual understanding of this triple heritage for his work.[44]

HEANEY'S REGIONALIZED *BEOWULF*

Heaney's fascination with his triple cultural heritage has resulted in his translations of major works from each tradition: *Sweeney Astray* (1983), *Beowulf* (2000), and Robert Henryson's Middle Scots poem *The Testament of Cresseid* (first published in a limited edition in 2004 and then published with seven of Henryson's fables in 2009). By 1997, in his introduction to his and Ted Hughes's edited collection *The School Bag*, he could confidently state that they included "poems in translation from the Irish, Welsh, and Scottish Gaelic languages" because "it is only in the relatively recent past that there has been any developed awareness of the deep value and high potential of the non-English poetries of Britain and Ireland."[45] This collection and these three major translations bespeak Heaney's continued attempt to recover a full range of regional voices in Britain and Ireland outside the dominant influence of London.

According to Walter Benjamin, translation itself constitutes a marginal act, one to which Heaney ineluctably was drawn as a member of a neglected region of Britain. Benjamin believed that "unlike a work of literature, translation does not find itself in the center of the language forest but on the outside facing the wooded ridge; it calls into it without entering, aiming at that single spot where the echo is able to give, in its own language, the reverberation of the work in the alien one."[46] Already committed to recovering the full range of "British" literature through reclaiming the work of regional writers across the Atlantic archipelago, by the early 1970s Heaney began to see translation itself as a metaregionalist endeavor by which he might call into "the center of the language forest" and produce resonant literary echoes that enlarged staid nationalist notions of English literature by placing such works as *Beowulf* in their proper transatlantic context.

Sweeney Astray constitutes a crucial intervention by Heaney on behalf of his theories of regionalism; as Rui Carvalho Homem has argued, "Heaney has performed an act of cultural devolution" with his translation of that Irish epic, "retrieving a text from the autochthonous tradition."[47] Heaney even chose to publish his translation first in Northern Ireland, under the Field Day imprint, telling Neil Corcoran, "I liked the idea of it being published in Derry. It's a kind of all-Ireland event situated just within the North, and there's a little bit of submerged political naughtiness in that."[48] Sweeney's medieval Ulster is a unifying cultural space for Heaney, as he believes unionists and nationalists could both identify with the places the exiled figure visits in his *Sweeney Astray*, published the year before *Station Island*, in 1983.[49] But I have come to believe that Heaney's formal reliance on the quatrain through much of *Sweeney Astray* (relieved only by several passages of prose) weakens its effect as a unifying regional text and even drags down its visionary quality inhering in its "otherness... as a poem from beyond."[50] Looking back on the poem in 1989, Heaney spoke of his modest hopes for *Sweeney Astray* being released by Field Day during a time of great strife in Northern Ireland in the wake of the IRA hunger strikes and their aftermath. Although he later stressed that by the time he finished the translation he had first begun in 1972 he was more interested in the poem as transcending "my own mournful bondings to the 'matter of Ulster,'" he nonetheless had originally hoped for *Sweeney* to "render a unionist audience more pervious to the notion that Ulster was Irish, without coercing them out of their cherished conviction that it was British. Also, because it reached back into a pre-colonial Ulster of monastic Christianity and Celtic kingship, I hoped the book might complicate that sense of entitlement to the land of Ulster which had developed so overbearingly in the Protestant majority as a result of various victories and acts of settlement over the centuries."[51] Sweeney the leaper thus would recover and restore an original sense of the old nine-county Ulster from its truncated, six-county form in most of the twentieth century. Imagining such an expanded but historically accurate area, unionists and nationalists might live better in harmony realizing the dual Irish-British identity of this region and, by extension, that of its inhabitants.

All three of these major translations sprang largely from two related struggles: Heaney's continuous attempt to reconcile the life of the mind with the pull and tug of outward experience, and with his urge to somehow unify Ulster/Northern Ireland through language invoking a reinvigorated sense of the imagination. This last maneuver perceives the North as a sort of mediating region between mainland Britain and Ireland.

Beowulf is dedicated "in memory of Ted Hughes,"[52] and Heaney's long affirmation of Hughes as an enabling regional writer accords with his attempts to make the poem resound with the voices of his father's relatives, men whom he has described, in his revealing introduction to the poem, as "big-voiced scullions" since they spoke with a "weighty distinctness," uttering "phonetic units as separate and defined as delph platters displayed on a dresser shelf."[53] His father's uncles, cattle dealers from Hexham in northern England, not far from where Hughes grew up in Yorkshire, spoke with a weightiness and "solemnity of utterance" that led Heaney deep into translating an epic that he "had always loved" for its "kind of foursquareness about the utterance, a feeling of living inside a constantly indicative mood."[54] *Beowulf* was published in 1999, and when, just a few months earlier, on November 3, 1998, Heaney spoke of Hughes in his funeral eulogy in Devon for the English poet as a "keep ... a strong tower of both tenderness and defense" and as a "keeper," noting "that there was something in him that we looked up to and loved and trusted, something that the word 'keeper' with all its biblical resonance and reliability still guaranteed," he subtly suggested that Hughes and his poetic language hearkened back to the weightiness and directness of the word-hoard of *Beowulf*.[55] Toward the end of this eulogy, Heaney again implies an affinity between Hughes and the Anglo-Saxon author of *Beowulf*, the latter of whom gives him "a feeling of living inside a constantly indicative mood," when he praises Hughes's "ongoingness, the hereness of his genius and nowness of his artistic aboveness and beyondness and undisfigurable beauty and truth."[56]

In translating the Old English *Beowulf*, implicitly in a dialectic with the Irish *Sweeney Astray* and the Scots *Testament of Cresseid*, Heaney spoke of his urge to ensure "that my linguistic anchor would stay lodged on the Anglo-Saxon sea-floor."[57] The example of Hughes (and an even earlier model, Gerard Manley Hopkins) certainly did much to ensure that anchorage. Heather O'Donoghue argues that Heaney's *Beowulf* translation is inherently a regional maneuver: "Though proudly conscious of writing and speaking from what is perceived by literary London as a linguistic and political margin, Heaney has himself centralized that margin, foregrounding the literature, languages and politics of Ulster. Heaney's translation of *Beowulf* is a dizzying amalgam of opposites: very distant meets very recent; centralized margin meets marginalized centre."[58] His *Beowulf* therefore functions, just as *The Cure at Troy* does, as a regionalist allegory where he recognizes the great violence endemic to such ancient cultures, yet chooses to somewhat downplay that violence in favor of rapprochement and fellowship between people groups, epitomized in *Beowulf* by the unity the titular hero secures between his Geats and King Hrothgar's Danes after he defeats Grendel and Grendel's mother for Hrothgar. In so doing, Heaney obliquely chronicles the reprisal violence that characterizes much ancient and recent history in the North of Ireland, yet shows the common ground and peace available to warring communities there. Finally, by advocating Beowulf's great martial prowess, Heaney allegorizes it so that it represents his own poetic power and poetic combat, an inner "violence" pressing back protectively against outer violence, implicitly affirming poetry's power to offer a site of possibility where opposed "tribes" might meet.

After some difficulty with translating the poem in the middle 1980s, Heaney put the project aside,[59] but he was lured back through a realization that some of his own poetry hewed to Anglo-Saxon metrics: "Without any conscious intent on my part certain lines in the first poem in my first book conformed to the requirements of Anglo-Saxon metrics. These lines were made up of two balancing halves, each half containing two stressed syllables—'The spade sinks into gravelly ground: / My father digging. I look down...'—and in the case of the second line there was alliteration linking 'digging' and 'down' across the caesura. Part of me, in other words, had been writing Anglo-Saxon from the start."[60] As I showed in my introduction, he had absorbed the Anglo-Saxon alliterative tradition from Hopkins and Hughes, two of his major poetic influences. Heaney goes on to discuss his discovery in the late 1950s at university that the name of the River Usk in England shared a common etymology with the Gaelic word *uisce*, for water, observing that this "was definitely a place where the spirit might find a loophole, an escape route from what John Montague has called 'the partitioned intellect,' away into some unpartitioned linguistic country, a *region* where one's language would not be simply a badge of ethnicity or a matter of cultural preference or an official imposition, but an entry into further language. And I eventually came upon one of these loopholes in *Beowulf* itself."[61] Here *region* signifies both Heaney's home region of Northern Ireland and its linguistic affinities with the substratum of the English language across the North and other regions.

Heaney's linguistic loophole arrived in the form of the word *tholian*, meaning "to cope." After he replaced the *thorn* symbol with its phonetic "th" sound, he realized that "it was the word that older and less educated people would have used in the country where I grew up. 'They'll just have to learn to thole,' my aunt would say about some family who had suffered an unforeseen bereavement."[62] Heaney's recognition after this example of the archipelagic journey the word must have made—from England north into Scotland, then over to Ulster with the planters, then to the native Irish, finally to the American South when the Scots Irish emigrated—seems to assure him of its universal connecting power in Britain, Ireland, even America. Heaney recalls, "When I read in John Crowe Ransom the line, 'Sweet ladies, long may ye bloom, and toughly I hope ye may thole,' my heart lifted again, the world widened, something was furthered. The far-flungness of the word, the phenomenological pleasure of finding it variously transformed by Ransom's modernity and *Beowulf*'s venerability made me feel vaguely something for which again I only found the words years later."[63] Heaney may not have known Ransom's 1940 essay on Thomas Hardy, "Honey and Gall," but he certainly valued Hardy's emphasis on the hearth world of his local English culture that he transformed into his fictional Wessex. Given this predilection, Heaney would surely agree with Ransom's assessment of Hardy's poetry that "a superior metaphysical validity belongs to his lyrics and little narratives in that the particularity of their detail is sharp and local."[64] And elsewhere, Heaney had succinctly identified Ransom as "a poet from a regional culture," articulating his dilemma in "affirming the centrality of the local experience to his own being" while recognizing that "this experience is likely to be peripheral to the usual life of his age."[65] By connecting what he terms "Ransom's modernity" in his introduction to *Beowulf* with that southern American poet's clear linguistic heritage drawn from the ancient word-hoard of the British and Irish archipelago, Heaney's traces of a unifying dialect in his regionally inflected translation of *Beowulf* continue to offer us moderns courage and strength in the face of adversity.

This transatlantic linguistic heritage recalls the "united Ulster mythology" he was seeking to create in his translation of *Sweeney Astray* and offers a glimmer of linguistic understanding in the midst of the darkness and violence that has pervaded these islands and that pervades *Beowulf* itself. The term *thole* or *tholian* denotes coping, something Beowulf and the Geats had to do, as have the citizens of Northern Ireland for most of the last century. Its resonance, then, spreads out from the translated epic into the waters surrounding the British and Irish archipelago. Discovering *tholian* gave Heaney the courage in this translation to employ Ulster dialect words "where a certain strangeness in the diction came naturally. In those instances where a local Ulster word seemed either poetically or historically right, I felt free to use it."[66] He goes on to discuss his usage of "graith" for "harness," "hoked" for "rooted about," and "bawn" in referring to Hrothgar's Hall.[67]

Even when he did not use particular dialect words, Heaney's translation of the great Anglo-Saxon epic was often inflected with his regional culture. In this regard, given his long-standing interest in bogs in his earlier poems such as "The Tollund Man," "The Grauballe Man," "Punishment," and "Strange Fruit," among others, his attraction to the tarn where Grendel and his mother live and his desire to render its depth as "bottomless" in an earlier, unpublished version of line 1366 reveals just how much his regional culture colored his approach to the poem. Heaney originally translated the second half of that line and line 1367 as "And the water is bottomless. / Nobody alive has ever fathomed it."[68] The reader for Norton, which would publish the Norton Critical Edition that contains Heaney's translation, objected to the use of *bottomless*, noting that "'it' in the next line [1367] must refer to some bottom."[69] Heaney eventually gave in, translating this line and a half as "And the mere bottom / has never been sounded by the sons of men."[70] Heaney recalls admitting, in his response to this reader, that the reader was correct in pointing out that he had taken liberties with "what the original warrants," but the reasons he gives for having used the adjective *bottomless* are revelatory: "At this point, I might have pleaded out that 'bottomless' occurs as the last word in an early poem of my own ["Bogland"], but even if I did not adduce the chapter and verse, I went on to say that for me 'bottomless' was a word 'with *merey* suggestions, since as a child I was always being warned away from bog pools in our district—because they had 'no bottom to them.'"[71]

Heaney had recalled this warning before, and his extended discussion of it in his essay "The Bog" is worth briefly considering because of its bearing on how his concept of regionalism is allied to a similarly rich sense of the imagination. When recalling in that earlier essay his parents' warning about the nearby bog being bottomless, Heaney muses that "they said it so often that I firmly believed it, and in a different way I believe it still. As a child I used to imagine my helpless body whistling down a black shaft forever and ever; now I imagine the imagination itself sinking endlessly down and under that heathery expanse."[72] Taken together, Heaney's statement in his 1999 essay on translating *Beowulf*, "The Drag of the Golden Chain," and his 1976 essay on the Irish bog suggest the bog's irresistible fascination for him as a site of danger when he was a child and as a symbol of the inexhaustible imagination once he became an adult. Such a multivalent symbol is grounded in the local ("our district"), the regional, in part because it also functions as a imaginative site of dialect: Heaney goes on to comment in "The Drag of the Golden Chain" that when translating the great Old English epic "I wanted my anchor to be lodged on the Anglo-Saxon sea-floors, down in the consonantal rock, but I had a second mooring down in the old soft vowel-bog of the local speech."[73]

Such a mooring is ineluctably linked for Heaney, as the second part of his sentence suggests, to the powerful presence bogs exert in his individual consciousness and in the Irish national consciousness. In discussing the origins of "Bogland" in "Feeling into Words," he mentions that "bogland . . . is a landscape that has a strange assuaging effect on me. . . . We used to hear about bog-butter, butter kept fresh for a great number of years under the peat. . . . So I began to get an idea of bog as the memory of the landscape, or as a landscape that remembered everything that happened in and to it."[74] He finally argues that "I had a tentative unrealized need to make a congruence between memory and bogland and, for the want of a better word, our national consciousness," which he went on to do in "Bogland."[75] The intertwined significance bogs came to have for him—as memory banks and as symbols of the active, unfathomable imagination—seems to have driven his perception of this Anglo-Saxon mere as "bottomless."

But finally, Heaney's abiding interest in local bogs that influenced his reading of the mere in *Beowulf* suggests how he perceives them as a unifying part of Irish national consciousness that rejects the border between South and North and, by extrapolation, sees such landscape as a potentially unifying factor across the island of Ireland and the United Kingdom. In "The Bog," Heaney cites Daniel Corkery's maxim that "our national consciousness is a quaking sod," immediately observing that "somewhere in his heart every one of us is a bogtrotter. The bog itself, or the moss, as we called it in Co. Derry, is our outback, a benign wilderness, that part of our landscape that has never fallen completely under human sway."[76] His embrace here of the pejorative tag *bogtrotter* is consistent with his lifelong affirmation of regionalism, sometimes understood negatively by others, as unifying. Similarly in *Beowulf*, Heaney seems to imply, the monsters' mere and its surroundings have never been ruled by humans and constitute an anarchic (if not benign) miniwilderness. Such a reclamation of this watery landscape as elemental and formative in the Old English consciousness suggests a common link between England and Ireland, demonstrating again how Heaney's conception of regionalism breaks boundaries and often attempts to reveal commonalities that might bridge cultural ruptures.

Heaney's *Beowulf* should thus be understood in the context of his regionalist, ongoing work as a potentially healing mediator between competing binaries such as abstract notions of Irish and British nationalism that have nothing to do with the lived realities of citizens in these countries. In his translation, he cites the moment when Beowulf leaves the country of the Danes, having united his people, the Geats, with King Hrothgar's, the Danes. Hrothgar proclaims,

> What you have done is to draw two peoples,
> the Geat nation and us neighbouring Danes,
> into shared peace and a pact of friendship
> in spite of hatreds we have harboured in the past.[77]

This language, when compared to another leading translation by Charles W. Kennedy, suggests just how much Heaney read such lines through his own hopes for peace in Northern Ireland:

> You have brought it to pass
> That between our peoples a lasting peace
> Shall bind the Geats to the Danish-born;
> And strife shall vanish, and war shall cease. . . .[78]

Kennedy's translation here, particularly the rhyme of "peace" and "cease," suggests too simple a process for any former enemies, while Heaney's lack of rhyme suggests the hard work of cultural understanding and gradual peace. Heaney's peace is "shared," while Kennedy's is "lasting." Heaney senses that hatreds may persist, and he indicates that lingering possibility through the use of the present perfect tense, while Kennedy (too optimistically) believes that "strife shall vanish, and war shall cease," and uses the future tense to signify what he thinks is that definite outcome. Heaney also points out in his introduction that as the poem concludes, "A world is passing away, the Swedes and others are massing on the borders to attack and there is no lord or hero to rally the defence."[79] The poem's conclusion, which Heaney links to the contemporary killing fields not of Northern Ireland but of Rwanda or Kosovo, testifies to the power of the well-sung artistic witness to suffering: "The Geat woman who cries out in dread as the flames consume the body of her dead lord could come straight from a late-twentieth-century news report, from Rwanda or Kosovo.... We immediately recognize her predicament and the pitch of her grief and find ourselves the better for having them expressed with such adequacy, dignity and unforgiving truth."[80] Sometimes all art can do is bear witness and in so doing, speak truth to power. While Heaney clearly views the unfolding story of Northern Ireland somewhat more positively than he does that of Rwanda or Kosovo, he nonetheless holds out hope that those histories can be narrated by members of suffering communities in Africa and Europe and perhaps eventually spoken in dialogue with others who have their own particular histories.

Citing a likely apocryphal tale about how the leaves of Irish books steeped in water helped heal snakebite according to the Venerable Bede in his *Ecclesiastical History of the English People*, he claims he is happy for his translation of *Beowulf* to "function in the world in the same way as the Venerable Bede tells us that books from Ireland functioned within the Britannic and Hibernian context of his times in the eighth century."[81] Heaney approvingly terms this tale "an example of a writer calling upon a fiction in order to cope with differences between two islands linked and separated in various degrees by history and geography, language and culture," noting immediately by invoking Yeats that "as such, it prefigures much of the work that would be done by Irish poets in the coming times and much that will continue to be done."[82] Moreover, in his introduction to *Beowulf* he implies something like an understanding of the intertwined history of Britain and Ireland through his discussion of "the destinies of three peoples ... [and] their interweaving histories in the story of the central character": the Danes, the Geats, and the Swedes.[83] As Seamus Deane has pointed out, Heaney's translation of *Beowulf* is both consistent with his entire career and particularly pertinent to the current peace process in the region of Northern Ireland:

> [The translation] reminded readers of the battle that lies at the heart of his work. The deadly combat between the dragon and Beowulf is not only a story of a fight with a monstrous and evil force. It is also an emblem of the struggle between civilization and its opposite. If freedom has the air as its natural habitat, violence clings to the ground. Yet, like the dragon, it can rise from its buried lair and infect the air: the "ground-burner" is also the "sky-roamer." Since his undergraduate days, Heaney has been fascinated by this poem. His translation is one further act of retrieval, taking an Old English poem into the ambit of Northern Ireland, where the ancient combat between monstrous violence and the search for peace is even now being refought at a political level.[84]

On the threshold of a new millennium, Heaney's newly rediscovered role as translator enabled him to render a fresh but classic commentary on this epic poem and the situation in contemporary Northern Ireland.

In February 1999, Heaney was asked by an interviewer, "Having not lived in Northern Ireland for a long time, having traveled all over the world and having received such worldwide acclaim, do you feel a greater sense of the universal in your poetry today?" Heaney's response is telling: "I don't think so. I mean, my way, and it's just my way, has been to enter through the local. Unless I am focused in, I can't reach out. Almost every metaphor that comes to me and satisfies me has a feeling of being hooked in but opening out."[85] His regionalism revels in local culture yet strives to transcend that culture and reach others across the spectrum of cultures and language, suggesting our shared desire for friendship and accord with other groups despite our propensity to discord and violence. In this way, the vigorous, even violent poetic power he finds and translates in *Beowulf* becomes an alternative to the world's outer violence where poetry's significance is reaffirmed and space for cultural understanding is cleared.

HEANEY'S RECOVERY OF SCOTTISH CULTURE FOR NORTHERN IRISH REGIONALISM

Heaney's interest in the vernacular, displayed in his modified terza rimas employed in much of "Station Island" and in his particular word choices in *Beowulf*, among other works, often attempts to connect cultures that seem isolated from each other but are not. His later essays on regional writers approve those such as John Clare and Hugh MacDiarmid who attempt through their regionalist endeavors to represent an entire culture. For example, in "Frontiers of Writing," he contrasts what he perceives finally as Hewitt's refusal to grant Irish Gaelic culture its due in his formulation of Ulster regionalism with MacDiarmid's attempt to include Scottish Gaelic culture along with his own Dissenting background in his literary vision of Scotland. He observes that

> in poems like the "Lament for the Great Music" and "Island Funeral" the Scottish poet made a big space for that whole other mode of Scottish belonging. His cradle culture was that of the Dissenters and his hearth language the Lallans Scots, but that did not preclude a sympathy for the Gaelic, Catholic culture of the Highlands and Islands. It did not matter to MacDiarmid that the Gaelic life was marginal or in decline. What mattered was its meaning, its necessity as part of the whole diverse Scottish possibility; it was only through acknowledging it and embracing it that a totally inclusive future could be prefigured.[86]

Heaney's own largely belated recovery project of the Scottish dimension of the Northern Ireland region is anticipated by his early essay on MacDiarmid (analyzed in chapter 3 above) and in such early poems as "Docker," "The Other Side," and "The Wool Trade." The first poem offers a wholly negative portrait of a Belfast dockworker, while the next two give a mixed picture of Ulster Scots in the province, although "The Other Side" tentatively shows how cultural relations in the province can proceed through deference and patience. Writing in 1995, John Wilson Foster could thus accurately claim that "Heaney is disinclined to explore the Scots-Irish, the majority population of Northern Ireland, and offers them as representations merely of 'the others,'" arguing further that "large tracts of Ulster, both literal and figurative, are simply missing from the sizable acreage of Heaney's two hundred-odd collected poems."[87] In coming to his eventual realization about Hewitt's relative erasure of Gaelic Irish culture in the province, Heaney likely realized the paucity of the Scots-Irish or Ulster Scots presence in his own work and strove to remedy it so that his own version of regionalism would represent the entirety of Northern Ireland's population.

"The Impact of Translation," which first had public life at the 1986 conference of the English Institute and was collected in *The Government of the Tongue* (1988), indirectly signals such a recommitment to incorporating the Scottish dimension into his linguistic and cultural conception of Northern Ireland regionalism in his analysis of the promise but relative failure of the Scottish Edwin Muir's vernacular poetry to reinvigorate English poetry. There, he recognizes that the work of Muir and other regional writers in the British and Irish archipelago suggested a viable third way between the neoromanticism of Dylan Thomas and the "tight formation-flying of the Empson/Auden division."[88] In that essay, he favorably reviews the young British poet Christopher Reid's volume *Katerina Brac*, "written in the voice of an apocryphal Eastern European poet."[89] For Heaney, Reid's volume signifies "the delayed promise, though not the complete fulfillment, of a native British modernism." He then bewails the direction English poetry took with the verse of the Movement poets, such as "Larkin, Davie, Enright and others, the inheritors in the Empson/Auden line . . . . Yet it could be thought a matter of regret that Edwin Muir—the poet who translated Kafka in the 1920s and who witnessed the Communist takeover in Czechoslovakia after the war . . . did not succeed better in bringing the insular/vernacular/British imagination into more traumatic contact with a reality of which *Katerina Brac* is the wistful and literary after-image."[90] Heaney concludes by arguing "that there was a road not taken in poetry in English in this century, a road traveled once by the young Auden and the middle-aged Muir. Further, because we have not lived the tragic scenario which such imaginations presented to us as the life appropriate to our times, our capacity to make a complete act of faith in our vernacular poetic possessions has been undermined."[91] And yet Heaney is being too hard on himself. For it is precisely in his later work that we see an "act of faith in our vernacular poetic possessions" through his incorporation of the varying rich dialects of his native province.

"The Impact of Translation" suggests one reason why Heaney has been so drawn to the work of eastern European poets such as Osip Mandelstam, Miroslav Holub, and composer Leoš Janáček—because he finds in these geographically and linguistically peripheral poets the same sort of poetic regionalist ethos, in a European sense, that he does in Northern Irish, Scottish, English regionalist, and Welsh poetry. As one brief example, see his two-page introduction to his translation of Janáček's *Diary of One Who Vanished,* where he notes his replacement of "fledglings" with "scaldies" and the "tree in the hedge" with "boor tree"—an Ulster Scots term.[92] Additionally, as Alan Robinson has ably pointed out in his discussion of Heaney's "increasing affinity with East European writers in exile," the poet "admires them" not so much for "their refusal to succumb to the pressures of a totalitarian regime, but instead . . . [for] champion[ing] the illusion of individual autonomy enshrined in art's 'free state of image and allusion.'"[93]

In a response to the Good Friday Agreement of 1998 that established the conditions for power sharing between Catholics and Protestants in Northern Ireland, Heaney would reflect again on the interpenetrations of dialect and culture—this time in the person of the Scottish writer Sorley MacLean, whom he had admired for years. Speculating on the implications of the phrase "totality of relations," in the agreement, Heaney suggests the inextricability of the cultures throughout the archipelago: "I thought, for example, of the complexities, religious and cultural, that might be recognised and the extensions that might be suggested if the achievement of Sorley MacLean, a Gaelic-speaking, free Presbyterian, socialist, ex-British soldier poet of the Western Scottish Isles, were to be studied in Ulster schools."[94] MacLean is a perfect example of the intertwined nature of religious practice, politics, and language in the Hebridean Islands; moreover, his language and religious affiliation as Free Presbyterian would be anomalous but salutary for Northern Ireland, where Ian Paisley's Free Presbyterian Church typically rejects all things associated with "Irishness," such as speaking Gaelic. Heaney was drawn to MacLean's example for a number of years and wrote the introduction to a volume of critical essays on him in 1986. He also translated into English MacLean's Gaelic poem "Hallaig" in 1999.[95]

In his introduction to the MacLean essay collection, Heaney notes that he drew on the Scottish writer as an early example of a poet uneasy about his role as author and citizen. He cites a MacLean quatrain reflecting on his decision finally not to fight in the Spanish Civil War as evidence of this dilemma: "'I who avoided the sore cross / and agony of Spain, / what should I expect or hope, / what splendid prize to win?' Such lines were both sustenance and example to somebody hugging his own secret uneases about the way a poet should conduct himself at a moment of public crisis—for I first read them in the days of the heavy bombing campaign in Belfast, a town I had left in order to make some more deliberate commitment to the life of poetry."[96] MacLean's indecision in such a historical moment confirmed Heaney's own tendency to castigate himself for not speaking out enough against atrocities in Northern Ireland occasionally and to reprove himself for being too publicly political at other times.

Another salutary Scottish influence upon Heaney's rich concept of a unifying regionalism is Robert Burns, as we have seen already in my discussion of Heaney's adoption of the Burns stanza in *An Open Letter* from chapter 7. In his 1997 essay "Burns's Art Speech," Heaney recalls the salutary effect of Burns's "To a Mouse" upon him as a student. The opening line, "Wee, sleekit, cowran, tim'rous beastie," affirmed Heaney's own vernacular speech: "The word 'wee' put its stressed foot down and in one preemptive vocative strike took over the emotional and cultural ground, dispossessing the rights of written standard English and offering asylum to all vernacular comers. To all, at least, who hailed from north of a line drawn between Berwick and Bundoran."[97] Heaney's equation of the province of historic Ulster (Bundoran is a southern County Donegal village in Ireland but close to the border of Northern Ireland) with Scotland is effected through a common vernacular heritage and constitutes one of his clearest expressions of the cultural and literary affinities he sees between Scotland and Ulster. He approvingly recalls the linguistic rightness of Burns's opening line, its "truth to the life of the language I spoke while growing up in mid-Ulster, a language where trace elements of Elizabethan English and Lowland Scots are still to be heard and to be reckoned with as a matter of pronunciation and even, indeed, of politics."[98]

His approval of Burns's verse is paired with his delighted reading of the Donegal Irish poet Cathal Buí Mac Giolla Ghunna's "An Bonnán Buí," "The Yellow Bittern," which he juxtaposes with Burns's "To a Mouse," citing their literary affinities. Heaney's yoking of these two poems further indicates his perception of himself as a regional poet and displays the kind of linguistic reconciliation he finds rife in literature from the province. Mac Giolla Ghunna, he says, was important for him because he wrote using the Ulster Irish Heaney had learned in school: "[He was] significant because he was a Northern voice and part of a group of Ulster poets [Seamus Dall Mac Cuarta and Art Mac Cumhaigh] whose work, like Burns's was sustained out of the past by a long and learned literary tradition.... Their words and intonations belonged to an Ulster Irish in which I felt completely at home, since it was the Ulster version of the language that had been taught in Derry."[99] He compares his experience reading these Ulster Irish poets to Hewitt's when the elder poet read the Rhyming Weavers, "those local bards of the late eighteenth and early nineteenth centuries who wrote in the Ulster Scots vernacular and who produced in Hewitt 'some feeling that, for better or worse, they were my own people.'"[100] Finally, after translating from the Irish of "An Bonnán Buí," Heaney notes, "It's another source of satisfaction to me that *och* reappears at the phonetic centre of this poem in the word *loch* and the word *deoch*—which happens to mean 'drink' in Irish"; this linguistic intermingling points "toward a future that is implicit in the mutually pronounceable elements of the speech of Planter and Gael. Even if we grant the deeply binary nature of Ulster thinking about language and culture, we can still try to establish a plane of regard from which to inspect the recalcitrant elements of the situation and reposition ourselves in relation to them. And that plane, I believe, can be reliably projected from poems and poetry."[101] Despite his unfortunate recourse to the binary terms "Planter and Gael," which reinforces the pervasive view of a province torn between competing cultures, Heaney is to be commended for his artistic regionalist urging of a transcultural linguistic and literary unity across the historic province of Ulster, which has always been the essential ground of any larger cultural and political reconciliation for him.

In his 1992 Oxford lecture on MacDiarmid, Heaney again praised the Scottish poet's linguistic contribution to his home country, just as he had in his essay on the poet twenty years before. Heaney claims that MacDiarmid "effected a reorientation of attitudes to the country's two indigenous languages, the Scots Gaelic of the Highlands and Islands and the vernacular Scots of the Borders and Lowlands.... MacDiarmid also more or less singlehandedly created a literature in one of those languages."[102] Despite realizing MacDiarmid's excessive output of poetry and its unevenness, Heaney clearly recognizes him as laying the groundwork for the great outpouring of Scottish literature fostered in part by Hobsbaum's Glasgow Group in the closing decades of the century: "There is a demonstrable link between MacDiarmid's act of cultural resistance in the Scotland of the 1920s and the literary self-possession of writers such as Alasdair Gray, Tom Leonard, Liz Lochhead and James Kelman in the 1980s and 1990s."[103] Once again, Heaney is implicitly placing his own regionalist work in the continuum of devolved literatures expressed in varying languages and dialects throughout the twentieth century in the British and Atlantic archipelago. In 2001, he would look back to his coediting of *The School Bag* with Ted Hughes in the early 1980s and realize that their approach to collecting poetry from different regions and nations in the archipelago was consistent with the thrust of historian Hugh Kearney's landmark work *The British Isles: A History of Four Nations* (1989).

Heaney points out that Kearney's "Britannic," not "British," approach to history is salutary and inclusive since it appropriately decenters British history and articulates it as a devolving process:

> "Britannic" works like a cultural wake-up call and gestures not only towards the past but also towards an imaginable future. Without insistence or contention, "Britannic" is a reminder of much that the term "British" manages to occlude. "Britannic" allows equal status on the island of Britain to Celt and Saxon, to Scoti and Cymri, to Maldon and Tintagel, to *Beowulf* and the *Gododdin*, and so it begins to repair some of the damage done by the imperial, othering power of "British." In fact, one way of describing the era of devolution is to think of it as the moment when Britain went Britannic.[104]

Heaney's embrace of the term *Brittanic* can be thought of as a second, belated response to his inclusion in the Morrison anthology of "British" poetry that he originally protested in *An Open Letter*. While that pamphlet poem was occasionally caustic in its rejection of the label *British*, "Through-Other Places, Through-Other Times" demonstrates that the poet considers himself in this "Brittanic" tradition. His use of the dialect word *through-other* in the title of the essay, "a compound in common use in Ulster, meaning physically untidy or mentally confused, and appropriately enough, it echoes the Irish-language expression *tré na céile*, meaning things mixed up among themselves," suggests that he sees the cultural confluences across the Irish and English archipelago—and by implication, in his own work—as being in a healthy flux of confusion.[105]

Writing in 1989, the often-prescient John Wilson Foster argued in his seminal essay "Radical Regionalism" that "current motions in the political culture of Scotland are of particular moment to Ulster people," noting that "Scottish autonomy appeals in Ulster to both nationalists and loyalists, and Scottish culture to both Gaelic-speakers and English-speakers of settler ancestry."[106] Scottish devolution and the role that literature had and would play in that process there and elsewhere in Britain was much on Heaney's mind at the turn of the millennium: in a 2001 interview, he noted that he perceived his reawakened interest in Scottish writing and translation from Robert Henryson's Middle Scots *The Testament of Cresseid* and his fables as part of the historical devolution going on politically across Britain. Heaney hopefully mused, "It's an interesting moment in British history because of the devolution of powers from Westminster to Edinburgh and Cardiff, and hopefully in some ongoing form to Northern Ireland. There's a kind of new sense of a fluid relationship, a new sense of east-west, if you like, between Northern Ireland and Scotland. A new necessity for even nationalists within Northern Ireland to concede Scottish as well as Irish roots, and English roots."[107] He went on to explicitly claim a common language for the inhabitants of Northern Ireland, just as he had in many of his poems from *Wintering Out* such as "Broagh" nearly thirty years before and in the preface to his translation of *Sweeney Astray*, nearly twenty years before:[108] "I would concede that there is a language we all speak. I was joking about it yesterday ... about everybody in Ulster being able to pronounce *-agh* or *-och*, and suggesting that in this one common phonetic possession there might be the beginnings of a commonweal or a common welfare, a *res publica*, or rather a *res phonetica* leading to the *res publica*."[109] Although seemingly lighthearted, such a statement offers a viable starting point for a unifying language that he has privileged often in his writing as part of his regionalist endeavor.

In his introduction to his translation of Robert Henryson's *The Testament of Cresseid and Seven Fables*, Heaney points out that "I enjoyed the work because Henryson's language led me back into what might be called 'the hidden Scotland' at the back of my own ear. The speech I grew up with in mid-Ulster carried more than a trace of Scottish vocabulary and as a youngster I was familiar with Ulster Scots idioms and pronunciations across the River Bann in County Antrim."[110] Elsewhere, he acknowledges how his reclamation of the North's Scottish heritage completes his tricultural recovery project, as it were, stating that "*Sweeney Astray* was my 'hidden Ireland,' *Beowulf* was my 'hidden England,' and now I have a 'hidden Scotland' coming up."[111] Heaney evoked the notion of a "hidden Ulster" first in "The Sense of Place" and returned to it in the course of *An Open Letter* and *Sweeney Astray* to evoke and recall the occluded Irish Gaelic presence in the province as part of a potentially unifying cultural heritage for its inhabitants. Moreover, he first moots the concept of a "hidden England" in his lecture "Englands of the Mind," and he returns to it in his *Beowulf* translation, seeking to establish commonalities between Ireland and England through language.

Thus, just as with both *Sweeney Astray* and *Beowulf*, Heaney believed that his recovery of the particular dialect or tongue in Henryson's work enabled him to present the narratives themselves as a potentially unifying repository of stories for a given populace, an artistically devolutionary maneuver. We see this urge in his recognition of Henryson's use of the Old English word *thole*, which, as Conor McCarthy has pointed out, has "previously appeared in Heaney's translation of *Sweeney Astray, The Midnight Verdict*, and *Beowulf*, and which makes an appearance here in Henryson's original," reminding us "that the original poem's 'vernacular edge,' as Heaney describes it ..., contains, like Heaney's own poetic vernacular, fragments of both Gaelic and Anglo-Saxon."[112] In speaking about Henryson's fables, Heaney argues for their vernacular, unifying function, noting that "these tales of tricky and innocent beasts and birds were part of the common oral culture of Europe, a store of folk wisdom as pervasive and unifying at vernacular level as the doctrines and visions of Christianity were in the higher realms of scholastic culture."[113]

Heaney's penchant for simple diction drawn from an Anglo-Saxon word-hoard and pitched for an oral, regional audience is evident from the opening of *The Testament of Cresseid*:

A gloomy time, a poem full of hurt
Should correspond and be equivalent.

Just so it was when I began my work
On this retelling, and the weather went
From close to frosty, as Aries, mid-Lent,
Made showers of hail from the north descend
In a great cold I could barely withstand.[114]

The full and slant rhymes work to impart a muscular, rippling energy to the poem's beginning, echoing the blustery weather outside. The "north" as a region of Britain figures twice in the opening stanzas and is characterized by its chilly and harsh atmosphere; Heaney's translation informs us in the third stanza that "the northern wind had purified the air / And hunted the cloud-cover off the sky."[115]

Another compelling reason that Heaney turned to Henryson stemmed from his conviction of the great Scottish poet's fitness as moral commentator in his own conflicted age and in ours as well. When he claims toward the opening of his introduction to these translations that Henryson "belongs to the eternal present of the perfectly pitched, a poet whose knowledge of life is matched by the range of his art, whose constant awareness of the world's hardness and injustice is mitigated by his irony, tender-heartedness, and ever-ready sense of humour," we realize that Henryson's humane outlook as *makar*, or poet, matches Heaney's own.[116] Casting Henryson as responding to "the world's hardness and injustice" with "tender-heartedness" among other qualities suggests that his art displays a deep vein of imaginative sympathy toward suffering that refuses the saccharine and instead instills a radical view of our common humanity in the reader.

Later in the introduction, Heaney suggests that "this was also the poetry of a man whose imaginative sympathy prevailed over the stock responses of his time," clarifying his point by going on to claim that, despite his impressive "intellectual attainments," "from our point of view he proves himself more by his singular compassion for the character of Cresseid. Available to him all along was the rhetoric of condemnation, the trope of woman as the daughter of Eve, temptress, snare, Jezebel. But Henryson eschews this pulpit-speak."[117] Heaney has consistently shown sympathy to the plight of the other, the marginalized, the wretched, in his poetry. His feelings of deep identification with the "little adulteress" of "Punishment" and the beheaded girl of "Strange Fruit" (*N*, 30, 32) provide perhaps the most compelling examples of such radical sympathy, even empathy in his work. Conor McCarthy has pointed out a series of such deeply felt recognitions of women in his poetry, observing, "'Mycenae Lookout' is one of a number of places where Heaney's post-ceasefire poetry has described the suffering of women against a background of conflict."[118] Particularly in "Punishment," Heaney condemns the patriarchal, lingering narrative of women as temptresses and entrappers of men, showing how a series of condemned women—the woman whose body was found in the bog, the adulteress from the Gospel of John, chapter 8, and contemporary Catholic women in Northern Ireland who consorted with British soldiers and were stripped, tarred, and feathered—act as moral mirrors in which we see our own shortcomings and predilection to visit guilt upon the other rather than accept responsibility.[119] His reclamation of Henryson's poetry in these translations becomes a deeply moral act, reminding us how the best regional writing transcends its milieu and speaks to cultures past, present, and to come.

GUTTURAL AND GLOBAL: "THE GUTTURAL MUSE IN A GLOBAL AGE" AND *DISTRICT AND CIRCLE*

The recovery of regional culture found in Heaney's translations of *Sweeney Astray*, *Beowulf*, and *The Testament of Cresseid and Seven Fables* remains significant despite the hectic pace of globalization and the resulting fragmentary nature of our contemporary lives. Heaney first moots this issue indirectly in his 1995 Nobel Prize speech, *Crediting Poetry*,[120] but he poses the question much more directly in his critically neglected 2003 essay "The Guttural Muse in a Global Age" when he asks, "Can the local be any longer viable? Is there anywhere left that is truly beyond the reach of the satellite signal or its deadly corollary, the cluster bomb? Nowadays, after all, everywhere is at the centre of the web; computer speaks to computer, stock market answers stock market with the mysterious speed that used to be the prerogative of angels."[121] Heaney's answer, given in the essay and in his subsequent volume, *District and Circle*, is a cautious "yes" based on what he sees as the continuing vibrancy of life in the local district.

He recalls his reaction over twenty years in the past when he was bemoaning the rock music booming from a hotel basement in the Irish countryside: even as he "was overcome by feelings of pathos and regret, and began to reflect on the sad erosion of the local life, the way the parish dancehall was being absorbed into the commercial culture of the music industry, the charts and the hype and the homogenization of it all," the discotheque opened and the young people scattered into the parking lot, "whooping and yelling, singing and taunting, making a right old hullabaloo."[122] He quickly realized "that in those country shouts, in those raucous and unruly vowels and consonants, what I was hearing was a guarantee of the resilience of the ... guttural life, of all that was resurgent and untameable at a local level ... the sound of a culture enjoying itself, celebrating itself and making a song and dance about itself."[123] And then he spied "the muse of that culture ... the moonlit figure of a girl in a white dress being cuddled by her boyfriend at the side of a car, giggling and muttering by turns, the guttural muse of the dialect and the district."[124] The poem Heaney wrote about this incident and an earlier one in the evening, when he went tench-fishing, became "The Guttural Muse," a poem collected in *Field Work*.

He argues that the logic of the poem pivots on the idea that "just as there is healing and curative power in the old muddy tench swimming along at the bottom of the lake, so there is a healing and curative power, a kind of immunization, available from the old guttural accents that underlie our standardized speech, and it is this heaviness of glottal underlife that will save us from the weightlessness of the global babble that surrounds us."[125] Lest we imagine that Heaney is simply waxing romantic in recalling his fishing trip and the moonlit girl that long-ago night, after quoting his poem he quickly goes on to argue that "the young girl in that poem, or somebody like her, will be laughing tonight in a car park in Africa or St. Lucia or Lithuania or even in Afghanistan. The neon lights of the Coca Cola ads will be blinking above her, the latest American rap group will be firing up on the tape deck of her car, her body will be decked out in Levis and Nike, and everything on the surface will proclaim her a citizen of the global world—everything, that is, except her local speech and her local accent. And even though she will always be susceptible to market forces and military forces and media forces, her speech and her accent will remain the vital elements in her at homeness on the earth."[126] I quote this passage at such length to demonstrate Heaney's continuing belief in the viability of regionalism as an energizing force not cowed or diminished by globalization and to show how his thinking about geographical and linguistic regionalism had long burst the bounds of Northern Ireland and become transregional, an empowering term that acts as a stay against the often vacuous, empty abstractions of globalization.

In this sense, Heaney's Irish/transregional, joyous girl complements the suffering women upon which he focuses in his poems such as "Punishment" and "Strange Fruit" and in the crucial passages from *Beowulf*, *Antigone*, and *The Cresseid* that I have discussed above. In this sense, the "guttural girls" around the world, coupled with their suffering antecedents elsewhere in Heaney's work, become the composite Janus-figure that epitomizes this strand of his regionalism. This regionalism is truly radical because it dwells on particular pain yet can also celebrate local, lilting happiness.

The figure of Heaney's transregional girl is worth dwelling on because she potentially shares qualities that some of our most astute commentators on globalization have identified in resistant local culture. Arjun Appadurai, for example, argues in his *Modernity at Large: Cultural Dimensions of Globalization* (1996) that "unlike the largely negative pressures that the nation-state places on the production of context by local subjects, the electronic mediation of community in the diasporic world creates a more complicated, disjunct, hybrid sense of local subjectivity."[127] Complementing the example that Heaney would give several years later of the transregional girl hearing "the latest American rap group . . . firing up on the tape deck of her car," which he imagines her listening to in her home region, Appadurai suggests that "global flows" of media can activate and create local culture for diasporic populations. For example, "A Sikh cabdriver in Chicago may not be able to participate in the politics of the Punjab by using the Internet [and this economic "restriction" is surely out of date by now, given the lowered cost and spread of the Internet since 1996], but he might listen to cassettes of fiery devotional songs and sermons delivered at the Golden Temple in the Punjab."[128] Appadurai wisely concludes after reeling off a catalog of such examples, "Thus the work of the imagination . . . through which local subjectivity is produced and nurtured is a bewildering palimpsest of highly local and highly translocal considerations."[129] Appadurai's comments on "virtual neighborhoods, no longer bounded by territory, passports, taxes, elections, and other conventional diacritics," that were even in 1996 being created by "large international computer networks" seems positively prophetic given the many such virtual neighborhoods that have sprung up in subsequent years and that are perhaps best symbolized by the rapid success of Facebook.[130]

Heaney's *District and Circle* is uncannily attuned to such virtual neighborhoods and the rapid speed of contemporary communication even as it celebrates the guttural pleasures of local life. The opening stanza of his sequence "The Tollund Man in Springtime" suggests as much:

> Into your virtual city I'll have passed
> Unregistered by scans, screens, hidden eyes,
> Lapping myself in time, an absorbed face
> Coming and going, neither god nor ghost,
> Not at odds or at one, but simply lost
> To you and yours, out under seeding grass
> And trickles of kesh water, sphagnum moss,
> Dead bracken on the spreadfield, red as rust.
>
> (*DC*, 53)

This creature, revived from Heaney's earlier poem "The Tollund Man," from *Wintering Out*, whose home Heaney revisited after the 1994 IRA and loyalist cease-fires in "Tollund" from *The Spirit Level*, somehow registers the advanced surveillance apparatuses in our "virtual city" but is himself "unregistered by scans, screens, hidden eyes." He now functions as a positive figure of local resistance to globalization, whereas earlier, in "The Tollund Man," he symbolized the deadly, sacrificial nature of tribal societies past and present.

Moreover, his resurrection comes from his poetic utterances to himself as "I gathered / From the display-case peat my staying powers," suggesting Heaney's belief in the continuing incantatory power of poetry even in our globalized age. He tells "my webbed wrists to be like silver birches, / My old uncallused hands to be young sward, / The spade-cut skin to heal, and got restored / By telling myself this." Post-resurrection, we are told by the Tollund Man, "Late as it was, / The early bird still sang, the meadow hay / Still buttercupped and daisied, sky was new." He seems now to be trying to re-enchant us, to revivify us, who are worn out with the cares of this frenetic world. The concluding line of this fourth sonnet in the sequence quickly lifts us out of this world and offers respite in a modern symbol—the "transatlantic flights stacked in the blue" (56). As the sequence concludes, he leaves behind "a bunch of Tollund rushes" he has carried "through every check and scan" and spits on his hands, "felt benefit, / And spirited myself into the street" (58). Heaney has argued recently that "he spits on his hands like a labourer ready to venture out to do the job, and in that way he stands for much that has been resolute in the country and remains admirably so—the commitment of young people to serving as aid workers abroad . . . then at home the annual flocks of teachers and nurses and civil servants ready to get out there and to give of their best for the common good."[131]

Moreover, in accommodating himself to this globalized new world without losing his lively lyrical powers, the Tollund Man shows a marked ambivalence to contemporary culture that anyone concerned with the regional must as well. Yet he keeps in touch with his roots, even though he throws away his comforting rushes, by retaining his guttural powers to enchant himself and us. As Heaney has noted, this figure "wagers his earthly creatureliness against consumerist vacuity."[132] His stance toward the global recalls Heaney's description of how his guttural muse survives and flourishes today: "In order to hold her own in the global world the guttural muse must be able at one and the same time to stand her ground and be ahead of the game, must keep faith with the local and be able for the challenges of the world beyond. She must maintain the specific gravity of first-hand experience and yet see herself and her situation as if from a satellite in orbit."[133] As the Tollund Man moves deliberately but lightly into our staggeringly empty world despite its promises to give us everything, he remains at home because "whatever it was I knew / Came back to me. Newfound contrariness" (57).

In 2001, Heaney articulated his apprehension at the near ubiquity and power of the Internet while admitting that we cannot and should not shut ourselves off from its influence entirely. Employing a memorable image, he suggested that "looking directly into the World Wide Web is like looking directly at an eclipse of the sun. Indeed, the experience is in danger of blinding the subject rather than illuminating him. What is required, therefore, is some equivalent of the pincard, something we can hold up while turning our back on the glare, something that lets through a picture of what is happening while at the same time preserving us from being merely dazzled and bewildered. The poem, and the cultural heritage in general, is such an equivalent."[134] This image is worth briefly unpacking: the Internet's blinding and authoritative dominance can be mitigated through our taking the time to develop the power of perceptual singularity. Attending to the quieter but still insistent power of poetry and other art from our cultural heritage by slowing down and allowing contemplation to creep into our observation will enable us to acquire something like the Tollund Man's "newfound contrariness."

The reborn Tollund Man's pleasures in lyrical speaking, sensory perception, and nature—some of the essences of dynamic regionalism—offer both rebuff and riposte to contemporary culture's speed and abstraction that militate against contemplation. As Susan Stewart has noted, "This relentless emphasis on rapidity contributes to a climate of frustration and delay. Creating an atmosphere of something happening (canned music; recorded messages; advertisements in every interstice of hesitation and pause) is more important than making something happen. Speed is the enemy of difficulty; it tends to absorb or erase every other phenomenal quality."[135] Because the Tollund Man and, through him, Heaney continue to wield enchanting lyrical powers, they establish temporary artistic spaces like the best "artworks, [which] can slow and even stop the frantic activity that characterizes most of the rest of contemporary existence . . . [because] they provide time for the evaluation of intention and consequence. Even more significantly, they provide time for those extensions of memory into the past and imagination into the future by means of which our lives acquire their genuinely intersubjective and moral dimension."[136]

The title *District and Circle* simultaneously connotes both speed and leisurely attention to daily life because it refers to both events in London of the recent past and the quotidian activities of Heaney's home district in the 1940s and 1950s. *District and Circle* signifies, first of all, these two well-traveled Underground lines in the metropole of London and thus implicitly commemorates the three terrorist bombings on the Underground, two of which were on Circle Line trains (the other was on another train line, while there was a fourth on a double-decker bus), on July 7, 2005. Through locating his volume, as it were, on the grid of the London Underground, Heaney pays homage to the bombings' victims in the context of their cartographic high-speed community. But the title also suggests the way in which Heaney circles back fully to his Ulster childhood, his local district, more fully than he had since his 1960s poetry. Finally, *District and Circle* also implies the dynamism in vacillating between contemporary, globalized London and back to Heaney's native district in 1940s County Derry.

Heaney's consistent ability to travel back into his native region marks his poetry as enablingly phenomenological in the terms articulated by Edward Casey in his recuperation of place as a dynamic, ongoing event. Casey believes that places gather memories and experiences and suggests that this

> gathering gives to place its particular perduringness, allowing us to return to it again and again as *the same place* and not just as the same position or site. For a place, in its dynamism, does not age in a systematically changing way.... Only its tenants and visitors, enactors and witnesses ... age and grow old in this way.... Place is the generatrix for the collection, as well as the recollection, of all that occurs in the lives of sentient beings, and even for the trajectories of inanimate things.... Its power consists in gathering these lives and things, each with its own space and time, into one arena of common engagement.[137]

This revelatory description of place helps us understand how Heaney continued to perceive the district where he had grown up: South County Derry in his region of Northern Ireland. Even as he aged, he retained the power to travel back into the ongoing life of that native place and, in so doing, to find and re-create many of his childhood experiences and to refind the inanimate objects, such as the turnip-snedder and the harrow-pin, in the poems that take their titles from those implements, gathered by the power of that place. In 2001, when asked whether many of the "the secret nests and spaces of your childhood" are "still your most treasured places," Heaney quickly took the question literally, then revised his answer midsentence to affirm the centripetal role that remembered place plays: "Those places aren't there any more to be treasured: hedges have been taken out, farmyards built over, the river drained and redirected, motorways have covered whole townlands. But even so, the tree that is written about in 'Oracle' reappears in *Electric Light*, in a passage in a poem called 'The Real Names' which begins with the line 'There is a willow grows aslant the brook.' So in your memory they are there as radiant spaces but actually the tree has gone and all of those things are gone."[138]

"The Turnip-Snedder" evokes the cycle of life for the lowly turnip in its solid emplacement that it occupies in Heaney's memory. The way in which "it dug its heels in among wooden tubs / and troughs of slops" animates, even humanizes the machine, lending it an obstinate obduracy reinforced by his martial description of it as "a barrel-chested breast-plate // standing guard / on four braced greaves" (*DC*, 3). As the speaker imagines statements issuing forth from the snedder along with chopped-up turnips, he hears it proclaim, "'This is the way that God sees life' / . . . 'from seedling-braird to snedder,'" concluding by hearing, "'This is the turnip-cycle,' // as it dropped its raw sliced mess, / bucketful by glistering bucketful" (4). Heaney expects us not only to enter into the imagined life of this machine but also to recall how he revisits two of his earlier poems, gathering them, as it were, into the life of this new poem: "A Sofa in the Forties" and the fourth sonnet from "Clearances." The authoritative announcements of the turnip-snedder recall the similarly authoritative announcement from the faraway BBC announcer in "A Sofa in the Forties"—"HERE IS THE NEWS—" and each implies that there can be no other news or life for the turnip, respectively (*SL*, 8). But this somewhat off-putting voice is mitigated by the last line, where the speaker remembers the mess of the ground-up turnips emerging "bucketful by glistering bucketful," an image of plenty and peacefulness that recalls the intimate, shining moments that the young Heaney would spend with his mother peeling potatoes, in the third sonnet from his sequence "Clearances," and dropping them, "things to share, gleaming in a bucket of clean water" (*HL*, 27). Thus "The Turnip-Snedder" demonstrates the gathering power of place to evoke not just a particular memory but congeries of memories drawing on earlier Heaney poems, creating a "mess" of intertwined memories, as it were.

The solidity of the turnip-snedder is echoed in the similar in-placeness of "The Harrow-Pin," which is described as "head-banged spike, forged fang, a true dead ringer // Out of a harder time" (*DC*, 25). The absence of an article before "head-banged spike," along with the compounding of that adjective and the alliteration in these lines, recalls the Anglo-Saxon language of *Beowulf* that Heaney has shown to be linked inextricably to Ulster dialect words. Heaney seems to be using the harrow-pin like the turnip-snedder, to pin down his memories with an iron fastness. The utility and seeming ubiquity of the harrow-pin, employed for the harrow itself used outside, whether in the fields or "lodged in the stable wall" for hanging "horses' collars lined with sweat-veined ticking, / Old cobwebbed reins and hames and eye-patched winkers," or, inside the house, for hanging "a shelf for knick-knacks, a picture-hook or -rail" (25) grant it and, just as important, the objects associated with it a permanence and radiance meant to linger in our minds. The turnip-snedder works violence upon turnips, while the harrow pin was forged in violent action, yet Heaney transforms them into aesthetically pleasing, even beautiful tools of production in their very solidity. Such poems allow Heaney to continue to revisit and revivify his first strand of regionalism in which he acted as anthropologist for vanishing traditions in poems such as "Digging," "Thatching," "The Diviner," and "The Forge" in the 1960s.

Heaney's description elsewhere of the furnishing and tools in the "drowsy circle" of the family kitchen as "a set of implements that were contemplated over the years until they became furnishings of the mind, objects of affection, symbols of home," suggests how objects such as the turnip-snedder and harrow-pin(s) became singularized and humanized through lingering and loving gazes across the years.[139] In his reading of Thomas Hardy's "The Garden Seat," he further argues that such objects can attain a spiritual life of their own, noting that "the poem is about the ghost-life that hovers over some of the furniture of our lives, about the way objects can become temples of the spirit."[140] For Heaney, Hardy's garden seat "has become a point of entry into a common emotional ground of memory and belonging. It transmits the climate of a lost world and keeps alive a domestic intimacy with a reality which might otherwise have vanished. The more we are surrounded by such things, the more feelingly we dwell in our own lives."[141]

Susan Stewart's apologia above for art's ability to keep and stay time so that we might muse upon memories and imagine the future helpfully opens up two sequences from *District and Circle*, "Found Prose" and the title poem, the first of which revels in memory and the second of which uses the speed of the London underground to read the future. By extrapolation from his reading of Hardy's "The Garden Seat," Heaney's decision to call his sequence from *District and Circle* "Found Prose" implies that these memories, like those of the turnip-snedder and harrow-pin and objects that became part of the domestic intimacy of his household, have been lying there as objects for ages and are now recovered and recalled. Each of the three prose pieces in "Found Prose" focuses on the journey motif from the familiar into the unknown. The first, "The Lagans Road," offers that road as a comforting, even womblike path toward the unknown of the young boy's school: "It was one of those narrow country roads with weeds in the middle, grass verges, and high hedges on either side, and all around it marsh and rushes and little shrubs and birch trees. For a minute or two every day, therefore, you were in the wilderness" (*DC*, 37). But as the speaker remembers his first sight of the school, he retrospectively casts it as comparable to "an account of how the Indians of the Pacific Northwest foresaw their arrival in the land of the dead—coming along a forest path where other travellers' cast-offs lay scattered on the bushes, hearing voices laughing and calling, knowing there was a life in the clearing up ahead that would be familiar, but feeling at the same time lost and homesick" (37). The schoolroom itself becomes "the strange room, where our names were new in the roll-book and would soon be called" (37). This passage recalls another sonnet from "Clearances," where the poet-speaker imagines his mother arriving in "New Row, Land of the Dead," a "shining room," "where grandfather is rising from his place / With spectacles pushed back on a clean bald head / To welcome a bewildered homing daughter" (*HL*, 26). This regionalized memory of Heaney's attending Anahorish School as a child, then, slides surreally backwards into the region of the dead with its double recall of Native Americans' and Margaret Heaney's arrivals in "the land of the dead" through which the poet reenters that long-ago classroom and a part of himself—the completely carefree, unschooled self—dies. In so doing, Heaney conflates two of his concepts of region—as a literal and remembered place and as an imagined, spiritual state—looking back to the concerns of the spirit region in *Station Island* and *Seeing Things* and forward to *Human Chain*.

The second lyric from "Found Prose," "Tall Dames," muses upon "'the gypsies,'" who "we knew ... were properly another race. They inhabited the land of Eros" (38). Although the more politically correct, grown poet admits that "we would now call [them] travelers . . . at that time in that place 'tinker' was an honorable term, signifying tin-smiths, white-smiths, pony keepers, regulars on the doorstep, squatters on the long acre" (38). The speaker strives to render their activities quotidian but cannot help resorting to the language of the fantastic—not only are they from "the land of Eros," but he admits that there was "always a feeling that they were coming towards you out of storytime," and that "every time they landed in the district, there was an extra-ness in the air, as if a gate had been left open in the usual life, as if something might get in or get out" (38). The gypsies or travelers thus inhabit the realm of potential and bring that realm into the ordinary life of "the district" when they "landed" there, like extraterrestrials coming to earth. Here again, the literally regional is charged with the excitement of the something beyond or other—from the spirit region.

Finally, in "Boarders," the last prose piece from "Found Prose," Heaney again recalls a seemingly ordinary activity—riding a bus—but quickly transforms it into a ride toward the region of eternity. He opens by musing that "there's no heat in the bus, but the engine's running and up where a destination should be showing it just says PRIVATE, so it must be ours. . . . This is a special bus, so there'll be no tickets, no conductor, and no fare collection until the load is full" (39). Even though "the stops are the same as every other time," this journey is different: for one thing, "There's no real hurry" (39). The speaker shows his fear about approaching the unknown when he urges, "Let the driver keep doing battle with the gearstick, let his revs and double-clutchings drag the heart, anything to put off that last stop when he slows down at the summit and turns and seems about to take us back" (39). In the last paragraph, the speaker imagines starting again and "the known country fall[ing] away behind us" but pauses in the present as the driver comes to collect the money and perceives everyone, "one by one," going "farther into ourselves, wishing we were with him on the journey back, flailing downhill with the windows all lit up, empty and faster and angrier bend after bend" (39). Much of the language of this last paragraph recapitulates the poems "The Journey Back" and "The Crossing," from *Seeing Things*, as we will see in my analysis of them in the next chapter. Crucially, Heaney here sees his local district, "the known country," as the physical region continuous with and from which he will depart for the region beyond our ken, the flickering realm of the afterlife. If "The Tollund Man in Springtime" captures both regional and global culture, and indicates how a properly grounded regionalism can traffic with globalism even while holding it at arm's length, then "Found Prose" complements the title poem, as both sequences focus on travel that attends to local rhythms, yet also carries us into a strange country, a region of the unknown.

While places, most especially rural places, gather memories and emotions of time past, as we have seen in these regionally oriented poems from *District and Circle*, urban centers have a tendency to scatter and potentially sow confusion in their centrifugal power, or so at least Heaney often implied. In the fifth and last lyric of the title sequence, the entirety of which focuses on an aspect of traveling through the London Underground, he even employs the phrase "a long centrifugal / Haulage of speed through every dragging socket" to convey the figuratively dismembering power of the Underground (*DC*, 21). In a lecture to a conference that took its theme as "humanizing the city," Heaney recalled familiar Western tropes of the city such as "the City set upon a hill as harbinger of a new heaven and a new earth, the soul as a besieged citadel, the consonance between good order in the mind and spirit, and good order in the well-regulated, well-disposed city."[142] He then proceeded to read a number of poems where the city is represented positively or negatively, observing, "I want to read them as texts which help us mediate between the pandemonium and myriad bewilderments of the actual urban phenomenon and the ache for coherence that is at the centre of the consciousness within us," and noting further, "This is the one thing that poetic work can provide: a momentary stay against confusion, a moment of mediation between everything that is out there and whatever is in here, between the uncontainable and the rage for order."[143] Reading the "District and Circle" sequence in this way, we can apprehend how Heaney's relative fear of the "pandemonium and myriad bewilderments," the "uncontainable," is set in dialectic with the "ache for coherence" and "the rage for order" that is within us.

"District and Circle" voices both Heaney's continued longing for a connection to more traditional conceptions of the region—"the light / Of all-overing, ... / ... / body-heated mown grass" (18)—and his realization that as he ages he is heading ineluctably toward the region of the dead. The third lyric in the sequence uneasily recalls Eliot's similarly urban crowd that flowed over London Bridge in "The Waste Land"—"A crowd flowed over London Bridge, so many, / I had not thought death had undone so many":[144] "A crowd half straggle-ravelled and half strung / Like a human chain" (19). Yet the speaker's realization that "I re-entered the safety of numbers" (19) in moving toward the open subway doors, coupled with the phrase "like a human chain" (19), which would become the title of his 2010 volume of poetry, suggests his continued dependence on community in this life, a community that would ebb and flow with departures of familiar friends like David Hammond, elegized in "'The Door Was Open but the House Was Dark,'" and the arrival of a new grandchild, who is welcomed at the conclusion of "Route 110," both in *Human Chain*. Keeping a weather eye on devolving Northern Ireland and himself contributing to those developments as the 1990s gave way to the new millennium, Heaney began exploring the spirit region more fully than ever in *Seeing Things* and subsequent volumes, especially *Human Chain*, through his complex usage of the tercet form.

Chapter Eleven

"MY SHIP OF GENIUS NOW SHAKES OUT HER SAIL"

The Spirit Region and the Tercet in
Seeing Things and *Human Chain*

Poetry is a ratification of the impulse towards transcendence.
—Heaney, *Stepping Stones*

The doublet is never enough, unless it breeds. War and peace need a third phase, as liquid and ice need vapor to fill out and judge the concept of water, as God the Father and God the Son need the Holy Ghost, or hell and heaven need purgatory, or act and place need time.
  The doublet needs what it makes. This is a habit of creative mind.
—R. P. Blackmur, "Wallace Stevens: An Abstraction Blooded"

FROM MILLET TO CHAGALL: THE PROGRESSION OF HEANEY'S TERCETS

In his seminal essay "The Regional Forecast," Heaney argues that regional writers like Joyce and presumably himself have a task before them that is essentially formal and visionary: "The writer's task will ultimately be visionary rather than social; the human rather than the national dream is his or her responsibility, a care for the logic and possibility of the medium rather than its utility and applicability; and it will be a personal task ... in the sense that it will begin in a deeply felt inner need not to be appeased in any way other than by the achievement of a right form of expression."[1] In his continued embrace and development of the tercet form, Heaney's medium essentially became his message as that form repeatedly opened the "visionary" spirit region that increasingly preoccupied his later poetry, culminating in the somewhat wintry but finally affirmative *Human Chain*.

A strong part of his impetus to recover, visit, and offer this spiritual region stemmed from his growing realization over the previous quarter century that the Christian heritage of both Ireland and the West more generally had been receding like the sea of faith in Matthew Arnold's "Dover Beach." While he had left the Catholic Church as an active communicant by this time, his parents' deaths in the 1980s convinced him that he had unwisely ignored his own spiritual heritage and vocabulary, to his own personal and poetic cost. Heaney believed that a rich spiritual life is inextricably bound to a strong regional culture: as he argues in "The Regional Forecast," from the 1920s through the 1940s "official Anglo-Saxon culture withdrew many of its deposits from what T. S. Eliot called 'the mind of Europe.' Its metaphysical and classical-humanist agenda contracted, [and] it gradually killed many of its support systems from biblical tradition and religious faith."[2] He recalls and then quotes a long passage from Eliot's lecture "The Social Function of Poetry," which was first given to the British-Norwegian Institute in 1943 and which argues that the decline of "religious sensibility" and the decline of "the feeling for poetry" are interconnected.[3] Heaney concludes that "against this emptying of the world's meaning and significance, the last ditch of defense which Eliot can envisage is the fidelity of a region or a nation to its indigenous language, its poetry, and its particular religious sensibility."[4] Such a characterization of Eliot's regionalist program reminds us why Heaney was so upset by the relatively abstract and deregionalized language of the tercet-driven passages from his "Little Gidding," particularly when he looked to them for inspiration on matters both regional and spiritual during the writing of "Station Island." Lest his listeners "think that Eliot sounds a bit too churchy," he quickly points out "the refusal of writers like Nadezhda Mandelstam or

Czeslaw Miłosz to lose their cultural memory or concede to the despiritualization of the world."[5] He affirms "the stirring faith of Joseph Brodsky in a civilization's capacity for survival at the extremes, in the provinces and regions," where there flourish "transfusions of energy which a language is capable of giving to itself and the renewals and sallies which can occur through the action of poetry."[6] Thus Heaney identifies the need for poetic language to transfuse spiritual concerns back into our culture—the focus of the third strand of his regionalism from at least *Station Island* onward, expressed with increasing urgency as the "despiritualization of the world" continued to accelerate.

He describes this problem as particularly acute in Ireland, and while on the one hand he praises "a gradual shift in the country's sense of itself, from being a self-denying, frugal republic, to being an equal consumer nation," as a benefit to "young middle-class people," who now have "a terrific sense of confidence, freedom, relish of it all," on the other hand, he bewails "an attendant problem over these 40 or 50 years, and that is that some kind of metaphysic has disappeared from the common life [in Ireland]. The religious life of the country has dwindled considerably."[7] One perennial measure of Ireland's spiritual life has always been attendance at the Catholic mass. Diarmaid Ferriter notes that it "had remained exceptionally high by international standards in the 1970s and 1980s, but a national survey revealed attendance had fallen to 78 per cent in 1992, with a figure as low as 65 per cent recorded for 1997; the decline was most pronounced among urban youth."[8] Ordinations to the priesthood plunged, many thousands fled the priesthood and religious orders, and a series of sexual scandals rocked the Catholic Church in Ireland. Even the radical journalist Vincent Browne bemoaned the rapid erosion of Irish trust in the church: Ferriter observes about Browne's reaction that "the sense of camaraderie and solace that had been experienced in communal religious devotion had been replaced, he mused, by the individual subscribing 'to the anonymous society, acquisitive, rootless, unbounded.'"[9] The confidence and freedom that Heaney identifies in "young, middle-class people" has been diminished, certainly, by Ireland's recent financial woes—the collapse of the vaunted Celtic Tiger economy has unquestionably led to a rise in young people's emigration again—yet there certainly has been an increase in the younger generations' confidence generally as they have taken more control of their lives. Heaney does not miss "this authoritarian church" and its "puritanism," but he misses "its sense of service and readiness to go on missions and so on"; he claims that "the dwindling of the faith and, secondly, the clerical scandals have bewildered things. I think we still are running on an unconscious that is informed by religious values, but I think my youngsters' youngsters won't have that. I think the needles are wobbling in that way."[10]

Thus, when Heaney argues in "Frontiers of Writing" that poetry can redress at least indirectly societal ills (as his own linguistic and cultural regionalist work long attempted to do), he immediately plumps for another, allied definition of poetry's redress, which "is to know it and celebrate it for its forcibleness as itself, as the affirming spiritual flame which W. H. Auden wanted to be shown forth. It is to know it and celebrate it not only as a matter of proffered argument and edifying content, but as a matter of angelic potential, a motion of the soul."[11] Employing Nadezhda Mandelstam's phrase in *Hope against Hope* about poetry being "a vehicle of world harmony," Heaney then posits poetry's double redress: "To be a source of truth and at the same time a vehicle of harmony: this expresses what we would like poetry to be and it takes me back to the kinds of pressures which poets from Northern Ireland are subject to. These poets feel with special force a need to be true to the negative nature of the evidence and at the same time to show an affirming flame, the need to be both socially responsible and creatively free."[12] Such a statement seems to contradict the statement with which I begin this chapter where Heaney claims that the writer is responsible for "visionary rather than social" matters, yet such vacillation is typical of his dialectical progressions. When he concludes this lecture by affirming that "within our individual selves we can reconcile two orders of knowledge which we might call the practical and the poetic" and also "that each form of knowledge redresses the other and that the frontier between them is there for the crossing," he has given us his triple regionalist agenda in miniature.[13] Citing his poem from "Lightenings" about the ghostly ship that caught its anchor on the altar rails at Clonmacnoise, Heaney suggests that the form of this poem, the modified tercet, enables a crossing of the frontier between the current, still-divided region of Northern Ireland and the imagined, more harmonious Northern Ireland of the future or the spirit region.

Heaney's model for moving across this epistemological frontier is, somewhat surprisingly, Patrick Kavanagh, better known for his antipastoral poems such as "The Great Hunger." In his 1985 lecture "The Placeless Heaven: Another Look at Kavanagh," he limns the older poet's career in terms that could apply equally to his own: "Where Kavanagh had once painted Monaghan like a Millet, with a thick and faithful pigment in which men rose from the puddled ground, all wattled in potato mould, he now paints like a Chagall, afloat above his native domain, airborne in the midst of his own dream place rather than earthbound in a literal field."[14] When he admits at the end of this piece that when he read a late Kavanagh poem such as "Prelude" in 1963 the appeal was its rhythm and its "skillful way with an octosyllabic metre," he just as quickly observes that "I was too much in love with poetry that painted the world in a thick linguistic pigment to relish fully the line-drawing that was inscribing itself so lightly and freely here."[15] By this time, he believed that "when he had consumed the roughage of his early Monaghan experience, he had cleared a space where, in Yeats's words, 'The soul recovers radical innocence.'"[16] Yeats's and Kavanagh's "radical innocence," a rooted and flourishing spiritual condition, had now become Heaney's own, and he sought to joyfully convey this third aspect of his regionalism to us ever more explicitly in his prose and poetry of his last years. By the time he wrote an essay to celebrate the centenary of Kavanagh's birth in 2004, Heaney felt so strongly about Kavanagh's spirituality that he would conclude, "Most of all, he was a poet of pure spiritual force, to the extent that many of his lyrics now belong in the common mind as if they were prenatal possessions—even, perhaps, prenatal necessities."[17]

This third manifestation of Heaney's regionalism has familiar shades hovering over it—Dante, Eliot, and another enabling regional poet for Heaney, Wordsworth. In his 2006 lecture "'Apt Admonishment': Wordsworth as an Example," Heaney discusses what he terms "poetic recognition scenes," noting that "the sense of visitation and rededication will often derive from meetings and occasions which are far less exalted [than meeting "some great poetic forebear"], but which are nevertheless bathed in an uncanny light, occasions when the poet has been, as it were, unhomed, has experienced the *unheimlich*."[18] Such scenes dominate the central section of *Station Island*, and they would increasingly feature in significant Heaney poems in the 1990s and beyond—particularly in *Seeing Things*

"My Ship of Genius Now Shakes Out Her Sail"   361

and *Human Chain*, Heaney's best two volumes after *Station Island* and in many ways that volume's natural complements and successors. When the poet allows himself to be ungrounded, "unhomed," he is penetrated by visionary experiences that eventually enable a regrounding, a homecoming, but with a new and transcendent sense of self.

As Heaney puts it in "'Apt Admonishment,'" "The poet typically comes away from such encounters with a renewed sense of election, surer in his or her vocation. What is being enacted or recalled is usually an experience of confirmation, of the spirit coming into its own, a door being opened or a path being entered upon. Usually also the experience is unexpected and out of the ordinary, in spite of the fact that it occurs in the normal course of events, in the everyday world."[19] The recourse of the language of this passage to spiritual terms is remarkable: for example, *election*, which would have been a pejorative term for Heaney growing up minority Catholic in Protestant-majority Northern Ireland, which was composed of many Presbyterians who believed in such a theological concept, gives a religious weight and charge to the concept of vocation. And "the spirit coming into its own" suggests that the soul may acquire additional agency after such encounters.

Significantly, the first two examples Heaney gives us of such encounters with the everyday that lead to "a renewed sense of election" for the poet and to "the spirit coming into its own" are from works by Dante and T. S. Eliot where they employ terza rima. Heaney cites the first canto of *The Divine Comedy*, "when Dante meets the shade of Virgil" but "is not immediately aware that heaven has intervened to send the Latin poet to be his guide, yet a high sense of mystery and destiny does nevertheless prevail."[20] And right after this passage, in the very same sentence, Heaney cites Eliot's "Little Gidding" where the poet meets "a familiar ghost in the dawn light after an air raid in wartime London—a ghost whom Eliot thought of as an emanation of the recently dead William Butler Yeats." Here Heaney does not criticize Eliot's tendency toward abstract language as he did in his 1985 essay on Dante, discussed in chapter 8 above. In fact, he compares this passage from Eliot's section of "Little Gidding," which employs a variation on Dantean terza rima, favorably with that first canto from Dante, noting "a similar feeling of mystery and destiny in surroundings that are entirely matter of fact."[21] He even argues that "in both cases, the sense of rare occasion is present in the way the language goes a little bit beyond its usual operations . . . by recourse to idioms and allusions drawn from the world of high culture."[22]

In all of the essay's cited examples of poetic encounters with the seemingly ordinary that become extraordinary—Hesiod (*Theogony*), Dante, Eliot, D. H. Lawrence ("The Snake"), Wordsworth ("Resolution and Independence"), and Elizabeth Bishop ("The Moose")—the poet or speaker receives an admonishment from the figure he encounters in a flickering realm. Heaney even links Bishop to Dante by noting "the big othering eyes of a moose that had come out of the *selva oscura* of the Maine woods,"[23] again emphasizing Dante's central influence on Heaney from the 1980s and beyond. This "admonishing agent is one who appears in a haunted, dreamy light, like a messenger 'from some far region sent' [quoting Wordsworth's "Resolution and Independence"]. We participate in an experience of absorption in an other life: in each case, the poet arrives on the scene either abstracted or disoriented, and is then brought more fully alive to his or her obligations and capacities—is helped, in fact, to get back in touch with his or her proper poetic gifts."[24] This essay, in which Heaney looks back to earlier poems such as "The Tollund Man" and to Dante and Eliot, among others, suggests strongly how much he continues to privilege Wordsworthian "spots of time" that lead not only to epiphanic insight but also to spiritual encounters.

Heaney's consistent emphasis on how the quotidian can become transcendent through a rich recovery of the region is borne out in interviews from the period under consideration here. For example, in a 1992 interview, Heaney would tell Richard Kearney, "You don't want to be promoting the local in its own right. I mean, the local has to be radiant with something you would call truth."[25] Although he makes this statement in the context of his use of a northern European geography for the poems of *North*, Heaney goes on to note fairly quickly in this interview that "I do think that you cut yourself off from enabling heritages and from *visionary forms* if you shut off what traditionally is European civilization," observing further that he sees in southern Europe "the possibility of a hopeful, other, renewable, nonutilitarian, joyful spirit of being. Those promises, hopes and invitations reside in that Graeco-Roman-Judaic heritage, I think."[26] Although he does not specifically raise Dante as an influence here, his use of "visionary forms" in the context of his affirmation of the southern European "Graeco-Roman-Judaic heritage" suggests he may well be thinking of Dantean terza rima.

The growing influence of Yeats on Heaney—recognized by the younger poet as he approached fifty in 1989, and signaled above in his citation in "The Placeless Heaven" of Kavanagh's recovery of a "radical innocence" and in "'Apt Admonishment'" of Eliot's speaker's recognition of the ghost of Yeats in "Little Gidding"—also contributed to his growing awareness and realization that some variation of terza rima would become his privileged later form to plumb his third region—the spirit world. Already, in his 1978 lecture "Yeats as an Example?," Heaney had analyzed Yeats's late poem "Cuchulain Comforted" in terms of how its terza rima form complemented its move toward death. He observes there that "it is written in *terza rima*, the metre of Dante's *Commedia*, the only time Yeats used the form, but the proper time, when he was preparing his own death by imagining Cuchulain's descent among the shades. We witness here a strange ritual of surrender, a rite of passage from life into death, but a rite whose meaning is subsumed into song, into the otherness of art."[27] Thus, by 1978, Heaney was arguing that terza rima was the form for last things, for meditating on death and its ghosts, a remark that anticipates his own use of a modified version of this form, as we have seen, in the many lyrics in which he meets shades from his past in "Station Island" and in the poems from "Sweeney Redivivus," where the speaker flits airily, buoyed by the tercet stanzas forming the architecture of those poems. Note too that Heaney suggests that the form aestheticizes death, "subsume[s] [it] into song, into the otherness of art," by virtue of its rhyme scheme.

Heaney's turn toward the tercet may also have been influenced by the later Wallace Stevens's ability to render a consciousness permeable to spirituality through groups of three sounds even in his nontercet poems, and particularly in his tercet poems such as "The River of Rivers in Connecticut." In his book review of Paul Muldoon's 1977 volume *Mules*, Heaney quotes Stevens in the context of his analysis of Muldoon's "Centaurs." After noting about Muldoon's poem that "the life of the thing is in the language's potential for generating new meanings out of itself, and it is this sense of buoyancy, this delight in the trickery and lechery that words are capable of, that is the distinguishing mark of the volume as a whole," he argues that his imagination "delights in its own fictions and has a right to them; or we might quote Wallace Stevens: 'Poetry creates a fictitious existence on an exquisite plane.'"[28] The next year, in "Yeats as an Example?", he would call Stevens "that other great apologist of the imagination," although he would fault him for not having the rich public life that Yeats did.[29] By 1990, during the writing of many of the tercet-driven poems that would become part of *Seeing Things*, and partly through the influence of Helen Vendler, Stevens was important enough to Heaney to mention in the first sentence and cite twice at the beginning of his first Oxford lecture, "The Redress of Poetry." The first citation employs Stevens to affirm Heaney's own high regard for the imagination, particularly given his own long exposure to violence previously in Northern Ireland: "The nobility of poetry, says Wallace Stevens, 'is a violence from within that protects us from a violence without.' It is the imagination pressing back against the pressure of reality."[30] As we have seen, Heaney's portraits of Philoctetes in both *The Cure at Troy* and his translation of *Beowulf* allegorize these heroes so that they represent the poetic imagination's inner violence pressing back against outer violence.

Heaney is consistently drawn, moreover, to the way in which Stevens unifies reality and spirit through triple clusters of phrases, images, and sounds. He has apprehended and embraced what R. P. Blackmur pointed out about Stevens's penchant for triadic thinking: "A triad makes a trinity, and a trinity, to a certain kind of poetic imagination, is the only tolerable form of unity. I think the deep skills of imagination . . . thrive best when some single, pressing theme or notion is triplicated."[31] Instances of Heaney's attraction to Stevens's "triplicated imagination" abound: Vendler, for example, has pointed out that his poem "Terminus" from *The Haw Lantern* is likely influenced by Stevens's lines from "Thirteen Ways of Looking at a Blackbird": "I was of three minds, / Like a tree / In which there are three blackbirds."[32] Moreover, in his analysis of Stevens's "The Irish Cliffs of Moher," which proceeds through groups of two lines (one cannot call them couplets), one long and the other much shorter, Heaney praises the "poem's body of sound," which is created by "the solemn march established in three-time at the beginning—'in this world, in this house, / At the spirit's base,' 'My father's father, his father's father, his—,' 'before thought, before speech, / At the head of the past'—all this contributes to a deep horn music, the rounded-out lengthened-back note of the *cor au fond du bois*;

and it is this musical amplitude that persuades the ear of the reality of an inner space where the dimension of time has been precipitated out of the dimension of space, where density streams toward origin."[33]

Clearly, although Stevens was admitted relatively late to Heaney's hall of poetic exemplars, his example has been a powerful one, particularly in his late, tercet-driven poems. Heaney has observed recently that although he is not "possessed" by Stevens's poems as by Robert Frost's, "every time I look at 'The River of Rivers in Connecticut' or 'The Plain Sense of Things' or any number of those late poems, I'm in thrall to their plain mystery, the way thingness and concept are plied together. It's a very hard, very clean poetic alloy" (*SS*, 433). He references "The River of Rivers" briefly in his introduction to his translation of *Beowulf* when he recalls his realization that the River Usk in Britain derives from "the Irish and Scots Gaelic word *uisce*, meaning water . . . and so in my mind the stream was suddenly turned into a kind of linguistic *river of rivers*."[34] He has also noted that "in certain great poets—Yeats, Shakespeare, Stevens, Milosz—you sense an ongoing opening of consciousness as they age, a deepening and clarifying and even a simplifying of receptivity to what might be awaiting on the farther shore" (*SS*, 466). Even though Heaney claimed of Stevens that "deep down, he's as bleak as the Larkin of 'Aubade,'" he learned to value his "ongoing opening of consciousness" in his late poetry (385).[35]

Other forms that feature a procession of tercets, such as the villanelle, have proven helpful for Heaney's evolving formal tendency toward the tercet and his sense that it is the proper form for shades crossing over to the spirit region. For example, his "Villanelle for an Anniversary" (1986), written for the 350th anniversary of Harvard, focuses on John Harvard's walking spirit: "A spirit moved, John Harvard walked the yard, / The atom lay unsplit, the west unwon, / The books stood open and the gates unbarred" (*OG*, 265). But the form here and elsewhere for Heaney is employed to portray a largely celebratory, garlanded sort of death. Heaney is likely drawn to the villanelle form because it contains five tercets and a concluding quatrain—a sort of halfway form between the dominant form (quatrains) of his 1970s poetry and that of his later poetry (tercets).

In his 1991 Oxford lecture, "Dylan the Durable? On Dylan Thomas," Heaney again links the tercet directly to death in discussing Thomas's famous villanelle about his dying father, "Do Not Go Gentle into That Good

Night." Heaney believes that this poem "fulfills its promise precisely because its craft has not lost touch with a suffered world. The villanelle form, turning upon itself, advancing and retiring to and from a resolution, is not just a line-by-line virtuoso performance. Through its repetitions, the father's remoteness—and the remoteness of all fathers—is insistently proclaimed, yet we can also hear, in an almost sobbing counterpoint, the protest of the poet's child-self against the separation."[36] After citing the poem and analyzing it, Heaney points out that it "is obviously a threshold poem about death.... The reflexiveness of the form is the right correlative for the reflexiveness of the feeling."[37] At the end of his discussion of this masterful example of the villanelle, Heaney finally claims that this form "both participates in the flux of natural existence and scans and abstracts existence in order to register its pattern. It is a living cross-section, a simultaneously open and closed form, one in which the cycles of youth and age, of rise and fall, growth and decay find their analogues in the fixed cycle of rhymes and repetitions."[38] He thus argues that the villanelle's form is so tightly interwoven into its content that they work harmoniously together to express such a cyclical pattern. We might say by extrapolation from this analysis that the villanelle, which begins with terza rima yet does not "forward" that form through a series of rhymes that proceed through the alphabet, constitutes a form that in its entirety is "natural" and earth-bound in the best sense of the word because of the relative rigidity of the same *aba* rhyme across its tercets and the three out of four rhymed lines in its concluding quatrain. It speaks to the mystery of death but does not go beyond it, while many of Heaney's tercet-driven poems do.

While Heaney clearly admires the villanelle form in the hands of such masters as Dylan Thomas, his relative dislike of the overly fixed rhyme of the villanelle in these essays, written in the first couple of years after *Seeing Things*, may have confirmed to him that his own modified versions of terza rima, without that form's fixed, progressive rhymes, might enable him to achieve a truthful form with a buoyancy that would match its spiritual subjects of departure and arrival.

Certainly, Heaney's essentially trinitarian thinking was most greatly shaped by his childhood and adolescent immersion in Irish Catholicism, aspects of which he would draw on again after the death of his parents in the 1980s, but his devotion to Dante, whom he saw as a great writer of both his region of Italy and the spirit region, confirmed the general importance to him of trinitarian thinking and the form of terza rima. His in-depth reading of *The Divine Comedy* would have helped him realize the ubiquity and significance of the number three throughout that epic: as Michael Hurley has pointed out, "The *Commedia* is itself made up of three *cantiche*, each of which consists of thirty-three canti . . . , as each of his *terzine* consists of thirty-three syllables."[39]

Heaney perceives terza rima (and variations on it) as the formal container capable of carrying and expressing insight into the spirit world, his third strand of regionalism. His tercet forms that flirt with but usually depart from the full rhymes of Dantean terza rima leave the consoling sonic rhymes of the couplet behind while also achieving an airiness that his 1970s quatrain-oriented poems do not.[40] This in-between form is married time and again to liminal moments of insight into the spiritual world that Heaney catches in his poetry and reveals to us. Poised lightly upon that form, he has made it his poetic house as his last poetry muses upon border crossings to the region we inhabit after death and the new life that babies experience.

In his discussion of Dante's end rhymes in his terza rima, Hurley observes that "B. I. Gilman describes this cycle as the sense of a '*perpetual beyond*'" that, he suggests, recalls ideas of the infinite: "And we may well believe that the poet who first dared to write on eternal themes in popular speech gladly recognized the preemiment [*sic*] right of a popular verse to become its metrical dress."[41] Although Heaney will use pararhymes in his modifications of Dantean terza rima, at other times he departs from any kind of regular rhyme scheme at all in his tercets; yet because he is using three-line stanzas, he sets up the expectation in his readers that he will be treating eternal themes drawn from the spirit region.

More particularly, in this treatment he draws on another association of terza rima that Dorothy Sayers has observed: its propulsive, wavelike quality. In her introduction to her masterful translation of *The Inferno*, she points out "the strong forward movement of the verse, which is like that of a flowing tide, each wave riding in on the back of the one before it."[42] Even though Heaney often eschews Dante's specific rhyme scheme in his modifications of terza rima in his later poetry, he almost certainly read and appreciated Sayers's remark here when he began seriously reading

Dante in the early 1970s, and thus he repeatedly turns to variations on terza rima when he writes of watery scenes and surroundings. Certainly, all of the central section of *Station Island* is aquatic, set on that famous island in Lough Derg; moreover, his initial meeting (with William Carleton) and his last one (with James Joyce) end with rain showers. In *Seeing Things*, Heaney repeatedly is drawn to cast ghostly encounters in his modified terza rima that is anchored in often watery settings—"The Journey Back," the conclusion of "The Settle Bed," "A Retrospect," "The Sounds of Rain," the "Squarings" section of Part II, and the entirety of "The Crossing," where the setting is Charon's barge in the underworld. Several tercet-driven poems from *Human Chain*, including "In the Attic," "Miracle," "Chanson d'Aventure," and "Human Chain," respond to these earlier poems and signal Heaney's anticipation of his own pending departure even as he celebrates the human chain of community that helped him recover from his first stroke.

BUOYANCY AND ANCHORAGE IN THE TERCET POEMS
OF *SEEING THINGS* AND *HUMAN CHAIN*

Heaney's recourse to the tercet as formally signifying the spirit region is symbolized most fully by the appearance of various watercraft in major poems from *Seeing Things* and *Human Chain*. As such, the opening terza rima stanza from canto 1 of the *Purgatorio* signifies Heaney's artistic declaration in *Seeing Things* and the volumes since then: "For better waters heading with the wind / My ship of genius now shakes out her sail / And leaves that ocean of despair behind."[43] Significantly, Heaney's favored form for his "ship of genius" to sail upon is the tercet, often in the twelve-liners he favors in *Seeing Things* and sporadically in *Human Chain*. Thus the basic unit of sound for Heaney's final concept of regionalism is the tercet, which suggests his commitment to exploring a wider spirit world beyond the bounds of the actual and imagined province of Northern Ireland, signified by his own transformation of Dantean terza rima.

Michael Cavanagh has remarked upon the preponderance of the boat image in *Seeing Things* and has noted that the American edition of the volume features a cover photograph of the gold boat from the Broighter

Hoard in Heaney's native County Derry mentioned in "The Biretta."[44] For Cavanagh, who reads this artifact through Heaney's 1993 essay "The Sense of the Past," "The Gold Boat forges a connection between us and our distant ancestors at the same time that it narrows the distance between us and our humbler neighbors. Its aureate sheen, its profane perfection, reattaches us to, while raising us slightly above, the life around us."[45] And yet the volume concludes with Charon's boat ferrying the damned across the River Styx in Heaney's version of Dante's canto 3 from *The Inferno*, suggesting an altogether more sinister complement to this image of the gold boat on the American edition. Moreover, the cover of the British edition of *Seeing Things* reproduces a portion of the Gundestrup Cauldron, the largest surviving piece of European Iron Age silver work, which was found in a peat bog in what is now Himmerland, Denmark, in 1891. This cover thus resonates with Heaney's bog poems of the 1970s but also registers a significant discontinuity: given the fantastic detail of this religious vessel and its great purity (the plates making up the vessel are 97 percent pure silver), it has an aura of perfection and otherness that Glob's bog bodies lack.[46] Its metallurgical purity links it to the similar purity of the gold boat from the Broighter Hoard on the American cover. Most important, the cauldron's purpose of holding liquid symbolically highlights Heaney's belief that poetic form is a near-perfect way to hold ethereal content and suggests that *Seeing Things* will dramatize that conviction even as it continues to admit the constraining pressure of the cares that weigh upon our lives.

Rather than focusing on the literal boats of this volume, then, one strand of my argument articulates how their appearance highlights Heaney's concern with form as boatlike, both airy and solid, and how that form enables us to enter the spirit region. He articulates a long analogy between lyric poetry and a boat at the end of his Nobel Prize Address, beginning by noting that "the passage of the poem calls into being" the "temple inside our hearing" (*CP*, 28). Then he calls attention to "the energy released by linguistic fission and fusion, with the buoyancy generated by cadence and tone and rhyme and stanza" (28). In returning to muse again upon Yeats's "Meditations in Time of Civil War," Heaney lauds "the sheer in-placeness of the whole poem as a given form within the language," holding immediately that "poetic form is both the ship and the anchor. It is at once a buoyancy and a holding, allowing for the simultaneous gratification of whatever is centrifugal and centripetal in mind and body" (29). Thus, for Heaney, by virtue of its form, Yeats's poem "does what the necessary poetry always does, which is to touch the base of our sympathetic nature while taking in at the same time the unsympathetic reality of the world to which that nature is constantly exposed" (29). Finally, he argues that "the form of the poem ... is crucial to poetry's power to do the thing which always is and always will be to poetry's credit: the power to persuade that vulnerable part of our consciousness of its rightness in spite of the evidence of wrongness all around it, the power to remind us that we are hunters and gatherers of values, that our very solitudes and distresses are creditable, in so far as they, too, are an earnest of our veritable human being" (29). I quote so heavily from *Crediting Poetry* here because I believe this is the most sincere and insightful statement Heaney has ever made about form. In this passage, he both concisely articulates form's bifocal nature, which enables it to be attuned to both the harsh outer world of reality and the tender inner world of our soul, and powerfully links form to human values. In light of this argument, the modified terza rima in *Seeing Things* shows how he continued to keep an eye on the region of Northern Ireland in the late 1980s and early 1990s while paying more explicit attention to the condition of our souls—the spirit region—in his poetry than he ever had. Even if his tercets here eschew Dante's interlocking rhyme scheme in favor of none at all or embrace the envelope rhymes of "The Crossing," Heaney's poems that feature versions of terza rima in *Seeing Things* bob along, beckoning us with their lightsome form that is matched only by their sublime content.

The open and unfinished-looking form for the twelve-liners (four tercets) in *Seeing Things* formally accords with Heaney's sense, in the mid- to late 1980s, that with the passing of his parents he was *unroofed*, exposed to a previously closed spiritual realm. The speaker of "A Haul," the third lyric in "Three Drawings," even describes Thor as "unroofed" after he misses catching the "world-serpent" and his "head / opened out there on the sea": "He felt at one with space, // unroofed and obvious—" (*ST*, 14). Heaney has pointed out that "the fact of having been present at the death beds of my parents in the previous years is certainly one of the reasons for the sense of the roof coming off, and my daring to speak about the big events" in the poems of *Seeing Things*.[47] Helen Vendler argues that their deaths led him to reverse his earlier artistic strategy: "His aim is now to turn the crystalline, or virtual, absent realm into a material one—to make it visible by metaphors so ordinary as to be indubitable."[48] As we will see in my analysis of seminal poems from this volume, Heaney admirably succeeds in this aim of rendering the invisible realm visible to us, often through the wavering form of the tercet or by recourse to a tripartite structure and the employment of tripled words and phrases.

In the seventh lyric of "Glanmore Revisited," "The Skylight," a poem to which I will return, he celebrates the literal unroofing of a portion of Glanmore Cottage, which was done once when he was at Harvard: "But when the slates came off, extravagant / Sky entered and held surprise wide open" (*ST*, 39). Elsewhere he described the new skylight in his Glanmore study as "a tremendous change for me; again something to do with getting near fifty: I lifted up my eyes to the heavens" (*SS*, 326). Heaney noted in multiple interviews that the openness of the twelve-line form formally bespoke his new receptiveness to spiritual matters: "I didn't think of those twelve-liners as sonnets, mind you; they were more arbitrary than that. The thing about the sonnet is that it tends to tie itself up and in a good sense tie itself off at the end, like tying a bow: even if you are trying to dodge closure, closure is very much on your mind with a sonnet. But the way the first two or three twelve-liners went, they seemed to be open at both ends and I liked that very much; I gave myself permission, as it were, to be more whimsical."[49] Later, he said that "I felt free as a kid skimming stones, and in fact the relationship between individual poems in the different sections has something of the splish-splash, one-after-anotherness of stones skittering and frittering across the water" (*SS*, 319). He also described how these poems came to him first in terms of form: "It felt given, strange and unexpected; I didn't quite know where it came from, but I knew immediately it was there to stay. It seemed as solid as an iron bar. . . . The form operated for me as a generator of poetry" (320–21). Inherent in these comments is a sense of the twelve-liner's airiness yet firmness, a conviction that aligns well with Heaney's assertion in *Crediting Poetry* that "poetic form is both the ship and the anchor." As Colm Toíbín pointed out in his review of *Human Chain*, Heaney's twelve-line form "offers a sort of looseness, a buoyancy, a refusal to close and conclude; it means that the endings of these poems can have a particular pathos, a holding of the breath, 'gleaning the unsaid off the palpable,' as Heaney has it in his poem 'The Harvest Bow.' "[50] His light and airy tercets are gathered into the solid twelve-lined form of a series of remarkable poems in *Seeing Things* that probe the deepest recesses of our souls while keeping us grounded.

The tercet is both particularized and local, expansive and transcendent, thus recalling Heaney's bifocal Joyce, who is grounded and cosmopolitan. It is finally a dwelling-place, a home, *a lasting region*—one that increasingly afforded him safe harbor as a form, yet allowed him to remain a risky, international voice. One of Heaney's former mentors, Philip Hobsbaum, claimed that after Heaney's variations on terza rima in *Station Island* he "has considerably developed this usage of the form in his later verse," particularly in *Seeing Things*, noting that "The Crossing" "achieves something of a *terza rima* effect by pararhyming the first and third lines of each tercet, and leaving each second line unrhymed," and finally observing that "the echo of the *terza rima* is fainter in a sequence of twelve-lined poems, each arranged as four tercets, called 'Lightenings.' Really, the form in Heaney's hands deserves a name of its own. It would seem to have left the essentially linked tercets of Wyatt and Shelley well behind."[51] Yet as we will see, Heaney establishes linkages to important human beings past and present through his sometimes unlinked tercets in *Seeing Things* and *Human Chain*, which volumes themselves are intricately connected.

Heaney's use of the tercet form in the four-part sequence "Squarings" and in "The Crossing" enacts a dialogue with a number of tercet-driven poems from *Human Chain* about regional concerns—both local culture and spiritual matters. Significant poems in *Human Chain* such as "Miracle" and "In the Attic" "reply," as it were, to poems in *Seeing Things* such as "The Skylight" and "The Settle Bed" and offer extended meditations both on those subjects and on the boundary crossings of birth and death.

In "The Journey Back," the second poem of *Seeing Things*, a tribute to Philip Larkin, the tercet form enables the poet to have an encounter with a soul who has crossed over. Since both Larkin and Dante are regional writers in the most enabling sense for Heaney and have been most exemplary for him, it follows that he would choose to write this elegy for Larkin and translation from Dante ("The Crossing") that nearly frames *Seeing Things* in his version of terza rim. But a crucial change is now evident in Heaney's usage of this form in this volume: Larkin and Dante have both previously represented particular geographic regions for Heaney—Larkin standing for isolated northeastern England (particularly Hull) and Dante representing his vernacular region of Italy—but now they signify the spirit region of death for Heaney, symbolizing poets who have crossed over into that nebulous landscape and who function as guides opening up the realm of the marvelous and spiritual to the poet. Dante certainly inspired the poet's encounters with ghosts from his past in "Station Island," but he now is looked to as a guarantor of the spiritual afterlife by the poet. Heaney's remark about Yeats's use of terza rima late in his life suggests how strongly he had come to associate the form with death and crossing over: "The very deliberately chosen and executed *terza rima* of 'Cuchulain Comforted,' for example, is like a passport he issued for himself just before he had to cross the dark water. It says that this particular body is ready to board the barge as a shade" (*SS*, 465–66).

Larkin's death in 1985, occurring between Heaney's mother's death in 1984 and his father's death in 1986, was clearly another, albeit less personally emotional, death for Heaney that also inspired him to write about things spiritual and "unroofed" in this volume. Cavanagh has pointed out that Heaney's obituary and "generous appreciation" for Larkin in the *Irish Times* in 1985 praises Larkin in terms of "transcendence, awe, sonority, severity, and the uncompromised somberness of his vision."[52] And even though Heaney had finished a very negative prose assessment of Larkin entitled "Joy or Night: Last Things in the Poetry of W. B. Yeats and Philip Larkin," he would not publicly deliver that essay as a lecture until 1993, and it would not be collected until 1995 in *The Redress of Poetry*. Thus, in the 1991 *Seeing Things*, Heaney's treatment of Larkin in "The Journey Back" is largely appreciative and even affectionate through his fourteen-lined poem composed in the main of four tercets.

Michael Molino has argued that in this poem Heaney "meets the final 'shade,' Philip Larkin," in the procession of shades that he first encounters in "Station Island."[53] For Molino, "Larkin blends Dante's words with his own so that Dante's task '*to face / The ordeal of my journey and my duty*' becomes Larkin's unsentimental, empirical vision of the drabness and enervation of modern life."[54] And yet this reading neglects both the continuity of the microunit of form common to both the "Station Island" lyrics and "The Journey Back"—the tercet—and the new macrounit of form that largely constitutes "The Journey Back"—the twelve-liner.

Because of this formal neglect, Molino misses the transcendental charge of the last line, "A nine-to-five man who had seen poetry" (*ST*, 9). Despite his emphasis on the ordinary and everyday (which, *contra* Molino, Larkin often rendered luminous and extraordinary, as he does at the end of "The Whitsun Weddings"), Heaney affirms Larkin's vision of poetry as the first "seen thing" in this aptly named volume. Further, the line suggests that if Larkin's head librarianship at the University of Hull was his daylight vocation, then poetry shaped his nighttime vocation and filled his vision with things beyond his normal ken.

While the rhyme scheme of "The Journey Back" certainly does not conform to the typical terza rima rhyme that runs *aba bcb cdc*, et cetera, it nonetheless offers a roughly alternating rhyme scheme after the opening line that runs *aba cd1/2c def ghg d* and has the typical dangling last line of Dante's terza rima that Heaney also included in some of the lyrics of "Station Island." Such a scheme deftly pays homage to Dante's original form and to the brilliant rhyming abilities of Larkin, grounds the poem in "the heartland of the ordinary" (9) that Larkin inhabited, and suggests his own tendency toward the transcendent and extraordinary, confirming Heaney's view of Larkin up until his unfair tirade against the English poet in his Oxford lecture "Joy or Night."[55]

Another poem composed of tercets in *Seeing Things*, "The Settle Bed," has no discernible rhyme scheme, yet its recourse to the tercet form in its departure from Dantean terza rima in every way except for its tripartite lineation again implies a lyrical lightness that enables the poem to finally lift away from the literal heaviness of the settle bed (and by implication the weighty matter of sectarianism in the North of Ireland) and enter the realm of imagination (and by extension an imagined new province). Heaney's return to the sectarian situation in the North is therefore achieved through the tercet form, his privileged form that corresponds to things regional and vernacular. He has described the bed as "vernacular furniture with a capital V" (*SS*, 326). The poem opens by rehearsing the bed's earthiness and gravity: "Willed down, waited for, in place at last and for good. / Trunk-hasped, cart-heavy, painted an ignorant brown. / And pew-strait, bin-deep, standing four-square as an ark" (*ST*, 30).[56] After noting that when he lies in it "my ear" is "shuttered up" (30), fairly quickly the speaker hears

an old sombre tide awash in the headboard:
Unpathetic *och ochs* and *och hohs*, the long bedtime
Anthems of Ulster, unwilling, unbeaten,

Protestant, Catholic, the Bible, the beads,
Long talks at gables by moonlight, boots on the hearth,
The small hours chimed sweetly away so next thing it was

The cock on the ridge-tiles.

(30)

The inheritance of this bed from his maiden aunt leads Heaney back into the matter of the North in a volume that purports to fly away from it. He puts the language of the Ulster-Scots settlers and their Bibles on an equal footing with that of the native Catholics and their rosary beads here and implies their equal convictions that they are "right" theologically and that the other is "wrong." The bed's "un-get-roundable weight" (30) and, by implication, the seemingly immovable positions taken by the two major communities in Northern Ireland appear too heavy to be shifted.

But the poem itself shifts right in the middle of the third line from the sixth stanza, immediately after the end-stopped half-line that ends with the "un-get-roundable weight." The rest of that stanza and indeed the rest of the poem now envision a lightness, a removal of heaviness—both for the bed and for the province by the early 1990s:

But to conquer that weight,

Imagine a dower of settle beds tumbled from heaven
Like some nonsensical vengeance on the people,
Then learn from that harmless barrage that whatever is
    given

Can always be reimagined, however four-square,
Plank-thick, hull-stupid and out of its time
It happens to be.

(31)

The original, now obsolete meaning of *dower* used as a noun is "burrow," which recalls early, subterranean Heaney and strengthens the earth-boundedness of the settle bed with which the poem begins.[57] But by also drawing on the more modern meaning of *dower*, an inheritance for a widow or a gift for a groom brought into a marriage by a bride-to-be, Heaney conveys the bounty implicit in such a term, which is heightened by its rhyme with "shower," what we would usually expect to fall from heaven. By urging his readers to indulge in such a fanciful speculation about a series of inherited settle beds tumbling down from heaven in a "harmless barrage," Heaney suggests that even other types of similarly fixed and weighty inheritances, such as cultural and religious ones, can be "reimagined" and reconceived and that through this process a new, freer sense of relationships might come into being in Northern Ireland. That new era is signaled by his employment of nautical imagery beginning with calling "whatever is given" "hull-stupid."

The final shift in the poem occurs again in the middle of a stanza's last line: here in the middle of the last line of the penultimate stanza, immediately after the end-stopped half-line "It happens to be" (31). That punctuation signals an end to the middle section of the poem and the beginning of the last, briefest section, in which the mere possibility of reimagining is replaced with an entrance into a chosen, imagined situation where "you are as free as the lookout . . . // Who declared by the time that he had got himself down / The actual ship had been stolen away from beneath him" (31). The lookout, "that far-seeing joker posted high over the fog" (31), nimbly occupies a fanciful narrative space that he uses to transform the given coordinates of his time and place—the "actual ship." In a similar way, Heaney suggests, the givenness of the Northern Irish ship of state might be not so much righted as "disappeared" away from its inhabitants and "sailors," citizens who within seven years after the publication of *Seeing Things* would indeed declare their dissatisfaction with the given state of the North and vote for a devolved political autonomy free from the grip of both the Republic of Ireland and the United Kingdom. Such a possibility is prefigured by the last three and a half lines of "The Settle Bed," the shortest portion of the poem and perforce the most speculative and fanciful. Thus the majority of the poem, the "heaviest" part by sheer number of lines, figuratively concerns the ongoing gravity of the situation in the North, while the succeeding six lines depict the possibility of change and the last three and a half lines the possibility for the province if the populace imagines such a process.

The unidentified lookout at the end of "The Settle Bed" springs to life again in "In the Attic," from *Human Chain*, where he is identified as Jim Hawkins from Robert Louis Stevenson's *Treasure Island*, yet this poem is altogether different in its vulnerable tone, as the poet mourns his aging through most of it. "In the Attic," composed entirely of tercets as well, begins *in medias res*: "Like Jim Hawkins aloft in the cross-trees / Of *Hispaniola*, nothing underneath him / But still green water and clean bottom sand" (*HC*, 82). The simile itself hovers there in front of us, unanchored, until, as the poem proceeds, we realize that the speaker himself feels like Hawkins, as he suggests in the second section: "At the attic skylight, a man marooned // In his own loft, a boy / Shipshaped in the crow's nest of a life" (82). The somewhat despairing tone of the speaker's feeling "marooned" in his attic study jars with the earlier, hopeful, and even miraculous associations Heaney's study acquired once opened to the sky, remembered in "The Skylight," from the "Glanmore Revisited" sequence in *Seeing Things*.

Yet as "In the Attic" proceeds, the inertia of its prepositional title, along with the poet's fears about aging and his diminishing memory, are finally overwhelmed by his concluding acknowledgment and affirmation of his still-potent imaginative powers. At the start of the fourth section, he portrays himself as returning to the "lightheadedness" of the naive cabin boy in the rigging with which the poem opens:

> As I age and blank on names,
> As my uncertainty on stairs
> Is more and more the lightheadedness
>
> Of a cabin boy's first time on the rigging,
> As the memorable bottoms out
> Into the irretrievable ...
> (84)

The repetition of "as" imparts a cumulative effect to these two tercets, implying Heaney's sense that he is returning to childhood's innocence through his aging and memory loss. More disturbingly, his last phrase in the second tercet somewhat gloomily revisits and revises his wonderful concluding line about the unplumbable depths of the imagination in "Bogland"—"The wet centre is bottomless" (*DD*, 42)—and his lines about fishing and the analogous work of the imagination in another signature poem, "Casualty": "To get out early, haul / Steadily off the bottom . . . / As you find a rhythm / Working you, slow mile by mile, / Into your proper haunt" (*FW*, 24). If in those two poems he figuratively casts his imagination as inexhaustible and full of images that could be retrieved, here he "hits bottom," as it were, and fears being unable to retrieve the "memorable."

Yet the final tercet, carrying on from the pause at the end of the second tercet following "irretrievable," suggests strongly the poet's ability to nevertheless figure the sails of his imaginative ship swelling with air when he needs them to: "It's not that I can't imagine still / That slight untoward rupture and world-tilt / As a wind freshened and the anchor weighed" (84). Even though the double negative construction mitigates the initial swelling of the imaginative sails in the following lines, Heaney seems to believe that his aging, while leading him into irretrievable losses, also might lead him back into the wondering mind of the child with his Wordsworthian innocence.

Returning to "The Skylight" from *Seeing Things*, which enacts a conversation with "Miracle" from *Human Chain*, the speaker, surely Heaney himself, recalls his opposition to "cutting into the seasoned tongue-and-groove / Of pitch pine," because "I liked it low and closed, / Its claustrophobic, nest-up-in-the-roof / Effect" (*ST*, 39). The attentive reader has already been alerted to the "dumb, tongue-and-groove worthiness" of the settle bed in the poem of that name (30); a similar worthiness and weightiness is attached to the pitch pine ceiling of the study here. Yet this sonnet's *volta* registers the speaker's astonishment "when the slates came off": "extravagant / Sky entered and held surprise wide open" (39). Rather than adorning the sky with superfluous article adjectives, Heaney simply and cleanly places the polysyllabic "extravagant" before it, and its pairing with the monosyllabic "Sky" itself startles in our sense of their initial incongruity, as does the agency he imparts to it: it both "entered" and "held." Formally, the last four lines of this sestet eschew both the alternating *abab* rhyme in the first quatrain of the octave and the successive *ccdd* couplets

"My Ship of Genius Now Shakes Out Her Sail"   379

of its second quatrain. Instead, the lack of end rhymes in the last four lines, which run *eghi*, itself surprises us but seems appropriate to the tone of delight and movement:

> For days I felt like an inhabitant
> Of that house where the man sick of the palsy
> Was lowered through the roof, had his sins forgiven,
> Was healed, took up his bed and walked away.
> (39)

The introduction of this narrative from Mark 2:1–12 and Heaney's likening of himself to an inhabitant of the house, not to the crippled man himself, create some of the final surprises of this startling poem. Mark makes clear in 2:5 that the man is forgiven because of his friends' faith: "When Jesus saw their faith, he said unto the sick of the palsy, Son, thy sins be forgiven thee."[58] He heals the man only when he hears the grumbling scribes argue that he is committing blasphemy by forgiving sins, thus equating himself to God (5:6–7). Therefore, in verse 10, Christ states, "But that ye may know that the Son of man hath power on earth to forgive sins (he saith to the sick of the palsy)," and he continues in verse 11, "I say unto thee, Arise, and take up thy bed, and go thy way into thine house." The palsied man now gains tremendous agency and is portrayed in a succession of three active verbs, fittingly for Heaney's growing commitment to tripled parts of speech and phrase, the tercet, and tripartite structures: "And immediately he arose, took up the bed, and went forth before them all" (Mark 2:12). The immediacy of the healing conveyed through these verbs must have shocked the gathered witnesses, and indeed their response in the second half of 2:12 is also instantaneous: "insomuch that they were all amazed, and glorified God saying, We never saw it on this fashion."[59]

Similarly, Heaney's reaction, which does not glorify God but revels in the revealed sky of his altered study, is shot through with gratefulness and wonder. This literal "unroofing" accords with his similar sense in the 1980s after the deaths of his parents that he had witnessed a spiritual transformation at their bedsides. But that sense of commingled gratefulness and wonder at their passing and at the opening of this skylight in his Glanmore cottage was compounded and heightened after his 2006 stroke, from which he recovered fully and rapidly with the help of his "human chain" of friends.

Thus, nearly twenty years later, in "Miracle," Heaney revisits Christ's healing narrative from Mark's Gospel and this time likens himself to the palsied man whose sins are forgiven and healed, who takes up his bed and walks away. Eamon Grennan's insightful comment about the title *Human Chain* reveals the transformative nature of the volume as a whole: "I like how the two words temper each other, turning an instrument of bondage into one of liberation, a sign of individual restriction into an image of mutual aid, dependency, community."[60] Like "The Skylight," which refuses to focus on the miraculous healing of the palsied man but instead dwells on the bystanders' wonder, "Miracle" unselfishly views the aftermath of Heaney's stroke from the point of view of his friends, who had gathered at the playwright Brian Friel's house in Donegal the night before for a party. Despite its title, much of the poem focuses on the hard, burdensome work they undertook to form a human chain in carrying the poet downstairs so he could be taken to the ambulance.

The title, "Miracle," belies its contents, since it begins and proceeds in a straightforward, determined fashion, and indeed its first eight lines focus on the physical labor of Heaney's friends after his stroke, not on their or his expectation of healing. Thus the first line, abruptly bringing us into the scene *in medias res*, runs, "Not the one who takes up his bed and walks" (*HC*, 16). Heaney instead calls our attention to "the ones who have known him all along / And carry him in—" (16). The rhythm of their transport of him is emphasized by the stanzas' deliberately ragged line lengths: the first tercet begins with two longer lines, followed by the short line just cited, while the next tercet reverses that pattern with its opening long line—"Their shoulders numb, the ache and stoop deeplocked"—followed by two shorter lines (16). And their focused aim in carrying his partially paralyzed body is underscored by the absence of verbs in this stanza; instead, nouns and adjectives follow pell-mell, and the resulting spareness of line implies his friends' determination. In the third tercet, the verbs reenter, and their use here draws our attention again to Heaney's friends' actions with the indirect effect that his own inertia is highlighted: "Until he's strapped on tight, made tiltable / And raised to the tiled roof, then lowered for healing, / Be mindful of them as they stand and wait" (16). We have been catapulted back into the narrative from Mark's Gospel about Jesus's forgiveness, then healing of the palsied man. But while Mark's Gospel focuses first on the friends' faith in carrying the sick man to Christ, then quickly moves on to the question of Christ's authority in matters of forgiveness and healing, Heaney's poem maintains its focus on his friends' dedication and faith—not to Christ, but to him.

Moreover, "Miracle" revises the hopeful last stanza of its predecessor poem, "The Skylight," which ends, as we have seen, with a series of verbs that encapsulate the hopeful heart of Mark's narrative: "the man sick of the palsy / Was lowered through the roof, had his sins forgiven, / Was healed, took up his bed and walked away" (*ST*, 39). "Miracle" instead offers one fairly prosaic final stanza from the viewpoint of the friends who "stand and wait": "For the burn of the paid-out ropes to cool, / Their slight lightheadedness and incredulity / To pass, those ones who had known him all along" (*HC*, 16). Their immediate hope is for quick physical and mental relief from their burden; only then can they look forward with trepidation and expectation to Heaney's healing. The near repetition in line 12 of the phrase from line 2—"But the ones who have known him all along"—is lovely, suggesting something like their continuity of care for Heaney throughout his life, not just in this moment of crisis, while the change from the present perfect tense of "have known" in that second line to "had known" in the last line subtly implies their fear that they may not know him in the future, when the effects of the stroke may change him.

In the two poems that frame "Miracle," "Chanson d'Aventure" and "Human Chain," we do get Heaney's perspective on his stroke, but even there he casts it in terms of its effect on his relationship with his wife, Marie, and puts it in the context of other important burdens that have been carried in the past. "Chanson d'Aventure," although it comes immediately before "Miracle" in the volume, narrates the ambulance trip to the hospital after Heaney's friends carry him downstairs. He attempts to lend the story a rollicking spirit, as the title suggests, and the opening stanza's stripped-down three lines packed with verbs at first convey this spirit: "Strapped on, wheeled out, forklifted, locked / In position for the drive, / Bone-shaken, bumped at speed" (*HC*, 13). But the subsequent stanzas quickly shift to the interior scene of the ambulance, where Heaney lies "flat on my back—" and communicates wordlessly with Marie in some of the most moving lines he has ever written:

> Our postures all the journey still the same,
>
> Everything and nothing spoken,
> Our eyebeams threaded laser-fast, no transport
> Ever like it until then, in the sunlit cold
>
> Of a Sunday morning ambulance.
> (13)

These lines closely recapitulate, revise, and reorder a series of lines from John Donne's "The Ecstasy." Donne's lines 19 and 20 are revisited in the first two lines here: "All day, the same our postures were, / And we said nothing all the day," while the third line recalls Donne's seventh and eighth lines: "Our eye-beams twisted, and did thread / Our eyes, upon one double string."[61] This emphasis on the physicality of the love between the Heaneys, given additional weight by the multiple Donne allusions, seems at first surprising in a volume that often focuses on the departed souls in Heaney's human chain of friends and family, but with the additional aid of this poem's epigraph from the last two lines of Donne's poem—"Love's mysteries in souls do grow, / But yet the body is his book"—we realize how Love writes its more quotidian realities in and on our bodies (13).

The further fear expressed in "When we might, O my love, have quoted Donne / On love on hold, body and soul apart" (13), imparts an additional poignancy to the poem as Heaney fears he may soon die and be apart from his body and apart from Marie. This double fear of sundering, tonally conveyed by the odal rhetoric and "O" vowel sounds in these two lines, carries over into the opening tercet of Part II, which quotes almost verbatim a famous line from Keats's "Ode to a Nightingale," "Forlorn: the very word is like a bell": "Apart: the very word is like a bell" (13).[62] "Apart" seems more hopeful than Keats's "Forlorn," but the possibility of "forlornness" hovers here, of course, unspoken, like all that is unvoiced on the Heaneys' wordless ambulance trip.

The rest of the poem turns on the image of a series of active and inactive hands, from the one implied through the image of "a bell / That the sexton Malachy Boyle outrolled," (13) to the bell Heaney "tolled in Derry in my turn / As college bellman" in the "heel of my once capable // Warm hand, hand that I could not feel you lift / And lag in yours throughout that journey / Where it lay flop-heavy as a bellpull" (14). That tolling bell recalls Donne's famous "Meditation 17," with its bells tolling death in the present and in the future, but it also recalls the great community Donne expresses there—"No man is an island entire of itself"—and Heaney's own supportive community that manifested itself during his stroke and its aftermath.[63] This reading is confirmed by two images from Part III—that of "the charioteer at Delphi" with "his left hand lopped // From a wrist protruding like an open spout" (14)—and that of Heaney's hand while he is recovering in physical therapy. He draws strength from the charioteer's stoicism and "his eyes-front, straight-backed postures like my own / Doing physio in the corridor" (14). As he works to regain his strength and mobility, likely using a walker, Heaney compares himself not only to this charioteer but also to his father's teaching him to plow as a boy:

As if once more I'd found myself in step

Between two shafts, another's hand on mine,
Each slither of the share, each stone it hit
Registered like a pulse in the timbered grips.
           (14–15)

Here the tercets emphasize the triple image of driving charioteer, hobbling older Heaney, and plowing younger Heaney. Older Heaney is held up by his memory of the mythical, stoic charioteer, by the more recent, realistic, fatherly hands of Patrick Heaney, and finally by the force of the tercets, which contain these images and release him, as it were, gradually back into his own walking rhythms in the present.

"Human Chain," the third poem in this triptych about Heaney's stroke, compounds an image of contemporary "bags of meal passed hand to hand / In close-up by the aid workers" in the first tercet with Heaney's childhood memory of lifting grain on the family farm "with a grip on two sack corners, / Two packed wads of grain I'd worked to lugs / To give me purchase, ready for the heave—" in the second tercet (17). In so doing, it also revisits two earlier Heaney poems in his chain of poetry, his life's work: "Summer 1969" and "The Barn." The brief phrase running from the end of line 2 through the beginning of line 3—"soldiers / Firing over the mob—" is borrowed from Heaney's "Summer 1969" in the sequence "Singing School" in *North* and reworked for "Human Chain." That earlier poem begins with Heaney's image from the early days of the Troubles in Northern Ireland while he spent time in Madrid, Spain: "While the Constabulary covered the mob / Firing into the Falls" (*N*, 63). And the image of Heaney lifting grain in the second stanza of "Human Chain" revisits lines from "The Barn," which opens with a positive image, "Threshed corn lay piled like grit of ivory / Or solid as cement in two-lugged sacks," but quickly articulates the boy Heaney's fear of the darkened barn and its negative and violent images of "piles of grain in corners, fierce unblinking" and "two-lugged sacks [that] moved in like great blind rats" (*DN*, 5). In this revisiting and revising of images of lifting grain sacks through references to a contemporary humanitarian crisis and poems from his past, Heaney conveys a sense of the difficulty of this physical action, which is heightened by our having just read of the immense physical effort expended by his friends in lifting his body in "Miracle." The second half of "Human Chain" employs the image of lifting grain bags and the welcome rest that floods in afterward to finally trope human life as work and then a final rest. The final tercet conveys that temporary rest and our eternal rest with a series of gradually diminishing lines, a lineation that suggests how a life shrinks down: "That quick unburdening, backbreak's truest payback, / A letting go which will not come again. / Or it will, once. And for all" (17).

Clearly, for Heaney in his early seventies, this letting go, this breaking of the human chain that has held him firmly for so many years, can be held in abeyance by his revisiting and his recasting of particular images from his earlier poetry in the tercets that temporarily retain them. The volume as a whole, then, celebrates the great strength of human presence, its interlocked hands, in Heaney's life and the corresponding chain of his poetry, even as it mourns his pending unlinking from this chain. But as we will see when I return to several more poems from *Human Chain* in the Afterword, it also exults in a projection of how the chain will continue in "Route 110" and "A Kite for Aibhín."

Like these related poems from *Human Chain* would, a series of poems from Part I of *Seeing Things* (including the title poem, which is not written in tercets) similarly focus on miraculous events, often through tercet-driven stanzas. The first part of "A Retrospect," for example, which depicts a countryside drenched in an extraordinary flood, marries the tercet form to the light and marvelous nature of its content. Its first line—"The whole county apparently afloat:"—surprisingly has no verb, almost as if it had been washed away too, and sets the tone of anticipation much as Yeats's recourse to the colon in visionary poems like "The Second Coming" does. Heaney's penchant for bogs crops up again here, but this bog is itself subsumed in the whelming flood:

> I had to
> Wade barefoot over spongy, ice-cold marsh
> (Soft bottom with bog water seeping through
>
> The netted weeds)
> (*ST*, 44)

The parenthesis works to contain the heretofore fantastic properties of the bog in Heaney's earlier poetry and prose and render it nearly continuous with the ubiquitous floodwater. When Heaney observes that "everything ran into water-colour. / The skyline was full up to the lip / As if the earth were going to brim over," and enjambs the second two lines of this stanza to linearly emphasize this abundance, his painterly poetic moves closer to the Chagall to whom he likened the late Kavanagh, not the Millet of early Kavanagh. Frost's shade, however, hovers most strongly over this poem of watery abundance: one of Heaney's essays on Frost, "Above the Brim," takes its title from a line in "Birches," from which he extrapolates to praise "the specifically upward waft of Frost's poems, and the different ways in which he releases the feeling, preeminent in the lines just quoted, of airy vernal daring, an overbrimming of invention and of what he once called 'supply.'"[64]

In other watery, flooded poems from *Seeing Things* such as "The Sounds of Rain," dedicated to the memory of Richard Ellmann, Heaney doubles the preferred tercet into sestets, but its overall structure is tripartite, reinforcing the tendency toward tripling in the volume as a whole.

The "all-night drubbing overflow on boards / On the verandah" (50) from Part I sets the aquatic series of tableaux that follow where Heaney remembers not just Ellmann but also Boris Pasternak and William Alfred's friend (another set of three). The bounty of the rising waters in the concluding section cannot compensate for these deaths, but the poet clearly takes delight in its movement, which he describes as "gathering from under, / Biding and boding like a masterwork / Or a named name that overbrims itself" (51). Thus he again links the content of rising water and buoyancy to a numerological structure derived from the number three.

The second half of *Seeing Things* is composed entirely of the "Squarings" sequence, which has become one of the most discussed swaths of his work. But even his most attentive critics such as Vendler and Peter McDonald have neglected how the tercet form lifts these spiritual poems out of the poet's "heaviness of being" (*ST*, 52). For instance, in her brilliant chapter on Heaney in *The Breaking of Style: Hopkins, Heaney, Graham*, Vendler convincingly argues that "the apparent bareness and simplicity of some recent poems in *Seeing Things* . . . . in some instances sprang from a poem's concentration on a single grammatical element."[65] Her example of such grammatical concentration is the "noun-poem," poem xxiv from "Squarings." To be fair, Vendler does note in passing that in the last stanza of poem xxiv, "The word 'known' rules over the last tercet here as it did over the last tercet of the earlier 'theory' sonnet, Poem xix,"[66] but her focus remains on the singular grammatical elements Heaney employs in particular poems, not how the form is married to and evokes their often marvelous content.

McDonald, whose remit, to be fair, is the influence of Yeatsian form on contemporary Irish poets such as Heaney, Longley, and Mahon, cites the crucial line of poem xxii in the "Squarings" sequence—"How habitable is perfected form?"—only to quickly turn to a meditation on Heaney's praise of Yeatsian ottava rima in his essay "The Place of Writing: W. B. Yeats and Thoor Ballylee" and conclude with an encomium for Heaney's praise of Yeats's formal and oracular authority in his introduction to the Yeats selection from *The Field Day Anthology of Irish Writing*.[67] Heaney's preference for the tercet in the poem under consideration does not fully suggest his growing comfort with "the idea of poetic form as the poet's 'redoubt,'"[68] as McDonald argues; rather, it suggests the poet's sense that the tercet form enables us to apprehend the habitable, permeable places where souls dwell. Heaney has even noted in an interview that the fundamental question of the poem that McDonald cites, which Heaney paraphrases as "What's the use of something formal that cannot be assailed for assurance?", implies that "one of the justifications for established form, whether it's poetical or sculptural, is that we can rebel against it; but we still want it to be there."[69] The finality of couplets would close such spaces down, while the solidity of quatrains would box them off from our view, as it were.

The forty-eight poems from "Squarings" both anchor us in particular memories and scenes from the past and point beyond them into the afterlife. It would be impossible to survey them all, but besides poems "xxii" and "xxiv," which Vendler and McDonald discuss, I will analyze "i," "viii," "ix," "xii," "xxi," "xxvii," and "xxxvi." Heaney's comment that the poems of "Squarings" form a "constellation around an unroofed space" invites us to read these lyrics as analogous to interstellar lights that collectively illumine the unknown that lies beyond this life, the marvelous visitations from the beyond into our lives, and the way particular events in our lives are retrospectively fantastical.[70]

The first of these, from the "Lightenings" sequence, conveys to us a sense of the ethereal region not only through its liminal tercets but also through its pared-down lines within those tercets, which are bereft of a verb until line 3: "Shifting brilliancies. Then winter light / In a doorway, and on the stone doorstep / A beggar, shivering in silhouette" (*ST*, 55). This first stanza suggests through its liminal setting of the "stone doorstep" a picture of the soul in transit, released from the body and waiting for judgment.[71] That judgment is imagined in the second stanza: "Bare wallstead and a cold hearth rained into— / Bright puddle where the soul-free cloud-life roams." The soul is portrayed as experiencing "nothing magnificent, nothing unknown. / A gazing out from far away, alone." Heaney's rejection of a fabulous afterlife full of opulence is thuddingly expressed here and in the last stanza, when the speaker admits, "There is no next-time-round," but by the twelfth line even this bleak knowledge imparts a slight lift in tone: "Unroofed scope. Knowledge-freshening wind" (55). If the scope of our vision is "Unroofed," unblinkered as it were, then our overall knowledge about things spiritual expands, even if the quotidian reality of the afterlife Heaney imagines here contracts.

Such a relatively bleak view of the afterlife is tempered, however, by later poems in the sequence that amply demonstrate the poet's continued and expanded openness to spiritual visitations in this life, such as the well-known lyric "viii," which narrates the story of a ghost ship that enters the earthly atmosphere of the monastery at Clonmacnoise. Even though Heaney leads into this marvelous vision by adverting to the authority of a putative history, "The annals say," this ghostly ship's penetration of reality clearly excites him, and he has repeatedly cited it in interviews and in the introduction to *The Redress of Poetry*. There he observes that "poems and parables about crossing from the domain of the matter-of-fact into the domain of the imagined had been among the work that appeared in *The Haw Lantern* in 1987, and the Clonmacnoisie [sic] poem was only one of several about being transported 'out to an other side' that had surfaced not long afterwards. What lay behind these poems was an interest in 'the frontier of writing.'"[72] He says that the best poetry can playfully create a space like that explored in Frost's "Directive," where he gives us "a draught of the clear water of transformed understanding and fills the reader with a momentary sense of freedom and wholeness."[73] Given what seems to be Heaney's desolate picture of the afterlife in lyric "i," he must have felt all the more responsibility to give us such drinks of "transformed understanding" and "freedom and wholeness" in other poems from "Squarings" such as "viii."[74] Daniel Tobin has convincingly argued that such poems as "viii" reveal Heaney's "eschatological perspective," which "constitutes a vision of 'super-abundant life,' a vision of transcendence that manifests itself, paradoxically, within our immanent lives.... As such, all of life is potentially vivid with advent, with the things of the world placed against the relief of an infinite field of vision."[75] This insightful characterization of the "Squarings" lyrics suggests in turn Heaney's hope that they will open our own eyes to the "vivid" visitations of the marvelous we experience through our own life-journeys.

The ninth poem in the sequence must articulate one of Heaney's earliest memories about an earthly boat whose memory grows more strange and fantastic over the years: "A boat that did not rock or wobble once / Sat in long grass one Sunday afternoon / In nineteen forty-one or -two" (*ST*, 63). The poem concludes by his recollection of "me cradled in an elbow like a secret // Open now as the eye of heaven was then / Above three sisters talking, talking steady / In a boat the ground still falls and falls from under" (63). This boat is seemingly being transformed, if not into a ghost ship, then into a lightsome craft where he perches and is gazed upon by "the eye of heaven."

After gazing back in tranquillity at that boat of levity seen by heaven, Heaney seems more receptive to exploring the Christian understanding of the afterlife; thus the twelfth lyric overall and the last in the "Lightenings" sequence offers hope, even Christian surety, as if to counterpoint the bleakness of the first lyric. He gives us one definition of "lightening" in the second tercet: "A phenomenal instant when the spirit flares / With pure exhilaration before death— / The good thief in us harking to the promise!" (66). Now he offers the dash tendered in line 5 as a punctuational representation of this "phenomenal instant," whereas in line 5 of "i" he employs it to convey the flatness and neutrality, finally the loneliness, of the nothingness beyond for the atheist. Moreover, the full stop of line 6 in "i" that indicates the finality of that version of the afterlife now is set in equipoise against the exclamation mark of line 6 in "xii." As this twelfth lyric proceeds, he imagines the last moments of the good thief, "Scanning empty space, so body-racked he seems / Untranslatable into the bliss // Ached for at the moon-rim of his forehead." But this lunar image itself begins "translating" the man with "nail-craters on the dark side of his brain" into Christian paradise, and indeed the poem resonantly concludes with Christ's promise to him because of his belief: "*This day thou shalt be with Me in Paradise*" (66). The operation of such resonant language through the form of this procession of tercets suggests that this and other lyrics from "Squarings" affirm life and then go beyond it, as Heaney argues that poetry at its best can do: "When language does more than enough, as it does in all achieved poetry, it opts for the condition of overlife, and rebels at limit," even, we might add, at the limits of the poet's own lack of belief in a Christian afterlife.[76]

Lyrics "xxi" and "xxvii" both explore Heaney's belief in the ongoing life of the soul across time and space. In "xxi," the speaker recalls firing a gun "at a square of handkerchief / Pinned on a tree about sixty yards away" (75). Although "it exhilarated me—" and led him to somatically apprehend "a whole new quickened sense of what *rifle* meant," he immediately lapses into language from the "Doxology," the traditional "praise-song" of

Christianity, to explain the revulsion he experienced after this shooting when the initial exhilaration wore off:

And then again as it was in the beginning
I saw the soul like a white cloth snatched away

Across dark galaxies and felt that shot
For the sin it was against eternal life—
Another phrase dilating in new light.

This shooting and his recollection of it seem to have ushered two phrases from his Catholic past back into his contemporary lexicon—"as it was in the beginning" and "eternal life," and he views them "in new light," admitting their viability for him as he ponders the advent of the ineffable into our quotidian lives.

The essential flux of our lives and the possibility of transformation of earthly matter into the divine drives "xxvii," one of many poems in *Seeing Things* that elegizes the poet's father Patrick Heaney. "Flow" and variations on this word characterize the metamorphizing possibilities hovering over this lyric. It opens with the speaker musing, "Everything flows. Even a solid man, / A pillar to himself and to his trade, / All yellow boots and stick and soft felt hat" (81). By the very next line, transformation occurs: "Can sprout wings at the ankle and grow fleet / As the god of fair-days, stone posts, roads and crossroads." Recalling his father's advice to "his sister setting out / For London," the speaker remembers his urging, "'Look for a man with an ash plant on the boat'" (81). The poet often associates an ashplant with Patrick Heaney himself: Joyce's ghost in section 12 of "Station Island" carries one and acts somewhat fatherly, if gruff, toward the poet, and it features also in Part 2 of "Two Stick Drawings" (*SL*, 51–52) and "The Strand," where he mentions "the dotted line my father's ashplant made" (62). His father must have thought that such a man would be a figure of trust, as he himself was. In the concluding tercet of "xxvii," the imagined boat journey of Heaney's aunt across the Irish Sea to England itself becomes transformed into an ecstatic metaphor of the passage of the soul through time and space: "Flow on, flow on, / The journey of the soul with its soul guide / And the mysteries of dealing-men with sticks!" (*ST*, 81).

"My Ship of Genius Now Shakes Out Her Sail" 391

Although not the last poem in the overall sequence of "Squarings," poem "xxxvi," the last poem in the internal sequence "Crossings," returns us to the realm of Dante's shades in the *Inferno*. In so doing, it prepares us for the crossing in the volume's last poem, Heaney's translation from Dante's canto 3 of that first part of the *Commedia*. This Dantesque meditation on Heaney's participation in a civil rights march, likely the one he went on with Michael Longley to Newry (a week after the atrocity of Bloody Sunday) on February 6, 1972, opens with a phrase from the Twenty-Third Psalm: "And yes, my friend, we too walked through a valley" (90).[77] The allusion conveys the deathly danger that surrounded the civil rights marchers then and at other marches—"the valley of the shadow of death," as the Psalmist has it. Their stuttering, surreptitious procession after "the march dispersed" is signified by the three full end-stops in line 2: "Once. In darkness. With all the streetlamps off." This "scene from Dante" allows the poet to cast the marchers as "herded shades who had to cross // And did cross, in a panic, to the car / Parked as we'd left it, that gave when we got in / Like Charon's boat under the faring poets." The relief at their safe passage is palpable and the car's "sinking" assures them that they are still alive, much as Charon's boat that sinks under the weight of the living poets did (90).

That long-ago crossing, already gathered into the mythology extended by the Dante allusions here, leads ineluctably to the concluding poem in *Seeing Things*, "The Crossing," based upon Dante and Virgil's trip on Charon's ferry in canto 3 of the *Inferno*.[78] Rui Carvalho Homem argues that this poem, like earlier ones bidding farewell to Heaney's father in *Seeing Things*, is "valedictory . . . a bid for the mourned soul of an immediate forebear to enjoy a good crossing onto brighter shores than those that one reaches with Charon."[79] Certainly, such a "bid" must be the driving force behind Heaney's inclusion of his translation here, contrasting as it does with Philip Larkin's "forewarned journey back / Into the heartland of the ordinary" in "The Journey Back" (*ST*, 9). But Heaney also employs his translation to cast himself as a late addition to Dante's duo of Virgil and himself, making a poetic trinity, and allowing him to view the damned while not becoming part of them. The relief expressed by the poets in "xxvi" returning safely to their car after the civil rights march now becomes something like eternal relief when the poet (and by extension,

Patrick Heaney) realizes that he is not one of the damned, who are "all naked and exhausted," and "bitterly weeping" (105, 106). Heaney chooses to conclude this passage with Virgil's comment that "no good spirits ever pass this way / And therefore, if Charon objects to you, / You should understand well what his words imply," rather than with the earthquake that occurs and shakes the riverbanks, making Dante swoon, in the full version of the original canto. Heaney's version of this passage in "The Crossing" thus pictures him standing alertly in the simultaneous present despair and future hope of Good Friday evening, the date on which this canto occurs.

Such poetic perspicacity has stood him in good stead in the volumes that flowed after *Seeing Things*, which show the penetration of the ineffable into the everyday in poems as different as the tercet-driven birth poem "Out of the Bag" (*Electric Light*) and "The Tollund Man in Springtime" (*District and Circle*). The concerns of "The Crossing" lead us into some of the most haunting—literally and figuratively—poems of *Human Chain*, and the Afterword explores "Route 110," "The Door Was Open but the House Was Dark," and "A Kite for Aibhín" as part of the stream of eschatological advent poems and elegies that glides past us in that magnificent volume, taking us ever deeper into Heaney's spirit region, yet showing us how his imagination roams out by first recognizing its anchor in his home region of Northern Ireland.

Afterword

VISITING THE DEAD AND WELCOMING NEWBORNS
Human Chain and Heaney's Three Regions

> *At the core of it [the Aeneid] is respect for the human effort to build, to sustain a generous polity—against heavy odds. Mordantly and sadly it suggests what the effort may cost, how the effort may fail. But as a poem it is carried onward victoriously by its own music.*
> —Robert Fitzgerald, Postscript to *The Aeneid*

If well over half the poems in *Seeing Things* were tercets— fifty-four of the eighty-one poems in that volume were fully in tercets and several more used the tercet form at least once—Heaney uses the form almost exclusively in the last major collection published before his death, *Human Chain*. Twenty-four of the twenty-nine poems in this volume employ only tercets, and several more use them at least once. There are still several twelve-liners, but more poems, such as "Album," "Chanson d'Aventure," "Eelworks," "Slack," "Route 110," "The Riverbank Field," "Loughanure," "Hermit Songs," "Lick the Pencil," and "In the Attic," employ the tercet across a series of ruminative sections. While Paul Fussell could still argue in 1979 that "we may inquire how well any three-line stanza, regardless of the talent of its practitioner, can ever succeed in English," Heaney's repeated recourse to the form over the course of the last thirty years and his adroit handling of it now suggest otherwise.[1] Of all the reviewers of *Human Chain*, Sean O'Brien has been the most insightful about Heaney's tercet. He notes that "Heaney makes frequent use of the tercet stanza, which posterity may indicate he has done much to render a contemporary *forma franca*. In his hands it has remarkable flexibility—see the dozen 12-line sections of 'Route 110.' The stanza moves as though between the epigrammatic hinge of a couplet and the more expansive quatrain, generating drama and extension (as though into the future of the imaginative act) through enjambed line- and stanza-endings. The triple line, with its echo of *terza rima*, reels in and out, re-gathering to achieve the tension of resolution—a movement clearly suited to the alert, considering melodies that Heaney so often plays."[2] Heaney's musical stanzas in the volume thus achieve their power and resolution through his most extensive use of the tercet form yet in his poetry—a form that refuses the finality of the couplet and the promise of extension inherent in the quatrain.

The Heaneyesque tercet brings together in this volume his life's exploration of the triple strains of regionalism in his work: the rural rhythms and later, the war-torn region of Northern Ireland; its imagined future state; and the spirit region that hovers tantalizingly close to the poet. In this way, his adaption of the terza rima into this form accords with his unambiguous declaration to Seamus Deane in 1977: "You have to make your own work your home."[3]

Heaney once mused, "I just happen to belong to the last generation that learned Latin, that read Virgil, that knew about the descent into the underworld," and book 6 of Virgil's *Aeneid* rivals Dante's *Commedia* in its influence on him and certainly predates his close reading of the great Italian master (*SS*, 295). He pointed out his great love for book 6 of the *Aeneid*: "I like that book of the *Aeneid* so much I'm inclined to translate it as a separate unit" (440). The great translator of *The Aeneid* in our time, Robert Fitzgerald, made comments that illuminate why Heaney might have been so drawn to book 6 of the epic: "In this half of *The Aeneid*, and it really begins with Anchises' review of Roman souls in Book VI—the poet was on home ground, his action at last ranging along the river and in the countrysides that he cared for, north, east, and south, among places named and folklore handed down by the fabulists and annalists of Rome. But during his century this land of Italy . . . had been torn by civil wars between big armies."[4] Having survived the Troubles and having largely successfully upheld his artistic integrity despite the demands upon his poetic regionalism from multiple quarters, Heaney similarly revels in being back on "home ground" in *District and Circle* and *Human Chain*. He has internalized this book from Virgil's epic, even observing, "There's one Virgilian journey that has . . . been a constant presence and that is Aeneas's venture into the underworld. The motifs of Book VI have been in my head for years—the golden bough, Charon's barge, the quest to meet the shade of the father" (*SS*, 389). He has been able to remake it in a stunningly lovely meditation upon his life and, more indirectly, upon the life of the province of Northern Ireland and its many deaths during the Troubles. But where the *Aeneid*'s book ends with the poet traveling back out of the underworld to his waiting men, Heaney's "Route 110" ends on the riverbank field of his personal Ulster Elysium, where he mourns past deaths in his home region and welcomes new life into this world.

"Route 110" should be read as a *summa* of Heaney's career, retrospectively looking back to his purchase of the *Aeneid*, book 6, in a dusty Belfast bookshop and using the trip by bus down "Route 110, Cookstown via Toome and Magherafelt" (*HC*, 51) to view his life's journey and, more indirectly, the journey of the province of Northern Ireland, toward the present, which concludes with the birth of his grandchild, "Anna Rose," to whom the sequence is dedicated (49). This poem is clearly the centerpiece of the volume: its historical and personal sweep, its vulnerability, and its adroit handling of the tercet stanza make it one of his most memorable. Such poems have led Colm Tóibín to state unequivocally in his review that *Human Chain* is "his best single volume for many years, and one that contains some of the best poems he has written."[5]

While readers new to Heaney can appreciate much of "Route 110," it gains in resonance and heft when we realize how it converses with the shades of his earlier works, just as the poet-speaker does throughout this long poem. If boats—particularly the golden, ethereal boat from the Broighter Hoard and the ghost ship that catches its anchor on the altar rail at Clonmacnoise from lyric "viii"—were the dominant symbol of *Seeing Things*, Charon's quotidian, rough ferryboat, troped as a local bus, is the guiding symbol of *Human Chain*. The haunting third section of "Found Prose" from *District and Circle* and its pending journey into the region of death anticipates Heaney's use of the bus on Route 110 here, as does John Montague's beginning his sequence *The Rough Field* with a bus journey,[6] but this bus ride is rendered buoyant and more memorable by virtue of the poem's lightsome handling of the now-familiar Heaney tercet—mostly unrhymed, lithe and limber like a green stick used to prod his mind into memories. In "The Riverbank Field," the poem immediately preceding "Route 110," the poet vows to "confound the Lethe in Moyola // By coming through Back Park down from Grove Hill / Across Long Rigs on to the riverbank—" and thus gains access to these memories that the long poem explores by going the back way around forgetfulness (*HC*, 47). Michael Parker argues that Heaney's use of "confound" in line 3 "invokes two meanings of the verb. In a sense, he is damning the river of oblivion, constructing an intricate verbal device as a stay against the erasure of personal memory that must inevitably come." But he is also "signaling how he intends to mix up features from the classical text . . . with ones from his birthplace, Castledawson, so as to render them indistinguishable."[7] This shorter poem thus draws upon book 6 of the *Aeneid*, lines 704–15 and 748–51 (48) but also upon Heaney's deep affinity with his home district. Dwelling on the riverbank of his past, Heaney moves into his personal Aenean Underground, where he surveys his past and that of the province of Northern Ireland, concluding by ending up back on that riverbank among the shades of the dead and the newly born, the spirit region, in "Route 110."

The opening tercets of "Route 110" suggest that Heaney's "plucking" of the *Aeneid*, book 6, from the bookshop shelves functions as his golden bough needed to transport him to rapturous visits to the shades of his past in his home region of Northern Ireland. After the speaker is given his "used copy of *Aeneid VI*," he inhales "as she slid my purchase / Into a deckle-edged brown paper bag," and he "hurried on, shortcutting to the buses," going through Smithfield Market in Belfast, past a series of objects for sale, including "racks of suits and overcoats that swayed / When one was tugged from its overcrowded frame / Like their owners' shades close-packed on Charon's barge" (*HC*, 49, 50). Such a scene recalls Heaney's translation of a portion of Dante's canto 3 from the *Inferno*, "The Crossing," in *Seeing Things*. But when he writes in his third section of "passengers [who] / Flocked to the kerb like agitated rooks / Around a rookery, all go // But undecided" (50), he is clearly drawing upon Virgil's description of the souls waiting to cross on Charon's barge in book 6 of *The Aeneid*: "Here a whole crowd came streaming to the banks. . . . Or as migrating birds from the open sea / That darken heaven when the cold season comes / And drives them overseas to sunlit lands."[8] After more avian imagery—"the inspector / Who ruled the roost in bus station and bus / Separated and directed everybody"—the stanzas of memories unroll as do the miles on Route 110 (50).

Lyric "vi" opens with the quiet proclamation "It was the age of ghosts," and ghosts populate this and the succeeding six sections (52). Moving ahead to lyric "ix," we are led, much like Aeneas in Elysium, through a series of meetings with named and unnamed victims of the Troubles. The first of these is John F. Lavery, who was a Catholic civilian killed December 21, 1971, while removing an IRA bomb from the pub he owned on the Lisburn Road in Belfast. He was horribly maimed as the bomb went off: as one account says judiciously, "the nature of the injuries suggesting he had been carrying the bomb when it exploded."[9] Heaney opens this stanza with a moving tribute to Lavery that mourns his material absence because of the manner of his death:

> And what in the end was there left to bury
> Of Mr. Lavery, blown up in his own pub
> As he bore the primed device and bears it still
>
> Mid-morning towards the sun-admitting door
> Of Ashley House?
> (55)

By starting the poem with the paratactic "And," Heaney imparts a storytelling, musing quality to it and suggests how such events are links in a chain preceded by similar ones in the previous stanzas. Lyrics "vi" and "vii" had recalled Michael Mulholland's wake, "the first / I attended as a full participant," and his premature death renders his parents and family "without the corpse of their own dear ill-advised / Sonbrother swimmer, lost in the Bristol Channel" (53). This double loss—first, Mulholland's death, and second, the lack of a recovered body—makes the wake strange and frustrating. Similarly, John Lavery's death and the terrible destruction of his body likely made his family unable to properly mourn him in his wake. The terrible intrusion by the IRA into a pub, where community is celebrated as people relax over drinks, is stylistically rendered all the more shocking by the terse, procession of monosyllabic words in the first three lines; moreover, the only polysyllabic words in those lines, "bury" and "Mr. Lavery," chime together and highlight his sacrifice that spared the lives of other workers in the pub.

The next victim, not a figure of sacrifice like Lavery, is Heaney's fisherman friend Louis O'Neill, whom he elegized in "Casualty," collected in *Field Work*. Heaney's poem does not blame O'Neill for his own death when he violated an IRA curfew because the man followed his natural inclinations toward drink and convivial company in pubs. Similarly, he simply asks here, carrying on from the opening question, "And what in the end was there left to bury . . . ?," "Or of Louis O'Neill / In the wrong place the Wednesday they buried // Thirteen who'd been shot in Derry?" (55). In both cases and in the many instances of the bodies that follow these two named men, there was simply nothing left of the person after the explosion; the unique individual was obliterated, leaving the families with no bodies to bury. Then immediately, these lesser-known murders in the Troubles are linked into the narrative after another conjunction: "Or of bodies / Unglorified, accounted for and bagged / Behind the grief cordons" (55). These bodies, and those of Lavery and O'Neill, are the ones whose lives we should really remember, the poet seems to imply, but instead, the ones who committed murder during the Troubles, including some British troops and many paramilitary members, get the state funeral and the annual commemorations, respectively: "not to be laid // In war graves with full honours, nor in a separate plot / Fired over on anniversaries / By units drilled and spruce and unreconciled" (55). These burials and commemorations work to keep the memory of the deceased green and glorified, while the "bodies / Unglorified" are relegated to bags and cut off from their relatives temporarily and in some cases, like that of Lavery and O'Neill and many others, are not recognized by any official organizations, only by friends and families.

Such despair is left behind in lyric "x," however, which turns back to Virgil's "happy shades," who

> ... in pure blanched raiment
> Contend on their green meadows, while Orpheus
> Weaves among them, sweeping strings, aswerve
>
> To the pulse of his own playing and to avoid
> The wrestlers, dancers, runners on the grass.
> Not unlike a sports day in Bellaghy.
>   (55–56)

These lines recall Aeneas's entrance to Elysium in the underworld after he leaves the golden bough as a ritual offering for Proserpina. Book 6 tells us that at this point Aeneas and the Sibyl "came / To places of delight, to green park land, / Where souls take ease amid the Blessed Groves."[10] The souls they see "train on grassy rings, others compete / In field games, others grapple on the sand. / Feet moving to a rhythmic beat, the dangers / Group in a choral pattern as they sing," while Orpheus accompanies them.[11] By turning to Virgil and then to "a sports day in Bellaghy," Heaney imparts an Elysian quality to his childhood memories of such games, with "teams of grown men stripped for action / Going hell for leather until the final whistle, / Leaving stud-scrapes on the pitch and on each other" (56). These Ulster warriors from his boyhood contend with each other in pitched battles that leave the crowds of spectators in awe.

Lyric "xi" returns us, however, from Elysium and its blessed groves to memories of "those evenings when we'd just wait and watch / And fish," as the "riverbank field" grows stranger, "as if we had commingled // Among shades and shadows stirring on the brink / And stood there waiting, watching, / Needy and ever needier for translation" (56–57). In retrospect, the poet recalls feeling commingled with the dead, after having surveyed the living athletes of his district, and, with his companions, wanting "translation" into the spirit region so they could converse with the dead.

But quickly, the twelfth lyric of twelve-lined tercets begins by again imparting continuity to this procession of deaths in the preceding stanzas: "And now the age of births," almost as if the bus driver on Route 110 had announced, "We are all stopping here." The poet recalls past births, when someone would bring in "fresh-plucked flowers // To quell whatever smells of drink and smoke / Would linger on where mother and child were due / Later that morning from the nursing home" (57). The quotidian beauty and scent of these flowers are here implicitly contrasted with the lovely golden bough Aeneas must pick from the tree early in book 6 to gain access to the underworld; they act as homemade disinfectants for the arriving mother and child. These earlier births are now linked to the new birth of the grandchild Anna Rose, to whom the poem is dedicated:

> So now, as a thank-offering for one
> Whose long wait on the shaded bank has ended,
> I arrive with my bunch of stalks and silvered heads
>
> Like tapers that won't dim
> As her earthlight breaks and we gather round
> Talking baby talk.

These stalks and their "silvered heads" recall Mrs. McNicholls's "votive jampot" in lyric "v," which contains "stalks / From . . . each head of oats / A silvered smattering, each individual grain / Wrapped in a second husk of glittering foil / They'd saved from chocolate bars" (52). Recalling at the conclusion of that earlier stanza the time when "old Mrs. Nick, as she was to us," gave him one of these silvered stalks, he remembers that "it as good as lit me home" (52). Heaney clearly wants to welcome his granddaughter into the "earthlight" of home with his "silvered heads" of flowers, his votive offering to her at the end of "Route 110." Although he and his wife also have silvered heads at this point in their lives, they rejoice in the shining new birth of this new link in their human chain. "Route 110" thus brings together the three regions Heaney has consistently explored in his life's work: the rural past and current region of Northern Ireland with its violence, an imagined future Northern Ireland where peace might reign, and the spirit region where new souls arrive and older ones depart.

These three regions are also evoked in his thirteen-line poem "'The Door Was Open and The House Was Dark,'" an elegy in memory of Heaney's friend and folksinger David Hammond, which not only remembers Hammond but also does so by revisiting one of Heaney's better-known poems, the sonnet "The Forge," along with lyric "xxvi" from "Squarings," thereby creating another human and poetic chain linking one of Heaney's lasting rural exemplars for poetry and the civil rights movement in Northern Ireland and Hammond's leavening work in it, respectively. Heaney's relationship with Hammond marks much of his work: he made the singer the co-dedicatee, along with Michael Longley, of *Wintering Out*; Hammond is the singer in Heaney's poem "The Singer's House" and features also in "September Song"; he was a director of the Field Day Theatre Company along with Heaney; Heaney's story about an aborted recording session one evening during the early part of the Troubles features at the beginning of the introductory essay to *The Government of the Tongue*; and Heaney contributed the script "Something to Write Home About," to a documentary for Hammond's Flying Fox film company (*SS*, 488). In "The Singer's House," Heaney's speaker likens Hammond's song to "a rowboat far out in evening," and concludes by urging, "Raise it again, man. We still believe what we hear" (*FW*, 27). He has recalled describing "David as a natural force masquerading as a human being" (*SS*, 53), and the trajectory of "'The Door Was Open'" moves from the doorway of Hammond's home, into the street, and imaginatively onto "a midnight hangar // On an overgrown airfield in late summer" (*HC*, 81). The poem thus suggests that Hammond's effervescent spirit, what Heaney calls elsewhere his association with "outbreak, a kicking over of traces, an impatience with the ordinary" (*SS*, 117), has simply burst his domestic bonds and bounds and penetrated the atmosphere of the outer world with his death.

Yet for all Heaney's former celebration of Hammond's joie de vivre, the poem itself is much quieter than the musician himself was. Kate Kellaway suggests in her review of the volume that the poem "is especially arresting because it refuses the dead man even the briefest afterlife in *poetry*. Instead, Heaney explores the silence after a death. It is a wonderful idea that silence should develop a life of its own, journeying through the second stanza and retiring into the street."[12] And so it is. Heaney's privileging of silence here is particularly remarkable given his vexed vacillations, rehearsed in "Punishment," "Whatever You Say Say Nothing," *An Open Letter*, and many other works, between speaking out against atrocities during the Troubles and keeping silent. Yet to elegize Hammond, who died at the advanced age of eighty, unlike many victims of the Troubles, who died far before their time, silence seems appropriate, even natural.

Intriguingly, the poem is musically closer to full terza rima than most other tercet poems Heaney has written. For instance, the concluding *b* rhyme at the end of line 2, "knew," sets up the first rhyme of the next stanza, as in traditional terza rima, the "grew" at the end of line 4 (*HC*, 81). Although "street" at the end of line 5 does not find an exact chime at the end of the first line in the third stanza, it is in a quarter rhyme with "out" there (the end of line 7). In that third stanza, the second line's concluding "stranger" perfectly sets the full rhyme of "danger" at the beginning of the fourth and last stanza (81). And the dangling thirteenth line resembles the common single closing line at the end of Dantean terza rima. Such full rhymes sonically recall Hammond's melodies, while the dangling last line, in its relative loneliness from the rest of the poem, suggests how Hammond's postdeath solitude finally separates him from Heaney.

Collectively, the thirteen lines of "'The Door Was Open,'" its emphasis on a singer, and especially the association of "door" and "dark" recall a touchstone poem for Heaney from his 1969 volume, *Door into the Dark*—the modified Petrarchan sonnet "The Forge," with its blacksmith as a musician working on the anvil, "an altar / Where he expends himself in shape and music" (*DD*, 7). But while that poem oscillates between the outside world and the inside world where the blacksmith creates "real iron" (7), the later poem hovers at the open door to Hammond's house and then retreats outside where silence "grew / Backwards and down and out into the street" (*HC*, 81). And where "The Forge" focuses on the music created within the smithy, "'The Door Was Open,'" by virtue of its silence, invites us to fill the poem with appropriate music of our own, as it were, for Hammond. If the blacksmith of the earlier poem materially and energetically exemplified regional rural artistry for Heaney as an analogue to his poetry, then the absent Hammond of this new poem suggests how his ineffable, silent absence creates a void in the North's artistic life and Heaney's own: "Only withdrawal, a not unwelcoming / Emptiness, as in a midnight hangar // On an overgrown airfield in late summer" (81).

Moreover, Heaney's elegy for Hammond revisits another of his poems, "xxvi," in *Seeing Things*. That poem recalls the poet's dangerous walk back to his car with Michael Longley after the civil rights march in Newry in early 1972: "Once. In darkness. With all the streetlamps off. / As danger gathered and the march dispersed" (*ST*, 90). Lines 1, 7, and 10 from the Hammond elegy revisit and finally revise particular words from that poem: "the house was dark"; "The streetlamps were out"; "Yet well aware that here there was no danger" (*HC*, 81). The effect memorializes Hammond's terrific work on behalf of ecumenism in the North and allows him a sort of rest after a busy and well-committed life. Besides lauding his joyful insouciance, Heaney has associated that spirit with this work: "In his professional life he's shown this powerful commitment to making life in Northern Ireland more salubrious and fulfilling on all sides . . . a wonderful inner freedom, a quality of liberation as if he had triumphed over the narrow-mindedness we'd all grown up with" (*SS*, 117). The open door of the title and the poem thus signify both Hammond's ecumenical attitude and his departure to a spiritual region where presumably such divisions as he experienced in his lifetime will disappear.

The somewhat enervated atmosphere at the end of "'The Door Was Open'" is offset, however, by the "air from another life and time and place, / Pale blue heavenly air" that opens *Human Chain*'s concluding poem, "A Kite for Aibhín," a translation that draws on all three of Heaney's strands of regionalism. In his essay on the poet Giovanni Pascoli, he has approvingly remarked that "the landscape of Pascoli's poem reminded me very much of the home ground of my childhood—open countryside with breezes blowing, flowers blooming, berries on briars, robins in hedges and a general feeling of fresh and airy life."[13] The poem is modeled upon yet departs from Pascoli's "*L'Aquilone*" ("The Kite") and in that adherence to, yet departure from a resonant ur-text Heaney's poem both celebrates the life of Aibhín, one of his granddaughters, and bids farewell to this life and its constraints as he imagines himself soaring into the spirit region.[14] The joy of this celebration and pending departure is signaled by exclamatory phrases such as "And yes, it is a kite!" in line 4 and the procession of active verbs in lines 10 through 12: "And now it hovers, tugs, veers, dives askew, / Lifts itself, goes with the wind until / It rises to loud cheers from us below" (85). Returned to his childhood home, the poet "take[s] his stand again, halt[s] opposite / Anahorish Hill to scan the blue," and feels buoyed by how "it rises to loud cheers from us below." As it "rises, and my hand is like a spindle / Unspooling," it is as if Heaney's life unspools before us and the kite, "climbing and carrying, carrying farther, higher / The longing in the breast and planted feet / And gazing face and heart of the kite flier," takes his aspirations aloft. Finally, "string breaks and—separate, elate— // The kite takes off, itself alone, a windfall" (85). Both the joy that Aibhín will figuratively soar in her life and his hope that his departure will be an unexpected "windfall" for him are signified in these pared-down lines.

As in other tercet-driven poems by Heaney, the tercets here reflect their airy contents as they hover between the closed couplets and overly expansive quatrain. The form keeps the stanzas open to the buffetings of the wind in the poem, as it were, while the purposely ragged lineation, of interspersed long and short lines, echoes the long swoops and dives of the kite and its suddenly short plunges and escalations, proving Colm Tóibín's argument about Heaney's lineation throughout the volume: "He uses a poetic line which sometimes seems complete and whole in its rhythm, and at others is stopped short, held, left hanging. It is as though to allow the rhythm its full completion would be untrue to the shape of the experience that gave rise to the poem, untrue to the terms of the struggle between the pure possibility that language itself can offer and a knowledge of the sad fixtures which the grim business of loss can provide."[15]

The irrepressible joy of the concluding lines suggests that Heaney now welcomes being "separate, elate," a positive reclamation and remaking of political and cultural intransigence in Northern Ireland that signifies the second strand of his regionalism—the imagined future of Northern Ireland. "Itself alone" revises the Sinn Fein motto of "Ourselves alone" and suggests how artistic solitude trumps groupthink and calcified identities, a theme Heaney had previously explored most movingly in "Casualty," where he celebrates the independent life of the loner fisherman Louis O'Neill. Yet the tercet form and the occasional reversions to full terza rima in "A Kite for Aibhín," as well as the entirety of *Human Chain*, show how we are linked together in a human chain of help and hope all our lives and beyond. Dwelling upon his native region consistently enabled Seamus Heaney to record its dying traditional culture and its despairs and despondencies even as his reconfigurations and reclamations of its plural linguistic and cultural heritage led him to dream a new province where new life might emerge as its heroes depart into the spirit region.

Notes

Introduction

The first epigraph, from Heaney's "Regional Forecast," is taken from p. 13; the second, from Heaney's "Place and Displacement," is taken from p. 4.

1. Heaney, "Gallery at the Abbey," n.p. The poem Keats was referring to specifically was his "Endymion" (*Letters*, 170).
2. Deane, "Artist and the Troubles," 47.
3. Heaney, *Place and Displacement*, 4.
4. Quoted in O'Driscoll, "Foreign Relations," 84.
5. Ibid.
6. Heaney, "Place, Pastness, Poems," 46.
7. Ibid., 46–47, 47.
8. Heaney, "Unhappy and at Home," 71.
9. Heaney, *Room to Rhyme*, 25.
10. S. Stewart, *Poetry*, 149.
11. E. Longley, "Edward Thomas," 32.
12. Frost, *Selected Letters*, 228; Heaney, "Threshold and Floor," 265. He does admit, however, that Frost influenced "a couple of monologues in women's voices in *Door into the Dark*" (266).
13. Heaney, "Conversation," 45.
14. Buttel, *Seamus Heaney*, 29.
15. Ross, "'Upward Waft,'" 97.
16. Heaney, *One on a Side*, 5.
17. Ibid., 10–11.
18. Heaney, "Threshold and Floor," 266.
19. Heaney, "Feeling into Words," 44.
20. Ibid.
21. Ibid.
22. Ibid., 45.
23. Heaney, "Fire i' the Flint," 85.
24. Ibid., 86, 87.

25. Heaney, "Art of Poetry," 123.
26. For a fuller discussion of Hopkins's influence on Heaney, see Russell, "Keats and Hopkins Dialectic."
27. Heaney, "Place, Pastness, Poems," 45.
28. Heaney, "Art of Poetry," 127.
29. Heaney, "Unhappy and at Home," 71.
30. Russell, *Poetry and Peace*, 253.
31. Murray, "Beall Poetry Festival."
32. See Kavanagh, "Parish and Universe," and for discussions of Kavanagh's positive reclamation of "parochialism"—and Heaney's approval of this term—see Russell, *Poetry and Peace*, 16–17, 48–49. The quote on Hughes is from Heaney, "Art of Poetry," 124.
33. Heaney, "Healing Fountain," 11.
34. Heaney, "Art of Poetry," 92.
35. Heaney, "Meeting Seamus Heaney," 73–74.
36. Heaney, "Englands of the Mind," 153, 154.
37. Heaney, "Conversation," 45.
38. Heaney, "Funeral Eulogy," n.p.
39. Ibid.
40. Hart, "Seamus Heaney," 81, 82.
41. Heaney, "Art of Poetry," 104.
42. Quoted in Keith, *Regions of the Imagination*, 4.
43. The important part of Massingham's quotation is as follows: "A specific quality manifests itself in the complete presentation of a region, in precisely the same way as it does in a work of art. A region thus presented *is* a work of art" (quoted in ibid., 5).
44. Paulin, *Minotaur*, 4.
45. Ibid., 1, 3.
46. See Burris, *Poetry of Resistance*, for a powerful reading of this poem through the lens of the pastoral: "The Irish maid backed against the tree, [*sic*] indicates that her spoiled innocence is a *fait accompli*, that pastoral dreams, hopeful though they may be, arise from a plundered world" (77). For the fullest and most historically grounded reading of this poem, see Moloney's chapter "Heaney's Love to Ireland" in her *Seamus Heaney*, 72–88.
47. See Hall's analysis of the three versions of this poem, *Seamus Heaney's Rhythmic Contract*, 98–103. He observes that the earliest form of the poem, composed in late 1972/early 1973, focused "not on British aggression but on an attempt to understand the [female] other" (99). As the violence on the ground in Northern Ireland accelerated and as Heaney settled into life in the Republic and gained some much-needed geographic distance from the North, he may have felt led to charge the poem with the explicitly colonizer/colonized context that drives the final version.
48. For instance, in his preface to *The Penguin Book of Irish Poetry* he points out, again employing sexual intercourse resulting in pregnancy as the driving

Notes to Pages 15–25   407

metaphor for Irish and English relations, that Paul Muldoon translates Nuala Ní Dhomhnaill's poem "'Ceist na Teangan' not as 'The Language Question' but as 'The Language Issue,' since 'issue' implies offspring from an ongoing intercourse between Irish and English rather than a barren stand-off" (xliv).

49. Heaney, "Poets on Poetry," 629.
50. See Russell, *Poetry and Peace*, 201–13, for this reading of *Wintering Out*.
51. Matthews, "Poet as Anthologist," 542.
52. Russell, *Poetry and Peace*, 167–290.
53. Hall, *Seamus Heaney's Rhythmic Contract*, 1.
54. Heaney, "Frontiers of Writing," 190. In this regard, see also Eugene O'Brien, *Seamus Heaney and the Place of Writing*, who cites an interview Richard Kearney conducted with Heaney where Heaney argues that the artist "can refuse history as a category, can say 'No. I prefer to dream possibilities'" ("Between North and South," 107). O'Brien argues for "the ethical effects of such dreaming of the possibilities of place" (*Seamus Heaney and the Place of Writing*, 162).
55. Barthes, *Mythologies*, 112.
56. Draper, *Introduction*, 2.
57. Falci, "Place, Space, and Landscape," 200, 201.
58. Ibid., 203, 204.
59. Ibid., 204.
60. For an illuminating brief discussion of the rise of writers on the margins of English literature such as William Blake, John Clare, and William Barnes, see Young, "At the Margins," 31–45.
61. Thurston, "Region and Nation," 72.
62. Keith, *Regions of the Imagination*, 9.
63. Ibid.
64. Dainotto, *Place in Literature*, 9.
65. B. O'Donoghue, "Heaney's Classics," 109. For a helpful survey of the development of pastoral, see the introduction to Potts's *Contemporary Irish Poetry*, 1–18, but especially 1–13.
66. Hart, *Seamus Heaney*, 31.
67. Heaney, "In the Country of Convention," 174.
68. Ibid., 175.
69. Ibid., 180; my emphasis.
70. Ibid.
71. Matthews, "Poet as Anthologist," 542.
72. Heaney, "Bags of Enlightenment," n.p.
73. Ibid.
74. McKittrick et al., *Lost Lives*, 375.
75. Heaney, "Vulgar Muse," 9. For a sense of Paulin's commitment to the vernacular, see his essay published as part of the Field Day Theatre Company's series of pamphlets issued in the 1980s, "New Look."
76. Heaney, "Vulgar Muse," 9.

77. Ibid. For a trenchant analysis of Harrison's poem "The Rhubarbarians," which was collected in his 1980 volume *Continuous*, see Crawford, *Devolving English Literature*, 282–84. Crawford argues that Harrison asserts "the strengths and independences of those who operate outside, against, or below the rule of standard English," in part by using "provincial demotic to question the cultural authority of an accredited standard English" (282, 284).

78. Heaney, "Vulgar Muse," 9.
79. Heaney, "Eclogues *in Extremis*," 1.
80. Ibid., 2.
81. Ibid.
82. See the discussion of how this process works in Longley's poetry in Russell, *Poetry and Peace*, 131–50.
83. Heaney, "Eclogues *in Extremis*," 7.
84. Miłosz, "The World," 41, quoted in Heaney, "Eclogues *in Extremis*," 8. My emphasis.
85. Heaney, foreword to *Lewis's Loughinsholin (1837)*, i.
86. Parker, "Past Master," 8, has pointed out that "Heaney shared Miłosz's pride in his origins on the margins of Europe, a region the latter had earlier described as 'situated beyond the compass of maps . . . where time flowed more slowly than elsewhere'" (*Native Realm*, 7).
87. Burris, *Poetry of Resistance*, ix. Besides O'Donoghue's excellent essay on the subject and Burris's book, see also Frawley's attempt to recover Heaney's pastoral as explicitly Irish in *Irish Pastoral*, 138–48, along with Potts's chapter on Heaney in *Contemporary Irish Poetry*, 45–74.
88. Nicolaisen, "Southern Agrarians," 691.
89. Ibid., 696.
90. Dainotto, *Place in Literature*, 17.
91. Frampton, "Towards a Critical Regionalism," 21.
92. Ibid.
93. Spivak employs the term *critical regionalism* repeatedly in her 2008 study *Other Asias*, unfortunately without attributing the term to Frampton. Her use of the term, however, is clearly indebted to Frampton. In writing, for example, of the need for "the new state in globalization . . . to secure itself socio-economically against the forces of globalization," she holds that "mere nationalism is no answer to this. Once again, we are looking at a *critical regionalism* where old disputes must be negotiated through genealogical deconstruction. The need for good regionalism in this area is well-known" (127; my emphasis).
94. Herr, *Critical Regionalism*, 18.
95. Whelan, "Bases of Regionalism," 13.
96. Ibid., 14.
97. The chapter "Regional, National, and Post-colonial (1)" in Draper, *Introduction*, 161.

98. Crawford, *Devolving English Literature*, 7.
99. Ibid.
100. Quoted in R. Stevenson, *Last of England?*, 255.
101. Whelan, "Bases of Regionalism," 49.
102. J. Foster, "Radical Regionalism," 290.
103. Heaney, "Regional Forecast," 13.
104. Lloyd, *Anomalous States*, 37, argues, taking Heaney's poetry as his example, that "the celebration of regionalism dulls perception of the institutional and homogenizing culture which has sustained its apparent efflorescence at the very moment when the concept of locality, enclosed and self-nurturing, has become effectively archaic, and, indeed, functions as such." But Lloyd merely foists such a stereotype of regionalism on Heaney, never taking seriously or trying to understand its rich and varied manifestations in his body of work.
105. Corcoran, *English Poetry since 1940*, 136.
106. Whelan, "Bases for Regionalism," 56.
107. Ibid., 27.
108. Evans, *Personality of Ireland*, 47.
109. Ibid., 77.
110. Whelan, "Bases of Regionalism," 11.
111. Keith, *Regions of the Imagination*, 11.
112. Evans, *Personality of Ireland*, 78.
113. Ibid.
114. Heaney, *Among Schoolchildren*, 6.
115. J. Foster, "Radical Regionalism," 290–91.
116. Parker, *Northern Irish Literature*, 126.
117. Ibid.
118. Ibid.
119. Ibid.
120. Ibid., 127.
121. McDonald, "'Our Lost Lives,'" 480.
122. Ibid.
123. J. Foster, "Radical Regionalism," 284.
124. Ibid.
125. Ibid., 285.
126. R. Kearney and Wilson, "Northern Ireland's Future," argue that

the idea of a "Europe of the regions" holds out the project, then, of a new, more modern Northern Ireland, in which pluralist, democratic and participatory institutions could acquire legitimacy, traditionally withheld by nationalists because of its association with the "unionist aspiration," through pragmatic acceptance of its status as the Northern Irish region of the evolving Europe.... It becomes possible, in this context, to present closer relations between north and south as pragmatically desirable in a single-market Europe without frontiers, where people, goods and capital move freely across former barriers. Such a focus could help modernize nationalist politics on the island in the process, away from the traditional emphasis on border change and territorial unity towards a stress on the unity of peoples, of "hearts and minds." (63–64)

127. J. Foster, "Radical Regionalism," 291, 292, 294.
128. Mantel, "No Passes or Documents," 104.
129. See, too, Dawe, "Telling a Story," 95, where in his discussion of understanding the interaction between region and nation in Northern Ireland and Ireland he argues, "This is one definite place where the writer has an important role to play, as Andre Brink suggests, 'of fighting to assert the most positive and creative aspects of his heritage'" (95).
130. E. Longley, "Multi-culturalism," 43.
131. Heaney, "Editor's Note," 6.
132. Deane, "Artist and the Troubles," 50.

Chapter One. The Development of Northern Irish Regionalism

1. J. Foster, "Was There Ulster Literary Life," 205.
2. Shovlin, *Irish Literary Periodical*, 1.
3. McNulty, *Ulster Literary Theatre*, 4. For an overview of McNulty's stimulating study, see Russell, "Eugene McNulty's *Ulster Literary Theatre*," 250–52.
4. Lyons, "Of Orangemen," 36.
5. The Field Day Theatre Company at century's end would attempt a reintegration of the Northern Irish state into the Republic, but on peculiarly Northern Irish terms. I address Heaney's pamphlet poem *An Open Letter* in the context of Field Day's ethos in chapter 7.
6. There is a dizzying array of books and articles on the subject. Two of the best are Bardon, *History of Ulster*, and A. Stewart's classic work, *Ulster Crisis*. The essays in Collins, *Nationalism and Unionism*, are detailed and helpful.
7. Kirkland, "Dialogues of Despair," 67.
8. C. O'Malley, *Poets' Theatre*, 104. For an insightful discussion of the *New Northman*, see Kirkland, "Poetics of Partition," 211, 216–18.
9. In Boyd's editorial for the third issue, he concludes by noting, "Finally, I should like to draw attention to the memorial essay on Joseph Campbell, the poet associated with our forerunner, *Uladh*" (J. Boyd, "Comment" [1945], 11).
10. J. Boyd, *Middle of My Journey*, 27.
11. J. Boyd, interview [Russell], n.p.
12. Ibid.
13. M. Longley, "Poetry," 95.

14. In his editorial for the second issue of the journal, Boyd repeats his initial claim that no Ulster artistic flourishing is under way but also suggests that certain Ulster poetry will be considered "major work" in the years to come: "When introducing the first collection of LAGAN the Editors disagreed with the theory that we were experiencing a renaissance in Ulster. Looking back, we have had no reason to regret our caution. Since then there has been an undoubted fruition in painting, music, and particularly theatre. In writing, several promising works have appeared. But a handful of blades is no more a harvest than a handful of 'slim volumes' is a renaissance. Instead of vaunting small beginnings we prefer to understand the word as it is interpreted by the rest of the world. But we feel confident that some of the poetry which will come out of Ulster will be considered major work in centres of appreciation abroad, just as the work of our southern fellow-countryman, forty years ago, resounded far beyond Ireland" (J. Boyd, "Comment" [1944], 11).

15. McIntosh, ever helpful in these matters, cites Boyd's first preface as evidence of this assertion: "A writer must be conscious of the changing attitudes of the common people, that is, of the governed to their governors; he must be conscious of the inherent contradictions in our society, and of the intricate relationship between a maladjusted society and a maladjusted individual; he must be conscious of the social use of literature as a drug or antiseptic: in short, he must be conscious that the struggle for a way of writing is part of the struggle for a way of life" (*Force of Culture*, 194). The regionalism of both Boyd and Hewitt is grounded in the socialism that each espoused.

16. J. Foster, "Post-war Ulster Poetry," 63, 63–64, 67.

17. See Kirkland, "Poetics of Partition," 217–18, for a discussion of *Poems from Ulster*. He notes, "Bearing a dramatic image by Leslie Owen Baxter of a bird rising over the dome of Belfast City Hall with a looming red hand in the background, its cover spoke of a poetry renaissance which was both rooted in Northern Ireland while seeking to be transcendent of it" (217).

18. Greacen, "Editor Says . . . ," n.p.

19. Ibid.

20. Shearman was a chief apologist for the Protestant Stormont regime for many years, and Greacen's approving inclusion of him here reveals his own thinly disguised Protestant bias, at least in his nonimaginative work. See McIntosh's interesting and informed discussion of Shearman's polemical writing versus his more sympathetic imaginative writing in *Force of Culture*, 185–94.

21. Greacen, "Editor Says . . . ," n.p.

22. Indeed, within the pages of this anthology, Rodgers's "Ireland" and Hewitt's "East Antrim Winter" represent much more inclusive visions of the province that are devoid of Greacen's recourse to easy stereotypes in his introduction (86–87, 89). Contemporary reviewer Keidryan Rhys did praise the collection for not being Protestant propaganda: "How nice to come across a Belfast publication which isn't an organ of the shipbuilding or linen industry" (quoted in McIntosh,

Force of Culture, 184–85). But Greacen's introduction and Shearman's contribution, "Ulster To-Day," referenced in the Greacen introduction above, lend a tinge of Ulster Protestant triumphalism to the anthology, despite its many thoughtful stories and poems. It is worth pointing out that Shearman's provocative essay is easily the longest in the *"Belles Lettres"* section of the collection, running to thirteen pages (John Hewitt's essay, "Painting in Ulster," is only eight pages long).

23. Kirkland, "Poetics of Partition," 215.
24. McDonald, *Mistaken Identities*, 24.
25. McIntosh, *Force of Culture*, 182.
26. Ibid.
27. Quoted in ibid., 181.
28. See J. Hewitt's poem "The Colony" for a somewhat strident example of his poetic efforts to write Northern Protestants into the landscape: "for we have rights drawn from the soil and sky; / . . . we would be strangers in the Capitol; / this is our country also, nowhere else; / and we shall not be outcast on the world" (*Collected Poems*, 79).
29. J. Foster, "Radical Regionalism," 281.
30. Kirkland, *Literature and Culture*, 29–30.
31. McFadden's view also does not square with official BBC Northern Ireland policy, which restricted Hewitt's speaking opportunities on-air. McIntosh, citing Ruby Hewitt, the poet's wife, notes that John Boyd told Hewitt "it was BBC policy not to have him on air too much" (*Force of Culture*, 209). This policy was presumably because the unionist BBC feared Hewitt's open-minded political views.
32. Hewitt was influenced early on by his socialist father, Robert Telford Hewitt, and attended various lectures by leading contemporary socialists in Belfast in the 1920s and 1930s. Socialist literary influences included William Morris's propagandist prose tale *A Dream of John Ball* (1888), about a medieval monk who dreamed of social justice, and Thomas Carnduff's *Songs from the Shipyards* (1924)—the first book of poems he ever bought (Ormsby, introduction to *Collected Poems of John Hewitt*, xlii, xliv). See "The Song of the Shipyard Men" in J. Hewitt, *Collected Poems*, 441, for a clear example of Carnduff's influence on Hewitt's incorporation of working-class dialect into his poetry.
33. Quoted in Ormsby, introduction to *Collected Poems of John Hewitt*, xlix. Hewitt's admission of his inward turn toward regionalism is a striking instance of the primary impetus behind the increasing promotion of Northern Irish culture in the 1940s; another impetus was undoubtedly the official declaration of the Irish republic in 1949 and the unionist impulse to define Northern Ireland in contrast to the South culturally and politically.
34. Walsh, "'Too Much Alone,'" 356.
35. Ibid. One of Hewitt's two poems Heaney included in his anthology of new Irish poetry, *Soundings '72*, was one that delved into the ritualistic practices—such as the carrying of candles "like ivory wands"—in a rural Italian Catholic church (J. Hewitt, "St Rosalie, Monte Pelligrino," 25).

Notes to Pages 51–53   413

36. J. Hewitt, "Bitter Gourd," 93.
37. Ibid.
38. Ibid., 94.
39. Ibid.
40. Ibid., 95.
41. In his list of sources at the end of the essay, Hewitt cites Ian Finlay's book *Scotland* (n.d.), which "is most emphatically to be recommended for the light which it throws upon problems closely analogous to our own" ("Bitter Gourd," 105).
42. Ibid., 96–97.
43. Ibid., 97, 97–98.
44. Ibid., 99.
45. Ibid., 101.
46. Ibid., 102.
47. Ibid.
48. Kersnowski, *Outsiders*, 115.
49. Clark, *Ulster Renaissance*, 117.
50. This bibliography is broadly inclusive, and all authors are represented who "were born in Ulster or were resident in Ulster during their effective period of writing. By 'Ulster' is meant the Nine Counties prior to 1922, and thereafter the Six Counties constituting Northern Ireland: but qualification for inclusion in the first category involves an author's having been engaged in writing before partition" ("Ulster Books and Authors," 55). The writers are divided into poets, playwrights, essayists, and novelists. The bibliography concludes with four lists: "Literary and Biographical Studies by or about Ulster Writers," "Works of Scholarship and General Interest," "Anthologies and Periodicals," and "Background Books."
51. Hunter and McFadden, introduction, 1.
52. See Adamson, *Cruithin*, *Identity of Ulster*, and *Ulster People*. His theories have been refuted by many historians. Strangely enough, while they provide an interesting insight into an attempt to create a separate preplantation Protestant Ulster, they actually share some features of nationalist narratives. For instance, Brian Graham points out that "somewhat ironically, Adamson's origin-myth adopts precisely the same foreshortening of time which McDonagh [*States of Mind*] (1983) identifies as a primary characteristic of traditional Irish nationalism, the distant past being used in both representations to validate and legitimate contemporary social order" ("Ulster," 49).
53. Shovlin, *Irish Literary Periodical*, 5. It is difficult to understand why Shovlin, in his introduction, offers such an assessment, which conflicts, to some degree, with his own reading of this last issue of *Rann* in his chapter on the journal. There he notes that "while Donegal writers like Patrick MacGill and Peadar O'Donnell are included, Monaghan's Patrick Kavanagh—arguably the archetypal Ulster regionalist—is omitted.... It was ... unfortunate that his particular ear for south-Ulster dialect could not find a more prominent place in the ranks of *Rann*'s 'Ulster' writers" (175–76). Certainly Kavanagh's omission is unfortunate, but the

inclusion of MacGill and O'Donnell alone suggests how fully the magazine looked beyond the political borders of the contemporary Northern Irish state; moreover, Kavanagh had settled in Dublin by 1939, even though he moved briefly to Belfast during the period 1946–49 and started writing his "Diary" entries for the Dublin magazine *Envoy* by 1949 and poetry set in Dublin by the time this last issue of *Rann* was published, which may have understandably led the editors to exclude him as an "Ulster" writer for their purposes.

54. Sergeant, "Ulster Regionalism," 3.
55. Ibid.
56. Ibid., 3–4.
57. Ibid., 4.
58. Ibid.
59. Ibid.
60. Fullwood and Edwards, "Ulster Poetry since 1900," 20. This characterization, without the term *Pseudonymous Generation*, accords with Hewitt's description of Ulster writers who emerged after the decline of the rhyming weavers in "Bitter Gourd": "finding themselves in an extroverted stubborn inarticulate society with well defined material values and, for the most part, a rigid creed, [they] revolted against their condition" and left the province (97–98). Fullwood and Edwards mention a continuation of this ethos in their critique of CEMA: "The attitude persists for instance, in an underground way, in the policy of a body such as the Council for the Encouragement of Music and the Arts, an organization set up in Belfast and supported from public funds (including taxes paid by poets), which deems it right to exclude poetry from the arts" (20).
61. Ibid., 34.
62. Ibid., 29.
63. J. Hewitt, "Course of Writing," 43.
64. Ibid., 44. Hewitt would later edit and publish *Rhyming Weavers* (1974).
65. J. Hewitt, "Course of Writing," 45.
66. Ibid.
67. Ibid.
68. Ibid., 47.
69. Boyd, "Ulster Novel."
70. J. Hewitt, "Course of Writing," 52.
71. C. O' Malley, *Poets' Theatre*, 105.
72. Ibid.
73. Ibid., 108, 111.
74. Ibid., 115.
75. Ibid., 117, 120, 119.
76. Ibid., 123–24.
77. Kersnowski, *Outsiders*, 109, 110. Strangely, though, Kersnowski refused to accept the journal's role in helping effect a literary community in Northern Ireland, arguing on the basis of one passage from Denis Ireland's essay in the second

issue of the journal in Autumn–Winter 1961 that "no real community exists in the North. The writers, though calling themselves Ulstermen, automatically call to mind Southern [Irish] writers when thinking about Irish literature" (110).
 78. Quoted in B. Stewart, "'Door,'" 167.
 79. Quoted in ibid.
 80. J. Hewitt, "Progress of a Poet," n.p.
 81. Ibid.
 82. Ibid.
 83. J. Hewitt, "Bitter Gourd," 99.
 84. Heaney, "Poetry of John Hewitt," 208.
 85. Ibid.
 86. Ibid., 210.
 87. The *Honest Ulsterman* was the successor to the short-lived Northern Ireland Arts Council magazine *Northern Review*, edited by Michael Mitchell and later by Michael Longley and Heaney.
 88. Kirkland, *Literature and Culture*, 65.
 89. See J. Foster, "Critical Condition of Ulster," 221.
 90. Kirkland, *Literature and Culture*, 67.
 91. Ibid., 75.
 92. Clark, *Ulster Renaissance*, 89. For the most thorough and perspicacious reading of the *Honest Ulsterman*, which also pays special attention to its regionalist ethos, see the entirety of Clark's discussion in *Ulster Renaissance*, 86–103.
 93. Quoted in Kirkland, *Literature and Culture*, 67.
 94. Clark, *Ulster Renaissance*, 89.
 95. Simmons, "Editorial," 5–6.
 96. M. Longley, "Poetry," 96.
 97. Simmons, "Honest Ulsterman," advertisement, inside front page of *Phoenix* 6/7.
 98. *Threshold*'s decline is much more typical of the pattern for Northern Irish literary journals than the long-running *Honest Ulsterman*. Conor O'Malley observes a decline in critical essays appearing in that journal by the 1980s. More disturbing to him is the increasing "geographical perspective which shows a gradual entrenchment behind the boundaries of the North" (*Poet's Theatre*, 123).
 99. Chambers, "Festival Poetry Pamphlets," 50.
 100. Ibid.
 101. E. Longley, "Northern House Pamphlet Poets," 55.
 102. Chambers is responsible for assembling and publishing the first collection of essays on Larkin's poetry, which appeared in *Phoenix* 11–12 (Autumn–Winter 1973–74).
 103. Irvine, *Ulster and Modern Thought*, 64.
 104. Heaney, preface to *Crane Bag Book*, 7.
 105. Morrison, *Seamus Heaney*, 31.
 106. Ibid., 30.

Chapter Two. Recording Bigotry and Imagining a New Province

1. Peacock, "Mediations," 235.
2. As he recalls in his Nobel Prize Address, "Without needing to be theoretically instructed, consciousness quickly realizes that it is the site of variously contending discourses. The child in the bedroom listening simultaneously to the domestic idiom of his Irish home and the official idioms of the British broadcaster while picking up from behind both the signals of some other distress—that child was already being schooled for the complexities of his adult predicament, a future where he would have to adjudicate between promptings variously ethical, aesthetical, moral, political, metrical, skeptical, cultural, topical, typical, post-colonial, and, taken all together, simply impossible" (*CP*, 15–16).
3. Heaney, "Out of London," 23.
4. Ibid., 24.
5. Ibid.
6. T. Kearney, "Poetry of the North," 67.
7. Vendler, *Seamus Heaney*, 175.
8. Anderson, *Imagined Communities*, 133.
9. McLoone, "Inventions and Re-imaginings," 10.
10. Ibid., 10–11.
11. Linfoot, "Origins of BBC Local Radio."
12. Ibid.
13. Quoted in Cathcart, *Most Contrary Region*, 61.
14. Ibid.
15. Ibid., 102.
16. Ibid., 267.
17. Quoted in ibid.
18. Heaney, "Conversation," 19.
19. The controlling powers at the BBC certainly distrusted Catholics. There was a long tradition of regarding Catholics as unfit for upper management positions in the organization. Curran notes in his study of the BBC, *Seamless Robe*, that when BBC director Reith left and recommended that his successor be Graves, a Roman Catholic, the story ran that the archbishop of Canterbury had complained about Graves's possible succession, while H. A. L. Fisher, a former director-general, was on record as saying that "if Graves were made Deputy Director-General it would be difficult ever to make him Director-General because he was a Roman Catholic. 'I think,' he wrote, 'it would be quite impossible that the supreme executive control of one of the most important organs of public education in this country should be placed in the hands of a Roman Catholic'" (345–46). When Curran himself became director-general in 1969, an objection was raised to his Catholicism (347).
20. J. Boyd, *Middle of My Journey*, 74.

21. For helpful discussions of the controversy surrounding Thompson's play, see Byrne, *Stage in Ulster*, 46–49. For Boyd's reaction in having *The Blood of Colonel Lamb* rejected for broadcast, see *Middle of My Journey*, 220–21. Boyd significantly revised it and retitled it *Assassins*; it became a hit at the 1969 Dublin Theatre Festival.

22. J. Boyd, "Personal Interview."
23. Mengel, *Sam Thompson*, 308.
24. McIntosh, *Force of Culture*, 70. See her sustained analysis of the subject on 69–102.
25. Quoted in Cathcart, *Most Contrary Region*, 267.
26. Richtarik, "Ireland, the Continuous Past," 257.
27. Ibid., 258.
28. Cathcart, *Most Contrary Region*, 200.
29. Ibid., 201.
30. Ibid.
31. De Paor, *Divided Ulster*, 162.
32. McIntosh, *Force of Culture*, 94.
33. Cathcart, *Most Contrary Region*, 263.
34. Parker, *Seamus Heaney*, 53.
35. Ibid.
36. Ibid., 55.
37. See my discussion of the Room to Rhyme tour in *Poetry and Peace*, 54–57.
38. Heaney, *Among Schoolchildren*, 4.
39. For a compelling analysis of the interactions between BBC Northern Ireland and Northern Irish poets in the decades leading up to the beginning of Heaney's association with the BBC, see Clark, "Regional Roots."
40. Mahony, "Memory and Belonging," 12.
41. Cathcart, *Most Contrary Region*, 181.
42. Ibid., 182.
43. Heaney, "Regional Forecast," 10.
44. Significantly, as Eamon Melaugh, an early march organizer, participant, and photographer, points out in *Derry*, 178, some posters for the October 5 march were printed in "red, white and blue in an attempt to attract Unionists to the march."
45. Heaney, "Untitled," 3.
46. Ibid., 4–5.
47. Ibid., 10.
48. "Frogman" was first published in *The Listener*, July 4, 1968, 11, and it was later collected in *Things Working*.
49. Heaney, "Untitled," 12.
50. The poem is essentially the same one as in his untitled piece for the *Explorations* series with only three minor punctuation changes.

51. Heaney, "Untitled," 12.
52. Ibid., 13.
53. Jung, "Two Kinds of Thinking," 16.
54. Ibid., 23.
55. Heaney, "Untitled," 13–14.
56. For example, he published an outraged essay in the *Listener* on October 24, 1968, "Old Derry's Walls," in which he complained about the beatings by the Royal Ulster Constabulary of the Derry protesters and concluded that "the Catholic minority in Northern Ireland at large, if it is to retain any self-respect, will have to risk the charge of wrecking the new moderation and seek justice more vociferously" (522).
57. Heaney is almost surely drawing upon Yeats's late theme of tragic gaiety that he explores so profoundly in poems such as "Lapis Lazuli."
58. Heaney, "William Butler Yeats," 787.
59. J. Foster, *Achievement of Seamus Heaney*, 3, 4.
60. E. Longley, "Poetry and Politics," 185.
61. Johnston, "Seamus Heaney and Violence," 114.
62. Heaney, "Place, Pastness, Poems," 35.
63. Ibid., 36.
64. Elliott, *Catholics of Ulster*, 258.
65. Ibid.
66. Dawson, "Henry Monro," n.p.
67. R. Foster, *Modern Ireland*, 266.
68. Elliott, *Watchmen in Sion*, 9, 8–9.
69. Ibid., 20.
70. Dawson, "Henry Monro," n.p.
71. Ibid.
72. Heaney, *Munro*, 60.
73. Ibid., 62.
74. Heaney in class discussion with Richard Rankin Russell's students, Baylor University, Waco, TX, March 4, 2013.
75. Heaney, *Munro*, 63.
76. See "Out of London." For an excellent analysis of this essay, see Parker, "Reckonings," 142–43. Parker points out that Heaney's somewhat strident rhetoric earlier in the poet's essay largely disappears when he discusses the arts, which suggests that Heaney saw art as the leavening agent so desperately needed among intransigent communities in the province. As Parker notes, "When Heaney's discussion focuses upon the arts, all religious and political labels disappear, as if to suggest that at least Belfast's artistic community possesses the grace and confidence to fly by the nets of 'ignorant and ugly bigotry' elsewhere in the province" (143).
77. R. Foster, *Irish Story*, 230. Foster's narrative throughout this chapter of his book, "Remembering 1798," is indebted to Ian McBride's seminal work *Scrip-

ture Politics. Foster further argues, drawing on McBride, that "for the Presbyterian radicals the new French dawn had seemed to promise the twilight of Romantic Catholic 'superstition.' Their own millennial surge had therefore very different roots from the Jacobite tradition clearly discernible in the polemic of the Southern rebels, and their civic republicanism was far from being proto-nationalism" (231).

78. Heaney, *Munro*, 65. Heaney cites these lines as part of his discussion about acting in the 1798 melodrama *The Hearts of Down*, recalling that they came from "this ballad where she appears in the last verse as the sister of the rebel leader, Harry Munro [he then recites the lines].... David Hammond used to sing it" (*SS*, 92).

79. Heaney, "Old Derry's Walls," 523.
80. Elliott, *Catholics of Ulster*, 263.
81. Ibid., 264.
82. Inside front cover of *Everyman: A Religio-Cultural Review*, no. 3, 1970.
83. Farrell, "Editorial," 5.
84. Ibid.
85. Ibid., 6.
86. Ibid., 8. Farrell then quotes John Lennon and Yoko Ono's "Give Peace a Chance," remarking that "perhaps it is a pity that we have not more hippies! Perhaps even the B men would have been disarmed by a flower! Now we will never know" (8). We can easily perceive how Heaney might appreciate an invocation of the American 1960s peace movement in Farrell's last paragraph, since he was living in Berkeley, California, by late 1970.
87. R. Foster, *Modern Ireland*, 265.
88. Heaney, *Munro*, 62.
89. Ibid.
90. Hobbs, "United Irishmen," 38.
91. Heaney, *Munro*, 62.
92. Ibid., 59, 64.
93. Quoted in Hobbs, "United Irishmen," 40.
94. Heaney, *Munro*, 64.
95. Russell, *Poetry and Peace*, 184. The relevant quotation from Heaney's "Our Own Dour Way" is "I only hope that their descendants of the 1960s follow their example—with the pen which is so much mightier than the pike" (15).
96. Heaney, "Englands of the Mind," 165.
97. Heaney, *Among Schoolchildren*, 5.
98. Bew and Gillespie, *Northern Ireland*, 24, 31.
99. Heaney, "Old Derry's Walls," 522. See Parker, "Reckonings," 150–52, for a trenchant analysis of this essay, which he terms "Heaney's second major foray into political journalism" (150) after his essay, "Out of London." As Parker argues, "Old Derry's Walls," coupled with an untitled ballad by Heaney satirizing the Royal Ulster Constabulary's brutalization of a Catholic civil rights march in Derry on October 5, 1968, the latter of which was "circulated anonymously within the nationalist

community," shows "the extent to which public concerns suffuse his writing at this time; explicit in their affiliations, they contrast markedly with the poems of *Wintering Out*, in which the poet generally adopts a much more oblique approach towards political questions" (150).

100. Bew and Gillespie, *Northern Ireland*, 33.
101. Cathcart, *Most Contrary Region*, 207.
102. Ibid., 209.
103. See, for example, Heaney, "Chester Pageant," his account of staging a portion of the Chester cycle of mystery plays while training secondary school teachers-to-be in the early 1960s.
104. Heaney, *Everyman*, 1.
105. See Corcoran, *Poetry of Seamus Heaney*, 26–27, for the full text of these lyrics.
106. Orange drums and the spirit of divisiveness they promote were much on Heaney's mind in the early to mid-1970s. For instance, his prose poem "July," from the 1975 pamphlet *Stations*, clearly criticizes the Orangemen who play drums in triumphalist parades every July that often process through Catholic neighborhoods (*S*, 15). See also similar passages from his poems "Whatever You Say Say Nothing" and "Orange Drums, Tyrone, 1966" (*N*, 52, 62).
107. Heaney, *Everyman*, 1–6.
108. Ibid., 6.
109. Ibid.
110. Ibid., 6–7.
111. Ibid., 7.
112. Ibid., 8.
113. Cathcart, *Most Contrary Region*, 207, emphasis in original. The 1949 policy on music, however, suggests at least a potential openness toward traditional music nearly two decades before the inception of *Orange and Green Folk*: "While Ulster music and musicians are the first charge, the body of Traditional Irish music is common to the whole island and therefore available to North, as well as South, as part of the living body of music of Western culture, so fully represented in BBC programmes" (267).
114. Heaney, *Everyman*, 9.
115. Ibid., 10.
116. Potter, *English Morality Play*, 57.
117. E. Longley, "Opening Up," 24–25.
118. Heaney was long drawn to harmonious music as a metaphor for improved relations between Catholics and Protestants. For instance, after the signing of the Good Friday Agreement in 1998, he offered his views on the peace settlement in an *Irish Times* column that drew on music's potential in this regard, "Unheard Melodies." See my analysis of this essay in *Poetry and Peace*, 308–10.
119. Heaney, "Out of London," 24.

Notes to Pages 99–104   421

120. Heaney, "Over the Bridge."
121. Ibid.
122. E. Longley, "Multi-culturalism," 42.

Chapter Three. Heaney's Essays on Regional Writers

1. See McGuinness, *Seamus Heaney*, 75–134; Corcoran, *Poetry of Seamus Heaney*, 209–33. See also Burris, "Reading Heaney Reading," and Baron, "Heaney," who specifically defend Heaney's prose criticism as upholding Virginia Woolf's theory of the radical, individual reader, and as inscribing a space for poetry's authority while nevertheless interacting with major social and ethical questions, respectively. Finally, Cavanagh's recent monograph *Professing Poetry* gives the most sustained attention yet to the prose.
2. E. O'Brien, *Seamus Heaney: Searches*, 10.
3. Heaney, "Regional Forecast," 22.
4. Heaney, "Mossbawn," 19, 20.
5. Heaney, "Belfast," 35.
6. Ibid., 36–37.
7. Duffy, *Exploring the History*, 18.
8. Ibid., 22.
9. Parker, *Seamus Heaney*, 36.
10. See Kirkland, "Dialogues of Despair," where he sweepingly claims that,

to use very broad brushstrokes, while a case can be made that Northern Protestant writing in this period finds itself preoccupied with questions of territory and space (the theme that connects such different writers as John Hewitt and Glenn Patterson), the Catholic imagination is, instead, dominated by the temporal; the possibility of inhabiting many historical locations beyond the fallen present. Protestant writing urges revision, redefinition, and assertion of presence, while Catholic writing is, instead, often circular—it returns repeatedly to the moment of the fall, it dwells on loss, and frequently finds the beginning of a new narrative to be a fraught and labored procedure. (66–67)

Besides Kirkland's bizarre hypostatizing of the existence of separate Protestant and Catholic imaginations, Northern Irish literature from throughout the century, as the last chapter demonstrated, shares many more aesthetic, cultural, and religious features than Kirkland's statement suggests. Most radically, its emphasis on the power of the imagination generally gives the lie to Kirkland's too-neat delineation of a difference between the pressing concerns of Protestants and Catholics.

11. As Fallon and Mahon claim there, "The Northern phenomenon remains, in Kinsella's phrase, 'largely a journalistic entity.' There was never, contrary to received opinion, a Northern 'School' in any real sense, merely a number of

individual talents. Too much has been made of the so-called Belfast 'Group.' Still, it is undeniable that in a traditionally philistine province, the individual talents of Heaney, Longley, Simmons and Mahon appeared more or less simultaneously and coincidentally with the present 'Troubles' " (xx). This is a shocking claim that misleadingly views the emergence of Northern Irish poetry as a body of work *ex nihilo* that was centered on individuals writing in isolation from each other. The current chapter and subsequent ones in this study prove its speciousness.

12. Fallon and Mahon, introduction to *Penguin Book*, xvii–xviii.
13. Heaney, "Belfast," 29.
14. Quoted in Parker, *Seamus Heaney*, 32.
15. Heaney, "From Monaghan," 116.
16. Duffy, *Exploring the History*, 204–5.
17. Ibid., 205.
18. Heaney, "From Monaghan," 116.
19. Ibid., 120.
20. Heaney, "Sense of Place," 137.
21. Ibid., 139.
22. Ibid., 140. See too, Heaney's essay, "Placeless Heaven," where he argues that Kavanagh's "early Monaghan poetry gives the place credit for existing, assists at its real topographical presence, dwells upon it and accepts it as the definitive locus of the given world" (4).
23. Heaney, "Lost Ulstermen," 550.
24. Heaney, "Sense of Place," 141.
25. Ibid., 141.
26. Kavanagh's influence was much stronger upon Heaney than it had been upon Montague. Michael Allen persuasively argues that Montague largely rejected Kavanagh's influence on him in favor of a supposedly larger cosmopolitanism but that Heaney stayed faithful to Kavanagh's parochial vision: "Heaney, on the other hand, has never shown any doubt about the social and artistic validity of his parish" ("Provincialism," 36).
27. Lucas, "Seamus Heaney," 124.
28. Heaney, "Poet as a Christian," 604–5.
29. See MacCana's essay "Early Irish Ideology" for an explanation of the origins of this syncretism. MacCana argues that the remarkable conservatism of Irish tradition and literature was able to continue after the introduction of Christianity because of this assimilative aspect of Irish ideology: "The subtle *modus vivendi* which had evolved during the first century and a half of the Christian mission ... permitted the complementary coexistence of two ideologies, one explicitly Christian, the other implicitly and essentially pagan" (58).
30. One recent example of a use of binaries to categorize Heaney's regionalism is Andrew Auge's attempt to import the distinction between arborescent and rhizomatic structures drawn by the theorists Gilles Deleuze and Felix Guattari into

a discussion of Heaney's regional ethos. Auge, citing Deleuze and Guattari's 1987 work *A Thousand Plateaus*, notes that "the arborescent signifies centralized hierarchical systems that privilege continuity and filiation" while the rhizomatic "constitutes an a-centered, non-hierarchical, proliferating multiplicity." Auge argues that Heaney's "aspiration toward an arborescent state of organic connectedness is repeatedly frustrated by disruptive encounters with the rhizomatic" ("Buoyant Migrant Line," 272). As evidence, he cites the uncontrollable, ambiguous, and unsettling qualities of poems from *Death of a Naturalist*, such as the title poem and "Personal Helicon" (272–74), that threaten the fixity and hierarchy of poems such as "Digging." But as Heaney's own prose and poetry make clear, he moves easily between the "arborescent" and the "rhizomatic" and actually obtains a certain groundedness from the profusion and variety of lore, myth, and religion attached to his local landscape. His work collapses the distinction between these two theoretical terms and renders them semantically and functionally useless in discussing his holistic regional worldview, an outlook that anchors him all the more firmly in his particularized landscape precisely through its multiplicity of meanings that he adroitly negotiates and claims in several passages from his "Poet as Christian" essay.

31. Heaney, "Indomitable Irishry," 104.
32. Montague, "Regionalism into Reconciliation," 113–14.
33. Ibid., 117.
34. Heaney, "Sense of Place," 141.
35. Ibid., 147.
36. B. Stewart, "'Door,'" 166, 169.
37. Ibid., 169.
38. Ibid., 166.
39. Heaney, "Poetry of John Hewitt," 209.
40. Allen, "Bleak Afflatus!," 84.
41. Clark, *Ulster Renaissance*, 123. She is quoting John Wilson Foster's judgment in "'Dissidence of Dissent'" that Hewitt's aesthetic is essentially "Calvinist, displaying as it does simplicity, sobriety and measure," and then Allen's "Parish and the Dream."
42. Allen, "Bleak Afflatus!," 85.
43. Kirkland, *Literature and Culture*, 32–33.
44. Clark, *Ulster Renaissance*, 125.
45. Ibid., 126.
46. J. Foster, "'Dissidence of Dissent,'" 123.
47. Dawe, "Parochial Idyll," 66.
48. M. Longley, introduction to *W. R. Rodgers*, 11.
49. Heaney, "Through-Other Places," 398. See McIntosh's "'Life Is a Series of Oppositions'" for an insightful study of Rodgers's extensive prose writings in the context of his postition as a Presbyterian minister and poet preaching and writing in his native Northern Ireland.

50. McDonald, *Mistaken Identities*, 29.
51. M. Longley, "Neolithic Night," 99. Indeed, the recovery of MacNeice as a major poet has been greatly aided by Longley himself. As Terence Brown has shown, Longley's 1967 review of E. R. Dodds's edition of *The Collected Poems of Louis MacNeice*, entitled "A Misrepresented Poet," "accurately establishes the overall shape of MacNeice's career. He notes the early lyric successes, the drab middle years, with the Second World War . . . read as a particularly fruitful period of MacNeice's life" ("Michael Longley," 3). See McIntosh, *Force of Culture*, 198–206, for a penetrating account of the critiques of Northern Ireland offered by Rodgers and MacNeice in the 1940s. And see McDonald's excellent account of Hewitt, Rodgers, and MacNeice's varying responses to and puncturings of identity discourse in *Mistaken Identities* (20–40).
52. See Heaney, "Frontiers of Writing," 198–200, in which he discusses this quincunx; I discuss this essay in some detail in chapter 10 of this study.
53. Their ascent and the lack of major volumes from poets like Robert Greacen and Roy McFadden resulted in a rejection of the romantic Celticism characterized by these more minor poets' verse. As John Wilson Foster points out, "The Ulster neo-Romantics of the 1940s fell silent around 1947 or 1948 and kept their heads down for a quarter of a century until the Movement was no longer recognizable as such. After *The Undying Day* (1948), Greacen did not publish a full-length volume of poetry until *A Garland for Captain Fox* (1975); after *The Heart's Townland* (1947), McFadden did not publish a full-length volume until *The Garryowen* (1971)" ("Post-war Ulster Poetry" 79).
54. Hewitt, "Progress of a Poet," n.p.
55. Heaney, "Obituary," 31.
56. Heaney, introduction to *Michael McLaverty*, 7.
57. Ibid., 8.
58. See Buxton, *Robert Frost*, 39–110, for her thoughtful and persuasive account of Frost's influence on Heaney.
59. Hewitt, "Bitter Gourd," 103.
60. Ibid., 104.
61. Heaney, "Frontiers of Writing," 197.
62. Heaney, "Above the Brim," 86.
63. Ibid.
64. E. Longley, "'Atlantic's Premises,'" 270–71.
65. Parker, *Seamus Heaney*, 42.
66. For a helpful essay on the regionalism of R. S. Thomas, see Hardy, "Region and Nation," 93–100.
67. Heaney, "R. S. Thomas Memorial," 11.
68. Parker, *Seamus Heaney*, 44
69. Heaney, "Norman MacCaig," 433. See, too, Heaney's approval of how MacCaig's regionally particular poems attain a universality in "Regional Forecast": "His deceptively simple late poems are testing the echo of the universe as authenti-

cally as even a persecuted poet could manage to.... But his skill in pretending—even to himself—to be a modest inscriber of glosses should not blind his native audience or any other audience to the modernity of his achievement in these lyrics which sing with the constancy and high nervousness of barbed wire on a moorland" (23).

70. Heaney, "Tradition," 195.
71. Ibid., 195–96.
72. Ibid., 196–97.
73. Heaney, "Celtic Fringe, Viking Fringe," 254–55.
74. Parker, *Seamus Heaney*, 78–79.
75. Holloway, "Literary Scene," 110.
76. Holloway specifically notes this quality in the Orcadian author's work: "Brown is clearly thinking in terms of *documenting* the distinctive society of which he writes. His vivid individualization is in part a kind of social study or very superior kind of literary reportage, with analogues in the fields of journalism, the TV or radio feature, and the documentary film" (ibid., 111).
77. Heaney, "Interview: Seamus Heaney, Poet."
78. Alexander, "Wordsworth," 25.
79. See, for instance, his 1988 volume for Faber, *William Wordsworth*, along with the opening discussion of Wordsworth in his 1984 lecture delivered at Grasmere, *Place and Displacement*; his linkage of Wordsworth and Japanese writers in his 2007 essay "Pathos of Things"; and his meditation on the romantic poet throughout his 2008 essay "'Apt Admonishment.'"
80. Quoted in Keith, *Regions of the Imagination*, 4.
81. Heaney, "Conversation," 53.
82. Ibid.
83. Heaney, preface to *Seamus Heaney*, xvii.
84. Ibid.
85. Heaney, "Place of Writing," 21.
86. See, for example, "Main of Light," 21, where Heaney holds that poems such as "At Grass," "MCMXIV," "How Distant," and "The Explosion" have the "light in them honeyed by attachment to a dream world that will not be denied because it is at the foundation of the poet's sensibility. It is the light that was on Langland's Malvern, 'in summer season, when soft was the sun,' at once local and timeless." And see too "Joy or Night," when Heaney states about Larkin's late poem "Aubade" that "it would be hard to think of a poem more opposed than this one to the life-enhancing symbolism of the Christ child in the Christmas crib" (155).
87. See, for an example of this first tendency, Booth's "Turf Cutter." Michael Cavanagh's very fine chapter "Fighting Off Larkin," in his *Professing Poetry*, 185–211, exemplifies this second trend, with extensive discussion of why Heaney's earlier admiration of Larkin had seemingly changed so much by the time he wrote "Joy or Night," particularly in the passage I have cited in the previous note about Heaney's rejection of the bleakness expressed in "Aubade."

88. Heaney, "Englands of the Mind," 151.
89. Ibid.
90. Ibid.
91. Ibid., 168.
92. Ingelbien, "Seamus Heaney," 473, quoting Heaney's "Englands of the Mind," 167.
93. Ingelbien, "Seamus Heaney," 473.
94. Ibid., 474.
95. Heaney, "Englands of the Mind," 151; my emphasis.
96. I am drawing on Parker, "'His Nibs,'" 328, who argues for this particular dating of this autobiographical sketch, and from whom I cite Heaney, "Biographical Sketch," n.p.
97. Heaney, "Fair (A Progress Report)," 7.
98. Heaney, "Bogland," 10.
99. Heaney, "Englands of the Mind," 152.
100. Ibid., 165.
101. Ibid., 168.
102. Draper, "Philip Larkin," 81.
103. Crawford, *Devolving English Literature*, 276–77. Draper, too, focuses on the participle *swerving* in Larkin's "Here," insightfully noting that this word helps establish a regional modernity in the poem: "The sense of direction conveyed by 'Swerving' is exact with regard to the geographical relationship of Hull to London and the industrial areas of the Midlands . . . but it is also a participle which builds up a telling syntactical suspension. The reader is taken through a countryside which might seem drearily nondescript, but in fact acquires a novel beauty and serenity not unlike that which Hardy in *The Return of the Native* attributes to Egdon heath as more appropriately modern than the traditional, classical beauty of the Mediterranean" (84–85).
104. Heaney, "Englands of the Mind," 169.
105. Ibid., 153.
106. Hughes, "Ted Hughes and Crow," 9. I am grateful to Henry Hart for pointing out these distinctions between Hughes and Heaney to me.
107. Ibid., 169. Heaney would emphatically affirm Hughes's seminal role in this process many years later, noting in 2001 that when he wrote the poem for Hughes "On His Work in the English Tongue," "My purpose . . . was to say 'fret no more.' 'Fret no more and walk abroad confirmed'—that's one of the lines. The walking abroad image came from the Pentecost story, of the apostles in the upper room being visited by the Holy Spirit and being inspired to go out and speak confidently in tongues. So that part is an act of gratitude for Ted's work in the English tongue, and the fact that it released my own poetic tongue" ("Interview with Seamus Heaney" [Gammage], 11).
108. Heaney, "Deep as England," 13; my emphasis.

109. Ibid.
110. Hart, "Seamus Heaney and Ted Hughes," 78.
111. E. Longley, "Poetics of Celt and Saxon," 82, 83.
112. Ibid., 83.
113. More convincingly than Longley's formulation of Heaney's hidden nationalism here, J. Foster's *Achievement of Seamus Heaney*, 56, argues that while this lecture could possibly reflect "Heaney's own *de facto* Britishness when it comes to literature, it could alternatively be said to have been a subtle shrinking of England to imaginative versions and mental regions of itself of the kind Irish writers have been driven in compensation and colonial division to create and inhabit."
114. E. O'Brien, *Seamus Heaney and the Place of Writing*, 159.
115. Frampton, "Towards a Critical Regionalism," 26.

Chapter Four. Wounds and Fire

The epigraph from Heaney's "Unhappy and at Home" is taken from p. 67.

1. Heaney, "Unhappy and at Home," 66.
2. Ibid., 68.
3. See my *Poetry and Peace*, 201–13.
4. See my analysis of "Digging" and "Requiem for the Croppies" in ibid., 179–85, and 191–92, respectively, for an exploration of how these poems explore the hope for reconciliation in 1960s Northern Ireland in the context of the 1798 rebellion.
5. Bardon, *History of Ulster*, 211–12.
6. Heaney, "Seamus Heaney—Poetry International."
7. Glassie, *All Silver*, 127.
8. Pearson, review of *Border-Crossing*.
9. Ibid.
10. Glassie, *All Silver*, 129.
11. Haggerty, "Mumming."
12. Just four years earlier, Heaney's participation in the Northern Ireland Arts Council tour, "Room to Rhyme," whose title derives from one of the opening demands of mummers when entering a household, had seemed to him a sign of a new, more promising era in divided Northern Ireland.
13. Heaney, *Room to Rhyme*, 7.
14. Corcoran, *Poetry of Seamus Heaney*, cites two stanzas of the poem, briefly observing that "it angrily bites out its resentment against the threatening Loyalist bonfires of the twelfth of July" (251), while Parker offers a short, compelling analysis of the poem in "From *Winter Seeds*," 132.
15. Heaney, "Interview with Seamus Heaney" [Randall], 16.

16. Heaney, "Intimidation," 34.
17. Ibid.
18. "Tumulus," *OED* online.
19. Heaney, "Intimidation," 34.
20. "Stour," *OED* online.
21. Heaney, "Intimidation," 34. The specific action of burning the "nests" of the triumphal Protestants and the association of them with the "Ghetto" suggest that the poem may well be a dramatized riposte on the part of a Catholic speaker to John Hewitt's "The Colony," whose Northern Irish Protestant speaker recalls "*smoking out the nests* / of the barbarian tribesmen, clan by clan," and notes that "one or two loud voices would restore / the rack, the yellow patch, the *curfewed ghetto*" (J. Hewitt, *Collected Poems*, 77, 78; my emphases).
22. Heaney, "Intimidation," 34; my emphasis.
23. Ibid.; my emphasis.
24. In another context, Heaney has used the term *ghetto* more positively. For example, over two decades after publishing "Intimidation," in his "Irish Society Michaelmas Dinner Address," delivered during the early to mid-1990s at Oxford University, he would characterize people of Irish descent in Britain as not having "the ghetto mentality that the Irish of earlier times necessarily developed, as a protection against a hostile social and economic environment. They are assimilated but not daunted; their ethnic background and separate cultural heritage are a resource, a positive aspect of their Britishness rather than a hindering circumstance."
25. Hall, *Seamus Heaney's Rhythmic Contract*, 64.
26. Heaney, "Nocturne," 35.
27. This erotic language is jettisoned from the subsequently revised poem in "A Northern Hoard," "Roots," replaced simply by "all": "And all shifts dreamily as you keen / Far off" (*WO*, 39).
28. In the later version of the poem, these sounds appear in line 7 of the second quatrain and are expanded to include gas: "Of gunshot, siren and clucking gas" (*WO*, 39).
29. In his sensitive brief reading of "Nocturne," Parker, "From *Winter Seeds*," 132, calls this a "[John] Montague-like 'fault,'" noting that the fifth section of Montague's long sequence, *The Rough Field*, entitled "The Fault," had been published the year before "in *Honest Ulsterman* 23 (May–June, 1970), 3–7."
30. Heaney, preface to *Stations*, 3.
31. See my discussion of this decision in *Poetry and Peace*, 196–201.
32. Heaney, "Nocturne," 35.
33. See my *Poetry and Peace*, 229–33, for an analysis of this poem in terms of Heaney's auditory imagination.
34. R. Kearney, "Language Play," 83.
35. Heaney, "Threshold and Floor," 267; my emphasis.
36. Heaney, "Mossbawn," 23.

37. Heaney, "Amputation."
38. Ibid.
39. Heaney, "On Hogarth's Engraving."
40. Despite the violence it portrays, "On Hogarth's Engraving," part of which was later incorporated into a longer poem about cockfighting, "Triptych for the Easter Battlers," actually suggests the existence of a secretive community across the cultural/political/religious divide in Northern Ireland. "Triptych" opens with the speaker noting that "it drew them compulsively as a lover" and observing that "five counties prepared themselves with caution." Heaney has pointed out that "all sides attended the fights. And because the fights were illegal, a special bond was created among the aficionados" (SS, 131).
41. Lloyd, *Anomalous States*, 21.
42. Heaney, "Odin's World," 82.
43. Ibid., 80.
44. H. O'Donoghue, "Heaney, *Beowulf*," 198.
45. Ibid., 200.
46. For a full account of Stone's attack on the funerals of three IRA members shot by the British Special Armed Services (SAS) in Gibraltar, and then the reprisal attack on British Army corporals Derek Wood and David Howe during the funeral of Kevin O'Brady, who was killed pursuing Stone after his onslaught, see McKittrick et al., *Lost Lives*, 1117–24.
47. Wood, *Yeats and Violence*, 24.
48. I discuss how the advice of the Viking longship to the speaker in "North" by using the compound "word-hoard" (*N*, 11) was "a kenning for the poet's vocabulary in Anglo-Saxon times" that "signals Heaney's recognition of his rich, archipelagic, truly northern geographical heritage and his desire to burrow into it for poetic inspiration" in my *Poetry and Peace*, 230, 230–32.
49. H. O'Donoghue, "Heaney, *Beowulf*," 195.
50. The much better known poem critiquing the Shankill Butchers is Michael Longley's "The Butchers," modeled on passages from the *Iliad*, books 22 and 24, where Odysseus murders the suitors. I discuss the sectarian context of this poem in *Poetry and Peace*, 113–16.
51. H. O'Donoghue, "Heaney, *Beowulf*," 194.
52. Joyce, *Portrait of the Artist*, 253.
53. B. O'Donoghue, *Seamus Heaney*, 72.
54. Russell, *Poetry and Peace*, 220–24.
55. Heaney, *Bog Poems*, title page.
56. Heaney, preface to *Bog Poems*, n.p.
57. Heaney, "Bogland," 6.
58. Heaney, "North" [typescript].
59. Heaney, "January Review."
60. Heaney, "Hughie O'Donoghue Exhibition."

61. Heaney, "Mossbawn," 18.
62. Ibid., 19.
63. Ibid.
64. Heaney, "Poem Is Landscape."
65. Heaney, "Feeling into Words," 57.

Chapter Five. Darkness Visible

1. Heaney, "Confessions and Histories," 22.
2. Ibid., 22–23.
3. Brannigan, *Race*, 6.
4. Ibid., 181. See his discussion of this process in America on 180–81.
5. See Heaney, "Murmur of Malvern," 5, his review of Walcott's 1979 volume, *The Star-Apple Kingdom*.
6. Heaney, "Irish Quest," 46.
7. Berry, *Hidden Wound*, 19.
8. Ibid.
9. Morrison, *Seamus Heaney*, 23.
10. Elliott, *Catholics of Ulster*, notes that journalist David McKittrick's study in March of 1993 revealed that half of the province's "residents lived in areas which were over 90 per cent one religion (often reflecting a three-fold increase during the Troubles), that less than 110,000 of its 1.5 million populace lived in truly mixed areas and that even these might be divided by the so-called peacelines" (432).
11. Heaney, "Belfast," 31.
12. Ibid., 33.
13. Intriguingly, Heaney's early poems "Digging," "Storm on the Island," and "Scaffolding" were published in the December 4, 1964, issue of *New Statesman* when Martin Luther King Jr. was advertised as speaking in London as part of an event sponsored by an English group called "Christian Action." I am grateful to Rosie Lavan for pointing out this connection to me. The ad for King's talk appears on p. 876 of that issue, while Heaney's poems appear on p. 880.
14. Heaney, "Views," 903.
15. Harris, *Exorcising Blackness*, 23–24.
16. His poem "Freedman" links Roman imperialism to Northern Irish Protestant/British imperialism but also critiques the imperialist cast of the Catholic Church. In that poem, employing language very similar to that used in the O'Driscoll interview just cited, Heaney's speaker recalls being "subjugated yearly under arches" and concludes his second stanza, after recalling having the cross impressed on his forehead on Good Friday, with "I was under the thumb too like all my caste" (*N*, 55).
17. Heaney, "Strange Fruit" [holograph and early typewritten drafts].

18. In ibid, an early holograph version of the poem is dated December 19, 1972.
19. Vendler, *Seamus Heaney*, 48.
20. E. Longley, "*North*," 45, 46. Corcoran, *Poetry of Seamus Heaney*, views the phrase positively too, observing that "the five adjectives there are simple and abjectly descriptive, aiming at nothing more than statement, standing up against any tendency to mythologization, whether religious or literary" (74).
21. B. O'Donoghue, *Language of Seamus Heaney*, 75.
22. Vendler, *Seamus Heaney*, 48.
23. Hall, *Seamus Heaney's Rhythmic Contract*, 84.
24. Heaney, "Strange Fruit" [holograph and early typewritten drafts].
25. Ibid.
26. Heaney, "Man and the Bog," n.p.
27. Heaney, "Strange Fruit" [holograph and early typewritten drafts].
28. Ibid.
29. Ibid.
30. See the section entitled "An Ulster Prophecy" in Montague, *Rough Field*: "A severed head speaking with a grafted tongue" (29). The entire fourth section of *The Rough Field* is also called "A Severed Head"; the section is introduced with a woodcut from John Derricke's *A Discovery of Woodkarne*, featuring a presumably English soldier holding a severed head of an Irishman and this rhyme: "And who ever heard / Such a sight unsung / As a severed head / With a grafted tongue?" (31). For the best reading of this section, see Parker, *Northern Irish Literature*, 158–62.
31. Heaney, *Personal Selection*, n.p.
32. Litton, *Celts*, 33.
33. Heaney, "Feeling into Words," 58.
34. Quoted in ibid., 59.
35. Ibid.
36. Heaney experienced a much more benign, even beneficent counterpart to such public spectacles when he went to Lourdes in 1958 on the Derry Diocesan Pilgrimage. While there, he and his cousin carried stretchers and pushed wheelchairs, and Heaney was often an altar boy (*SS*, 288). His remarks suggest his strong awareness even as a teenager about the power that a religiously inspired crowd was capable of generating: "I was susceptible, of course, to the surge of crowd emotions, the big choral responses to the rosary, the hymns, and the druggy fragrance off flowers and candles in the grotto itself" (289).
37. Sanburn, "All Time 100 Songs."
38. Hall, *Seamus Heaney's Rhythmic Contract*, 84.
39. Meeropol, "Strange Fruit."
40. Curtis, *Apes and Angels*.
41. See my analysis of the poem in *Poetry and Peace*, 204, 206–7. See also Heaney's discussion of the school in *Stepping Stones*, 242–47.

42. See, for example, Heaney's essay "Old Derry's Walls," where he equates the two civil rights movements after the participants in the October 5, 1968, march were beaten by the Royal Ulster Constabulary and after Protestants and Catholics united in a subsequent protest march at Queen's University on October 9: "The new 'Londonderry Air' sounds very much like 'We shall overcome'" (523). For the postcolonial approach, see Kiberd's *Inventing Ireland*, passim; Kiberd employs Fanon's *Wretched of the Earth* as one of his guiding theories, for example, in his analysis of John Synge's *Playboy of the Western World*.

43. Heaney, "Strange Fruit" [holograph and early typewritten drafts].

44. Ibid.

45. Fanon, *Black Skin, White Masks*, 110.

46. Ibid., 112.

47. DuBois, *Souls of Black Folk*, argues that "the Negro is . . . born with a veil, and gifted with second-sight in this American world,—a world which yields him no true self-consciousness, but only lets him see himself through the revelation of the other world. It is a peculiar sensation, this double-consciousness, this sense of always looking at one's self through the eyes of others, of measuring one's soul by the tape of a world that looks on in amused contempt and pity. One ever feels his twoness,—an American, a Negro; two souls, two thoughts, two unreconciled strivings; two warring ideals in one dark body, whose dogged strength alone keeps it from being torn asunder" (214–15).

48. For a thorough explanation of how this process occurred in the American South and how the southern writer William Faulkner portrayed it, see my essay "Black Passages."

49. Fanon, *Black Skin, White Masks*, 134.

50. Heaney, "Strange Fruit" [holograph and early typewritten drafts].

51. I would like to thank the graduate students in my seminar on Brian Friel, Seamus Heaney, and Bernard MacLaverty at Baylor University in the spring of 2011 for helping me to perceive how these three parts of the poem are shaped.

52. Harris, *Exorcising Blackness*, 23.

53. Heaney was drawn repeatedly to the image of rotten or dead fruit. In his television script "Bogland," he recalls that the pots, pans, and kettles "hung like black fruit in the mouth of the chimney" in the traditional Irish cottage kitchen (9–10). After writing "Strange Fruit," he would describe "a black rat / [that] Sways on the briar like infected fruit" in the ninth lyric of "Glanmore Sonnets" (*FW*, 41), an image that itself recalls the "rat-grey fungus" of the spoiled blackberries when "the fruit fermented, the sweet flesh would turn sour" in "Blackberry-Picking" (*DN*, 8). An early draft of what would become "Strange Fruit" refers to the girl's head as "this bog-fruit" ("Strange Fruit" [holograph and early typewritten drafts]).

54. Harris, *Exorcising Blackness*, 23.

55. Ibid., 2, notes that "burning, mutilation, *gathering trophies*, and initiating children" were all part of the lynching ritual (my emphasis).

56. Siculus, *Diodorus Siculus*, bk. 1, ch. 83, 287. Hart, *Seamus Heaney*, notes that Diodorus's history had a "didactic purpose ... to snub democracy and applaud the strong man in history, as well as the 'good life' made possible by him" (96).

57. Litton, *Celts*, cites Siculus on this issue: "They embalm in cedar-oil the heads of the most distinguished enemies and preserve them carefully in a chest and display them with pride to strangers saying that for this head one of their ancestors, or his father, or the man himself, refused the offer of a large sum of money. They say that some of them boast that they refused the weight of the head in gold" (quoted on 33).

58. I cannot find the passage in Siculus where he makes this admission, but Litton, *Celts*, cites the similar confession by Posidonius, that Strabo, a near-contemporary of Siculus, gives in his *Geography*, where he discusses the tendency of the northern tribes to cut off their enemies' heads, hang them from their horses' necks, and then, having arrived at home, nail them to their doors: "At any rate Posidonius says that he himself saw this spectacle in many places, and that, although at first he loathed it, afterwards through his familiarity with it, he could bear it calmly" (34).

59. Corcoran, *Poetry of Seamus Heaney*, 75.

60. Sontag, *Regarding the Pain of Others*, 91.

61. Cunliffe, *Ancient Celts*, 210.

62. Žižek, *Violence*, 61.

63. Longenbach, *Resistance to Poetry*, 10.

64. Ibid., 97.

65. See Heininger, "Making a Dantean Poetic," 50 (52–60 for his reading of "Ugolino") and McCarthy, *Seamus Heaney*, 53 (53–85 for his reading of Dante's importance to Heaney).

66. Cavanagh, *Professing Poetry*, notes that Heaney started reading Dante seriously in 1972, after he moved to the Republic (145).

67. McCarthy, *Seamus Heaney*, 57–58, argues that Heaney added the lines about "sweet fruit" and like "some spattered melon" to connect this concluding poem with the opening poem of the volume: "The narrative of one man eating another in the world below in revenge for crimes committed in the world above counterpoints the opening poem of the book, 'Oysters,' with its explicit reminder that the oysters being eaten are alive."

68. Heininger, "Making a Dantean Poetic," 56.

69. Harmon, "Seamus Heaney," 11.

Chapter Six. Border Crossings

1. Heaney noted "that at first he had considered reading his prose poem 'The Wanderer,' which recalls the day he won a scholarship to St. Columb's College in Derry—'a lifetime achievement award I received at the age of 12'" (Flood, "Seamus Heaney").

2. Hall, *Seamus Heaney's Rhythmic Contract*, 117.
3. Murphy, *Tradition of Subversion*, 85–86.
4. Fredman, *Poet's Prose*, 3.
5. Hart, *Seamus Heaney*, 100–101. The passage he cites is from a personal letter Heaney wrote him on August 17, 1988.
6. Heaney, "Threshold and Floor," 267.
7. Edson, "Interview," n.p.
8. Hart, *Seamus Heaney*, 115.
9. Jones, preface to *In Parenthesis*, xv.
10. Jones's strange, fragmentary poetry was certainly on Heaney's mind at this time: he concludes his review of *The Penguin Book of Pastoral Verse*, originally published as "In the Country of Convention" in the *Times Literary Supplement* in 1975, with a series of suggestions of poets whose work should have been included, citing two poems from Jones's *The Sleeping Lord and Other Fragments* (1974) as potential candidates for inclusion in this collection of pastoral verse—"The Sleeping Lord" and "The Tutelar of the Place" (180).
11. Heaney, preface to *Stations*, 3.
12. Brandes and Durkan, *Seamus Heaney*, 314. These prose poems were published in *Exile* 2, nos. 3 and 4 (1975): 107–20. Brandes and Durkan note that "all of the poems appear with revisions in *Stations* except 'Ballad' and 'Turas.' 'Turas' was collected as 'Stations of the West' in *Stations* and *Selected Poems 1966–1987*. 'Alias' was collected with revisions as 'Incertus' in *Stations* and *Selected Poems 1966–1987*" (314).
13. Brandes and Durkan, *Seamus Heaney*, 313.
14. Quoted in ibid.
15. See Heaney, "Interview with Seamus Heaney" [Randall], 16: "With *North* and *Wintering Out* I was burrowing inwards and those thin small quatrain poems, they're kind of drills or augers for turning in and they are narrow and long and deep."
16. Fredman, *Poet's Prose*, vii–viii.
17. See Heaney, "North" [typescript].
18. Ibid.; *North*, 56.
19. See Heaney, *Seamus Heaney*, 29–31.
20. In making changes from their appearance in Fiacc's anthology for their publication in *North*, Heaney rendered "Whatever You Say, Say Nothing" without the medial comma and retitled "From Singing School" as "The Ministry of Fear," making it the first section of the larger poem "Singing School."
21. Heaney, "Romanist," 44.
22. I am citing the English Standard Version.
23. Ibid.
24. Even in 2013, he is still pondering the Golden Rule in his poem "On the Gift of a Fountain Pen," when he muses, "All that 'Do unto others / As you would have done unto you'? / Mistaken? Virtue?"

25. Parker, "From *Winter Seeds*," 130.
26. Russell, "Exorcising the Ghosts," 53. The cuts to power and other utilities launched by the Ulster Workers' Council in mid- to late May of 1974 led Northern Irish prime minister Brian Faulkner to resign on May 28, which effectively dissolved the nascent Assembly set up by the December 1973 Sunningdale Agreement. Heaney specifically identifies the collapse of Sunningdale in his Nobel Prize address as the moment when his hopes and those of others for a peaceful solution to Northern Ireland's violence died for twenty years:

> Until the British government caved in to the strong-arm tactics of the Ulster loyalist workers after the Sunningdale Conference in 1974, a well-disposed mind could still hope to make sense of the circumstances, to balance what was promising with what was destructive and do what W. B. Yeats had tried to do half a century before, namely, "to hold in a single thought reality and justice." After 1974, however, for the twenty long years between then and the ceasefires of August 1994, such a hope proved impossible. The violence from below was then productive of nothing but a retaliatory violence from above, the dream of justice became subsumed into the callousness of reality, and people settled in to a quarter century of life-waste and spirit-waste, of hardening attitudes and narrowing possibilities that were the natural result of political solidarity, traumatic suffering and sheer emotional self-protectiveness. (*CP*, 17)

27. See Hufstader, *Tongue of Water*, on the issue of Heaney's recasting of what Hufstader sees as unblemished Wordsworthian spots of time in these prose poems. In his reading of the prose poem "Patrick and Oisin," Hufstader holds that Heaney "proposes the traditional Christian view that underneath the camouflage of cultural discourse we must look within universal human experience for the realities of moral behavior. The reason why spots of spotless time cannot be found is that we are always spotted" (29). For an example of Heaney's continuing interest in Wordsworthian spots of time, see his 2008 essay "'Apt Admonishment,'" particularly his observation about poetic encounters with the uncanny, which he terms "an experience of confirmation, of the spirit coming into its own, a door being opened or a path being entered upon. . . . A strange thing happens. A spot of time becomes a spot of the timeless, becomes . . . one of 'the hiding places of power'" (21).
28. I would note that although I came to this reading of Heaney on my own, Hart invokes Blake's statement that "without Contraries is no progression" in the title of his study *Seamus Heaney* and at one point in the body of that work describes his entire study as Blakean in this sense (119).
29. Heaney, "Irish Quest," 46.
30. Meek, "Commentaries," n.p.
31. Young, "Commentaries," n.p.
32. Ibid.
33. Caws, "Prose Poem," 977.
34. Benedikt, introduction to *Prose Poem*, 48.

35. Marcus, "Essay," n.p. Caws agrees with both Benedikt and Marcus, arguing that "the prose poem aims at knowing or finding out something not accessible under the more restrictive conventions of verse" ("Prose Poem," 978).

36. Indeed, returning to *Stations* after many years of reading Heaney's canonical poems, I was startled to realize that Heaney borrowed and recast his own phrase—"it never could be toppled"—for the end of his explicitly political poem "The Toome Road," which features a speaker who meets and is annoyed by presumably British soldiers in "armoured cars" but then concludes by musing, ode-like, "O charioteers, above your dormant guns, / It stands here still, stand vibrant as you pass, / The invisible, *untoppled* omphalos" (*FW*, 15; my emphasis). Tobin, *Passage to the Center*, 151–52, has pointed out this self-borrowing.

37. G. Boyd, "Commentaries," n.p.; Benedikt, introduction to *Prose Poem*, 47.

38. Calinescu, *Rereading*, 18.

39. Ibid., 19.

40. Simon Sweeney's bow saw that he carries symbolizes the lyre of the poet; Heaney also increasingly likened himself to the Irish mythological figure of Sweeney during the 1980s through his translation of the Irish epic *Sweeney Astray* in 1983 and in Part III of *Station Island*, where he identifies with the figure of Sweeney Redivivus.

41. See "Faith of Our Fathers."

42. See Barr, "Catholics in England," n.p., who mentions Ralph Thomas Campion Stonor, the seventh Lord Camoys, "a title bestowed on an ancestor for valor in the Battle of Agincourt in 1415."

43. Murphy, *Tradition of Subversion*, 3.

44. Hufstader, *Tongue of Water*, 29.

45. Ibid., 30; Hufstader's emphasis.

46. Murphy, *Tradition of Subversion*, 4.

47. "Kerne," *OED* online.

48. See Heaney, "Lost Ulstermen," for his review of Montague's volume. The illustrations on the original cover of *The Rough Field* and the ones that introduce each section of the poem "are details from John Derricke's *A Discoverie of Woodkarne* (1581). Captioned in doggerel verse, these twelve woodcut plates depict the life of the Irish in Ulster and Sir Henry Sidney's campaigns [over three years] against them" (87).

49. "Glib," *OED* online. Denis Donoghue, "Literature of Trouble," 189, points out that Heaney uses *glib* in this way in describing the way the "blanket bog" in "Belderg" is "stripped off": then "The soft-piled centuries // Fell open like a glib" (*N*, 4).

50. "Glib," *OED* online. Under part "b" of the first definition of *glib* as a noun in the *OED*, a quotation from J. Nott's *Dekker's Gulls Horn-book* is given to illustrate its adaptation as an adjective: "These wood-karne went with glibbed heads, or wearing long bushy hair over their eyes."

51. In the later prose poem "Ballad," which concerns the death of a young boy at the hands of the local police, a similar conflation of water and blood imagery opens the first paragraph: "Blood ran a jeweled delta down the back of the lorry..." (*S*, 21).

52. Heaney later identifies these returned neighbors in this prose poem as "the demobbed Evans brothers arriving on our doorstep with the rosary beads for my father" (*SS*, 180). The Evans brothers appear again in "Edward Thomas on the Lagans Road" (*DC*, 36).

53. Hart, *Seamus Heaney*, 115. Vendler, *Seamus Heaney*, 81, notes that while "the [sectarian] stereotypes are still present ... something else 'dips and lifts' in the passage—the fact that the Protestant neighbor has thought of Patrick Heaney when he was away at war, that he has brought back as a gift something he thought the recipient would like—a rosary, and a generously big one. The two men will not be able to go farther into amiability than their awkward joking; but the son hails it none the less as the marking out of an intermediate territory where Catholic and Protestant might feel neighborly good will for each other rather than enmity."

54. See Heaney's use of comparable avian language in "Viking Dublin: Trial Runs," which also employs the word *trial* in its title: first, he gives the more positive phrase about writing, equating it to "a bill in flight" (*N*, 12), and then the beckoning invitation to "Come fly with me" (14) to see how a series of hate-mongers "spread out your lungs / and made you warm wings for your shoulders" (15).

55. Hart, *Seamus Heaney*, 105, 118. Anne Stevenson, however, dismissively terms them "twenty-one ... self-conscious entries in a diary of personal memories.... We are left wanting either more autobiography or more art; or perhaps *less* art and more context, more 'reality'" ("*Stations*," 50). If Heaney has left behind the sense of himself as "Incertus," Stevenson sees this as a sign that *Stations* is "a stage in the progress of the poet towards mastery of all the material he calls experience." But she is not convinced that he has, holding that "there is enough evidence, even in *North* and *Field Work*, to suggest that 'Incertus' is Heaney's worst enemy" (51). Stevenson's antipathy toward ambiguity and toward the form of the prose poem indicates a typically Western desire for control over the workings of our subconscious minds and over the artistic process. Why is it so bad for Heaney to retrospectively admit that he was a shy, uncertain writer when he began? Why is it so bad, by extension, for him to admit uncertainty about the role of the artist in a time of violence, and further, to uncertainty in writing in a new genre at such a time?

56. Calinescu, *Rereading*, xiii.
57. Casey, *Remembering*, 286.
58. Fredman, *Poet's Prose*, 3.
59. Terdiman, *Discourse/Counter-Discourse*, 343, quoted in Murphy, *Tradition of Subversion*, 202.

60. Murphy, *Tradition of Subversion*, 202. Murphy explores William Carlos Williams's *Kora in Hell* and John Ashbery's *Three Poems* in different chapters of her study and believes they function to open up such democratic vistas.

Chapter Seven. Joyce, Burns, and Holub

1. Heaney, "Place of Writing," 20. Kay, *In Gratitude*, instead maintains that "Heaney's visionary turn exists in response to poetic developments on the other side of Europe [eastern Europe]" (4). While Kay's study is truly groundbreaking in its assessment of the importance of eastern European poets for Heaney's development of artistic independence and his so-called visionary turn, she does not give enough credence to the Irish poets such as Yeats and Kavanagh, whose late, spiritual work was also exemplary for Heaney.
2. Russell, *Poetry and Peace*, 266; the Heaney quotation occurs in "Place of Writing," 20.
3. Heaney, "Regional Forecast," 13.
4. Ibid.
5. Heaney, *Place and Displacement*, 16; my emphasis.
6. Russell, *Poetry and Peace*, 210; the Heaney passage is from *WO*, 37.
7. Heaney, *Among Schoolchildren*, 10.
8. Ibid.
9. Ibid., 11.
10. Ibid.
11. Ibid., 12.
12. Ibid., 13.
13. Ibid.
14. Heaney, "Tradition," 196.
15. Ibid.
16. Ibid., 196, 197.
17. Johnston, *Irish Poetry after Joyce*, 31.
18. See, too, the portion of Heaney's review of *An Duanaire* concerned with Thomas Kinsella's translation of these Gaelic poems into English, where he links the urban Kinsella with the urban Joyce. Pointing out that Kinsella has found "a denser, more laconic, more indigenous way with the poetic line," he notes further that "when I say 'indigenous,' I do not mean the alternative charm of some kind of 'Irish note' but rather something genetic at the roots of Kinsella's own Dublin speech. In fact, the rhythms of Joyce's prose are finally more relevant to his endeavour than the metrics and assonances of the native tradition" ("Poems of the Dispossessed," 32).
19. Crawford, *Devolving English Literature*, 262.
20. Ibid., 262–63. Heaney is certainly capable of his own "demotic language" too: Vendler argues that he "bursts into demotic language in 'Whatever You Say, Say Nothing' and 'Station Island'" (*Breaking of Style*, 68).

21. Heaney, introduction to *Padraic Fallon*, 13. In *An Open Letter*, Heaney again resorts to the image of holding course between these mythical monsters in attempting to assert his Irishness without causing too much fuss: "So let's not raise a big hubbub. / Steer between Scylla and Charyb / A middle way that's neither glib / Nor apocalyptic" (*AOL*, 12).

22. Heaney, "Joyce's Poetry," 423.
23. See Richtarik, *Acting between the Lines*, 146–64, passim.
24. Ibid., 147.
25. Ibid., 147–48.
26. Heaney, "Frontiers of Writing," 201–2.
27. Tange, "Regional Redemption," 77.
28. Heaney, "Through-Other Places," 400–401.
29. Heaney, speaking on the BBC radio program "Whatever You Say Say Nothing."
30. Richtarik, *Acting between the Lines*, 157.
31. Quoted in ibid., 159.
32. A. O'Malley, *Field Day*, 7.
33. Heaney, *Place and Displacement*, 9; my emphasis.
34. Brandes, "Seamus Heaney's Working Titles," 26.
35. Heaney, "Frontiers of Writing," 201.
36. "Heaney to Publish Epic Poem," 8.
37. Heaney, "Joyce's Poetry," 424.
38. Joyce, "Gas from a Burner," 103. In his brief reading of adulterous betrayal in Joyce's *Ulysses*, David Lloyd argues that Joyce's obsession with Parnell's betrayal "underlines the extent to which adultery is also an historical and political issue for Irish nationalism. The common tracing of the first Anglo-Norman conquest of Ireland in 1169 to the adulterous relationship between Diarmaid Mac-Murchadha, King of Leinster, and Dearbhghiolla, the High King's wife, establishes adulteration as a popular myth of origins for Irish nationalist sentiment" (*Anomalous States*, 106). Indeed, Heaney addresses this very myth in stanza 25, where he states that "the cuckold's impotent in Leinster / House" (*AOL*, 12).
39. Crawford, *Devolving English Literature*, 103.
40. Ibid., 99. See Crawford's discussion on 99–100 of Burns's mocking attitude toward the Church of Scotland ministers and rhetoric professors William Greenfield and Hugh Blair.
41. B. O'Donoghue, *Seamus Heaney*, vii. O'Donoghue cites "Meeting Seamus Heaney," 63.
42. Henry Hart has pointed out to me that Robert Frost and Ted Hughes were also strong antiacademic models for Heaney, with Hughes famously calling academia "academentia."
43. Brogan, "Burns Stanza," 153.
44. B. O'Donoghue, *Seamus Heaney*, 27.

45. Heaney, "Open Letter," n.p.; henceforth cited parenthetically in the text as "AOL."

46. Even if Heaney's protest was more of a secondary issue in the poem, O'Driscoll, "Heaney in Public," believes that "recent anthologies from major United Kingdom publishing houses bear titles and subtitles which take account of Heaney's protest. *The Firebox*, Sean O'Brien's anthology from Picador in 1998, was subtitled *Poetry in Britain and Ireland* after 1945, while the same year saw publication of the *Penguin Book of Poetry from Britain and Ireland* since 1945, edited by Simon Armitage and Robert Crawford" (57). Certainly, Heaney himself seems to prefer such a nomenclature: Richtarik, *Acting between the Lines*, notes that "he later assigned the Morrison and Motion anthology to a class he taught at Harvard—'British and Irish Poetry, 1930–1980'" (148).

47. See my discussion in *Poetry and Peace*, 208–9, of why Heaney has Macmorris voice the question, "What ish my nation?" and then has Joyce's Leopold Bloom answer, "'Ireland'. . . / 'I was born here. Ireland'" (*WO*, 32) in that poem.

48. Dolan, *Dictionary of Hiberno-English*, 95, 120.

49. Donaghmore Historical Society, "Words and Expressions."

50. Dolan, *Dictionary of Hiberno-English*, 210.

51. See Joyce's "The Dead," in *Dubliners*, 188, 190.

52. Richtarik, *Acting between the Lines*, 148; O'Driscoll, "Heaney in Public," 57.

53. "So rudely forc'd" occurs on lines 100 and 205, and "Tereu" occurs in line 206 of "The Waste Land" (*T. S. Eliot*, 56, 61).

54. In his image of the twins here, Heaney may well have been remembering not only Yeats's "Leda and the Swan" but also Paul Muldoon's playful poem "The Mixed Marriage," which revisits the myth of Leda's rape. In his 1978 review of Muldoon's volume *Mules* Heaney cites "The Mixed Marriage," and its second stanza, along with Muldoon's suggestion about the potentially troubled outcome of a mixed religious marriage, may have stayed with Heaney and influenced him in his depiction of Leda's twins and the image of twins in "the hurt North": "My mother was the school mistress, / The world of Castor and Pollux, / There were twins in her own class. / She could never tell which was which" (quoted in Heaney, "Mixed Marriage," 211).

55. See Kiberd, *Inventing Ireland*, 315, where he claims "the possibility of interpreting the swan as the invading English occupier and the girl as a ravished Ireland," partly because of the date given by Yeats at the end of his poem, 1923, during which the so-called civil war in Ireland continued to rage between those forces who recommended Ireland be satisfied with its newly independent twenty-six counties (the Free-Staters) and those who still wanted the six counties in the North to be part of the new Free State (the Die-Hards). Kiberd goes on to speculate that the poem's debate about Leda's consent recalls the cliché "that the Irish were colonizable because they secretly wished others to take command of their lives. The poem might then be read as a study of the calamitous effects of the

original rape of Ireland and of the equally precipitate British withdrawal" (315). See my essay "W. B. Yeats," 113–15, for a critique of Kiberd's position here.

56. B. O'Donoghue, *Seamus Heaney*, 93.

57. Joyce, *Ulysses*, 1.135–36, 1.146. Joyce is referencing, through Stephen, Oscar Wilde's statement in "The Decay of Lying": "I can quite understand your objection to art being treated as a mirror. You think it would reduce genius to the position of a cracked looking-glass." See Thornton, *Allusions in "Ulysses,"* 14.

58. Heaney, "Sense of Place," 141: "Both Kavanagh and Montague explore a hidden Ulster, to alter Daniel Corkery's suggestive phrase, and Montague's exploration follows Corkery's tracks in a way that Kavanagh's does not."

59. Heaney, *Among Schoolchildren*, 10.

60. Heaney, "Sense of Place," 141.

61. In the first draft of *An Open Letter*, Heaney privileges the issue of naming more by featuring the Holub narrative much earlier—in stanzas 8 through 12—and by also including along with the epigraph from Bachelard a second epigraph from Holub's statement in "On the Necessity of Truth": "The right name is the first step toward the truth which makes things things and us us" ("AOL").

62. Further evidence that Heaney was thinking of *An Open Letter* in the context of both Field Day and Joyce's broadside poems comes from his remarks preceding his poetry reading celebrating the publication of the *Field Day Anthology of Irish Literature*. In his "Holograph Notes," Heaney read a series of poems from the *Field Day Anthology* and concluded with Joyce's "Gas from a Burner," which was reproduced in the *Anthology*.

63. Molino, *Questioning Tradition*, 124.

64. Heaney, "Fully Exposed Poem," 50.

65. Kay, *In Gratitude*, 25; Kay's emphasis.

66. Heaney, "Poems of the Dispossessed," 31.

67. Heaney, "Interesting Case," xx.

Chapter Eight. Affirming and Transcending Regionalism

1. B. O'Donoghue, *Seamus Heaney*, 151–52.
2. J. Foster, *Forces and Themes*, 18.
3. Ibid., 17.
4. Heaney, "Tale of Two Islands," 11.
5. Ibid., 12.
6. Ibid.
7. Similarly, Heaney told Deaglan de Breadun in a 1984 interview, "Comfortable Image," that Carleton's autobiography "still stands in some way for the experience of people in the 20th-Century Ulster" (13).

8. For a sustained reading of "Casualty" that considers O'Neill an exemplary artistic figure who rejects what Heaney came to see as a restrictive Northern Irish Catholic solidarity, see my *Poetry and Peace*, 239–45.

9. See ibid., 233, for an analysis of this line. Heaney would employ a close variant of the adjective again in "Parable Island," a poem that examines the issue of the border in Northern Ireland from a mythological standpoint, from his next volume, *The Haw Lantern*, to refer to the "forked-tongued natives" (*HL*, 10).

10. In "From the Canton of Expectation" in *The Haw Lantern*, Heaney recalls in his second stanza this generally passive nationalism he was exposed to in his youth:

> Once a year we gathered in a field
> of dance platforms and tents where children sang
> songs they had learned by rote in the old language.
> An auctioneer who had fought in the brotherhood
> enumerated the humiliations
> we always took for granted, but not even he
> considered this, I think, a call to action.
> Iron-mouthed loudspeakers shook the air
> yet nobody felt blamed. He had confirmed us.
> (*HL*, 46)

11. Joyce, *Portrait of the Artist*, 180.
12. Russell, *Poetry and Peace*, 259.
13. For my quote, see ibid., 260.
14. For an exemplary interpretation of Stephen's unconscious understanding of himself as Icarus, see Thornton, *Antimodernism*, 144–45.
15. Ludwig, "Province and Metropolis," 62–63.
16. Ibid., 64.
17. Heaney, "Redress of Poetry," 6–7.
18. Ibid., 7.
19. McCarthy, *Seamus Heaney*, 70–71.
20. Heaney, "Regional Forecast," 17–18. Notice his emphasis again on the "indigenous" tradition, which Heaney argued Kinsella had tapped through Joyce in his essay on Kinsella's translations of Irish poetry cited in the previous chapter.
21. Homem, *Poetry and Translation*, 50.
22. Heaney, *Poems and a Memoir*, 7, 8.
23. In "Feeling into Words," Heaney argues that the word *undine* itself was transformative, "a field of force that called up other images," going on to term the myth "as being about the liberating, humanizing effect of sexual encounter" (53).
24. Homem, *Poetry and Translation*, 49, observes that Heaney's translations of these three cantos were "considerably less provocative than his 'Ugolino,'

and rhetorically much closer to a conventionally scholarly translation," although Heaney aligns these translations with his earlier work at times, as when he translates the second line of the *Inferno* as "I found myself astray in a dark wood." As Homem argues, "This description of Dante's anxiety at losing his way retroactively emphasizes the wanderings of Sweeney [Heaney's translation of *Buile Suibhne*] . . . while it also reminds readers of Heaney's concern with continuity and coherence in his writing" (49).

25. Cavanagh, *Professing Poetry*, 158.
26. S. Stewart, "Dante," 39.
27. Ibid.
28. Cavanagh, *Professing Poetry*, 145, cites this interview, "*Pausa per la riflessione*," 72, as evidence of Heaney's interest in Dante through Sayers's translation.
29. Heaney, "Note about 'Belderg,'" 129. Earlier in this note, he states that Caulfield "was like one of those guardian figures in myths and fairy tales whose function is to lead the quester across the frontier into a new world, as Virgil leads Dante into the land of the dead in *The Divine Comedy*."
30. Canto 1, lines 100–102; Heaney's parenthetical identification misstates that the epigraph is from lines 100–103.
31. Parker, *Seamus Heaney*, 259 n. 26.
32. Quoted in Hurley, "Interpreting Dante's *Terza Rima*," 326–27.
33. Carson, introduction to *Inferno*, xi–xii.
34. Sayers, introduction to *Comedy [Hell]*, 34. Heaney almost certainly knew this long and rich introduction, since he had read Sayers's translation of *The Divine Comedy* so thoroughly.
35. Ibid., 37. Although I independently arrived at the conclusions that Heaney was drawn to Dante because of that poet's exilic condition and his ability to see both sides of political issues, I was pleased to find confirmation in Cavanagh, *Professing Poetry*, 146, who argues, "What was appealing to Heaney in Dante was his exile and the fact that in exile Dante was, though political, ostentatiously nonpartisan between Guelph and Ghibelline."
36. On this point, see B. O'Donoghue, *Seamus Heaney*, 154, where he observes that Heaney's "passing discussion of Eliot's Dante in 'Envies and Identifications' . . . gives as much clue to the essence of his own aesthetic philosophy as anything he writes. For example, his puzzlement that Eliot did not make more of the Guelf/Ghibelline side of Dante—his reconciliation of Church and State—is itself puzzling: Eliot's political-cultural pronouncements were never revealing. But the point is, Heaney's *are* revealing."
37. Heaney, "Heaney on Dante," 16.
38. Ibid.
39. See Heaney, "Canto I, Canto II, Canto III," 3–15. Some passages of these three cantos are closer to the original terza rima than others. The opening three tercets of canto 2, for example, all feature full rhymes in their first and third lines,

and the end word of the second line of the second tercet, "duty," does set the end rhymes of "me" and "faculty" in the next tercet (7).

40. Sayers, introduction to *Comedy [Purgatory]*, 9.
41. Ibid., 10.
42. Heaney and Hass, *Sounding Lines*, 4.
43. Corcoran, *Poetry of Seamus Heaney*, 124–25.
44. Heaney, "Government of the Tongue," 94.
45. Ibid. See the very similar language in the opening essay from *Government of the Tongue*, "Interesting Case," where Heaney asserts that Mandelstam believed that "the essential thing for the lyric poet was . . . a condition in which he was in thrall to no party or programme, but truly and freely and utterly himself. . . . Mandelstam implied that *it was the poet's responsibility to allow poems to form in language inside him, the way crystals formed in a chemical solution*. He was the vessel of language" (xix; my emphasis). Heaney uses similar language about crystals in "Envies and Identifications" (1985), 18: "Dante is not perceived [by Mandelstam] as the mouthpiece of an orthodoxy but rather as the apotheosis of free, natural, biological process, as a hive of bees, *a process of crystallization*, a hurry of pigeon flights, a focus for all the impulsive, instinctive, non-utilitarian elements in the creative life" (my emphasis). In his revised and truncated version of "Envies and Identifications" for *Finders, Keepers* (2002), 178, he significantly retains almost verbatim this entire sentence. All other references to "Envies and Identifications" in this chapter refer, however, to the original 1985 essay.
46. Quoted in Heaney, "North" [typescript].
47. Cuda, "Use of Memory," 153.
48. Heaney, "Place, Pastness, Poems," 47.
49. Ibid.
50. Hart, *Seamus Heaney*, 161–62.
51. Heaney, "Impact of Translation," 43.
52. See my discussion of this ethical issue in Russell, *Poetry and Peace*, 214–27.
53. Heaney, "Impact of Translation," 38.
54. See Corcoran, *Poetry of Seamus Heaney*, 115–16. Corcoran, *Poets of Modern Ireland*, does mention again Heaney's essay on Dante, terming it (as of 1999), "probably Heaney's most significant uncollected essay" (111). See Corcoran's discussion there of Heaney's reaction to Joyce in the twelfth section of "Station Island," 107–8 and 110–20, and particularly on Eliot's use of Yeats in "Little Gidding," 119–20.
55. Heaney, "Envies and Identifications," 8.
56. Ibid.
57. Ellis, introduction to *Dante Alighieri: Hell*, x.
58. Ibid.
59. Carson, introduction to *Inferno of Dante Alighieri*, xxi.

60. Hurley, "Interpreting Dante's *Terza Rima*," 329.
61. Heaney, "Envies and Identifications," 14–16.
62. Hurley, "Interpreting Dante's *Terza Rima*," 322.
63. See Heaney, "Makings of a Music," 65, where after reading a passage from Hazlitt on Wordsworth's penchant for composing as he walked, he notes about "the motion of Wordsworth's blank verse" that "the swing of the poet's body contributed as well to the sway of the voice." Shortly after this, he observes about "The Ruined Cottage" that "there is a cumulative movement in the Pedlar's lines that does not so much move the narrative forward as intensify the lingering meditation, just as the up and down walking does not forward a journey but habituates the body to a kind of dreamy rhythm." And he finally characterizes the skating passage in book 1 of *The Prelude* as having a "pacing" stemming from "a slow, gathering but not climactic movement, repetitive but not monotonous, a walking movement," further holding that "we might say, in fact, that Wordsworth at his best . . . is a pedestrian poet" (68).
64. Heaney, "Regional Forecast," 22; "Envies and Identifications," 12.
65. Heaney, "Sense of Place," 136–37.
66. "Envies and Identifications," 13.
67. Ibid., 12.
68. Heaney, "Fire i' the Flint," 85. See my essay "Keats and Hopkins Dialectic" for an exploration of this aspect of Hopkins.
69. B. O'Donoghue, *Seamus Heaney*, 151.
70. Corcoran, *Poetry of Seamus Heaney*, 124.
71. Ibid., 124 n. 7.
72. See also Heaney's affirmation of Eliot's regionalism in "Learning from Eliot," when he speaks of Eliot's use of Dante in "Ash Wednesday" (1930): "They are not hostages taken from *The Divine Comedy* and held by Eliot's art in the ascetic compound of his poem. They actually sprang up in the pure mind of the twentieth-century poet and their in-placeness does not derive from their having a meaning transplanted from the iconography of the medieval one" (31).
73. Heaney, "Regional Forecast," 22. The use of *indigenous* in reference to language is always a term of approval for Heaney.
74. Eliot, "Social Function of Poetry," 19.
75. Eliot, "Music of Poetry," 29.
76. Ibid., 31.
77. Ibid. Heaney must have approved of Eliot's memory of hearing Yeats read his own poetry as a proof case for his theory of poetry's necessity for remaining in contact with the living rhythms of speech (31–32).
78. Eliot, *Notes toward a Definition*, 128.
79. Ibid., 127.
80. Heaney, "Learning from Eliot," 35.
81. McCarthy, *Seamus Heaney*, 71.

82. Zillman and Scott, "*Terza Rima*," 1271.

83. This is another departure from Dante's heavy use of end-stopped stanzas: according to Robey, "*Terza Rima*," 809, "The vast majority of the poem's lines are end-stopped; the opposite feature of *enjambment* is comparatively rare."

84. B. O'Donoghue, *Seamus Heaney*, 100, has pointed out that "the end of the Strathearn apparition—'and he trembled like a heatwave and faded' [*SI*, 80]—is a reworking of Eliot's 'and faded on the blowing of the horn,' which in turn is a modernization of the form of a canto's typical last line in *Inferno*."

85. See Ellmann, "Heaney Agonistes," 165, where he argues about the appropriateness of Heaney meeting Joyce's shade, not Yeats's, here: "It seems fitting that Heaney should find his model not in Yeats, constantly trying to break through the façade of what is, but in Joyce, who 'found the living world enough' if sufficiently epiphanized. Joyce's message is a reaffirmation, with the authority of an immortal, of what Heaney has meant in speaking of himself as 'an inner émigré' and claiming a migrant solitude."

86. B. O'Donoghue, *Seamus Heaney*, 99.

87. Corcoran, *Poets of Modern Ireland*, 114.

88. Heaney has stated that he intended the pilgrim to "leave the island renewed, with liberating experience behind him and more ahead. The pattern always was the simple one of setting out, encountering tests[,] and getting through to a new degree of independence; on such matters, Joyce is our chief consultant" (*SS*, 249). Notice that Heaney affirms Joycean independence here but qualifies it with the preceding phrase "a new degree of." Similarly, in his interview with Deaglan de Breadun, "Comfortable Image," Heaney states approvingly that "Joyce, I would say, is politically, in terms of an independent Ireland, the most important writer we have, because he establishes forms for saying what we are," but then immediately states, "He is a kind of intellectual *Sinn Feiner*," a remark that suggests Joyce's extreme autonomy, as does his later comment, "The intonations of his work, the shapes, the modes.... They are discovered entirely by himself, for himself" (13).

89. Corcoran, *Poets of Modern Ireland*, 205 n. 18.

90. Hart, *Seamus Heaney*, 163.

91. Molino, *Questioning Tradition*, 168.

92. Ibid., 168–94.

93. Heaney, "Impact of Translation," 43–44.

94. Heaney, "Cornucopia and Empty Shell," 54.

95. Corcoran, *Poetry of Seamus Heaney*, 148; Helen Vendler, *Seamus Heaney*, 115.

96. Heaney, "Cornucopia and Empty Shell," 55.

97. Ibid.

98. Johnston, *Irish Poetry after Joyce*, 29; For Manganiello's point, see his *Joyce's Politics*, 232.

99. Crawford, *Devolving English Literature*, 287.

Chapter Nine. The Northern Irish Context and Owen and Yeats Intertexts in The Cure at Troy

The epigraph from the interview "Seamus Heaney (January 2010)" is taken from p. 207.

1. Heaney, "Seamus Heaney" [interview by Faller et al.], 50. For a compelling earlier discussion of how Heaney widens his native cultural and linguistic ambit to include Joyce and Greek culture, specifically through Heaney's use of *omphalos* in his early essay "Mossbawn," see E. O'Brien, *Seamus Heaney and the Place of Writing*, 31–44.
2. Heaney, "Drag of the Golden Chain," 14.
3. Heaney, "*Cure at Troy*," 175; my emphasis.
4. Heaney, "Drag of the Golden Chain," 16.
5. Ibid., 14; my emphasis.
6. In a further sign of his desire to emphasize the process of translation, Heaney at one point had planned to substitute the last dialogue between Carbery and King Cormac in Kuno Meyer's translation of the ninth-century Irish piece "The Instructions of King Cormac" for Auden's "As I Walked Out One Evening" as epigraph to the play (Heaney, "Alternative Epigraph"). He finally retained Auden's lines about loving "your crooked neighbor / With your crooked heart" (*CT*, n.p.).
7. Turner, "Sophocles or Heaney," 133.
8. Peacock, "Mediations," 237–38. Heaney narrated the script and Stephen Rea voiced the character of Sweeney.
9. Ibid., 233.
10. Heaney, "Extending the Alphabet," 20–22.
11. Ibid., 29.
12. Heaney, "Chester Pageant," 58–60.
13. Heaney, "On Poetry and Professing," 74.
14. Ibid., 73.
15. Heaney, *Among Schoolchildren*, 7.
16. Friel, "Brian Friel," 187.
17. Ibid.
18. Ibid., 190.
19. Ibid., 185.
20. Heaney, "Sparks," 3.
21. Cavanagh, *Professing Poetry*, 57.
22. Heaney, "Healing Fountain," 8.
23. Corcoran, *Poetry of Seamus Heaney*, 188.
24. Wilson, "Philoctetes," 224.
25. Corcoran, *Poetry of Seamus Heaney*, 188.
26. Quoted in Heaney and Hass, *Sounding Lines*, 23.

27. Richtarik, *Acting between the Lines*, 13.
28. Although Whelan, "Between the Politics," points out, citing Heaney's *Cure*, that "the Philoctetes figure since the eighteenth century has become a symbol of Catholic Ireland, amputated from the body politic by the Penal Laws, which deprived them of political participation from the Glorious Revolution (1688) until Catholic Emancipation (1829)," Heaney's representation of him and comments about him elsewhere show that he considers his Philoctetes to clearly represent both unionist and nationalist communities in Northern Ireland.
29. Scarry, *Body in Pain*, 53.
30. But Heaney, in his poem "In Memoriam Francis Ledwidge," collected in *Field Work*, does signify the Catholic Ledwidge's estrangement while alive from "true-blue" Northern Irish Protestants who also fought in World War I: "You were not keyed or pitched like these *true-blue* ones / Though all of you consort now underground" (*FW*, 60; my emphasis).
31. Heaney, "The Cure at Troy," 175. Cavanagh argues in *Professing Poetry*, 103, that "Heaney has spoken critically of writing inspired by what he considers victimage; his sardonic reference in the 1997 *Paris Review* interview to the 'swank of deprivation' as something that annoys him about modern writing would seem to preclude a poetry that enumerates colonial oppressions." Heaney's use of the word *swank* in relation to victimhood and deprivation suggests he has no patience for those who wallow in their suffering.
32. Parker, *Seamus Heaney*, 270 n. 161.
33. Peacock, "Mediations," 234.
34. Scarry, *Body in Pain*, 161, 162.
35. McBride, *Siege of Derry*, 18.
36. Ibid., 72–73.
37. Heaney, "Frontiers of Writing," 187.
38. Elliott, *Catholics of Ulster*, 427.
39. Heaney, "Envies and Identifications," 5.
40. Owen, preface to *Poems*, 192.
41. Yeats, introduction to *Oxford Book*, xxxiv.
42. Owen, preface, 192. Heaney, "Interview with Seamus Heaney" [Brandes], 8. He quotes the same sentence from Owen in his essay "Sounding Auden," 112.
43. Brandes and Durkan, *Seamus Heaney*, B129 and C594, respectively. For a critical essay treating Heaney and Ledwidge, see Lojek, "Man, Woman, Soldier."
44. Haughey, "Partitioned Memories," 184.
45. See Russell, "Owen and Yeats," 177, for a close reading of Heaney's "Exposure" through Owen's poem of the same name, and 177–78, for many other examples of Owen references in Heaney's poetry.
46. Owen, *Poems*, 126.
47. Ibid.
48. Heaney, "Redress of Poetry," 2–3.
49. Ibid., 8.

50. See McKenna, "Green Fire," 116, for a thoughtful metrical reading of how Neoptolemus's desire to deceive Philoctetes, represented by "a pentameter or hexameter, mostly iambic rhythm," later changes to "short lines" including the "excited spondees" employed by Heaney when Philoctetes allows Neoptolemus to touch the bow.

51. Owen, *Poems*, 123.

52. Heaney, "Atlas of Civilization," 177.

53. Owen, *Poems*, 123.

54. Taplin, "Sophocles' Philoctetes," notes that "here Heaney turns three lines of Greek anapests (a semi-lyric metre) into two six-line stanzas and a pendent extra line" (166).

55. C. P., "Poems by Wilfred Owen."

56. Heaney, "Envies and Identifications," 6.

57. Owen, preface to *Poems*, 192.

58. Heaney, "Interesting Case," xvi. The citations of Owen's lines occur on pp. xiv and xv.

59. Yeats, *Collected Poems*, 181.

60. Ibid., 181.

61. For more on Yeatsian fluidity, see Bedient, *Yeats Brothers*, passim.

62. Heaney, "Yeats's Nobility," 12.

63. A. O'Malley, *Field Day*, 120. Both O'Malley, 120, and the present author, in *Poetry and Peace*, 303–8, chart numerous specific instances of how and in what context these lines have been quoted.

64. Heaney, "Healing Fountain," 7.

65. Russell, *Poetry and Peace*, 306.

66. A. O'Malley, *Field Day*, 131.

67. Although I arrived at this reading on my own, I was pleased to find it confirmed in E. O'Brien, *Seamus Heaney and the Place of Writing*. From reading Heaney's adaptation through Derrida's *Acts of Literature*, and his essay "On Responsibility," O'Brien suggests that "translation . . . is the vehicle that allows us to achieve this putative transformation, becoming a way not of erasing the original but of keeping the original alive. It is a way of 'translating oneself into the other language without giving up one's own language.' . . . It is . . . a way of transforming the temporal orientation of a culture from the past to the present, as the old tongue becomes transformed into the new tongue, which points toward a politics of the future" (125). See also A. O'Malley, *Field Day*, who, drawing on John Caputo and Richard Kearney's critique of Derrida's concept of hospitality, gift economy, and forgiveness (129–31), masterfully argues how, "through the act of forgiveness, history is replaced with the temporality of hope, and so hope comes to rhyme with hope" (130). O'Malley concludes that "it is only if hope and history are understood as containing the possibility of rhyming that the utopian drive of this idea (and of the 'fifth province') has meaning and stays relevant to political discourse" (131).

68. Auden, *Collected Poems*, 134.
69. Ibid.
70. Ibid., 135.
71. Heaney, *Place and Displacement*, 22.
72. Heaney, "Interview with Seamus Heaney" [Gammage], 5.
73. Bew and Gillespie, *Northern Ireland*, 104, 212, 246.
74. Deane, introduction to *Birmingham Six*, 11; my emphasis.
75. Ibid., 10.
76. Heaney, "Hope Is Something," n.p.

Chapter Ten. Guttural and Global

The epigraph from Heaney's "The Guttural Muse in a Global Age" is taken from p. 13.

1. Draper, *Introduction*, 185.
2. J. Foster, "Crediting Marvels," 223 n. 14.
3. Cavanagh, *Professing Poetry*, 44.
4. Heaney, "Further Language," 13.
5. Anderson, *Imagined Communities*, 44.
6. Ibid., 44, 45.
7. Corcoran, *Poetry of Seamus Heaney*, 210.
8. Heaney, "John Clare's Prog," 63.
9. Ibid.
10. Ibid.
11. Ibid., 64.
12. Ibid., 65.
13. Ibid., 68; my emphasis.
14. Heaney, "Frontiers of Writing," 195.
15. Ibid., 196.
16. Hewitt, *Collected Poems*, 303.
17. Ibid., 540. The title of this late poem comes from Hewitt's "The Colony," where the speaker disturbingly notes of Catholics in the North that "they breed like flies. The danger's there; / when Caesar's old and lays his scepter down, / we'll be a little people, well outnumbered" (78). Hewitt himself, however, is clearly dramatizing a common fear among Protestants in the province; his own position is expressed in the last stanza: "I think these natives human, think their code, / though strange to us, and farther from the truth, / only a little so," and desires to "make amends / by fraternizing, by small friendly gestures," to convince others that "if [we are] not kin," then we are "co-inhabitants" (79).
18. Ibid., 541.

19. Heaney, "Frontiers of Writing," 198.
20. Heaney, "Through-Other Places," 406.
21. Ibid., 407.
22. Ibid.
23. Heaney, "Through-Other Places," 409, and "Poetry of John Hewitt," 210.
24. For a more generous view of the implications of Hewitt's regionalism, see J. Foster, "Radical Regionalism," where he draws a fascinating comparison, not between Northern Ireland and French Quebec as Hewitt does here, but between Northern Ireland and the Canadian West, following George Melnyk's 1981 book, *Radical Regionalism.* Foster argues that "Hewitt's belief that Ulster culture should be 'no mere echo of the thought and imagination of another people or another land' is echoed in Melnyk's claim that 'a whole people's consciousness of itself is repressed (therefore inauthentic) when its identity is determined elsewhere, when it comes from without rather than from within. A culture is inauthentic when it is the expression of the other, rather than the self.' Melnyk's region, like Hewitt's, must be no mere hinterland" (293–94).
25. Quoted in Schuchard, introduction to *Place of Writing,* 9–10.
26. Mahon, *Collected Poems,* 17.
27. See M. Longley, "Neolithic Night," and MacNeice, *Louis MacNeice.*
28. Clark, *Ulster Renaissance,* 133.
29. Heaney, "Pre-natal Mountain," 43.
30. Ibid., 44.
31. Ibid., 46.
32. Heaney, "Frontiers of Writing," 198–99.
33. Corcoran, *Poetry of Seamus Heaney,* 216.
34. Heaney, "Pre-natal Mountain" (44–45; my emphases).
35. The poem appeared in the *New Yorker.* See Brandes and Durkan, *Seamus Heaney,* 359.
36. Heaney, preface to *Derry and Londonderry,* xxiii.
37. Heaney, "Frontiers of Writing," 199.
38. Ibid.
39. Ibid.
40. Ibid., 200.
41. Joyce, *Dubliners,* 172. For "quincunx," the *OED* also gives as its third definition of the word an even more Catholic connotation: "A reliquary having a folding construction on a quincuncial pattern."
42. Heaney, "Frontiers of Writing," 200.
43. Yet Corcoran, *Poetry of Seamus Heaney,* 218–19, is right to point out that "the attempt at inclusiveness in the figure [of the quincunx] and the liberality of its recognitions and invitations are, however, to some degree vitiated by the fact that the actual architecture of the quincunx is a military architecture: the towers, castles and keeps are the permanent reminders, in the Irish landscape and

in the Irish literary tradition, that this is ground that has been fought over, and that the battles, still going on, have left permanent scars."
44. Heaney, "Through-Other Places," 398.
45. Heaney, foreword to *School Bag*, xvii.
46. Benjamin, "Task of the Translator," 76.
47. Homem, *Poetry and Translation*, 50.
48. Heaney, quoted in Corcoran, *Student's Guide*, 40.
49. Russell, *Poetry and Peace*, 250–52. Hart's chapter, "Heaney's Sweeney," in his very fine study, *Seamus Heaney*, 138–58, remains compulsory reading for those wishing to fully appreciate the complexity of Heaney's affinity for Sweeney. For instance, after surveying Heaney's recognition of many landmarks that the mythical figure flits among in *Buile Suibhne*, Hart elegantly observes, in a compelling section on Heaney's own unease and sense of exile after moving to the Republic of Ireland, that "topographical affinities aside, Heaney must have felt a profound psychological bond with the Celtic king who fled from battles in Ulster to take up the more solitary ardors of contemplation and poetry in the South" (140). And Homem, *Poetry and Translation*, 41, has intelligently pointed about Heaney's *Sweeney Astray* that "the avowed ambition that a new version of a medieval tale of events in Ulster might contribute to a better intercultural and intersectarian understanding brings it into line with the strategy of juxtaposing present and past adversities that defined *North*."
50. Heaney, "Earning a Rhyme," 70. He admits as much on p. 68 of this same essay: although he claims that "a certain intensity gathered through the steadier, more lexically concentrated gaze at individual words" when he started reshaping "stanzas from scratch," his statement that "the unit of composition now became the quatrain itself and the metrical pattern became more end-stopped and boxed in" suggests the "new asceticism" Heaney mentions shortly after (69).
51. Ibid., 70, 65.
52. Heaney, *Beowulf*, n.p.
53. Heaney, introduction to *Beowulf*, xxvi.
54. Ibid., xxvii.
55. Heaney, "Funeral Eulogy," n.p.
56. Heaney, introduction to *Beowulf*, xxvii; "Funeral Eulogy," n.p.
57. Heaney, introduction to *Beowulf*, xxii.
58. H. O'Donoghue, "Heaney, *Beowulf*," 202.
59. Heaney, introduction to *Beowulf*, xxii.
60. Ibid., xxiii.
61. Ibid., xxv; my emphasis.
62. Ibid.
63. Ibid.
64. Ransom, "Honey and Gall," 123.
65. Heaney, "Place, Pastness, Poems," 47.
66. Heaney, introduction to *Beowulf*, xxix.

67. Ibid., xxix–xxx. As he explains, "In Elizabethan English, bawn (from the Irish *bó-dhún*, a fort for cattle) referred specifically to the fortified dwellings that the English planters built in Ireland to keep the dispossessed natives at bay, so it seemed the proper term to apply to the embattled keep where Hrothgar waits and watches. Indeed, every time I read the lovely interlude that tells of the minstrel singing in Heorot just before the first attacks of Grendel, I cannot help thinking of Edmund Spenser in Kilcolman Castle, reading the early cantos of *The Faerie Queene* to Sir Walter Raleigh, just before the Irish would burn the castle and drive Spenser out of Munster back to the Elizabethan court. Putting a bawn into *Beowulf* seems one way for an Irish poet to come to terms with that complex history of conquest and colony, absorption and resistance, integrity and antagonism, a history that has to be clearly acknowledged by all concerned in order to render it ever more 'willable forward / again and again and again'" (xxx).

68. Heaney, "Drag of the Golden Chain," 15.
69. Quoted in ibid.
70. Heaney, *Beowulf*, 45.
71. Heaney, "Drag of the Golden Chain," 15–16.
72. Heaney, "Bog," 21.
73. Heaney, "Drag of the Golden Chain," 16.
74. Heaney, "Feeling into Words," 54.
75. Ibid., 54–55.
76. Heaney, "Bog," 21.
77. Heaney, *Beowulf*, 60.
78. Kennedy, *Beowulf*, 60.
79. Heaney, introduction to *Beowulf*, xv.
80. Ibid., xxi.
81. Heaney, "Through-Other Places," 414.
82. Ibid., 415.
83. Heaney, introduction to *Beowulf*, xiv; see xiv–xv for the full discussion.
84. Deane, "Famous Seamus," 66.
85. Heaney, "Interview with Seamus Heaney" [Wylie and Kerrigan], 134.
86. Heaney, "Frontiers of Writing," 196.
87. J. Foster, *Achievement of Seamus Heaney*, 34.
88. Heaney, "Impact of Translation," 40.
89. Ibid.
90. Ibid., 41.
91. Ibid., 44. Heaney's stance here borrows heavily from the language and argument of Hobsbaum, "Road Not Taken."
92. Heaney, introduction to *Diary*, n. p.
93. Robinson, *Instabilities*, 123. For excellent treatments of Heaney's affinities with Russian and eastern European poets, see Kay, *In Gratitude*, and Bugan, *Seamus Heaney*.

94. Heaney, "Unheard Melodies," n.p.

95. See McCarthy, *Seamus Heaney*, 130–31, for a discussion of Heaney's translation of this poem, specifically how he perceives the commonality between the lingering presence of the Gaelic *aisling* or dream vision in "Hallaig" and the medieval "dream-vision tradition" of Langland's Middle English *Piers Plowman*, which demonstrates how he refuses "the separation of Gaelic and English-language literary traditions" (131).

96. Heaney, introduction to *Sorley Maclean*, 2.

97. Heaney, "Burns's Art Speech," 378.

98. Ibid., 379.

99. Heaney, "Burns's Art Speech," 384.

100. Ibid.

101. Ibid., 386. For the complete translation of "An Bonnán Buí," see Heaney, "Yellow Bittern."

102. Heaney, "Torchlight Procession," 103.

103. Ibid., 104. Space does not permit even a cursory discussion of the development and devolution of twentieth-century Scottish literature, but helpful treatments are available in D. Hewitt, "Scoticisms and Cultural Conflict"; in Kimpel, "Beyond the Caledonian Antisyzygy"; in the chapter "Regional, National, and Post-Colonial" in Draper's *Introduction*; throughout Crawford's enormously far-ranging and thoughtful *Devolving English Literature*, which focuses on Scottish literature as his case study; and in Thurston's "Region and Nation," 81–86. Kimpel is especially helpful for her overview of Muir, MacDiarmid, MacLean, MacCaig, and Edwin Morgan.

104. Heaney, "Through-Other Places," 411–12. Not everyone is as convinced of the viability of the "Four Nations" approach as Kearney, other historians, and Heaney are. For instance, Colley, "Britishness and Otherness," argues that "such an approach can reduce Britishness to the interaction of four organic and invariably distinct nations.... As such, it can sit comfortably not only with Welsh, Scottish, and Irish nationalism, but also with a newly assertive English nationalism.... The Four Nations approach, if pushed too hard or too exclusively, is an incomplete and anachronistic way to view the British past and, also, a potentially parochial one. It conceals, if we are not too careful, the fact that the four parts of the United Kingdom have been connected in markedly different ways and with sharply varying degrees of success.... There is considerable evidence that at grass-roots level the Welsh, the Scottish, and the English saw (and often still see) the Irish as alien in a way that they did not regard each other as alien" (314).

105. Ibid., 398. In this regard, Heaney has endorsed the schoolmaster Hugh's line, "My friend, confusion is not an ignoble condition," which he utters toward the end of Brian Friel's play *Translations*. See his "Brian Friel," 239.

106. J. Foster, "Radical Regionalism," 284.

107. Heaney, "On Elegies, Eclogues," 27.

108. I discuss the potentially unifying tongue that Heaney articulates in "Broagh" and in other poems from *Wintering Out* and in Heaney's preface to *Sweeney Astray* in *Poetry and Peace*, 202–10 and 250–52.

109. Heaney, "On Elegies, Eclogues," 27.

110. Heaney, introduction to *Robert Henryson*, xiii–xiv.

111. Heaney, "On Elegies, Eclogues," 27.

112. McCarthy, *Seamus Heaney*, 134, 135.

113. Heaney, introduction to *Robert Henryson*, xiv.

114. Heaney, *Robert Henryson*, 3.

115. Ibid.

116. Heaney, introduction to *Robert Henryson*, vii.

117. Ibid., xii.

118. McCarthy, *Seamus Heaney*, 140. McCarthy cites Heaney's discussion of the keening Geat woman at the end of *Beowulf* in Heaney's introduction to his translation of the poem along with Heaney's pointing out that his motivation for translating *Antigone* in 2004 was his recall of "the opening lines of Eibhlín Dubh Ní Chonaill's lament, an outburst of grief and anger from a woman whose husband had been cut down and left bleeding on the roadside in Co. Cork, in much the same way as Polyneices was left outside the walls of Thebes, unburied, desecrated, picked at by the crows. . . . I made a connection between the wife traumatized by the death of her husband at the hands of the English soldiery at Carriganimma and the sister driven wild by the edict of a tyrant in Thebes" (140, citing Heaney's "Story That Sings," n.p.).

119. See my reading of "Punishment" through the lens of Christian ethics and Elaine Scarry's theory of ethical beauty in *Poetry and Peace*, 219–27.

120. See Burris, "Reading Heaney Reading," 69–70, for an analysis of the passage in *Crediting Poetry* about atrocities in "Ulster and Israel and Bosnia and Rwanda and a host of other wounded spots on the earth" (*OG*, 457–58). Burris argues that widespread media dissemination of such images "threatens to overwhelm the artist's traditional capacity for celebration. . . . He fears that with the world so much with us, so emblazoned across our TV screens, the evidence for the destructive potential of human nature has nearly outweighed the informing hope of all art: the hope that our constructive capacity will finally prevail, and that poetry, in Heaney's case, will stand as an eloquent testimony to the expressive and ennobling side of human endeavor."

121. Heaney, "Guttural Muse," 11.

122. Ibid., 12.

123. Ibid.

124. Ibid.

125. Ibid., 13.

126. Ibid., 13–14.

127. Appadurai, *Modernity at Large*, 197.

128. Ibid.
129. Ibid., 198.
130. Ibid., 195.
131. Heaney, "Seamus Heaney (January 2010)," 205.
132. Ibid.
133. Heaney, "Guttural Muse," 15.
134. Heaney, "Time and Again," 23.
135. S. Stewart, *Poetry*, 330.
136. Ibid.
137. Casey, "How to Get from Space," 26.
138. Heaney, "Interview with Seamus Heaney" [Gammage], 7.
139. Heaney, "Bog," 22.
140. Heaney, "Place, Pastness, Poems," 30.
141. Ibid., 30–31.
142. Heaney, "Seamus Heaney" [in *Humanizing the City*], 87–88.
143. Ibid., 88.
144. Eliot, *T. S. Eliot*, 39. Although I articulated this reading independently, I find it confirmed in Homem's *Poetry and Translation*, 32.

Chapter Eleven. "*My Ship of Genius Now Shakes Out Her Sail*"

The first epigraph, from Heaney's *Stepping Stones*, is taken from p. 470; the second, from R. P. Blackmur's "Wallace Stevens: An Abstraction Blooded," is taken from p. 213.

1. Heaney, "Regional Forecast," 19.
2. Ibid., 20.
3. Ibid., 21.
4. Ibid., 21–22.
5. Ibid., 22.
6. Ibid.
7. Heaney, "Hope Is Something," n.p.
8. Ferriter, *Transformation of Ireland*, 733.
9. Quoted in ibid., 739.
10. Heaney, "'Hope Is Something,'" n.p.
11. Heaney, "Frontiers of Writing," 192.
12. Ibid., 193.
13. Ibid., 203.
14. Heaney, "Placeless Heaven," 13.
15. Ibid., 13, 13–14.
16. Ibid., 14.

17. Heaney, "In the Light," 14.
18. Heaney, "'Apt Admonishment,'" 21.
19. Ibid.
20. Ibid.
21. Ibid.
22. Ibid., 21–22.
23. Ibid., 25.
24. Ibid.
25. Heaney, "Between North and South," 103.
26. Ibid., 104; my emphasis.
27. Heaney, "Yeats as an Example?," 113.
28. Heaney, "Mixed Marriage," 213. Heaney is quoting Stevens's statement in *Sur Plusieurs Beaux Sujets*, excerpted in *Wallace Stevens: Collected Poetry and Prose*, 915.
29. Heaney, "Yeats as an Example?," 100.
30. Heaney, "Redress of Poetry," 1. He also cites Stevens shortly thereafter, when he approvingly states that Stevens believed "the poet to be a potent figure because the poet 'creates the world to which we turn incessantly and without knowing it, and . . . gives life to the supreme fictions without which we are unable to conceive of [that world]'" (2).
31. Blackmur, "Wallace Stevens," 213.
32. Vendler, *Seamus Heaney*, 122.
33. Heaney, "Place, Pastness, Poems," 40.
34. Heaney, introduction to *Beowulf*, xxiv; my emphasis.
35. Vendler, *Seamus Heaney*, notes, when discussing how Heaney's stoicism in a cluster of poems from *The Spirit Level* such as "Keeping Going" differed from Stevens's stoicism in poems such as "The Snow Man," that "Heaney's temperament is more sanguine than Stevens's, more social, more wedded to the possibilities of hope and trust and mutual help" (158).
36. Heaney, "Dylan the Durable?," 137.
37. Ibid., 138, 139.
38. Ibid., 139.
39. Hurley, "Interpreting Dante's *Terza Rima*," 322.
40. Booth, "Turf Cutter," 378, believes, however, that calling these units of sounds "tercets" is misleading: "The audible narrative flow of *terza rima*, with its interwoven rhymes . . . disappears with the general abandonment of the middle rhyme of each tercet, leaving (usually) a half-rhyme on the first and third lines. If the ear succeeds in picking up the pararhymes, what is heard is a sequence of baggy couplets of irregular line length. In the "Squarings" sequence [from *Seeing Things*], the 'tercet' divisions are even more purely typographical since rhyme is absent, and stanzas are regularly enjambed into each other."
41. Hurley, "Interpreting Dante's *Terza Rima*," 322.

42. Sayers, introduction to *Comedy [Hell]*, 56.
43. Alighieri, *Comedy [Hell]*, 73.
44. Cavanagh, *Professing Poetry*, 212–13.
45. Ibid., 237.
46. Lee, "Gundestrup Cauldron."
47. Heaney, "Seeing Things," 28.
48. Vendler, *Seamus Heaney*, 114–15.
49. Heaney, "Seeing Things," 29–30.
50. Tóibín, review of *Human Chain*, n.p.
51. Hobsbaum, *Metre, Rhythm*, 125.
52. Cavanagh, *Professing Poetry*, 194.
53. Molino, *Questioning Tradition*, 165.
54. Ibid.
55. This is not the place to rehearse Heaney's ill-judged argument against Larkin and in favor of Yeats in that essay, but at this point (in 1990) he does not seem to have been aware of Larkin's negative comments about him in his *Selected Letters*, which were not published till 1992.
56. As Daniel Donoghue, "Philologer Poet," 240, has pointed out, this procession of compound words in the poem suggests Heaney's links to two literary exemplars I have earlier argued are deeply regional: Gerard Manley Hopkins and the *Beowulf* poet.
57. "Dower," *OED* online.
58. King James translation.
59. Ibid.
60. Grennan, "Seamus Heaney's Book," n.p.
61. Donne, *Complete English Poems*, 54, 53.
62. Keats, *Poems*, 371.
63. Donne, "XVII. Meditation," 68.
64. Heaney, "Above the Brim," 74.
65. Vendler, *Breaking of Style*, 41.
66. Ibid., 43.
67. McDonald, *Serious Poetry*, 149, 149–52.
68. Ibid., 152.
69. Heaney, "Seamus Heaney: The Words Worth Saying," 104. My argument follows that of Cavanagh, *Professing Poetry*, who offers the more accurate image for Heaney's sense of form than McDonald does with his incomplete image of a fortified building. After dwelling on the same passage from Heaney on Yeatsian ottava rima that McDonald does (227), Cavanagh turns to Heaney's argument about poetic form being both the ship and the anchor in *Crediting Poetry*, concluding, "The image of a vessel bobbing on the water is a remarkable complication of the image of the poem as anchor—or, indeed, as a room or tower, but a complication expected in a writer who wants to communicate poetry's intimate contact with ex-

perience, its lightness, grace, and fragility, as well as its power to sustain and the sense it offers of enclosure or fixity" (229).
70. Heaney, *Stepping Stones* (Audiobook).
71. Heaney notes in ibid. that "a beggar shivering" is the soul waiting for judgment.
72. Heaney, introduction to *Redress of Poetry*, xiii.
73. Ibid., xv.
74. I discuss the implications of this poem for Heaney's aesthetic much more fully in *Poetry and Peace*, 267–68.
75. Tobin, *Passage to the Center*, 258–59.
76. Heaney, "Joy or Night," 158.
77. Parker, *Seamus Heaney*, 118, dates Heaney and Longley's participation in this march.
78. Heaney may also have been influenced to write about this passage from his reading of Wallace Stevens's "The River of Rivers in Connecticut," which clearly draws on and revises Dante's passage with lines like "There is a great river this side of Stygia," and "But there is no ferryman" (*Collected Poems*, 533).
79. Homem, *Poetry and Translation*, 51.

Afterword. Visiting the Dead and Welcoming Newborns

The epigraph from Fitzgerald's "Postscript" to *The Aeneid* is taken from p. 417.

1. Fussell, *Poetic Meter*, 132.
2. S. O'Brien, review of *Human Chain*, n.p.
3. Heaney, "Unhappy and at Home," 72.
4. Fitzgerald, "Postscript," 408.
5. Toíbín, review of *Human Chain*, n.p.
6. See the first line proper of Montague, *Rough Field*: "Catching a bus at Victoria Station" (10). Heaney remarks upon this narrative device in his review of Montague's volume "Lost Ulstermen": "The poem begins with a bus journey out of Belfast into the outback of upland Tyrone" (550).
7. Parker, "'Back in the Heartland,'" 376.
8. Virgil, *Aeneid* 6.414, 421–23.
9. McKittrick et al., *Lost Lives*, 134.
10. Virgil, *Aeneid* 6.854–56.
11. Ibid., 860–63.
12. Kellaway, review of *Human Chain*, n.p.
13. Heaney, "On Home Ground," 21.
14. A more immediate source for the translation was Heaney's own poem "A Kite for Michael and Christopher," written for his two sons in 1979 and collected

in *Station Island*. See "On Home Ground," 19–20, for a discussion of how he was inspired to undertake the Pascoli translation by the birth of Michael's daughter and a recollection of his kite poem for his sons. Pascoli became a major influence on Heaney's last poems: while this book was in production, Peter Fallon's Gallery Press published in December 2013 a posthumous collection of Heaney's translations from Pascoli entitled *The Last Walk*.

15. Toíbín, review of *Human Chain*, n.p.

Bibliography

Adamson, Ian. *Cruithin: The Ancient Kindred.* Newtonards: Nosmada, 1974.

———. *The Identity of Ulster: The Land, the Language and the People.* Belfast: Pretani, 1982.

———. *Ulster People: Ancient, Medieval, and Modern.* Belfast: Pretani, 1991.

Alexander, J. H. "Wordsworth, Regional or Provincial? The Epistolary Context." In *The Literature of Region and Nation*, edited by R. P. Draper, 24–33. New York: St. Martin's Press, 1989.

Alighieri, Dante. *The Comedy of Dante Alighieri the Florentine. Cantica I: Hell.* Translated by Dorothy L. Sayers. London: Penguin, 1965.

———. *The Comedy of Dante Alighieri the Florentine. Cantica II: Purgatory.* Translated by Dorothy L. Sayers. London: Penguin, 1980.

Allen, Michael. "Bleak Afflatus!" Review of *Poets from the North of Ireland*, edited by Frank Orsmby. *Threshold*, no. 31 (Autumn–Winter 1980): 82–87.

———. "The Parish and the Dream: Heaney and America, 1969–1987." *Southern Review* 31, no. 3 (1995): 726–38.

———. "Provincialism and Recent Irish Poetry: The Importance of Patrick Kavanagh." In *Two Decades of Irish Writing: A Critical Survey*, edited by Douglas Dunn, 23–36. Chester Springs, PA: Dufour, 1975.

Anderson, Benedict. *Imagined Communities.* Rev. ed. 1991. Reprint, London: Verso, 1996.

Appadurai, Arjun. *Modernity at Large: Cultural Dimensions of Globalization.* Minneapolis: University of Minnesota Press, 1996.

Auden, W. H. *Collected Poems.* Edited by Edward Mendelson. New York: Vintage, 1991.

Auge, Andrew. "'A Buoyant Migrant Line': Seamus Heaney's Deterritorialized Poetics." *LIT: Literature Interpretation Theory* 14, no. 4 (2003): 269–88.

Bardon, Jonathan. *A History of Ulster.* Belfast: Blackstaff Press, 1992.

Baron, Michael. "Heaney and the Functions of Prose." In *Seamus Heaney: Poet, Critic, Translator*, edited by Ashby Bland Crowder and Jason David Hall, 74–91. New York: Palgrave, 2007.

Barr, Robert. "Catholics in England Suffered Long Repression." *Free Republic*, September 11, 2010. www.freerepublic.com/focus/f-religion.

Barthes, Roland. *Mythologies.* Translated by Annette Lavers. New York: Hill and Wang, 1994.

Bedient, Calvin. *The Yeats Brothers and Modernism's Love of Motion.* South Bend, IN: University of Notre Dame Press, 2009.
Benedikt, Michael. Introduction to *The Prose Poem: An International Anthology*, edited by Michael Benedikt, 39–50. New York: Dell, 1976.
Benjamin, Walter. "The Task of the Translator: An Introduction to the Translation of Baudelaire's *Tableaux Parisiens*." In *Illuminations: Essays and Reflections*, edited and introduced by Hannah Arendt, 69–82. New York: Schocken, 1969.
Berry, Wendell. *The Hidden Wound.* San Francisco: North Point Press, 1989.
Bew, Paul, and Gordon Gillespie. *Northern Ireland: A Chronology of the Troubles, 1968–1999.* Dublin: Gill and Macmillan, 1999.
Blackmur, R. P. "Wallace Stevens: An Abstraction Blooded." In *Form and Value in Modern Poetry*, 213–17. Garden City, NY: Doubleday, 1952.
Booth, James. "The Turf Cutter and the Nine-to-Five Man: Heaney, Larkin, and 'the Spiritual Intellect's Great Work.'" *Twentieth-Century Literature* 43, no. 4 (Winter 1997): 369–93.
Boyd, Greg. "Commentaries: Edouard's Nose." *The Prose Poem: An International Journal* 8 (1999): n.p. http://digitalcommons.providence.edu/prosepoem/vol8/iss1/67/.
Boyd, John. "Comment." *Lagan* 2 (1944): 11–12.
———. "Comment." *Lagan* 3 (1945): 11.
———. Interview by Richard Rankin Russell. March 11, 2000, Belfast. Typescript.
———. *The Middle of My Journey.* Belfast: Blackstaff Press, 1990.
———. "The Ulster Novel." *Rann: An Ulster Quarterly* 20 (June 1953): 35–38.
Brandes, Rand. "Seamus Heaney's Working Titles: From *Advancement of Learning* to *Midnight Anvil.*" In *The Cambridge Companion to Seamus Heaney*, edited by Bernard O'Donoghue, 19–36. Cambridge: Cambridge University Press, 2009.
Brandes, Rand, and Michael J. Durkan. *Seamus Heaney: A Bibliography, 1959–2003.* London: Faber and Faber, 2008.
Brannigan, John. *Race in Modern Irish Literature and Culture.* Edinburgh: Edinburgh University Press, 2009.
Brogan, T. V. F. "Burns Stanza." In *The New Princeton Encyclopedia of Poetry and Poetics*, edited by Alex Preminger and T. V. F. Brogan, 153. New York: MJF Books; Princeton, NJ: Princeton University Press, 1993.
Brown, Terence. "Michael Longley and the Irish Poetic Tradition." In *The Poetry of Michael Longley*, edited by Alan J. Peacock and Kathleen Devine, 1–12. Gerrards Cross, UK: Colin Smythe, 2000.
Bugan, Carmen. *Seamus Heaney and East European Poetry in Translation: Poetics of Exile.* London: Legenda, 2013.
Burris, Sidney. *The Poetry of Resistance: Seamus Heaney and the Pastoral Tradition.* Athens: Ohio University Press, 1990.
———. "Reading Heaney Reading." In *Seamus Heaney: Poet, Critic, Translator*, edited by Ashby Bland Crowder and Jason David Hall, 59–73. New York: Palgrave, 2007.

Buttel, Robert. *Seamus Heaney*. Lewisburg, PA: Bucknell University Press, 1975.
Buxton, Rachel. *Robert Frost and Northern Irish Poetry*. Oxford: Oxford University Press, 2004.
Byrne, Ophelia. *The Stage in Ulster from the Eighteenth Century*. Belfast: Linen Hall Library, 1997.
Calinescu, Matei. *Rereading*. New Haven: Yale University Press, 1993.
Carson, Ciaran. Introduction to *The Inferno of Dante Alighieri*, translated by Ciaran Carson, xi–xxi. New York: Granta, 2004.
Casey, Edward. "How to Get from Place to Space in a Fairly Short Stretch of Time: Phenomenological Prolegomena." In *Senses of Place*, edited by Steven Feld and Keith H. Basso, 13–52. Santa Fe, NM: School of American Research Press, 1996.
———. *Remembering: A Phenomenological Study*. Bloomington: Indiana University Press, 1987.
Cathcart, Rex. *The Most Contrary Region: The BBC in Northern Ireland, 1924–1984*. Belfast: Blackstaff Press, 1984.
Cavanagh, Michael. *Professing Poetry: Seamus Heaney's Poetics*. Washington, DC: Catholic University Press of America, 2009.
Caws, Mary Ann. "Prose Poem." In *The New Princeton Encyclopedia of Poetry and Poetics*, edited by Alex Preminger and T. V. F. Brogan, 977–79. New York: MJF Books; Princeton, NJ: Princeton University Press, 1993.
Chambers, Harry. "Festival Poetry Pamphlets." *Phoenix* 1 (March 1967): 50–55.
"Christian Action: Martin Luther King, Nobel Peace Prize Winner, 1964, Public Meeting, Holborn Circus, E. C. 1, Chairman, Canon L. John Collins, Monday, 7th December, 7:30 P.M." *New Statesman* 68, no. 1760 (December 4, 1964): 876.
Clark, Heather. "Regional Roots: The BBC and Poetry in Northern Ireland, 1945–55." *Eire-Ireland* 38, nos. 1–2 (Spring–Summer 2003): 87–105.
———. *The Ulster Renaissance: Poetry in Belfast, 1962–1972*. Oxford: Oxford University Press, 2006.
Colley, Linda. "Britishness and Otherness: An Argument." *Journal of British Studies* 31, no. 4 (October 1992): 309–29.
Collins, Peter, ed. *Nationalism and Unionism: Conflict in Ireland, 1885–1921*. 1994. Corrected reprint, Belfast: Institute for Irish Studies, 1996.
Corcoran, Neil. *English Poetry since 1940*. London: Longman, 1993.
———. *The Poetry of Seamus Heaney: A Critical Study*. London: Faber and Faber, 1998.
———. *Poets of Modern Ireland: Text, Context, Intertext*. Cardiff: University of Wales Press, 1999.
———. *A Student's Guide to Seamus Heaney*. London: Faber and Faber, 1986.
C. P. "The Pity of War." Review of *Poems*, by Wilfred Owen. *Guardian*, December 29, 1920. www.guardian.co.uk/books/1920/dec/29/fromthearchives.poetry/print.

Crawford, Robert. *Devolving English Literature.* 2nd ed. Edinburgh: Edinburgh University Press, 2001.
Cuda, Anthony. "The Use of Memory: Seamus Heaney, T. S. Eliot, and the Unpublished Epigraph to *North.*" *Journal of Modern Literature* 28, no. 4 (Summer 2005): 152–75.
Cunliffe, Barry. *The Ancient Celts.* New York: Oxford University Press, 1997.
Curran, Charles. *A Seamless Robe: Broadcasting—Philosophy and Practice.* London: Collins, 1979.
Curtis, L. Perry, Jr. *Apes and Angels: The Irishman in Victorian Caricature.* Rev. ed. Washington, DC: Smithsonian Institution Press, 1997.
Dainotto, Roberto M. *Place in Literature: Regions, Cultures, Communities.* Ithaca, NY: Cornell University Press, 2000.
Dawe, Gerald. "The Parochial Idyll: W. R. Rodgers." In *False Faces: Poetry, Politics, and Place,* 62–68. Belfast: Lagan Press, 1994.
———. "Telling a Story: On 'Region' and 'Nation.'" In *A Real Life Elsewhere,* 88–98. Belfast: Lagan Press, 1993.
Dawson, Kenneth L. "Henry Monro, Commander of the United Irish Army of Down." Down County Museum. Down Surveys, 1998 ed. www.downcountymuseum.com/template.aspx?parent=114&parent2=169&pid=171&area=12.
Deane, Seamus. "The Artist and the Troubles." In *Ireland and the Arts: A Literary Review Special Issue,* edited by Tim Pat Coogan, 42–50. London: Namara Press, n.d.
———. "The Famous Seamus." *New Yorker,* March 20, 2000, 54–69.
———. Introduction to *The Birmingham Six: An Appalling Vista, An International Anthology of Support by 55 Writers and Artists,* edited by Oscar Gilligan, 10–11. Dublin: Litéreire Publishers, 1990. Henry C. Pearson Collection of Seamus Heaney, University of North Carolina–Chapel Hill.
De Paor, Liam. *Divided Ulster.* Baltimore: Penguin, 1970.
Dolan, Terence Patrick. *A Dictionary of Hiberno-English.* 2nd ed. Dublin: Gill and Macmillan, 2006.
Donaghmore Historical Society. "Words and Expressions." n.d. Living History: Social and Economic Transformation in Rural Northern Ireland. www.donaghmorelivinghistory.com/downloads/documents/Words%26Expressions.pdf.
Donne, John. *The Complete English Poems.* Edited by A. J. Smith. London: Penguin, 1971.
———. "XVII. Meditation." In *Seventeenth-Century Prose and Poetry,* 2nd Ed., selected and edited by Alexander M. Witherspoon and Frank J. Warnke, 68–69. San Diego, CA: Harcourt Brace, 1982.
Donoghue, Daniel. "The Philologer Poet: Seamus Heaney and the Translation of *Beowulf.*" In *Beowulf: A Verse Translation,* edited by Daniel Donoghue and translated by Seamus Heaney, 237–47. New York: Norton Critical Edition, 2002.

Donoghue, Denis. "The Literature of Trouble." In *We Irish: Essays on Irish Literature and Society*, 182–94. New York: Knopf, 1986.
Draper, R. P. *An Introduction to Twentieth-Century Poetry in English*. New York: St. Martin's Press, 1999.
———. "Philip Larkin: Provincial Poet." In *The Literature of Region and Nation*, edited by R. P. Draper, 81–92. New York: St. Martin's Press, 1989.
DuBois, W. E. B. *The Souls of Black Folk*. In *Three Negro Classics*, introduced by John Hope Franklin, 207–389. New York: Avon Books, 1965.
Duffy, Patrick J. *Exploring the History and Heritage of Irish Landscapes*. Dublin: Four Courts Press, 2007.
Edson, Russell. "Interview: The Art of the Prose Poem." By Peter Johnson. *The Prose Poem: An International Journal* 8 (1999): n.p. http://digitalcommons.providence.edu/prosepoem/vol8/iss1/63/.
Eliot, T. S. "The Music of Poetry." In *On Poetry and Poets*, 26–38. London: Faber and Faber, 1957.
———. *Notes toward a Definition of Culture*. In *Christianity and Culture: The Idea of a Christian Society and Notes towards the Definition of Culture*, 79–202. San Diego, CA: Harcourt Brace, 1988.
———. "The Social Function of Poetry." In *On Poetry and Poets*, 15–25. London: Faber and Faber, 1957.
———. *T. S. Eliot: Collected Poems, 1909–1962*. New York: Harcourt Brace, 1991.
Elliott, Marianne. *The Catholics of Ulster*. New York: Basic Books, 2001.
———. *Watchmen in Sion: The Protestant Idea of Liberty*. Field Day Pamphlet no. 8. Derry, Northern Ireland: Field Day Theatre Company, 1985.
Ellis, Steve. Introduction to *Dante Alighieri: Hell*, translated by Steve Ellis, ix–xx. London: Vintage, 1995.
Ellmann, Richard. "Heaney Agonistes." In *Seamus Heaney: Modern Critical Views*, edited and introduced by Harold Bloom, 159–65. New Haven, CT: Chelsea House, 1986.
Evans, E. Estyn. *The Personality of Ireland: Habitat, Heritage, and History*. Dublin: Lilliput Press, 1996.
"Faith of Our Fathers." www.traditionalmusic.co.uk/folk-song-lyrics/Faith_Of_Our_Fathers.htm.
Falci, Eric. "Place, Space, and Landscape." In *A Concise Companion to Postwar British and Irish Poetry*, edited by Nigel Alderman and C. D. Blanton, 200–220. Malden, MA: Wiley-Blackwell, 2009.
Fallon, Peter, and Derek Mahon, eds. Introduction to *The Penguin Book of Contemporary Irish Poetry*, xvi–xxii. New York: Penguin, 1990.
Fanon, Frantz. *Black Skin, White Masks*. Translated by Charles Lam Markmann. New York: Grove Press, 1967.
Farrell, Cyril. "Editorial." *Everyman: An Annual Religio-Cultural Review* 3 (1970): 5–8.

Ferriter, Diarmaid. *The Transformation of Ireland, 1900–2000*. London: Profile Books, 2005.
Fitzgerald, Robert. "Postscript." In *The Aeneid*, by Virgil, translated by Robert Fitzgerald, 403–17. New York: Vintage Classics, 1990.
Flood, Alison. "Seamus Heaney Chooses Two Poems to Sum Up His Lifetime Achievement." *Guardian*, March 19, 2009. www.theguardian.com/books/2009/mar/19/david-cohen-seamus-heaney.
Foster, John Wilson. *The Achievement of Seamus Heaney*. Dublin: Lilliput Press, 1995.
———. "Crediting Marvels: Heaney after 50." In *The Cambridge Companion to Seamus Heaney*, edited by Bernard O'Donoghue, 206–23. Cambridge: Cambridge University Press, 2009.
———. "The Critical Condition of Ulster." In *Colonial Consequences: Essays in Irish Literature and Culture*, 215–33. Dublin: Lilliput Press, 1991.
———. "'The Dissidence of Dissent': John Hewitt and W. R. Rodgers." In *Colonial Consequences: Essays in Irish Literature and Culture*, 114–32. Dublin: Lilliput Press, 1991.
———. *Forces and Themes in Ulster Fiction*. Totowa, NJ: Rowman and Littlefield, 1974.
———. "Post-war Ulster Poetry." In *Colonial Consequences: Essays in Irish Literature and Culture*, 60–80. Dublin: Lilliput Press, 1991.
———. "Radical Regionalism." In *Colonial Consequences: Essays in Irish Literature and Culture*, 278–95. Dublin: Lilliput Press, 1991.
———. "Was There Ulster Literary Life before Heaney?" In *Between Shadows: Modern Irish Writing and Culture*, 205–18. Dublin: Irish Academic Press, 2009.
Foster, Roy. *The Irish Story: Telling Tales and Making It Up in Ireland*. Oxford: Oxford University Press, 2002.
———. *Modern Ireland, 1600–1972*. London: Penguin, 1988.
Frampton, Kenneth. "Towards a Critical Regionalism: Six Points for an Architecture of a Resistance." In *The Anti-aesthetic: Essays on Postmodern Culture*, edited by Hal Foster, 16–31. Seattle, WA: Bay Press, 1983.
Frawley, Oona. *Irish Pastoral: Nostalgia and Twentieth-Century Irish Literature*. Dublin: Irish Academic Press, 2005.
Fredman, Stephen. *Poet's Prose: The Crisis in American Verse*. Cambridge: Cambridge University Press, 1983.
Friel, Brian. "Brian Friel and Field Day." In *Brian Friel in Conversation*, edited by Paul Delaney, 178–94. Ann Arbor: University of Michigan Press, 2000.
Frost, Robert. *Selected Letters of Robert Frost*. Edited by Lawrance Thompson. London: Jonathan Cape, 1965.
Fullwood, Daphne, and Oliver Edwards. "Ulster Poetry since 1900." *Rann: An Ulster Quarterly, Poetry and Comment* 20 (June 1953): 19–34.
Fussell, Paul. *Poetic Meter and Poetic Form*. Rev. ed. New York: McGraw Hill, 1979.

Glassie, Henry. *All Silver and No Brass: An Irish Christmas Mumming.* Dingle, Ireland: Brandon Press, 1983.
Graham, Brian. "Ulster: A Representation of Place Yet to Be Imagined." In *Who Are "the People"? Unionism, Protestantism, and Loyalism in Northern Ireland,* edited by Peter Shirlow and Mark McGovern, 34–54. London: Pluto Press, 1997.
Greacen, Robert. "The Editor Says . . ." In *Northern Harvest: An Anthology of Ulster Writing,* n.p. Belfast: Derrick MacCord, 1944.
Grennan, Eamon. "Seamus Heaney's Book of Resurrections." Review of *Human Chain,* by Seamus Heaney. *Irish Times,* August 28, 2010. www.irishtimes.com/newspaper/weekend/2010/0828/1224277733017_pf.html.
Haggerty, Bridget. "Mumming—a Yuletide Tradition." August 22, 2013. www.irishcultureandcustoms.com/ACalend/Mummers.html.
Hall, Jason David. *Seamus Heaney's Rhythmic Contract.* Basingstoke, UK: Palgrave Macmillan, 2009.
Hardy, Barbara. "Region and Nation: R. S. Thomas and Dylan Thomas." In *The Literature of Region and Nation,* edited by R. P. Draper, 93–107. New York: St. Martin's Press, 1989.
Harmon, Maurice. "Seamus Heaney: Divisions and Allegiances." *Colby Quarterly* 30, no. 1 (March 1994): 7–16.
Harris, Trudier. *Exorcising Blackness: Historical and Literary Lynching and Burning Rituals.* Bloomington: Indiana University Press, 1984.
Hart, Henry. "Seamus Heaney and Ted Hughes: A Complex Friendship." *Sewanee Review* 120, no. 1 (Winter 2012): 76–90.
———. *Seamus Heaney: Poet of Contrary Progressions.* Syracuse, NY: Syracuse University Press, 1992.
Haughey, James P. "Partitioned Memories: The Great War in Irish Poetry." *LIT: Literature, Interpretation, Theory* 10, no. 2 (October 1999): 181–91.
Heaney, Seamus. "Above the Brim." In *Homage to Robert Frost,* by Joseph Brodsky, Seamus Heaney, and Derek Walcott, 61–88. New York: Farrar, Straus, Giroux, 1996.
———. "Alternative Epigraph" [to *The Cure at Troy*]. Seamus Deane Papers, Manuscript, Archives, Rare Book Library, Emory University.
———. *Among Schoolchildren.* John Malone Memorial Lecture. Queen's University of Belfast, June 9, 1983. Belfast: John Malone Memorial Committee, 1983.
———. "Amputation." Worksheets, Belfast Group, October 1963 to March 1966. Philip Hobsbaum Collection, Manuscript, Archives, Rare Book Library, Emory University.
———. "'Apt Admonishment': Wordsworth as an Example." *Hudson Review* 61, no. 1 (Spring 2008): 19–33.
———. "The Art of Poetry: Interview with Seamus Heaney." By Henri Cole. *Paris Review* 75 (Fall 1997): 88–138.

———. "Atlas of Civilization." In *Finders Keepers: Selected Prose, 1971–2001*, 167–83. New York: Farrar, Straus, Giroux, 2002.
———. "Bags of Enlightenment." *Guardian*, October 24, 2003. www.guardian.co.uk/books/2003/oct/25/poetry.highereducation/print.
———. "Belfast." In *Preoccupations: Selected Prose, 1968–1978*, 28–37. London: Faber and Faber, 1980.
———, trans. *Beowulf*. London: Faber and Faber, 1999.
———. "Between North and South: Poetic Detours." Interview by Richard Kearney. In *States of Mind: Dialogues with Contemporary Thinkers on the European Mind*, edited by Richard Kearney, 101–8. Manchester: Manchester University Press, 1995.
———. "Biographical Sketch." Supplied to the BBC by Rosemary Allen of Faber and Faber, September 4, 1973, to the producers of *New Horizons: Poets on Poetry*, BBC Northern Ireland, transmission date October 8, 1973; recorded June 19, 1973. BBC Written Archive Centre, Caversham, UK, folder T69/88/1.
———. "The Bog." In *Ireland of the Welcomes*, 20–25. Dublin: *Bord Faílte* / Irish Tourist Board, May–June 1976.
———. "Bogland." In *Ulster in Focus* series, BBC Television. Unknown broadcast date. Broadcast number 175665003. Transcript, 1–11. Seamus Heaney Papers, Manuscript, Archives, Rare Book Library, Emory University.
———. *Bog Poems*. Illustrations by Barrie Cooke. Devon, UK: Rainbow Press, 1975. Henry C. Pearson Collection of Seamus Heaney, Rare Book Collection, University of North Carolina–Chapel Hill.
———. "Brian Friel and the Use of Memory." In *The Achievement of Brian Friel*, edited by Alan Peacock, 229–40. Gerrards Cross, UK: Colin Smythe, 1993.
———. "Burns's Art Speech." In *Finders Keepers: Selected Prose, 1971–2001*, 378–95. New York: Farrar, Straus, Giroux, 2002.
———. "Canto I, Canto II, Canto III." In *Dante's Inferno: Translations by Twenty Contemporary Poets*, introduced by James Merrill and edited by Daniel Halpern, 3–15. Hopewell, NJ: Ecco Press, 1993.
———. "Celtic Fringe, Viking Fringe." *Listener*, October 24, 1968, 254–55.
———. "A Chester Pageant." *Use of English* 17, no. 1 (Autumn 1965): 58–60.
———. "Comfortable Image Belies the Serious Poet." Interview by Deaglan de Breadun. *Irish Times*, September 13, 1984, 13.
———. "Confessions and Histories." Review of *Confessions and Histories*, by Edward Lucie-Smith; *Selected Poems*, by Anne Sexton; *77 Dream Songs*, by John Berryman; *The Arctic Ox*, by Marianne Moore. *Outposts* 65 (Summer 1965): 21–23. Henry C. Pearson Collection of Seamus Heaney, Rare Book Collection, University of North Carolina–Chapel Hill.
———. "The Conversation." In *Seamus Heaney in Conversation with Karl Miller*, 17–56. London: Between the Lines, 2000.
———. "Cornucopia and Empty Shell: Variations on a Theme from Ellmann." In *The Place of Writing*, 54–72. Atlanta, GA: Scholar's Press, 1989.

———. *Crediting Poetry*. Loughcrew, Ireland: Gallery Press, 1996.
———. *The Cure at Troy: A Version of Sophocles' Philoctetes*. New York: Noonday, 1990.
———. "*The Cure at Troy*: Production Notes in No Particular Order." In *Amid Our Troubles: Irish Versions of Greek Tragedy*, edited by Marianne McDonald and J. M. Walton, 171–80. London: Methuen, 2002.
———. *Death of a Naturalist*. London: Faber and Faber, 1966.
———. "Deep as England." Review of *Selected Poems: 1957–1967*, by Ted Hughes. *Hibernia*, December 1, 1972, 13.
———. "Digging," "Storm on the Island," and "Scaffolding." *New Statesman*, December 4, 1964, 880.
———. *District and Circle*. New York: Farrar, Straus, Giroux, 2006.
———. *Door into the Dark*. London: Faber and Faber, 1969.
———. "The Drag of the Golden Chain: How the Translator 'Gropes Along,' Transmitting Meaningful Signals 'from the Hoard to the Herd.'" *Times Literary Supplement*, November 12, 1999, 14–16.
———. "Dylan the Durable? On Dylan Thomas." In *The Redress of Poetry: Oxford Lectures*, 124–45. London: Faber and Faber, 1995.
———. "Earning a Rhyme." In *Finders Keepers: Selected Prose, 1971–2001*, 63–70. New York: Farrar, Straus, Giroux, 2002.
———. "Eclogues *in Extremis*: On the Staying Power of Pastoral." *Proceedings of the Royal Irish Academy* 103 C, no. 1 (2003): 1–12. Henry C. Pearson Collection of Seamus Heaney, University of North Carolina–Chapel Hill.
———. "Editor's Note." In *Soundings: An Annual Anthology of New Irish Poetry*, edited by Heaney, 5–6. Belfast: Blackstaff Press, 1972.
———. "Edwin Muir." In *Finders Keepers: Selected Prose, 1971–2001*, 269–80. New York: Farrar, Straus, Giroux, 2002.
———. *Electric Light*. New York: Farrar, Straus, Giroux, 2001.
———. "Englands of the Mind." In *Preoccupations: Selected Prose, 1968–1978*, 150–69. London: Faber and Faber, 1980.
———. "Envies and Identifications: Dante and the Modern Poet." *Irish University Review* 15, no. 1 (Spring–Summer 1985): 5–19.
———. "Envies and Identifications: Dante and the Modern Poet." In *Finders Keepers: Selected Prose, 1971–2001*, 184–96. New York: Farrar, Straus, Giroux, 2002.
———. *Everyman*. Typescript. BBC Northern Ireland Schools Department. Transmitted March 11, 1971. Michael Longley Collection, Manuscript, Archives, and Rare Book Library, Emory University.
———. "Extending the Alphabet: On Christopher Marlowe's 'Hero and Leander.'" In *The Redress of Poetry: Oxford Lectures*, 17–37. London: Faber and Faber, 1995.
———. "Fair (A Progress Report)." *Universities' Poetry Five*, May 1963, 7. Henry C. Pearson Collection of Seamus Heaney, University of North Carolina–Chapel Hill.

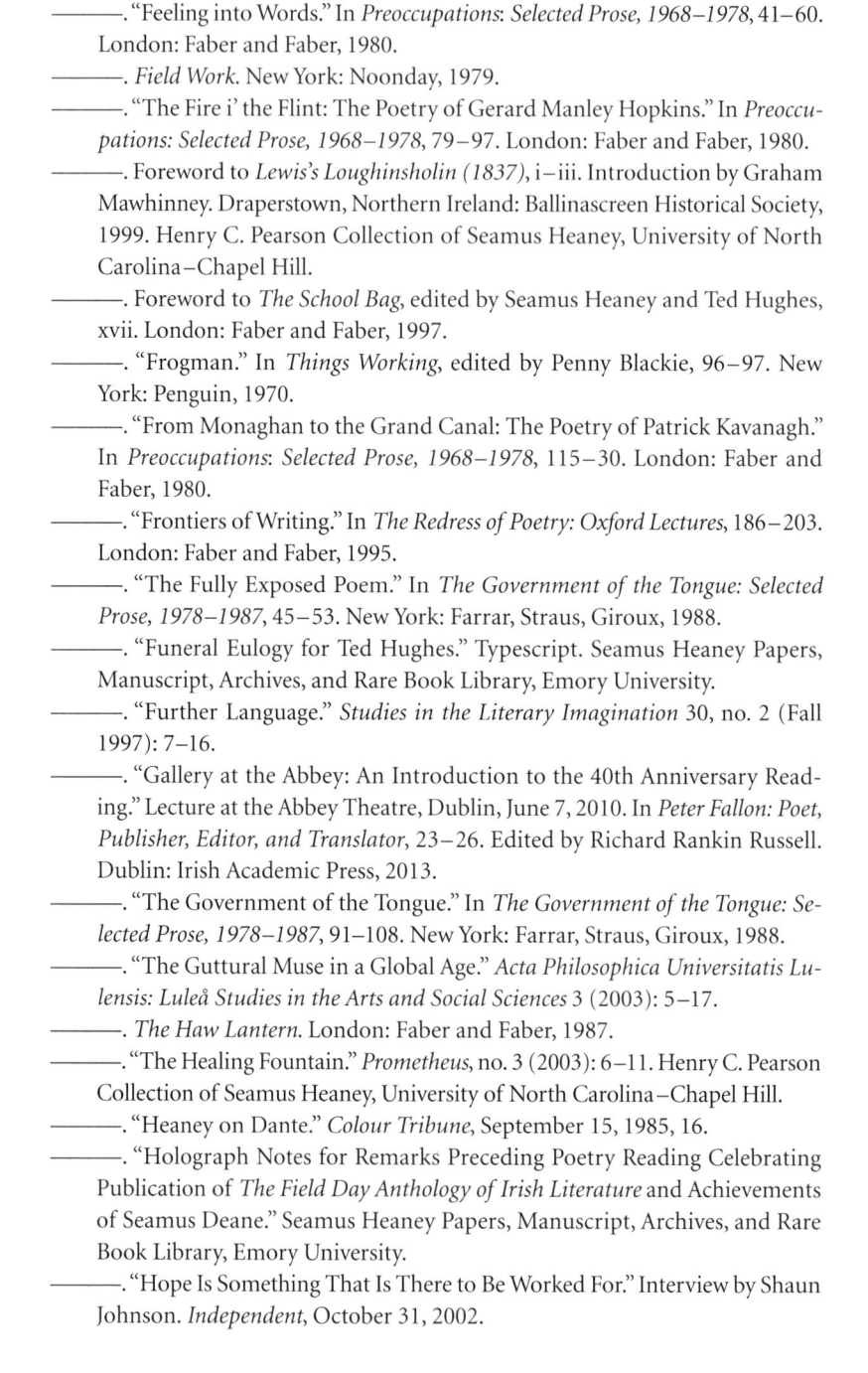

———. "Feeling into Words." In *Preoccupations: Selected Prose, 1968–1978*, 41–60. London: Faber and Faber, 1980.
———. *Field Work*. New York: Noonday, 1979.
———. "The Fire i' the Flint: The Poetry of Gerard Manley Hopkins." In *Preoccupations: Selected Prose, 1968–1978*, 79–97. London: Faber and Faber, 1980.
———. Foreword to *Lewis's Loughinsholin (1837)*, i–iii. Introduction by Graham Mawhinney. Draperstown, Northern Ireland: Ballinascreen Historical Society, 1999. Henry C. Pearson Collection of Seamus Heaney, University of North Carolina–Chapel Hill.
———. Foreword to *The School Bag*, edited by Seamus Heaney and Ted Hughes, xvii. London: Faber and Faber, 1997.
———. "Frogman." In *Things Working*, edited by Penny Blackie, 96–97. New York: Penguin, 1970.
———. "From Monaghan to the Grand Canal: The Poetry of Patrick Kavanagh." In *Preoccupations: Selected Prose, 1968–1978*, 115–30. London: Faber and Faber, 1980.
———. "Frontiers of Writing." In *The Redress of Poetry: Oxford Lectures*, 186–203. London: Faber and Faber, 1995.
———. "The Fully Exposed Poem." In *The Government of the Tongue: Selected Prose, 1978–1987*, 45–53. New York: Farrar, Straus, Giroux, 1988.
———. "Funeral Eulogy for Ted Hughes." Typescript. Seamus Heaney Papers, Manuscript, Archives, and Rare Book Library, Emory University.
———. "Further Language." *Studies in the Literary Imagination* 30, no. 2 (Fall 1997): 7–16.
———. "Gallery at the Abbey: An Introduction to the 40th Anniversary Reading." Lecture at the Abbey Theatre, Dublin, June 7, 2010. In *Peter Fallon: Poet, Publisher, Editor, and Translator*, 23–26. Edited by Richard Rankin Russell. Dublin: Irish Academic Press, 2013.
———. "The Government of the Tongue." In *The Government of the Tongue: Selected Prose, 1978–1987*, 91–108. New York: Farrar, Straus, Giroux, 1988.
———. "The Guttural Muse in a Global Age." *Acta Philosophica Universitatis Lulensis: Luleå Studies in the Arts and Social Sciences* 3 (2003): 5–17.
———. *The Haw Lantern*. London: Faber and Faber, 1987.
———. "The Healing Fountain." *Prometheus*, no. 3 (2003): 6–11. Henry C. Pearson Collection of Seamus Heaney, University of North Carolina–Chapel Hill.
———. "Heaney on Dante." *Colour Tribune*, September 15, 1985, 16.
———. "Holograph Notes for Remarks Preceding Poetry Reading Celebrating Publication of *The Field Day Anthology of Irish Literature* and Achievements of Seamus Deane." Seamus Heaney Papers, Manuscript, Archives, and Rare Book Library, Emory University.
———. "Hope Is Something That Is There to Be Worked For." Interview by Shaun Johnson. *Independent*, October 31, 2002.

---. "Hughie O'Donoghue Exhibition, Kilkenny, Address for Exhibition Opening." Typescript. Seamus Heaney Papers, Manuscript, Archives, and Rare Book Library, Emory University.
---. *Human Chain*. New York: Farrar, Straus, Giroux, 2010.
---. "The Impact of Translation." In *The Government of the Tongue: Selected Prose, 1978–1987*, 36–44. New York: Farrar, Straus, Giroux, 1988.
---. "The Indomitable Irishry." *Poetry Ireland* 3 (Spring 1964): 104.
---. "The Interesting Case of Nero, Chekhov's Cognac, and a Knocker." In *The Government of the Tongue: Selected Prose, 1978–1987*, xi–xxiii. New York: Farrar, Straus, Giroux, 1988.
---. "Interview: Seamus Heaney, Poet." By Susan Mansfield. *Scotsman*, March 14, 2010. http://thescotsman.scotsman.com/features/Interview-Seamus-Heaney-poet.6148896.jp.
---. "An Interview with Seamus Heaney." By Rand Brandes. *Salmagundi* 80 (Fall 1988): 4–21.
---. "Interview with Seamus Heaney." By Nick Gammage. *Thumbscrew* 19 (Autumn 2001): 2–11.
---. "An Interview with Seamus Heaney." By James Randall. *Ploughshares* 5, no. 3 (1979): 7–22.
---. "An Interview with Seamus Heaney." By J. J. Wylie and John C. Kerrigan. *Nua: Studies in Contemporary Irish Writing* 2, nos. 1–2 (Autumn 1998–Spring 1999): 125–37.
---. "In the Country of Convention: English Pastoral Verse." In *Preoccupations: Selected Prose, 1968–1978*, 173–80. London: Faber and Faber, 1980.
---. "In the Light of the Imagination." *Irish Times*, October 21, 2004, 14.
---. "Intimidation." *Malahat Review* 17 (January 1971): 34.
---. Introduction to *Beowulf*, ix–xxx. London: Faber and Faber, 1999.
---. Introduction to *Diary of One Who Vanished: A Song Cycle by Leoš Janáček of Poems by Ozef Kalda in a New Version by Seamus Heaney*. London: Faber and Faber, 1999.
---. Introduction to *Michael McLaverty: Collected Short Stores*, 7–9. Dublin: Poolbeg Press, 1978.
---. Introduction to *Padraic Fallon: Collected Poems*, 11–17. Manchester: Carcanet, 1990.
---. Introduction to *The Redress of Poetry: Oxford Lectures*, xiii–xviii. London: Faber and Faber, 1995.
---. Introduction to *Robert Henryson: The Testament of Cresseid and Seven Fables*, translated by Seamus Heaney, vii–xvi. New York: Farrar, Straus, Giroux, 2009.
---. Introduction to *Sorley Maclean: Critical Essays*, edited by Raymond J. Ross and Joy Hendry, 1–7. Edinburgh: Scottish Academic Press, 1986.
---. Introduction to *Sweeney Astray*. n.p. London: Faber and Faber, 1983.

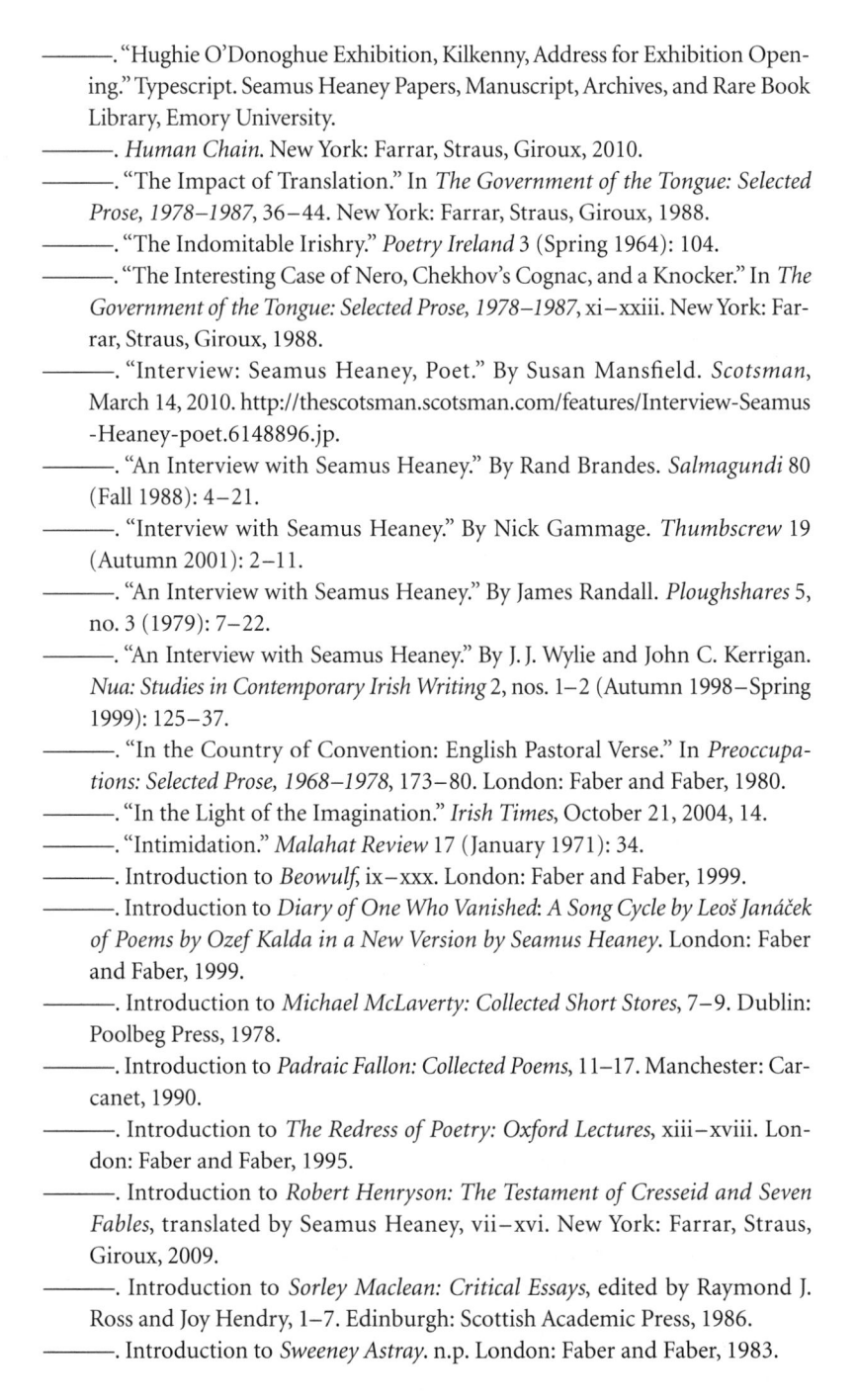

———. "The Irish Quest." Reprinted in *Seamus Heaney*, edited by Edward Broadbridge, 46–48. Denmark: Skoleradioen, 1977. Originally published in *Guardian*, November 2, 1974, n.p.

———. "Irish Society Michaelmas Dinner Address." Oxford University, November 30, 1992. Seamus Heaney Papers, Manuscript, Archives, Rare Book Library, Emory University.

———. "January Review, 'The Arts in Ireland.'" Typescript. Tuesday, January 23, 1973, 12:25–12:55 P.M. Northern Ireland Home Service, Radio 4. Seamus Deane Papers, Manuscript, Archives, Rare Book Library, Emory University.

———. "John Clare's Prog." In *The Redress of Poetry: Oxford Lectures*, 63–82. London: Faber and Faber, 1995.

———. "Joyce's Poetry." In *Finders Keepers: Selected Prose, 1971–2001*, 422–24. New York: Farrar, Straus, Giroux, 2002.

———. "Joy or Night: Last Things in the Poetry of W. B. Yeats and Philip Larkin." In *The Redress of Poetry: Oxford Lectures*, 146–63. London: Faber and Faber, 1995.

———, trans. *The Last Walk: Translations from the Italian of Giovanni Pascoli*. Loughcrew, Ireland: Gallery Press, 2013.

———. "Learning from Eliot." In *Finders Keepers: Selected Prose, 1971–2001*, 28–41. New York: Farrar, Straus, Giroux, 2002.

———. "Lost Ulstermen." Review of *The Rough Field*, by John Montague. *Listener*, April 26, 1973, 550.

———. "The Main of Light." In *The Government of the Tongue: Selected Prose, 1978–1987*, 15–22. New York: Farrar, Straus, Giroux, 1988.

———. "The Makings of a Music: Reflections on Wordsworth and Yeats." In *Preoccupations: Selected Prose, 1968–1978*, 61–78. London: Faber and Faber, 1980.

———. "The Man and the Bog." Opening Speech to the Exhibition of Bog Bodies: "Face to Face with Your Past," Silkeborg Museum, Denmark, August 2, 1996. Henry C. Pearson Collection of Seamus Heaney, University of North Carolina–Chapel Hill.

———. "Meeting Seamus Heaney: An Interview." By John Haffenden. In *Viewpoints: Poets in Conversation with John Haffenden*, 57–75. London: Faber and Faber, 1981.

———. "The Mixed Marriage: Paul Muldoon." In *Preoccupations: Selected Prose, 1968–1978*, 211–13. London: Faber and Faber, 1980.

———. "Mossbawn." In *Preoccupations: Selected Prose, 1968–1978*, 17–27. London: Faber and Faber, 1980.

———. *Munro*. Everyman: An Annual Religio-Cultural Review 3 (1970): 58–65.

———. "The Murmur of Malvern." In *The Government of the Tongue: Selected Prose, 1978–1987*, 23–29. New York: Farrar, Straux, Giroux, 1988.

———. *New Selected Poems, 1966–1987*. London: Faber and Faber, 1990.

———. "Nocturne." *Malahat Review* 17 (January 1971): 35.

---. "Norman MacCaig, 1910–1996." In *Finders Keepers: Selected Prose, 1971–2001*, 433–36. New York: Farrar, Straus, Giroux, 2002.
---. "North." Typescript. Seamus Deane Papers, Manuscript, Archives, Rare Book Library, Emory University.
---. *North*. London: Faber and Faber, 1975.
---. "A Note about 'Belderg.'" In *The Mayo Anthology*, edited by Richard Murphy, 129. Castlebar, Ireland: Mayo County Council, 1990.
---. "Obituary: Michael McLaverty: Part of His Own Posterity." *Fortnight*, no. 306 (May 1992): 31.
---. "Odin's World." *Trowel* 10 (2005): 80–84. Henry C. Pearson Collection of Seamus Heaney, Rare Book Collection, University of North Carolina–Chapel Hill.
---. "Old Derry's Walls." *Listener*, October 24, 1968, 521–23.
---. "On Elegies, Eclogues, Translations, Transfusions: An Interview with Seamus Heaney." By Rui Carvalho Homem. *European English Messenger* 10, no. 2 (Autumn 2001): 24–30.
---. *One on a Side: An Evening with Seamus Heaney and Robert Frost*, October 26, 2002. Edited by Kevin O'Connor and Mark Schorr. Robert Frost Foundation. Lawrence, MA: Bookmarkpress, 2008.
---. "On Hogarth's Engraving 'Pit Ticket for the Royal Sport.'" Worksheets, Belfast Group, October 1963 to March 1966. Michael Longley Papers and Philip Hobsbaum Collection, Manuscript, Archives, Rare Book Library, Emory University. http://beck.library.emory.edu/BelfastGroup/browse.php?id=heaney1_1041#.
---. "On Home Ground." Address to "Pascoli e l'immaginario degli italiani," Convegno Internazionale di Studi, Bologna, Italy, April 2–4, 2012. *Rivista Pascoliana* 24–25 (2012–13): 19–26.
---. "On Poetry and Professing." In *Finders Keepers*, 71–79. London: Faber and Faber, 2002.
---. "On the Gift of a Fountain Pen." Broadside. Baylor University, Beall Poetry Festival, March 4, 2013.
---. "An Open Letter." Typescript. Seamus Deane Papers, Manuscript, Archives, Rare Book Library, Emory University.
---. *An Open Letter*. Derry: Field Day Publications, 1983.
---. "Our Own Dour Way." *Hibernia*, April 1963, 15.
---. "Out of London: Ulster's Troubles." *New Statesman*, July 1, 1966, 23–24.
---. "Over the Bridge." Holograph manuscript, ca. 1973. *Explorations* series, BBC Northern Ireland, transmission date unknown, but likely 1973. Seamus Heaney Papers, Manuscript, Archives, Rare Book Library, Emory University.
---. "The Pathos of Things." *Guardian*, November 24, 2007, "Features and Reviews," 20.
---. "*La pausa per la riflessione: Incontro con Seamus Heaney*." Conducted by Carla de Petris. *Linea d'Ombra, Milano Massmedia* 42 (1989): 69–73.

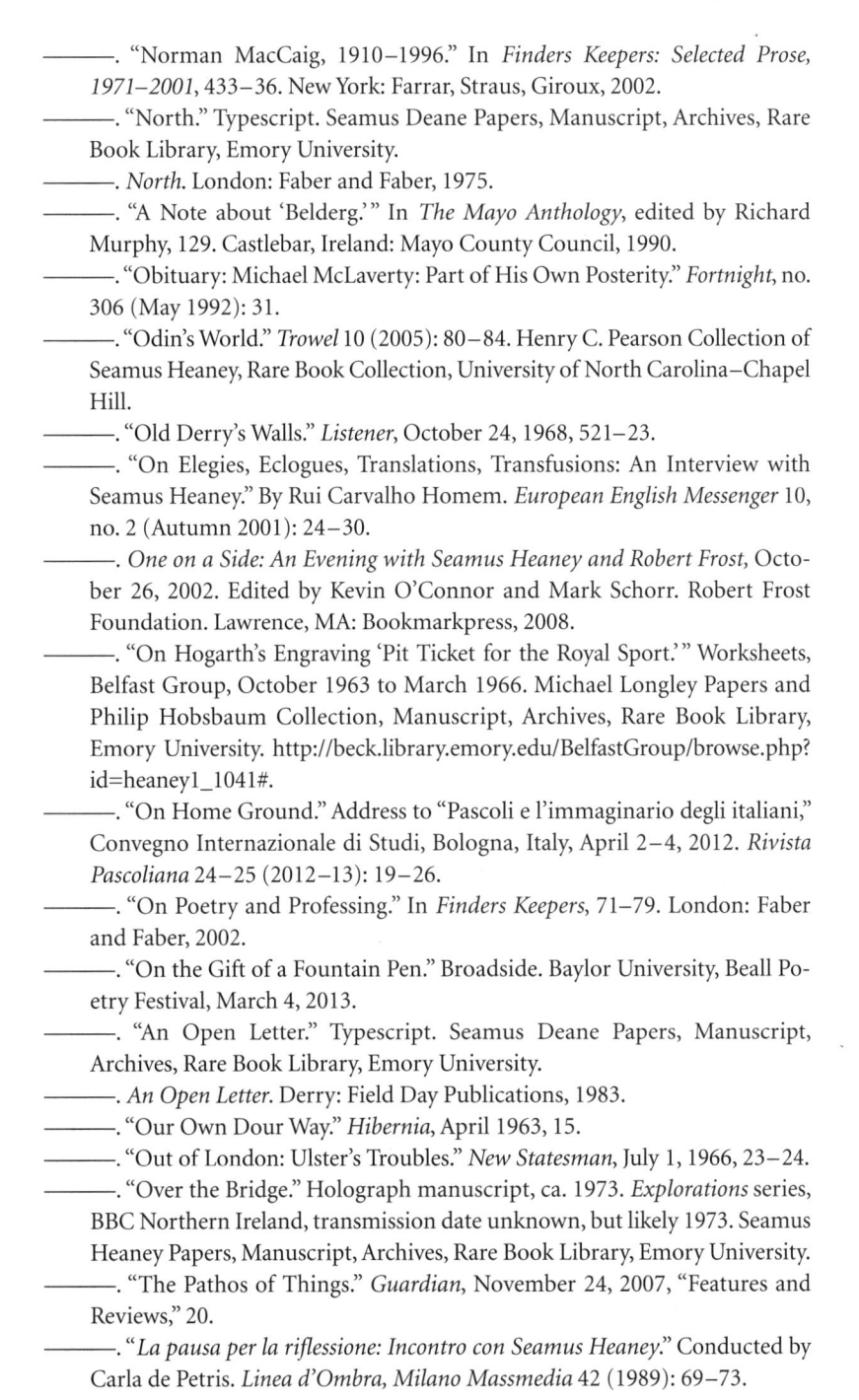

———. *A Personal Selection: Seamus Heaney*. Exhibition catalogue for an Exhibit of Art Chosen by Heaney from the Ulster Museum's Holdings, August 20–October 24, 1982. Publication No. 248. Belfast: Ulster Museum, 1982.

———. *Place and Displacement: Recent Poetry of Northern Ireland*. Grasmere, UK: Trustees of Dove Cottage, 1984.

———. "The Placeless Heaven: Another Look at Kavanagh." In *The Government of the Tongue: Selected Prose, 1978–1987*, 3–14. New York: Farrar, Straus, Giroux, 1988.

———. "The Place of Writing: W. B. Yeats and Thoor Ballylee." In *The Place of Writing*, 18–35. Atlanta, GA: Scholar's Press, 1989.

———. "Place, Pastness, Poems: A Triptych." *Salmagundi* 68–69 (Fall 1985–Winter 1986): 30–47.

———. "A Poem Is Landscape." Typescript with holograph revisions. Likely mid-1990s. Seamus Heaney Papers, Manuscript, Archives, Rare Book Library, Emory University.

———. *Poems and a Memoir*. New York: Limited Editions Club, 1982.

———. "The Poems of the Dispossessed Repossessed." In *The Government of the Tongue: Selected Prose, 1978–1987*, 30–35. New York: Farrar, Straus, Giroux, 1988.

———. "The Poet as a Christian." *Furrow* 29, no. 10 (October 1978): 603–6.

———. "The Poetry of John Hewitt." In *Preoccupations: Selected Prose, 1968–1978*, 207–10. London: Faber and Faber, 1980.

———. "Poets on Poetry." Interview by Patrick Garland. *Listener*, November 8, 1973, 629.

———. Preface to *Bog Poems*. Devon, UK: Rainbow Press, 1975.

———. Preface to *The Crane Bag Book of Irish Studies* (1977–1981), edited by Mark Patrick Hederman and Richard Kearney, 7–8. Dublin: Blackwater, 1982.

———. Preface to *Derry and Londonderry, History and Society: Interdisciplinary Essays on the History of an Irish County*, edited by Gerard O'Brien, xxii–xxiii. Dublin: Geography Publications, 1999. Henry C. Pearson Collection of Seamus Heaney, University of North Carolina–Chapel Hill.

———. Preface to *The Penguin Book of Irish Poetry*, edited by Patrick Crotty, xliii–xlvi. New York: Penguin, 2010.

———. Preface to *Seamus Heaney: Poems and a Memoir*, xvii–xviii. New York: Limited Editions Club, 1982.

———. Preface to *Stations*, 3. Belfast: Ulsterman Publications, 1975.

———. "The Pre-natal Mountain: Vision and Irony in Recent Irish Poetry." In *The Place of Writing*, 36–53. Atlanta, GA: Scholar's Press, 1989.

———. "The Redress of Poetry." In *The Redress of Poetry: Oxford Lectures*, 1–16. London: Faber and Faber, 1995.

———. "The Regional Forecast." In *The Literature of Region and Nation*, edited by R. P. Draper, 10–23. New York: St. Martin's Press, 1989.

---, trans. and introd. *Robert Henryson: The Testament of Cresseid and Seven Fables.* New York: Farrar, Straus, Giroux, 2009.
---. "Romanist." In *Wearing of the Black*, edited by Padraic Fiacc. Belfast: Blackstaff Press, 1974.
---. *Room to Rhyme.* Commencement Address, University of Dundee, Scotland, July 2003. Dundee: University of Dundee, 2004.
---. "R. S. Thomas Memorial." Delivered at Westminster Abbey, March 28, 2001. *Poetry Ireland Review*, no. 69 (Summer 2001): 11–14.
---. *Seamus Heaney.* Edited by Edward Broadbridge. Denmark: Skoleradioen, 1977.
---. "Seamus Heaney." In *Humanizing the City: Politics, Religion, the Arts in Critical Conversation*, edited by Patrick Primeaux, 87–105. San Francisco: International Scholars Publications, 1997.
---. "Seamus Heaney." Interview by Stephen Faller, Nathan Ligo, Chris Hass, Ashley Payne, Anne Stringfield, Ellie Brown, Harry Thomas, Courtney Robertson, Christopher Kip, Carey Morton, and Mark Overcash. In *Talking with Poets*, 42–69. New York: Handsel Books, 2002.
---. "Seamus Heaney (January 2010)." Interview by Jody Allen Randolph. In *Close to the Next Moment: Interviews from a Changing Ireland*, edited by Jody Allen Randolph, 201–12. Manchester: Carcarnet, 2010.
---. "Seamus Heaney—Poetry International." Museum no. 908. Transmission date October 15, 1972. BBC Northern Ireland Radio Archives. Cultra, Northern Ireland.
---. "Seamus Heaney: The Words Worth Saying." Interview by Steven Ratiner. In *Giving Their Words: Conversations with Contemporary Poets*, 95–107. Amherst: University of Massachusetts Press, 2002.
---. *Seeing Things.* London: Faber and Faber, 1991.
---. "Seeing Things: John Breslin Interviews Seamus Heaney." *Critic* 46 (Winter 1991): 26–35.
---. "The Sense of Place." In *Preoccupations: Selected Prose, 1968–1978*, 131–49. London: Faber and Faber, 1980.
---. "Sounding Auden." In *The Government of the Tongue: Selected Prose, 1978–1987*, 109–28. New York: Farrar, Straus, Giroux, 1988.
---. "Sparks in the Tin Hut." In *Irish Theatre on Tour*, edited by Nicholas Grene and Chris Morash, 1–5. Dublin: Carysfort Press, 2005.
---. *The Spirit Level.* London: Faber and Faber, 1996.
---. *Station Island.* New York: Farrar, Straus, Giroux, 1985.
---. *Stations.* Belfast: Ulsterman Publications, 1975.
---. *Stepping Stones* (Audiobook). London: Faber and Faber / Penguin, 1995.
---. *Stepping Stones: Interviews with Seamus Heaney.* By Dennis O'Driscoll. New York: Farrar, Straus, Giroux, 2008.
---. "A Story That Sings Down the Centuries." *Sunday Times*, March 21, 2004, 41–42.

———. "Strange Fruit." Holograph and early typewritten drafts. Seamus Heaney Papers, Manuscript, Archives, and Rare Book Library, Emory University.
———. "A Tale of Two Islands: Reflections on the Irish Literary Revival." In *Irish Studies*, edited by P. J. Drudy, 1–20. Cambridge: Cambridge University Press, 1980.
———. "Threshold and Floor." *Metre* 7–8 (Spring–Summer 2000): 265–68.
———. "Through-Other Places, Through-Other Times: The Irish Poet and Britain." In *Finders Keepers: Selected Prose, 1971–2001*, 396–415. New York: Farrar, Straus, Giroux, 2002.
———. "Time and Again: Poetry and the Millennium." *European English Messenger* 10, no. 2 (Autumn 2001): 19–23.
———. "A Torchlight Procession of One: On Hugh MacDiarmid." In *The Redress of Poetry: Oxford Lectures*, 103–23. London: Faber and Faber, 1995.
———. "Tradition and an Individual Talent: Hugh MacDiarmid." In *Preoccupations: Selected Prose, 1968–1978*, 195–98. London: Faber and Faber, 1980.
———. "Triptych for the Easter Battlers." Worksheets, Belfast Group, October 1963 to March 1966. Michael Longley Papers and Philip Hobsbaum Collection, Manuscript, Archives, Rare Book Library, Emory University. http://beck.library.emory.edu/BelfastGroup/browse.php?id=heaney1_10163.
———. "Unhappy and at Home: Interview with Seamus Heaney by Seamus Deane." In *The Crane Bag Book of Irish Studies (1977–1981)*, edited by Mark Patrick Hederman and Richard Kearney, 66–72. Dublin: Blackwater Press, 1982.
———. "Unheard Melodies." *Irish Times*, April 14, 1998, 1.
———. "Untitled." Series Title: *Explorations*. Typescript. BBC Northern Ireland Schools Department. Transmitted May 1, 1968. Michael Longley Collection, Manuscript, Archives, Rare Book Library, Emory University.
———. "Views." *Listener*, December 31, 1970, 903.
———. "The Vulgar Muse." Review of *The Faber Book of Vernacular Verse*, edited by Tom Paulin. *Sunday Times*, December 23, 1990, "Books," 9.
———. "William Butler Yeats." In *The Field Day Anthology of Irish Literature*, general editor, Seamus Deane, vol. 2, 783–90. Derry, Northern Ireland: Field Day Publications, 1991.
———. *Wintering Out*. London: Faber and Faber, 1972.
———. "Yeats as an Example?" In *Preoccupations: Selected Prose, 1968–1978*, 98–114. London: Faber, 1980.
———. "Yeats's Nobility." *Four Quarters* 3, no. 2 (Fall 1989): 11–14.
———. "The Yellow Bittern." Translation of *An Bonnán Buí* by Cathal Buí Mac Giolla Ghunna (c. 1680–1756). Broadside. Keough–Notre Dame Centre, Dublin. Fourth Irish Seminar, July 2002. Designed by Caroline Moloney.
Heaney, Seamus, and Robert Hass. *Sounding Lines: The Art of Translating Poetry*. Edited by Christina M. Gillis. Occasional Papers Series No. 20. Berkeley:

Doreen B. Townsend Center for the Humanities, University of California, Berkeley, 2000.

"Heaney to Publish Epic Poem." *Derry Journal*, September 6, 1983, 8.

Heininger, Joseph. "Making a Dantean Poetic: Seamus Heaney's 'Ugolino.'" *New Hibernia Review* 9, no. 2 (Summer 2005): 50–64.

Herr, Cheryl. *Critical Regionalism and Cultural Studies: From Ireland to the American Midwest*. Gainesville: University of Florida Press, 1996.

Hewitt, David. "Scoticisms and Cultural Conflict." In *The Literature of Region and Nation*, edited by R. P. Draper, 125–35. New York: St. Martin's Press, 1989.

Hewitt, John. "The Bitter Gourd: Some Problems of the Ulster Writer." *Lagan* 3 (1945): 93–105.

———. *The Collected Poems of John Hewitt*, edited by Frank Ormsby. Belfast: Blackstaff Press, 1992.

———. "The Course of Writing in Ulster." *Rann: An Ulster Quarterly* 20 (June 1953): 43–52.

———. "The Progress of a Poet." *Belfast Telegraph*, May 19, 1966. n.p.

———, ed. *Rhyming Weavers and Other Country Poets of Antrim and Down*. Foreword by Tom Paulin. 1974. Reprint, Belfast: Blackstaff Press, 2004.

———. "St Rosalie, Monte Pelligrino." In *Soundings '72: An Annual Anthology of New Irish Poetry*, edited by Seamus Heaney, 25. Belfast: Blackstaff Press, 1972.

Hobbs, John. "United Irishmen: Seamus Heaney and the Rebellion of 1798." *Canadian Journal of Irish Studies* 21, no. 2 (December 1995): 38–43.

Hobsbaum, Philip. *Metre, Rhythm, and Verse Form*. London: Routledge, 1996.

———. "The Road Not Taken." *Listener*, November 23, 1961, 860–63.

Holloway, John. "The Literary Scene." In *The New Pelican Guide to English Literature Guide to English Literature*, vol. 8, *The Present*, edited by Boris Ford, 65–125. New York: Penguin, 1983.

Homem, Rui Carvalho. *Poetry and Translation in Northern Ireland: Dislocations in Contemporary Writing*. New York: Palgrave, 2009.

Hufstader, Jonathan. *Tongue of Water, Teeth of Stones: Northern Irish Poetry and Social Violence*. Lexington: University Press of Kentucky, 1999.

Hughes, Ted. "Ted Hughes and Crow." Interview by Ekbert Faas. *London Magazine*, January 1971, 5–20.

Hunter, Barbara, and Roy McFadden. Introduction. *Rann: An Ulster Quarterly* 20 (June 1953): 1.

Hurley, Michael D. "Interpreting Dante's *Terza Rima*." *Forum for Modern Language Studies* 41, no. 3 (July 2005): 320–31.

Ingelbien, Raphaël. "Seamus Heaney and the Importance of Larkin." *Journal of Modern Literature* 34, no. 1 (Summer 2000): 471–82.

Irvine, Gilbert Marshall. *Ulster and Modern Thought: A Philosophy of Literature*. Belfast: Strain, 1929.

Johnston, Dillon. *Irish Poetry after Joyce.* 2nd ed. Syracuse, NY: Syracuse University Press, 1997.
———. "Seamus Heaney and Violence." In *The Cambridge Companion to Contemporary Irish Poetry*, edited by Matthew Campbell, 113–32. Cambridge: Cambridge University Press, 2003.
Jones, David. Preface to *In Parenthesis*, ix–xv. New York: New York Review of Books, 2003.
Joyce, James. *Dubliners.* Edited by Robert Scholes and A. Walton Litz. New York: Viking/Penguin, 1976.
———. "Gas from a Burner." In *James Joyce: Poems and Shorter Writings*, edited by Richard Ellmann, A. Walton Litz, and John Whittier-Ferguson, 103–5. London: Faber and Faber, 1991.
———. *A Portrait of the Artist as a Young Man.* Edited by Chester Anderson. New York: Viking Penguin, 1977.
———. *Ulysses.* Edited by Hans Walter Gabler. New York: Vintage, 1986.
Jung, C. G. "Two Kinds of Thinking." In *The Basic Writings of C. G. Jung*, translated by R. F. C. Hull, 12–38. Princeton, NJ: Princeton University Press, 1990.
Kavanagh, Patrick. "The Parish and the Universe." In *Collected Pruse*, 281–83. London: Macgibbon and Kee, 1967.
Kay, Magdalena. *In Gratitude for All the Gifts: Seamus Heaney and Eastern Europe.* Toronto: University of Toronto Press, 2012.
Kearney, Richard. "Language Play: Brian Friel and Ireland's Verbal Theatre." In *Brian Friel: A Casebook*, edited by William Kerwin, 77–116. New York: Garland, 1997.
Kearney, Richard, and Robin Wilson. "Northern Ireland's Future as a European Region." *Irish Review* 15 (Spring 1994): 51–69.
Kearney, Timothy. "The Poetry of the North: A Post-modernist Perspective." In *The Poetry of Seamus Heaney*, edited by Elmer Andrews, 64–68. New York: Columbia University Press, 1998.
Keats, John. *The Letters of John Keats, 1814–1821.* Vol. 2. Edited by Hyder Edward Rollins. Cambridge, MA: Harvard University Press, 1958.
———. *The Poems of John Keats.* Edited by Jack Stillinger. Cambridge, MA: Harvard University Press, 1978.
Keith, W. J. *Regions of the Imagination: The Development of British Rural Fiction.* Toronto: University of Toronto Press, 1988.
Kellaway, Kate. Review of *Human Chain*, by Seamus Heaney. *Observer*, August 22, 2010.
Kennedy, Charles W., trans. *Beowulf: The Oldest English Epic.* 1940. Reprint, Oxford: Oxford University Press, 1978.
Kersnowski, Frank. *The Outsiders: Poets of Contemporary Ireland.* Fort Worth: Texas Christian University Press, 1975.
Kiberd, Declan. *Inventing Ireland: The Literature of the Modern Nation.* Cambridge, MA: Harvard University Press, 1997.

Kimpel, Ursula. "Beyond the Caledonian Antisyzygy: Contemporary Scottish Poetry in between Cultures." In *Poetry in the British Isles: Non-metropolitan Perspectives*, edited by Hans-Werner Ludwig and Lothar Fietz, 135–56. Cardiff: University of Wales Press, 1995.

Kirkland, Richard. "Dialogues of Despair: Nationalist Cultural Discourse and the Revival in the North of Ireland, 1900–20." *Irish University Review* 33, no. 1 (Spring–Summer 2003): 64–78.

———. *Literature and Culture in Northern Ireland since 1965: Moments of Danger*. London: Longman, 1996.

———. "The Poetics of Partition: Poetry and Northern Ireland in the 1940s." In *The Oxford Handbook of Modern Irish Poetry*, edited by Fran Brearton and Alan Gillis, 210–24. Oxford: Oxford University Press, 2012.

Lee, Kee-Lee. "Gundestrup Cauldron." Essay in catalogue for virtual exhibition "Celtic Art and Cultures" produced by students in the course of the same name (Art 111), University of North Carolina–Chapel Hill, Fall 1998. www.unc.edu/celtic/topicsindex.html.

Linfoot, Matthew. "The Origins of BBC Local Radio." n.d. www.bbc.co.uk/historyofthebbc/resources/in-depth/local_radio.shtml.

Litton, Helen. *The Celts: An Illustrated History*. Dublin: Wolfhound, 1997.

Lloyd, David. *Anomalous States: Irish Writing and the Post-colonial Moment*. Durham, NC: Duke University Press, 1993.

Lojek, Helen. "Man, Woman, Soldier: Heaney's 'In Memoriam Francis Ledwidge' and Boland's 'Heroic.'" *New Hibernia Review* 10, no. 1 (Spring 2006): 123–38.

Longenbach, James. *The Resistance to Poetry*. Chicago: University of Chicago Press, 2004.

Longley, Edna. "'Atlantic's Premises': American Influences on Northern Irish Poetry in the 1960s." In *Poetry and Posterity*, 259–79. Newcastle, UK: Bloodaxe, 2000.

———. "Edward Thomas and Robert Frost." In *Poetry in the Wars*, 22–46. Newcastle, UK: Bloodaxe, 1986.

———. "Multi-culturalism and Northern Ireland: Making Differences Fruitful." In *Multi-culturalism: The View from the Two Irelands*, edited by E. Longley and Declan Kiberd, 1–44. Cork, Ireland: Cork University Press / Armagh, Northern Ireland: Centre for Cross-Border Studies, 2001.

———. "*North*: 'Inner Émigré' or 'Artful Voyeur?'" In *The Art of Seamus Heaney*, edited by Tony Curtis, 65–95. 1985. Reprint, Chester Springs, PA: Seren Books, 1994.

———. "Northern House Pamphlet Poets." *Phoenix* 1 (March 1967): 55–58.

———. "Opening Up: A New Pluralism." *Fortnight* 256 (1987): 24–25.

———. "The Poetics of Celt and Saxon." In *Poetry and Posterity*, 52–89. Newcastle, UK: Bloodaxe, 2000.

———. "Poetry and Politics in Northern Ireland." In *Poetry in the Wars*, 185–210. Newcastle upon Tyne: Bloodaxe, 1986.

Longley, Michael. Introduction to *W. R. Rodgers: Poems*, edited by Michael Longley, 11–22. Loughcrew, Ireland: Gallery Press, 1993.

———. "The Neolithic Night: A Note on the Irishness of Louis MacNeice." In *Two Decades of Irish Writing: A Critical Survey*, edited by Douglas Dunn, 98–104. Chester Springs, PA: Dufour, 1975.

———. "Poetry." In *Causeway: The Arts in Ulster*, edited by Michael Longley, 95–117. Belfast: Arts Council of Northern Ireland, 1971.

Lucas, John. "Seamus Heaney and the Possibilities of Poetry." In *Seamus Heaney: A Collection of Critical Essays*, edited by Elmer Andrews, 117–38. New York: St. Martin's Press, 1992.

Ludwig, Hans-Werner. "Province and Metropolis, Centre and Periphery: Some Critical Terms Re-examined." In *Poetry in the British Isles: Non-metropolitan Perspectives*, edited by Hans-Werner Ludwig and Lothar Fietz, 47–69. Cardiff: University of Wales Press, 1995.

Lyons, Laura E. "Of Orangemen and Green Theatres: The Ulster Literary Theatre's Regional Nationalism." In *A Century of Irish Drama: Widening the Stage*, edited by Stephen Watt, Eileen Morgan, and Shakir Mustafa, 34–53. Bloomington: Indiana University Press, 2000.

MacCana, Proinsias. "Early Irish Ideology and the Concept of Unity." In *The Irish Mind: Exploring Intellectual Traditions*, edited by Richard Kearney, 56–78. Dublin: Wolfhound Press, 1985.

MacNeice, Louis. *Louis MacNeice: Poems Selected by Michael Longley*. London: Faber and Faber, 2001.

Mahon, Derek. *Collected Poems*. Loughcrew, Ireland: Gallery Press, 1999.

Mahony, Christina Hunt. "Memory and Belonging: Irish Writers, Radio, and the Nation." *New Hibernia Review* 5, no. 1 (Spring 2001): 10–24.

Manganiello, Dominic. *Joyce's Politics*. London: Routledge, 1980.

Mantel, Hilary. "No Passes or Documents Are Needed: The Writer at Home in Europe." In *On Modern British Fiction*, edited by Zachary Leader, 93–106. Oxford: Oxford University Press, 2002.

Marcus, Morton. "Essay: The *Fu*: China and the Origins of the Prose Poem." *The Prose Poem: An International Journal* 8 (1999): n.p. http://digitalcommons.providence.edu/prosepoem/vol8/iss1/64/.

Massingham, H. J. *Remembrance: An Autobiography*. London: Batsford, 1942.

Matthews, Steven. "The Poet as Anthologist." In *The Oxford Handbook of Modern Irish Poetry*, edited by Fran Brearton and Alan Gillis, 534–47. Oxford: Oxford University Press, 2012.

McBride, Ian. *Scripture Politics: Ulster Presbyterianism and Irish Radicalism in Late Eighteenth-Century Ireland*. Oxford: Oxford University Press, 1998.

———. *The Siege of Derry in Ulster Protestant Mythology*. Dublin: Four Courts Press, 1997.

McCarthy, Conor. *Seamus Heaney and Medieval Poetry*. Cambridge: D. S. Brewer, 2008.

McDonagh, Oliver. *States of Mind: A Study of Anglo-Irish Conflict, 1780–1980.* New York: Routledge, 1985.
McDonald, Peter. *Mistaken Identities: Poetry and Northern Ireland.* Oxford: Oxford University Press, 1997.
———. "'Our Lost Lives': Protestantism and Northern Irish Poetry." In *The Oxford Handbook of Modern Irish Poetry*, edited by Fran Brearton and Alan Gillis, 473–91. Oxford: Oxford University Press, 2012.
———. *Serious Poetry: Form and Authority from Yeats to Hill.* Oxford: Oxford University Press, 2002.
McGuinness, Arthur E. *Seamus Heaney: Poet and Critic.* New York: Peter Lang, 1994.
McIntosh, Gillian. *The Force of Culture: Unionist Identities in Twentieth-Century Ireland.* Cork, Ireland: Cork University Press, 1999.
———. "'Life Is a Series of Oppositions': The Prose Work of W. R. Rodgers." *Irish Studies Review* 8, no. 2 (August 2000): 205–16.
McKenna, Bernard. "'Green Fire into the Frozen Branch': Violence and the Recovery of Identity in Vincent Woods's *At the Black Pig's Dyke* and Seamus Heaney's *The Cure at Troy*." In *That Other World: The Supernatural and the Fantastic in Irish Literature and Its Contexts*, vol. 2, edited by Bruce Stewart, 97–119. Gerrards Cross, UK: Colin Smythe, 1998.
McKittrick, David, Seamus Kelters, Brian Feeney, Chris Thornton, and David McVea. *Lost Lives: The Stories of the Men, Women, and Children Who Died as a Result of the Northern Ireland Troubles.* Rev. and updated ed. Edinburgh: Mainstream, 2007.
McLoone, Martin. "Inventions and Re-imaginings: Some Thoughts on Identity and Broadcasting in Ireland." In *Culture, Identity, and Broadcasting in Ireland: Local Issues, Global Perspectives*, edited by Martin McLoone, 2–30. Belfast: Institute of Irish Studies, 1991.
McNulty, Eugene. *The Ulster Literary Theatre and the Northern Revival.* Cork, Ireland: Cork University Press, 2008.
Meek, Jay. "Commentaries: Travel Notes." *The Prose Poem: An International Journal* 8 (1999): n.p. http://digitalcommons.providence.edu/prosepoem/vol8/iss1/72/.
Meeropol, Abel. "Strange Fruit." www.ladyday.net/stuf/vfsept98.html.
Melaugh, Eamon. *Derry: The Troubled Years.* Derry, Northern Ireland: Guildhall Press, 2005.
Mengel, Hagal. *Sam Thompson and Modern Drama in Ulster.* New York: Peter Lang, 1986.
Miłosz, Czesław. *Native Realm: A Search for Self-Definition.* New York: Farrar, Straus, Giroux, 2002.
———. "The World." Translated by Robert Hass and Robert Pinsky. *Ironweed* 9, no. 2 (Fall 1981): 41.
Molino, Michael. *Questioning Tradition, Language, and Myth: The Poetry of Seamus Heaney.* Washington, DC: Catholic University of America Press, 1994.

Moloney, Karen. *Seamus Heaney and the Emblems of Hope.* Columbia: University of Missouri Press, 2007.
Montague, John. "Regionalism into Reconciliation: The Poetry of John Hewitt." *Poetry Ireland* 3 (Spring 1964): 113–18.
———. *The Rough Field.* Loughcrew, Ireland: Gallery Press, 1989.
Morrison, Blake. *Seamus Heaney.* London: Methuen, 1982.
Murphy, Margueritte S. *A Tradition of Subversion: The Prose Poem in English from Wilde to Ashbery.* Amherst: University of Massachusetts Press, 1992.
Murray, Les. "Beall Poetry Festival Panel Discussion." Baylor University, Waco, TX, April 6, 2013.
Nicolaisen, Peter. "The Southern Agrarians and European Agrarianism." *Mississippi Quarterly* 49, no. 4 (Fall 1996): 683–700.
O'Brien, Eugene. *Seamus Heaney and the Place of Writing.* Gainesville: University Press of Florida, 2002.
———. *Seamus Heaney: Searches for Answers.* London: Pluto Press, 2003.
O'Brien, Sean. Review of *Human Chain*, by Seamus Heaney. *Independent*, September 3, 2010. www.independent.co.uk/.
O'Donoghue, Bernard. "Heaney's Classics and the Bucolic." In *The Cambridge Companion to Seamus Heaney*, edited by Bernard O'Donoghue, 106–21. Cambridge: Cambridge University Press, 2009.
———. *Seamus Heaney and The Language of Poetry.* Hemel Hempstead, UK: Harvester Wheatsheaf, 1994.
O'Donoghue, Heather. "Heaney, *Beowulf*, and the Medieval Literature of the North." In *The Cambridge Companion to Seamus Heaney*, edited by Bernard O'Donoghue, 192–205. Cambridge: Cambridge University Press, 2009.
O'Driscoll, Dennis. "Foreign Relations: Irish and International Poetry." In *Troubled Thoughts, Majestic Dreams: Selected Prose Writings*, 80–91. Loughcrew, Ireland: Gallery Press, 2001.
———. "Heaney in Public." In *The Cambridge Companion to Seamus Heaney*, edited by Bernard O'Donoghue, 56–72. Cambridge: Cambridge University Press, 2009.
OED Online. Oxford English Dictionary Online. www.oed.com/.
O'Malley, Aidan. *Field Day and the Translation of Irish Identities: Performing Contradictions.* New York: Palgrave, 2011.
O'Malley, Conor. *A Poet's Theatre.* Dublin: Elo Press, 1988.
Ormsby, Frank. Introduction to *The Collected Poems of John Hewitt*, edited by Frank Ormsby, xli–lxxiv. Belfast: Blackstaff Press, 1992.
Owen, Wilfred. *The Poems of Wilfred Owen.* Edited by Jon Stallworthy. New York: Norton, 1986.
———. Preface to *The Poems of Wilfred Owen*, edited by Jon Stallworthy, 192. New York: Norton, 1986.
Parker, Michael. "'Back in the Heartland': Seamus Heaney's 'Route 110' Sequence in *Human Chain*." *Irish Studies Review* 21, no. 4 (2013): 374–86.

———. "From *Winter Seeds* to *Wintering Out*: The Evolution of Heaney's Third Collection." *New Hibernia Review* 11, no. 2 (Summer 2007): 130–41.

———. "'His Nibs': Self-Reflexivity and the Significance of Translation in Seamus Heaney's *Human Chain*." *Irish University Review* 42, no. 2 (Autumn–Winter 2012): 327–50.

———. *Northern Irish Literature, 1956–1975: The Imprint of History.* New York: Palgrave, 2007.

———. "Past Master: Czesław Miłosz and His Impact on the Poetry of Seamus Heaney." *Textual Practice* 27, no. 5 (2013): 825–50.

———. "Reckonings: The Political Contexts for Northern Irish Literature 1965–68." *Irish Studies Review* 10, no. 2 (2002): 133–58.

———. *Seamus Heaney: The Making of the Poet.* Iowa City: University of Iowa Press, 1993.

Paulin, Tom. *Minotaur: Poetry and the Nation State.* Cambridge, MA: Harvard University Press, 1992.

———. "A New Look at the Language Question." In *Ireland's Field Day: Field Day Theatre Company*, 3–17. Notre Dame, IN: University of Notre Dame Press, 1986.

Peacock, Alan. "Mediations: Poet as Translator, Poet as Seer." In *Seamus Heaney: A Collection of Critical Essays*, edited by Elmer Kennedy-Andrews, 233–55. New York: St. Martin's Press, 1992.

Pearson, Mike. Review of *Border-Crossing: Mumming in Cross-Border and Cross-Community Contexts*, edited by Anthony D. Buckley, Críostóir Mac Cárthaigh, Séamas Ó Catháin, and Séamus Mac Mathúna. July 16, 2008. www.mastermummers.org/articles/Review-Border-Crossing.htm.

Potter, Robert. *The English Morality Play: Origins, History, and Influence of a Dramatic Tradition.* Boston: Routledge and Kegan Paul, 1975.

Potts, Donna. *Contemporary Irish Poetry and the Pastoral Tradition.* Columbia: University of Missouri Press, 2011.

Ransom, John Crowe. "Honey and Gall." In *Selected Essays of John Crowe Ransom*, edited by Thomas Daniel Young and John Hindle, 112–27. Baton Rouge: Louisiana State University Press, 1984.

Richtarik, Marilynn J. *Acting between the Lines: The Field Day Theatre Company and Irish Cultural Politics, 1980–1984.* Oxford: Oxford University Press, 1994.

———. "'Ireland, the Continuous Past': Stewart Parker's Belfast History Plays." In *A Century of Irish Drama: Widening the Stage*, edited by Stephen Watt, Eileen Morgan, and Shakir Mustafa, 256–74. Bloomington: Indiana University Press, 2000.

Robey, David. "*Terza Rima*." In *The Dante Encyclopedia*, edited by Richard Lansing, 808–10. New York: Garland, 2000.

Robinson, Alan. *Instabilities in Contemporary British Poetry.* London: Macmillan, 1998.

Ross, Daniel W. "'The Upward Waft': The Influence of Frost and Eliot on Heaney's Later Phase." In *Seamus Heaney: Poet, Critic, Translator*, edited by Bland Crowder and Jason David Hall, 92–102. New York: Palgrave, 2007.

Russell, Richard Rankin. "Black Passages through White Spaces: The Masking of Faulkner's African-American Characters in *Go Down, Moses*." *CEA Critic* 73, no. 1 (Winter 2010): 86–109.

———. "Eugene McNulty's *The Ulster Literary Theatre and the Northern Revival*." *Modern Drama* 52, no. 2 (Summer 2009): 250–52.

———. "Exorcising the Ghosts of Conflict in Northern Ireland: Stewart Parker's *The Iceberg* and *Pentecost*." *Eire-Ireland* 41, nos. 3–4 (Fall–Winter 2006): 42–58.

———. "Imagining a New Province: Seamus Heaney's Creative Work for BBC Northern Ireland Radio, 1968–1971." *Irish Studies Review* 15, no. 2 (Spring 2007): 137–62.

———. "The Keats and Hopkins Dialectic in Seamus Heaney's Early Poetry: 'The Forge.'" *ANQ* 25, no. 1 (January–March 2012): 44–50.

———. "Owen and Yeats in Heaney's *The Cure at Troy*." *Essays in Criticism* 61, no. 2 (April 2011): 173–89.

———. *Poetry and Peace: Michael Longley, Seamus Heaney, and Northern Ireland*. Notre Dame, IN: University of Notre Dame Press, 2010.

———. "Seamus Heaney's Regionalism." *Twentieth-Century Literature* 54, no. 1 (Spring 2008): 47–74.

———. "W. B. Yeats and Eavan Boland: Postcolonial Poets?" In *W. B. Yeats and Postcolonialism*, edited by Deborah Fleming, 101–32. West Cornwall, CT: Locust Hill Press.

Sanburn, Josh. "All Time 100 Songs: 'Strange Fruit.'" *Time*, October 21, 2011. http://entertainment.time.com/2011/10/24/the-all-time-100-songs/slide/strange-fruit-billie-holiday/.

Sayers, Dorothy. Introduction to *The Comedy of Dante Aligheri: The Florentine. Cantica I: Hell*, translated by Dorothy Sayers, 9–69. Baltimore: Penguin, 1949.

———. Introduction to *The Comedy of Dante Aligheri: The Florentine. Cantica II: Purgatory*, translated by Dorothy Sayers, 9–71. Baltimore: Penguin, 1955.

Scarry, Elaine. *The Body in Pain: The Making and Unmaking of the World*. New York: Oxford University Press, 1985.

Schuchard, Ronald. Introduction to *The Place of Writing*, by Seamus Heaney, 2–16. Atlanta, GA: Scholar's Press, 1989.

Sergeant, Ben. "Ulster Regionalism." *Rann: An Ulster Quarterly, Poetry and Comment* 20 (June 1953): 3–7.

Shovlin, Frank. *The Irish Literary Periodical, 1923–1958*. Oxford: Oxford University Press, 2003.

Siculus, Diodorus. *Library of History*. Book 1. Translated by C. H. Oldfather. Loeb Classical Library. Cambridge, MA: Harvard University Press, 1935. http://penelope.uchicago.edu-LacusCurtius.

Simmons, James. Editorial. *Honest Ulsterman* 1 (May 1968): 2–6.
———. "The Honest Ulsterman." Advertisement. Inside front page of *Phoenix* 6/7 (Summer 1970).
Sontag, Susan. *Regarding the Pain of Others.* New York: Picador, 2004.
Spivak, Gayatri Chakravorty. *Other Asias.* Malden, MA: Blackwell, 2008.
Stevens, Wallace. *The Collected Poems of Wallace Stevens.* New York: Vintage, 1982.
———. *Wallace Stevens: Collected Poetry and Prose.* New York: Library of America, 1997.
Stevenson, Anne. "*Stations*: Seamus Heaney and the Sacred Sense of the Sensitive Self." In *The Art of Seamus Heaney*, 3rd ed., edited by Tony Curtis, 45–51. Chester Springs, PA: Dufour, 1994.
Stevenson, Randall. *1960–2000: The Last of England?* Vol. 12 of *The Oxford English Literary History.* Oxford: Oxford University Press, 2004.
Stewart, A. T. Q. *The Ulster Crisis: Resistance to Home Rule, 1912–1914.* 1967. Reprint, Belfast: Blackstaff Press, 1997.
Stewart, Bruce. "'The Door and What Came through It': Aspects of Influence." In *Patrick Kavanagh*, edited by Stan Smith, 163–87. Dublin: Irish Academic Press, 2009.
Stewart, Susan. "Dante and the Poetry of Meeting." *American Poetry Review* 35 (July–August 2006): 39–42.
———. *Poetry and the Fate of the Senses.* Chicago: University of Chicago Press, 2002.
Tange, Hanne. "Regional Redemption: Graham Swift's *Waterland* and the End of History." *Orbis Litterarum* 59, no. 2 (2004): 75–89.
Taplin, Oliver. "Sophocles' *Philoctetes*, Seamus Heaney's, and Some Other Recent Half-Rhymes." In *Dionysus since 69: Greek Tragedy at the Dawn of the Third Milennium*, edited by Edith Hall, Fiona Macintosh, and Amanda Wrigley, 145–68. New York: Oxford University Press, 2004.
Terdiman, Richard. *Discourse/Counter-discourse: The Theory and Practice of Symbolic Resistance in Nineteenth-Century France.* Ithaca, NY: Cornell University Press, 1985.
Thornton, Weldon. *Allusions in "Ulysses": An Annotated List.* Chapel Hill: University of North Carolina Press, 1968.
———. *The Antimodernism of Joyce's "A Portrait of the Artist as a Young Man."* Syracuse, NY: Syracuse University Press, 1994.
Thurston, Michael. "Region and Nation in Britain and Ireland." In *A Concise Companion to Postwar British and Irish Poetry*, edited by Nigel Alderman and C. D. Blanton, 72–91. Malden, MA: Wiley-Blackwell, 2009.
Tobin, Daniel. *Passage to the Center: Imagination and the Sacred in the Poetry of Seamus Heaney.* Lexington: University Press of Kentucky, 1999.
Toíbín, Colm. Review of *Human Chain*, by Seamus Heaney. *Guardian*, August 21, 2010. www.guardian.co.uk/books/2010/aug/21/seamus-heaney-human-chain-review/print.

Turner, Paul. "*The Cure at Troy*: Sophocles or Heaney?" In *Seamus Heaney: Poet, Critic, Translator*, edited by Bland Crowder and Jason David Hall, 121–35. New York: Palgrave, 2007.
"Ulster Books and Authors: 1900–1953." *Rann: An Ulster Quarterly* 20 (June 1953): 55–73.
Vendler, Helen. *The Breaking of Style: Hopkins, Heaney, Graham*. Cambridge, MA: Harvard University Press, 1995.
———. *Seamus Heaney*. Cambridge, MA: Harvard University Press, 1995.
Virgil. *The Aeneid*. Translated by Robert Fitzgerald. New York: Vintage, 1983.
Walsh, Patrick. "'Too Much Alone': John Hewitt, Regionalism, Socialism, and Partition." *Irish University Review* 29, no. 2 (Autumn–Winter 1999): 341–57.
"Whatever You Say Say Nothing." Museum number 4010. Transmission date July 24, 1994. BBC Northern Ireland Radio Archives. Cultra, Northern Ireland.
Whelan, Kevin. "The Bases for Regionalism." In *Culture in Ireland—Regions: Identity and Power*, edited by Proinsias O'Drisceoil, 5–64. Proceedings of the Cultures of Ireland Group Conference. Belfast: Institute for Irish Studies, 1993.
———. "Between the Politics of Culture in Friel's *Translations*." *Field Day Review* 6 (2010): 7–27.
Wilson, Edmund. "Philoctetes: The Wound and the Bow." In *The Wound and the Bow: Seven Studies in Literature*, 223–42. New York, Farrar, Straus, Giroux, 1978.
Wood, Michael. *Yeats and Violence*. Oxford: Oxford University Press, 2010.
Wordsworth, William. *William Wordsworth: Poems Selected by Seamus Heaney*. London: Faber and Faber, 1988.
Yeats, W. B. *The Collected Poems of W. B. Yeats: A New Edition*. Edited by Richard J. Finneran. New York: Scribner, 1996.
———. Introduction to *The Oxford Book of Modern Verse, 1892–1935*, v–xlii. Oxford: Clarendon Press, 1936.
Young, Gary. "Commentaries: A Woman Leans." *The Prose Poem: An International Journal* 8 (1999): n.p. http://digitalcommons.providence.edu/prosepoem/vol8/iss1/74/.
Young, Robin. "At the Margins: Outsider-Figures in Nineteenth-Century Poetry." In *Poetry in the British Isles: Non-metropolitan Perspectives*, edited by Hans-Werner Ludwig and Lothar Fietz, 31–45. Cardiff: University of Wales Press, 1995.
Zillman, Lawrence J., and Clive Scott. "Terza Rima." In *The New Princeton Encyclopedia of Poetry and Poetics*, edited by Alex Preminger and T. V. F. Brogan, 1271. New York: MJF Books; Princeton, NJ: Princeton University Press, 1993.
Žižek, Slavoj. *Violence*. New York: Picador, 2008.

Index

activism, 225, 295, 311
Alighieri, Dante, 2, 4, 17, 40, 184, 185, 215, 240–42, 247–57, 259–63, 265–68, 271, 273, 275, 279–80, 295, 360–63, 366–70, 372–74, 391–92, 394, 396, 433, 443–46, 457, 459

Barthes, Roland, 20
Benjamin, Walter, 324
biblical allusion/inspiration, 141, 142, 160, 196–97, 379, 381
birth imagery, 171–72, 233–34
blackness/American civil rights movement, 16, 161, 162–86
boundary (real or fictitious), 189, 214, 241, 287, 320, 330, 346, 410n129
Boyd, John, 43, 44, 48, 51, 57, 73, 77, 410n9, 411n14
British colonization/imperialism, 14, 42, 70, 112, 128, 161, 164, 177, 196, 220, 226, 234, 252, 269, 430n16
Brown, George Mackay, 5, 16, 102, 120
Burris, Sydney, 27
Buttel, Robert, 6

Caedmon, 5
Catholicism/Catholic Church, 225–26, 242–43, 271, 293, 358–59, 416n19, 430n10
community, 383, 404
Corcoran, Neil, 33, 102, 138, 182, 248, 256, 260, 261, 264, 265, 270, 271, 272, 275, 287, 314, 320, 324, 427n14, 431n20, 444n54, 451

Crawford, Robert, 30, 126, 217, 226, 227, 277, 408n77, 426n103
critical regionalism, 28–29, 129, 408n93

Dainotto, Roberto M., 22, 27, 28, 29, 33
deracination, 142, 289
direct language, 6, 232
Draper, R. P., 20, 29, 30, 126, 311
dual identity, 219–20, 221, 223, 225, 226, 228, 231, 237, 320, 325

ecumenism, 91, 92, 93, 115, 173, 243, 307, 403
Eliot, T. S., 204, 234, 241, 250, 256–61, 263, 265–68, 271, 273, 335, 360–63, 440n53, 443n36, 444n54, 445n72, 445nn74–75, 445nn77–78, 445n80, 446n84, 456n144
empathy, 299, 342–43
eternity/eternal rest, 384, 387–88, 389, 390, 392, 401, 404
Evans, E. Estyn, 30, 31, 34, 35, 65
exile, 252, 253–54, 325, 452n49

Falci, Eric, 20–21, 28
fictional place, 121–22
food imagery/images of consuming, 171, 181, 185
Foster, John Wilson, 31, 32, 33, 35, 36, 38, 39, 41, 45, 49, 60, 85, 113, 114, 241, 311, 334, 340, 418n77, 423n41, 424n53, 427n113, 451n24

487

Frampton, Kenneth, 28, 29, 129, 408n93
Frost, Robert, 5–7, 32, 102, 116–18, 163, 319–20, 365, 385, 388, 405n12, 425n58, 439n42
Fussell, Paul, 393–94

Garland, Patrick, 15
gaze/gazing, 182–83, 194
gendered place (Ireland and Britain), 13–15, 60–61, 140–41, 161, 234, 236, 252, 406n48
genre, 188–89, 191, 193, 200, 206, 207
geographical place/space, 34, 49, 51, 56, 80, 103–4, 106, 107, 108, 109, 113, 114, 115–16, 121–22, 124, 129, 141, 151, 152, 158, 200, 212, 263, 269, 272, 273, 275, 280, 312, 315, 321, 322, 325, 329, 330, 345, 349, 350–51, 372–73, 407n54

Haffenden, John, 10
Hall, Jason David, 19, 170, 188, 248, 406n47
Hart, Henry, 11, 22, 128, 188, 189, 190, 208, 209, 259, 273, 435n28, 437n55, 439n42, 452n49
Heaney, Seamus
  and critical reception, 102, 222–23, 316, 334–35
  and English language, 10, 24, 51, 59, 119–20, 123, 126, 146–47, 151, 192, 213, 214, 215, 246, 260, 283
  film script by, 401
  interviews, 7, 112, 120–21, 130, 279, 316, 318, 333, 340, 356
  love for drama/dramatic readings, 283–84
  and other regional authors, 4, 7–8, 9, 10–11, 23, 25, 28, 29, 32, 39, 41, 45, 49–50, 56–57, 58–59, 63–64, 76–77, 84–85, 101–29, 214, 216, 224, 226, 237, 247, 258–59, 284, 318–19, 336, 337–38, 367, 372, 401, 445n72
  reflecting provincial/local dialect, 7, 8, 9, 16, 23–25, 53, 71, 119–20, 121, 131, 215
  tour "Room to Rhyme," 78, 427n12
Heaney, Seamus, anthologies
  Rattle Bag, The, 11, 22, 23–24
  School Bag, The, 11, 324, 339
Heaney, Seamus, biography
  actor, 86, 283, 284
  beginning poet, 130
  Belfast Group, 32, 42, 52, 73, 101, 144
  birth of grandchild, 400
  Catholic "countryside" poet, 4–5, 8–9, 81, 109, 158–59, 177, 200, 201, 227, 243, 330, 349–50
  Catholicism, 172–73, 254, 357, 366, 390, 431n36
  collaborations, 1, 11, 22, 23–24, 77–78, 324, 339
  eulogizer at Ted Hughes's funeral, 11
  family's move to Republic of Ireland, 141–42
  Field Day Theatre Company member, 17, 211, 218–19, 222, 223–24, 280, 282–83, 284–85, 286, 287, 288, 291, 401
  leaving Northern Ireland, 186, 254
  literary influences/inspirations, 4, 5, 6, 7–8, 9–10, 11, 16, 17, 18, 25, 105–6, 108–9, 110–29, 145, 157, 174, 176, 184, 189, 191, 198, 212, 213–15, 225, 232, 238, 246, 273, 279, 306, 317, 326, 327, 360, 438n1
  memorial service eulogy for R. S. Thomas, 118
  Nobel Prize, 2, 8, 32, 276, 312, 416n2, 435n26
  poetic "calling," 5
  radio broadcaster, 16, 19, 66, 68–73, 78–82, 84–100

rural labor/delight in rural labor,
  6–7, 252, 383
stroke, 2, 18, 381–82
student at Anahorish School, 177,
  352
student at Queen's University, 7, 8,
  73, 116, 177, 283
teacher at St. Thomas's School 9, 79,
  115
trained as a teacher at St. Joseph's
  School, 79, 283
year at University of California,
  Berkeley, 141, 164, 167, 189,
  191
Heaney, Seamus, essays
  "Above the Brim," 117, 385
  "'Apt Admonishment': Wordsworth
    as an Example," 360–62, 363,
    435n27
  "Belfast," 166
  "Bog, The," 329
  "Cornucopia and Empty Shell:
    Variations on an Theme from
    Ellmann," 274, 276–77
  Crediting Poetry, 12, 312, 343,
    369–70, 371
  "Drag of the Golden Chain, The,"
    330
  "Dylan the Durable? On Dylan
    Thomas," 365–66
  "Eclogues in Extremis: On the
    Staying Power of Pastoral," 22,
    25–26
  "Englands of the Mind," 63, 94,
    123–27, 128, 341
  "Envies and Identifications: Dante
    and the Modern Poet," 259,
    260–61, 262–63
  "Feeling into Words," 7, 107, 161,
    277, 330, 442n23
  "From Monaghan to the Grand
    Canal: The Poetry of Patrick
    Kavanagh," 106, 111

"Frontiers of Writing, The," 18,
  19–20, 113, 117, 219, 225, 275,
  316, 318, 320–23, 334, 359
"Fully Exposed Poem, The," 238
"Further Language," 313
"Government of the Tongue, The,"
  257
"Guttural Muse in a Global Age,
  The," 18, 310, 343
"Humanizing the City," 354
"Impact of Translation, The,"
  259–60, 335–36
"Interesting Case of Nero,
  Chekhov's Cognac, and a
  Knocker, The," 444n45
"John Clare's Prog," 312, 314–16
"Joyce's Poetry," 218, 225
"Joy or Night: Last Things in the
  Poetry of W. B. Yeats and Philip
  Larkin," 122–23, 373, 374
"Learning from Eliot," 257
"Main of Light, The," 122
"Mossbawn," 103, 104, 107, 147,
  158, 190
"Old Derry's Walls," 90, 94, 419n99,
  432n42
"Omphalos," 103
"Our Own Dour Way," 58, 93
"Out of London: Ulster's Troubles,"
  68
Place and Displacement: Recent
  Poetry of Northern Ireland, 1, 213,
  224
"Placeless Heaven, The," 107, 111,
  363, 422n22
"Place of Writing, The," 122, 212,
  386
"Poet as a Christian, The," 109
"Pre-natal Mountain: Vision and
  Irony in Recent Irish Poetry,"
  319–20
"Redress of Poetry, The," 298, 364,
  373, 388, 457n30

Heaney, Seamus, essays (*cont.*)
  "Regional Forecast, The," 1, 17, 32, 79, 102, 212, 215, 245, 247, 260, 265, 356
  "Room to Rhyme," 5, 11, 427n13
  "Sense of Place, The," 107–12, 127, 236, 263, 319, 341
  "Through-Other Places, Through Other Times," 220–21, 224, 339
Heaney, Seamus, poetry
  "Act of Union," 14, 16, 17, 140, 141, 207, 233, 291
  "Album," 393
  "Alias," 192
  "Amputation," 144, 179
  "Autobiographical Borings," 192
  "Ballad," 192, 434n12, 437n51
  "Barn, The," 384
  "Belderg," 131, 146, 152
  "Boarders," 353
  "Bogland," 106, 137, 159, 315, 329, 330
  Bog Poems, 11, 152–55, 174
  "Bog Queen," 152, 171
  "Bone Dreams," 131, 151, 152
  "Casualty," 119, 398, 404, 442n
  "Cauled," 192
  "Chanson d'Aventure," 368, 381, 393
  "Clearances," 350
  "Cloistered," 187, 192
  "Come to the Bower," 152
  "Constable Calls, A," 193, 194
  "Corncake," 249
  "Crossing, The," 353, 368, 370, 372, 391, 392, 396–97
  "Daylight Art, A" 274
  "Death of a Naturalist," 82, 198
  Death of a Naturalist, 3, 9, 41, 59, 63, 82, 105–6, 115, 124, 198, 248, 249, 291, 298, 314, 316, 384, 423n30, 432
  "Digging," 9, 82, 93, 117, 118, 135, 160, 248, 351, 430n
  "Disappearing Island, The," 274–76
  District and Circle, 19, 311, 312, 315, 343, 346–55, 392, 395, 437n52
  "District and Circle," 312, 354–55
  "Diviner, The," 106, 351
  "Docker," 334
  Door into the Dark, 3, 64, 82, 106, 137, 145, 146, 159, 249, 298, 315, 378, 402
  "'Door Was Open and the House Was Dark, The'" 18, 392, 400–403
  "Dream," 145
  "Eelworks," 393
  Electric Light, 26, 295, 311, 350, 392
  "England's Difficulty," 187, 189, 192
  "Exposure," 206, 296
  "Fair (A Progress Report)," 124
  Field Work, 17, 24, 119, 149, 184–86, 251–52, 253, 271–72, 296, 344, 378, 398, 401, 432n53, 436n36, 437n55, 448n30
  "Field Work," 251–52
  "Follower," 314
  "Forge, The," 298, 351, 401, 402
  "Fosterage," 115
  "Found Prose," 312, 351, 352, 354, 396
  "Freedman," 194, 195, 196, 197, 209
  "Frogman," 82
  "From Singing School," 194, 434n20
  "From the Canton of Expectation," 442n10
  "From the Frontier of Conscience," 275
  "From the Frontier of Writing," 275, 276
  "From the Republic of Conscience," 274, 276
  "Funeral Rites," 131, 147, 149, 157

Index 491

"Gents, The," 192
"Given Note, The," 249
"Glanmore Eclogue," 26
"Glanmore Revisited," 371, 377
"Grauballe Man, The," 152, 171, 329
"Guttural Muse, The," 344
"Hailstones," 274
"Harrow-Pin, The," 312, 350–51
"Harvest Bow, The," 372
"Haul, A" 370
Haw Lantern, The, 27, 151, 274–76, 311, 350, 352, 388, 442n9, 442n10
"Hedge-School," 192
"Hermit Songs," 393
Human Chain, 2, 18, 40, 276, 352, 355, 356, 357, 361, 368, 371–72, 377–78, 380–84, 392, 393–404
"Human Chain," 368, 381, 383, 384
"Incertus," 187, 188, 434n12
"Indomitable Irishry, The," 110
"In Memoriam Francis Ledwidge," 297, 448n30
"Inquisition," 193, 198, 199, 204, 206, 208
"In the Attic," 368, 372, 377–78, 393
"Intimidation," 16, 96, 131, 138–40, 144, 186, 205, 428n21, 428n24
"Journey Back, The," 353, 368, 372–74, 391
"July," 187, 193, 194, 204, 206, 207, 208
"Kernes," 192, 204, 205–6, 207, 208
"Kinship," 131, 152, 157, 159
"Kite for Aibhín, A," 18, 384, 392, 403, 404
"Lagans Road," 352
"Last Mummer, The," 131, 134, 135, 136, 138, 167
"Lick the Pencil," 393
"Lightenings," 359, 372, 387
"Linen Town," 131–34, 252
"Loughanure," 393

"Lough Neagh Sequence," 106
"May Day," 249
"Miracle," 368, 372, 378, 380–81, 384
"*Mo Thuras Go Rann Na Feirste*," 192
"My Reverence," 173, 174, 178
"Nesting Ground," 187, 192
New Selected Poems, 1966–1987, 187, 272
"Nocturne," 131, 138, 140–43, 144
"No Man's Land," 143
"North," 127, 143, 149, 151, 157
North, 3, 13, 14, 16, 17, 69, 84, 106, 115, 127, 128, 130–61, 162–86, 187, 188, 189, 190, 192, 193, 194, 198, 199, 206, 207, 221, 384, 437n55
"Northern Hoard, A," 131, 138, 140, 143–44, 162, 163, 185
"No Sanctuary," 144, 185
"Ocean's Love to Ireland," 13, 14, 233, 252
"October Thought," 7, 176
"On His Work in the English Tongue," 11, 295, 297, 426n107
"On the Gift of a Fountain Pen," 434n24
Opened Ground: Selected Poems, 1966–1996, 187, 204, 214, 272
Open Letter, An, 17, 211, 212–39, 260, 285, 286, 308, 337, 339, 341
"Orange Drums, Tyrone, 1966," 193, 207
"Other Side, The," 249, 334
"Out of the Bag," 392
"Parable Island," 274, 275, 276, 442n9
"Patrick and Oisin," 192
"Peninsula, The," 113
"Personal Helicon," 82, 106, 298
"Plantation, The," 82, 83, 84

Heaney, Seamus, poetry (*cont.*)
"Postcard from Iceland, A," 274, 275
"Postcard from North Antrim: In Memory of Sean Armstrong, A," 24, 274
"Punishment," 84, 127, 152, 161, 169, 171, 180, 181, 183, 185, 194, 221, 250, 273, 308, 342, 343, 401
"Reliquary," 172, 178
"Retrospect, A," 385, 386
"Riverbank Field, The," 18, 393, 396
"Roots," 138, 162
"Route 110," 2, 18, 355, 384, 392–96, 400
"Sabbath-Breakers, The," 192, 201–4, 205, 206, 208
"Scaffolding," 430
"Seed-Time," 193
Seeing Things, 18, 356, 360–61, 364, 368–69, 370–77, 378–80, 381, 385–92
"September Song," 401
"Servant Boy," 131, 168
"Settle Bed, The," 368, 372, 374–77
"Shoreline," 146
"Singer's House, The," 401
"Singing School," 106, 115, 185, 193, 194, 199, 296, 384, 434n20
"Sinking the Shaft," 192, 200–201
"Skylight, The," 371, 372, 377, 378–80, 381
"Slack," 393
"Sofa in the Forties, A," 67–68, 70, 350
"Song of the Bullets, The," 297
"Sounds of Rain," 368, 385
Spirit Level, The, 12, 67, 321, 346, 350
"Squarings," 368, 372, 386–90, 391, 401, 457n40
Station Island, 17, 52, 201, 215, 240–74, 352, 361, 368, 446n84, 459n14

"Station Island," 17, 214, 218, 240–73, 444n54
Stations, 17, 141, 187–211
"Stations of the West, The," 187–88, 434n12
"St. Francis and the Birds," 249
"St. Kevin and the Blackbird," 12
"Storm on the Island," 430n13
"Stone Grinder, The," 274
"Strand at Lough Beg, The," 184, 251, 252, 253, 255, 390
"Strange Fruit," 17, 152, 162, 165, 167, 169–85, 329, 343, 345
"Stump," 143, 144, 163, 179
"Summer 1969," 185, 384
"Sweeney Redivivus," 17, 247, 257, 272, 274, 363
"Sweet William," 192, 193, 204, 205, 206–7
"Tall Dames," 352–53
"Thatching," 135, 351
"Three Drawings," 370
"Tinder," 144
"Tollund Man, The," 58, 127, 137–38, 149, 163, 169, 174, 183, 194, 312, 329, 346, 354, 362, 392
"Tollund Man in Springtime, The," 312, 346–48, 354, 392
"Toome Road, The," 436n36
"Trial Runs," 187, 208–9
"Triceps," 169, 178
"Turas," 192, 200, 434n12
"Turnip-Snedder, The," 312, 350
"Two Quick Notes," 274
"Two Stick Drawings," 390
"Ugolino," 17, 169, 184–85, 251, 252, 297, 442n24
"Ulster Twilight," 192
"Unacknowledged Legislator's Dream," 194
"Undine," 249, 442n23

"Viking Dublin: Trial Pieces," 131, 148–51
"Villanelle for an Anniversary," 365
"Virgil: Eclogue IX," 26
"Visitant," 187, 192
"Wanderer, The," 187, 188, 192
"Water Babies," 192
"Welcome Home Ye Lads of the Eighth Army," 198, 199, 204, 208
"Whatever You Say Say Nothing," 165, 194, 207, 221, 250, 281, 308, 401, 434n20
Wintering Out, 3, 16, 71, 112, 120, 127, 131–38, 139, 140, 143–44, 146, 149, 161, 162–63, 168, 174, 177, 183, 188, 189, 192, 197, 214, 231, 236, 249, 277, 340, 346, 401, 428n27, 428n28, 440n47
"Wishing Tree, The," 274
"Wool Trade, The," 214, 215, 252, 334
Heaney, Seamus, radio scripts
Everyman, 16, 68, 69, 94–98, 208, 284
Munro, 68, 69, 86–94, 131, 284
Over the Bridge, 68, 69, 98–99
"Untitled," BBC *Explorations* series, 16, 19, 49, 66, 68, 69, 71, 78, 80–86
Heaney, Seamus, translations
Beowulf, 8, 18, 280, 312, 315, 324–28, 330, 331–41, 345, 351, 364–65, 455n118
Cresseid, Testament of, The, 18, 312, 324, 326, 340–43, 345
Cure at Troy, The, 17, 66, 139, 144, 145, 278, 279–309, 310, 311, 322, 326, 364, 448n28
Inferno, 250, 253, 273, 442n24
Midnight Verdict, The, 341
Sweeney Astray, 282, 324–25, 326, 328, 340, 341, 343

Herr, Cheryl, 29
Hewitt, John, 16, 38–39, 41, 46, 45, 47–52, 54–60, 63, 69, 76–77, 102, 104, 110–17, 128, 312, 316–20, 334–35, 338, 411n15, 412n22, 412n23, 412nn31–33, 412n35, 413n36, 413n41, 414n60, 414n64, 423n41, 424n51, 428n21, 450n17, 451n24, 454n103
Hill, Geoffrey, 63, 123–25, 191
historical context, 15, 27, 28, 30–31, 32, 33, 35, 36, 37, 38, 39, 41, 42, 44, 45, 48, 50, 52–53, 55, 58–59, 68, 69, 70, 71, 74, 75–76, 78, 80, 84, 86–87, 90–91, 92, 94–95, 97, 99, 101, 102, 113, 114, 115, 117, 121, 130, 131, 134, 135, 137, 138, 139, 141, 144, 146, 147, 148, 149, 163, 164, 167, 168, 173, 176, 177, 181, 183, 191, 197, 198, 214–15, 221, 223, 238, 242, 247, 252, 253, 279, 283, 284, 292, 293, 298, 304, 305, 307–9, 313, 325, 335, 336, 340, 348, 358–59, 369, 391–92, 402–3, 448n28
and political conflict, 254, 271, 288–89, 440n55
historical allusion/imagery, 202, 203, 204, 205, 251, 271, 275, 281–82, 293
"Britannic," 339
historical potential, 131, 132–33
historical violence, 3, 14, 43, 69, 115, 131, 134, 137, 145, 146, 148, 151, 157, 161, 164–65, 169, 175, 176, 180, 181, 182–83, 222, 253, 278, 280, 281, 282, 288, 298, 305, 332, 348–49, 395
Hopkins, Gerard Manley, 5, 7–9, 23, 263, 326–27, 386, 406n26, 445n68, 458n56

Hughes, Ted, 5, 7, 9–11, 16, 22–24, 30–31, 102, 117, 121, 123–28, 130, 152, 295, 324–27, 339, 406n32, 426nn106–7, 439n42
imagination, 43, 67–68, 70, 78, 80–81, 82, 83–84, 107, 120, 133–34, 147, 212, 285, 321, 322, 329–30, 345, 364, 378
individualism/independence, 61, 245, 267, 270, 271–72, 273, 274, 277, 282, 287, 301, 302–3, 404
Internet, the, 345, 346, 347–48
isolation, 289, 291, 295, 334

Jones, David, 191
journeying, 84, 192, 273
Joyce, James, 41–42, 119, 145, 149–50, 212–19, 225–26, 228, 231–35, 237–38, 240–41, 243–47, 269–74, 276–77, 279–80, 322–23, 356, 368, 372, 391, 438n18, 439n38, 440n47, 441n57, 441n62, 442n20, 444n54, 446n85, 446n88, 447n1

Kavanagh, Patrick, 5, 7, 9, 16, 21, 23, 25, 41, 55, 59, 101, 104, 105, 106, 107, 108, 111, 112, 115, 116, 117, 119, 122, 126, 127, 243, 244, 319, 360, 363, 385, 406n32, 413n53, 422n22, 438n1, 441n58
Keith, W. J., 13, 21, 22, 35
Kirkland, Richard, 43, 48, 49, 50, 60, 61, 104, 113, 411n17, 421n10

Larkin, Philip, 16, 64, 102, 121–26, 335, 365, 372–74, 391, 415nn86–87, 426n103, 458n55
linguistic technique, 203, 264
 formal vs. colloquial language, 264
 language as exchange, 264

literary allusion, 150, 151, 202, 230, 231, 233, 234, 235, 240, 247, 272, 279–80, 285, 302, 332, 355, 357, 365, 377, 382, 383, 391, 453n67, 454n95
Longley, Edna, 40, 63, 64, 85, 98, 100, 117, 128, 169
Longley, Michael, 25–26, 38, 45, 51, 55, 62, 78, 114, 128, 319, 391, 402, 415n87

MacNeice, Louis, 16, 44, 53, 55–56, 58, 105, 114–15, 318–22, 424n51
Mantel, Hilary, 39–40
marginalization, 240, 324, 342, 407n60, 408n86
Matthews, Steven, 18–19
McDonald, Peter, 38, 48, 114, 386, 387, 424n51, 458n69
McLaverty, Michael, 3, 9, 47, 55, 59, 79, 104, 115–16, 244
McLoone, Martin, 70–71
McNulty, Eugene, 42–43
meaning-making, 5, 146
memory, 349, 350, 352, 357, 377, 387, 388–89, 396, 397, 399–400
modernization, 125
Montague, John, 3–4, 38, 102, 104, 108–9, 110, 111, 127, 174, 206, 236, 244, 319, 327, 396, 422n26, 431n30, 436n48, 441n58, 459n6
Morgan, F. W., 12
multiple meanings, 138–39, 376, 396
mythology/allusions to mythology, 142, 146, 147, 150, 164, 174, 175, 203, 215–16, 245, 274, 278, 279–80, 282, 287, 290, 296, 305, 345, 368, 370, 383, 391–92, 394–95, 396–97, 399, 442n9

Nairn, Tom, 77
national identity, 39, 42, 46, 49, 70,
    79, 113–14, 143, 215, 218, 221,
    224–25, 226, 232, 236–37,
    238–39, 269, 316, 331, 454n104
    and literature, 238–39, 241
nationalism/national sentiment,
    54–55, 70, 90, 121, 126–28,
    133, 220, 225–26, 235, 271–72,
    319–20, 427n113
nature imagery, 244
Nicolaisen, Peter, 27–28
numerology, 257, 364, 385–86

O'Brien, Sean, 30, 394, 440n46
O'Donoghue, Bernard, 22, 151, 170,
    227, 241, 248, 263–64, 271,
    408n87, 443n36, 446n84
O'Driscoll, Dennis, 4, 7, 134, 164, 168,
    189, 190, 210, 214, 226, 233, 236,
    242, 288, 295, 300, 430n16,
    440n46
oppression, 226, 246
otherness/minority, 167, 168, 169,
    177, 179, 183, 217, 233, 312, 316,
    353, 361
Owen, Wilfred, 18, 282, 286, 291,
    294–302, 303

paganism, 173–75, 183
Parker, Michael, 36–37, 38, 77, 118,
    119, 120, 138, 197, 252, 291,
    396, 418n76, 419n99, 426n96,
    427n14
parochialism, 406n32, 422n26
Pascoli, Giovanni, 18, 403, 459n14
Paulin, Tom, 13, 24–25, 219, 407n75
peripheral regions, 4, 27, 71, 110
personification, 13–15
pilgrimage, 262, 266, 431n36
Plunkett, Oliver, 17, 173, 177–79,
    183

"poet as witness," 301–2
poetic forms
    blank verse, 89, 274
    "buried" tercet, 251, 253
    "macro-form," 249
    pastoral, 22–23, 26, 360, 406n46
    pastoral versus "regional," 22–23,
        25, 27
    Petrarchan sonnet, 170, 180
    prose poems, 187–211, 434n12
    tercet variant, 2, 13, 18, 40, 247, 249,
        252, 274, 275–76, 355, 357, 372,
        373, 385, 393
    terza rima, 2, 17, 40, 241, 247,
        248–49, 250, 251, 252, 254,
        255–56, 257, 259, 260, 261, 262,
        263, 264, 265, 266, 267, 268, 269,
        270, 271, 272, 275, 276, 334, 361,
        363, 366, 367, 368, 370, 372, 373,
        374, 394, 402, 404, 443n39,
        457n40
    terza rima and relation to Dante
        and Eliot, 264–65
poetic image, 265–66, 364, 368–69,
    370, 376, 383, 385, 395, 432n53,
    458n69
poetic imitation, 257
poetic influence/inspiration, 246–47,
    250, 276–77, 282, 297, 300, 301,
    322, 329, 363, 364–66, 382, 403,
    405n12, 440n54
    and political discourse, 295–96,
        303, 309
poetic language (importance of),
    268–69, 270, 292, 306, 326, 328,
    332, 363, 401
poetic metaphor, 252–53, 262, 270,
    271, 274, 302, 321, 342, 354,
    376–77, 380–81, 382, 383, 390,
    401
poetic punctuation, 389
poetic quality, 268

poetic rhyme/rhythm, 249, 251–52, 256, 262, 265, 267, 274–75, 286, 301, 304–5, 331–32, 342, 351, 367, 374, 377–78, 378–79, 402
poetic technique/form, 107, 138, 141, 157–58, 169, 176–77, 180–81, 184, 185, 188, 189, 194–95, 196, 199, 200, 202, 213, 224, 226, 227, 232, 241, 247, 248–49, 250, 251, 252, 254, 255, 257, 265–66, 268, 269, 271, 274, 275–76, 286, 365, 366–67, 377, 386, 393–94
  as reflecting/preserving regionalism, 125, 254–55, 261, 262–63, 269, 272, 334
poetic transformation, 252, 261–62, 284, 299, 300, 304, 308, 384, 390
poetic voice/tone, 127–28, 169–70, 211, 227–28, 229, 233, 252, 256, 270, 375, 377
poetry as healing, 306–7, 310, 346–47
poetry as intermediary, 313
progress, 133
prophetic sight/"reading," 352
provincial dialect/imagery, 67, 92–93, 107, 117–19, 126–27, 136, 139, 215, 226–27, 228–29, 232–33, 242, 250, 259, 261, 263, 272, 279, 314, 315, 328–29, 335, 338, 340–41, 344, 351, 376, 408n77, 453n67
public vs. private genre, 66

quincunx, the, 320–23, 424n52

racism, 163–64, 166, 168, 171, 176, 179
reading/ways of reading, 201, 421n1, 422n30
"the city," 354
reanimation, 163

reconciliation, 68, 69, 91, 97, 197, 249, 277–78, 311, 327, 333, 359
regionalism
  and the arts, 117, 235, 258, 259, 406n43, 418n76
  development of, 41–65, 110, 113, 117, 278, 310–12
  Heaney's imagined Northern Ireland, 2, 4, 13–14, 15, 16, 19, 34, 38, 40, 42, 65, 70, 80, 82, 159, 166, 188, 211, 213, 215, 235–36, 243, 277, 313, 321, 330, 359, 392, 394, 400, 404, 420n118
  Heaney's Northern Ireland and conflict/sectarianism, 2, 14, 15, 16, 17, 24, 26, 33, 35, 73, 80, 94, 98, 100, 120, 130, 131, 132, 134, 135, 139, 142, 145, 146, 148, 157, 160, 164, 166, 167, 169, 175, 185, 193, 198, 199, 202, 203–4, 205, 206, 207, 208, 209, 221, 237, 240, 244, 253, 278, 284, 286, 304, 311, 394, 397, 398, 400, 402, 418n56, 435n26
  Heaney's Northern Ireland and rural regionalism, 2, 6–10, 18, 26, 27, 100, 106, 108, 111, 112, 117, 120, 127, 156, 188, 198, 230–31, 311, 368, 394
  importance of, 1, 11–12, 27, 33, 122, 212–13, 315
  and language, 232–33, 235, 243, 247–48, 268, 280, 312, 313, 314, 331, 341, 357
  and local culture, 12, 15–16, 31, 33, 34, 36, 41–42, 46, 48, 49, 51–52, 73–74, 75, 76, 78, 79, 101, 108, 115, 129, 134, 252, 258, 269–70, 312, 332, 343–44, 347, 348, 409n104, 411n15
  —*Honest Ulsterman*, 57, 60, 61–62, 63, 64, 192, 415n87

—*Lagan*, 44, 48, 51, 53, 57, 411n14
—New Literary Dinner Club, 48
—*New Northman*, 44, 46, 48, 57
—*Phoenix*, 62–63, 64
—*Rann*, 52–55, 57
—*Threshold*, 57, 58, 59, 60, 61, 111, 415n98
—*Uladh*, 44, 47, 57, 117, 118
—Ulster literary theatre, 42–43, 417n21
and preservation of, 123, 268, 315, 404
and relational nature of, 29, 65, 198
and religious belief, 50–51, 68, 70, 73, 77–78, 80, 85, 90, 95, 96–97, 114, 128, 150, 165, 201, 242, 278, 310–11, 317, 336, 357, 421n10, 450n17
and Scots-Irish/Ulster Scots culture, 317, 318, 320, 323, 325, 328–29, 334–36, 338, 340–41
and Scottish Gaelic culture, 313, 316, 334, 335, 336, 337, 338, 340, 341, 342, 375
and surrounding influence, 269–70, 311, 316, 327
spirit region, the, 2, 13, 18, 27, 40, 209–10, 212, 240, 244, 251, 255, 256, 311, 351, 352, 353, 357, 359, 362, 363, 368, 370, 386–87, 392, 394, 399, 400, 401, 403–4
and unification, 49–50, 70, 76, 81, 98, 100, 128–29, 130, 134, 137, 211, 215, 325, 330, 337, 341, 410n129
religious imagery, 172, 173, 178–79, 182, 203, 209, 223, 259, 271, 293–94, 323, 389–90
republicanism, 222
rural imagery, 124, 200, 252, 349–50, 351, 384, 399

Sayers, Dorothy, 250, 251, 254, 255, 256, 367, 443n34
sectarianism
and artistic/literary engagement, 2–3, 26, 42–43, 47, 57–58, 68–69, 73–74, 77, 84–85, 86, 88–89, 91, 94, 99–100, 108, 114, 116, 134–36, 137, 139–40, 143, 144, 167, 185, 188, 189, 190, 191, 193, 194, 199, 201, 216, 221, 223, 249, 264, 266, 277, 281, 283–84, 287–88, 289, 292, 303, 318, 320, 342, 374, 395
and class division, 80, 90–91
and color, 90, 138, 148, 161, 162, 163, 167, 168, 170, 175, 177, 207
and music, 95–96, 97, 176, 206, 207–8, 420n118
self-reflection, 81–82, 84, 221, 306
sexual imagery, 13–15, 141, 161, 171–72, 175, 179–82, 229
Shearman, Hugh, 47, 411n20, 412n22
Shovlin, Frank, 41–42, 53, 413n2
silence, 250–51, 402
sinfulness, 186
solitude, 224, 404
"standard" English, 56, 67, 227, 280, 344, 408n77
and English education, 56
"standard" Irish, 314
Stewart, Susan, 250, 348
sympathetic recognition, 78–79

translation/role of translator, 281–82, 324–25, 326, 327, 333, 447n6, 449n67
trans-regionalism/globalization, 344–45, 346, 347
typography, 200–201

uncanny, 360
unionism, 75, 216, 288, 291, 325
  and bigotry, 73–74, 98, 138–42,
  144–45, 188, 197, 205, 211

victimhood, 286, 289–90, 294, 302,
  448n31
violent imagery, 127, 130–31, 140,
  143–45, 149–50, 151, 152,
  156, 160, 162, 166, 169, 170,
  171, 173–74, 177–79, 180,
  181–82, 183, 185, 200, 207,
  253, 259, 260, 279, 290–92,
  297, 326–27, 364, 397–98,
  429n46

Whelan, Kevin, 29, 30–31, 33–34,
  34–35, 448n28
Williams, Raymond, 21, 22

Wordsworth, William, 6, 16, 23, 102,
  119, 121, 160, 188, 191, 193–94,
  197, 200, 262, 360, 362, 425n79,
  435n27, 445n63
writer/passion for writing, 93, 356–57
writing process, 191, 196, 228–29,
  231–32, 272, 281, 288, 303–4,
  305–6, 314–15, 392, 445n63

Yeats, William Butler, 12, 18–20,
  23–24, 41–42, 84–85, 105, 107,
  121–23, 126, 145, 193, 212–13,
  215, 234, 236, 256, 263, 265, 271,
  276–77, 282, 286, 295–96,
  298–300, 302–3, 306, 322, 332,
  360–61, 363–65, 369–70, 373,
  385–86, 418n57, 435n26, 438n1,
  440n54, 440n55, 444n54, 445n77,
  446n85, 448n45, 458n55, 458n69

RICHARD RANKIN RUSSELL

is professor of English and 2012 Baylor Centennial Professor at Baylor University. He is the author of a number of books, including *Poetry and Peace: Michael Longley, Seamus Heaney, and Northern Ireland* (University of Notre Dame Press, 2010).